Human
Development

Human Development

ROBERT V. KAIL
Purdue University

JOHN C. CAVANAUGH
University of Delaware

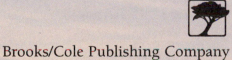

Brooks/Cole Publishing Company
An International Thomson Publishing Company

Pacific Grove • Albany • Bonn • Boston • Cincinnati • Detroit • London • Madrid • Melbourne
Mexico City • New York • Paris • San Francisco • Singapore • Tokyo • Toronto • Washington

Sponsoring Editor: *Jim Brace-Thompson*
Project Developmental Editor: *Eileen Murphy*
Marketing Team: *Margaret Parks, Gay Meixel*
Marketing Representatives: *Jay Honeck, Ronald V. Shelly*
Editorial Associate: *Cathleen S. Collins*
Production Editor: *Marjorie Z. Sanders*
Manuscript Editor: *David Hoyt*
Permissions Editor: *Cathleen S. Collins*
Interior and Cover Design: *E. Kelly Shoemaker*

Interior Illustration: *Suffolk Technical Illustrators; Wayne Clark*
Page Layout: *Terri Wright Design*
Cover Photo: *Scott Barrow*
Art Editor: *Lisa Torri*
Photo Coordinator: *Larry Molmud*
Photo Researcher: *Robin Sterling*
Typesetting: *Graphic World Inc.*
Printing and Binding: *Von Hoffman Press, Inc.*

For more information, contact:

BROOKS/COLE PUBLISHING COMPANY
511 Forest Lodge Road
Pacific Grove, CA 93950
USA

International Thomson Publishing Europe
Berkshire House 168-173
High Holborn
London WC1V 7AA
England

Thomas Nelson Australia
102 Dodds Street
South Melbourne, 3205
Victoria, Australia

Nelson Canada
1120 Birchmount Road
Scarborough, Ontario
Canada M1K 5G4

International Thomson Editores
Campos Eliseos 385, Piso 7
Col. Polanco
11560 México D. F. México

International Thomson Publishing GmbH
Königswinterer Strasse 418
53227 Bonn
Germany

International Thomson Publishing Asia
221 Henderson Building
#05-10 Henderson Building
Singapore 0315

International Thomson Publishing Japan
Hirakawacho Kyowa Building, 3F
2-2-1 Hirakawacho
Chiyoda-ku, Tokyo 102
Japan

Printed in the United States of America

10 9 8 7 6 5 4 3 2 1

Library of Congress Cataloging-in-Publication Data
Kail, Robert V.
    Human development / Robert V. Kail, John C. Cavanaugh.
        p.   cm.
    Includes bibliographical references and index.
    ISBN 0-534-22224-2
    1. Developmental psychology.   I. Cavanaugh, John C   II.   Title.
BF713.K336 1996
155—dc20   95-2840
                                    CIP

To Dea and Patrice

ROBERT V. KAIL is Professor of Psychological Sciences at Purdue University. His undergraduate degree is from Ohio Wesleyan University and he received his Ph.D. from the University of Michigan. Kail has served as Associate Editor of the journal *Child Development,* received the McCandless Young Scientist Award from the American Psychological Association, is a fellow of the American Psychological Association and the American Psychological Society, and was named the Distinguished Sesquicentennial Alumnus in Psychology by Ohio Wesleyan University. Kail has also written *The Development of Memory in Children,* and, with Rita Wicks-Nelson, *Developmental Psychology.* His research interests are in the area of cognitive development during childhood and adolescence. Away from the office, he enjoys flying, working out, and arguing with his teenage sons about the relative musical contributions of the Beatles and Nirvana.

JOHN C. CAVANAUGH is Professor of Individual and Family Studies at the University of Delaware. He received his undergraduate degree from the University of Delaware, and his Ph.D. from the University of Notre Dame. Cavanaugh is a fellow of the American Psychological Association, the American Psychological Society, and the Gerontological Society of America. He has been an American Council of Education Fellow, and has been elected President of the Adult Development and Aging Division (Division 20) of the APA. Cavanaugh has also written *Adult Development and Aging.* His research interests in gerontology concern family caregiving as well as the role of beliefs in older adults' cognitive performance. For enjoyment he backpacks, writes poetry, and, while eating chocolate, ponders the relative administrative abilities of James T. Kirk, Jean-Luc Picard, Kathryn Janeway, and Benjamin Sisko.

CONTENTS

CHAPTER 3

Growth and Development of Physical and Perceptual Skill   79

CHAPTER 4

The Emergence of Thought and Language   109

PART II
School-Age Children and Adolescents 177

C H A P T E R 6
Off to School 179

PART IV
Later Adulthood   443

"To boldly go where no one has gone before" is a phrase familiar to millions of "Star Trek" fans around the world. It is a fundamental characteristic of being human to explore the unknown in order to further our knowledge and understanding. Boldly going into the unknown is also what each of us does in the course of our development; none of us has been to where we are headed. Indeed, in a real sense, we create our own destinies.

Good starship captains rely on computer data banks and technical manuals to help guide them through the galaxy. Likewise, *Human Development* serves as a resource to help you understand aspects of your past and point you toward your future. Human development is a most fascinating and complex science; this text introduces the issues, forces, and outcomes that make us who we are.

Contemporary research and theory on human development emphasize a multidisciplinary approach. Such an approach is needed to describe and explain how people change (and how they stay the same) over time. Moreover, because people are so diverse, there must be an appreciation for individual differences in the course of development. *Human Development* incorporates both. The book aims to address three specific goals:

*   To provide a comprehensive yet highly readable account of human development across the life span.
*   To build theoretical and empirical foundations that enable students to become educated and critical interpreters of developmental information.
*   To present a blend of basic and applied research, as well as controversial topics and emerging trends, to demonstrate connections between the laboratory and life and the dynamic nature of the science of human development.

Organization

The great debate among authors and instructors in the field of human development is whether to approach the topic from a chronological approach (focusing on functioning at specific stages of the life span, such as infancy, adolescence, and middle adulthood) or from a topical approach (following a specific aspect of development, such as personality, throughout the life span). Both approaches have their merits. We have chosen a modified chronological approach, which we believe combines the best aspects of both. The overall organization of the text is chronological; we trace development from conception through late life in sequential order, dedicating several chapters to issues at particular points in the life span (such as infancy and early childhood, adolescence, young adulthood, middle adulthood, and late life).

However, the developmental continuity of topics such as social and cognitive development gets lost with narrowly defined, artificial age-stage divisions.

Therefore, we dedicate some chapters to tracing their development over larger segments of the life span. These chapters give a much more coherent description of important developmental changes, make clear that the course of development is not easily divided into "slices," and provide students with understandable explications of developmental theories.

A primary difference between *Human Development* and similar texts is that this book provides a richer and more complete description of adult development and aging. Six chapters focus on this topic, as compared with seven on childhood and adolescence. Theories of adult development and aging are included in the theory overview in Chapter 1. This more even treatment reflects the rapid emergence of adult development and aging as a major emphasis in the science of human development, as well as a recognition that roughly three-fourths of most people's lives occurs beyond adolescence.

As a reflection of our modified chronological approach, *Human Development* is divided into four main parts. After an introduction to the science of human development (Chapter 1), Part I discusses the biological foundations of life (Chapter 2) and development during infancy and early childhood (Chapters 3–5). Part II focuses on development during middle childhood and adolescence (Chapters 6–8). Part III (Chapters 9–12) discusses young and middle adulthood. Part IV examines late life (Chapters 13–14) and concludes by discussing dying and bereavement (Chapter 15).

Content

Our text provides comprehensive, up-to-date coverage of research and theory from conception through old age and death. We explicitly adopt the biopsychosocial framework as an organizing theme, integrating it throughout the text, along with many developmental theories. Emerging trends in research and theory are also incorporated throughout.

At several points, we communicate our personal involvement with the issues being discussed, to illustrate how human development plays itself out in people's lives. For instance, Rob Kail provides several examples of his children's developmental experiences, and John Cavanaugh shares his and his wife's experience with miscarriage. Additionally, we open each chapter with vignettes and include many other examples of people's experiences with development. Some of these are showcased in Real People features. We also encourage students to do their own research into developmental issues through the See for Yourself features. These illustrations help make the transition from classroom to life.

In addition to personalizing the material, we have included many topics and features that are unique. Two of the most important are the following.
- The diversity (both in the United States and around the world) in ethnicity, culture, gender, race, age, ability, and sexual orientation is thoroughly integrated in the text, in both the content and the photo program.
- Explicit connections between the theories introduced in Chapter 1 and later topics are made by including graphics reminding students about these ties in subsequent chapters. Separate features illustrating the biopsychosocial framework in action are included in each chapter.

Pedagogical Features

Among the most important aspects of *Human Development* is its exceptional integration of pedagogical features aimed at helping students maximize their learning. Because a more complete description of these features is provided at the end of Chapter 1, we will only highlight them here.

Our text is written with the student in mind. We deliberately adopted a relaxed, engaging writing style (without sacrificing scientific rigor), as a way to hold students' interest. All figures, tables, and photos that are explicitly discussed in the text are fully integrated, eliminating the need for students to turn pages in search of a graphic. Likewise, box-like feature material is also fully integrated; each feature type is set off by a unique icon. Learning objectives are provided for each major section; concept checks conclude each major section; and each chapter ends with a set of "thought" questions, as well as a summary, a list of key terms (with page numbers indicating where they are defined), and an annotated list of suggested readings. Within the text, definitions of key terms are printed in boldface type, with the key term in boldface italics. End-of-book features include a glossary, subject and author index, and a complete reference list.

Supplementary Materials

Human Development is accompanied by a complete teaching and learning package. The package consists of:

- **Instructor's Manual**
  Written by Dina L. Anselmi of Trinity College and Anne L. Law of Rider University, this extensive manual contains a general introduction to teaching human development and fostering critical thinking; instructional goals and teaching strategies for each chapter; chapter summaries and outlines; learning objectives for the study guide; extended lecture topics, including gender issues and ideas for integrating cross- and multicultural issues into classes; in-class and out-of-class activities; video guide; over 50 transparency masters; and suggested answers to end-of-chapter thought questions.

- **Concordance**
  Daniel R. Bellack of Trident Technical College has prepared a concordance that highlights the benefits of our four-part structure, and includes suggestions for how to adjust syllabi and tests to accommodate this structure, with suggested syllabi for quarter and semester courses.

- **Transparency Acetates**
  A set of approximately 100 full-color acetates, 70% drawn from figures in the book, 30% test-independent.

- **Test Items**
  The test bank of more than 1500 items written by Bradley J. Caskey and Richard W. Seefeldt, both of the University of Wisconsin–River Falls, includes true/false, multiple-choice, fill-in-the-blank, short-answer, and essay questions. The items are labeled as factual or conceptual with level of difficulty indicated; all are keyed to the main test with page references. An electronic version of the test bank is available for Mac, DOS, and Windows.

- **Videos**
  Adopters may select complimentary videos from Films for the Humanities and Sciences, Inc., and the Annenberg/PCB Discovering Psychology Series. To request complimentary videos, contact Brooks/Cole marketing at 1-800-354-0092.

- **Study Guide**

  This study guide written by Dea K. DeWolff of Purdue University and Terri L. Combs of Indiana University–Purdue University at Indianapolis contains chapter and section outlines; learning objectives; fill-in-the-blank, true/false, and multiple-choice questions with answers; essay questions with suggested answers; and test yourself summary tests consisting of multiple-choice questions. An electronic version of the study guide is available for Mac and DOS. It provides questions and answers in an interactive format, reinforcing students for correct answers and providing helpful cues for incorrect answers.

Acknowledgements

Textbook authors do not produce books on their own. We would like to thank the many people who have generously given their time and effort to help us sharpen our thinking about human development and shape the development of this text. We are especially grateful to the following people who reviewed various aspects of our manuscript: Polly Applefield, University of North Carolina at Wilmington; Daniel R. Bellack, Trident Technical College; David Bishop, Luther College; Lanthan Camblin, Jr., University of Cincinnati; Ken Elliott, University of Maine at Augusta; Martha Ellis, Collin County Community College; Linda Flickinger, St. Clair County Community College; Steve Fulks, University of Tennessee; Rebecca Glover, University of Arkansas; J. A. Greaves, Jefferson State Community College; Patricia Guth, Westmoreland County Community College; Phyllis Heath, Central Michigan University; Myra Heinrich, Mesa State College; Sandy Hellyer, Indiana University-Purdue University at Indianapolis; Shirley-Anne Hensch, University of Wisconsin Center; Thomas Hess, North Carolina State University; Kathleen Hurlburt, University of Massachusetts-Lowell; Heidi Inderbitzen, University of Nebraska at Lincoln; Sanford Lopater, Christopher Newport University; Bill Meredith, University of Nebraska at Omaha; Maribeth Palmer-King, Broome Community College; Harve Rawson, Franklin College; and Virginia Wyly, State University of New York College at Buffalo.

We also deeply appreciate the strong support we received from our Brooks/Cole team. Jay Honeck and Ron Shelly urged the two of us to collaborate. Jim Brace-Thompson made the collaboration possible and helped to give us a vision of what this book should be. (Consequently, any flaws in that vision are Jim's fault.) Our developmental editor, Eileen Murphy, taught us much about writing, doing so with wit and grace. Kelly Shoemaker designed what we think is a gorgeous book. Marjorie Sanders skillfully used a good supply of carrots and sticks to guide the book through production, consistently meeting deadlines with good cheer. Cat Collins made the legal side of obtaining permission to use copyright material almost enjoyable. Beyond the friendly confines of Brooks/Cole's building in Pacific Grove, California, Robin Sterling found the beautiful photographs that appear throughout the book. Terri Wright and Sharon Powell did a masterful job of assembling, page by page, the text, photographs, and graphs. To all of these people, many thanks. They are the best.

Robert V. Kail
John C. Cavanaugh

A Guide through the Book

A life span human development text—by its very
nature—presents difficult challenges to its authors.
*Should the material be organized chronologically
or topically? How much of the book should focus
on childhood and adolescence, how much on adulthood and aging?
How should theory and research be integrated?*

In this book, authors Robert Kail (an expert in child development)
and John Cavanaugh (an expert in adult development) offer a text
that is briefer, more integrated, and more balanced than other
texts for the course. In addition, the book's fresh organization
(see next page), its even-handed coverage of both childhood and
adulthood, and its relaxed, engaging style all combine to give
readers an experience of life span development that is meaningful,
memorable, and easy to retain.

The pages that follow demonstrate how the authors have structured their text to "tell the story of life span" in a way that will
remain with readers long after specific theories and research
studies are forgotten.

A four-part modified chronological structure demonstrates the "unfolding" of development.

Kail and Cavanaugh "tell the story of life span" in a narrative that is intuitive and holistic—eliminating the redundancy of describing the life span via the traditional 5 x 3 or similar organizational structure used by many texts for the course.

The book's four-part structure reflects "early childhood," "the school years," "the working/raising children years," and "later life"—a structure that makes sense to students and more accurately depicts the developmental process.

> *"Kail and Cavanaugh deviate from the formula, presenting topical and transitional issues within four major chronological segments. There is a more realistic picture of how development proceeds. I really like that."*
>
> **Daniel Bellack**
>
> **Trident Technical College**

Note age-specific chapters where essential (prenatal development, adolescence, entering adulthood, middle age, later life) and more topical chapters where appropriate to reflect the continuity of development (entering the social world, the school years, relationships, work in adulthood, and dying and bereavement).

The authors provide comparatively more emphasis on adulthood and aging than other texts for the course. Of the 13 chapters covering age-related material, 6 cover adulthood and aging.

"This text deviates from the norm of presenting the typical chronological sequence and depicts the study of human development to be truly a life span approach, as opposed to the usual review of the glories of childhood, and 'oh, yes, these things happen in adulthood.'"
Rebecca J. Glover
University of North Texas

"The authors have presented the chronological qualities of development in the traditional step-by-step fashion, but they have also nicely described major 'sea changes' in the life path where dramatic changes in perspective, cognition, emotion, and behavior are all occurring at the same time. They have very nicely offered these two perspectives concurrently."
Sanford Lopater
Christopher Newport University

Chapter opening and section pedagogy makes the material easy to learn.

In these excerpts from Chapter 8, note how the authors draw readers into key concepts of the chapter and consistently reinforce active learning of the material.

Every chapter opens with several *vignettes* that get readers thinking about some aspect of development. This opening vignette (one of five for Chapter 8) provides a real example of a developmental issue (in this case, eating disorders) that will be explored in the chapter.

> Linda just celebrated her 12th birthday and is eagerly looking forward to the greater independence of adolescence. At the same time, Linda is concerned that she has gained weight and that her body is no longer as lean as it was during her childhood years. Linda is thinking about going on a diet, an idea that seems reasonable to her because her mother diets constantly to remain a size 4.

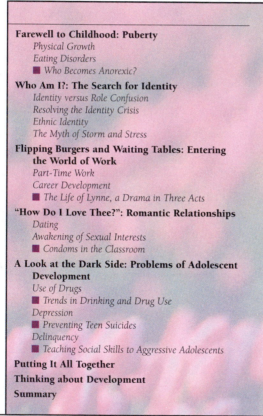

Farewell to Childhood: Puberty
Physical Growth
Eating Disorders
■ *Who Becomes Anorexic?*

Who Am I?: The Search for Identity
Identity versus Role Confusion
Resolving the Identity Crisis
Ethnic Identity
The Myth of Storm and Stress

Flipping Burgers and Waiting Tables: Entering the World of Work
Part-Time Work
Career Development
■ *The Life of Lynne, a Drama in Three Acts*

"How Do I Love Thee?": Romantic Relationships
Dating
Awakening of Sexual Interests
■ *Condoms in the Classroom*

A Look at the Dark Side: Problems of Adolescent Development
Use of Drugs
■ *Trends in Drinking and Drug Use*
Depression
■ *Preventing Teen Suicides*
Delinquency
■ *Teaching Social Skills to Aggressive Adolescents*

Putting It All Together

Thinking about Development

Summary

Chapter opening outlines help students organize material and are an excellent way for them to make sure they've understood the chapter's "big picture." Mini-outlines in each section list heads within the major subheading of the section.

Farewell to Childhood: Puberty

LEARNING OBJECTIVES

- *What changes define puberty? When do they occur?*
- *What are the effects of maturing early or late? Are they the same for boys and girls?*
- *What are some of the causes of eating-related disorders, such as obesity and anorexia nervosa?*

Each section's *Learning Objectives* orient students to what they will be learning in that section and provide focus for students preparing for exams.

eting. She said she felt good knowing she had enough self-control to stay on her diet even though she was hungry. . . .

As a child, Wendy had been a good student, but she did not do as well at school as her older brothers did. Thus her parents praised her brothers more than they praised her. But as her weight dropped, her schoolwork suffered and she became more isolated from her classmates.

Wendy's parents said she had been a pleasant, obedient child. When they set limits on her activities, she complied willingly. Therefore, they were surprised and upset when they could not get her to abandon her diet and resume eating normally. Because they and her doctor feared for her life, they finally placed her in the hospital for treatment (Leon & Dinklage, 1989).

This persistent refusal to eat, accompanied by an irrational fear of being overweight, typifies a condition known as *anorexia nervosa*. As was the case with Wendy and the girl in the photograph, anorexia primarily affects females and usually begins with the onset of adolescence (Attie, Brooks-Gunn, & Petersen, 1990). Adolescents with anorexia tend to be well-behaved, conscien-

tious, good students from middle-class families. Their body image is distorted: Despite being painfully thin, they claim to be overweight Brooks-Gunn, & Petersen, 1990). The disorder is quite serious: Damag heart is common, and without treatment, as many as 15% of adolescen anorexia die (Wicks-Nelson & Israel, 1991).

Full-color figures, tables, and photos are fully integrated with the text, supporting the narrative flow and eliminating the need for students to turn pages in search of a graphic. Here, the photograph graphically reinforces student understanding of anorexia.

Test Yourself questions at the end of each section provide readers with a quick way to assess their mastery of important concepts. Answers are provided for immediate reinforcement.

The authors integrate theories (including emerging life span theories) throughout the book, rather than isolating them in a separate chapter that can be read and forgotten.

In Chapter 1, readers will find a brief theory overview as well as a summary table that lists 10 major theories, their characteristics, and their positions on developmental issues.

As students move through the book, appropriate portions of the summary table are repeated in context, with discussion of theory integrated with chapter topic coverage, as shown here.

Throughout the text, definitions of *Key Terms* are printed in boldface type, with the key term itself in boldface italics.

> *"I like the fact that the present book does not include a separate chapter on theories. I think the short introductions to major theories provided in Chapter 1 are sufficient to get the student going. I like the more extensive elaborations that occur within chapters as appropriate topics are produced."*
>
> *Thomas M. Hess*
>
> *North Carolina State University*

Note how the table section supports the flow of information as Kail and Cavanaugh effectively integrate the discussion of theory with the topic of achieving generativity.

Joyce is not alone. Despite the evidence that personality traits change little during adulthood, many middle-aged people like the man in the photograph report that they are increasingly concerned with helping younger people achieve rather than with getting ahead themselves. **In his psychosocial theory, Erikson argued that this shift in priorities reflects** *generativity,* **or being productive by helping others in order to ensure the continuation of society by guiding the next generation.**

Achieving generativity can be very enriching. It is grounded in the successful resolution of the previous six phases of Erikson's theory. The basic idea, summarized in the table, is that generativity is the next stage of psychosocial development, which has proceeded in sequence since birth. There are many avenues for generativity, such as through mentoring (see Chapter 11), volunteering, foster grandparent programs, and many other activities.

Perspective	Examples of Theories	Main Ideas	Emphases in Biopsychosocial Framework	Positions on Developmental Issues
Psychodynamic	Erikson's psychosocial theory	Personality develops through sequence of stages	Biological, social, and life-cycle forces crucial; less emphasis on psychological	Nature–nurture interaction, discontinuity, universal sequence but individual differences in rate

Some adults do not achieve generativity. Instead, they become bored, self-indulgent, and unable to contribute to the continuation of society. **Erikson referred to this state as** *stagnation,* **in which people are not able to deal with the needs of their children or are unable to provide mentoring to younger adults.**

Some theorists question whether Erikson's description of generativity is adequate to describe adulthood. For example, Kotre (1984) contends that adults experience many opportunities to express generativity that differ in importance, and that most adults do not show generativity all the time. Rather, he believes that generativity is more like a set of impulses felt at different times in different settings, such as at work or in grandparenting. Only rarely is generativity continuous in adulthood.

LIFE TRANSITION THEORIES

Although Erikson's notion of generativity provided much insight into adulthood, many theorists believe that middle adulthood includes other important changes. Indeed, Carl Jung, one of the founders of psychoanalytic theory, believed that adults may experience a midlife crisis. **In general, a** *midlife crisis* **is considered to be a time of psychological upheaval, during which people reevaluate their lives.**

Some theorists, such as Levinson and colleagues (1978), Gould (1978), and Vaillant (1977) have developed more precise stage theories. They account for personality change in adulthood by studying fairly exclusive and nonrepresentative groups of adults (in some cases only men) over several decades. All of these theories postulate that adults go through a series of predictable stages of growth and transition (including some version of a midlife crisis) in a universal sequence. Much of the data was gathered through interviews and personal reflections of the study participants.

What Determines Quality of Attachment?

The answer to this question begins with biological forces. Remember infants' biological heritage includes behaviors such as clinging and smiling that are designed to elicit caregiving from adults. Along with their appearance, such behaviors make it clear that babies are dependent on others, which prods adults to care for them.

FORCES IN ACTION

Once caregiving is underway, the quality of attachment reflects the quality of interaction between parents and their babies (van IJzendoorn et al., 1992). A secure attachment is most likely when parents respond to their infants predictably and appropriately. For example, Fabio always notices when his son, Sasha, smiles or talks. When Sasha cries, gestures, or tries to communicate in other ways, Fabio attempts to understand Sasha's intent and tries to respond appropriately. Behaviors like Fabio's evidently help to convey to babies that social interactions are predictable and satisfying. Apparently, they instill in infants the trust and confidence that is the hallmark of secure attachment.

Of course, not all caregivers react to babies in a reliable and proper manner. Some respond intermittently or only after the infant has cried long and hard. When these caregivers finally do respond, they are sometimes annoyed by the infant's demands and may misinterpret the baby's intent. Over time, these babies tend to see social relationships as erratic and often frustrating. Such conditions do little to foster trust and confidence.

Longitudinal studies attest to how important a caregiver's sensitivity is for the quality of attachment. In a study by Cox and her colleagues (1992), mothers and fathers were observed at home as they interacted with their 3-month-olds. Then, when the infants were 12 or 13 months old, they were tested in the Strange Situation twice, once with each parent.

Several aspects of parents' behaviors with their 3-month-olds predicted the security of the infants' attachment at 1 year. For both mothers and fathers, babies were more likely to form secure attachments when their parents

*   were sensitive, responding quickly and appropriately to their infant's signals;
*   expressed much positive emotion toward the baby;
*   enjoyed playing with the infant, especially play in which parent and infant both participated actively; and,
*   were frequently physically affectionate with the infant.

When parents respond predictably and sensitively to their infants, as this mother is doing, secure attachments are the likely result.

How does predictable and responsive parenting promote secure attachment relationships? To answer this question, we need to consider psychological factors. Think for a moment about your own friendships or romantic relationships. Such relationships are most satisfying when we believe that we can trust others—that we can depend upon them in times of need. Much the same formula seems to hold for infants. An infant needs to learn that a caregiver is concerned about his or her needs and will try to meet them. When parents are dependable and caring, babies come to trust them and to know that they can be relied on for comfort in times of stress. **This expectation is called an *internal working model*; it is thought to affect close relationships throughout the person's life (Bretherton, 1992).**

The formation of attachment well illustrates the combined influence of the different components of the biopsychosocial framework. Many infant behaviors that elicit caregiving in adults—smiling and crying, for example—are biological in origin. When the caregiver is responsive to the infant (a sociocultural force), then a secure attachment forms in which the infant trusts caregivers and knows that they can be relied upon in stressful situations (psychological force). 🌸

Throughout the text, the authors use a biopsychosocial framework as an organizing theme. This theme is reinforced in every chapter with short *Forces in Action* sections that explore how the biopsychosocial framework is used to help understand a particular issue in development.

Featured sections in every chapter flow directly from the text

Set off with marginal icons—but not boxed off from the narrative flow of the text—are five fascinating features that help expand readers' understanding of some aspect of development.

The Cost of Raising a Child

YOU MAY
BE WONDERING

You've just discovered that you're going to be a parent! Once the cheering and excitement begin to die down, you realize that you need to start putting some money aside for the child. Never having had children before, you may be wondering just how much will be enough. "I can almost guarantee you anybody having their first child will be surprised," says F. Stephen Wershing, Jr., a certified financial planner and father of a 1-year-old son (Johnston, 1993). Why, you ask?

Well, it turns out that for children born in 1992, middle-income families will spend a total of $224,800 per child by the time the child graduates from high school. Lower-income families will spend $161,620, and upper-income families will spend $314,550. That's for *each* child, and it assumes a two-

Integrating Sight and Sound

SPOTLIGHT
ON RESEARCH

When Darla hears her son waking, she greets him with cheerful morning chatter and reaches into the crib to pick him up. In so doing, Darla provides two cues that she is getting closer: Her image gets larger, and her voice sounds louder. We already know that older infants use sights and sounds independently to judge distance, but have infants integrated these rules from different sensory systems? Do infants know that an approaching object looks larger *and* sounds louder, whereas a departing object looks smaller *and* sounds quieter?

To answer these questions, Jeffrey Pickens (1994) created the setup shown in the drawing. He presented pairs of 25-second videotapes on two video monitors placed side by side. In one pair, the first video showed a toy train that appeared to be coming toward the viewer; the second video showed a train going away from the viewer. These videos were shown eight times simultaneously. On four of the presentations, the soundtrack consisted of an engine getting louder; on the other four presentations, the engine was getting quieter. Research assistants wearing headphones (so that they couldn't hear the soundtrack) recorded which video the infant was watching.

What should the 5-month-old infants that Pickens (1994) tested do when they see these videos? If infants know the rules

getting closer = larger and louder
getting farther = smaller and quieter

then perhaps they will look at the video that matches the sound: They'll watch the video of the arriving train when the engine gets louder and the video of the departing train when the engine gets quieter. Infants might also do just the opposite—look at the mismatching sounds because they find them so peculiar. In either case, there is a strong link between what they hear and where they look.

You May Be Wondering features explore answers to common questions people have about development. Here, the authors offer practical information on "The Cost of Raising a Child."

Spotlight on Research features demonstrate connections between the laboratory and life and the dynamic nature of the science of human development.

Here, in "Integrating Sight and Sound," readers get a fascinating, behind-the-scenes account of a recent research study. Note how the integrated illustration clarifies a key aspect of the experimental design.

Schindler's List

The outbreak of war typically provides shrewd business people the chance to profit from the increased demand for manufactured goods relating to military needs. The outbreak of World War II in Europe in 1939 was no exception. Oskar Schindler was an entrepreneur who saw an opportunity to make a great deal of money by working for the Germans in Poland after they had taken over the country. His flamboyant demeanor brought him to the attention of the local German commanders, for whom Schindler did favors. Motivated by the potential for personal profit at the expense of others, he opened a factory in which he employed Jews.

Schindler's company was quite successful. But as the war continued, official German policy toward Jews changed to one of extermination. Jewish citi-

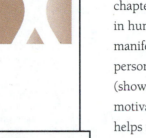

REAL PEOPLE

Preschoolers on the Witness Stand

Remember Cheryl, the 4-year-old who claimed that a neighbor had touched her "private parts?" Regrettably, episodes like this one are all too common in America today. When abuse is suspected, the victim is usually the sole eyewitness. To prosecute the alleged abuser, the child's testimony is needed. Can preschool children like Cheryl be trusted on the witness stand?

CURRENT CONTROVERSIES

Dealing with Physical Aging

How do people deal with the signs of physical aging? Find out for yourself by doing the following exercises.

SEE FOR YOURSELF

1. Look through popular fashion magazines such as *Vogue, Cosmopolitan, GQ,* and *Elle,* and watch television programs. Pay attention to advertisements and articles dealing with wrinkles, hair, and weight. How many can you find that give the message that these natural signs of aging are acceptable? Do you detect a difference between messages aimed at men and women?
2. Talk to men and women you know who are over 40. Ask them how they feel about the physical changes that have happened to them. Do you detect any gender differences?
3. Talk to someone from a culture other than your own. Find out how people in another culture view the physical changes associated with aging. Are the changes that accompany aging looked upon in the same way around the world?

These exercises should provide you with some insights into how people and corporations (through their advertisements) view the physical changes that occur in middle age. Compare your findings with other students' results and discuss any gender differences you uncovered. Do people ignore these changes? See for yourself. ❧

Another physical change is loss of bone mass. Especially in women, loss of bone mass is a potentially serious problem. The changes shown in the diagram begin in the 30s and accelerate in the 50s; the result can be a dramatic reduc-

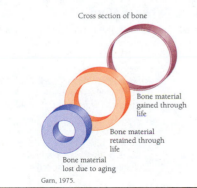

Cross section of bone

Bone material gained through life

Bone material retained through life

Bone material lost due to aging

Garn, 1975.

Real People features in every chapter illustrate how an issue in human development is manifested in the life of a real person. In "Schindler's List" (shown here), the changing motivation of Oskar Schindler helps readers understand Kohlberg's theory.

Current Controversies features offer thought-provoking questions about difficult issues, such as the section shown here, "Preschoolers on the Witness Stand"

See for Yourself features provide readers with ways to explore issues in human development on their own. Here, in "Dealing with Physical Aging," readers are encouraged to explore how individuals and corporations (through their advertising) view the physical changes that occur in middle age.

Note how seamlessly the *See for Yourself* material is integrated into the main flow of the text.

Superlative end-of-chapter pedagogy

At the end of each chapter, you'll find material designed to help students test their mastery of the chapter's ideas and concepts:

Putting It All Together sections provide a chapter capstone by revisiting each of the chapter-opening vignettes. Unlike the point-by-point detail offered in the *Summary*, the *Putting It All Together* section is designed to help readers focus on the "big picture" and relate that chapter's material to the whole of life span development.

Thinking About Development questions are thought questions designed to help readers go beyond simple retention of chapter material.

A list of the chapter's *Key Terms,* annotated with the page number on which the term is defined, can be used as a "quick check" of chapter mastery as well as a practical study aid.

If You'd Like to Learn More sections include additional reading on the chapter's topics, ranging from research-based resources to self-help books and popular fiction.

Putting It All Together

Is it any wonder why middle age gets bad press? There's a lot to face: signs of biological aging, children leaving, cognitive abilities changing, and parents dying. But middle age also has much going for it, from many people's perspective: generally good relationships with children, grandparenthood, and accumulated experience. We saw how middle age is partly a continuation of previous developmental trends (for example, in aspects of cognitive development and personality) and partly a time of new challenges (such as getting used to physical changes and dealing with different generations in the family).

We learned that Dean, the Type A individual, is well positioned to recover from his heart attack if he reduces his anger and hostility. Kesha's expertise in social work is typical of middle-aged adults, many of whom become experts in one area or another. We saw that Jim's behav-

ior is not a reflection of a universal midlife crisis. Esthe joy and relief when her youngest daughter moved out the reaction of most middle-aged parents who acquire empty nest (at least until their adult children decide move back).

Judging from the information in this chapter and Chapters 10 and 11, middle age has many positive a pects—relatively good health, the best financial secur most people ever have, stable relationships with pa ners, good relations with children, expertise in sor area, and the prospect of rewarding relationships wi grandchildren. It has its challenges, too. Getting used physical aging can be hard, as is caring for an aging pa ent. But for many people, on balance these are the be years of their lives.

Thinking about Development

1. The experience of undergoing the physical changes related to aging, such as gray hair, reflects the interaction of biological, psychological, social, and life-cycle factors. How so?

2. How are the cognitive developmental changes discussed in this chapter related to those discussed in Chapter 9, with regard to primary and secondary mental abilities and postformal thought?

4. As noted in Chapter 10 (p. 353), marital satisfa tion improves as children leave home. Based on the d cussion in this chapter, why does this happen?

5. How do family relationships in middle age fit in Duvall's model, discussed in Chapter 10 (pp. 361-362

Key Terms

aerobic exercise (415)	filial obligation (433)	osteoporosis (410)
agreeableness (424)	formal style (435)	practical intelligence (418)
appraise (414)	fun-seeking style (435)	processes of thinking (420)
climacteric (411)	generativity (426)	products of thinking (420)
conscientiousness (424)	hassles (414)	sandwich generation (429)
coping (414)	hormone replacement	stagnation (426)
cultural conservator (438)	therapy (411)	stress and coping paradigm (413)
dispenser of family	kinkeepers (432)	surrogate parents (435)
wisdom (436)	menopause (411)	Type A behavior pattern (414)
distant style (435)	midlife crisis (426)	Type B behavior pattern (414)
encapsulated (420)	neuroticism (423)	unexercised ability (418)
extraversion (423)	openness to experience (424)	
fictive grandparents (438)	optimally exercised ability (418)	

If You'd Like to Learn More

BRODY, E. M. (1990). *Women in the middle: Their parent-care years.* New York: Springer. This description of the experiences of women who provide care for their parents is research-based but contains many good examples.

CHERLIN, A. J., & FURSTENBERG, F. F. (1986). *The new American grandparent.* New York: Basic Books. This is a very readable overview of research on the meanings and styles of grandparenthood.

ESTES, C. P. (1992). *Women who run with the wolves.* New York: Ballantine Books. Femininity is discussed from a Jungian point of view, as revealed through story and myth.

KEEN, S. (1991). *Fire in the belly: On being a man.* New York: Bantam Books. This very readable book pre sents a new model of masculinity in contemporar society.

TAN, A. (1989). *The Joy Luck Club.* New York: Putnam This novel explores the bond among four Chines American women and their adult daughters.

WHITBOURNE, S. K. (1985). *The aging body.* New York Springer. This excellent resource covers the biolog cal and physiological changes that occur in adul hood, with the psychological implications of thes changes discussed in detail.

Summary

Physical Changes and Health

Changes in Appearance

■ Some of the signs of aging appearing in middle age include wrinkles, gray hair, and weight gain. An important change, especially in women, is loss of bone mass, which in severe form may result in the disease osteoporosis.

Reproductive Changes

■ The climacteric (loss of the ability to bear children by natural means) and menopause (cessation of menstruation) occur in the 40s and 50s and constitute a major change in reproductive ability in women. Most women do not have severe physical symptoms associated with the hormonal changes.

■ Reproductive changes in men are much less dramatic; even older men are usually still fertile. Physical changes do affect sexual response.

Stress and Health

■ In the stress and coping paradigm, stress results from a person's appraisal of an event as taxing his or her resources. Daily hassles are viewed as the primary source of stress.

■ The types of situations people appraise as stressful change through adulthood. Family and career issues are more important for young and middle-aged adults; health issues are more important for older adults.

■ Type A behavior pattern is characterized by intense competitiveness, anger, hostility, restlessness, aggression, and impatience. It is linked with a person's first heart attack and with cardiovascular disease. Type B behavior pattern is the opposite of Type A; it is associated with lower risk of first heart attack, but poorer prognosis afterward if an attack should occur. Following an initial heart attack, Type A behavior pattern individuals have a higher recovery rate.

■ Whereas stress is unrelated to serious psychopathology, it is related to social isolation and distrust.

Exercise

■ Aerobic exercise has numerous benefits, especially to cardiovascular health and fitness. The best results are obtained through a moderate exercise program maintained throughout adulthood.

Cognitive Development

Practical Intelligence

■ Research on practical intelligence reveals differences between optimally exercised ability and unexercised ability. This gap closes during middle adulthood. Practical intelligence appears not to decline appreciably until late life.

Becoming an Expert

■ People tend to become experts in some areas and not in others. Experts tend to think in more flexible ways than novices and to be able to skip steps in solving problems. Expert performance tends to peak in middle age.

Lifelong Learning

■ One must teach adults differently than children and youth. Older students learn differently and are motivated differently.

Personality

Stability Is the Rule:
Costa and McCrae's Model of Personality

■ Costa and McCrae postulate five dimensions of personality: neuroticism, extraversion, openness to experience, agreeableness, and conscientiousness. Several longitudinal studies indicate that personality traits show long-term stability.

■ There is some evidence that gender role identity converges in middle age, to the extent that men and women are more likely to endorse similar self-descriptions. However, these similar descriptions do not necessarily translate into similar behavior.

Change Is the Rule:
Changing Priorities at Midlife

■ Erikson believed that middle-aged adults become more concerned with doing for others and passing social values and skills to the next generation—a set of behaviors and beliefs he labeled *generativity*. Those who do not achieve generativity are thought to experience stagnation.

■ For the most part, there is little support for theories based on the premise that all adults go through predictable life stages at specific points in time. Individuals

Each chapter's *Summary,* organized by major section headings, offers a point-by-point summary of the main ideas and key concepts of the chapter.

Human Development

The Study of Human Development

 You are about to begin the most exciting personal journey of your life. In this course, you will have the opportunity to ask some of the most basic questions there are: How did your life begin? How did you go from a single cell, about the size of the period at the end of a sentence in this text, to the fully grown, complex adult person you are today? Will you be the same or different by the time you reach late life? How do you influence other people's lives? How do they influence yours? How do the various roles you have throughout life—child, teenager, partner, parent, worker, grandparent—shape your development? How do we deal with our own and others' deaths?

These are examples of the questions that create the scientific foundation of *human development*, the multidisciplinary study of how people change (and how they remain the same) over time. Answering them requires us to draw on many physical and social sciences, including biology, genetics, chemistry, medicine, psychology, sociology, demography, ethnography, economics, and anthropology. The science of human development reflects the complexity and uniqueness of each person and each person's experiences.

Before our journey begins, there are some things you need to have to make the trip more rewarding. In this chapter, we pick up the necessary road maps that point us in the proper direction: a framework to organize theories and research, common issues and influences on development, the methods developmentalists use to make discoveries, and tips on how to use this book. Pack well, and bon voyage.

Thinking about Human Development

LEARNING OBJECTIVES

❧ *What are the fundamental issues of development that scholars have addressed throughout history?*

❧ *What are the basic forces in the biopsychosocial framework? How does the timing of these forces make a difference in their impact?*

The journey of development, like any great adventure, is filled with interesting people. Let's look ahead at some of the people we will meet along the way. There is Nancy, a 14-month-old in Chapter 2 who is a world-class crawler, and Roberto, a 7-year-old in Chapter 7 who spends hour after hour watching action-adventure cartoons on TV. You'll share the despair of Jalen, a teen in Chapter 8 who abandoned his dream of a college education when his father died. Along with Marcus and Deb, newlyweds in Chapter 10, we'll wonder how long their honeymoon bliss will last. We will meet Jim, a middle-aged man in Chapter 12 who behaves rather strangely by divorcing his wife and buying a little red sports car, and Betty, a woman in Chapter 15 who discovers that she has terminal breast cancer.

These are just some of the people that you'll meet. Our descriptions of them illustrate a few of the many facets of life that are illuminated by the modern science of human development. These topics are interesting in their own right, but they are important for another reason: They bear on general issues of human development that have intrigued philosophers and scientists for centuries. In the next few pages, we introduce some of these issues, which surface no matter which specific aspect of development is being investigated.

Recurring Issues in Human Development

Do genes or experience really determine how smart a person becomes? If a 5-year-old is outgoing, does this mean that the child will be outgoing as an adult? Is human development much the same everywhere around the world? These and similar questions have occupied some of the greatest philosophers in history: Plato, Aristotle, René Descartes, John Locke, John Stuart Mill, and Ludwig Wittgenstein, among many others. Three main issues in human development have captured the most attention: nature versus nurture, continuity versus discontinuity, and universal versus context-specific development. These issues cut across virtually all of the topics that we'll discuss in this book, so let's examine each one briefly.

NATURE VERSUS NURTURE

Think for a minute about a particular feature that you and several people in your family have, such as intelligence, good looks, or a friendly, outgoing personality. Why do you think this trait is so prevalent? Do you think it's because you inherited the trait from your parents? Or is it because of where and how you and your parents were brought up?

Various answers to these questions illustrate different positions on the *nature–nurture issue,* **which involves the degree to which genetic or hereditary influences (nature) and experiential or environmental influences (nurture) determine the kind of person you are.** Scientists once hoped to answer these questions by identifying either heredity or environment as *the* cause of a particular aspect of development. The goal was to be able to say, for example, that intelligence was due to heredity or that personality was due to experience. Today, however, we know that virtually no features of life-span development are due exclusively to either heredity or environment. Instead, development is always shaped by both; nature and nurture are mutually interactive influences. For example, in Chapter 2 we'll see that some individuals inherit a disease that leads to mental retardation if they eat dairy products. However, if their environment contains no dairy products, they develop normal intelligence. Similarly, in Chapter 9 you'll learn that one risk factor for cardiovascular disease is heredity, but that lifestyle factors such as diet and smoking play important roles in determining who has heart attacks.

As these examples illustrate, a major aim of modern developmental science is to understand how heredity and environment codetermine the development of thought, personality, and social behavior. Throughout this text, we will provide numerous examples of how the interaction between nature and nurture shapes our lives.

This student's performance could be explained in part by arguing that she has inherited good math skills that were fostered by a supportive environment, a nature–nurture interaction approach. Additionally, her level of thinking could reflect merely that she knows more than she used to (continuity), or that her thinking has undergone qualitative shifts since childhood (discontinuity).

CONTINUITY VERSUS DISCONTINUITY

Think of some ways in which you remain similar to how you were as a 5-year-old. Maybe you were outgoing and friendly at that age and remain outgoing and friendly today. Perhaps you were very bright then and remain so today. Examples like these suggest a great deal of continuity in development. Once a person begins down a particular developmental pathway—for example, toward friendliness or intelligence—he or she stays on that path throughout life. According to this view, friendly and smart 5-year-olds become friendly and smart 25- and 75-year-olds.

However, some theorists would claim that development is not always continuous, as illustrated by these examples. People can change from one developmental path to another, perhaps several times in their lives. Consequently, smart and friendly 5-year-olds may be smart but obnoxious as 25-year-olds and wise but aloof as 75-year-olds!

The *continuity–discontinuity issue* **concerns whether a particular developmental phenomenon represents a smooth progression throughout the life span (continuity) or a series of abrupt shifts (discontinuity).** Throughout this book, we'll find examples of both continuities and discontinuities in development. For example, in Chapter 5, we'll see evidence of continuity: Infants who have satisfying emotional relationships with their parents typically become children with satisfying peer relationships. But in Chapter 14 we'll see an instance of discontinuity: After spending most of adulthood trying to ensure the success of the next generation and to leave a legacy, older adults turn to evaluating their own lives, in search of closure and a sense that what they have done has been worthwhile.

UNIVERSAL VERSUS CONTEXT-SPECIFIC DEVELOPMENT

The *universal versus context-specific development issue* concerns whether there is just one path of development or several. In some cities in Brazil, 10-to-12-year olds like this boy sell fruit and candy to pedestrians and passengers on buses. They purchase and sell goods, make change for customers, and monitor their sales. Yet they have little formal education and often cannot identify the numbers on the money that they handle so proficiently (Saxe, 1988).

Life for Brazilian street vendors seems so different from childhood in the United States, where 10-to-12-year-olds are formally taught at home or school to identify numbers and to perform the kinds of arithmetic needed to handle money. Is it possible for one theory to explain development in both groups of children? Perhaps. Some theorists would argue that despite what look like differences in development, there is really only one fundamental developmental process, which is the same for everyone. According to this view, differences in development are simply variations on a fundamental developmental process, in much the same way that cars as different as a Chevrolet, a Honda, and a Porsche are all products of fundamentally the same manufacturing process.

The opposing view, of course, is that differences among people may not be just variations on a theme. Advocates of this view argue that human development is inextricably intertwined with the context within which it occurs. A person's development is a product of complex interaction with the environment, and that interaction is *not* fundamentally the same in all environments. Each environment has its own set of unique procedures that shape development, just as the "recipes" for cars, milkshakes, and fly swatters have little in common.

Putting all three issues together, and using personality to illustrate, we can ask how heredity and environment interact to influence the development of personality, whether the development of personality is continuous or discontinuous, and whether personality develops in much the same way around the world. Of course, *answers* to these questions are what really interest us; let's begin our search for answers by looking at the forces that combine to shape development.

Basic Forces in Human Development: The Biopsychosocial Framework

We've seen that developmentalists deal with three fundamental issues in an effort to frame the general discussion of human development. These issues are fundamental, because they set the stage for asking much grander questions: What specific forces make us who we are? Why do some people become creative artists, whereas others work on assembly lines? Why are some people conservatives and others liberals? How can siblings who grow up in the same family turn out very different from each other? What creates the wonderful range of diversity that is humanity? To provide cohesive explanations of people's characteristics and behaviors across the life span, developmentalists usually consider combinations of four interactive forces:

- *Biological forces* include all genetic and health-related factors that affect development.
- *Psychological forces* include all internal perceptual, cognitive, emotional, and personality factors that affect development.
- *Sociocultural forces* include interpersonal, societal, cultural, and ethnic factors that affect development.
- *Life-cycle forces* reflect differences in how the same event affects people of different ages.

Each person is a product of a unique combination of these forces. No two individuals, even in the same family, experience these forces in the same way; even identical twins eventually have different friendship networks, partners, and occupations.

To see why each of these forces is important, let's imagine that you wanted to know how a mother decides whether to breast-feed her infant. You would need to consider a number of biologically based variables, such as the mother's general health and the quality and amount of milk she produces. You would also want to ask about the mother's beliefs and attitudes about the virtues of breast feeding. You would want to know the influences of other people (the father, for example) and what the mother's culture says about appropriate ways to feed infants. Additionally, you would want to know how old the mother is, because she might have been influenced by the beliefs of a certain period. Focusing on only one of these forces would give you an inadequate, distorted view of the mother's decision.

One useful way to organize the biological, psychological, and sociocultural forces on human development is with the *biopsychosocial framework.* As you can see in the figure, the biopsychosocial framework emphasizes that human development is more than any one of the basic forces considered alone. Rather, each force interacts with the others to make up development. Let's look at the different elements of the biopsychosocial model in more detail.

BIOLOGICAL FORCES

Did you ever wonder why members of the same family have different color eyes? Or why you don't seem to do as well on exams when you are not feeling well? Or how eating the right diet may help you live longer? Questions such as these highlight the important role that biological forces play in shaping the course of human development.

Biological forces include such diverse events as the sequence of prenatal development, brain maturation, puberty, menopause, facial wrinkling, and

Looking at the children in this photo, you can see that they resemble their parents, which shows biological influences on development. At the same time, the fact that they look different from each other illustrates the influence of genetic variations as a type of biological force on development.

changes in the cardiovascular and other major body systems. Many of these biological forces are determined by our genetic code, which is discussed in Chapters 2, 3, 8, and 13. But biological forces also include the effects of lifestyle factors, such as diet and exercise; these and other examples will be explored in Chapters 2, 8, and 9.

As is true of all forces, some biological forces are experienced universally—either by all people or, in the case of reproductive changes, by all males or all females. **Forces like these that affect people at a similar point in the life span, and have done so across generations, are termed *normative age-graded influences.*** One example of a normative age-graded influence would be puberty, which occurs in early to mid-adolescence in virtually all people. Another would be menopause, which occurs between the ages of 40 and 55 in most women. These normative age-graded influences create markers that are used to divide the life span into different segments.

Sometimes, though, forces act on only a specific generation. **Forces that only influence people in a certain generation at a particular point in historical time are termed *normative history-graded influences.*** One example of a normative history-graded biological influence was the worldwide flu epidemic in the years immediately after World War I. People who survived this epidemic had lifelong memories of seeing people die from what typically is a less serious illness.

Still other influences are rare, affecting only a handful of people. **When a force is experienced by only a few people, it is called a *nonnormative influence.*** For example, a progressive and fatal brain disease called kuru occurs only on certain islands in the South Pacific.

Collectively, biological forces can be viewed as providing the raw material necessary (in the case of genetics) and as setting the boundary conditions (in the case of one's general health) for development.

PSYCHOLOGICAL FORCES

You probably have an intuitive understanding of psychological forces, because they are the ones used most often to describe the characteristics of a person. For example, think about how you respond when asked to describe yourself when you meet someone new. Most of us say that we have a nice personality and are intelligent, honest, self-confident, or something along those lines. Concepts such as these reflect psychological forces.

In general, psychological forces are all of the internal cognitive, emotional, personality, perceptual, and related factors that influence behavior. Psychological forces have received the most attention of the three main developmental forces. Much of what we will discuss throughout the text will reflect psychological forces. For example, we will see how the development of intelligence enables individuals to experience and think about their world in different ways. We'll also see how the emergence of self-esteem is related to the beliefs people have about their abilities, which in turn influence what they do.

Like biological forces, different psychological forces have different types of effects. Some, such as language, have normative age-graded influences; children around the world begin to acquire language during their second year of life, as discussed in Chapter 4. Other psychological forces, such as expertise in certain computer programs, may be specific to a particular generation. Still others, such as depression or other mental disorders, may affect only a relatively small number of people.

Collectively, psychological factors provide the things we notice most about what makes people the way they are, as well as the interesting variations that make us individuals.

SOCIOCULTURAL FORCES

People develop in the world, not in a vacuum. If we want to understand human development, we need to know how people and their environments interact and relate to each other. In other words, we need to view an individual's development as part of a much larger system, in which no part of the system can act without influencing all other aspects of the system. This larger system includes one's parents, children, and siblings as well as important individuals outside of the family, such as friends, teachers, and co-workers. The system also includes institutions that influence development, such as schools, television, and the workplace.

Although these children were born into different cultures, they will learn how to talk at about the same age. This phenomenon leads some researchers to claim that language development may be biologically based.

All of these people and institutions fit together to form a person's *culture*—the knowledge, attitudes, and behavior associated with a group of people. Culture can be linked to a particular country or people (e.g., French culture), to a specific point in time (e.g., popular culture of the 1990s), or to groups of individuals who maintain specific, identifiable cultural traditions (e.g., African Americans). Knowing the culture from which a person comes provides some general information about important influences that may appear throughout the life span. The United States, for example, includes many different ethnic groups, creating a diverse population that has a wide variety of experiences across the life span. By looking at human development in these different groups (and in other groups around the world), we can understand how sociocultural forces influence human development.

As is the case with biological and psychological forces, many sociocultural forces influence all people at a particular age. A good example of such a normative age-graded influence would be the fact that, throughout the United States, children begin kindergarten at approximately 5 years of age. Other sociocultural forces are specific to a particular generation: Growing up in the United States during the Great Depression is an example of such a normative history-graded influence. Finally, some sociocultural influences are nonnormative: A small percentage of American children, for instance, are educated at home rather than in school.

In trying to describe sociocultural influences on development, we confront a practical problem. Most investigators tend to study groups of people who are relatively easy to contact, and much of the research we describe in this text was conducted on middle-class European Americans. Accordingly, we must be careful *not* to assume that findings from this group necessarily apply to people in other groups. You may find yourself feeling frustrated at times, wondering whether a particular set of results obtained with one group is applicable to other groups as well. Indeed, there is a great need for research on different cultural groups. Perhaps, as a result of taking this course, you will help fill this need by becoming a developmental researcher yourself.

These individuals from Honduras and Cuba are of Hispanic heritage. However, their cultural backgrounds vary on several important dimensions, meaning that we should not view them as being from one homogeneous group.

Another practical problem that we face is deciding the most appropriate term to describe each group. Terminology changes over time. For example, the terms *colored people*, *Negroes*, *black Americans*, and *African Americans* have all been used to describe Americans of African ancestry. In this book, we will use the term *African American* because it emphasizes the unique cultural heritage of that group of people. Following the same line of reasoning, we will use the terms *European American* (instead of *Caucasian* or *white*), *Native American* (instead of *Indian* or *American Indian*), *Asian American*, and *Hispanic American*.

These labels are not perfect. In some cases, they blur distinctions within ethnic groups. For example, the term *European American* ignores differences between individuals of northern or southern European ancestry; the term *Asian American* blurs variations among people whose heritage is, for example, Japanese, Chinese, or Korean. Whenever researchers have identified the subgroups in their research sample, we will use the more specific terms in describing results. When we use the more general terms, you should remember that conclusions may not apply to all subgroups within the more general term.

The sociocultural forces in development provide most of the labels we use to identify people, whether referring to the kind of occupation a person has ("She's an engineer, and you know what *they're* like") or to a person's ethnicity or other demographic category. In sum, sociocultural forces provide the broader context or backdrop for development. In a real sense, they provide the stage upon which development gets played out.

THE FORCES INTERACT

So far, we've described biological, psychological, and sociocultural forces in the biopsychosocial framework as if they were independent of the others. But as we pointed out earlier in introducing the notion of the biopsychosocial framework, each shapes the others. Consider eating habits. When the authors of this text were growing up, a "red meat and potatoes" diet was typical fare. Based on dietary evidence of the day, such a diet was thought to be healthy. Subsequently, it became known that high-fat diets can lead to cardiovascular disease and some forms of cancer. (We'll consider this in greater depth in Chapter 9.) Consequently, social pressures were brought to bear to change what people eat; advertising campaigns were begun; and restaurants began to indicate which menu items were low in fat. Thus, the biological forces of fat in the diet were influenced by the social forces of the times, whether in support of (or in opposition to) having steak every evening. Finally, as your authors became more educated about the whole issue of diets and their effects on health, the psychological forces of thinking and reasoning also influenced their choice of diets. (We must confess, however, that chocolate remains a passion for one of us!)

This example illustrates that no aspect of human development can be fully understood by examining only one or two of the forces. All three must be considered in interaction. In order to understand the effects of genetic variation, we may need to examine some specific aspect of behavior in a particular social context. Or to understand the effects of a sociocultural force such as poverty, we may need to look at how poverty affects people's health. In fact, we'll see later in this chapter that integration across the three major forces of the biopsychosocial framework is one criterion by which the adequacy of a developmental theory can be judged. Before we do that, however, there is one more aspect of this framework that we need to consider: The point in life at which a specific combination of biological, psychological, and sociocultural forces operates matters a great deal.

TIMING IS EVERYTHING: LIFE-CYCLE FORCES

Consider the following two versions of the same situation. In the first version, Jacqui is a 24-year-old woman who has been happily married for a year. She and her husband have a comfortable income. After talking it over, they decide to start a family, and a month later, Jacqui finds out that she is pregnant. In the second version, Jacqui is a 14-year-old girl who spends most of her time on the street. She has been sexually active for about six months but is not in a stable relationship. After missing her period, Jacqui takes a pregnancy test and discovers that she is pregnant.

Despite the fact that Jacqui became pregnant in both versions of the story, you probably would not conclude that the pregnancies had the exact same effect. Rather, you would probably conclude that the outcome would be affected by the other factors in Jacqui's situation. And you probably would be right.

The example illustrates another key fact in the process of human development: The same event can have different effects, depending on when it happens. The term *life-cycle forces* refers to the fact that the meaning of any event depends on the person and the timing of the event. In the two examples with Jacqui, the same event—pregnancy—may be a happy and anticipated event in the first scenario but produce anxiety and concern in the second.

Jacqui's different experiences show how life-cycle forces help shape the effects of the remaining three forces. One way to depict this influence is to show the biological, psychological, and sociocultural forces as a unified spiral. The diagram illustrates how a particular issue or event may recur, as indicated by the X's on the spiral, and how a person's accumulated experience comes into play. For example, trust is an issue that is addressed throughout life (Erikson, 1982). From its beginnings as the trust infants have in their parents, it develops into progressively more complex forms of trust for friends and for lovers, as Jacqui can attest. Each time a person revisits trust issues, he or she builds on past experiences in light of intervening development. This accumulated experience means that the person will deal with trust in a new way.

The younger mother-to-be will likely react differently to her pregnancy than will the middle-aged woman. This example illustrates the importance of life cycle forces on development.

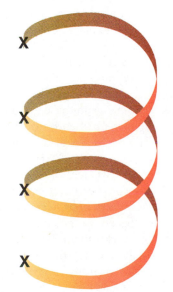

By combining the four developmental forces, we can take a view of human development that encompasses the life span, appreciating the unique aspects of each phase of life. Indeed, the remainder of the book is based on this combination.

TEST YOURSELF

1. The nature–nurture issue involves the degree to which _____ and the environment influence human development.
2. Azar remarked that her 14-year-old son is incredibly shy and has been ever since he was a little baby. This illustrates the _____ of development.
3. _____ forces include genetic and health factors.

4. How does the biopsychosocial framework provide insight into the recurring issues of development (nature–nurture, continuity–discontinuity, universal–context-specific)?

Developmental Theories

LEARNING OBJECTIVES

❧ *How do psychodynamic theories account for development?*

❧ *What is the focus of learning theories of development?*

❧ *How do cognitive-developmental theories explain changes in thinking?*

❧ *What are the main points in the ecological and systems approach?*

❧ *What are the major tenets of life-span and life-cycle theories?*

Just as lumber, bricks, pipes, and wires can be used to build an incredible variety of houses, the basic elements of the biopsychosocial framework have been assembled to form an incredible assortment of theories. **Developmental theories use the elements of the biopsychosocial framework to organize knowledge so as to provide testable explanations of human behaviors and the ways in which they change over time.** By "testable," we mean that theories have to generate hypotheses that can be falsified; that is, you must be able to show that a theory is wrong. The falsifiability requirement is what sets theory apart from mere descriptions of behavior, making it the most important ingredient.

Developmental theories derived from the biopsychosocial framework serve several purposes. First, they offer descriptions and explanations of various aspects of behavior, helping to distinguish between those that are central to development and those that are not. In this regard, theories differ in their breadth. No modern theories of human development are truly comprehensive in attempting to cover all aspects of human behavior throughout the life span (Cavanaugh, 1981). However, some theories attempt to explain a range of behaviors, whereas others focus on specific aspects. Additionally, some theories only consider development at particular points in the life span, while others take a more holistic view.

Second, as noted earlier, any developmental theory must provide falsifiable hypotheses about the course of development. Hypotheses are evaluated by using the research designs described later in this chapter in order to obtain evidence that either confirms them or fails to do so. On the basis of such evidence, theories are revised so as to provide the most complete account of development possible. Revised theories then provide the basis for new hypotheses, leading to new research, and so on. Thus, no theory of development is ever complete. The theories are constantly being evaluated and modified; the science of human development itself is constantly evolving.

Over the years, many theories have been proposed to account for development. In general, these can be grouped into several different perspectives, based on the fundamental assumptions they espouse. The table on page 11 lists

How will this father bond with his child? Answering this question requires a theory of development.

Perspective	Examples of Theories	Main Ideas	Emphases in Biopsychosocial Framework	Positions on Developmental Issues
Psychodynamic	Erikson's psycho-social theory	Personality develops through sequence of stages	Biological, social, and life-cycle forces crucial; less emphasis on psychological	Nature–nurture interaction, disconti-nuity, universal sequence but indi-vidual differences in rate
Learning	Behaviorism (Watson, Skinner) Social-learning theory (Bandura)	Environment controls behavior People learn through modeling and observing	In all theories, some emphasis on biological and psychological, major focus on social, little recog-nition of life cycle	In all theories, strongly nurture, continuity, and universal principles of learning
Cognitive	Piaget's theory (and extensions) Kohlberg's moral reasoning theory	For Piaget and Kohlberg, think-ing develops in sequence of stages	For Piaget and Kohlberg, main emphasis on bio-logical and social forces, less on psychological, little on life cycle	For Piaget and Kohlberg, strongly nature, discontinuity, and universal sequence of stages
	Information-processing theory	Thought develops by increases in efficiency at handling information	Emphasis on biological and psychological, less on social and life cycle	Nature–nurture interaction, continu-ity, individual differ-ences in universal structures
Ecological and Systems	Bronfenbrenner's theory	Developing person embedded in series of inter-acting systems	Low emphasis on biological, moder-ate on psychologi-cal and life cycle, heavy on social	Nature–nurture interaction, continu-ity, context-specific
	Competence-environmental press (Lawton and Nahemow)	Adaptation is opti-mal when ability and demands are in balance	Strong emphasis on biological, psy-chological, and social; moderate on life cycle	Nature–nurture interaction, continu-ity, context-specific
Life Span and Life Cycle	Riley's life-span perspective	Development is multiply determined	Strong emphasis on the interaction of all four forces; cannot consider any in isolation	Nature–nurture in-teraction, continuity and discontinuity, context-specific
	Family life-cycle theory (Duvall)	Families go through series of stages	Strong emphasis on all except biological	Nature–nurture in-teraction, continuity and discontinuity, universal series of stages

five perspectives that guide contemporary thinking and research about development and provides a capsule version of key aspects of each perspective. It also gives examples of theories, their main points, what aspects of the biopsychosocial framework they emphasize, and their positions on the recurring developmental issues (nature–nurture, continuity–discontinuity, and universal–context-specific). In the next few pages, we'll introduce the five perspectives briefly. As we describe each of them, keep in mind that they were designed to provide broad frameworks for understanding development and stimulating insightful research questions. As we revisit each of the main theories in later chapters in the text, we will reintroduce the appropriate row of the table on page 11 as a reminder of these main points.

Psychodynamic Theory

Psychodynamic theories propose that human behavior is largely governed by motives and drives that are internal and often unconscious. These hidden forces influence all aspects of our behavior, thought, and personality, essentially shaping every part of our lives. Psychodynamic theories postulate that development occurs in a sequence of universal stages. This perspective underlies the oldest of the modern theories of human development, tracing its roots to Freud's work in the late 19th and early 20th centuries. It also led to the development of the first comprehensive life-span view, Erik Erikson's psychosocial theory.

FREUD'S THEORY

Psychodynamic theory argues that we are driven by unconscious motives and emotions, shaped by experiences very early in life. Historically, the originator

of this view was Sigmund Freud (1856–1939), perhaps the most famous person in the history of psychology. He was convinced that people mature psychologically according to principles that apply universally, but also that each individual personality is shaped by experience in a social context. Freud insisted that early experiences establish patterns that endure through the entire life span.

Freud's psychoanalytic theory of personality focuses on three components: the id, ego, and superego. **The *id*, a reservoir of primitive drives, is present at birth; it is the force that presses for immediate gratification of bodily needs and wants. The *ego* is the practical, rational component of personality.** The ego begins to emerge during the first year of life, in response to the fact that the infant cannot always have what it wants. An example of the emerging ego is the child's learning other means for communicating one's needs when crying does not work. **Between the third and fourth years of life, the *superego* or "moral agent" of personality develops as the child begins to incorporate adult standards of right and wrong.**

Freud also proposed that development occurs in universal stages that do not vary in sequence. These stages are largely determined by an innate tendency to reduce tension and achieve a pleasurable experience. Each stage is given its unique character by the development of sensitivity in a particular part of the body or *erogenous zone*—that is, an area that is particularly sensitive to erotic stimulation—at a particular time in the developmental sequence. Freud characterized these stages as *psychosexual*. In his theory, development results from successively focusing on, and reducing tension in, the erogenous zones that predominate at different times in life.

Freud believed that development proceeds best when children's psychosexual needs at each stage, which are summarized in the table, are met but not exceeded. Children whose needs are not met adequately become frustrated and reluctant to move to other, more mature forms of stimulation. If children find one source of stimulation *too* satisfying, they see little need to progress to more advanced stages. In Freud's view, parents have the difficult task of satisfying children's needs without indulging them.

Stage	Ages	Description
Oral	Birth to 1 year	Psychosexual needs are gratified orally (by sucking), which can foster attachment to the mother.
Anal	1 to 3 years	Youngsters are urged to control their bladder and bowels, creating a conflict between biological urges and social demands for control.
Phallic	3 to 6 years	Psychosexual energy is directed to the genitals, prompting desires for the opposite sex parent. Fear of retaliation from the same-sex parent causes children to identify with that parent and, in the process, vicariously satisfy the attraction to the opposite-sex parent.
Latency	6 to 12 years	A "quiet time" in which psychosexual energy is channeled into socially acceptable activities such as schoolwork and play with same-sex peers.
Genital	12 years and beyond	A period of sexual maturation in which psychosexual needs are directed toward heterosexual relationships.

Another of Freud's important insights is that humans are not always conscious of their own motives. Unconscious impulses possess great strength, durability, and motivational properties. Freud warned that the rational and the rationalizing person are not easy to tell apart.

ERIKSON'S THEORY

In Freud's view, development is largely complete by adolescence. In contrast, one of Freud's students, Erik Erikson (1902–1994) believed that development continues throughout life. Erikson took the foundation laid by Freud and extended it through adulthood and into late life.

In his *psychosocial theory*, Erikson proposed that personality development is determined by the interaction of an internal maturational plan and external societal demands. He proposed that the life cycle is composed

(Handwritten margin note:) CRITICISM — development complete when sexually mature usually late adolescence

According to Erikson, trust is an issue that will face this couple as they develop their relationship.

of eight stages (shown in the table) and that the order of the stages is biologically fixed. Each stage is marked by a struggle between two opposing tendencies, both of which are experienced by the person. The names of the stages reflect the issues that form the struggles. The struggles themselves are resolved through an interactive process involving both inner psychological and outer social influences. Successful resolutions establish the basic areas of psychosocial strength; unsuccessful resolutions impair ego development in a particular area and adversely affect the resolution of future struggles. Thus, each stage of Erikson's theory represents a kind of crisis, which involves a personal and deep-felt need to reexamine old values.

Psychosocial Stage	Age	Description	Psychosocial Strength
Basic trust vs. mistrust	Birth to 12–18 months	Infant develops a sense of whether the world can be trusted	Hope
Autonomy vs. shame and doubt	12–18 months to 3 years	Child develops first sense of self as independent or as shameful and doubtful	Will
Initiative vs. guilt	3–6 years	Child develops ability to try new things and learns how to handle failure	Purpose
Industry vs. inferiority	6 years–puberty	Child learns basic skills within his or her culture and learns to combat feelings of inferiority	Competence
Identity vs. identity confusion	Puberty to young adulthood	Adolescent determines own sense of self	Fidelity
Intimacy vs. isolation	Young adulthood	Person makes commitment to another; isolation and self-absorption occur if unsuccessful	Love
Generativity vs. stagnation	Middle adulthood	Person seeks to guide the next generation or risks feelings of personal incompleteness	Care
Integrity vs. despair	Late life	Older adult seeks a sense of personal accomplishment with life and accepts death, or falls into despair	Wisdom

The sequence of stages in Erikson's theory is based on the *epigenetic principle*, which means that each psychosocial strength has its own special time of ascendancy or period of particular importance. The eight stages represent the order of this ascendancy. Because the stages extend across the whole life span, it takes a lifetime to acquire all of the psychosocial strengths. Moreover, Erikson realizes that present and future behavior must have its roots in the past, because later stages are built on the foundation laid in previous ones.

We will examine each of Erikson's stages in more detail later in the book. In general, we can view them as a cycle that repeats (Logan, 1986): from basic trust vs. mistrust to identity vs. identity confusion, and from intimacy vs. isolation to integrity vs. despair. In this view, the developmental progression is trust → achievement → wholeness. Throughout life, we first establish that we can trust others and ourselves, represented by the first two stages. In the second cycle, we search for a person whom we can trust enough to establish a close relationship. In achievement, we have a need to create something of our own, seen in the first cycle in the initiative vs. guilt and industry vs. inferiority stages, and in the second cycle in the generativity vs. stagnation stage. Finally, we seek to answer the question of who we are, which in the first cycle is the identity vs. identity confusion stage, and in the second cycle the integrity vs. despair stage. From Erikson's perspective, there are only a few issues that face us in life, and we periodically return to them in order to reach higher resolutions of them.

Learning Theory

In contrast to psychodynamic theory, learning theory concentrates on what can be observed and measured objectively. Consequently, learning theories focus on how behaviors come to be acquired and maintained. Two influential theories in this tradition are behaviorism and social learning theory.

BEHAVIORISM

At about the same time in the early 20th century that psychodynamic theory was attracting increased attention, John Watson (1878–1958) was among the first psychologists to champion the English philosopher John Locke's view that the infant's mind is a blank slate on which experience writes. Watson held that the child learns to be what he or she becomes, usually in a social context. He believed that with the correct techniques, anything could be learned by almost anyone. **B. F. Skinner (1904–1990) took this view one step further, explaining learning on the basis of external reward and punishment within the paradigm of** *operant conditioning.*

In operant conditioning, the consequences of a behavior determine whether the behavior is likely to be repeated in the future. **If the behavior is followed by a consequence that increases the likelihood of the behavior in the future, this is called** *reinforcement.* Positive reinforcement consists of giving a reward—like chocolate, gold stars, or paychecks—to increase the likelihood of the desired behavior. Negative reinforcement consists of taking away unpleasant things to achieve the same goal, such as opening an umbrella to block the rain, or turning down someone's stereo to remove loud music. **If the goal is to lower the future likelihood of a particular behavior, then** *punishment* **is used.** Punishment suppresses a behavior by either adding something aversive (like spanking a child) or withholding a pleasant event (such as television or sex).

Reinforcement is the best way to change behavior, and it is most effective when it immediately follows the target behavior. **If a behavior is not rein-**

Skinner's notion that behavior is determined in part by reinforcement and punishment helps explain many situations. Many people argue that it is the reward of a paycheck that keeps people working.

forced, it will eventually stop through the process known as *extinction*. Intermittent reinforcement will create more durable behaviors that will last longer and be more resistant to extinction. That is why, for example, occasionally paying attention to a child who is pestering you only makes matters worse; you would actually be better off if you paid attention every time and then abruptly stopped. In contrast, punishment is ineffective over the long run, because the person knows only what he or she is *not* supposed to do and is never shown what the proper behavior should be.

Operant conditioning is a powerful explanation of how people develop the behaviors they do. For example, we will see in Chapter 7 that it is a cornerstone for much of parental discipline. It also plays a pervasive role in our lives as adults, from the intermittent reinforcement of grades and paychecks to the hugs our loved ones give us for doing something nice.

SOCIAL LEARNING THEORY

Behaviorism offers powerful insights, but it cannot explain the amount of learning that occurs with no apparent reward or punishment; *social learning theory* **was developed to explain this phenomenon.** Albert Bandura (1977, 1986) accepted the idea that conditioning, reward, and punishment all

contribute to social development. But he questioned whether all (or even most) of what actually goes on during childhood learning can be explained in these terms. Children learn by observation, he argued, and this type of learning can take place without any direct reward or punishment at all. This approach, which directly addresses processes of social development, has inspired a large body of research, as we will see especially in Chapter 7.

Social learning theory differs from behaviorism in that it views the learner as an active participant, not as a pawn at the mercy of external contingencies. People work to create situations in which they learn, rather than passively being subject to situations set up by others. Bandura's social learning theory also emphasizes the importance of thinking, especially personal beliefs. **In particular, Bandura points out that the extent to which people believe they are capable of performing a certain task, which he calls** *self-efficacy,* **is a major determinant in how well they will perform if they must attempt the task, or even whether they will try at all.**

Cognitive-Developmental Theory

Still another way to approach development is to focus on thought processes and knowledge. In cognitive-developmental theory, the key is how people think and how these processes change over time. Two distinct approaches have developed. One approach postulates that thinking develops in a universal sequence of stages; Piaget's theory of cognitive development (and its recent extensions) and Kohlberg's theory of moral reasoning are two examples. The other approach proposes that people process information much like computers, becoming more efficient over much of the life span; information-processing theory is an example of this view.

PIAGET'S THEORY

Much of the way we now conceptualize children's and adolescents' thinking is due to the work of Jean Piaget (1896–1980). Piaget believed that changes in thinking reflect fundamental changes in the way people understand and organize knowledge. These are based on the four basic periods of cognitive development shown in the table below, each characterized by more sophisticated types of reasoning. These four periods apply to both cognitive and social development, for Piaget believed that development in these domains could not be separated.

In Piaget's theory, biological forces and experience work together to produce developmental change through self-initiated interactions with the environment. Biology provides humans with the basic machinery to profit from experience. **One fundamental mechanism is** *assimilation,* **the process of taking in information in such a way as to make it compatible with what one already knows. Another is** *accommodation*—**changing what one already knows based on new knowledge.** Beginning in infancy and continuing throughout life, assimilation and accommodation allow people to interpret and understand their experiences. However, assimilation and accommodation depend on a constant supply of novel experiences to propel people through the four stages. For example, a preschool boy may believe that the amount of milk in a short, wide beaker increases merely by pouring it into a tall, thin one. He will overcome his misconception only when he is sufficiently mature to appreciate the underlying principle of the trade-off between height and diameter (termed *conservation* by Piaget) and has had an opportunity to explore the effects of pouring for himself.

Piaget's theory has had an enormous influence on how developmentalists and practitioners conceptualize cognitive development. The theory has been applied in many ways—from the creation of children's discovery learning toys

Stage	Approximate Age	Characteristics
Sensorimotor	Birth to 2 years	Infant's knowledge of the world is based on senses and motor skills; by the end of the period, uses mental representations
Preoperational thought	2–6 years	Child learns how to use symbols such as words and numbers to represent aspects of the world, but relates to the world only through his or her perspective
Concrete operational thought	7 years to early adolescence	Child understands and applies logical operations to experiences, provided they are focused on the here and now
Formal operational thought	Adolescence and beyond	Adolescent or adult thinks abstractly, deals with hypothetical situations, and speculates about what may be possible

to the ways teachers plan lessons. However, his theory has also been criticized. Some say that Piaget underestimated infants' and young children's abilities. Also, the universality of his sequence of stages is not entirely supported by evidence from different cultures. More recently, Piaget's theory has been extended to include important cognitive changes in adulthood. We will consider these issues in more detail later in Chapters 4, 6, and 9.

KOHLBERG'S THEORY

Because Piaget's theory attempts to tie together maturation and experience on the one hand and cognitive and social development on the other, it has inspired developmentalists with a wide variety of interests. One of the most influential of these was Lawrence Kohlberg, who built his theory of moral reasoning on the foundation of Piaget's theory of overall cognitive development.

As we will see in greater detail in Chapter 9, Kohlberg described a sequence of fixed stages that reflect the different ways people think about moral dilemmas. Kohlberg's theory is an excellent example of how a general theory of development (Piaget's theory) can be more narrowly focused to deal with a more circumscribed issue (moral reasoning). Kohlberg's stages map fairly well onto Piaget's stages, but they involve levels of thinking beyond Piaget's final stage. In this respect, Kohlberg's theory constitutes an extension of Piaget's work. We will consider other extensions of Piaget's stages in detail in Chapter 9.

INFORMATION-PROCESSING THEORY

Rather than viewing cognitive development as a sequence of stages, many theorists adopt alternative approaches. One of these, information-processing theory, draws heavily on the workings of computers to explain people's thinking and its development across the life span. The computer metaphor encompasses both hardware (disk drives, random-access memory, and central processing unit) and software (the programs we use). **Information-processing theory proposes that human cognition uses both mental hardware and mental software.** Human cognition consists of built-in mental and neural structures that allow the mind to operate. However, thought also involves mental software; writing poetry, solving algebra problems, and playing the flute are just a few examples. In the information-processing view, acquiring skills like these can be understood as the acquisition of ever more complex and efficient software designed to accomplish an ever-increasing array of tasks and functions. At any point in development, thinking consists of an organized set of cognitive processes, many of which can be broken down into even more elementary processes, just as computer software consists of modules that can be broken down into other modules or individual commands. Thinking at different phases of development is distinguished by the amount, complexity, efficiency, and power of this mental software.

Some researchers also point to deterioration of the mental hardware (along with declines in the mental software) as explanations of cognitive aging. We will see in Chapter 13, for example, that normal aging brings with it significant changes in people's ability to process information.

The information-processing approach is the dominant view in the study of processes such as memory and attention. Like Piaget, theorists in these fields

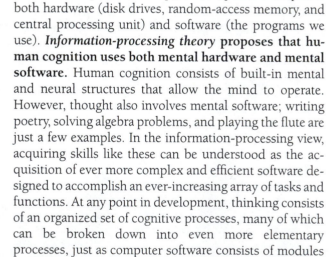

According to information-processing theory, people handle information in much the same way as a computer. Doing well on an exam consists of encoding information during study, storing it, then retrieving it on the test.

view people as active; unlike Piaget, they do not propose a sequence of stages. The strength of this approach lies mostly in its relative simplicity and ease of understanding, which lead to parsimonious explanations of how and why people's cognitive abilities change with age. Its major drawbacks relate to the view that cognitive processes can be reduced to their constituent parts, isolated, and studied separately. Many would argue that such a reductionist approach cannot encompass the complexity of human thinking.

The Ecological and Systems Approach

Most developmentalists agree that the environment is an important force in many aspects of development. However, only ecological theories have focused on the complexities of environments and their links to development. **For *ecological theory*, which gets its name from the branch of biology dealing with the relation of living things to their environment and to one another, human development is inseparable from the environmental contexts in which a person develops.** The ecological approach is broad; it proposes that all aspects of development are interconnected, much like the threads of a spider's web are all intertwined. Interconnectedness means that no aspect of development can be isolated from others and understood independently. We will consider two examples of the ecological and systems approach: Bronfenbrenner's theory and the competence–environmental press framework.

BRONFENBRENNER'S THEORY

The best-known proponent of this approach is Urie Bronfenbrenner (1979, 1989), who proposes that the developing individual is embedded in a series of progressively more complex and interactive systems, which jointly produce development. **Like many other theorists, Bronfenbrenner notes that development is strongly influenced by people and objects in an individual's immediate environment, which he terms the *microsystem*.** The microsystem at any point in life consists of the people closest to an individual, such as an infant's parents or an adult's partner and children. Moreover, individuals have more than one microsystem; for example, a young child might have the microsystems of the family and of the day care setting, and an adult might have microsystems of family, work, and a social club.

Unique to the ecological approach is recognition that the environmental influence on development extends beyond these factors in the immediate environment, or microsystems. **To understand development, we must also understand how the microsystems themselves are interrelated in what Bronfenbrenner calls the *mesosystem:* what happens in one setting is likely to influence others.** A good example of this is a topic we will explore in more detail in Chapter 11—the interaction of work and family life. You have probably found that if you have a stressful day at work, you may be somewhat grouchy at home, or vice versa. This is an indication that your mesosystem is alive and well; your microsystems of home and work are indeed interconnected emotionally for you.

Bronfenbrenner's theory also includes the *exosystem*, a social setting that a person may not experience firsthand but that can still influence de-

Understanding why adolescents behave the way they do requires considering the many different systems that influence them. Parents, peers, teachers, the neighborhood, and social policy all exert effects that shape behavior.

velopment. To continue with the previous example, a child may experience greater attention from his mother if the mother's work situation is going well, but less attention when the mother is under a great deal of work-related stress. Or frail older adults may experience major changes in their home meals program after voters in their district refuse to pass a tax levy. In short, although the influence of the exosystem is at least secondhand, the effects are no less real on the developing person.

The broadest environmental context for Bronfenbrenner is the macrosystem, the subcultural and cultural contexts in which the microsystem, mesosystem, and exosystem are embedded. This level is similar to what we earlier called *sociocultural forces* in the biopsychosocial framework. However, Bronfenbrenner explicitly recognizes that the macrosystem itself evolves over time; what is true about a particular culture today may or may not have been true in the past and may or may not be true in the future. Thus, each successive generation develops in a unique sociocultural period. We will return to this notion later in this chapter when we discuss cohort effects in developmental research.

The various interactive systems Bronfenbrenner proposed are depicted in the figure. The primary advantage of his approach is that it makes us realize

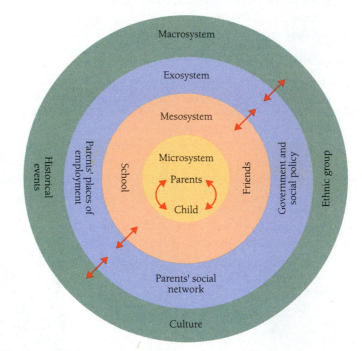

Adapted from Kopp and Krakow, 1982

that people do not develop in a vacuum; they are part of increasingly complex and embedded systems. However, because of this explicit recognition of the complexity of development, ecological theory makes it very difficult to understand how development happens. It is all but impossible to adequately represent all of the various embedded systems in a research project. From this view, the best we can do is to create approximations of the developmental process. We will never manage a complete explanation of how a given person's development occurs.

COMPETENCE–ENVIRONMENTAL PRESS THEORY

A second, less complex approach that also emphasizes the interaction of individuals with their environment is Lawton and Nahemow's (1973) competence–environmental press theory. As we will see in greater detail in Chapter 14, this theory was originally proposed to account for the ways in which older adults function in their environment. Basically, according to the theory, how well people adapt is a function of the match between their competence, or abilities, and the environmental press, or the demands put on them by the environment.

This notion of "best match" or "best fit" leading to adaptation could be extended across the life span. For example, how well a child's social skills match her peer group's demands could account for whether she will be accepted by the peer group or not. As with Bronfenbrenner's theory, competence–environmental press theory emphasizes that in order to understand people's functioning, it is essential to understand the systems in which they live.

Life-Span and Life-Cycle Theories

One criticism of most of the theories of human development we have considered thus far is that they pay little or no specific attention to the adult years of the life span. Historically, adulthood was downplayed due to the belief that it was a time when abilities had reached a plateau (rather than continuing to develop) and that adulthood was followed by inevitable decline in old age. However, the field of adult development and aging has evolved greatly since the late 1940s. As a result, new theoretical perspectives emphasize the importance of viewing human development as a lifelong process. Life-span and life-cycle theories view development in terms of where a person has been and where he or she is heading.

LIFE-SPAN PERSPECTIVE

According to the *life-span perspective,* human development is multiply determined and cannot be understood within the scope of a single framework. Matilda Riley, the person most responsible for developing the life-span perspective, insists that human development must be viewed from the biopsychosocial framework. The basic premises of the life-span perspective, in which aging is viewed in the context of the rest of the life span, are as follows (Riley, 1979).

• Aging is a lifelong process of growing up and growing old, beginning with conception and ending with death. No single period of a person's life (such as childhood, adolescence, or middle age) can be understood apart from its origins and its consequences. To understand a specific period, we must know what came before and what comes after.

• How one's life gets played out is affected by social, environmental, and historical change. Thus, the experiences of one generation may not be the same as those of another.

• New patterns of development can cause social change. For example, the realization over the past few decades that severe physical punishment harms psychological development resulted in the passage of laws restricting parents' rights to use this form of punishment. Thus, not only does social change influence people's development, but patterns of development influence society.

Many older adults return to colleges and universities to further their education. As pointed out in the life span perspective, development never stops.

The fact that human aging is a lifelong process means that human development never stops (Brim & Kagan, 1980). From this perspective, development involves the processes necessary to reach a person's potential in any domain (such as physical prowess, intellectual abilities, or social skills). This view is similar to Maslow's (1968) *humanistic theory*, a nondevelopmental theory postulating that people are guided by a variety of needs, from basic physiological ones to self-actualization, the need to achieve one's full potential.

The life-span perspective is important because it argues for a holistic view of development by explicitly incorporating the biopsychosocial framework. In this holistic view, behaviors are *emergent*—that is, they cannot be understood or predicted by examining only their constituent parts. One cannot predict what a 67-year-old person will be like by only knowing what she was like in the past, or by breaking her behavior down into smaller units (such as cognitive or personality components). Rather, some aspects of behavior will be consistent, whereas others will be new, reflecting discontinuities in development. The life-span perspective views nature and nurture as interactive. Individual differences in development are the rule; thus, development is context-specific.

FAMILY LIFE-CYCLE THEORY

A key to the life-span perspective is knowing when during life certain events occur. This aspect emphasizes the importance of the life-cycle force in the biopsychosocial framework. This focus has led some researchers to develop life-cycle theories of development. One example of these theories, which we will explore in more detail in Chapter 10, is Duvall's (1977) family life-cycle theory. This theory postulates that families go through a universal series of changes related to the ages of the children, not to the ages of the parents. Although each stage has its own characteristics (which indicates discontinuous development), families also show certain consistencies in all the stages in terms of how they deal with situations. This theory maintains that family development is multiply determined and that inherited abilities and experience interact to shape behavior.

Overall, life-span and life-cycle theories have greatly enhanced the general body of developmental theory by drawing attention to the role of aging in the broader context of human development. These theories have played a major role in conceptualizing adulthood and have greatly influenced the research we will consider in Chapters 9–14.

The Big Picture

Each of the theories provides ways of explaining how the biological, psychological, sociocultural, and life-cycle forces create human development. But because no single theory provides a complete explanation of all aspects of development, we must rely on the biopsychosocial framework to help piece together an account based on many different theories. Throughout the remainder of this text, you will read about many theories that differ in focus and in scope. To help you understand them better, each theory will be introduced in the context of the issues that it addresses.

Because one of the criteria for a theory is that it be testable, developmentalists have adopted certain methods to help accomplish this. The next section provides an overview of the methods by which developmentalists conduct research and test their theories.

TEST YOURSELF

1. _____ organize knowledge in order to provide testable explanations of human behaviors and the ways in which they change over time.
2. The _____ perspective proposes that people are governed by unconscious motives.
3. According to social learning theory, children learn mainly through _____ .
4. Piaget's theory and _____ theory are examples of the cognitive-developmental perspective.
5. According to Bronfenbrenner, development occurs in the context of the _____ , mesosystem, exosystem, and macrosystem.
6. A belief that understanding any given point in development requires knowing where a person has been and where the person is going is fundamental to the _____ perspective.
7. How are the psychodynamic perspective and Piaget's theory similar? How are they different?

Doing Developmental Research

Doing Developmental Research
*Age, Cohort, and Time of
Measurement*
*Ways of Gathering Developmental
Data*
Research Methods
Conducting Research Ethically

LEARNING OBJECTIVES

❧ **What are age, cohort, and time-of-measurement effects? Why are they important in human development research?**

❧ **In what ways are developmental data gathered?**

❧ **What research methods are used in human development?**

❧ **What ethical procedures must researchers follow?**

Suppose you would like to know whether a particular parenting style is better than another. Although the approach in the Calvin and Hobbes cartoon is amusing, to satisfy your curiosity properly, you would have to follow the principles of scientific inquiry used by developmentalists. These are based on the

CALVIN AND HOBBES © 1990 Watterson. Reprinted with permission of Universal Press Syndicate. All rights reserved.

methods used in the social sciences, such as sociology and psychology. Additionally, because of the biopsychosocial framework, any research must examine multiple influences on behavior. The goals of scientific inquiry in human development are to describe and explain the change and stability that characterize people's lives (Maddox & Campbell, 1985).

Age, Cohort, and Time of Measurement

Every study of human development is built on combinations of three fundamental effects: age, cohort, and time of measurement (Schaie, 1984). **Age effects involve differences due to underlying biological, psychological, or sociocultural processes in the biopsychosocial model.** Usually, researchers use chronological age (the time elapsed since a person was born) as a general index of age effects. Chronological age provides a shorthand method for organizing events by using the commonly understood measurement of calendar time.

It is important to realize that no index variable, including age, causes behavior directly. For example, iron left outside for a long time will rust, but rust is not caused simply by time. Rather, rust, like human behavior, is a time-dependent process: Time (or age) is a measure of the rate at which the process in question occurs. What we study in human development is the result of age-dependent processes, not the result of age itself.

A more precise way to depict time-dependent processes is to use definitions that reflect the biopsychosocial framework (Birren & Renner, 1977). For example, measures of biological age (such as the functioning of various organ systems), psychological age (such as intellectual skills), and social age (such as how maturely one behaves with one's peers) would each measure age more precisely than simply the number of birthdays one has celebrated.

The key point is that simply knowing a person's chronological age tells us very little about what he or she is really like. Think about the many differences among individuals in your peer group. To describe all of you merely using chronological age would yield inaccurate information and imply a sameness that may not be true. Nevertheless, most investigators continue to make use of chronological age, because it is the best single index variable available for developmental research.

"No, Grandma, I'm never asked to clap the erasers. My job is wiping off the computer screens."

FAMILY CIRCUS, © 1993. Reprinted with special permission of King Features Syndicate.

Cohort effects **are differences due to experiences and circumstances unique to the particular generation to which a person belongs.** In general, cohort effects reflect normative history-graded influences (described on page 6). The Family Circus cartoon illustrates a cohort effect resulting from differences in the grandmother's and the grandson's experiences at school. One difficulty is deciding how to define a cohort. Sometimes a cohort may be all the people born in a particular year. At other times, a cohort may consist of people born during a range of years; for example, the Baby Boom cohort includes anyone born between 1946 and 1964.

To see why cohort effects are important, think about the following example. Suppose you are given the assignment to write a research paper on your favorite topic in human development. You would probably begin by going to the library and checking one of the terminals to find out what books were available on your topic. You might go to another terminal and conduct a search of a database such as *Psych Lit* for articles that have been published in journals. By printing the abstracts from the database and gathering the books you found in the catalog, you could complete your primary search in a few hours. Finally, you would likely gather your materials and head for a computer to write your paper (using a spell-checker and grammar-checker to guard against errors, of course).

Now consider how different the process was when the authors of this book were college students in the late 1960s to the mid-1970s. We would begin by searching the card catalog (where books were listed on small index cards), as well as each journal, by hand. We took notes on each article we found, because photocopy machines were rare and expensive. The library work you were able to do in a few hours would have taken us several days. To write the paper, we headed for a typewriter, but only after first writing everything down by hand. What's more, in those days, the spell-checker was the dictionary on the shelf, and we needed to have all the rules of grammar in our heads.

The example highlights differences in the ways that our two generations experience the world. The widespread availability of personal computers in the 1990s makes education a very different experience for you compared to what it was for previous generations. This may result in your acquiring different learning strategies, broader knowledge bases, and different intellectual skills. These are the kind of cohort effects that are important in interpreting developmental research. As we will see, researchers must be careful about generalizing research findings from studying one generation.

Time-of-measurement effects **reflect differences due to the social, environmental, historical, or other events at the time the data are collected.** For example, suppose you compared infant feeding practices in two different periods. Women in one period tended to feed their babies formula, whereas more women in the other period breast-fed. It would be a time-of-measurement effect if child care experts advocated different infant-feeding practices in the two periods. The differences you observed in feeding might have had to do with these changes in expert opinion, rather than mothers simply changing their minds about feeding habits.

In conducting human development research, investigators have tried to identify and separate these three effects. This is not easy, because the effects are related. For example, if you want to study a group of 18-year-olds in 1998, then you have no choice but to find people born in the 1980 cohort. In this case, age and cohort effects are confounded. The behaviors you observe may be due to the fact that the research participants are 18 years old; or they may be due to the specific life experiences they have had because they were born at a particular point in historical time. **In general,** *confounding* **refers to any situation in which you cannot determine which of two or more effects is responsible for the behaviors you observe.** Confounding is a serious problem in human development research.

Ways of Gathering Developmental Data

What makes human development different from other sciences is a basic interest in understanding how people change during their lives. This interest is reflected in the three main ways of gathering developmental data: cross-sectional, longitudinal, and sequential.

The table will help you visualize these designs and show how each of them is related. The matrix shown contains each of the major effects: age, cohort, and time of measurement. Cohort is represented by the years down the left column. Time of measurement is represented by the years across the bottom. Age is represented by the numbers in the body of the table.

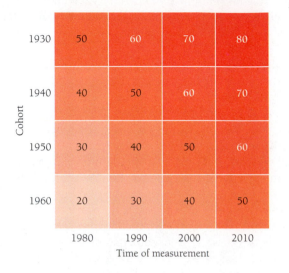

A *cross-sectional design* compares groups of people of varying ages at one point in time. A single column in the table represents a cross-sectional study. For example, a researcher may compare how 4-, 8-, 12-, and 16-year-olds learn and remember information by giving all of the participants a memory task. Because time-of-measurement effects are eliminated (all of the data are collected at one point in time), only age and cohort effects remain. But because age groups are automatically formed when specific cohorts are selected (or vice versa), these two effects are confounded and cannot be separated. Thus, in cross-sectional research, it is unclear whether any observed age differences are due to age or to cohort. This means that cross-sectional data describe only *age differences* in behavior. To establish whether there are *age changes* in behavior requires another approach, the longitudinal design.

Longitudinal designs study a single cohort over multiple times of measurement. Any row in the table is an example of a longitudinal design. For example, a researcher may follow people born in 1960 for ten years in order to trace some aspect of development. Because only a single cohort is studied, only age and time-of-measurement effects are available to explain age changes; the latter two effects are confounded.

Longitudinal designs also have several other problems. Over time, the people who remain in a longitudinal study tend to have different characteristics from the people who drop out; this makes it difficult to draw conclusions from the research. Additionally, there may be *practice effects*; that is, people may improve because they are repeatedly tested over time, not because the underlying ability is improving. Finally, because only one cohort is involved, the findings from a longitudinal study may not apply to other cohorts. Despite these limitations, longitudinal studies provide major insights into the processes responsible for individuals' development; we will consider several later in this book.

Sequential designs build on the designs we have already considered. *Cross-sequential designs* consist of two or more cross-sectional studies that are conducted at two or more times of measurement. Cross-sequential designs are represented by two columns in the table. *Longitudinal sequential designs* consist of two or more longitudinal studies that include two or more cohorts. Longitudinal sequential designs are represented by two rows in the table. Sequential designs provide a way to examine various combinations of the three basic developmental effects, and these designs provide the most complete view of human development (Schaie, 1977). However, this completeness comes at a price; sequential designs are very expensive to conduct. Consequently, few sequential studies exist; we will consider one of the best, Schaie's study of adults' intelligence, in Chapter 9.

Research Methods

Suppose some friends of yours have a healthy 10-month-old baby girl. Unfortunately, your friends' daughter tends to get fussy each night, and they have trouble getting her to sleep. How could you, a human developmentalist, figure out the best thing to do to get the girl to sleep?

Questions like this call for scientific research. **Like researchers in any physical or social science, developmentalists use the *scientific method*, which entails systematic observation, testing alternative explanations or hypotheses about the phenomena under study, and sharing of one's results with the scientific community so that other researchers can learn from, repeat, and extend your investigation.** Researchers use two general scientific methods: experimental and nonexperimental.

EXPERIMENTAL METHODS

An *experiment* is a systematic manipulation of the key factor (or factors) believed to cause a particular behavior. The factor that is manipulated is called the *independent variable*; the behavior that is observed is called the *dependent variable*. In our example, you may believe that the baby is fussy because she has been fed right before going to bed. In this case, you may want to manipulate feeding (making it the independent variable) and observe whether the baby goes to sleep (making sleeping the dependent variable).

To find out if feeding matters, you will want to compare groups of infants: an *experimental group* that is fed right before bedtime and a *control group* that is not. These groups of babies should be formed by randomly assigning infants to one or the other. Random assignment provides a way to eliminate the influence of other factors, such as ethnicity and socioeconomic status, that could explain behavioral differences between the groups. This approach leaves only the independent variable as the best reason for group differences, should they be found.

Such systematic comparison across groups of otherwise comparable babies will allow you to make conclusions about whether feeding causes babies to be fussy at bedtime. Being able to draw such conclusions confidently is a major advantage of using experimental methods. However, experimental methods have their drawbacks. One of the most important is that the conditions necessary for experiments are often artificial compared to the natural setting. This artificiality sometimes limits the applicability of experimental data to real-world settings.

Why is this baby being fussy? One way to find out would be to conduct an experiment with different feeding times to see if that makes a difference.

NONEXPERIMENTAL METHODS

Nonexperimental methods **do not involve the systematic manipulation of factors; they involve only observation of phenomena. Thus, these methods do not provide information about what causes specific behaviors.** Several nonexperimental methods are used in human development research.

Observational studies **are careful investigations of individuals that provide useful, detailed information about a person.** For example, you could take notes on your friends' parenting styles and their daughter's bedtime behaviors by observing them for a period of time. Alternatively, you could interview your friends or have them complete paper-and-pencil questionnaires about what they do when they put their daughter to bed; in either case, you would provide specific questions about bedtime behavior as a way of gathering the necessary information. Interviews and surveys are often used to gather descriptive information from many people about a particular topic.

A common nonexperimental method in human development research involves establishing whether there is a relation between two phenomena. For example, you could establish whether there is a statistical relation between bedtime and whether parents report that their child is fussy. **Statistical relations such as this one are usually measured by calculating a *correlation coefficient*, abbreviated *r*, which expresses the strength and direction of a relation between two variables.** Correlations can range from -1.0 to 1.0:

- When $r = 0$, the two variables are completely unrelated: Later bedtimes are equally likely for fussy and nonfussy children.
- When r is greater than 0, the variables are related positively: Later bedtimes are associated with fussier children.
- When r is less than 0, the variables are related, but inversely: Later bedtimes are associated with less fussy children.

Correlational studies often examine issues similar to those in experiments. For example, we could conduct an experiment on bedtimes with different types of children. However, because potential explanatory factors are not manipulated in correlational studies, no conclusions about cause and effect can be drawn. In our present example, a correlational study would not tell us whether later bedtimes *caused* children to be fussier; we would need to conduct an experiment to determine if this was the case.

In general, nonexperimental methods provide important descriptive information about human development. Indeed, much of the data we will discuss in this text come from nonexperimental studies.

In sum, human development investigators have several options at their disposal for conducting research. Their choices depend on the research question being asked and the context in which the study is being done. To illustrate how and why these decisions are made, and how discoveries about development come about, each chapter includes a Spotlight on Research feature that provides more insights into the human development research enterprise.

Conducting Research Ethically

Conducting research on human development requires that investigators be very careful about what they are doing and treat their research participants with respect. Professional organizations, such as the American Psychological Association, and government research funding agencies, such as the National Institutes of Health, have adopted strict guidelines for the protection of research participants. Such guidelines have been adopted for both human and nonhuman participants.

In general, ethical principles require investigators to submit their research proposals to ethics review panels before beginning the project. Review panels examine the proposal to make sure that the researcher will obtain *informed consent* from human participants before collecting data from them, and to see whether any potential risks or harm could occur in the project. Only when the review panel has given the investigator permission to proceed can research begin.

The requirement for informed consent is especially important. Prospective participants must be told the purpose of the project, what they will be asked to do, whether there are any risks or potential harm, any benefits they may receive, that they are free to discontinue participation at any time without penalty, that they are entitled to a complete debriefing at the end of the project, and any other relevant information the review panel deems appropriate. If prospective participants cannot complete the informed consent procedure themselves (perhaps because they are young children or have a disease, such as Alzheimer's disease, that causes intellectual impairment), someone else must give consent. However, researchers must be particularly sensitive to these individuals. For example, if it becomes apparent that the participant does not like the procedures, the researcher must stop collecting data from that individual.

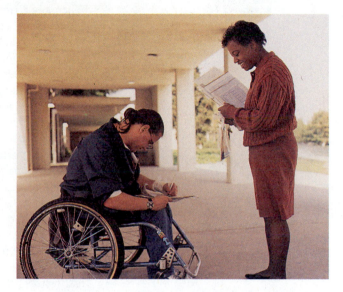

Protecting the rights of research participants is an important ethical issue for all investigators. This person is completing an informed consent document that spells out the procedures to be used in the upcoming study.

TEST YOURSELF

1. _____ effects are due to experiences or circumstances unique to the particular generation to which a person belongs.
2. _____ designs involve studying several different groups of people from different cohorts at the same point in time.
3. The factor that is manipulated in an experiment is called the _____ .
4. Researchers are required to obtain _____ from research participants, after describing all procedures involved in the project.
5. How could a longitudinal design be used to test Piaget's theory?

How to Use This Book

Human Development is written with you, the student, in mind. We have used several techniques that will make it easier for you to learn. At the beginning of each subsequent chapter, you will find chapter-opening vignettes that introduce some of the topics to be covered in the chapter. These brief stories provide examples of the developmental issues that people face, translating the issues discussed in the text to real-life situations. The vignettes are followed by a detailed outline of the chapter.

Answers: (1) cohort, (2) cross-sectional, (3) independent variable, (4) informed consent

We have included several other distinctive features to help you learn the material and organize your studying.

- Each section includes a mini-outline that lists the major subheadings of the section and a set of learning objectives.
- When key terms are introduced in the text, they appear in ***boldfaced italics like these.*** The definition of the key term appears in **bold face like this.** This should make key terms easier to find and learn.
- Data tables, photographs, and cartoons are integrated into the text where they are discussed, eliminating the need to search for them on other pages. This integration will help you tie the graphic material with the text.
- Because key developmental theories are introduced in Chapter 1 and at other points in the text, a theories graphic is used to make explicit connections between these discussions. This will help you make explicit ties between the general discussion of developmental theory and more detailed considerations presented throughout the text.
- The end of each section includes a feature called Test Yourself, which will help you to check your knowledge of major ideas you just read about. The Test Yourself questions serve two purposes. First, they give you a chance to spot-check your understanding of the material. Second, at times the questions will relate the material you have just read to other facts, theories, or the biopsychosocial framework you read about earlier.
- Text features that expand or highlight a specific topic are integrated with the rest of the material. This book includes six different types of features, each identified by a distinctive icon. The list below describes the types of features and shows the respective icons.

SPOTLIGHT ON RESEARCH elaborates a specific research study discussed in the text and offers more details on the design and methods used.

CURRENT CONTROVERSIES offers thought-provoking questions about difficult issues that warrant further discussion.

REAL PEOPLE is a case study that illustrates how an issue in human development is manifested in the life of a real person.

YOU MAY BE WONDERING gives answers to common questions people have about development, often based in everyday experiences.

SEE FOR YOURSELF provides ways for you to explore issues in human development on your own.

FORCES IN ACTION describes how the biopsychosocial framework is used to understand a particular issue in development.

- The end of each chapter includes a concluding section, some thought questions that will help you integrate the information, a summary organized by major section headings, a list of the key terms that appear in the chapter, and some books and articles that you can read for more information. The concluding section, called Putting It All Together, provides a capstone for each chapter by revisiting each of the chapter opening vignettes. The organization of the chapter summaries matches the major sections of the chapter, providing another study tool that will help you organize the material.

We strongly encourage you to take advantage of these learning and study helps as you read the book. Use the chapter-opening outlines, mini-outlines, and learning objectives to help orient yourself to the upcoming material. The boldface sentences will help guide your highlighting and direct your attention to important terms. The text features will help you expand your understanding of the text material and get you to think about related issues. Although they are not meant to replace the Study Guide, the Test Yourself and Thinking about Development questions will help you spot-check your retention of information that you have just read. The organization of the chapter summaries will help you make connections to the appropriate sections of the chapter. We have also left room in the margins for you to make notes to yourself about the material, so you can more easily integrate the text with your class and lecture material.

A few last words about terminology before we cast off. We mentioned earlier the terms that we would use to refer to several different cultural groups. Likewise, certain terms will be used to refer to different periods of the life span. Although you may already be familiar with the terms, we would like to clarify how they will be used in this text. The following terms will refer to a specific range of ages:

Newborn	birth to 1 month
Infant	1 month to 1 year
Toddler	1 year to 2 years
Preschooler	2 years to 6 years
School-age child	6 years to 12 years
Adolescent	12 years to 20 years
Young adult	20 years to 40 years
Middle-aged adult	40 years to 60 years
Young-old adult	60 years to 80 years
Old-old adult	80 years and beyond

Sometimes, for the sake of variety, we will use other terms that are less tied to specific ages, such as babies, youngsters, and older adults. When we do, you will be able to tell from the context what groups we are describing.

Organization

Authors of textbooks on human development always face the problem of deciding how to organize the material into meaningful segments across the life span. This book is organized in four parts. We believe that this organization achieves two major goals. First, it divides the life span in ways that relate to those encountered in everyday life. Second, it allows this book to provide a more complete account of adulthood than other books do.

Because some developmental issues pertain only to a specific point in the life span, some chapters are organized around specific ages. Overall, the text begins with conception and proceeds through childhood, adolescence, adulthood, and old age to death. But because some developmental processes unfold over longer periods of time, some of the chapters are organized around specific topics.

Part I covers prenatal development, infancy, and early childhood. Here we will see how genetic inheritance operates and how the prenatal environment affects a person's future development. During the first two years of life, the rate of change in both motor and perceptual arenas is amazing. How young children acquire language and begin to think about their world is as intriguing as it is rapid. Early childhood also marks the emergence of social relationships, as well as an understanding of gender roles and identity. By the end of this period, a child is reasonably proficient as a thinker, uses language in sophisticated ways, and is ready for the major transition into formal education.

Part II covers the years from elementary school through high school. In middle childhood and adolescence, the cognitive skills formed earlier in life evolve to adultlike levels in many areas. Family and peer relationships expand. During adolescence, there is increased attention to work, and sexuality emerges. The young person begins to learn how to face difficult issues in life. By the end of this period, a person is on the verge of legal adulthood. The typical individual uses logic and has been introduced to most of the issues that adults face.

Part III covers young adulthood and middle age. During this period, people achieve their most advanced modes of thinking, achieve peak physical performance, form intimate relationships, start families of their own, begin and advance within their occupations, manage to balance many conflicting roles, and begin to confront aging. Over these years, you go from breaking away from your family to having your children break away from you. You redefine the relationship with your parents, and you experience the pressure of being caught between the younger and the older generations. By the end of this period, most people have shifted focus from time since birth to time until death.

Part IV covers the last decades of life. The biological, physical, cognitive, and social changes associated with aging become apparent. It must be remembered that many aspects of old age represent positive elements: wisdom, retirement, friendships, and family relationships. We conclude this section, and the text, with a discussion of the end of life. Through our consideration of death, we will gain additional insights into the meaning of life and human development.

We hope that the organization and learning features of the text are helpful to you—that they make it easier for you to learn about human development. After all, this book tells the story of people's lives, and understanding the story is what it's all about.

Thinking about Development

1. Think of some common, everyday behaviors, such as getting together with your friends. Analyze these behaviors in terms of the nature–nurture, continuity–discontinuity, and universal–context-specific issues in development.

2. How are the five major theoretical perspectives similar and different? What commonalities can you find across these perspectives?

3. Explain how each of the major developmental research designs could be used to test a particular theory of human development.

Summary

Thinking about Human Development

Recurring Issues in Human Development

■ Three main issues are prominent in the study of human development. The nature–nurture issue involves the degree to which genetics and the environment influence human development. In general, theorists and researchers view nature and nurture as mutually interactive influences; development is always shaped by both. The continuity–discontinuity issue concerns whether the same explanations (continuity) or different explanations (discontinuity) must be used to explain changes in people over time. Continuity approaches emphasize quantitative change; discontinuity approaches emphasize qualitative change. In the issue of universal versus context-specific development, the question is whether development follows the same general path in all people or is fundamentally different, depending on the sociocultural context.

Basic Forces in Human Development: The Biopsychosocial Framework

■ Development is based on the combined impact of four primary forces. Biological forces include all genetic and health-related factors that affect development. Some biological forces, such as puberty and menopause, are universal and affect people across generations, whereas others, such as diet or diseases, affect people in specific generations or occur only in a small number of people.

■ Psychological forces include all internal cognitive, emotional, perceptual, and personality factors that influence development. Like biological forces, psychological forces may affect all individuals, only specific generations, or only a few individuals.

■ Sociocultural forces include interpersonal, societal, cultural, and ethnic factors that affect development. Culture consists of the knowledge, attitudes, and behavior associated with a group of people. Overall, sociocultural forces provide the context or backdrop for development.

■ The biopsychosocial framework emphasizes that the four forces are mutually interactive; development cannot be understood by examining the forces in isolation. Furthermore, the same event can have different effects, depending on when it happens. Life-cycle forces provide a context for understanding how people perceive their current situation and its effects on them.

Developmental Theories

Developmental theories organize knowledge so as to provide testable explanations of human behaviors and the ways in which they change over time. Current approaches to developmental theory focus on specific aspects of behavior. At present, there is no single unified theory of human development.

Psychodynamic Theories

■ Psychodynamic theories propose that behavior is determined by unconscious motives. Freud claimed that development proceeds in a universal sequence of stages and that personality development is essentially complete by adolescence. Erikson proposed a life-span theory of psychosocial development, consisting of eight universal stages, each characterized by a particular struggle.

Learning Theory

■ Learning theory focuses on the development of observable behavior. Operant conditioning is based on the notions of reinforcement, punishment, and environmental control of behavior. Social learning theory proposes that people learn by observing others.

Cognitive-Developmental Theory

■ Cognitive-developmental theory focuses on thought processes. Piaget proposed a four-stage universal sequence, based on the twin mechanisms of assimilation and accommodation. According to information-processing theory, people deal with information like a computer does; development consists of increased efficiency in handling information.

The Ecological and Systems Approach

■ Bronfenbrenner proposed that development occurs in the context of several interconnected systems of increasing complexity. The competence–environmental press theory postulates that there is a "best fit" between a person's abilities and the demands placed on that person by the environment.

Life-Span and Life-Cycle Theories

■ According to the life-span perspective, development must be viewed in terms of all four forces in the biopsychosocial framework. Understanding any point in development requires knowing where the person came from and where the person is heading. In the life-cycle approach, the meaning of certain events depends on when in a person's life they are experienced.

Doing Developmental Research

Age, Cohort, and Time of Measurement

■ Every study of human development is built on three effects. Age effects involve differences due to underlying biological, psychological, or sociocultural processes; chronological age serves as a general index. Cohort effects are differences due to experiences and circumstances unique to the particular generation of people. Time-of-measurement effects reflect differences due to social, environmental, historical, or other events at the time the data are collected.

Ways of Gathering Developmental Data

■ Most developmental researchers gather data in one of three ways. Cross-sectional designs compare groups of people of varying ages at one point in time. These studies uncover only age differences. Longitudinal studies examine a single cohort over multiple times of measurement. These studies have several limitations, such as participant dropout and practice effects. Sequential designs are multiple cross-sectional or longitudinal studies.

Research Methods

■ Two general research methods are used. Experimental methods involve systematically manipulating an independent variable (which the researcher thinks causes the behavior being studied) and measuring the dependent variable (the behavior). Nonexperimental methods include observational studies, interviews and questionnaires, and correlational methods.

Conducting Research Ethically

■ Investigators must follow strict ethical codes in doing human development research. This includes having the project reviewed by ethics boards and obtaining informed consent from participants.

Key Terms

accommodation   (17)
age effects   (24)
assimilation   (17)
biological forces   (5)
biopsychosocial framework   (5)
cohort effects   (24)
confounding   (25)
continuity–discontinuity
   issue   (3)
correlation coefficient   (28)
cross-sectional design   (26)
cross-sequential design   (27)
culture   (7)
dependent variable   (27)
developmental theories   (10)
ecological theory   (19)
ego   (12)
epigenetic principle   (14)
exosystem   (19)
experiment   (27)

extinction   (16)
human development   (1)
id   (12)
independent variable   (27)
information-processing
   theory   (18)
life-cycle forces   (5)
life-span perspective   (21)
longitudinal design   (26)
longitudinal sequential
   design   (27)
macrosystem   (20)
mesosystem   (19)
microsystem   (19)
nature–nurture issue   (3)
nonexperimental methods   (28)
nonnormative influence   (6)
normative age-graded
   influences   (6)

normative history-graded
   influences   (6)
observational studies   (28)
operant conditioning   (15)
psychodynamic theories   (12)
psychological forces   (5)
psychosocial theory   (13)
punishment   (15)
reinforcement   (15)
scientific method   (27)
self-efficacy   (16)
sequential design   (27)
social learning theory   (16)
sociocultural forces   (5)
superego   (12)
time-of-measurement
   effects   (25)
universal–context-specific
   development issue   (4)

If You'd Like to Learn More

BALTES, P. B. (1987). Theoretical propositions of life-span developmental psychology: On the dynamics between growth and decline. *Developmental Psychology, 23,* 611–626. This is an excellent overview of what it means to take a holistic view of life-span development. Written by one of the leading proponents of this approach, the text is moderately difficult reading.

BALTES, P. B., REESE, H. W., & NESSELROADE, J. R. (1977). *Life-span developmental psychology: Introduction to research methods.* Pacific Grove, CA: Brooks/Cole. This is one of the classic texts on developmental research methods. It's very readable and an easily understood presentation of research designs and methods.

LERNER, R. M. (1986). *Concepts and theories of human development* (2nd ed.). New York: Random House. Lerner's book is a very readable overview of the various philosophical assumptions underlying developmental theories. It includes summaries of several theories.

Prenatal Development, Infancy, and Early Childhood

❧ Leslie and Glenn are excited at the thought of starting their own family. At the same time, they're nervous because Leslie's grandfather had sickle-cell anemia and died when he was just 20 years old. Some days, Leslie is terrified that her baby could inherit the disease that killed her grandfather.

❧ Eun Jung has just learned that she is pregnant with her first child. Like many other parents-to-be, she and her husband Kinam are ecstatic. But Eun Jung rapidly realizes how little she knows about "what happens when" during pregnancy. She's eager to visit her obstetrician to get some answers to her many questions.

❧ Marlena is about to attend the first of six classes designed to help prepare her for her baby's birth. Marlena is relieved that the classes are finally starting—this means that the end of pregnancy is in sight. But all the talk she has heard about "breathing exercises" and "coaching" sounds pretty silly to her. She'd prefer to get knocked out for the delivery and wake up when everything is over.

Biological Foundations

If you ask parents to name some of the most memorable experiences of their lives, many will mention the events associated with childbirth. From the initial exciting news that a woman is pregnant through birth nine months later, the entire experience of pregnancy and birth evokes awe and wonder in a way that is unique.

This time is crucial for human development, as it is the foundation on which all later development is built. This foundation is the focus of this chapter. We begin with genetics. A child represents the merger of two people's hereditary material. We will examine how this merger takes place and, in the process, learn about inherited factors such as the sickle-cell anemia that so frightens Leslie. The second part of the chapter traces the events that transform sperm and egg into a living, breathing human being. We'll learn about the timetable that governs development before birth and, along the way, get answers to Eun Jung's questions about the timing of events during pregnancy. We'll also talk about some of the problems that can occur during development before birth. In the last section of the chapter, we turn to birth and the newborn baby. We'll find out how a mother-to-be like Marlena can prepare for birth and what her newborn will be like.

In the Beginning: 23 Pairs of Chromosomes

LEARNING OBJECTIVES

ᔧ *What are chromosomes and genes? How do they carry hereditary information from one generation to the next?*

ᔧ *What are common problems involving chromosomes and what are their consequences?*

ᔧ *How is children's heredity influenced by the environment in which they grow up?*

Blood gets its red color from cells like those in the photograph on the left. **You may remember that red blood cells are called *erythrocytes* and that they carry oxygen and carbon dioxide through the body.** When a person has sickle-cell anemia, the red blood cells are distorted and stiff. In the photograph on the right, you can see that they are long and curved, like a sickle. Cells that are distorted like these do not flow through small capillaries easily, so oxygen cannot reach parts of the body where it is needed. Because of these circulatory problems, individuals with sickle-cell anemia—including Leslie's grandfather in the opening vignette and many other African Americans—often die from infections. The sickle-shaped cells block the way of the white blood cells that are the body's natural defense against bacteria.

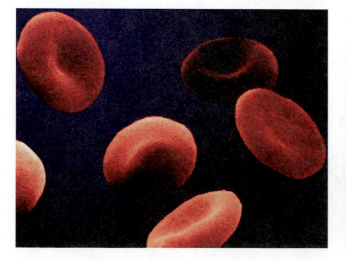

Sickle-cell anemia is inherited. Because Leslie's grandfather had the disorder, it apparently runs in her family. To know whether her baby could inherit the disease, we need to examine the mechanisms of heredity.

Mechanisms of Heredity

At conception, egg and sperm unite to create a new organism that incorporates some of each parent. As recently as 200 years ago, scientists believed that egg and sperm each contained an adult in miniature. **Today we know that each egg and sperm cell has 23** *chromosomes,* **threadlike structures in the nucleus that contain genetic material.** When a sperm penetrates an egg, their chromosomes combine to produce 23 pairs of chromosomes. The photograph shows all 46 chromosomes, organized in pairs ranging from the largest to the

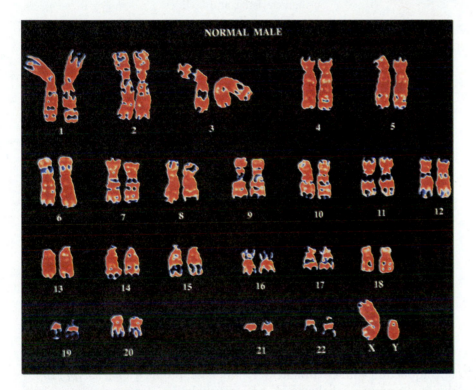

smallest. **The first 22 pairs of chromosomes are called** *autosomes;* **the chromosomes in each pair are about the same size.** In the 23rd pair, however, the chromosome labeled X is much larger than the chromosome labeled Y. **The 23rd pair determines the sex of the child, so these are known as the** *sex chromosomes.* When the 23rd pair consists of an X and a Y chromosome, the result is a boy; two X chromosomes produce a girl.

Each chromosome actually consists of one molecule of *deoxyribonucleic acid*—**DNA for short.** To understand the structure of DNA, imagine four different colors of beads placed on two strings. The strings complement each other precisely: Wherever a red bead appears on one string, a blue bead appears on the other; wherever a green bead appears on one string, a yellow one appears on the other. DNA is organized this way, except that the four colors of beads are actually four different nucleotide bases—adenine, thymine, guanine,

Strands of
phosphate
and sugars

Nucleotide bases
(A = Adenine,
T = Thymine,
G = Guanine,
C = Cytosine)

and cytosine. The strings, which are made up of phosphates and sugars, wrap around each other, creating the double helix shown in the drawing.

The order in which the nucleotide "beads" appear is really a code that causes the cell to create specific amino acids, proteins, and enzymes—important biological building blocks. For example, three consecutive thymine nucleotides make up the instruction to create the amino acid phenylalanine. **Each group of nucleotide bases that provides a specific set of biochemical instructions is a *gene*.** Thus, genes are the functional units of heredity, because they determine production of chemical substances that are, ultimately, the basis for all human characteristics and abilities.

Remember that human chromosomes are organized in pairs. The DNA in each pair of chromosomes typically consists of matched sequences of genes. For example, inheritance of red blood cells is controlled by genes that are found on the shorter (upper) arm of the two chromosomes that make up the 11th pair. **However, genes come in different variations or *alleles*.** In the case of red blood cells, there are two alleles. One allele has instructions for normal red blood cells; another allele has instructions for sickle-shaped red blood cells. **The alleles in the pair of chromosomes are sometimes the same, which is known as being *homozygous*.** If Leslie's baby were homozygous, she would have two alleles for normal cells *or* two alleles for sickle-shaped cells. **The alleles sometimes differ, which is known as being *heterozygous*.** Leslie's baby might have one allele for normal cells and one for sickle-shaped cells. Thus, a person's heredity actually consists of the different alleles that appear on all 46 chromosomes. *Genotype* **is the technical term used to denote a person's hereditary makeup.**

We've seen that genes initiate chemical reactions that ultimately produce physical structures and that influence human behavior. **Genetic instructions, in conjunction with environmental influences, produce a *phenotype*, an individual's physical, behavioral, and psychological features.** How does a genotype produce a phenotype? The answer is simple if a person is homozygous. When both alleles are the same—and thus have chemical instructions that would lead to the same phenotype—that phenotype results. If Leslie's baby has two alleles for normal red blood cells, the baby is almost guaranteed to have normal cells. If, instead, the baby has two alleles for sickle-shaped cells, her baby will almost certainly suffer from the disease.

When a person is heterozygous, the process is more complex. **Often one allele is *dominant*, which means that its chemical instructions are followed and those of the other, *recessive* allele are ignored.** In the case of sickle-cell anemia, the allele for normal cells is dominant, and the allele for sickle-shaped cells is recessive. This is good news for Leslie: As long as either she or Glenn contributes the allele for normal red blood cells, their baby will not develop sickle-cell anemia.

The diagram at the top of page 43 summarizes what we've learned about

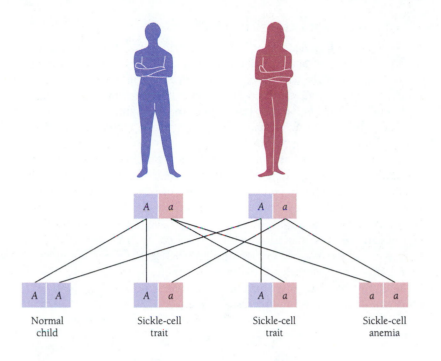

sickle-cell anemia: *A* denotes the allele for normal blood cells and *a* denotes the allele for sickle-shaped cells. Depending on the alleles in Leslie's egg and in the sperm that fertilizes that egg, three outcomes are possible. Only if the baby inherits two recessive alleles for sickle-shaped cells is it likely to develop sickle-cell anemia. But this is unlikely in Glenn's case: He is positive that no one in his family has had sickle-cell anemia, so he almost certainly has the allele for normal blood cells on both of the chromosomes in his 11th pair.

The simple genetic mechanism responsible for sickle-cell anemia, involving a single gene pair in which one allele is dominant and the other recessive, is common. Some of the many characteristics determined by this form of inheritance are shown in the chart. A number of disorders are also inherited in this way, including cystic fibrosis, phenylketonuria, congenital deafness, and albinism. In each case, individuals with the disorder have two recessive alleles, one from each parent.

Some Common Traits Associated with Single Pairs of Genes	
Dominant Trait	*Recessive Trait*
Curly hair	Straight hair
Thick lips	Thin lips
Cheek dimples	No dimples
Immunity to poison ivy	Susceptibility to poison ivy

One final word about sickle-cell anemia: **Sometimes one allele does not dominate another completely, a situation known as** *incomplete dominance.* The phenotype that results often falls between the two phenotypes associated with either allele. This is the case for the genes that control red blood cells. **Individuals with one dominant and one recessive allele have** *sickle-cell trait:* **In most situations they have no problems, but if they are seriously short of oxygen, they suffer a temporary, relatively mild form of the anemia.** Sickle-cell trait is likely to manifest itself when the person exercises vigorously or is at high altitudes (Sullivan, 1987).

Sickle-cell anemia and sickle-cell trait, as well as the phenotypes listed in the chart, involve genes located on the autosomes. Now, let's look at the sex chromosomes, where inheritance is more complicated because the Y chromosome has almost no genes.

VICTORIA'S SECRET: SEX-LINKED INHERITANCE

Victoria, Queen of England from 1837 to 1901, gave birth to four daughters and five sons. One of her sons had hemophilia, a disease in which the blood does not clot properly, leading to uncontrolled bleeding. This son, Leopold, died at 31 years of age. Queen Victoria had ten grandchildren. None of the granddaughters had hemophilia, but three of the six grandsons did. Among her great-grandchildren, none of the seven great-granddaughters had hemophilia, but five of the ten great-grandsons did.

This pattern of inheritance, in which males are affected but females are not, is common. Traits that are inherited in this manner usually involve recessive alleles that are found on the X chromosome. Because the Y chromosome has very few genes, the single allele on the X chromosome determines the phenotype. Boys are affected, of course, because only they have the Y chromosome.

You can see these mechanisms of sex-linked inheritance in the diagram. The mother is heterozygous for hemophilia: She has the dominant allele, B, on one of her X chromosomes but the recessive allele, b, on the other. The father has the dominant allele, B, on his only X chromosome. His Y chromosome has neither the dominant nor the recessive allele.

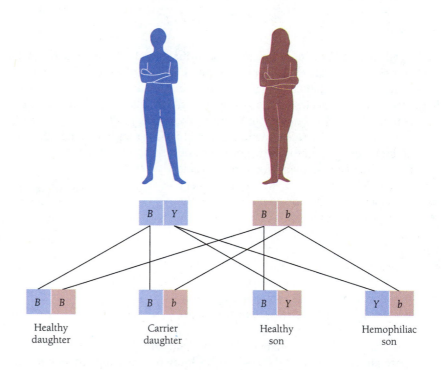

| B | B | | B | b | | B | Y | | Y | b |
| Healthy daughter | | | Carrier daughter | | | Healthy son | | | Hemophiliac son | |

If the egg that is fertilized has the X chromosome with the dominant allele, B, the baby will be healthy. Why can we be so sure? The sperm that fertilizes the egg could contain the X chromosome with the dominant allele, B. The resulting baby girl would have the genotype BB, which is associated with normal clotting. The sperm might also contain a Y chromosome that has neither the dominant nor the recessive allele. The resulting baby boy would have the genotype B, which is also associated with normal clotting.

The situation is more complicated if the egg that is fertilized has the X chromosome with the recessive allele, b. If the sperm that fertilizes the egg carries the X chromosome, the result is a baby girl who is heterozygous, Bb. Her blood will clot normally, but she could pass along the disorder to her children, because she carries the recessive allele, *b*. If the sperm that fertilizes the egg carries a Y chromosome, the result is a son who has only the recessive allele from his mother's X chromosome, *b*. Consequently, he will have hemophilia, and his blood will not clot normally.

Girls can inherit sex-linked disorders. How? If a male who has a sex-linked disorder mates with a female who carries the gene for the same disorder, they could produce a daughter with the genotype *bb*. Because girls can inherit a sex-linked disorder only when both parents contribute a recessive allele, girls are much less likely to inherit these disorders than boys (who can be afflicted based solely on the mother's allele).

Hemophilia is just one of many disorders carried on the X chromosome. Others include one type of muscular dystrophy, red-green color blindness, night blindness, and one form of diabetes. Add these to the disorders that are carried on the autosomes (see page 43) and the power of recessive alleles to disturb development is clear. Heredity can also disrupt development when individuals have the wrong number of chromosomes, which is the topic of the next section.

Extra or Missing Chromosomes

You have probably seen individuals with Down syndrome. Like the boy in the photograph, persons with Down syndrome have almond-shaped eyes and a fold over the eyelid. Also, their head, neck, and nose are usually smaller than normal. During roughly the first six months of life, development of Down-syndrome babies seems to be normal. Thereafter, their mental and behavioral development begins to lag behind that of an average child. By childhood, moderate to severe mental retardation is typical. In addition, Down-syndrome children often suffer from heart and respiratory problems.

Down syndrome is an example of a disorder that can be linked to an abnormal number of chromosomes. Sometimes a person does not receive the normal complement of 46 chromosomes. Individuals may be born with extra, missing, or damaged chromosomes, and their development is invariably abnormal. Persons with Down syndrome usually have an extra 21st chromosome, commonly provided by the egg (Antonarakis et al., 1991). Why the mother provides two 21st chromosomes is unknown. However, the odds that a woman will bear a child with Down syndrome increase markedly as she gets older, particularly once she is past 40 years of age. Consequently, some scientists speculate that a woman's eggs are prone to deteriorate over time. Another interpretation focuses on hazards in the environment, such as X rays. An older mother often has a longer history of exposure to these hazards, and this exposure may damage her eggs.

Regardless of its source, the extra, 47th chromosome in individuals with Down syndrome disrupts the normal sequence of genetic instructions. The result is physical and behavioral development that is dramatically different than the norm. (However, we'll see in Chapter 6 that many mentally retarded persons lead fulfilling lives nonetheless.)

An extra autosome (as in Down syndrome), a missing autosome, or a damaged autosome always has far-reaching consequences for development, because each autosome contains huge amounts of genetic material. In fact, nearly half of all fertilized eggs are aborted spontaneously within two weeks, the chief cause being abnormal autosomes. Thus, most eggs that could not develop normally are removed naturally (Moore & Persaud, 1993).

Abnormal sex chromosomes can also disrupt development. The chart lists four of the more frequently occurring disorders associated with atypical numbers of X and Y chromosomes. Keep in mind that *frequent* is a relative term; the chart shows that most are rare. You'll notice that there are no disorders associated solely with Y chromosomes. The presence of an X chromosome appears to be necessary for life. A Y chromosome without an X is lethal.

Common Disorders Associated with the Sex Chromosomes			
Disorder	*Sex Chromosomes*	*Frequency*	*Characteristics*
Klinefelter's syndrome	XXY	1 in 500 male births	Tall, small testicles, sterile, below-normal intelligence, passive
XYY complement	XYY	1 in 1000 male births	Tall, some cases apparently have below-normal intelligence
Turner's syndrome	X	1 in 2500–5000 female births	Short, limited development of secondary sex characteristics, problems perceiving spatial relations
XXX syndrome	XXX	1 in 500–1200 female births	Normal stature but with delayed motor and language development

Polygenic Inheritance

Traits that are controlled by single genes are usually "either-or" phenotypes. A person either has dimpled cheeks or not; a person either has normal color vision or red-green color blindness; a person's blood either clots normally or it does not. The genotypes are usually associated with two (or sometimes three) well-defined phenotypes.

Many important behavioral and psychological characteristics are *not* "either-or" cases. Instead, an entire range of different outcomes is possible. Take extroversion as an example. Imagine trying to classify ten people that you know well as either extroverts or introverts. This would be easy for a few extremely outgoing individuals and a few intensely shy persons. Most are probably neither extroverts nor introverts, but "in between." The result is a distribution of individuals like the one shown in the chart, ranging from one extreme of the continuum—introversion—to the other—extroversion.

Many behavioral and psychological characteristics are distributed in this fashion, including intelligence, activity level, memory ability, and impulsivity (Plomin, 1990). **In many of these cases, these phenotypes reflect the combined activity of a number of separate genes, a pattern known as** *polygenic inheritance.*

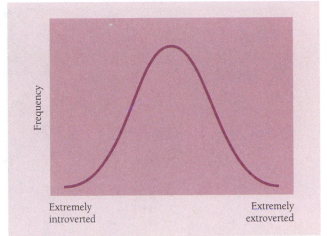

Because many genes are involved in polygenic inheritance, we usually cannot trace the effects of each gene. However, the following *hypothetical* example shows how various genes could work together to produce a behavioral phenotype that spans a continuum. Let's suppose that extroversion is an inherited trait, that eight pairs of genes contribute to extroversion, and that the allele for extroversion is dominant. Thus, a person could inherit as many as 16 alleles for extroversion or as few as 0. Of course, these extremes would be rare, for the same reason that if you toss a coin 16 times, you rarely get 16 heads or 16 tails. Because each allele is equally likely to be present, most people will inherit about 8 dominant alleles for extroversion and 8 recessive alleles for introversion. The result is the distribution of extroversion shown in the diagram.

Remember, this example is completely hypothetical. Extroversion is *not* based on the combined influence of eight pairs of genes. However, the sample shows how several genes working together *could* produce a continuum of phenotypes. Something like our example is probably involved in the inheritance of many human behavioral traits, except that many more pairs of genes are involved. Moreover, the environment also influences the phenotype.

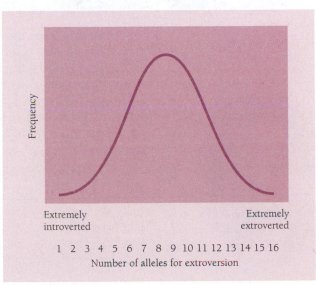

If many behavioral phenotypes involve countless genes, how can we hope to unravel the influence of heredity? Twins and adopted children provide some of the clues.

STUDYING TWINS AND ADOPTED CHILDREN

Identical twins like these look the same because they have the same genes controlling body structure, height, facial features, and the like. **Identical twins are also called *monozygotic twins,* because they come from a single fertilized egg that splits in two.** Because monozygotic twins come from the same fertilized egg, their genes are identical.

Do monozygotic twins act, think, or feel alike? If they did, this would suggest that their behavior, like their looks, is rooted in their genes. **In twin studies, scientists compare monozygotic twins with fraternal or *dizygotic twins,* which come from two separate eggs fertilized by two separate sperm.** Genetically, dizygotic twins are just like any other siblings— on average, about half of their genes are the same. Consequently, by comparing monozygotic and dizygotic twins, we can measure the influence of heredity. If monozygotic twins are more alike than are dizygotic twins, heredity must be implicated.

Much of this same logic is used in adoption studies, in which adopted children are compared with their biological parents and their adoptive parents. The idea here is that biological parents provide their child's genes, but adoptive parents provide the child's environment. Consequently, if a behavior has important genetic roots, then adopted children should behave more like their biological parents than like their adoptive parents.

These and other methods are not foolproof. Maybe you thought of a potential flaw in twin studies: Parents and other people may treat monozygotic twins more similarly than they treat dizygotic twins. This would make monozygotic twins more similar than dizygotic twins in their experiences as well as in their genes. However, because each method has its unique pitfalls, when different methods converge on the same conclusion about the influence of heredity, we can be confident of that result.

Heredity Is Not Destiny: Genes and Environments

Many people mistakenly view heredity as a set of phenotypes unfolding automatically from the genotypes that are set at conception. Nothing could be further from the truth. Although genotypes are fixed when the sperm fertilizes the egg, phenotypes are not. Instead, phenotypes depend on both the genotypes and the environment in which the child develops.

THE CASE OF PKU

PKU is short for *phenylketonuria,* an inherited disorder in which babies are born lacking an important liver enzyme. This enzyme converts phenyl-

ROBERT PLOMIN
". . . the answer to the question 'How much does heredity affect behavior?' is 'a lot.'"

alanine—found in dairy products, bread, and fish—into tyrosine, an amino acid that is responsible for skin pigmentation. Without this enzyme, phenylalanine accumulates and produces toxins that harm the nervous system, resulting in mental retardation.

Today, most American newborns are tested for PKU with a blood test. Newborns who have the disease are immediately placed on a diet that limits the intake of phenylalanine. The result is that mental retardation is avoided. Thus, a child who has the genotype for PKU becomes mentally retarded when exposed to phenylalanine but has normal intelligence when phenylalanine is avoided. (This explains the warning that appears on many products, such as diet soda: "Phenylketonurics: contains phenylalanine.") PKU illustrates that development depends on heredity *and* environmental factors such as medical care, educational opportunities, and diet.

RANGE OF REACTION

PKU is *not* an isolated example. The general rule is that heredity and environment jointly determine the direction of development. **The term** *reaction range* **refers to the fact that a genotype can lead to a range of phenotypes, in reaction to the environment in which development takes place.** The graph illustrates this fact by showing how phenotypic intelligence might vary, depending on the environment. Look first at genotypic intelligence *A*, which has the smallest reaction range. This genotype leads to much the same phenotypic intelligence, no matter whether development takes place in an enriched environment filled with stimulation from parents, siblings, and books or

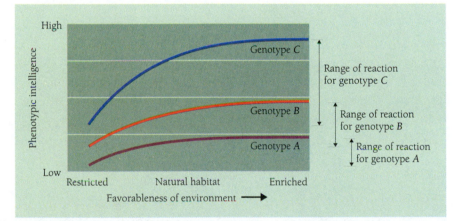

Gottesman, 1963.

in an impoverished environment that lacks all such stimulation. In contrast, genotype *C* has the largest reaction range: The enriched environment leads to a much greater phenotypic intelligence than does the impoverished environment. Thus, a single genotype can lead to a range of phenotypes, depending on the quality of the rearing environment.

Of course, what makes a "good" or "rich" environment is not the same for all facets of behavioral or psychological development. Throughout this book, we will see how specific kinds of environments influence very particular aspects of development (Wachs, 1983).

GENE–ENVIRONMENT CORRELATION

We have emphasized that experience can determine the impact of heredity. As strange as it may seem, the reverse is also true: Heredity can affect experience!

SANDRA SCARR
" . . . given a wide range of opportunities, individuals make their own environments, based on their own heritable characteristics."

Specifically, genotypes can determine the types of experiences that children have (Scarr & McCartney, 1983). For example, different genotypes may evoke different responses from the environment. Children with one genotype may be outgoing and friendly with their peers, which leads them to have rewarding social interactions. Children with another genotype who are less outgoing may feel awkward around their peers and find the same social interactions much less satisfying. **Furthermore, as children get older, they may deliberately seek environments that fit their heredity, a process known as *niche-picking*.** Extroverted youngsters will tend to seek environments in which they can socialize with others; shy youngsters will tend to seek quiet, private environments. The Real People feature shows such niche-picking in action.

REAL PEOPLE

Ben and Matt Pick Their Niches

Ben Kail and Matt Kail were born 25 months apart. Even as a young baby, Ben was always a "people person." He relished contact with other people and preferred play that involved others. From the beginning, Matt was different. He was more withdrawn and was quite happy to play alone. The first separation from parents was harder for Ben than for Matt, because Ben relished parental contact more. When they entered school, Ben enjoyed increasing the scope of his friendships; Matt liked all the different activities that were available and barely noticed the new faces. These differences reveal heredity in action, because sociability is known to have important genetic components (Braungart et al., 1992).

As Ben and Matt have grown up (they're now adolescents), they have consistently sought environments that fit their differing needs for social stimulation. Ben has been involved in team sports, and he plays the drums in the school band. Matt has taken a series of art and photography classes. Ben avoids spending his free time alone; he is always doing something with friends. Matt enjoys the company of a few long-time friends, but he's also just as happy to be drawing, making models, or playing computer games. Ben and Matt have chosen very different niches, and their choices have been driven in part by the genes that regulate sociability. ❧

Much of what we have said about genes, environment, and development is summarized in the diagram. Parents are the source of children's genes and, at least for young children, are also the primary source of children's experiences. Children's genes also influence the experiences that they have and the impact of those experiences on them. Together, heredity and environment determine behavioral and psychological development.

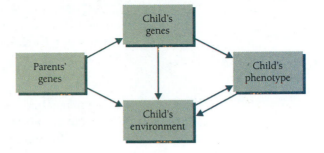

Most of this book is devoted to explaining the links between nature, nurture, and development. We can first see the interaction of nature and nurture during prenatal development, which we examine in the next section of this chapter.

TEST YOURSELF

1. The first 22 pairs of chromosomes are called _____.
2. Sex-linked traits are usually passed from mothers to their _____.
3. _____ reflects the combined activity of a number of distinct genes.
4. Individuals with _____ have an extra 21st chromosome, usually inherited from the mother.
5. When a fertilized egg has defective autosomes, the usual result is that _____.
6. Children who inherit PKU can develop normal intelligence if _____.
7. The term _____ refers to the fact that the same genotype can be associated with many different phenotypes.
8. Explain how niche-picking might work in the domain of intelligence.

The Many Wonders of Prenatal Development

LEARNING OBJECTIVES

❧ **What are the stages of development before birth? What type of changes occur in each stage?**

❧ **What are some of the factors that can harm development before birth?**

❧ **How can abnormal development before birth be detected and treated?**

Let's go with Eun Jung, the pregnant woman in the second chapter-opening vignette, on her first visit to the obstetrician. Here are just a few of the many questions that she asks:

"When will I be able to feel the baby moving?"

Answers: (1) autosomes, (2) sons, (3) Polygenic inheritance, (4) Down syndrome, (5) the fertilized egg is aborted spontaneously, (6) they have a special diet that is low in phenylalanine, (7) reaction range

"I'm 38. I know that older women are more likely to give birth to mentally retarded babies. Is there any way that I can know if my baby will be mentally retarded?"

"I spend much of my day at work sitting in front of a computer monitor. Is there radiation from this machine that could be harmful to my baby?"

"When my husband and I get home from work, both of us are often on edge, so we'll have a glass of wine just to help us to unwind from the stress of the day. Is drinking like this, in moderation, okay?"

If you're sure that you can answer *all* of these questions, skip this next section and go directly to page 65. Otherwise, read on to learn about how pregnancy usually proceeds, as well as some of the problems that sometimes arise.

Periods of Prenatal Development

Prenatal development begins when a sperm successfully fertilizes an egg. For nearly all of recorded history, sexual intercourse was the only way for sperm and egg to unite and begin the development that results in a human being. This is no longer the only way, as we see in the Current Controversies feature.

CURRENT CONTROVERSIES

Making Babies, 1990s Style

About 20 years ago, Louise Brown captured the world's attention as the first test-tube baby—conceived in a petri dish instead of in her mother's body. Today, this reproductive technology is no longer experimental; it is a multibillion-dollar business in the United States (Beck, 1994). Many new techniques are available to couples who cannot conceive a child through sexual intercourse. **The best known, *in vitro fertilization,* involves mixing sperm and egg together in a petri dish and then placing several fertilized eggs in the mother's uterus, with the hope that they will become implanted in the uterine wall.**

The sperm and egg usually come from the prospective parents, but sometimes they are provided by donors. Typically, the fertilized eggs are placed in the uterus of the prospective mother, but sometimes they are placed in the uterus of a surrogate mother, who will carry the baby to term. This means that a baby could have as many as five "parents": the man and woman who provided the sperm and egg; the surrogate mother who carried the baby; and the mother and father who will rear the baby.

For the many couples who have long yearned for a child, these techniques offer new hope. At the same time, they have led to much controversy because of some complex ethical issues associated with their use. One concerns the prospective parents' right to select particular egg and sperm cells; another involves who should be able to use this technology.

Pick your egg and sperm cells from a catalog? Until recently, prospective parents have known nothing about egg and sperm donors. Today, however, they are sometimes able to select egg and sperm based on physical and psychological characteristics of the donors, including appearance and race. Some claim that such prospective parents have a right to be fully informed about the person who provides the genetic material for their baby. **Others argue that this smacks of *eugenics,* which is the effort to improve the human species by allowing only certain people to mate and pass along their genes to subsequent generations.**

Available to all? Most couples who use *in vitro* fertilization are in their 30s and 40s, but a number of older women have begun to use the technology. Many of these women cannot conceive naturally, because they have gone through menopause and no longer ovulate. Some argue that it is unfair to a child to have parents who may not live until the child reaches adulthood. Others point out that people are living longer and that middle-aged (or older) adults make better parents. (We discuss this in more depth in Chapter 12.)

What do you think? Should prospective parents be allowed to browse a catalog of potential donors that includes photos and complete biographies? Should new reproductive technologies be available to all, regardless of age?   ❧

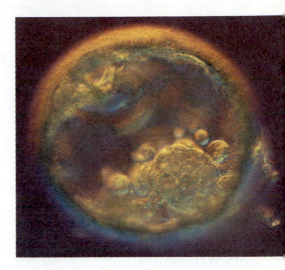

This zygote is approximately four days old. It now contains about 100 cells that create a hollow, fluid-filled ball. The cells on the inside of the ball will develop into the baby.

After a sperm fertilizes an egg, an average of 38 weeks will pass before a baby is born. **The many changes that transform the fertilized egg into a newborn human constitute *prenatal development*.** You may have heard the terms *first trimester*, *second trimester*, and *third trimester* used to describe pregnancy. These terms are useful in explaining the general changes that a woman will experience over the course of nine months of pregnancy. However, scientists divide prenatal development into the periods of the zygote, the embryo, and the fetus. Each period gets its name from the scientific term used to describe the baby-to-be at that point in prenatal development.

PERIOD OF THE ZYGOTE (1–2 WEEKS)

The teaspoon or so of seminal fluid produced during a male's ejaculation contains from 200 to 500 million sperm. Of the sperm released into the vagina, only a few hundred will actually complete the 6- or 7-inch journey to the fallopian tubes. Here, an egg arrives monthly, hours after it is released by an ovary. If an egg is present, many sperm will simultaneously begin to burrow their way through the cluster of nurturing cells that surround the cell. Two sperm cells are doing just this in the photograph. Their tails can be seen clearly, but one sperm has burrowed so deeply that the head is barely visible. When this or some other sperm finally penetrates the cellular wall of the egg, chemical changes occur in the wall immediately, blocking out all other sperm. Then the nuclei of the egg and sperm fuse and the two independent sets of 23 chromosomes are interchanged. The development of a new human being is underway!

The fertilized egg is called a *zygote*. This period of prenatal development lasts two weeks, ending when the zygote implants itself in the wall of the uterus. The zygote travels down the fallopian tube toward the uterus. Within hours, the zygote divides for the first time, then continues to do so every 12 hours. Occasionally, the zygote separates into two clusters that will develop into twins; because they come from a common sperm and egg, they will be identical in appearance. Fraternal twins, which are more common than identical twins, are created when two ova are released and each is fertilized by a different sperm cell.

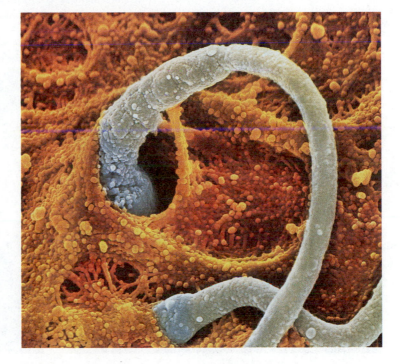

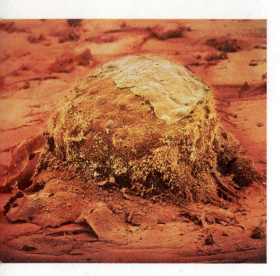

During the second week after conception, the zygote, now consisting of a few thousand cells, becomes implanted in the wall of the uterus.

After about four days, the zygote, which is now a hollow ball of about 100 cells, enters the uterus. The inner part of the ball is destined to become the new individual. The cells in the outer layer form a number of structures that will provide a life-support system throughout prenatal development. **The individual will rest in two sacs, an outer sac called the** *chorion* **and an inner sac called the** *amnion.* **The** *placenta,* **which develops from the chorion, will be the structure through which nutrients and wastes are exchanged between the mother and the developing individual. Finally, the** *umbilical cord,* **composed of veins and arteries, will connect the developing child to the placenta.** Each of these structures will emerge from the outer layer of cells on the zygote.

By the end of week, the zygote ends its travels by coming in contact with the lining of the uterus. The zygote gradually becomes enveloped by an elaborate set of blood vessels in the uterine wall. This process is complete by the end of the second week. The zygote, now consisting of a few thousand cells and measuring no more than 1 millimeter in diameter, is completely embedded in the uterine wall and has established working connections with the mother's blood supply. This connection triggers hormonal changes that prevent menstruation, providing the woman with the first clue that a baby is in the making.

PERIOD OF THE EMBRYO (3–8 WEEKS)

The start of the third week marks a new period in prenatal development, the period of the embryo, which will last until the end of the eighth week after conception. During the third week after conception, three layers begin to form in the embryo. **The outer layer or** *ectoderm* **will become hair, the outer layer of skin, and the nervous system; the middle layer or** *mesoderm* **will form muscles, bones, and the circulatory system; and the inner layer or** *endoderm* **will form the digestive system and the lungs.**

One dramatic way to see these changes is to compare a 3-week-old embryo with an 8-week-old embryo. The 3-week-old embryo shown in the photograph on the left is about 2 millimeters long. Differentiation of cells is underway, but the organism looks more like a salamander than a human being. However,

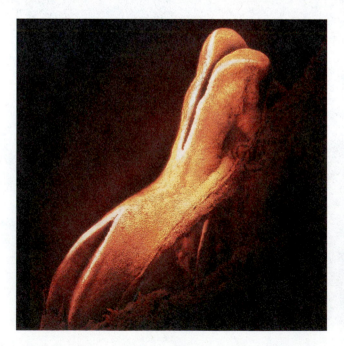

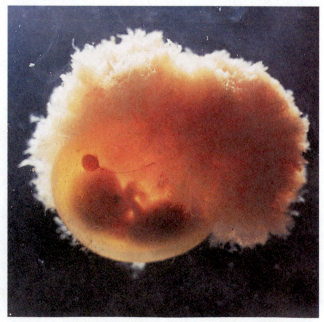

growth and differentiation proceed so rapidly that the 8-week-old embryo in the photograph on the right looks very different: You can see eyes, jaw, arms, and legs. The brain and the nervous system are developing rapidly, and the heart has been beating for nearly a month. Most of the organs found in a mature human are in place, in some form. (The sex organs are a notable exception.) Yet, being only an inch long and weighing a fraction of an ounce, the embryo is much too small for the mother to feel its presence.

Growth in this phase follows two important principles. First, the head develops before the rest of the body. **Such growth from the head to the base of the spine illustrates the *cephalocaudal principle*.** Second, arms and legs develop before hands and feet. **Growth of parts near the center of the body before those that are more distant illustrates the *proximodistal principle*.** In Chapter 3, we'll see that growth after birth also follows these principles.

PERIOD OF THE FETUS (WEEKS 9–38)

The final and longest phase of prenatal development, the *period of the fetus,* extends from the ninth week after conception until birth. Over the course of these seven months, the fetus becomes *much* larger—from less than an ounce at the beginning of this period to 7 or 8 pounds at birth. At about four months, the fetus weighs roughly 4 to 8 ounces, which is finally large enough for the mother to feel its movements.

Just as important are the changes that occur in the different body systems. The testes and ovaries are present at the beginning of the third month. During this month, the testes secrete the male hormone testosterone, which causes a group of cells to develop into the penis, scrotum, and seminal vesicles. In the absence of testosterone, the same cells develop into the fallopian tubes, uterus, and vagina.

By the fifth month, the billions of cells that make up the brain are in place and the brain has begun to function. Some simple reflexes like sucking and swallowing are present, and the mother can sometimes feel the fetus hiccupping!

Gradually, the finishing touches are placed on the many systems that are essential to human life: respiration, digestion, vision, and the like. The chart, which depicts the fetus at about $\frac{1}{8}$ of its actual size, shows some of the highlights of this period.

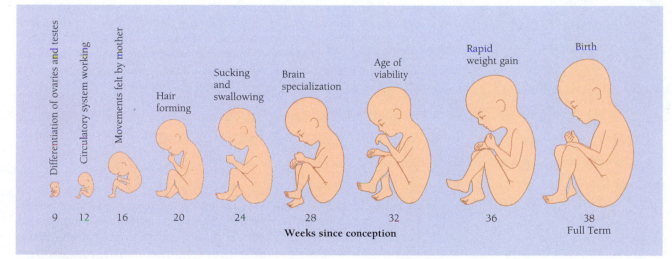

Moore and Persaud, 1993.

You can see that by about 7 months, most systems function well enough that a fetus born at this age has a chance to survive, which is why 7 months is often called the *age of viability*. Babies born this early (or earlier) have trouble breathing, because their lungs are not yet fully mature. Also, they cannot regulate their body temperature very well, because they lack the insulating layer of fat that appears in the eighth month after conception. With modern neonatal intensive care, infants born this early can survive, but they face other challenges, as we'll see later in this chapter.

By the last two months of prenatal development, the fetus is so well developed that it registers experiences. Of course, there's not much in the way of visual experience in the dark world of the uterus, but sounds abound. Microphones placed in the uterus reveal a noise level of about 75 decibels, which is roughly the loudness of a normal conversation. Of course, every second or so the noise level increases as the mother's heart beats (Birnholz & Benacerraf, 1983).

Remarkably, newborns can apparently recognize some of the sounds that they have experienced during prenatal development. DeCasper and Spence (1986) had pregnant women read aloud the famous Dr. Seuss story *The Cat in the Hat*. Mothers did this twice a day for the last $1\frac{1}{2}$ months of pregnancy, which means that, as newborns, their babies had heard *The Cat in the Hat* for more than three hours. These newborns were then allowed to suck on a mechanical nipple connected to a tape recorder in such a way that the baby's sucking could turn the tape on or off. The investigators discovered that babies would suck to hear a tape of their mother reading *The Cat in the Hat* but not to hear her reading other stories. Newborns evidently recognized the familiar, rhythmic quality of *The Cat in the Hat* from the twice-daily "story time" during prenatal development.

Findings like these tell us that the last few months of prenatal development leave the fetus remarkably well prepared for independent living as a newborn baby. Unfortunately, not all babies arrive well prepared, because their prenatal development has been disrupted. Let's see how prenatal development can sometimes go awry.

Influences on Prenatal Development

Take a moment and reread the questions that Eun Jung asked her obstetrician (on pages 51–52). You'll notice that except for the first, her questions concern the potential for harm to her baby-to-be. She wonders about her age and about the safety of computer monitors and drinking a glass of wine. Her concern is well founded. Many general factors, such as a woman's nutritional level, affect the odds that prenatal development may not proceed normally. Also, many specific factors, such as drugs or environmental hazards, are potential sources of harm. Let's look at each of these types of prenatal influence.

GENERAL RISK FACTORS

As the name implies, these factors can have widespread effects on prenatal development.

- *Parental age.* The age of both the mother and the father can affect prenatal development. For women, the prime childbearing years are the 20s and early 30s. Teenage mothers as well as middle-aged (and older) mothers are more likely to have babies with birth defects, including mental retardation. For teenage mothers, problems are usually linked to poor health and to poor prenatal care (Culp et al., 1988). For older mothers, problems typically appear among women who are in poor health (Ales et al., 1990).

Paternal age is also important; the odds that a damaged sperm will fertilize the egg increase steadily as men enter their 30s and 40s. For example, older men are more likely than younger men to contribute the extra 21st chromosome that leads to Down syndrome.

- *Maternal nutrition.* The mother is the sole source of nutrition throughout prenatal development, so a proper diet is vital. Proteins, vitamins, and iron are particularly important for pregnant women. When prenatal nourishment is not adequate, the baby is more likely to be born prematurely and to be underweight. Also, a poor diet can affect the development of the central nervous system and may leave babies vulnerable to illness (Guttmacher & Kaiser, 1986).

- *Maternal stress.* Pregnant women who experience severe, prolonged stress often give birth to premature and irritable babies (Norbeck & Tilden, 1983). This may be because stress causes the secretion of hormones that reduce the flow of oxygen to the fetus while increasing its heart rate and activity level.

We can summarize these general factors by saying that prenatal development is most likely to proceed normally when women are in their 20s and 30s, have adequate health care and adequate nutrition, and lead lives that are free of chronic stress. However, even in these optimal cases, prenatal development can be disrupted by other, more specific influences.

TERATOGENS

In the late 1950s, many pregnant women in Germany took thalidomide, a drug that helped them to sleep. Soon, reports began to emerge that mothers who had taken thalidomide were giving birth to an unusually large number of babies with deformed arms, legs, hands, or fingers (Jensen, Benson, & Bobak, 1981). **Thalidomide was proving to be a powerful *teratogen,* an agent that causes abnormal prenatal development.** Ultimately, more than 7000 babies worldwide were harmed before thalidomide was withdrawn from the market (Moore & Persaud, 1993).

Prompted by the thalidomide disaster, scientists began to study teratogens extensively. Today, we know much about many specific teratogens that cause harm during prenatal development. Most potent teratogens fall into one of three categories: drugs, diseases, and environmental hazards. Let's look at each.

Thalidomide illustrates the harm that drugs can cause during prenatal development. The chart lists several other drugs that are known teratogens. You'll notice that most of the drugs in the list are substances that people use routinely—alcohol, aspirin, caffeine, nicotine. When consumed by pregnant women, they present special dangers. Alcohol is a good example. Women who drink regularly throughout pregnancy often have babies with cognitive and motor deficits (Barr et al., 1990). **Pregnant women who consume large quantities of alcoholic beverages often give birth to babies who are afflicted with *fetal alcohol syndrome.*** Children with this syndrome usually grow more slowly than normal, have heart problems, and are mentally retarded. As you can see in the photo-

Teratogenic Drugs and Their Consequences	
Drug	*Potential Consequences*
Alcohol	Fetal alcohol syndrome, cognitive deficits, heart damage, growth retardation
Aspirin	Deficits in intelligence, attention, and motor skill
Caffeine	Lower birth weight and decreased muscle tone
Cocaine and heroin	Retarded growth, irritability in newborns
Marijuana	Lower birth weight and less motor control
Nicotine	Retarded growth, facial deformities

graph, their faces are usually deformed—the head is small, the upper lip is thin, the nose is short, and the eyes are widely spaced. The syndrome is most likely when pregnant women drink 3 or more ounces of alcohol daily, but even women who drink 1 ounce daily have a 10% risk of giving birth to a baby with fetal alcohol syndrome (Abel, 1980).

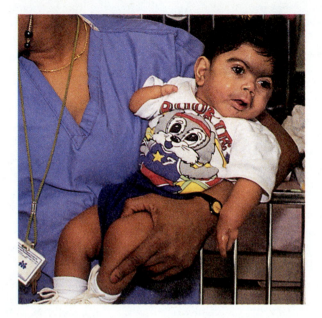

Diseases form another category of teratogens; several are listed in the chart. Acquired Immune Deficiency Syndrome—commonly known as AIDS—is a recent addition to the list. When women with AIDS become pregnant, about one-third of the time they give birth to babies who have the disease. Although adults often don't show symptoms of AIDS until years after they have been infected, infants who are infected usually show symptoms by approximately 6 months of age. The virus attacks the brain, leading to seizures and retarded mental development. After symptoms appear, most infants die in less than a year (Chamberlain et al., 1991; Schmitt et al., 1991).

Teratogenic Diseases and Their Consequences	
Disease	*Potential Consequences*
AIDS	Frequent infections, neurological disorders, death
Cytomegalovirus	Deafness, blindness, abnormally small head, mental retardation
Genital herpes	Encephalitis, enlarged spleen, improper blood clotting
Rubella	Mental retardation; damage to eyes, ears, and heart
Syphilis	Damage to the central nervous system, teeth, and bones

AIDS is unlike other teratogenic diseases in always being fatal, but otherwise it shares a common feature. The only way to guarantee that these diseases will not harm development is for the pregnant woman to be sure that she does not contract the disease. Medicines that may help to treat a woman after she has become ill do not prevent the disease from damaging the developing individual.

Environmental hazards create the third category of teratogens. A byproduct of life in an industrialized world is that people are often exposed to toxins in the food they eat, fluids they drink, and the air they breathe. The table lists several environmental hazards that are known teratogens. You'll notice that X rays are included in the list, but radiation associated with computer monitors or video-display terminals (VDTs) is not. Several major studies have examined the impact of exposure to the electromagnetic fields that are generated by VDTs. For example, Schnorr and her colleagues (1991) compared the outcomes of pregnancies in telephone operators who worked at VDTs at least 25 hours weekly with operators who never used VDTs. For both groups of women, about 15% of their pregnancies ended in miscarriages. Other studies have found no links between exposure to VDTs and birth defects (Parazzini et al., 1993). Evidently, VDTs can be used safely by pregnant women.

Environmental Teratogens and Their Consequences

Hazard	Potential Consequences
Lead	Mental retardation
Mercury	Retarded growth, mental retardation, cerebral palsy
X rays	Retarded growth, leukemia, mental retardation

Most environmentally based teratogens are chemicals associated with industrial wastes. The quantities involved are usually minute. However, as is the case with many teratogens, amounts that go unnoticed by an adult can cause serious damage to prenatal development. We discuss such an example, polychlorinated biphenyls (PCBs), in our Spotlight on Research.

Industrial Toxins and Mental Development

SPOTLIGHT ON RESEARCH

For many years, polychlorinated biphenyls (PCBs) were used in electrical transformers and in paints. PCBs were banned by the U.S. government in the 1970s. However, like many industrial byproducts, they have seeped into the waterways, where they can contaminate fish and wildlife.

The amount of PCBs in a typical contaminated fish does not affect adults, but extensive exposure to PCBs during prenatal development *is* harmful. Sandra Jacobson, Joseph Jacobson, and their colleagues (1985, 1990, 1992) have studied a sample of more than 200 children whose mothers consumed, before and during their pregnancies, large quantities of PCB-contaminated salmon and trout from Lake Michigan. The PCBs accumulated in the women's bodies and were transferred through the placenta to the fetus. To estimate prenatal exposure to PCBs, the Jacobsons measured concentrations of PCBs in (a) blood obtained from the umbilical cord, and (b) for mothers who were breast-feeding, a sample of breast milk.

By accepted clinical standards, the babies were normal at birth. Yet when the Jacobsons first tested them at 7 months of age, infants who had had the greatest exposure to PCBs had poorer memory skills than babies with the least exposure. When the children were tested again, at 4 years of age, memory

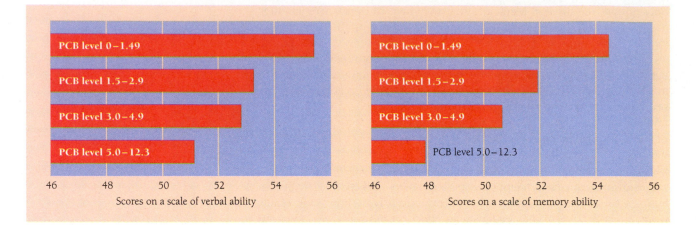

deficits were still present and were accompanied by deficits in verbal ability. Looking at the graph, you can see that verbal and memory scores are lowest for the 4-year-olds who had the greatest prenatal exposure to PCBs. All of these scores *are* in the normal range—compared with thalidomide or rubella, exposure to PCBs produces relatively mild defects. Nevertheless, because of their reduced verbal and memory skills, these youngsters will probably have some trouble in school, such as in learning to read.   🐾

By putting together all of the information about harm caused by drugs, diseases, and environmental hazards, we can identify some important general principles about how teratogens usually work (Vorhees & Mollnow, 1987; Wilson, 1977).

- *The impact of teratogens depends on the genotype of the organism.* Thalidomide produces deformities in developing humans but not in developing rats or rabbits, which had been used in some of the tests to evaluate the safety of thalidomide. Also, some women who took thalidomide gave birth to babies with normal limbs. Others, taking comparable doses of thalidomide at the same time in their pregnancies, gave birth to babies with deformed arms and legs. Apparently, heredity can make some individuals more susceptible than others to a teratogen.
- *The impact of teratogens changes over the course of prenatal development.* This principle shouldn't surprise you. As we learned earlier in the chapter, different kinds of growth occur in each of the three periods of prenatal development, so teratogens typically have different consequences during each period. Exposure to teratogens during the period of the zygote usually results in spontaneous abortion of the fertilized egg. Exposure during the period of the embryo produces major defects in bodily structure, like the ill-formed or missing limbs that were common in thalidomide babies. Finally, exposure to thalidomide during the period of the fetus can produce minor defects in bodily structure or can cause body systems to function improperly.

    The chart on page 61 illustrates the relation between the timing of exposure to a teratogen and its impact on prenatal development. The chart also shows phases at which different structures or systems are most susceptible to teratogens. Red shading indicates a time of maximum vulnerability; yellow shading indicates a time when the developing organism is

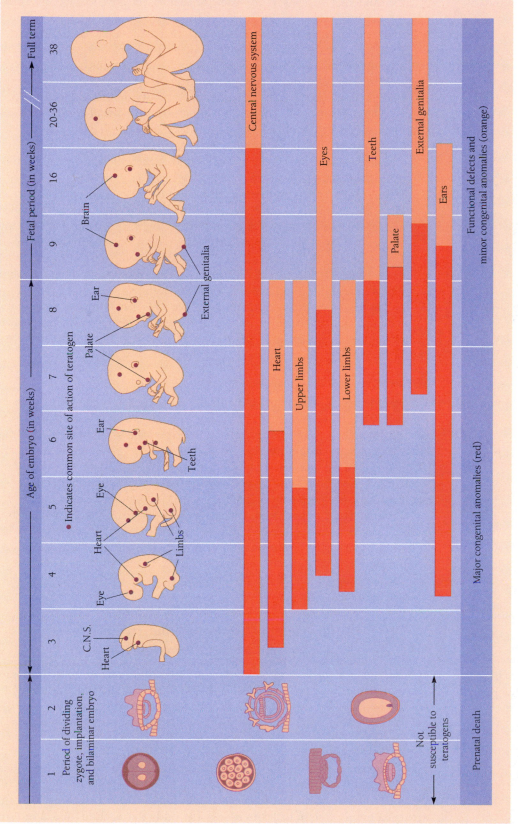

Moore and Persaud, 1993.

less vulnerable. The heart, for example, is most sensitive to teratogens during the first half of the embryonic period. Exposure to teratogens before this time rarely produces heart damage; exposure after results in milder damage. In the case of thalidomide, women who took the drug 34–38 days after the start of their last menstrual period often gave birth to babies with missing ears. When women took the drug 38–42 days after their last period, their babies typically had an outer ear, but one that was deformed.

- *Each teratogen affects a specific aspect (or aspects) of prenatal development.* Teratogens do not harm all aspects of development. Exposure to rubella (German measles), for example, produces problems with the eyes, ears, and heart, whereas exposure to thalidomide damaged the limbs and sometimes the heart and kidneys.

- *Damage from teratogens is not always evident at birth but may appear later in life.* Some miscarriages occur because a pregnant woman does not produce enough of the hormone progesterone. Between 1947 and 1971, many women who were prone to miscarriages took a drug—diethylstilbestrol or DES—that was thought to increase the body's production of progesterone. Their babies were apparently normal at birth. However, as adults, daughters are more likely to have a rare cancer of the vagina and to have difficulties becoming pregnant themselves; the sons may have abnormal seminal fluid and are at risk for cancer of the testes (Meyers, 1983). This is a case in which the impact of the teratogen is not evident until decades after birth.

THE REAL WORLD OF PRENATAL RISK

We have discussed risk factors individually, as if each were the only potential threat to prenatal development. In reality, teratogens and general risk factors can act in concert to influence the course of prenatal development. The sad news is that many infants are exposed to multiple risks. Pregnant women who drink often smoke and drink coffee (Barr et al., 1990). Many of these same women may have poor nutrition and lead stressful lives. When all of these risks are combined, unfortunately, prenatal development will rarely be optimal.

From what we've said here, you may think that the developing child has little chance of escaping harm. But most babies *are* born in good health. Of course, a good policy for pregnant women is to avoid drugs, diseases, and environmental hazards that are known teratogens. This, coupled with thorough prenatal medical care and adequate nutrition, is the best recipe for normal prenatal development.

Preventing, Diagnosing, and Treating Abnormal Prenatal Development

"I really don't care whether I have a boy or girl, just as long as it's healthy." Legions of parents worldwide have felt this way, but until recently, all they could do was hope for the best. Today, however, advances in technology mean that parents can have a much better idea whether their baby will develop normally.

GENETIC COUNSELING

Like Leslie and Glenn in the first chapter-opening vignette, many people at risk for a hereditary disorder are afraid of passing it on to their children. **These individuals often benefit from *genetic counseling,* in which a counselor constructs a family tree in order to assess the odds that a child would inherit**

the disorder. If the family tree suggests that a prospective parent is likely to be a carrier of the disorder, blood samples can be used to determine his or her genotype for some disorders. Such testing could determine if Leslie (or Glenn) carries the recessive allele associated with sickle-cell anemia. Genes associated with cystic fibrosis, PKU, Duchenne muscular dystrophy, and hemophilia can also be detected through testing.

Armed with this information, a genetic counselor can advise prospective parents about their choices, which would include conceiving a child "naturally," conceiving a child with the new technologies discussed in the Current Controversies feature, or adopting a child.

PRENATAL DIAGNOSIS

Traditionally, obstetricians tracked the progress of prenatal development by feeling the size and position of the fetus through a woman's abdomen. This technique was not very precise and, of course, couldn't be done at all until the fetus was large enough to feel. Today, several new techniques have revolutionized prenatal diagnosis. **The most common is *ultrasound,* in which sound waves reflected from the fetus are used to generate an image of the fetus like the one in the photograph.** Ultrasound can be used to determine the position and sex of the fetus, to detect multiple pregnancies, and to identify gross physical deformities. Typically, it can be used as early as 4 or 5 weeks after conception; before this time the fetus is not large enough to generate an image that can be interpreted.

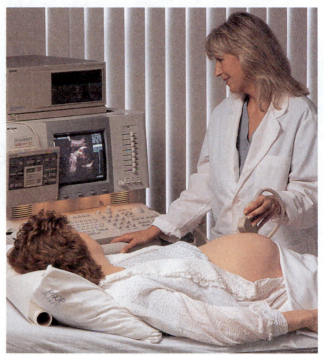

Ultrasound is often a standard element of modern prenatal care. In pregnancies where a genetic disorder is suspected, two other techniques are particularly valuable, because they provide a sample of fetal cells that can be analyzed. **In *amniocentesis,* a needle is inserted through the mother's abdomen into the amnion to obtain a sample of the amniotic fluid that surrounds the fetus.** As you can see in the diagram, ultrasound is used to guide the needle into the uterus. The fluid contains skin cells that can be cultured and then analyzed.

A drawback to amniocentesis is that although the amniotic fluid is extracted at about 16 weeks after conception, another 3 weeks must pass for the individual cells to grow sufficiently to allow testing. **A procedure that can be used much earlier in pregnancy is *chorionic villus sampling,* in which a sample of tissue is obtained from parts of the chorion that form the placenta.** The diagram on page 64

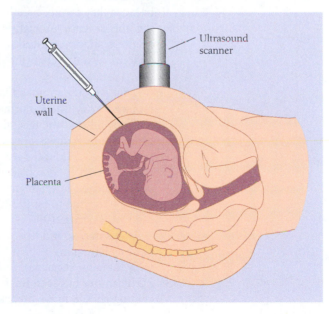

Ultrasound scanner

Uterine wall

Placenta

shows that a small tube is inserted through the vagina and into the uterus. This procedure can be used within 8 or 9 weeks after conception, and results are available within 24 hours.

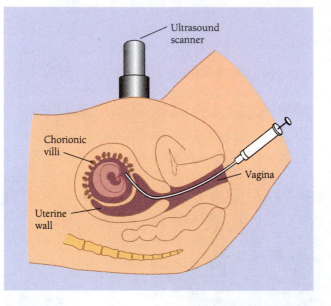

With the samples that are obtained from either amniocentesis or chorionic villus sampling, roughly 200 different genetic disorders can be detected. These procedures are virtually error-free, but there is a price. Miscarriages are slightly more likely—1 or 2%—after amniocentesis or chorionic villus sampling (Cunningham, MacDonald, & Gant, 1989). Women must balance the benefit of more information about their baby-to-be against the slight risk of a possible miscarriage.

TREATMENT

Diagnostic tools like ultrasound, amniocentesis, and chorionic villus sampling have made it much easier to determine whether prenatal development is progressing normally. When it is not, until recently a woman's options have been limited: She could continue the pregnancy or end it. However, the list of options is expanding because of progress in the new field of prenatal treatment. Some prenatal disorders are being treated medically, by administering drugs or hormones to the fetus. In one case, a fetus had an enlarged thyroid gland that would have made delivery difficult. The hormone thyroxine was injected into the amniotic fluid, which caused the thyroid gland to shrink, allowing a normal delivery (Davidson et al., 1991).

Another path is fetal surgery, in which the fetus is partially removed from the uterus, operated on, and then returned to the uterus. One example involves repair of the diaphragm, which separates the lungs from other organs in the abdomen. If the diaphragm does not develop properly, babies often die at birth because they cannot breathe properly. To correct an abnormal diaphragm, during the seventh or eighth month of pregnancy, surgeons cut through the mother's abdominal wall to expose the fetus. Then they cut through the fetal abdominal wall, repair the diaphragm, and return the fetus to the uterus (Kolata, 1990a).

Yet another approach is genetic engineering, in which defective genes are replaced by synthetic normal genes. Take PKU as an example. Remember that if a baby inherits the recessive allele for PKU from both parents, it lacks the enzyme to break down phenylalanine. In theory, it should be possible to take a sample of cells from the fetus, remove the recessive genes from the 12th pair of chromosomes, and replace them with the dominant genes. These "repaired" cells could be injected into the fetus, where they would multiply and cause enough enzyme to be produced to break down phenylalanine, thereby avoiding PKU (Verma, 1990).

This may sound like science fiction, but each of these techniques *has* been used with humans. Each is highly experimental—the first efforts at "gene repair" with humans began in 1990. Failures are common. However, the end of the 20th century has seen huge progress in prenatal diagnosis, and the turn of the century should make prenatal treatment a reality.

Postscript: Answers to Eun Jung's Questions

Now you can return to Eun Jung's questions (pages 51–52) and answer them for her. If you're not certain, we'll help by giving you the pages in this chapter where the answers appear:

- Question about baby's movement—page 55
- Questions about alcohol and radiation from VDTs—page 59
- Question about mental retardation—page 56

TEST YOURSELF

1. The period of the zygote ends _____.
2. The heart begins to beat during the _____.
3. Exposure to a teratogen during the period of the _____ usually results in minor defects in body structure or body systems that don't function properly.
4. Important general risk factors include maternal age, maternal nutrition, and _____.
5. The primary techniques of prenatal diagnosis used today include ultrasound, amniocentesis, and _____.
6. From the general risk factors and teratogens described on pages 56–62, select an example that represents a normative age-graded influence on development, one that represents a normative history-graded influence, and another that represents a nonnormative influence.

Happy Birthday!

LEARNING OBJECTIVES

- *What are the phases of labor and delivery? What is natural childbirth and what are its benefits?*
- *What are some complications associated with childbirth?*
- *How do reflexes help newborns interact with the world?*
- *What behavioral states are common among newborns?*

In the last several weeks of pregnancy, many women find that sleeping and breathing become more difficult, that they tire more rapidly, that they become constipated, and that their legs and feet swell. Women look forward to birth, both to relieve their discomfort and, of course, to see their baby.

Labor and Delivery

Labor is an appropriate name for childbirth, which is the most intense, prolonged physical effort that humans experience. Labor is usually divided into the three stages shown in the diagram on page 66.

Answers: (1) *at 2 weeks after conception,* (2) *period of the embryo,* (3) *fetus,* (4) *maternal stress,* (5) *chorionic villus sampling*

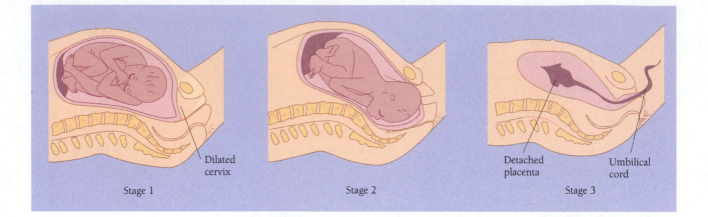

Stage 1 — Dilated cervix

Stage 2

Stage 3 — Detached placenta — Umbilical cord

- In stage 1, which may last from 12 to 24 hours for a first birth, the uterus starts to contract. The first contractions are weak and irregular. Gradually, they become stronger and more rhythmic, enlarging the cervix (the opening from the uterus to the vagina) to approximately 10 centimeters.
- In stage 2, the baby passes through the cervix and enters the vagina. The mother helps to push the baby along by contracting muscles in her abdomen. **Soon the top of the baby's head appears, an event known as** *crowning.* Within about an hour, the baby is delivered.
- In stage 3, which lasts only minutes, the mother pushes a few more times to expel the placenta (also called, appropriately, the *afterbirth*).

The times given for each of the stages are only approximations; the actual times vary greatly among women. For most women, labor with their second and subsequent children is much more rapid. Stage 1 may last 4 to 6 hours, and stage 2 may be as brief as 20 minutes.

CHILDBIRTH ALTERNATIVES

Among the Jarara of South America, the birth of a child is a public event. In this tribal culture, the entire community—adults and children alike—watches as a woman gives birth (Jordan, 1980). In industrialized countries like the United States, by contrast, birth is usually a private affair that takes place in a hospital. For much of the 20th century, only the mother and medical personnel were present during labor and delivery. Since the 1960s, however, many people have tried more "natural" or prepared approaches to childbirth, in which labor and delivery are seen as life events to be celebrated, not medical procedures to be endured. Fathers and other relatives are often present, and unnecessary medical procedures are avoided. Labor and delivery occur in a birthing center—homelike hospital rooms that encourage women to be more relaxed.

Childbirth classes play an important role in prepared approaches. The basic idea is that birth is more likely to be rewarding and less likely to be frightening if both mothers and fathers are well prepared. In these classes, (a) participants learn the basic facts about labor and delivery, (b) women learn breathing techniques that help them relax as the contractions become more and more intense, and (c) people learn how to "coach" the mother-to-be through labor, offering support and encouragement (Broome & Koehler, 1986).

Although Marlena, the pregnant woman in the last chapter-opening vignette, may have her doubts about childbirth classes, research shows that they *are* useful (Hetherington, 1990). For example, compared to mothers who do not attend childbirth classes, mothers who do attend report less pain and use less medication during delivery.

For the most part, even women who do attend childbirth classes will use some form of medication to reduce the pain of labor. Typically, such medications cross the placenta and affect the baby. If a woman receives large doses of pain-relieving medication, her baby may seem withdrawn or irritable for days or even weeks (Brazelton, Nugent, & Lester, 1987). These effects are temporary; nevertheless, mothers may get the unfortunate impression that they have a difficult baby. The best advice is to use as little medication during delivery as possible.

BIRTH COMPLICATIONS

Birth requires that the newborn adjust rapidly to a new environment outside the uterus. Breathing is the most important of the many changes that the newborn must make. Within moments after birth, babies must draw oxygen from their own lungs instead of from blood supplied from their mother, via the placenta. **If the umbilical cord connecting the baby to the placenta is pinched or tangled during delivery, or if the newborn's lungs do not react properly, the result is *anoxia,* lack of oxygen.** Lacking oxygen, cells begin to die, particularly those in the brain. Severe anoxia can cause mental retardation and cerebral palsy (Apgar & Beck, 1974).

Problems also arise when babies are born too early or too small. Normally, a baby spends about 38 weeks developing before being born. **Babies born before the 36th week are called *preterm* or *premature*.** In the first year or so, premature infants often lag behind full-term infants in many facets of development. However, by 2 or 3 years of age, such differences have vanished, and most premature infants develop normally (Greenberg & Crnic, 1988).

Prospects are usually not as bright for babies who are small for their age. Though born after a normal-length pregnancy, they are much smaller than normal, usually because the mother's nutrition was inadequate or because of congenital infections (Allen, 1984). **Newborns who weigh 2500 grams (5.5 pounds) or less are said to have *low birth weight*; newborns weighing less than 1500 grams (3.3 pounds) are said to have *very low birth weight*; and those weighing less than 1000 grams (2.2 pounds) are said to have *extremely low birth weight*.**

Babies with very or extremely low birth weight do not fare well. Many do not survive; those who live often lag behind in the development of intellectual and motor skills (Klein, Hack, & Breslau, 1989). The odds are better for newborns who weigh more than 1500 grams. Most survive. Some will develop normally, but others will always lag behind. Why? The Forces in Action feature provides some clues.

What Determines Life Outcomes for Low-Birth-Weight Babies?

FORCES IN ACTION

Low birth weight is an example of a biological force that apparently does not always influence development in the same way for all children. Why do some low-birth-weight babies seem to recover completely, whereas others do not? A sociocultural force turns out to be critical: the quality of care that these babies receive in the hospital and at home. Low-birth-weight babies can thrive *if* they receive excellent medical care and their home environment is supportive and stimulating. Unfortunately, not all low-birth-weight babies have such optimal experiences. Many receive inadequate medical care because their families are living in poverty. Others experience stress or disorder in their family life. In such cases, development is usually delayed in low-birth-weight babies.

The importance of a supportive environment for low-birth-weight babies is underscored by the results of a 30-year longitudinal study by Werner (1989), covering all children born on the Hawaiian island of Kauai in 1955. The key to a successful outcome turns out to be the influence of a stable family environment, which Werner defined as the presence of two supportive, mentally healthy parents throughout childhood. Low-birth-weight children who grew up in stable homes were indistinguishable from children born without birth complications. However, when low-birth-weight children experienced an unstable family environment—due, for example, to divorce, parental alcoholism, or mental illness—they lagged behind their peers in intellectual and social development.

Thus, when biological and sociocultural forces are both harmful—low birth weight *plus* inadequate medical care or family stress—the prognosis for babies is grim. The message to parents of low-birth-weight newborns is clear: They need not despair, because excellent caregiving can usually compensate for all but the most severe birth problems (Werner & Smith, 1992).

The Newborn

Only doting parents can honestly call their newborn baby "beautiful." In reality, the newborn is homely, as shown in this photograph of Ben Kail when he was 20 seconds old. Like many newborns, he is covered with blood and vernix, a white-colored "grease" that protected his skin during the months of prenatal development. Ben's head is temporarily distorted from the journey through the birth canal; he has a beer belly; and he is bow-legged. Of course, Ben's appearance is characteristic of most newborns, as we'll learn in the See for Yourself feature.

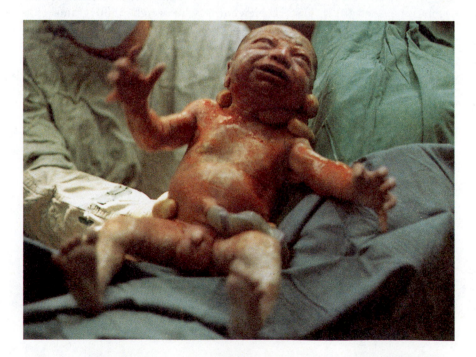

Visit a Newborn Nursery

Words can hardly capture the miracle of a newborn baby. If you have never seen a newborn, you need to see one—or even better, a roomful. Arrange to visit the maternity ward of a local hospital, which will include a nursery for newborns. Through a large viewing window, you will be able to observe as many as 15 or 20 newborns. Almost all will be less than 3 days old because health insurance usually pays for only two nights in a hospital following child-birth. These babies will no longer be covered with blood or vernix, but you will be able to see how the newborn's head was distorted in its journey from the uterus.

As you watch the babies, look for reflexive behavior and changes in states (topics that we cover in the next few pages). Watch while a baby sucks its fingers. Find a baby who seems to be awake and alert, then note how long the baby stays this way. When alertness wanes, watch for the behaviors that replace it. Finally, be sure to observe how the newborns look and act differently from each other. Do all babies respond similarly to stimulation such as light and sound? When they're awake, are some babies more active than others? A recurring theme in this book is an appreciation of the wonderful variety and diversity found among human beings, and this is already evident in humans who are hours or days old. See for yourself!   ❧

ASSESSING THE NEWBORN

To evaluate the newborn baby's condition, medical personnel will compute an *Apgar score,* named after the physician who devised the test in 1953. Five vital signs are evaluated 1 and 5 minutes after birth: heart rate, respiration, muscle tone, color, and reflex irritability (which refers to sneezing and coughing). Each vital sign receives a score of 0, 1, or 2, with 2 being the optimal score. For example, a newborn whose muscles are completely limp receives a 0; a baby who shows strong movements of arms and legs receives a 2. The five scores are added together, with a score of 7 or more indicating a baby who is in good physical condition. A score of 4 to 6 means that the newborn will need special attention and care. A score of 3 or less signals a life-threatening situation that requires emergency medical care (Apgar, 1953).

The Apgar provides a quick, approximate assessment of the newborn's status, primarily if the baby is in immediate danger. For a thorough, comprehensive evaluation of the newborn's well-being, pediatricians and other child-development specialists may administer the Neonatal Behavioral Assessment Scale or NBAS for short (Brazelton, 1984). This test measures a broad range of newborn abilities, including reflexes, hearing, vision, alertness, irritability, and consolability. The NBAS, in conjunction with a thorough physical examination, is an effective way to determine whether the newborn is functioning normally. Scores from the NBAS can, for example, be used to diagnose disorders of the central nervous system (Brazelton, Nugent, & Lester, 1987).

NEWBORN REFLEXES

Most newborns are well prepared to begin interacting with their world. **The newborn is endowed with a rich set of *reflexes*—unlearned responses that are triggered by a specific form of stimulation.** The chart on page 70 shows the variety of reflexes commonly found in newborns. Some reflexes are designed to pave the way for newborns to get the nutrients that they need to grow: The rooting and sucking reflexes ensure that the newborn is well prepared to begin

Some Major Reflexes Found in Newborns		
Name	Response	Significance
Babinski	A baby's toes fan out when the sole of the foot is stroked from heel to toe.	Unknown
Blink	A baby's eyes close in response to bright light or loud noise.	Protects the eyes
Moro	A baby throws its arms out and then inward (as if embracing) in response to loud noise or when its head falls.	May help a baby to cling to its mother
Palmar	A baby grasps an object placed in the palm of its hand	Precursor to voluntary grasping
Rooting	When a baby's cheek is stroked, it turns its head toward the cheek that was stroked and opens its mouth.	Helps a baby to find the nipple
Stepping	A baby who is held upright by an adult and is then moved forward begins to step rhythmically.	Precursor to voluntary walking
Sucking	A baby sucks when an object is placed in its mouth.	Permits feeding
Withdrawal	A baby withdraws its foot when the sole is pricked with a pin.	Protects a baby from unpleasant stimulation

Adapted from Berk, 1994, Table 4-1.

a new diet of life-sustaining milk. Other reflexes seem designed to protect the newborn from danger in the environment. The eyeblink and withdrawal reflexes, for example, help newborns to avoid unpleasant stimulation.

Still other reflexes serve as the foundation for larger, voluntary patterns of motor activity. For example, look at the baby in the photograph, who is showing us the stepping reflex. These motions look like precursors to walking, so it probably won't surprise you to learn that babies who practice the stepping reflex often learn to walk earlier than those who don't practice this reflex (Zelazo, 1993).

Reflexes are also important because they can be a useful way to determine whether the newborn's nervous system is working properly. For example, infants with damage to the sciatic nerve, which is found in the spinal cord, do not show the withdrawal reflex. As another example, infants who have problems with the lower part of the spine do not show the Babinski reflex. If these or other reflexes are weak or missing altogether, a thorough physical and behavioral assessment is called for.

NEWBORN STATES

Tired new parents are generally grateful that newborns sleep as much as they do: 16 to 18 hours a day is a common total, with several brief waking periods between long naps. If you've ever seen newborns asleep, you know that they can be extraordinarily active. **Instead of just lying there peacefully, their arms and legs may move, they may grimace, their eyes may dart beneath their eyelids; together, these features define** *irregular* **or** *rapid-eye-movement (REM) sleep.* Roughly half of newborns' sleep is REM sleep, a time when the body is quite active. Brain waves register fast activity, the heart beats more rapidly, and breathing is more rapid. *Regular* **or** *non-REM sleep* **is much closer to our image of sleep as restful and peaceful: Breathing, heart rate, and brain activity are steady, and newborns lie quietly, without the twitching associated with REM sleep.**

The function of REM sleep is still debated. Older children and adults dream during REM sleep, and brain waves during REM sleep resemble those of an alert, awake person. Consequently, many scientists believe that REM sleep provides the brain with stimulation that helps to foster growth in the nervous system (Roffwarg, Muzio, & Dement, 1966).

Newborns spend most of their waking hours in one of three states (Berg & Berg, 1987; Wolff, 1987):

- *Alert inactivity.* The baby is calm, with eyes open, and attentive; the baby appears to be deliberately inspecting the environment.
- *Waking activity.* The baby's eyes are open but seem unfocused; the baby moves arms or legs in bursts of uncoordinated motion.
- *Crying.* The baby cries vigorously, usually accompanied by agitated but uncoordinated motion.

Of these states, crying captures the attention of parents and researchers alike. If you haven't spent much time around newborns, you might think that all crying is pretty much alike. In fact, scientists and parents can identify three distinctive types of cries (Holden, 1988). **A** *basic cry,* **starting softly and gradually becoming more intense, usually occurs when a baby is hungry or tired; a** *mad cry* **is a more intense version of a basic cry; and a** *pain cry* **begins with a sudden, long burst of crying, followed by a long pause, and gasping.** Thus, crying represents the newborn's first venture into interpersonal communication; by crying, babies can tell their parents that they are hungry or tired, angry, or hurt. By responding to these cries, parents are encouraging their newborn's efforts to communicate.

Transitions between crying and other states occur frequently in newborns (though sometimes not quickly enough for parents, as we see in the You May Be Wondering feature). Newborns typically go through a cycle of wakefulness and sleep about every four hours. That is, they will be awake for about an hour, sleep for three hours, then start the cycle anew. During the hour when newborns are awake, they move between the different waking states several times. Cycles of alert inactivity, waking activity, and crying are common.

As babies grow older, the sleep-wake cycle gradually begins to correspond to the day-night cycle. By three or four months of age, most babies will sleep through the night—a major milestone for their bleary-eyed parents. When babies are awake, periods of alert inactivity become more common and last longer; infants are rapidly progressing from a reflexive, sleeping creature to one who deliberately explores the environment.

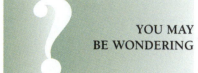

YOU MAY BE WONDERING

How to Calm a Crying Baby

Newborns spend 2–3 hours each day crying or on the verge of crying. Of course, parents are concerned when their baby cries. If they can't quiet a crying baby, their concern mounts and can easily give way to frustration and annoyance.

For centuries, mothers have relied on a number of different tricks for soothing their babies. Science hasn't contributed many new techniques, but it has told us which techniques work best and why.

The first step should always be to determine why the baby began to cry. Is it hungry? Is its diaper wet? Addressing the needs that caused the crying will often quiet a baby. If crying persists, the best method is to lift the baby to the shoulder and rock it or walk with it. Being upright, restrained, and in physical contact with a person, while moving—this combination helps to calm babies. Also effective is swaddling—wrapping the baby tightly in a blanket—and then rocking it in a cradle or taking it for a ride in a baby carriage. Here, too, the key seems to be the combination of bodily restraint and movement. (As the cartoon suggests, a modern variant is to strap the newborn into a car seat and go on a

HI AND LOIS, © 1994. Reprinted with special permission of King Features Syndicate.

drive. This technique was used once as a last resort when Ben Kail was 10 days old and had been crying uncontrollably for more than an hour. After about the 12th time around the block, he finally fell asleep!) Babies can also be soothed by giving them a pacifier; sucking apparently allows them to control their own level of arousal (Campos, 1989).

None of these techniques is foolproof. Some will work well for one baby but not for another. Sometimes you may need to combine techniques, such as holding a swaddled baby to your shoulder. If all of these fails, just put the baby down. Every so often, just to make you wonder, a baby will stop crying spontaneously and go right to sleep! 🦋

TEMPERAMENT

If you've seen a number of babies together, did you notice some who were quiet most of the time, alongside others who cried often and impatiently? Maybe you saw some infants who responded warmly to strangers next to others who seemed shy? **These characteristics of infants indicate a consistent style or pattern to an infant's behavior and, collectively, they define an infant's *temperament*.**

According to one important theory, proposed by Buss and Plomin (1984), temperament includes three dimensions:

- *Emotionality* **refers to the strength of the infant's emotional response to a situation, the ease with which that response is triggered, and the ease with which the infant can be returned to a nonemotional state.** At one extreme are infants whose emotional responses are strong, easily triggered, and not easily calmed; at the other are infants whose responses seem subdued, relatively difficult to elicit, and readily soothed.
- *Activity* **refers to the tempo and vigor of a child's actions.** Active infants are always busy exploring their environment, and they enjoy vigorous play. Inactive infants have a more controlled behavioral tempo and are more likely to enjoy quiet play.
- *Sociability* **refers to a preference for being with other people.** Some infants relish contact with and attention from other people and prefer play that involves others; other infants enjoy solitude and are quite content to play alone with toys.

Not all developmentalists agree that these are the only dimensions of temperament (Goldsmith et al., 1987), but it is clear that temperament consists of a handful of biologically based dimensions.

Is an emotional newborn likely to be emotional as a 12-month-old and as a 12-year-old? Yes, at least to some extent. Studies of temperamental dimensions reveal reasonable stability. For example, Stifter and Fox (1990) studied responses in two situations known to be moderately stressful to infants: As newborns, they were allowed to suck briefly on a pacifier, which was then taken away from them. Later, as 5-month-olds, mothers gently restrained their infant's arms, prohibiting all movement. Of the newborns who cried when the pacifier was removed, 53% cried when their hands were restrained; of the newborns who did not cry, 72% did not cry when their hands were restrained. In other words, emotional reactivity, as indicated by crying, was consistent from birth to 5 months of age.

This study is typical of research showing that emotionality, like other temperamental dimensions, is fairly stable (Bates, 1987). However, the stability is not perfect. In the Stifter and Fox study, for example, about one-third of the infants cried on one occasion but not the other. Perhaps it is best to think of temperament as a predisposition. Some infants are naturally predisposed to be sociable, emotional, or active; others *can* act in these ways, too, but only if the behaviors are nurtured by parents and others (Wachs, 1987).

Temperamental characteristics remind us that, although infants have many features in common, each baby also seems to have its own unique personality from the very start. From these early differences, development can proceed along many different routes. This theme will emerge in many parts of this book, including Chapter 3.

TEST YOURSELF

1. _____ occurs in stage 3 of labor.
2. Childbirth classes provide information about labor and delivery, _____, and show men how to be supportive coaches during labor.
3. When preterm and full-term infants are compared at 2 or 3 years of age, _____.
4. Two reflexes that make it easier for babies to get milk from a nipple are the _____ and the sucking reflexes.

5. The _____ is based on five vital functions and provides a quick indication of a newborn's physical health.

6. A baby lying calmly with its eyes open and focused is in a state of _____.

7. Max, a father-to-be, said, "I'm sure I'll worry a lot about our baby, because babies are so helpless; they can't do anything." What could you say to Max about factors that contribute to healthy prenatal development? What could you tell Max about newborns' skills that would convince him that, all things considered, newborns are quite talented?

Putting It All Together

Since the beginning of this chapter, we've gone from conception, through 38 weeks of prenatal development, to a newborn baby. We saw the mighty impact of the shuffling of genes that occurs at conception. Sometimes single genes influence development, as in the case of the sickle-cell anemia that so frightens Leslie. More often, many genes work together to influence growth, with the outcome depending strongly on the impact of the environment. We learned that structures and processes unfold in a predictable sequence during prenatal development. Knowing this sequence, we can understand how and why prenatal development sometimes goes wrong. We used this knowledge to answer some of Eun Jung's questions about her pregnancy. Finally, we looked at labor and delivery, where we saw some of the advantages of a prepared childbirth such as Marlena plans to have. We learned that newborn babies are endowed with reflexes that prepare

them well for life outside the uterus and that their behavior is already organized into a number of distinct waking and sleeping states.

This chapter, more than most of the others in this book, has emphasized the biological components of the biopsychosocial framework. Even here, however, biological forces do not operate in isolation but in interaction with the other elements of the framework. Phenotypes depend on the genotype *and* the environment to which the genotype is exposed. Prenatal development reflects biologically programmed events inside the uterus as well as the experiences that the child-to-be has in the uterus.

The development that we have traced in this chapter serves as a prelude to the remainder of life-span human development. Each succeeding movement builds on the themes established in the prelude, as we'll see in the next chapter, which is devoted to infancy.

Thinking about Development

1. How does the concept of reaction range help to explain how and why nature *and* nurture are almost always involved in the developmental equation?

2. In Chapter 1, we asked you to imagine how Jacqui's pregnancy might be different if she were a married 24-year-old instead of a 14-year-old living on the street. Now that you know more about influences on prenatal development, describe in detail how the pregnancies could differ.

3. Do studies on the long-term effects of prematurity and low birth weight provide evidence for continuity in development or for discontinuity in development?

4. Explain how niche-picking could lead newborns of different temperaments to have very different experiences as they grow up.

Summary

In the Beginning: 23 Pairs of Chromosomes

Mechanisms of Heredity

■ Humans have 23 pairs of chromosomes—22 pairs of autosomes plus the sex chromosomes. Each chromosome includes many genes, which are the functional units of heredity.

■ Different forms of the same gene are called *alleles*. A person who inherits the same allele on a pair of chromosomes is homozygous; in this case, the biochemical instructions on the allele are followed. A person who inherits different alleles on a pair of chromosomes is heterozygous; in this case, the instructions of the dominant allele are followed, and those of the recessive allele are ignored.

■ In sex-linked inheritance, characteristics that are influenced by genes on the X chromosome are passed from mothers to sons. Hemophilia and red-green color blindness are examples of sex-linked disorders.

Extra or Missing Chromosomes

■ Most fertilized eggs that do not have 46 chromosomes (44 autosomes and 2 sex chromosomes) are aborted spontaneously, soon after conception. One exception is Down syndrome, in which individuals usually have an extra 21st chromosome. Persons with Down syndrome have a distinctive appearance and are mentally retarded.

■ Disorders of the sex chromosomes are more common because these chromosomes contain much less genetic material. Common examples include Klinefelter's syndrome, XYY complement, Turner's syndrome, and XXX syndrome.

Polygenic Inheritance

■ Many behavioral and psychological phenotypes, such as intelligence and extroversion, show differences along a continuum. These phenotypes often involve polygenic inheritance, in which the phenotype reflects the combined activity of a number of distinct genes. The influence of heredity and environment on these phenotypes can be revealed by studying twins and adopted children.

Heredity Is Not Destiny: Genes and Environments

■ PKU is an inherited disorder in which phenylalanine accumulates in the body, damaging the nervous system.

The mental retardation that usually results can be avoided through a diet that is low in phenylalanine. This demonstrates the concept of reaction range—the outcome of heredity depends on the environment in which development occurs.

■ Heredity can influence the types of experiences that children have. People seek environments that fit their genotype; this process is known as niche-picking.

The Many Wonders of Prenatal Development

Periods of Prenatal Development

■ Prenatal development consists of three periods. The first, the period of the zygote, begins with fertilization of the egg by the sperm and ends when the zygote becomes implanted in the wall of the uterus at about two weeks after conception. The second, the period of the embryo, is a period of rapid growth, in which most of the major body structures are created. It ends at 8 weeks after conception and is followed by the period of the fetus. In this stage, which lasts until birth, the fetus becomes much larger, and many of the bodily systems necessary for life begin to function.

Influences on Prenatal Development

■ Prenatal development can be influenced by general factors, including a mother's age, her nutrition, and the amount of stress that she experiences. In addition, specific hazards known as *teratogens* can cause prenatal development to go awry. Major categories of teratogens are drugs (such as alcohol and cocaine), diseases (such as AIDS and rubella), and environmental hazards (such as PCBs and X rays).

■ The impact of teratogens depends on the genotype of the organism, the period of prenatal development at which the organism is exposed to the teratogen, and the amount of exposure. Teratogens usually affect a specific aspect of prenatal development, but their impact may not be evident until later in life.

Preventing, Diagnosing, and Treating Abnormal Prenatal Development

■ Techniques that can be used to determine whether prenatal development is progressing normally include ultrasound, amniocentesis, and chorionic villus sampling. Prenatal treatment remains largely experimental, but the field is progressing rapidly.

Happy Birthday!

Labor and Delivery

■ Labor consists of three stages: an initial phase in which the cervix enlarges, the baby's journey from the uterus into the world, and the delivery of the placenta. Today, many couples prefer natural childbirth; one of the aims of this approach is to reduce labor pain (and, consequently, medication) by relaxing.

■ One complication at birth is that some newborns experience lack of oxygen because the umbilical cord is pinched closed during delivery or because their lungs do not work properly. Another complication is that babies are born prematurely or with low birth weight. Premature babies lag behind full-term babies during the first year, but they soon catch up. Newborn babies with low birth weight can develop normally when they have excellent medical care and a supportive environment; babies with very or extremely low birth weight do not fare well.

The Newborn

■ Newborns are often assessed with an Apgar score, which consists of an evaluation of five vital functions. It provides a measure of a newborn baby's physical well-being. The Neonatal Behavioral Assessment Scale pro-

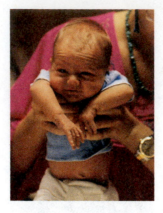

vides a more comprehensive evaluation of a baby's behavioral and physical status.

■ Babies are born with a number of different reflexes. Some, like the rooting and sucking reflexes, help them adjust to life outside the uterus. Others, like the eye-blink and withdrawal reflexes, help protect them from danger. Still others, like the stepping reflex, serve as the basis for later voluntary motor behavior.

■ Newborns spend approximately two-thirds of every day asleep. Half of their sleep is REM sleep, which is characterized by active brain waves and frequent movements of the eyes and limbs. REM sleep may stimulate growth in the nervous system. The waking hours are spent in states of alert inactivity, waking activity, and crying. Newborns go through a complete sleep-wake cycle once every four hours.

■ The term *temperament* refers to a consistent style or pattern to an infant's behavior. Dimensions of temperament include emotionality, activity, and sociability. Temperament is a reasonably stable characteristic of infants and young children.

Key Terms

activity (73)

age of viability (56)

allele (42)

amniocentesis (63)

amnion (54)

anoxia (67)

autosomes (41)

basic cry (71)

cephalocaudal principle (55)

chorion (54)

chorionic villus sampling (63)

chromosomes (41)

crowning (66)

deoxyribonucleic acid
    (DNA) (41)

dizygotic twins (48)

dominant (42)

ectoderm (54)

emotionality (73)

endoderm (54)

erythrocytes (40)

eugenics (52)

extremely low birth weight (67)

fetal alcohol syndrome (57)

gene (42)

genetic counseling (62)

genotype (42)

heterozygous (42)

homozygous (42)

incomplete dominance (43)

in vitro fertilization (52)

low birth weight (67)

mad cry (71)

mesoderm (71)

monozygotic twins (48)

niche-picking (50)

non-REM sleep (71)

pain cry (71)

period of the fetus (55)

phenotype (42)

phenylketonuria (48)

placenta (54)

polygenic inheritance (47)

prenatal development (53)

preterm (premature) (67)

proximodistal principle (55)

rapid-eye-movement (REM)
    sleep (71)

reaction range (49)

recessive (42)

reflexes (69)

sex chromosomes (41)

sickle-cell trait (43)

sociability (73)

temperament (72)

teratogen (57)

ultrasound (63)

umbilical cord (54)

very low birth weight (67)

zygote (53)

If You'd Like to Learn More

BRAZELTON, T. B. (1983). *Infants and mothers: Differences in development*. New York: Delta/Seymour Lawrence. The author, a well-known pediatrician and creator of the NBAS, illustrates striking differences among babies by examining a few case studies in detail.

KOPP, C. (1993). *Baby steps: The "whys" of your child's behavior in the first two years*. New York: Freeman. As the title indicates, this book is not only about newborns. However, we recommend the book because the author begins with newborn babies and traces the changes that occur in physical, motor, mental, and social-emotional development.

NILSSON, L., & HAMBERGER, L. (1990). *A child is born*. New York: Delacorte. This book is the source of many of the photographs in the second part of this chapter. Nilsson developed a variety of techniques to photograph the fetus as it was developing; Hamberger provides an entertaining and informative text to accompany the photos.

PLOMIN, R. (1990). *Nature and nurture*. Monterey, CA: Brooks/Cole. This brief book provides a very readable introduction to modern research on the role of genetics in human behavior, written by one of the leading researchers in the field.

CHAPTER 3

❧ While crossing the street, 4-year-old Martin was struck by a passing car. He was in a coma for a week but then gradually became more alert. Now he seems to be aware of his surroundings. Needless to say, Martin's mother is grateful that he survived the accident, but she wonders what the future holds for her son.

❧ Nancy is 14 months old and a world-class crawler. Using hands and knees, she can get just about anywhere she wants to go. Nancy does not walk and seems to have no interest in learning how. Nancy's dad, Dave, wonders whether he should be doing something to help Nancy progress beyond crawling. Deep down, he worries that perhaps he has been negligent in not providing more exercise or training for Nancy when she was younger.

❧ Darla adores her 3-day-old son. She loves holding him, talking to him, and simply watching him. Darla is certain that her baby is, in his own way, already getting to know her, coming to recognize her face and the sound of her voice. Darla's husband, Tony, thinks she is crazy: "Everyone knows that babies are born blind, and they probably can't hear much either." Darla doubts what Tony says and wishes someone could tell her the truth about babies' vision and hearing.

Growth and Development of Physical and Perceptual Skill

 Think about what you were like two years ago. Whatever you were doing, you probably look, act, think, and feel in much the same way today that you did then. Two years in an adult's life usually don't result in profound changes. But two years do make a big difference early in life. The changes that occur in the first few years after birth are incredible. An infant is transformed from a seemingly helpless newborn into a talking, walking, havoc-wreaking toddler in less than two years. No changes at any other point in the life span come close to the drama and excitement of these early years.

In this chapter, we'll look at three facets of change in this period. We'll begin with physical growth—changes in the body. We'll look at how the brain develops and learn what the future holds for Martin, the boy in the chapter-opening vignette who was struck by a car.

In the second part of the chapter, we focus on motor skills. We'll discover how babies learn to walk and, in the process, determine whether Dave, the father of the world-class crawler in the chapter-opening vignettes, should be concerned that his daughter is not yet walking. We'll also see how infants learn to use their hands to hold and then manipulate objects.

In the last part of the chapter, we'll examine changes in infants' sensory abilities that allow them to comprehend their world. When we've finished, we'll be able to answer questions about infants' hearing and sight that Darla asked in the last vignette.

Growing Bigger Every Day

LEARNING OBJECTIVES

- *How do height and weight change from birth to 2 years of age?*

- *What nutrients do infants and young children need? How are they best provided?*

- *What are the consequences of malnutrition? How can it be treated?*

- *What are the parts of a nerve cell? How are neurons organized in the brain?*

- *When is the brain formed in prenatal development? When do different regions in the brain begin to function?*

Physical Growth

For parents and youngsters alike, physical growth is a topic of great interest and a source of pleasure. Parents marvel at the speed with which babies add pounds and inches; 2-year-olds proudly proclaim, "I bigger now!" In fact, growth is more rapid in infancy than during any other period of life. Typically, infants double their birth weight by 3 months of age and triple it by their first birthday. This rate of growth is so rapid that if it continued throughout childhood, a typical 10-year-old boy would be nearly as long as an airliner and weigh almost as much (McCall, 1979).

The growth charts shown at the top of page 81 depict changes in height and weight over the first three years of life. Notice that an average girl weighs about 7 pounds at birth, about 21 pounds at age 1, and about 26 pounds at age 2. If perfectly average, she would be 19–20 inches long at birth, grow to 29–30 inches at age 1, and 34–35 inches at age 2. Figures for an average boy are similar, but weights are slightly larger at ages 1 and 2.

These charts also highlight how much children of the same age vary in weight and height. At age 1, for example, normal weights for boys range from about 19 to 27 pounds. This means that an extremely light but normal boy would weigh only two-thirds as much as his extremely heavy but normal peer!

The important message here is that average height and normal height are not one and the same. Many children are much taller or shorter than average but are still perfectly normal. This applies to all of the age norms that we mention in this book. Whenever we provide a typical or average age for a developmental milestone, remember that the normal range for passing the milestone is much wider.

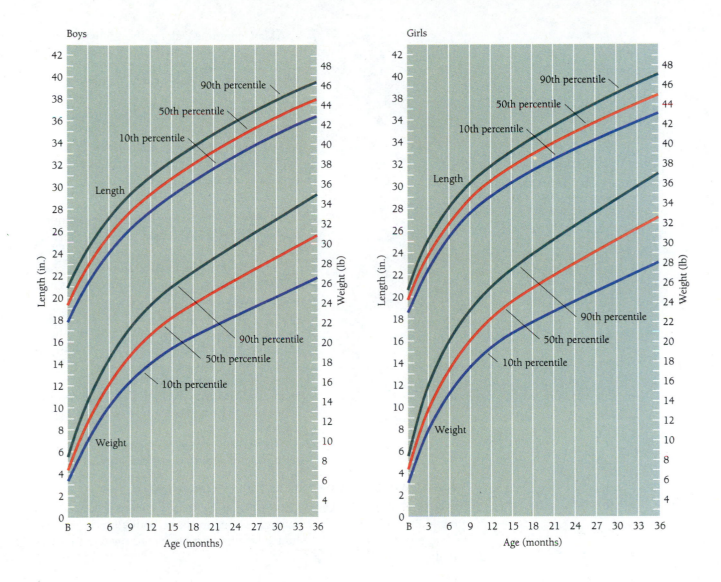

Whether an infant is short or tall depends largely on heredity. Both parents contribute to their children's height. In fact, the correlation between the average of the two parents' heights and their child's height at 2 years of age is about .7 (Plomin, 1984). As a general rule, two tall parents will have tall offspring; two short parents will have short offspring; and, as the Real People feature shows, one tall parent and one short parent will have offspring of medium height.

See Matt Grow

Matt Kail was born October 17, 1980. At birth and at regular intervals thereafter, his height and weight were recorded during visits to a pediatrician. As an infant, his height was measured while he was lying down; beginning at about 2 years of age, standing height was recorded. The measurements are shown on the chart at the top of page 82. You can see that Matt was about 19 inches long at birth, which put him at about the 25th percentile for boys. This is about the length that would be expected for a baby whose father is around the 55th percentile for height and whose mother is near the 15th percentile.

REAL PEOPLE

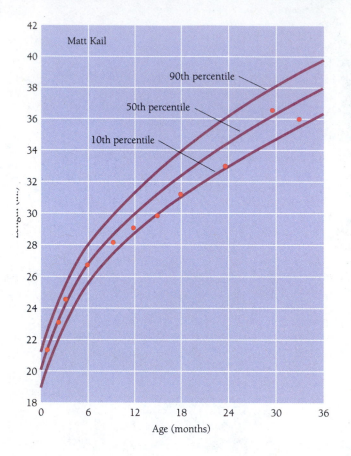

Matt continued along the 25th percentile trajectory. On his first birthday, Matt was 29 inches long. At 2 years, he was 33 inches long—this figure is interesting. A rule of thumb is that doubling a boy's height at age 2 gives a rough estimate of his height as an adult. (For girls, the rule is to double the height at 18 months of age.) In Matt's case, $2 \times 33 = 66$, or 5 feet 6 inches. You'll need to read a later edition of this book to check the accuracy of this prediction! 🐾

So far, we have emphasized the quantitative aspects of growth, such as height. This ignores an important fact: Infants are not simply scaled-down versions of adults. The chart below shows that compared to adolescents and adults, infants and young children look top-heavy because their heads and trunks are disproportionately large. As growth of the hips, legs, and feet catches up later in childhood, their bodies take on more adult proportions. This pattern of growth, in which the head and trunk develop first, follows the cephalocaudal principle introduced in Chapter 2 (page 55).

Growth of this sort requires energy. Let's see how food and drink provide the fuel to grow.

"YOU ARE WHAT YOU EAT"—NUTRITION AND GROWTH

In a typical 2-month-old, roughly 40% of the body's energy is devoted to growth. Most of the remaining energy is used for basic bodily functions such as digestion and respiration. A much smaller portion is consumed in physical activity.

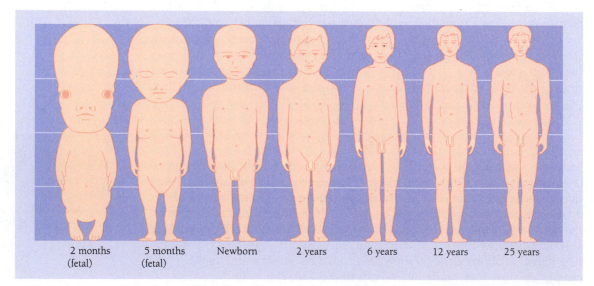

| 2 months (fetal) | 5 months (fetal) | Newborn | 2 years | 6 years | 12 years | 25 years |

Based on Eichhorn, 1969.

Because growth requires so much high energy, young babies must consume an enormous number of calories relative to their body weight. A typical, 12-pound 3-month-old, for example, should ingest about 600 calories daily, representing about 50 calories per pound of body weight. An adult, by contrast, needs to consume approximately 15–20 calories per pound, depending on the person's level of activity (National Research Council, 1989).

A young baby's dietary needs are amply met by human milk, which contains the proper amounts of carbohydrates, fats, and protein, as well as necessary vitamins and minerals. Breast feeding has other advantages as well: Breast milk contains antibodies that help to fight disease; infants are less likely to develop allergies; and they are less likely to overeat than infants who are bottle-fed (Whitney, Cataldo, & Rolfes, 1987). Bottle feeding does allow other family members to experience the intimacy of feeding the baby, and modern formula does contain essentially the same proportion of nutrients as human milk. Consequently, a mother can choose either method—or use them both—knowing that they will meet her baby's nutritional needs.

MALNUTRITION

Unfortunately, an adequate diet is only a dream to many of the world's children. **The World Health Organization of the United Nations estimates that 10 million children under 5 years of age are severely *malnourished*—that is, their body weight is less than 60% of the average for their age.** Many are from Third World countries. However, malnutrition is regrettably common in industrialized countries, too. For example, many American children growing up homeless and in poverty are also malnourished.

Millions of children throughout the world are malnourished. Treating them requires an improved diet as well as training their parents to provide a stimulating environment.

Malnourished children tend to develop less rapidly than their peers. Malnourishment is especially damaging during infancy, because growth is ordinarily so rapid during these years. This is well illustrated by a longitudinal study conducted in Barbados in the West Indies (Galler & Ramsey, 1989; Galler, Ramsey, & Forde, 1986). Included were more than 100 children who had been severely malnourished as infants, as well as 100 children whose family environments were similar but who had adequate nutrition as infants. The children who had experienced malnutrition during infancy were indistinguishable from their peers physically—they were just as tall and weighed just as much. However, children with a history of infant malnutrition had much lower scores on intelligence tests. Also, many of the children who had been malnourished during infancy had difficulty maintaining attention in school; they were easily distracted. Many similar studies suggest that malnutrition during rapid periods of growth may cause substantial and potentially irreversible damage to the brain (Morgane et al., 1993).

Malnutrition would seem to have a simple cure—an adequate diet. But as we see in the Forces in Action feature, the solution is more complex than you might expect.

Fostering Development in Malnourished Children

Malnourished children are often listless and inactive (Ricciuti, 1993). Such behavior is useful to children whose diet is inadequate, because it helps conserve their limited energy. However, this behavior may also deprive youngsters of experiences that would further their development. For example, when children are routinely unresponsive and lethargic, parents may come to believe that their actions have little impact on the children. Over time, parents may provide fewer experiences that foster their children's development. The result is a self-perpetuating cycle in which malnourished children are forsaken by parents

FORCES IN ACTION

who feel as if they can do little to change their children's fate. A biological force (lethargy stemming from insufficient nourishment) causes a profound change in the sociocultural forces (parental teaching) that influence a child's development.

An improved diet, alone, will not break the vicious cycle. In addition, parents need to be taught how to foster their children's development, and parents must be encouraged to do so. The key is to address both biological and sociocultural forces. Programs that combine dietary supplements with parent training offer promise in the treatment of malnutrition (Super, Herrera, & Mora, 1990).   ❧

The Emerging Nervous System

The physical changes that we see as infants grow are impressive. Even more awe-inspiring are the changes that we cannot see—those involving the brain and the nervous system. An infant's feelings of hunger or pain, its smiles or laughs, and its efforts to sit upright or to hold a rattle all reflect the functioning of the brain and the rest of the emerging nervous system.

How does the brain accomplish these many tasks? To begin to answer this question, we need to look at the organization of the brain. **The basic unit in the brain and the rest of the nervous system is the *neuron*, a cell that specializes in receiving and transmitting information.** Neurons have the three basic elements that are shown in the diagram. **The *cell body*, in the center of**

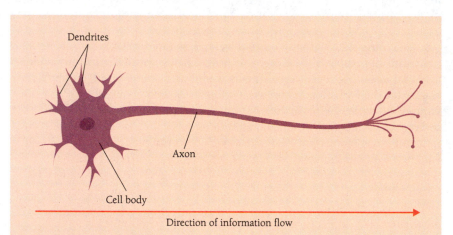

Dendrites

Axon

Cell body

Direction of information flow

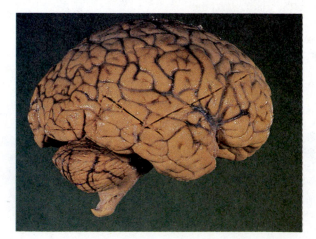

the cell, contains the basic biological machinery that keeps the neuron alive. The receiving end of the neuron, the *dendrite*, looks like a tree with its many branches.** This structure allows one neuron to receive input from thousands of other neurons (Morgan & Gibson, 1991). **The tube-like structure that emerges from the other side of the cell body, the *axon*, transmits information to other neurons.**

Take 50 to 100 billion neurons like these, and you have the beginnings of a human brain. An adult's brain, like the one in the photograph, weighs a little less than 3 pounds and would easily fit into your hands. (Just why you would be holding a human brain in your hands is another question.)

The wrinkled surface of the brain is the *cerebral cortex;* made up of 10^{10} neurons, the cortex regulates many of the functions that we think of as distinctly human. The cortex consists of left and right halves, called *hemispheres,* linked by a thick bundle of neurons called the *corpus callosum.* The characteristics that you value the most—your engaging personality, your "way with words," or your uncanny knack for "reading" others' emotions—are all controlled by specific regions in the cortex. **For example, your personality and your ability to make and carry out plans are largely centered in an area in the front of the cortex that is called (appropriately enough) the *frontal cortex.*** Your ability to produce and understand language is mainly housed in neurons in the left hemisphere of the cortex. When you recognize that others are happy or sad, neurons in your right hemisphere are at work.

Now that we know a bit of the organization of the mature brain, let's look at how the brain grows and begins to function.

THE MAKING OF THE WORKING BRAIN

If you were to look at an embryo roughly 3 weeks after conception, you could see a group of cells that form a flat structure known as the *neural plate.* In the next week, the neural plate folds to form a tube that is open at the ends. One end of this tube becomes the spinal cord; the other becomes the brain.

Virtually all of the neurons that the brain will ever have are produced in the third and fourth months after conception. During these months, neurons are formed at the incredible rate of more than 4000 per second (Kolb, 1989). By the sixth month of prenatal development, neurons are in their proper location in the brain.

The brain weighs only three-quarters of a pound at birth, which is roughly 25% of the weight of an adult brain. You can see from the graph, however, that the brain grows rapidly during infancy and the preschool years. At 3 years of age, the brain has achieved 80% of its ultimate weight.

Because the brain grows so rapidly, it may not surprise you to learn that many areas of the cortex begin to function early in life. Take the left hemisphere's influence on language as an example. When children suffer damage to the brain, damage to the left hemisphere of the cortex typically produces greater loss of language ability than does a comparable injury to the right hemisphere of the cortex (Witelson, 1987).

Do you remember Martin, the preschooler in the chapter-opening vignette, who was struck

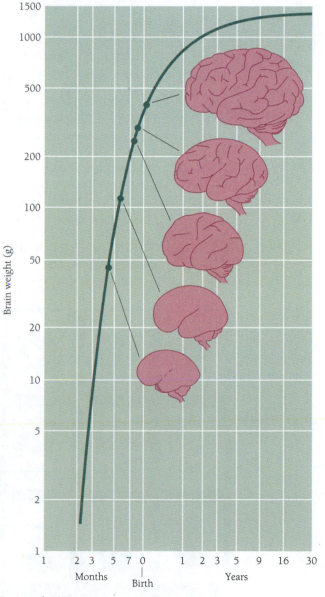

Lemire et al., 1975.

Electrodes have been attached to this baby's scalp so that electrical activity can be recorded on an electroencephalogram.

by a car? The only lasting effect of the accident seems to be to Martin's speech, which is now slow and deliberate. This is not surprising; a neurologist determined that the left hemisphere of Martin's brain had absorbed much of the force of the collision. Cases like Martin's indicate that by early childhood, the left hemisphere specializes in language processing.

Fortunately for children, such cases of brain damage are relatively uncommon. Consequently, scientists have devised other methods to study brain functioning in healthy children. One approach is to record the brain's ongoing electrical activity. To do this, several metal electrodes are placed on an infant's scalp. **The combined output of the electrodes yields a pattern of waves known as an *electroencephalogram*—or simply an EEG.** Typically, a newborn infant's left hemisphere generates more electrical activity in response to speech than does the right hemisphere (Molfese & Burger-Judisch, 1991). Apparently, at birth, the left hemisphere of the cortex is uniquely prepared to process language. As we'll see in Chapter 4, this specialization allows language to develop rapidly during infancy.

Is the right hemisphere equally well prepared to function at birth? This is a difficult question to answer, in part because the right hemisphere influences so many different nonlinguistic functions. In addition to recognizing emotions, the right hemisphere influences understanding of spatial relations, identifying faces, and perceiving nonspeech sounds such as music (Kinsbourne, 1989). Music does elicit greater electrical activity in the infant's right hemisphere than in the left hemisphere. Other functions, such as understanding spatial relations and recognizing faces, are under the right hemisphere's control by the preschool years (Hahn, 1987).

The frontal cortex also begins to function early. **Mapping the areas of activity and energy in the frontal cortex is possible with *positron emission tomography* or PET scan.** The energy that the brain needs to function is provided by glucose, a form of sugar. Consumption of glucose in different regions of the brain is related to the level of brain activity in those regions: Areas that are particularly active need more glucose than areas that are less active. The brain's consumption of glucose is measured by injecting a radioactive form of glucose into a person's bloodstream. The levels of radioactivity measured in different regions of the brain indicate levels of glucose, which relate to the levels of brain activity in those regions. The photograph shown here, in which a computer has generated color codes for the different levels of activity, reveals little activity in the frontal cortex of 5-day-old babies. Activity has increased considerably by 11 weeks of age and reaches adult levels by 7 to 8 months (Chugani & Phelps, 1986).

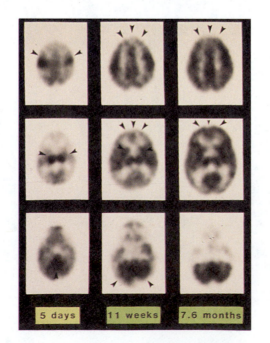

5 days   11 weeks   7.6 months

What is the frontal cortex regulating in PET scans like this one? Deliberate goal-oriented behavior is a good bet. To understand research that leads to this conclusion, think back to a time when you had to make a permanent change in your regular routine. At the start of a new school year, perhaps you had a new locker, located in a different hallway in school. Nevertheless, for several days you may have turned down the old hallway, following last year's habit. To overcome this error, maybe you deliberately reminded yourself to turn at the new hallway, not the old one.

Overriding old responses that are now incorrect or inappropriate is an important part of deliberate, goal-directed behavior. Adults with damage to the frontal cortex often have great difficulty inhibiting responses that are no longer appropriate. The frontal cortex begins to regulate such inappropriate responses around the first birthday and gradually achieves greater control through the preschool and school years (Welsh, Pennington, & Groisser, 1991).

Not only does the frontal cortex regulate old, irrelevant responses; it also regulates our feelings of happiness, sadness, and fear. By distinguishing emotions associated with approaching or exploring a stimulus from those associated with avoiding or withdrawing from stimuli, we can pinpoint the regions of the frontal cortex that govern emotional responding. Among adults, the left frontal cortex regulates emotions stemming from the tendency to approach an object; the right frontal cortex regulates those stemming from avoidance.

Are these emotions regulated by the infant's frontal cortex? To answer this question, Fox and Davidson (1988) simultaneously videotaped 10-month-olds and recorded their EEGs. They discovered that when babies were joyful, EEG revealed more activity in the left frontal cortex than in the right; when babies cried because they were angry or sad, the right frontal cortex was more active.

In each of the regions of the brain that we have examined, the conclusion has been the same: Many of the distinguishing features of the mature brain can be recognized early in life. Language processing is associated primarily with the left hemisphere; recognizing nonspeech sounds, emotions, and faces is associated with the right hemisphere; and regulating emotions and intentional behavior is a function of the frontal cortex. Of course, this early specialization does not mean that the brain is functionally mature. Over the remainder of childhood and into adulthood, these and other regions of the brain continue to become more specialized. In Chapter 13, we'll see that some regions of the brain continue to develop into old age, whereas others are sometimes destroyed by diseases associated with aging.

When babies are angry, their right frontal cortex is particularly active.

TEST YOURSELF

1. Compared to older children and adults, an infant's head and trunk are _____.
2. Because of the high energy demands of growth, infants need _____ calories per pound than adults.
3. The most effective treatment for malnutrition is improved diet and _____.
4. The _____ is the part of the neuron that contains the basic machinery that keeps the cell alive.
5. The frontal cortex is the seat of personality and regulates _____.
6. Human speech typically elicits the greatest electrical activity from the _____ of an infant's brain.
7. By measuring consumption of glucose, a _____ reveals activity in the frontal cortex by 3 months of age.
8. How does malnutrition illustrate the influence on development of life-cycle forces in the biopsychosocial framework?

Answers: (1) disproportionately large, (2) more, (3) parent training, (4) cell body, (5) goal-directed behavior, (6) left hemisphere, (7) PET scan

Moving And Grasping—Early Motor Skills

LEARNING OBJECTIVES

🥀 *What are the component skills involved in learning to walk? At what age do infants master them?*

🥀 *How do infants learn to coordinate the use of their hands?*

🥀 *When do most children begin to prefer using one hand? What factors determine this preference?*

🥀 *How do maturation and experience influence children's acquisition of motor skills?*

Do you remember what it was like to learn to type, to drive a car with a stick shift, to play a musical instrument, or to play a sport? **Each of these activities involves** *motor skills*—**coordinated movements of the muscles and limbs.** Success demands that each movement be done in a precise way, in exactly the right sequence, and at exactly the right time. For example, if you don't give the car enough gas as you let out the clutch, you'll kill the engine. With too much gas, the engine races and the car lurches forward.

These activities are demanding for adults, but think about similar challenges that infants face. **Infants must learn to move about in the world: to** *locomote.* Newborns are relatively immobile, but infants soon learn to crawl, to stand, and to walk. Once the child has learned to move through the environment upright, the arms and hands are free. To take full advantage of this arrangement, the human hand has fully independent fingers (instead of a paw), with the thumb opposing the remaining four fingers. **Infants must learn the** *fine motor skills* **associated with grasping, holding, and manipulating objects.** In the case of feeding, for example, infants progress from being fed by others, to holding a bottle, to feeding themselves with their fingers, to eating with a fork and spoon.

Together, locomotion and fine motor skills give children access to an enormous variety of information about shapes, textures, and features in their environment. Thus, acquiring motor skills is a valuable asset in human development. Let's begin by looking at how children learn to move themselves.

Locomotion

Advances in posture and locomotion transform the infant in little more than a year. No longer a motionless piece of humanity, he or she stands upright in a mature manner and walks through the environment. The chart on page 89 shows some of the important milestones in motor development and the age by which most infants have achieved them. By about 5 months of age, most babies will have rolled from back to front and will be able to sit upright with support. By 7 months, infants can sit alone, and by 10 months, they can creep. A typical 14-month-old is able to stand alone briefly and walk with assistance. **In light of this accomplishment, youngsters at this age are called** *toddlers,* **after the toddling manner of early walking.** Of course, not all children walk at exactly the same age. Some walk before their first birthday; others, like Nancy, the world-class crawler in the chapter-opening vignettes, may take their first steps as late as 18 or 19 months of age. By 24 months, most children can climb steps, walk backwards, and kick a ball.

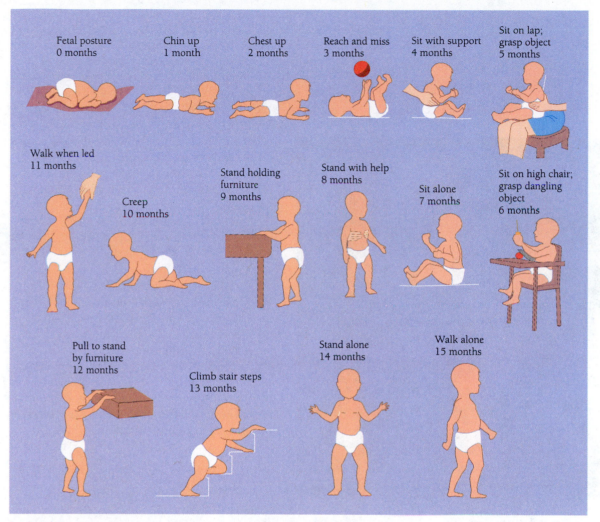

Based on Shirley, 1931 and Bayley, 1969.

This sequence of milestones fails to do justice to the truly remarkable nature of the infant's accomplishments in learning to walk. Walking involves the maturity and coalescence of many essential skills. For example, the ability to maintain an upright posture is fundamental to walking. This is virtually impossible for newborns and young infants because of the shape of their body. Due to cephalocaudal growth, the infant is top-heavy and, consequently, inherently unstable: As soon as young infants start to lose their balance, they tumble over because of their topheaviness. Only with growth of the legs and muscles can infants maintain an upright posture (Thelen, Ulrich, & Jensen, 1989).

When an infant can stand upright, he or she must continuously adjust posture to avoid falling down. By four months of age, infants are able to use cues from their inner ears to help them stay upright. If a 4-month-old is propped in a sitting position and starts to lose balance, he or she will nevertheless keep the head upright, using the muscles in the back of the neck. This happens even when the infant is blindfolded, which tells us that the essential clues are from the inner ears, not the eyes (Woollacott, Shumway-Cook, & Williams, 1989).

Another essential element in walking is moving the legs alternately—constantly transferring the weight of the body from one foot to the other. Children don't step spontaneously until approximately 10 months of age, because they must be able to stand in order to step. Can younger children step if they are held upright? Thelen and Ulrich (1991) devised a clever procedure to answer this question. Infants were placed on a treadmill and were held upright by an adult. When the belt on the treadmill started to move, infants could have done several things. They might have simply let both legs be dragged rearward by the belt. Or they might have let their legs be dragged briefly, then moved them forward together in a hopping motion. Instead, some 3-month-olds and many

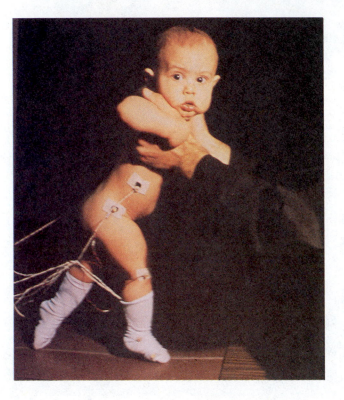

6- and 7-month-olds demonstrated the mature pattern of alternating steps on each leg, shown in the photograph. Even more amazing is that when the treadmill was equipped with separate belts for each leg, moving at different speeds, the babies adjusted, stepping more rapidly on the faster belt. Apparently, the alternate stepping motion that is essential for walking is present long before infants walk alone.

Findings like these remind us that each of the different motor milestones—from learning to sit to learning to walk—is not a unitary event. Instead, each demands the orchestration of many individual skills. Each must first be mastered alone and then integrated with the other skills, which is a general principle of motor development (Werner, 1948). **That is, mastery of intricate motions involves both *differentiation* of individual motions and their *integration* into a coherent, working whole.** In the case of walking, not until 12 to 15 months of age has control of component skills reached such a level of precision that they can be coordinated to allow independent, unsupported walking.

The first tentative steps are followed by others that are more skilled. Walking is joined by jumping, hopping, running, and skipping—a multitude of methods of locomotion that exhilarate children and parents alike. If you can recall the feelings of freedom that accompanied your first driver's license, you can imagine how the world expands for infants and toddlers as they learn to move independently. Much of youngsters' enthusiasm for their growing locomotive skills is because they are so useful (Bertenthal, Campos, & Kermoian, 1994). Now toddlers can get to desired objects like toys, food, and books alone, without depending upon a parent. Of course, once the desired object is reached, another set of motor skills is called for. These we discuss next.

Fine Motor Skills

Soon after birth, infants begin to use their hands to grasp objects (Karniol, 1989). Initially, infants use one hand only, first holding an object and later moving it. By 3 months, they perform more complicated motions, such as shaking a toy. At about 4 months, infants use both hands. At first, these motions are not coordinated, as if each hand has a mind of its own. A toy may be held motionless in one hand while the other hand is used to shake a rattle. Soon, however, infants use both hands together in common actions, such as holding a large toy.

At roughly 5 months of age, infants can coordinate the motions of their hands. The hands can now perform different actions that serve a common goal. A typical example would be grasping an object with one hand and manipulating it with the other. An infant might hold a toy animal in the right hand while petting it with the left.

These gradual changes in fine motor coordination are well illustrated by the ways children feed themselves. Beginning at roughly 6 months of age, many parents allow their infants to experiment with "finger foods" such as sliced bananas and green beans. Infants can easily pick up such foods, but getting them into their mouths is another story. The hand grasping the food may be raised to the cheek, then moved to the edge of the lips, and finally shoved into the mouth. Mission accomplished, but only after many detours along the way! However, infants' eye/hand coordination improves rapidly, and foods varying in size, shape, and texture are soon placed directly in the mouth.

The next time that your spouse, friends, or parents complain about your manners at the dining room table, show them this photograph and remind them of how far you've progressed!

At about the first birthday, many parents allow their children to try eating with a spoon. Youngsters first simply play with the spoon, dipping it in and out of a dish filled with food or sucking on an empty spoon. Soon they learn to fill the spoon with food and place it in their mouth, but the motions are awkward. For example, most 1-year-olds will fill a spoon by first placing it directly over a dish. Then they lower it until the bowl of the spoon is full. In contrast, typically 2-year-olds will scoop food from a dish by rotating their wrist, which is the same motion that adults use.

Fine motor skills continue to progress beyond infancy. Most 18-month-olds can scribble with a pencil and build with blocks. During the preschool years, youngsters typically learn to draw simple geometric figures (e.g., circle, square) and the human body (Frankenburg & Dobbs, 1969). Soon, they master using scissors, buttoning shirts and coats, and tying shoelaces.

Each of these actions illustrates the principles of differentiation and integration that were introduced in our discussion of locomotion. Complex acts involve many constituent movements. Each must be performed correctly and in the proper sequence. Development involves first mastering the separate elements and then assembling them into a smoothly functioning whole.

HANDEDNESS

Are you right-handed or left-handed? If you're right-handed, you're in the majority. About 90% of the people worldwide prefer to use their right hand, although this figure varies somewhat from place to place, reflecting cultural influences. Most of the remaining 10% are left-handed; a relatively small percentage of people are truly ambidextrous.

A preference for one hand over the other does not seem to emerge until after the first birthday. Most 6- and 9-month-olds, for example, use their left and right hands interchangeably (McCormick & Maurer, 1988). They may shake a rattle with their left hand, but, moments later, pick up blocks with their right.

The emergence of handedness soon after the first birthday is illustrated in a study in which infants and toddlers were videotaped as they played with toys that could be manipulated with two hands, such as a pinwheel (Cornwell, Harris, & Fitzgerald, 1991). The 9-month-olds used their left and right hands equally. However, by 13 months of age, most of the infants and toddlers acted like the girl in the photograph: They first grasped the toy with their right hand, then used their left hand to steady the toy while the right hand manipulated the object.

This early preference for one hand becomes stronger and more consistent throughout the preschool years. By the time children are ready to enter kindergarten, handedness is well established and is very difficult to reverse (McManus et al., 1988). To observe the development of handedness firsthand (apologies for the pun), administer some of the tasks in the See for Yourself feature to preschool children.

Determining the Onset of Handedness

SEE FOR YOURSELF

How can we decide if a preschooler is left- or right-handed? With adults, we can simply ask, and their response will reflect which hand they use in writing or throwing. We need a more concrete approach with preschoolers, few of whom even know left from right. With the permission of a local nursery school or day care center, you could ask several preschoolers to do the following tasks (from McManus et al., 1988):

1. Draw a face with a pen
2. Color a square
3. Throw a ball
4. Thread a bead onto a wire
5. Turn over cards placed on a table

6. Show how they use a spoon to eat
7. Brush their teeth with an imaginary toothbrush
8. Comb their hair with an imaginary comb
9. Blow their nose with a tissue
10. Pick a piece of candy from a bag

You should see that younger preschoolers—2½-year-olds, for example—will use their left hand on some tasks and their right on others. However, by the time children are 5 years old, most will do at least eight of these activities with one hand, showing that handedness is now well established. See for yourself!   ❧

Whether children become left- or right-handed is based, in part, on heredity. Parents who are both right-handed tend to have children who are right-handed. Children who are left-handed generally have a left-handed parent or grandparent. But experience also contributes to handedness. Many aspects of modern industrial cultures favor right-handedness. School desks, scissors, and can openers, for example, are usually designed for right-handed people and can be used by left-handers only with difficulty. In some cultures, social values influence handedness. Islam dictates that the left hand is unclean, so its use is forbidden in eating and greeting others. Writing with the left hand is a cultural taboo in China, so virtually no Chinese youngsters write with the left hand. Nevertheless, when children of Chinese parents grow up in cultures that lack this prohibition, about 10% of them write with their left hand, which is a typical figure worldwide (Harris, 1983). In the United States, elementary school teachers used to encourage left-handed children to use their right hands; as this practice has diminished in the last 50 years, the percentage of left-handed children has risen steadily (Levy, 1976). Thus, handedness seems to involve a biological force (heredity) in conjunction with sociocultural forces (social values and experiences).

Woe is the left-handed child in a world designed for right-handers!

Maturation and Experience Both Influence Motor Skill

For locomotion and fine motor skill, the big picture is much the same. Infants' motor skills develop rapidly during the first year as fundamental skills are mastered; these are combined with other skills to generate even more complex behaviors. Are the changes that we observe primarily due to maturation? Are we simply watching a gradual unfolding of skill that depends little on training, practice, or experience? As you might imagine, both maturation and experience contribute.

Let's begin with the impact of maturation on motor development, which is well documented. The sequence of motor development that we have described for locomotion and fine motor skill holds for most cultures. That is, despite enormous variation in child-rearing practices across cultures, motor development proceeds in much the same way and at roughly the same rate worldwide.

In some African cultures, mothers often carry their babies in a "piggy-back" style. This seems to strengthen the infant's muscles, which may be why babies carried in this manner learn to walk at an earlier age than most babies growing up in North America.

This general point is well illustrated in a classic study of Hopi children by Dennis and Dennis (1940). Traditionally, infants in the Hopi culture are secured to cradle boards like the one shown in the photograph. Cradle boards prevent them from moving their hands or legs, rolling over, or raising their bodies. Infants feed and sleep while secured to the board; they are removed only for a change of clothes. This practice begins the day the infant is born and continues for the first three months. For the next several months, infants are allowed time in which they are not secured to the boards and are free to move about. This time increases gradually, but for most of the first year, infants sleep on cradle boards and are left there for some part of their waking hours.

Obviously, the cradle board strictly limits the infant's locomotion during much of the first year—a time when other infants are learning to sit, creep, and crawl. Nevertheless, the infants in this study learned to walk at approximately 15 months—about the same age as other Hopi children reared by parents who had adopted Western values and no longer used cradle boards.

More than 40 years later, the story remained the same. Chisholm (1983) studied Navajo infants who spent much of their infancy secured to cradle boards. They, too, learned to walk at about the same age as infants whose parents did not use cradle boards.

In both of these studies, a restrictive environment that massively reduced opportunities for practice had no apparent effect on the age at which children began walking. This suggests that the timing of an infant's first steps is determined more by an underlying genetic timetable than by specific experiences or practice. Thus, Dave, the worried father of the world-class crawler in the opening vignette, can be reassured that his daughter's motor development is perfectly normal.

Maturation and experience are not, of course, mutually exclusive. The fact that maturation has been shown to figure in motor development does not imply that experience plays no role. In fact, as the cartoon suggests, practice and training do affect children's mastery of motor skills. Here, too, studies of other cultures are revealing. In some African countries, young infants have daily exercise sessions, in which they practice walking under the tutelage of a parent or sibling. In addition, many infants are carried by their parents piggy-back style, which helps to develop muscles in the infants' trunk and legs. Apparently because of such experiences, these infants sometimes learn to walk months earlier than would be expected otherwise (Super, 1981).

The effect of these experiences tends to be specific to particular muscle groups. You wouldn't expect daily practice kicking a soccer ball to do much to improve your golf game. By the same token, infants who receive concentrated practice on one motor skill usually don't improve on other skills. This is shown by experiments in which scientists train infants in one skill, then test them on that skill plus another in which they have had no special training. Research by Zelazo and her colleagues (1993) with 6-week-olds illustrates this phenomenon. Some infants had daily sessions in which, with parents' help, they practiced stepping. Other infants had daily sessions in which they practiced sitting. After 7 weeks of practice, these infants, as well as a control group of children who had received no practice, were tested on their ability to step and to sit. The graph tells the whole story. For both stepping and

"Ryan's walking two months earlier than most other kids, thanks to these training shoes that Gary made in the basement."

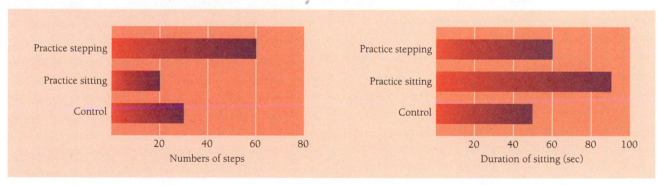

Zelazo et al., 1993.

sitting, infants improved the skill they had practiced. When infants were tested on the skill that they had not practiced, they did no better than infants in the control group. Clearly, the impact of motor skill practice is specific, not general.

Experience becomes even more important in complex actions, in which discrete skills must be connected in the correct sequence and timed properly. Many of the games that older babies enjoy, like pat-a-cake and peek-a-boo, involve such complex actions. Mastering these games depends on a number of critical experiences, such as observing others play the game, practicing the game with a skilled partner, and receiving feedback when errors are made. Experiences of this sort build on maturational changes to allow youngsters to enjoy a wide range of motor behaviors: kicking a soccer ball, playing a violin, signing to communicate with people who do not hear, or, as in the You May Be Wondering feature, toilet training.

**YOU MAY
BE WONDERING**

Toilet Training ·

Learning to walk and to eat with a spoon are surely important milestones of infancy, but many parents just as eagerly look forward to the day when the last diaper is changed! (They should: 5 diapers a day for 2½ years makes more than 4500 diaper changes!) Parents and children alike take pride when children learn to control their bladder and bowels. Training pants are worn proudly, as a sign that the child is a "big" girl or boy.

Today, control of the bladder during the day is achieved by about 50% of American 2-year-olds but by nearly 90% of 4-year-olds. Bladder control during the night is typically achieved a few months later (Erickson, 1987).

Controlling the bladder and bowels involves regulating the muscles that surround the openings to these organs. How do infants learn this all-important motor skill? Most do so through a combination of observing others, direct instruction from parents, and, unfortunately, trial and error. One popular approach, devised by Nathan Azrin and Richard Foxx, is described in their book, *Toilet Training in Less than a Day* (1974). Azrin and Foxx based their approach on learning theories, which we've described in Chapter 1 and are summarized in the chart. They reasoned that the key principles of learning, including im-

Perspective	Examples of Theories	Main Ideas	Emphases in Biopsychosocial Framework	Positions on Developmental Issues
Learning	Behaviorism (Watson, Skinner) Social-learning theory (Bandura)	Environment controls behavior People learn through modeling and observing	In all theories, some emphasis on biological and psychological, main focus on social, little recognition of life cycle	In all theories, strongly emphasize nurture, continuity, and universal principles of learning

itation, feedback, and reward, could be used to toilet-train children. In this program, youngsters must first show their readiness for toilet training. Among the necessary signs are:

1. *Bladder control*: The child stays dry for several hours, then urinates in large quantities.
2. *Physical maturation*: The child picks up objects easily and walks easily (requires no parental support, seldom falls).
3. *Instructional readiness*: The child readily responds to simple requests and commands (e.g., to sit down, to imitate, to bring an object).

A child who passes all of these tests is probably ready for toilet training, which involves several steps:

1. Parents use a doll that wets to teach the sequence involved in using the toilet (e.g., sitting on the potty seat, lowering pants, urinating).
2. Children are taught the difference between dry and wet pants; they are

praised for the former and rewarded with a drink of a sweet beverage (thereby giving the child more opportunities to urinate).

3. About every 15 minutes, children are led to the potty, where they are encouraged to sit quietly so that they may urinate. When they are successful, parents show their approval verbally and nonverbally (e.g., hugging, smiling, clapping) and provide rewards.

This is just a quick sketch of the program. The basic idea is that youngsters learn to make a particular motor response in the presence of a distinctive stimulus. Imitation is used to illustrate what is desired; reward, feedback, and practice allow children to master the response. As the name suggests, most children taught in this way master the essentials of toilet training in 24 hours or less.

TEST YOURSELF

1. When 4-month-olds tumble from a sitting position, they usually try to keep their head upright. This happens even when they are blindfolded, which means that the important cues to balance come from _____.

2. When many 6- and 7-month-olds are held upright by an adult and placed on a treadmill, they _____.

3. Akira uses both hands simultaneously, but not in a coordinated manner; each hand seems to be "doing its own thing." Akira is probably _____ months old.

4. Before the age of _____, children show no signs of handedness; they use their left and right hands interchangeably.

5. Compared to infants reared in less restrictive environments, infants reared on cradle boards learn to walk _____.

6. When infants practice motor skills, the impact of this practice is _____.

7. Describe how the mastery of a fine motor skill such as learning to use a spoon or a crayon illustrates the integration of biological, psychological, and sociocultural forces in the biopsychosocial framework.

Coming to Know the World: Perception

LEARNING OBJECTIVES

- *Are infants able to smell, to taste, and to experience pain?*
- *Can infants hear? How do they use sound to locate objects in space?*
- *How well can infants see? Can they see color?*
- *What visual cues do infants use to perceive depth?*
- *How do infants coordinate information between different sensory modalities, such as between vision and hearing?*

Do you remember Darla, the adoring mother of the 3-month-old in the last chapter-opening vignette? She savors the full experience of her newborn son—how he looks, his sounds, and the warmth of his skin on hers. Darla wonders

Answers: (1) *the inner ear,* (2) *show the mature pattern of moving the legs alternately,* (3) *4,* (4) *1 year,* (5) *at about the same age,* (6) *not generalized, but limited to the skill practiced*

what her son experiences. What does he see? Can he hear her voice? Does he feel the warmth of her body? Darla's husband, Tony, is confident that the answer to each of her questions is no.

To answer Darla's questions, we need to define what it means for an infant to experience or sense the world. Humans have several kinds of sense organs, each of which is receptive to a different kind of physical energy. For example, the retina at the back of the eye is sensitive to some types of electromagnetic energy, and sight is the result. The eardrum detects changes in air pressure, and hearing is the result. Cells at the top of the nasal passage detect the passage of airborne molecules, and smell is the result. In each case, the sense organ translates the physical stimulus into nerve impulses that are sent to the brain. **The processes by which the brain receives, selects, modifies, and organizes these impulses is known as *perception*.** This is simply the first step in the complex process of accumulating information that eventually results in "knowing."

Darla's questions are really about her newborn son's perceptual skills. By the end of this section, you'll be able to answer her questions, because we're going to look at how infants use different senses to experience the world. We begin with smell and taste, which are often known as the *chemical senses*, because they are among the most mature senses at birth.

Smell and Taste

Newborns have a highly developed sense of smell. They will respond to some odors but not others. For example, very young infants will look in the direction of a pad that is saturated with breast odor from a nursing woman but not in the direction of one with her underarm odor (Porter et al., 1992). Some newborns apparently recognize their mothers based on odor. In one study

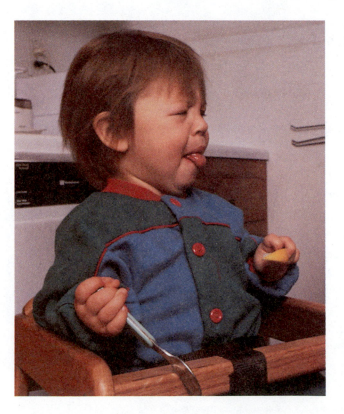

(Cernoch & Porter, 1985), mothers wore a gauze pad in their underarm overnight. The following morning, this pad was placed next to the cheek of the mother's 15-day-old baby; a pad from another mother was placed next to the baby's other cheek. Breast-fed babies consistently turned in the direction of the pad worn by their mothers, but bottle-fed babies did not. Breast-fed babies apparently recognized their mothers' odor because of repeated skin contact while nursing.

Infants also have a highly developed sense of taste. They readily differentiate salty, sour, bitter, and sweet tastes (Crook, 1987). Most infants seem to have a "sweet tooth"—they react to sweet substances by smiling, sucking, and licking their lips. In contrast, like the youngster in the photograph, they respond negatively to bitter and sour substances (Rosenstein & Oster, 1988).

This early sensitivity to odor and taste is valuable to an infant. Feeding is simplified, because infants favor odors and tastes associated with feeding, and sensitivity to odor and taste allows babies to recognize their mothers.

Touch and Pain

Newborns are sensitive to touch. As you remember from Chapter 2, many areas of the newborn's body respond reflexively when touched. For example, if you stroke the sole of a newborn's foot, the toes spread apart, and the big toe moves upward. This response is known as the Babinski reflex. Behaviors such as these prove that infants perceive touch.

Whether babies perceive pain is more difficult to answer, because pain has such a subjective element to it. The same pain-eliciting stimulus may lead some adults to complain of mild discomfort, whereas others report that they are in agony. Infants cannot express their pain to us directly, of course, so our conclusions about their experience of pain are based on indirect evidence.

The infant's nervous system is definitely capable of transmitting pain; receptors for pain in the skin are just as plentiful in infants as they are in adults (Anand & Hickey, 1987). Furthermore, babies' behavior in response to apparent pain-provoking stimuli also suggests that they experience pain. For example, when newborns receive an injection, they cry in a way that is associated with pain: The cry occurs rapidly, is high-pitched, and is not easily soothed. Furthermore, their facial expression changes systematically in response to the injection. They lower their eyebrows, purse their lips, and, of course, open their mouths (Grunau, Johnston, & Craig, 1990).

Such sensitivity to touch and pain is useful in maintaining contact with a caregiver, especially the mother, and in helping the infant to avoid dangerous stimuli.

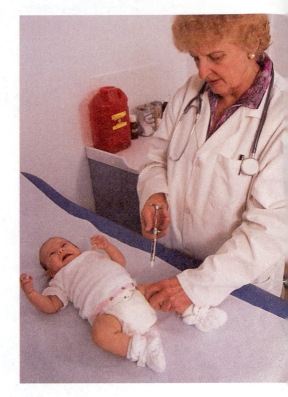

If this baby could talk, it looks as if she would be telling us, "That hurts!"

Hearing

Do you remember, from Chapter 2, the study in which mothers read aloud *The Cat in the Hat* late in pregnancy? This research showed that the fetus can hear by 7 or 8 months after conception. Evidence that newborns can hear comes from their responses to sounds. If a parent is quiet but then coughs, infants may startle, blink their eyes, and move their arms or legs. These responses, typical for many infants, indicate that infants are sensitive to sound.

However, detecting a noise is simply the beginning of auditory perception. Sound is a particularly lush source of stimulation; in addition to carrying a message through words or music, sound can reveal much about its source. When we hear a person speak, the pitch of the speech can be used to judge the age and sex of the speaker; if the speech contains many relatively lower-pitched sounds, then the speaker is probably a man. The loudness of the speech tells us about the speaker's distance; if it can barely be heard, the speaker is far away. Also, differences in the time it takes sound to travel to the left and right ears tells us about the speaker's location; if the sounds arrive at exactly the same time, the speaker must be directly ahead or directly behind us.

Even infants can extract much of this information in sound. Young babies can distinguish sounds of different pitches; 6-month-olds do so nearly as accurately as adults (Spetner & Olsho, 1990). They are also able to differentiate speech sounds, such as different vowel and consonant sounds (a topic that we examine in more detail in Chapter 4).

Like adults, infants use sound to locate objects, looking toward the source of sound (Morrongiello, Fenwick, & Chance, 1990). Infants also use sound to decide whether objects are near or far. In one study (Clifton, Perris, & Bullinger, 1991), 7-month-olds were shown a rattle. Next, the experimenters darkened the room and shook the rattle, either 6 inches away from the infant

RACHEL CLIFTON

" . . . infants use sound to evaluate environmental events and objects at a very young age, integrating this auditory information with their motor activity and cognitive functioning."

or about 2 feet away. Infants would often reach for the rattle in the dark when it was 6 inches away but not when it was 2 feet away. These 7-month-olds were quite capable of using sound to estimate distance—in this case, distinguishing a toy that they could reach from one they could not.

Thus, by the middle of the first year, infants are responding to much of the information that is provided by sound. In Chapter 4, we will reach the same conclusion when we examine the perception of language-related sounds.

Seeing

If you've ever watched infants, you've probably noticed that they spend much of their waking time looking around. Sometimes they seem to be generally scanning their environment, and sometimes they seem to be focusing on nearby objects. What do they see as a result? Perhaps their visual world is a sea of confusing gray blobs. Or maybe they see the world essentially as adults do. Actually, neither of these descriptions is entirely accurate, but the second is closer to the truth.

The various elements of the visual system—the eye, the optic nerve, and the brain—are relatively well developed at birth. Newborns respond to light and can track moving objects with their eyes. How well do infants see? **The clarity of vision, called *visual acuity,* is defined as the smallest pattern that can be distinguished dependably.** You've undoubtedly had your acuity measured, probably by being asked to read rows of progressively smaller letters or numbers from a chart. The same approach is used to assess newborns' acuity, adjusted to compensate for the fact that we can't use words to explain to infants what we'd like them to do. Most infants will look at patterned stimuli instead of plain, patternless stimuli. For example, if we were to show these two stimuli to an infant, most babies would look longer at the striped pattern than at

the gray pattern. As we make the lines narrower (along with the spaces between them), there comes a point at which the black and white stripes become so fine that they simply blend together and appear gray—just like the other pattern.

To estimate an infant's acuity, we pair the gray square with squares in which the widths of the stripes differ, like these: When infants look at the two

stimuli equally, this indicates that they are no longer able to distinguish the stripes of the patterned stimulus. By measuring the width of the stripes and their distance from an infant's eye, we can estimate acuity, with detection of thinner stripes indicating better acuity. Measurements of this sort indicate that newborns and 1-month-olds see at 20 feet what normal adults would see at 200 to 400 feet. By the first birthday, infants' acuity is essentially the same as that of an adult with normal vision (Banks & Dannemiller, 1987).

Now that we know that infants can see, an obvious next question is "What do they look at?" Videotapes of babies' eyes as they scan objects reveal that newborns and 1-month-olds often gaze at some conspicuous feature of an object, such as an edge (Bronson, 1991). Beginning at about 2 or 3 months, infants start to inspect the interior of objects, too (Aslin, 1987).

This general sequence also applies to how infants look at faces. Newborns and 1-month-olds typically gaze at the outer edges of faces and at the eyes. By 2 months, infants begin to fixate on other facial features in addition to the eyes. By age 3 months, infants recognize facial features as a unique configuration of elements. They know that the eyes, nose, and mouth are not arranged haphazardly but always appear in approximately the same relative positions (Aslin, 1987).

Thus, long before the first birthday, infants are scanning objects thoroughly. Their skill allows them to recognize some features that coincide consistently, forming familiar objects.

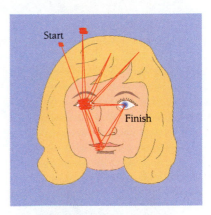

Salapatek, 1975.

This diagram shows the movements of a 3-month-old's eyes while scanning a face. Notice that the baby looks primarily at the lips and eyes.

COLOR

By today's standards, the first color televisions were primitive. Balancing the colors correctly, so that people didn't look green, for example, was extraordinarily difficult. Nevertheless, these televisions were immensely popular (as were the people who owned them), because adding color makes objects more engrossing, more enjoyable, and more beautiful. But color is more than pleasing; it is functional, too. Color helps us recognize objects and people, and it alerts us to danger.

How do we perceive color? The wavelength of light is the basis of color perception. In the diagram, light that we see as red has a relatively long wavelength, whereas violet, at the other end of the color spectrum, has a much

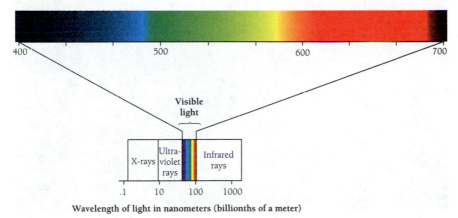

Goldstein, 1994.

shorter wavelength. **Concentrated in the back of the eye, along the retina, are specialized neurons called *cones*.** Some cones are particularly sensitive to short-wavelength light (blues and violets). Others are sensitive to medium-wavelength light (greens and yellows); still others are sensitive to long-wavelength light (reds and oranges). These different kinds of cones are linked together by complex circuits of neurons, and this circuitry is responsible for our ability to see the world in colors.

These circuits begin to function gradually in the first few months after birth. Apparently, newborns perceive few colors. However, 1-month-olds can differentiate blue from gray, which means that the short-wavelength circuit is functioning (Maurer & Adams, 1987). At this age, babies can also differentiate red from green, but not yellow from green or yellow from red. Apparently, the medium- and short-wavelength circuits are functioning (because infants discriminate red and green) but not with complete fidelity (because they cannot distinguish yellow). However, 3- and 4-month-olds perceive colors in much the same way that adults do, despite the fact that their visual acuity is not yet fully developed (Adams, 1989).

ELEANOR GIBSON
"The trends in perceptual development emerge as the product of both experience with an environment and the maturing powers of an individual."

DEPTH

People see objects as having three dimensions: height, width, and depth. The retina of the eye is flat, so height and width can be represented directly on its two-dimensional surface. But the third dimension, depth, cannot be represented directly on this flat surface, so how do we perceive depth? We use perceptual processing to *infer* depth.

Depth perception tells us whether objects are near or far, which was the basis for some classic research by Eleanor Gibson and Richard Walk (1960) on the origins of depth perception. **In their work, babies were placed on the glass-covered platform shown in the photograph, a device known as the *visual cliff*.** On one side of the platform, a checkerboard pattern appeared directly under the glass; on the other side, the pattern appeared several feet below the glass. The result was that the first side looked shallow but the other looked deep, like a cliff.

Mothers stood on each side of the visual cliff and tried to coax their infants across the deep or the shallow side. Most babies willingly crawled to their mothers when they stood on the shallow side. In contrast, almost every baby refused to cross the deep side, even when the mothers called them by name and tried to lure them with an attractive toy. Clearly, infants can perceive depth by the time they are old enough to crawl.

What about younger babies who cannot yet crawl? When babies as young as 1½ months are simply placed on the visual cliff, their hearts beat more slowly when they are placed on the deep side of the cliff. Heart rate often decelerates when people notice something interesting, so this would suggest that 1½-month-olds notice that the deep side is different. At 7 months, infants' heart rate accelerates, a sign of fear. Thus, although young babies can detect a difference between the shallow and the deep sides of the visual cliff, only older, crawling babies are actually afraid of the deep side (Campos et al., 1978).

How do infants infer depth? They rely upon many sources of information. **One is *retinal disparity*: When a person views an object, the retinal images in the left and the right eyes differ.** When objects are distant, the retinal images are nearly identical; when they are nearby, the images differ. Thus, greater disparity in retinal images signifies that an object is close. By 4–6 months of age, infants use retinal disparity as a depth cue, correctly inferring that objects are nearby when disparity is great (Yonas & Owsley, 1987).

Motion can also provide information about depth. When an object such as a person or vehicle moves away, it looks smaller. Knowing that the object is not really getting smaller, we interpret the change to mean that the object is becoming more distant. Also, moving objects often pass in front of or behind other objects. When one object is partially obscured by another, we infer that the obscured object is farther away than the unobscured object. By 5 months of age, infants use both of these motion cues to deduce depth (Craton & Yonas, 1988).

Not only do infants use visual cues to judge depth, they also use sound. Remember that infants correctly judge quieter objects to be more distant than louder objects. Given such an assortment of cues, it is not surprising that infants gauge depth so accurately.

We've seen that infants use both auditory and visual information to estimate distance. This represents an important process in perception—integrating information from different senses. Let's look at this more carefully.

When babies pick up toys, they integrate information received by touch and from vision.

Integrating Sensory Information

We have described the infants' sensory systems separately, but their experiences are usually "multimedia events." A nursing mother provides visual and taste cues to her baby. A rattle may stimulate vision, hearing, and touch. From experiences like these, infants learn to coordinate information provided by different senses. Infants can integrate information from vision and touch. For example, if 6-month-olds are allowed to feel unfamiliar toys that they cannot see, they later look at these toys longer than unfamiliar toys that they have not felt previously. Infants can come to know objects through touch and later recognize them visually (Rose & Orlian, 1991).

Infants also coordinate sights and sounds. For example, by the first birthday, infants have linked the characteristic sounds of male and female voices with the characteristic appearances of male and female faces (Poulin-Dubois et al., 1994). Another example of integration from vision and hearing, judging distance, is the topic of the Spotlight on Research feature.

Integrating Sight and Sound

When Darla hears her son waking, she greets him with cheerful morning chatter and reaches into the crib to pick him up. In so doing, Darla provides two cues that she is getting closer: Her image gets larger, and her voice sounds louder. We already know that older infants use sights and sounds independently to judge distance, but have infants integrated these rules from different sensory systems? Do infants know that an approaching object looks larger *and* sounds louder, whereas a departing object looks smaller *and* sounds quieter?

SPOTLIGHT ON RESEARCH

To answer these questions, Jeffrey Pickens (1994) created the setup shown in the drawing. He presented pairs of 25-second videotapes on two video monitors placed side by side. In one pair, the first video showed a toy train that appeared to be coming toward the viewer; the second video showed a train going away from the viewer. These videos were shown eight times simultaneously. On four of the presentations, the soundtrack consisted of an engine getting louder; on the other four presentations, the engine was getting quieter. Research assistants wearing headphones (so that they couldn't hear the soundtrack) recorded which video the infant was watching.

What should the 5-month-old infants that Pickens (1994) tested do when they see these videos? If infants know the rules

getting closer = larger and louder
getting farther = smaller and quieter

then perhaps they will look at the video that matches the sound: They'll watch the video of the arriving train when the engine gets louder and the video of the departing train when the engine gets quieter. Infants might also do just the opposite—look at the mismatching sounds because they find them so peculiar. In either case, there is a strong link between what they hear and where they look. If, in contrast, infants don't know these rules, then the soundtrack should not influence what they watch; they should watch the videos equally.

The top bar of the graph, labeled approach/retreat, shows the percentage of time that these 5-month-olds looked at the video that corresponded to the soundtrack. You can see that infants spent nearly two-thirds of the time watch-

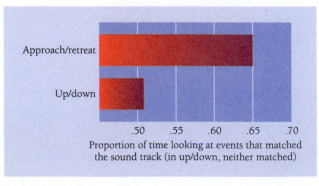

Based on data from Pickens, 1994.

ing the video that matched the soundtrack; evidently they knew the rules for integrating visual and auditory cues to grasp distance.

The second bar in the graph is from a control condition in which two other videos were shown. One video showed a train moving from the top of the video monitor to the bottom; the other showed a train moving from the bottom to the top. The soundtrack was the same—the sound of an engine getting louder or quieter. Neither video corresponded to the soundtrack, because the train remained a constant distance from the viewer. Consequently, the infants should look equally at the two videos—and they did.

These findings, plus similar results from other studies (Morrongiello & Fenwick, 1991), provide strong evidence that infants coordinate sight and sound to determine whether objects are getting closer or farther.   ❧

Skillful integration of sight and sound is yet another indication that babies have extraordinary perceptual skill. Young infants perceive the world with impressive precision in each of the sensory systems that we have examined. Darla's son can smell, taste, and feel pain; he can distinguish sounds; and, in a few months, he will use sounds to locate objects. His vision is blurry now but will improve rapidly; in a few months, he'll see the full range of colors and perceive depth. In short, Darla's son, like most infants, is exceptionally well prepared to begin to make sense out of his environment.

TEST YOURSELF

1. Taste and _____ are the chemical senses.
2. Infants respond negatively to substances that taste sour or _____.
3. A high-pitched cry that is not readily soothed is part of the infant's response to _____.
4. If an infant seated in a completely darkened room hears the sound of her favorite rattle nearby, she will reach for it; this demonstrates _____.
5. By the time an infant is _____ old, his or her visual acuity approximates that of an adult with normal vision.
6. _____ are specialized neurons in the retina that are sensitive to color.
7. The term _____ refers to the fact that the images of an object in the left and right eyes differ for nearby objects.
8. Infants integrate information between sight and touch and between sight and _____.
9. What features of infants' perceptual skill show the influence of nature? What features show the influence of nurture?

Putting It All Together

The first three years of life produce remarkable change in human beings. The rate of physical growth is extraordinary but can be slowed when children are malnourished. Different regions of the infant's brain are already regulat-

ing distinct functions, such as goal-directed behavior. This pattern of specialization helps to explain the impact of Martin's injury on his language.

We also looked at improvements in motor skill. Infants gradually become more mobile during the first year. Most begin to walk soon after their first birthday, reflecting biological maturation and integration of the different component skills involved in walking. Babies vary in terms of when they take their first steps. Like Nancy, the world-class crawler, some won't walk until 15 or 16 months of age. Paralleling changes in locomotion are changes in fine motor skills: During the first year, infants become more skilled at grasping and manipulating objects.

In the last section of the chapter, we saw that infants are endowed with powerful perceptual skills. Even new-born babies can smell, taste, feel, hear, and see—in some cases with remarkable accuracy. Because of these skills, infants like Darla's son are well prepared to experience the world; and these skills are the basis for the first steps of intellectual and social development, as we'll see in Chapters 4 and 5.

Thinking about Development

1. In Chapter 2, we explained how polygenic inheritance is often involved when phenotypes form a continuum. Height is such a phenotype. Propose a simple polygenic model to explain how height might be inherited.

2. What features of research on locomotion support the idea of development as a universal process? What features support the idea of development as a context-specific process?

3. Psychologists often refer to "perceptual-motor skills," which implies that these two types of skills are interrelated. Based on what you learned in this chapter, how might motor skills influence perception? How does perception influence motor skills?

Summary

Growing Bigger Every Day

Physical Growth

■ Physical growth is particularly rapid during infancy, but babies of the same age differ considerably in their heights and weights. Size at maturity is largely determined by heredity.

■ Growth follows the cephalocaudal principle, in which the head and trunk develop before the legs. Consequently, infants and young children have disproportionately large heads and trunks.

■ Infants must consume a large number of calories, relative to their body weight, primarily because of the energy that is required for growth. Breast feeding and bottle feeding both provide babies with adequate nutrition.

■ Malnutrition is a worldwide problem that is particularly harmful during infancy, when growth is so rapid. Treating malnutrition adequately requires improving children's diet and training their parents to provide stimulating environments.

The Emerging Nervous System

■ A nerve cell, called a *neuron,* includes a cell body, a dendrite, and an axon. The mature brain consists of billions of neurons, organized into nearly identical left and right hemispheres connected by the corpus callosum. The

cerebral cortex regulates most of the functions that we think of as distinctively human. The frontal cortex is associated with personality and goal-directed behavior; the left hemisphere of the cortex with language; and the right hemisphere of the cortex with nonverbal processes such as perceiving music and regulating emotions.

■ Case studies of children with brain injury and EEG records all suggest that the left hemisphere specializes in language processing early in life, probably by birth.

■ The right hemisphere controls some nonverbal functions, such as perception of music, very early in infancy; control of other functions, such as understanding spatial relations, is achieved by the preschool years. The frontal cortex has begun to regulate goal-directed behavior and emotional responding by the first birthday.

Moving and Grasping—Early Motor Skills

Locomotion

■ Infants acquire a series of motor skills during their first year, culminating in walking a few months after the first birthday. Like most motor skills, learning to walk involves differentiation of individual skills, such as maintaining balance and using the legs alternately, and then integrating these skills into a coherent whole.

Fine Motor Skills

■ Infants first use only one hand at a time, then both hands independently, then both hands in common actions, and, finally, at about 5 months of age, both hands in different actions with a common purpose.

■ Most people are right-handed, a preference that emerges after the first birthday and becomes well established during the preschool years. Handedness is determined by heredity but can also be influenced by cultural values.

Maturation and Experience Both Influence Motor Skills

■ Biology and experience both shape the mastery of motor skills. On the one hand, the basic developmental timetable for motor skills is similar around the world, which emphasizes underlying biological causes. On the other hand, specific experience can accelerate motor development, particular for complex motor skills.

Coming to Know the World: Perception

Smell and Taste

■ Newborns are able to smell, and some can recognize their mother's odor; they also taste, preferring sweet substances and responding negatively to bitter and sour

tastes.

Touch and Pain

■ Infants respond to touch. They probably experience pain, because their responses to painful stimuli are similar to those of older children.

Hearing

■ Babies can hear. More importantly, they can distinguish different sounds and use sound to locate objects in space.

Seeing

■ A newborn's visual acuity is relatively poor, but 1-year-olds can see as well as an adult with normal vision. Color vision develops as different sets of cones begin to function, a process that seems to be complete by 3 or 4 months of age. Infants perceive depth, based on retinal disparity and cues from motion.

Integrating Sensory Information

■ Infants coordinate information from different senses. They can recognize, by sight, an object that they've felt previously. They look at a woman's face when they hear a woman's voice or look at an object that is becoming more distant when a sound becomes softer.

Key Terms

axon   (84)
cell body   (84)
cerebral cortex   (85)
cones   (101)
corpus callosum   (85)
dendrite   (84)
differentiation   (90)
electroencephalogram
   (EEG)   (86)
fine motor skills   (88)

frontal cortex   (85)
hemispheres   (85)
integration   (90)
locomotion   (88)
malnourished   (83)
motor skills   (88)
neural plate   (85)
neuron   (84)
perception   (98)

positron emission tomography
   (PET scan)   (86)
retinal disparity   (103)
toddlers   (88)
visual acuity   (100)
visual cliff   (102)

If You'd Like to Learn More

ASLIN, R. N. (1987). Visual and auditory discrimination in infancy. In J. D. Osofsky (Ed.), *Handbook of infant development* (2nd ed.). New York: Wiley. This text is a comprehensive but technical account of recent research on infant perception.

KEOGH, J., & SUGDEN, D. (1985). *Movement skill development.* New York: Macmillan. This textbook explores

all facets of motor skill development in a thorough and readable fashion.

TANNER, J. M. (1978). *Fetus into man.* Cambridge, MA: Harvard University Press. Tanner is a leading authority and presents a straightforward account of human growth.

☙ Three-year-old Jamila loved talking to Grandma Powell on the telephone. Sometimes these conversations were not very successful because Grandma Powell would ask questions, to which Jamila would reply by nodding her head "yes" or "no." Jamila's dad had explained that Grandma Powell (and others on the phone) couldn't see her nodding—that she needed to *say* "yes" or "no." But Jamila would invariably return to head-nodding. Her dad couldn't see why such a bright and talkative child didn't realize that nodding was meaningless over the phone.

☙ A few days ago, 4-year-old Cheryl told her mother a disturbing story. Several months ago, she said, Mr. Johnson, a neighbor and long-time family friend, had taken down her pants and touched her "private parts." Her mother was shocked. She had always believed Mr. Johnson to be an honest, decent man, which made her wonder if Cheryl's imagination had simply run wild. Yet Mr. Johnson *had* always seemed a bit peculiar, so her daughter's claim did have a ring of truth.

☙ Victoria, a 4-year-old, enjoys solving jigsaw puzzles, coloring, and building towers with blocks. While busy with these activities, she often talks to herself. For example, once as she was coloring a picture, she said, "Where's the red crayon? Stay inside the lines. Color the blocks blue." These remarks were not directed at anyone else; after all, Victoria was alone. Why did she say these things? What purpose did they serve?

☙ Nabina was just a few weeks away from her first birthday. For the past month, she had seemed to understand much of her mother's speech. If her mom asked, "Where's Garfield?" (the family cat), Nabina would scan the room and point toward Garfield. Yet Nabina's own speech was still gibberish: she "talked" constantly, but her mom couldn't understand a word of it. If Nabina apparently could understand others' speech, why couldn't she speak herself?

The Emergence
of Thought and Language

 In the movie *Look Who's Talking,* we are privy to an infant's adult-like thoughts about his birth, diaper changes, and his mother's boyfriends. Of course, few of us believe that babies are capable of this sophisticated thinking. But what thoughts occupy the mind of an infant who is not yet speaking? How does cognition develop during infancy and early childhood? What makes these changes possible?

These questions provide the focus of this chapter. We begin with what has long been considered the definitive account of cognitive development, Jean Piaget's theory. According to this theory, thinking progresses through distinct stages, one of which holds the explanation for Jamila's persistent head-nodding while she's on the phone.

The next two sections of the chapter concern alternative accounts of cognitive development. We'll look at the information-processing perspective. This approach has traced children's emerging cognitive skills in many specific domains, among them the memory skills necessary for Cheryl to recall events from her past. We'll also examine Lev Vygotsky's theory, which emphasizes the cultural origins of cognitive development and explains why children like Victoria sometimes talk to themselves as they play or work.

In the last section, we'll study how children master the sounds, words, and grammar of their native language. In the process, we'll learn how Nabina can understand some language even though she does not yet speak it.

The Onset of Thinking: Piaget's Account

LEARNING OBJECTIVES

🐦 *According to Piaget, how do assimilation, accommodation, and organization provide the foundation for cognitive development throughout the life span?*

🐦 *How do schemes become more advanced as infants progress through the six stages of sensorimotor thinking?*

🐦 *What are the distinguishing characteristics of thinking during the preoperational stage?*

🐦 *What are some of the shortcomings of Piaget's account of cognitive development?*

Imagine that you are the adult seated at the table in the drawing. You ask the child, a preschooler, to select the photograph that shows how the mountains on the table look to you. Which photograph do you think the preschooler will pick? One photo shows the mountains as they would actually look to you; many preschoolers pick the photo that shows how the mountains look to them!

Why do preschoolers act this way? What do such mistakes tell us about their thinking? For many years, the most convincing answers to these questions were provided by a theory developed by the Swiss psychologist Jean Piaget (1896–1980). Piaget began work on his theory of mental development in the 1920s, and it remains influential today. In Chapter 1, we saw that, in Piaget's theory, thinking progresses through four qualitatively different stages. This and other important features of the theory are highlighted in the chart that appears at the top of page 111. In this section, we'll begin by describing some of the general features of Piaget's theory. In the next section, we'll examine Piaget's account of thinking during infancy and during the preschool years. We end this section by discussing some criticisms of the theory.

Perspective	Examples of Theories	Main Ideas	Emphases in Biopsychosocial Framework	Positions on Developmental Issues
Cognitive	Piaget's theory	Thinking develops in sequence of stages	Main emphasis on biological and social forces, less on psychological, little on life cycle	Strongly nature, discontinuity, and universal sequence of stages

Basic Principles of Cognitive Development

Biologists have long known that living things must adapt to their environments if they are to survive. Cattle seek new pastures when grass becomes scarce; animals stand motionless to blend into the background and thereby hide from predators; and corn plants roll up their leaves in a drought to conserve water. Adaptation of a similar sort occurs in thinking, according to Piaget. Throughout the life span, people adjust their ways of thinking, responding to new experiences. For example, a baby who has just begun to pick up objects soon learns that some are too heavy or too slippery to lift.

Successful intellectual adaptation requires two processes working together: assimilation and accommodation. To learn more about these processes, let's return to our example of the baby picking up objects. **Piaget would call this activity a *scheme*, which is a mental structure similar to a concept that is used to organize information and regulate behavior. *Assimilation* occurs when new experiences are readily incorporated into existing schemes.** If our infant first formed a scheme based on picking up a rattle, she would soon discover that the same scheme also works well on blocks, toy cars, and other small objects. ***Accommodation* occurs when schemes are modified based on experience.** Soon our infant will learn that some objects can only be lifted with two hands and that some can't be lifted at all. These experiences produce changes in schemes. For example, infants may develop a new scheme involving actions for lifting heavy objects.

Another of Piaget's principles of cognitive development is based on the fact that schemes do not exist in isolation. Instead, they always form a cohesive, integrated mental structure. For babies, schemes for grasping, sucking, and waving make up an organized whole. In the same way, for toddlers, schemes for climbing, jumping, and throwing all fit together in a unified cognitive structure. It is as if the child is a little scientist trying to formulate a grand theory of how the world works. Each scheme is part of the theory, and the child, like a good scientist, tries to fit all of the pieces together. **This *organization* of schemes is another key principle in Piaget's account of cognitive development.**

Periodically, however, shortcomings in a child's way of thinking appear; experiences are no longer easily assimilated into a scheme. For example, preschoolers' concept of death resembles their concept of sleep: Death is characterized by closed eyes and lack of movement (Carey, 1985). We will have more to say about conceptions of death in Chapter 15; for now, the important fact is that the preschoolers' scheme for death is wrong. When youngsters learn that, unlike sleep, death is a permanent state from which one cannot return, their scheme for death must be changed substantially.

Many experiences like these can shake the foundation of a child's cognitive

Piaget believed that infants have a scheme for grasping objects, which helps them to organize information and regulate their behavior.

structure. Because schemes form an inseparable whole, massive accommodation can produce an overall state of cognitive disorganization. To restore the balance, the current but now outmoded way of thinking is replaced by a qualitatively different, more advanced structure. Faced with the fact that his or her grand theory of the world is fundamentally wrong because it is at odds with too much of the evidence, a youngster abandons the old theory in favor of one that is new and better.

According to Piaget, these revolutionary changes in cognitive organization occur three times over the life span: at approximately 2, 7, and 11 years of age. This divides cognitive development into the following four periods:

Period of Development	Age Range
Sensorimotor period	Infancy (0 to 2 years)
Preoperational period	Preschool and early elementary school years (2 to 7 years)
Concrete operational period	Middle and late elementary school years (7 to 11 years)
Formal operational period	Adolescence and adulthood (11 years and up)

The ages listed here are only approximate. Some youngsters may move through the periods more rapidly than others, depending on their ability and their experience. However, all children go through all four periods and in exactly this sequence. Sensorimotor thinking always gives rise to preoperational thinking; a child cannot "skip" preoperational thinking and move directly from the sensorimotor to the concrete operational period.

In the next few pages of this chapter, we will consider Piaget's account of sensorimotor and preoperational thinking, the periods from birth to approximately 7 years of age. In Chapter 6, we will return to Piaget's theory to examine his account of concrete and formal operational thinking in older children and adolescents.

Sensorimotor Thinking

Before examining Piaget's description of infancy, let's review some of the facts of infancy that we've already learned. In Chapter 3, we saw that infants' locomotor skills improve rapidly during the first year, culminating in walking at 14 or 15 months of age; fine motor skills develop rapidly during this same period; and perceptual skills, already powerful in early infancy, improve quickly.

Piaget proposed that this period of rapidly changing perceptual and motor skills forms a distinct phase in human development. **The *sensorimotor period*, from birth to roughly 2 years of age, is the first of Piaget's four periods of cognitive development.** Piaget divided this period into six stages. All infants progress through the six stages in the same order, but they may do so at different rates, so the ages we list here are only approximations.

1. *Exercising reflexes (roughly 0–1 month).* We know, from Chapter 2, that newborns respond reflexively to many stimuli. As infants use these reflexes during the first month, they become much more coordinated. For example, just as major-league players swing a bat with greater power and strength than do Little Leaguers, 1-month-olds suck more strongly and steadily than do newborns. Reflexes like this one provide the foundation for much cognitive growth during infancy.

2. *Learning to adapt: Primary circular reactions (roughly 1–4 months).* During these months, reflexes become modified by experience. **The chief mechanism for change is the *primary circular reaction*, in which an infant accidentally produces some pleasing event and then tries to recreate the event.** For example, an infant may inadvertently touch her lips with her thumb, thereby initiating sucking and the pleasing sensations associated with sucking. Later, the infant tries to recreate these sensations by guiding her thumb to her mouth. Sucking no longer occurs only when the mother places a nipple at the infant's mouth; instead, the infant has found a way to initiate sucking herself.

3. *Making interesting events (roughly 4–8 months).* Primary circular reactions are centered on the infant's own body—they typically involve such reflexes as sucking or grasping. However, beginning in Stage 3, the infant begins to show greater interest in the world. Now objects are more often the focus of circular reactions. For example, the infant shown in the photograph accidentally shook a new rattle. Hearing the interesting noise, the infant grasped the rattle anew, tried to shake it, and expressed great pleasure when the noise resumed. This sequence was repeated several times.

Novel actions that are repeated with objects characterize the *secondary circular reaction*. They are significant because they represent an infant's first efforts to learn about objects in the environment, to explore their properties. No longer are infants grasping objects "mindlessly," simply because something is in contact with their hands. Instead, they are learning about the sights and sounds associated with the objects.

4. *Behaving intentionally: Separating means from ends (roughly 8–12 months).* This stage marks the onset of deliberate, intentional behavior. For the first time, the means and the ends of activities are distinct. For example, if a father places his hand in front of a toy, an infant will move his hand to be able to play with the toy. The "move the hand" scheme is the means to achieve the end of activating the "grasp the toy" scheme. Combining schemes in this way is the first solid evidence of deliberate, purposeful behavior during infancy.

5. *Experimenting (roughly 12–18 months).* The infant at this stage is an active experimentalist. **An infant will repeat old schemes with novel objects— which Piaget called a *tertiary circular reaction*—as if trying to understand why different objects yield different outcomes.** A Stage 5 infant may deliberately shake a number of different objects, trying to discover which produce sounds and which do not. Or an infant may decide to drop different objects to see what happens. An infant in a crib discovers that stuffed animals land quietly, whereas harder toys often make a more satisfying "clunk" when they hit the ground.

Tertiary circular reactions represent a significant extension of the intentional behavior that emerged in Stage 4. Now babies repeat actions with different objects *solely* for the purpose of seeing what will happen.

6. *Using symbols (roughly 18–24 months)*. By 18 months, most infants have begun to talk and gesture (the subject of the last section of this chapter). These actions are significant because they illustrate toddlers' emerging capacity to use symbols. Words and gestures are symbols that stand for something else: Waving and saying "bye-bye" are both ways to indicate that you're leaving. Pretend play, which we'll examine in more detail in Chapter 5, also shows a youngster's use of symbols. For example, a 20-month-old may move her hand back and forth in front of her mouth, pretending to brush her teeth.

Once infants can use symbols, they can begin to anticipate the consequences of actions mentally, instead of having to perform them. Imagine that an infant and parent have constructed a tower of blocks next to an open door. Leaving the room, a Stage 5 infant might well close the door, knocking over the tower. This infant is unable to foresee the predictable outcome of closing the door. In contrast, a Stage 6 child could anticipate the consequence of closing the door and might well move the tower beforehand.

Using symbols is the crowning achievement of the sensorimotor period. In just two years, the infant has progressed from reflexive responding to symbolic processing. A summary of these changes is shown in the table.

Stage	Age (months)	Accomplishment	Example
1	0–1	Reflexes become coordinated.	Sucking a nipple
2	1–4	Primary circular reactions appear—an infant's first learned adaptations to the world.	Thumb sucking
3	4–8	Secondary circular reactions emerge, allowing infants to explore the world of objects.	Shaking a toy to hear it rattle
4	8–12	Means-end sequencing of schemes is seen, marking the onset of intentional behavior.	Moving an obstacle to reach a toy
5	12–18	Tertiary circular reactions develop, allowing children to experiment.	Shaking different toys to hear the sounds they make
6	18–24	Symbolic processing is revealed in language, gestures, and pretend play.	Eating pretend food with a pretend fork

The ability to use mental symbols marks the end of sensorimotor thinking and the beginning of preoperational thought, which we'll examine next.

Preoperational Thinking

Once they have crossed into preoperational thinking, the magic power of symbols is available to young children. Of course, mastering this power is a lifelong process; the preschool child's efforts are tentative and sometimes incorrect. Piaget identified a number of characteristic shortcomings in preschoolers' fledgling symbolic skills. Let's look at three.

EGOCENTRISM

Preoperational children typically believe that others see the world—both literally and figuratively—exactly as they do. **Egocentrism is difficulty in seeing** the world from another's outlook. When youngsters stubbornly cling to their own way, they are not simply being contrary. Preoperational children simply do not comprehend that other people differ in their ideas, convictions, and emotions.

One of Piaget's famous experiments, the three-mountains problem, demonstrates preoperational children's egocentrism (Piaget & Inhelder, 1956, chapter 8). Youngsters were seated at a table like the one shown in the drawing on page 110. When preoperational children were asked to choose the photograph that corresponded to another person's view of the mountains, they usually picked the photograph that showed their own view of the mountains, not the other person's. Preoperational youngsters evidently suppose that the mountains are seen the same way by all; they presume that theirs is the only view, not one of many conceivable views. According to Piaget, only concrete operational children fully understand that all people do not experience an event in exactly the same way.

Recall that in the first chapter-opening vignette, 3-year-old Jamila would nod her head during phone conversations with her grandmother. This, too, reflects preoperational egocentrism. Jamila assumes that because she is aware that her head is moving up and down (or side-to-side), her grandmother must be aware of it, too. In the Real People feature, we see yet another manifestation of this egocentrism.

Preschoolers are egocentric, which can make for some frustrating conversations, because they don't understand that there are other points of view!

REAL PEOPLE

Christine, Egocentrism, and Animism

Because of their egocentrism, preoperational youngsters often attribute their own thoughts and feelings to others. **They may even credit inanimate objects with life and lifelike properties, a phenomenon known as** *animism* **(Piaget, 1929).** A 3½-year-old we know, Christine, illustrated this in a conversation we had with her recently on a dreary, rainy day when she was forced to stay indoors.

> *Us:* Is the sun happy today?
> *Christine:* No. It's sad today.
> *Us:* Why?
> *Christine:* Because it's cloudy. He can't shine. And he can't see me!
> *Us:* What about your trike? Is it happy?
> *Christine:* No, he's very sad, too.
> *Us:* Why is that?
> *Christine:* Because I can't ride him. And because he's all alone in the garage, where it's dark.

Caught up in her egocentrism, preoperational Christine believes that objects like the sun and her tricycle think and feel as she does. 🐚

IRREVERSIBILITY

Logical and mathematical operations usually have inverses—operations that "undo" or reverse the effect of an operation. If you start with 5 and add 3, you obtain 8; by subtracting 3 from 8, you can reverse your steps and return to 5. For Piaget, reversibility of this sort also applied to psychological operations. Mature individuals can reverse their thinking if necessary. However, an inability to reverse thinking is one characteristic of preoperational youngsters.

Piaget demonstrated such irreversibility in another famous experiment, involving conservation of liquid quantity. Children were shown two identical

beakers filled with exactly the same amount of juice, like those in the photo-graph. After the children had agreed that the juice in the two beakers was the same, juice was poured from one of the beakers into a third beaker. This beaker was thinner than the original two, which meant that the juice rose higher in the beaker. Children were then asked if the two beakers still contained the same amount of juice. "Yes," older children would reply. Commonly, they justified their answer by explaining that the juice can always be poured back into the original container and that the amounts will be the same. In contrast, preoper-ational children argued that the thinner beaker contains more juice; unable to reverse their mental operations to return to the original equality, they re-sponded on the basis of level of the juice.

APPEARANCE AS REALITY

Many a 3-year-old has watched an older brother or sister slip on a ghoulish Halloween costume and become frightened when the sibling's face is hidden by a dreadful mask. For the youngster, the scary mask is re-ality, not just something that looks frightening but isn't real.

You shouldn't conclude that confusion between ap-pearance and reality is specific to costumes and masks. It is a general characteristic of preoperational thinking. To see how, think about some common instances where ap-pearances and reality may conflict:

Preschoolers are often frightened by scary costumes because they are unable to dis-tinguish appearances from reality.

- A boy is angry because a friend is being mean. Nev-ertheless, he smiles because he's afraid the friend will leave if he reveals his anger.
- A glass of milk looks brown when viewed through sunglasses.
- A piece of hard rubber looks like food (for example, like a piece of pizza).

Older children and adults know that the boy *looks* happy, the milk *looks* brown, and the object *looks* like food—but that the boy is *really* angry, the milk is *re-ally* white, and the object is *really* rubber. Preoperational children, however, readily confuse appearance and reality.

You can see evidence of this confusion in the results of a study by Friend and Davis (1993). Stories were presented in which a person's outward appearance conflicted with his or her underlying feelings. For example, children were told about Sally, a school-age child who was sad because her uncle gave her a baby rattle for her birthday. Sally didn't want to hurt her uncle's feelings, so she smiled as she took the gift out of the box. A photograph showed Sally smiling at her uncle. Children in the study were asked if Sally *looks* happy or sad and if she *really* is happy or sad.

The graph shows how accurately children answered the questions. Questions about Sally's appearance were easy for all children; 4- and 7-year-olds readily judged that Sally looked happy. Questions about her real feelings were

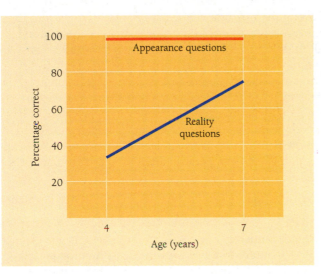

much more difficult; most 4-year-olds answered the questions incorrectly, and even some 7-year-olds did. Thus, when presented stories about people who feel sad but look happy, preoperational youngsters claim not only that the people look happy but that they are really and truly happy! In contrast, 7-year-olds are more likely to have progressed to concrete operational thinking. Consequently, they respond much more accurately.

Are you skeptical of these findings? Do you doubt that young children are confused so easily? When these findings were first reported, many researchers shared your skepticism. They went to great lengths to show that the children were somehow being misled by some minor aspects of the experiment. Surprisingly enough, they were unable to disprove the original results. Rewording the instructions, using different materials, and even training children all had relatively little impact (Flavell, Green, & Flavell, 1986). Confusion about appearance and reality is simply a deep-seated characteristic of preoperational thinking, especially in the early years of this period.

Some Faults of the Theory

Piaget's theory is our single most comprehensive account of cognitive development during infancy, childhood, and adolescence. It has stimulated extensive research, in which some of the theory's predictions have not been supported by research findings. Let's examine some of these gaps.

ALTERNATIVE EXPLANATIONS FOR PERFORMANCE

As we have seen, Piaget explained cognitive development by using constructs like accommodation, assimilation, and schemes. However, subsequent researchers have found that children's performance on Piaget's tasks is often better explained by other theoretical constructs. For example, preoperational children's performance on the conservation task appears to reflect, at least in part, their growing sensitivity to the nuances of language, rather than purely their lack of reversibility. The phrasing of the questions concerning the amount of water turns out to be critical (Winer, Craig, & Weinbaum, 1992). Remember that in this procedure, youngsters are twice asked if the amount of water in the two beakers is the same—once before the water is poured and once after. In everyday conversation, a question is usually repeated like this because the answer was wrong the first time. Or it may be repeated because the answer was correct at first but something has changed so that it is now wrong. Both of these rules about questions would lead young children who had answered "yes" to the first question to wonder if they were wrong and perhaps say "no" the second time. In fact, when the procedure is changed (for example, by asking the question only once) preschoolers are more likely to answer correctly.

Thus, children's performance on conservation problems is based partly on language development, not just the concepts that Piaget included in his theory. As we see in the Spotlight on Research feature, alternate explanations have also been proposed for children's performance on other Piagetian tasks.

SPOTLIGHT ON RESEARCH

When Do Infants Understand That Objects Are Permanent?

According to Piaget, one of the milestones of infancy is the understanding that objects exist independently of oneself and one's actions. He claimed that 1-to-4-month-olds—who are in Stage 2 of the sensorimotor period—believe that objects no longer exist when they disappear from view (out of sight, out of mind). As astounding as this may seem, if you take a favorite toy from a 3-month-old and hide it under a cloth directly in front of her, she will not look for it. This is true even though the shape of the toy is clearly visible under the cloth and within reach!

Beginning at about 4 or 5 months, Piaget found that infants would search for objects. Understanding of objects is far from complete, because even older infants are sometimes unable to find hidden objects. If 9-month-olds see an object hidden under one container, then see it hidden under a second container, most of them routinely look for the toy under the first container. Piaget claimed that this showed 9-month-olds' fragmentary understanding of objects. Infants do not distinguish the object per se from the actions they used to locate it, such as lifting a particular container. Not until approximately 18 months of age do infants apparently have full understanding of the permanence of objects.

Other investigators have questioned Piaget's interpretations. To understand the logic of their research, imagine a magician who has taken an object and wrapped it in a silk scarf. After a few waves of the magic wand and the usual magic words, the scarf is unwrapped. Presto! The object has vanished. We enjoy these tricks, of course, because they violate what we know to be true of objects—they can't really disappear into thin air.

A similar sleight of hand is the key to experimentation by Renée Baillargeon (1987, 1994). Her way of measuring object permanence is shown in the drawing on page 119. Infants first saw a silver screen that appeared to be

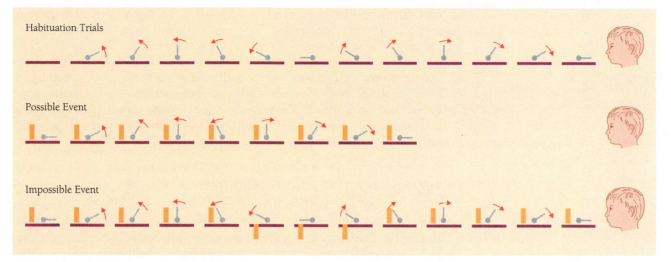

Habituation Trials

Possible Event

Impossible Event

Kail and Wicks-Nelson, 1993.

rotating back and forth. When they were familiar with this display, one of two new displays was shown. In the *possible event,* a yellow box appeared in a position behind the screen, making it impossible for the screen to rotate as far back as it had previously. Instead, the screen rotated until it made contact with the box, then rotated forward. In the *impossible event,* the yellow box appeared, but the screen continued to rotate as before. The screen rotated back until it was flat, then rotated forward, again revealing the yellow box. The illusion was possible because the box was mounted on a movable platform that allowed it to drop out of the way of the moving screen. However, from the infant's perspective, it appeared as if the box vanished behind the screen, only to reappear.

The disappearance and reappearance of the box violates the idea that objects exist permanently. Consequently, an infant who understands the permanence of objects should find the impossible event a truly novel stimulus and look at it longer than the possible event. Baillargeon found that 4½-month-olds consistently looked longer at the impossible event than the possible event. Infants apparently thought that the impossible event was novel, just as we are surprised when the object vanishes from the magician's scarf.

Evidently, infants have some understanding of the permanence of objects at a much younger age than Piaget's theory would predict. Why the difference? Remember that Piaget usually based his assessments on tasks in which infants had to search for missing objects. Search requires locomotor skills—reaching and grasping, for example—and apparently it is these skills that are limited in younger infants, not their understanding that objects are permanent. ❧

The contrary findings regarding infants' understanding of object permanence and conservation do not mean that Piaget's theory is fundamentally wrong. In some cases, the theory needs to be revised to include important constructs that Piaget overlooked.

CONSISTENCY IN PERFORMANCE

In Piaget's view, each stage of intellectual development consists of a unified set of mental structures that pervades children's thinking. For example, preoperational thinking should leave its mark on all of a child's activities. On conservation and three-mountains tasks, a 4-year-old should always respond in a preoperational way: He should claim that the water is not the same after pouring and believe that the other person sees the mountains as he does. In fact, research reveals some consistency in performance on various tasks, but exceptions are common, too (Siegler, 1981). A youngster may be advanced on the conservation task, perfectly average on the three-mountains task, and somewhat delayed on other Piagetian tasks. This variability is not readily incorporated into Piaget's view of uniform stages that should leave the same characteristic imprint in all domains.

THE IMPACT OF CULTURE ON COGNITION

Piaget believed that children, through accommodation and assimilation, construct their own image of the world. This construction of reality is said to be largely the child's own doing, uninfluenced by others. The four periods of cognitive development are said to apply to children and adolescents everywhere, regardless of the culture in which they live. Although Piaget recognized that children's thinking is influenced by parents, siblings, school, and other elements of their culture, he insisted that these elements had relatively little impact on children's progression through his four periods. As we'll see in the next section of the chapter, not all theorists share Piaget's view that culture has little impact on cognitive development.

These criticisms do not mean that Piaget's theory is invalid or should be ignored. As noted earlier, it remains the most complete account of cognitive development. However, in recent years, researchers have attempted to round out our understanding of cognitive development, using other theoretical perspectives such as the information-processing approach that is examined in the next section.

TEST YOURSELF

1. The term _____ means modification of schemes based on experience.
2. According to Piaget's principle of _____, schemes are always integrated to form a cohesive mental structure.
3. A _____ is an event that infants try to repeat because it produces interesting outcomes with objects.
4. The climax of the sensorimotor period occurs in Stage 6 when infants _____.
5. Preschoolers are often _____, meaning that they are unable to take another person's viewpoint.
6. Preoperational children sometimes attribute thoughts and feeling to inanimate objects. This is called _____.
7. In contrast to the prediction of Piaget's theory, when children are tested on different Piagetian tasks, their performance _____.
8. What forces in the biopsychosocial framework can you see in an infant's progression through the six stages of the sensorimotor period?

Answers: (1) *accommodation,* (2) *organization,* (3) *secondary circular reaction,* (4) *begin to use symbols,* (5) *egocentric,* (6) *animism,* (7) *is not always consistent from one task to the next*

Information Processing during Infancy and Early Childhood

LEARNING OBJECTIVES

❧ *What is the basis of the information-processing approach?*

❧ *How well do young children pay attention?*

❧ *Do infants and preschool children remember?*

❧ *What are the shortcomings of preschoolers' eyewitness testimony? What can we do to make it more reliable?*

❧ *Can infants discriminate different quantities?*

❧ *How do preschoolers count?*

Information Processing during Infancy and Early Childhood
Attention
Memory
■ *Preschoolers on the Witness Stand*
Quantitative Knowledge

A few weeks ago, a friend of ours, Jim, bought a new microcomputer for his office. After a few hours dominated by oaths that aren't fit to print in a G-rated textbook, Jim finally had the hardware—computer, keyboard, monitor, and printer—connected properly. He turned on the power, fully expecting the computer to be ready to handle his correspondence, prepare graphs for sales meetings, and when his boss wasn't looking, play a few games. Jim, who is quite naive about personal computers, was shocked to discover that, fresh out of the box, his computer could do none of the tasks for which he had purchased it. Instead, he needed to make another trip to the local computer store and fork over several hundred more dollars for software to make his computer function as he had intended.

This simple distinction between computer hardware and computer software is the basis of an approach to human thinking known as the *information-processing view.* Begun in the 1960s, it is now one of the principal approaches to cognitive development (Kail & Bisanz, 1992). You may remember from Chapter 1 that in the information-processing view, human thinking is based on both mental hardware and mental software. The term *hardware* refers to mental and neural structures that are built-in and that allow the mind to operate. The term *software* refers to mental programs that are the basis for performing particular tasks. According to information-processing psychologists, it is the combination of mental hardware and mental software that allows children to accomplish a specific task. As the chart reminds us, information-processing psychologists claim that as children develop, their mental software becomes more complex, more powerful, and more efficient.

Perspective	Examples of Theories	Main Ideas	Emphases in Biopsychosocial Framework	Positions on Developmental Issues
Cognitive	Information-processing theory	Thought develops by increases in efficiency at handling information	Emphasis on biological and psychological, less on social and life cycle	Nature–nurture interaction, continuity, individual differences in universal structures.

Information-processing psychologists believe that solving tasks successfully usually requires some general processes. Attention and memory, for example, are essential for most tasks, because they allow children to store information and retrieve it later. Of course, successful performance often requires processes and knowledge that are specific to particular domains. For example, to subtract 37 from 58, to find your way from school to home, and to decide what time it is, attention and memory are not enough; you need specialized procedures and knowledge. In the next few pages, we'll begin by looking at attention and memory, then take a glimpse at some of the particular processes involved as children develop quantitative skill.

Attention

Have you ever been in a class where you knew you should be listening and taking notes, but the lecture was just so boring that you started to notice other things—the smell of popcorn cooking, the sound of construction outside, or an attractive person seated two rows ahead of you? After a while, maybe you had to tell yourself, "Pay attention!" **Attentional processes determine which information will be processed further.** In a class, the key is to direct attention to the lecture or discussion, not to other stimuli that are irrelevant to the task at hand.

As you might suspect, young children do not direct their attention very effectively, particularly when compared to older children and adults (Enns, 1990). Preschoolers are more easily distracted by extraneous information. However, we can help children to pay attention better. One straightforward approach is to make the relevant information more salient than the irrelevant information. For example, closing a classroom door may not eliminate competing sounds and smells entirely, but it does make them less noticeable. When preschoolers are working at a table or desk, we can remove other objects that are not necessary for the task. Another useful tack, particularly for young children, is to remind them to pay attention to relevant information and ignore the rest.

Young children are not skilled at regulating their attention, so they often attend to salient stimuli that are not relevant to the task at hand.

In Chapter 6, we'll see that some children experience a disorder in which they have particular difficulty paying attention. Now let's look at another process that is central to most cognitive tasks: memory.

Memory

Nearly six months had passed since 2½-year-old Clark had last visited this playground, where he had fallen off a teeter-totter and badly scraped his chin. Nevertheless, as soon as he saw the teeter-totter, his face clouded and he remarked soberly, "Clark had big owie on that board." Parents of preschoolers are often astounded by cases like this one, in which their youngsters obviously remember events that the parents themselves may have forgotten.

The roots of memory are laid down in the first few months after birth. Young babies remember events for days or even weeks at a time. Some of the studies that revealed the infant's ability to remember were conducted by Carolyn Rovee-Collier (1987). The centerpiece of her method is the mobile shown in this photograph. A ribbon from the mobile is attached to a baby's leg; within a few minutes after the ribbon is attached, the mobile is moving constantly, because the baby has learned to kick to produce motion in the mobile. Rovee-Collier found that when she returned to the infant's home several days or a few weeks later, the baby remembered to kick to make the mobile move. Of course, babies eventually forgot that kicking made the mobile move. However, if Rovee-Collier gave them a reminder—showing them the mobile without attaching the ribbon to their foot—the next day they would kick. Thus, in a 3-month-old's kicking to move a mobile, we see three important features of memory: (1) an event from the past is remembered successfully, (2) over time, the event can no longer be recalled, and (3) a cue can serve to recover a memory that seemed to have been forgotten.

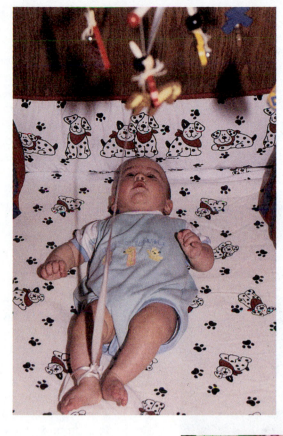

By the preschool years, children's memories of events can be surprisingly strong. In one study (Hamond & Fivush, 1991), 4-year-olds were asked about a trip that they had taken to Disney World nearly 18 months previously, when they were only 2½ years old. These youngsters spontaneously recalled an average of about ten features of the trip, such as "Minnie Mouse liked my brother," or "My sister saw Captain Hook."

A trip to Disney World is special. More common are events that infants and toddlers experience repeatedly, such as going to bed, taking a bath, and going to a fast-food restaurant. These experiences include many elements that occur in a predictable sequence. At a fast-food restaurant, the sequence of events would include ordering the food, paying, getting the food, sitting down, eating, throwing away the trash, and leaving. **Typically, after a few experiences with these events, preschool children have abstracted the common, essential elements, which are stored in memory as a *script*.**

When experiences consist of a common sequence of elements, such as eating at a fast-food restaurant, children store the common elements in memory as a script.

Preschoolers can use scripts to help them remember the individual elements in an activity. However, scripts can also distort children's recall. Sometimes children confuse what actually happened with what is specified in the script. For example, a young girl may remember throwing trash in the receptacle at McDonald's because this is part of the after-dinner script for fast-food restaurants, not because she actually did so (Hudson, 1988). Inaccurate memory may not be critical in a situation like this, but it can be pivotal in court cases, as we see in the Current Controversies feature.

Preschoolers on the Witness Stand

Remember Cheryl, the 4-year-old who claimed that a neighbor had touched her "private parts?" Regrettably, episodes like this one are all too common in America today. When abuse is suspected, the victim is usually the sole eyewitness. To prosecute the alleged abuser, the child's testimony is needed. Can preschool children like Cheryl be trusted on the witness stand?

CURRENT CONTROVERSIES

Answering this question is not as easy as it might seem. In legal proceedings, children are often interviewed repeatedly, sometimes as many as 10 or 15 times. Over the course of repeated questioning, people of all ages sometimes confuse what actually happened, what they think might have happened, and what others have suggested may have happened. Preschoolers are particularly prone to confusion of this sort. Their actual memory for the event may be more fragile than older children's and adults' memories. Also, preschoolers are less able to distinguish the source of memories and thoughts. Finally, if a preschooler has begun to doubt his or her memory of an event, and a person in authority suggests another version, the preschool child often decides that the adult's account is correct simply because the adult is an authority figure (Kail, 1990).

Do you doubt that skilled professionals would be misled by a preschooler's fabrications? After all, TV lawyers usually have a cold, penetrating stare that seems to bore right through a witness who might try to violate the oath "to tell the truth, the whole truth, and nothing but the truth." Surely it must be a simple matter to tell when a young child is unintentionally describing events that never happened? Law enforcement officials and child protection workers *believe* that they can usually tell if children are telling the truth (Brigham & Spier, 1992), but research points to a different conclusion. Leichtman and Ceci (1995) had experts watch videotapes of preschoolers who were telling the truth, as well as other preschoolers who were telling imaginary stories. Law enforcement officials, case workers, and developmental psychologists could not distinguish the truthful children from the fabricators.

Preschool children *can* provide reliable testimony, but many commonly used legal procedures tend to undermine the credibility of that testimony. What can we do to improve the reliability of child witnesses? Here are some guidelines:

- Warn children that interviewers may sometimes try to trick them or suggest things that didn't happen.
- Use questions that evaluate alternative hypotheses instead of questions that imply a single correct answer.
- Avoid questioning children repeatedly on a single issue.

Following these guidelines can foster the conditions under which preschoolers (and older children, too) are more likely to provide accurate testimony. More importantly, with greater understanding of the circumstances that give rise to abuse—a topic of Chapter 7—we should be able to prevent its occurrence altogether.   ❧

If children doubt the accuracy of their memory of an event, they will often go along with an authority figure's version.

One of the benefits of growing youngsters' improving attention and memory is that they are better able to acquire knowledge in particular domains. Information-processing psychologists have traced these changes in a number of areas, including learning to read, learning to find one's way, learning to solve problems, and learning about numbers. We'll look at the last of these—quantitative skill—in some detail. It effectively illustrates the information-processing approach, and it also helps set the stage for Chapter 6, where we will evaluate the level of American students' mathematical skill.

Quantitative Knowledge

At 2 years of age, when Laura Kail was asked how old she would be on her next birthday, she usually held up five fingers and proudly said, "Three!" At about this same time, she would count, saying, "1, 2, 3, 4, 5, 5, 8, 10." These anecdotes illustrate her emerging, if imperfect, understanding that a number name corresponds to a certain number of objects and that counting involves a sequence of number names in a specific order.

The origins of these basic number skills can be traced to early infancy. Many babies experience daily variation in quantity. They play with two blocks and see that another baby has three; they watch as a father sorts laundry and finds two black socks but only one blue sock, and they eat one hot dog for lunch while an older brother eats three.

From these experiences, babies apparently come to appreciate that quantity or amount is one of the ways in which objects in the world can differ. This conclusion is based on research in which babies are shown pictures like these.

The objects in the pictures differ, as do their size, color, and position in the picture. The only common element is that each of the first three pictures depicts two of something. When the first of these pictures is shown, an infant looks at it for several seconds; after several such pairs have been shown, an infant glances at the picture briefly, then looks away, as if to say, "Enough of these pictures of two things—let's move onto something else." In fact, if a picture of a single object or of three objects is shown next, infants will again look for several seconds, their interest apparently renewed. Because the only systematic change is the number of objects depicted in the picture, it is clear that babies can distinguish stimuli on the basis of number. Typically, 5-month-olds can distinguish two objects from three and, less often, three objects from four (van Loosbroek & Smitsman, 1990).

Several months later, babies say their first words. Names of numbers are not among the first words, but by 2 years of age, youngsters will know some number words and will have begun to count. Usually, their counting is full of mistakes. In Laura Kail's counting sequence that we mentioned earlier—"1, 2, 3, 4, 5, 5, 8, 10"—she repeats 5 and skips 6, 7, and 9. But if we ignore her mistakes momentarily, the counting sequence also reveals that she does understand a great deal.

Charting this understanding during the preschool years has been the aim of research by Rochel Gelman and her colleagues (Gelman & Meck, 1986). They simply placed various numbers of objects in front of a child and then asked, "How many?" By analyzing children's answers to many of these questions, Gelman and her coworkers discovered that by age 3, most children have mastered three basic principles of counting, at least when it comes to counting up to five objects.

Preschoolers often make mistakes when they count. Nevertheless, their counting usually follows the one-to-one, stable-order, and cardinality principles.

> **One-to-one principle: There must be one and only one number name for each object that is counted.** A child who counts three objects as "1, 2, A" understands this principle, because the number of number words matches the number of objects to be counted.

Stable-order principle: **Number names must be counted in the same order.** A child who counts in the same sequence most of the time—for example, consistently counting four objects as "1, 2, 4, 5"—shows understanding of this principle.

Cardinality principle: **The last number name differs from the previous ones in a counting sequence in that it denotes the total number of objects.** Typically, 3-year-olds reveal their understanding of this principle by repeating the last number name, often with emphasis: "1, 2, 4, 8, . . . EIGHT!"

During the preschool years, more children master these basic principles and apply them to ever larger sets of objects. By age 5, most youngsters apply them consistently when counting as many as nine objects.

Learning to count beyond 9 is somewhat easier, because the counting words can be generated based on rules for combining decade number names (20, 30, 40) with unit names (1, 2, 3, 4). Later, similar rules are used for hundreds, thousands, and so on. By 4 years of age, most youngsters can count as high as 20 and sometimes as high as 99. Usually, they stop counting at a number ending in 9 (such as 29 or 59), apparently because they don't know the next decade name (Siegler & Robinson, 1982).

Learning to count this high is quite complicated in English. For example, *eleven* and *twelve* are completely irregular names, following no rules. Also, the remaining "teen" number names differ from the 20s, 30s, and the rest in that the decade number name comes after the unit (thir-*teen*, four-*teen*) rather than before (*twenty*-three, *thirty*-four). Also, except for the teens, the decade names only loosely correspond to the unit names on which they are based: *twenty* and *thirty* resemble two and three but are not the same. In contrast, the Chinese, Japanese, and Korean number systems are almost perfectly regular: *Eleven* and *twelve* are expressed as *ten-one* and *ten-two*. There are no special names for the decades: *Two-ten* and *two-ten-one* are the names for 20 and 21. These simplified number names help to explain why youngsters growing up in Asian countries count more accurately than U.S. preschool children of the same age (Song & Ginsburg, 1988). Furthermore, the direct correspondence between the number names and the base-ten system makes it easier for Asian youngsters to learn base-ten concepts (Miura et al., 1988).

In Chapter 6, we will return to the development of quantitative skill, and we will find more evidence of cultural differences in mathematics. Let's turn now to a theory developed by Vygotsky, who believed that cognitive development has its roots in social interactions.

TEST YOURSELF

1. One way to improve preschool children's attention is to make irrelevant stimuli _____.
2. Four-month-old Tanya has forgotten that kicking moves a mobile. To remind her of the linking between kicking and the mobile's movement, we could _____.
3. The term _____ denotes the sequence in which routine activities occur.
4. Preschoolers' testimony is more likely to be reliable if interviewers test alternate hypotheses and avoid repeated questioning, and if we warn the children that _____.

5. When a child who is counting a set of objects repeats the last number, usually with emphasis, this indicates the child's understanding of the _____ principle of counting.

6. Think back to the changes in attention and memory that we've described in this section. Were the changes all quantitative in nature, or were some qualitative, like those emphasized by Piaget?

Mind and Culture: Vygotsky's Theory

Mind and Culture: Vygotsky's Theory
The Zone of Proximal Development
Scaffolding
Private Speech

LEARNING OBJECTIVES

❧ *What is the zone of proximal development? How does it help explain how children accomplish more when they collaborate with others?*

❧ *What is a particularly effective way of teaching youngsters new tasks?*

❧ *When and why do children talk to themselves as they solve problems?*

Human development is often referred to as a journey that can take people along many different paths. For Piaget and for information-processing psychologists, children make the journey alone. Other people (and culture in general) certainly influence the direction that children take, but fundamentally the child is a solitary adventurer-explorer, boldly forging ahead. Lev Vygotsky (1896–1934), a Russian psychologist, proposed a very different account: Development is an apprenticeship, in which children advance when they collaborate with others who are more skilled. According to Vygotsky (1978), children rarely make much headway on the developmental path when they walk alone; they progress when they walk hand in hand with an expert partner.

Vygotsky died of tuberculosis at the age of 37, so he never had the opportunity to develop his theory fully. He did not provide a complete theory of cognitive development throughout childhood and adolescence (as Piaget did), nor did he give definitive accounts of cognitive change in specific domains (as information-processing theorists do). However, many of his ideas are influential, largely because they fill in some gaps in the Piagetian and information-processing accounts. In the next few pages, we'll look at three of Vygotsky's most important contributions: the zone of proximal development, scaffolding, and private speech.

The Zone of Proximal Development

Four-year-old Ian and his father often make cars and planes from Lego blocks. Ian does most of the work, his father encourages him, sometimes finds a part that he needs, or shows Ian how to put parts together. When Ian tries to build the same objects by himself, he can rarely complete them. **The difference between what Ian can do with assistance and what he does alone defines his *zone of proximal development.*** That is, the zone is the area between the level of performance a child can achieve when working independently and a higher level of performance that is possible when working under the guidance or direction of more skilled adults or peers (Wertsch & Tulviste, 1992).

This boy can accomplish more on the puzzle with his father's help than he can alone, a difference that Vygotsky called the zone of proximal development.

For example, think about toddlers who are asked to clean their bedroom. Few will succeed, often because they simply don't know where to begin. By structuring the task for them—"start by putting away your books, then your toys, then your dirty clothes"—adults help children to accomplish what they could not do by themselves. Thus, just as training wheels help children learn to ride a bike by allowing them to concentrate on certain aspects of bicycling, collaborators help children perform more effectively by providing structure, hints, and reminders.

The idea of a zone of proximal development follows naturally from Vygotsky's basic premise: Cognition develops first in a social setting and only gradually comes under the child's independent control. What factors aid this shift? This leads us to the second of Vygotsky's key contributions.

Scaffolding

Have you ever had the good fortune to work with a master teacher, one who seemed to know exactly when to say something to help you over an obstacle but otherwise let you work uninterrupted? **Scaffolding is a style in which teachers gauge the amount of assistance they offer to match the learner's needs.** Early in learning a new task, children know little, so teachers give much direct instruction about how to do all of the different elements of a task. As the children catch on, teachers need to provide much less direct instruction; they are more likely to be giving reminders.

Scaffolding can be seen in a study in which mothers were asked to help their 3-year-olds solve jigsaw puzzles (McNaughton & Leyland, 1990). Some easy puzzles had only a few, readily distinguishable pieces. Others were more complicated—they had many more pieces, many of which were similar. The graph shows how mothers changed their help, depending on the level of difficulty of the puzzle. The term *direction maintenance* refers to remarks intended

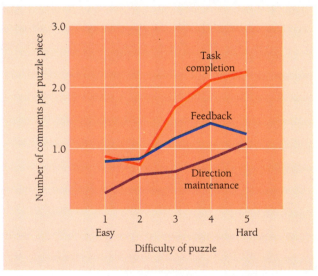

to keep children paying attention to the task; *feedback* refers to noninformative remarks of praise, like "Good job"; *task completion* refers to remarks that helped children place a piece of the puzzle, such as "Try it here." As the figure shows, all three forms of help were used more frequently as the puzzles became more difficult. The mothers spontaneously adjusted the level and detail of instruction, depending on the success their youngsters were having.

The sensitive adjustments that characterize scaffolding clearly promote learning. Youngsters do not learn readily when they are constantly told what to do or when they are simply left to struggle through a problem unaided. When teachers collaborate with them, allowing them to take on more and more of a task as they master its different elements—children learn more effectively (Pacifici & Bearison, 1991). Thus, scaffolding is an important element in transferring the control of cognitive skills from others to the child.

Private Speech

Remember Victoria, the 4-year-old who talked to herself as she colored? **Her behavior demonstrates *private speech*: comments that are not intended for others but are designed to help children regulate their own behavior (Vygotsky, 1934/1986).** Thus, Victoria's remarks are simply an effort to help herself color the picture.

Vygotsky viewed private speech as an intermediate step toward self-regulation of cognitive skills. At first, children's behavior is regulated by speech from other people that is directed toward them. When youngsters first try to control their own behavior and thoughts, without others present, they instruct themselves by speaking aloud. Finally, as children gain ever greater skill, private speech becomes *inner speech,* which was Vygotsky's term for thought.

If private speech functions in this way, can you imagine when a child would be most likely to use it? We should see children using private speech more often on difficult tasks than on easy tasks. Also, children should be more likely to use private speech more often after a mistake than after a correct response. These predictions are generally supported by research (Berk, 1992), which suggests the power of language in helping children learn to control their own behavior and thinking.

Like this little girl, many children talk to themselves while they perform difficult tasks. According to Vygotsky, this is an intermediate step in the transfer of control of thinking from others to the self.

Thus, Vygotsky's work has characterized cognitive development not as a solitary undertaking but as a collaboration between expert and novice. His work reminds us of the importance of language, which we'll examine in detail in the last section of this chapter.

TEST YOURSELF

1. The _____ is the difference between the level of performance that youngsters can achieve with assistance and the level they can achieve alone.
2. The term _____ refers to a style in which teachers adjust their assistance to match a child's needs.
3. According to Vygotsky, _____ is an intermediate step between speech from others and inner speech.
4. Compare the role of sociocultural influences in Piaget's theory, the information-processing approach, and Vygotsky's theory.

Answers: (1) zone of proximal development, (2) scaffolding, (3) private speech

Language

LEARNING OBJECTIVES

❧ *How well do infants hear speech sounds?*

❧ *How do cooing and babbling set the stage for the first words?*

❧ *Why do most infants say their first words soon after their first birthday?*

❧ *What are the rules that youngsters use to learn the meanings of words? What experiences foster word learning?*

❧ *How do young children progress from two-word speech to more complex sentences?*

❧ *How well do youngsters communicate?*

An extraordinary human achievement occurs soon after the first birthday: Most children speak their first word, which is followed in the ensuing months by several hundred more. This marks the beginning of a child's ability to communicate orally with others. Through speech, youngsters can impart ideas, beliefs, and feelings to family, friends, and others.

Actually, the first spoken words represent the climax of a year's worth of language growth. To tell the story of language acquisition properly, we must begin with the months preceding the first words.

The Road to Speech

The photograph depicts a common situation: A baby is upset and a concerned mother is trying to console it. The scene is overflowing with language-related

information. The infant, not yet able to talk, is conveying its displeasure by one of the few means of communication available to it—crying. The mother, for her part, is using both verbal and nonverbal measures to cheer her baby, to send the message that the world is really not as bad as it may seem now.

The scene raises two questions about infants as nonspeaking creatures. First, can babies who are unable to speak understand any of the speech that is directed at them? Second, how do infants progress from crying to more effective methods of oral communication, such as speech? Let's start by answering the first question.

PERCEIVING SPEECH

We learned in Chapter 3 that even newborn infants hear remarkably well. But can babies distinguish speech sounds? To answer this question, we first need to know more about the elements of speech. **The basic building blocks of language are *phonemes*, which are unique sounds that can be joined to create words.**

Phonemes include consonant sounds, such as the sound of "t" in *toe* and *tap,* along with vowel sounds such as the sound of "e" in *get* and *bed.* Infants can distinguish many of these sounds, some of them as early as one month after birth.

How do we know that infants can distinguish different vowels and consonants? A number of clever techniques have provided hints; most involve determining whether babies respond differently to distinct sounds. In one approach, a rubber nipple is connected to a tape recorder in such a way that sucking turns on the tape and sound comes out a loudspeaker. In just a few minutes, 1-month-olds learn the relation between their sucking and the sound: They suck rapidly in order to hear a tape that consists of nothing more than the consonant sound "p" (as in *pin, pet,* and *pat*), pronounced "puh." **After a few more minutes, infants seemingly tire of this repetitive sound and suck less often, a phenomenon known as** *habituation.* But if the tape is changed to a different sound—such as the sound of "b" (as in *bed, bat,* or *bird*), pronounced "buh"—babies begin sucking rapidly again. Evidently, they recognize that the sound of "b" is different from "p," because they suck more often to hear this new sound (Jusczyk, 1981).

Surprisingly, young infants can discriminate speech sounds that they have never heard! Not all languages use the same set of phonemes; a distinction that is important in one language may be ignored in another. For example, unlike English, the French and Polish languages differentiate between nasal and nonnasal vowels. To hear the difference, say the word *rod.* Now repeat it, but holding your nose. The subtle difference between the two sounds illustrates a nonnasal vowel (the first version of *rod*) and a nasal one (the second). Babies growing up in homes where English is spoken have no systematic experience with nasal and nonnasal vowels. Nevertheless, they can hear differences like this one. Interestingly, toward their first birthday, infants apparently lose this competence and no longer readily distinguish sounds that are not part of their own language environment (Werker & Lalonde, 1988).

What should we conclude from findings like these? Apparently newborns are biologically capable of hearing the entire range of phonemes that are used in all languages worldwide. As babies grow and have greater exposure to a particular language, they notice only those linguistic distinctions that are meaningful in that environment.

Infants' mastery of language sounds may be aided by a distinctive style of speaking that parents use with babies. **This style, known as** *caregiver speech,* **involves speaking more slowly to babies than to adults, and speaking with exaggerated changes in pitch and loudness.** (Caregiver speech was once known as *motherese,* until it became clear that most caregivers, not just mothers, talk this way.) Adults using this style alternate between soft and loud volume and high and low pitches. Caregiver speech attracts infants' attention more than speech directed toward adults (Pegg, Werker, & McLeod, 1992). This may be because its slower pace and accentuated changes may provide more salient language clues, just as understanding a person speaking in a foreign language is easier when that person talks slowly and carefully.

From exposure to speech of this type, infants approach their first birthday with striking skill in the perception of speech sounds that are essential to their language. Are infants as talented when it comes to producing speech? Let's see.

PUBLIC SPEAKING IN A FEW EASY STEPS

As new parents know all too well, newborns and young babies are experts when it comes to crying. For young infants, the cry is usually a distress signal of some sort. As you remember from Chapter 3, the type of cry varies somewhat with the nature of the distress. The high pitch of the pain cry, for example, distinguishes it from the cry of a baby who is hungry or tired.

The first sounds that are clearly linked to language come at about 3 months of age. **Babies begin to produce vowel-like sounds, such as "ooooooo" or "ahhhhhh," a phenomenon known as** *cooing.* Sometimes infants become quite excited as they coo, perhaps reflecting the joy of simply playing with sounds.

After cooing comes *babbling,* **which is speechlike sound that has no meaning.** A typical 4- or 5-month-old might say "dah" or "bah," utterances that sound like a single syllable consisting of a consonant and a vowel. Over the next several months, babbling becomes more elaborate. Apparently this is a form of experimentation with ever more complex speech sounds. Older infants sometimes repeat a sound, as in "bahbahbah," or combine different sounds, "dahmahbah" (Oller, 1986).

Beginning at roughly 7 months of age, infants' babbling includes *intonation,* **a pattern of rising or falling pitch.** In English declarative sentences, for example, pitch first rises, then falls toward the end of the sentence. In questions, however, the pitch is level, then rises toward the end. Older babies' babbling reflects these patterns: Babies who are brought up by English-speaking parents will have both the declarative and question patterns of intonation in their babbling. Babies who are brought up by parents who speak other languages with different patterns of intonation, such as Japanese or French, usually babble in ways that mimic their parents' use of intonation (Levitt & Utman, 1992).

The appearance of intonation in babbling clearly indicates a strong link between perception and production of speech: Infants' babbling is influenced by the characteristics of the speech that they hear. If perception of speech is indeed crucial for the development of babbling, then deaf children should learn to babble much more slowly than hearing children. This is the case. One-year-old deaf infants rarely babble repetitively (e.g., "bababa") in the manner that is common among hearing 7-to-10-month-olds (Oller & Eilers, 1988). Because of deaf children's limited exposure to human speech, their babbling emerges very slowly. However, the fact that deaf children babble at all shows that babbling also reflects maturational change.

For infants with normal hearing, the way in which babbling becomes progressively more complex suggests that it represents an infant's efforts to master the sounds of language, if not its meaning. Hearing *dog,* an infant may first say "dod," then "gog," before finally saying "dog" correctly. Just as beginning typists gradually link movements of their fingers with particular keys, through babbling infants learn how to use their lips, tongue, and teeth to produce specific sounds, gradually making sounds that approximate real words (Poulson et al., 1991). Fortunately, the task is easier for most babies than in the cartoon!

B.C. © 1993. Reprinted by permission of Johnny Hart and Creators Syndicate, Inc.

These developments in production of sound, coupled with the 1-year-old's advanced ability to perceive speech sounds, clearly set the stage for the infant's first true words. Let's see how this happens.

First Words and Many More

Remember that Nabina, the 1-year-old in the chapter-opening vignette, would look at the family cat when hearing its name. This phenomenon is common in 10-to-14-month-olds. They appear to understand what others say, despite the fact that they have yet to speak. In response to "Where is the book?" children will go find the book. They grasp the question, even though their own speech is limited to advanced babbling (Oviatt, 1982). Evidently, children have made the link between speech sounds and particular objects, even though they cannot yet manufacture the sounds themselves. As fluent adult speakers, we forget that speech is a motor skill requiring perfect timing and tremendous coordination.

A few months later, most youngsters utter their first words. Typically, these words have a structure borrowed from their advanced babbling, consisting of a consonant-vowel pair that may be repeated. *Mama* and *dada* are common examples of this type of construction. Other common words in early vocabularies denote animals, food, and toys (Nelson, 1973). Also common are words that denote actions (for example, *go*). By the age of 2, youngsters have a vocabulary of a few hundred words; by 6, a typical child's vocabulary includes more than 10,000 words (Anglin, 1993). However, children differ markedly in the size of their vocabulary (Fenson et al., 1994). At 16 months, vocabularies can range from as few as 10 words to as many as 150; at $2\frac{1}{2}$ years, from 375 words to 650.

As youngsters expand their vocabulary, some adopt a distinctive style of learning language (Bates, Bretherton, & Snyder, 1988). **Some children adhere to a *referential style*; their vocabularies tend to be dominated by words that are the names of objects, persons, or actions. Other children use an *expressive style*; their vocabularies include some names but also many social phrases that are used like a single word, such as "Go away," "What'd you want?," and "I want it."**

For children with the referential style, language seems to be primarily an intellectual tool—a means of talking about objects. For children with an expressive style, in contrast, language is more of a social tool—a way of enhancing interactions with others. Of course, both of these functions—intellectual and social—are important ingredients of language; as you might expect, most children adopt a blend of the referential and expressive styles of learning language.

THE GRAND INSIGHT: WORDS AS SYMBOLS

To make the transition from babbling to real speech, infants need to learn that speech is more than just entertaining sound. They need to know that particular sounds form words that can refer to objects, actions, and properties. Put another way, infants must recognize that words are symbols, entities that can stand for other entities.

A vivid account of this insight came from Helen Keller, an American essayist shown here in middle age. Born in 1880 and left blind and

KATHERINE NELSON
"The child comes to language learning with a range of organizing hypotheses about the world in the form of schemata, categories, or concepts."

deaf from an illness during infancy, she had no means to communicate with other people. When Helen was 7 years old, a tutor attempted to teach her words by spelling them in her hands. For Helen, the hurdle was to link the finger spelling with concepts she already knew; in her case, awareness came suddenly (Keller, 1965, p. 21):

> Someone was drawing water and my teacher placed my hand under the spout. As the cool stream gushed over one hand she spelled into the other the word *water,* first slowly, then rapidly. I stood still, my whole attention fixed upon the motions of her fingers. Suddenly I felt a misty consciousness as of something forgotten—a thrill of returning thought; and somehow the mystery of language was revealed to me. I knew then that "w-a-t-e-r" meant the wonderful and cool something that was flowing over my hand. That living word awakened my soul, gave it light, hope, joy, set it free!

When do youngsters who can hear and see have this insight? Piaget believed that it occurred roughly at 18 months of age and that it marked the transition into the sixth (and final) stage of sensorimotor thought (see pages 113–114). However, a glimmer of understanding of symbols occurs earlier, soon after the first birthday. By this age, children have already formed concepts such as "round, bouncy things" or "furry things that bark," based on their own experiences. With the insight that speech sounds can denote these concepts, infants begin to identify a word that goes with each concept (Reich, 1986).

WHAT'S WHAT? FAST MAPPING OF WORDS

Having the insight that a word can symbolize an object or action, the young talker now faces a formidable task. Matching a word with its exact referent is challenging, because most words have many plausible but incorrect referents. To illustrate, imagine trying to teach a child the word *phone*. You might point to a telephone and say: "Phone. This is a phone. See the phone." This all seems crystal clear to you and incredibly straightforward. But what might a child learn from this episode? Perhaps the correct referent for "phone." But a youngster could, just as reasonably, conclude that "phone" refers to the dial, to the color of the phone, or to your actions in demonstrating the phone.

Surprisingly, most youngsters learn the proper meanings of simple words in just a few presentations. **By *fast mapping,* children make connections between new words and referents so rapidly that they cannot be considering all possible meanings for the new word.** Children must be using rules to link words with their meanings (Carey, 1978).

What are the rules that guide children to discover a word's meaning? One of them is suggested in a study by Au and Glusman (1990). These investigators first taught preschoolers that a *mido* was a stuffed animal with pink horns that otherwise resembled a monkey. *Mido* was then repeated several times, always referring to the monkey-like stuffed animal with pink horns. Later, these same youngsters were asked to find a "theri" in a set of stuffed animals that included several mido. Never having heard the word theri before, what did the children do? They never picked a mido; instead, they selected other stuffed animals. Knowing that *mido* referred to monkey-like animals with pink horns, they evidently decided that *theri* had to refer to one of the other stuffed animals.

Apparently, the children were following this simple but effective rule for learning new words:

- If an unfamiliar word is heard in the presence of objects that already have

Young children often overextend the meaning of words. For example, at first they may call all four-legged animals "dogs."

names and those that don't, the word refers to one of the objects that doesn't have a name.

Can you think of other simple rules that might help children match words with the correct referent? Here are two more that scientists have discovered (Taylor & Gelman, 1989):

- A name refers to a whole object, not its parts or its relation to other objects, and it refers not just to this particular object but to all objects of the same type.
- If an object already has a name and another name is presented, the new name denotes a subcategory of the original name.

Rules like these are invaluable, for they help children substantially reduce the number of possible meanings for a word. Of course, the rules are not foolproof. **A common mistake, known as *overextension*, is defining a word too broadly.** Young children may use *car* to refer to buses and trucks or *ball* to denote all round objects. **Sometimes children make the opposite error, *underextension*, by defining a word too narrowly.** For instance, a child might use *car* to refer only to the family car or *ball* to a favorite toy ball. These errors disappear gradually as youngsters refine their meanings for words, broadening and narrowing them based on the feedback they receive from parents and others.

ENCOURAGING LANGUAGE GROWTH

For children to expand their vocabularies, they need to hear others speak. Not surprisingly, children learn words more rapidly if their parents speak to them frequently, particularly when the parents' speech responds to and encourages the child's own speech (Hoff-Ginsberg, 1991).

Watching television can help word learning, under some circumstances. For example, preschool children who frequently view *Sesame Street* often have larger vocabularies by the time they enter kindergarten than do preschoolers who watch *Sesame Street* less often (Rice et al., 1990). Other kinds of television programs—notably cartoons—do not have this positive influence.

What accounts for the difference? The key to success is encouraging children to become actively involved in language-related activities. Video segments like the one shown in the photo encourage youngsters to name objects, to sing, and to count. Apparently, the fundamental principle is much the same for television and parents: Children expand their vocabularies when they have experiences that engage and challenge their emerging language talents.

Speaking in Sentences: Grammatical Development

Within months after children say their first words, they begin to form simple sentences composed of two words. Such sentences are based on "formulas" that children figure out from their own experiences (Braine, 1976). Armed with a handful of formulas, children can express an enormous variety of ideas:

Formula	Example
actor + action	Mommy sleep, Timmy run
action + object	gimme cookie, throw ball
possessor + possession	Kimmy pail, Maya shovel

Each child develops a unique repertoire of formulas, reflecting his or her own experiences. However, the formulas listed here are commonly used by many children growing up in different countries around the world.

FROM TWO WORDS TO COMPLEX SENTENCES

Children rapidly move beyond two-word sentences, first doing so by linking two-word statements together: "Rachel kick" and "Kick ball" become "Rachel kick ball." Even longer sentences soon follow; sentences with ten or more words are common in 3-year-olds' speech. For example, at 1½ years, Laura Kail would say, "Gimme juice" or "Bye-bye Ben." As a 2½-year-old, she had progressed to "When I finish my ice cream, I'll take a shower, okay?" and "Don't turn the light out—I can't see better!"

Children's two- and three-word sentences often fall short of adults' standards of grammaticality. Youngsters will say, "He eating" rather than "He is eating," or "two cat" rather than "two cats." **This sort of speech is called *telegraphic* because, like the telegrams of days gone by, children's speech includes only words directly relevant to meaning, and nothing more. The missing elements, *grammatical morphemes*, are words or endings of words (such as *-ing, -ed,* or *-s*) that make a sentence grammatical.** During the preschool years, children gradually acquire the grammatical morphemes, first mastering those that express simple relations like *-ing,* which is used to denote that the action expressed by the verb is ongoing. More complex forms, such as appropriate use of the various forms of the verb *to be,* are mastered later.

Children's use of grammatical morphemes is based on their growing knowledge of grammatical rules, not simply memory for individual words. This was first demonstrated in a landmark study by Berko (1958), in which preschoolers were shown pictures of nonsense objects like the one in the figure. The experimenter labeled it, saying, "This is a wug." Then youngsters were shown pictures of two of the objects, and the experimenter said, "These are two

This is a wug.

Now there is another one.
There are two of them.
There are two _____.

Berko, 1958.

_____." Most children spontaneously said, "wugs." Because both the singular and plural forms of this word were novel for these youngsters, they could have generated the correct plural form only by applying the familiar rule of adding -s.

Children growing up in homes where English is spoken face the problem that their native tongue is highly irregular, with many exceptions to the rules. Such irregularities give rise to some intriguing errors in children's speech when children apply rules inappropriately. In the case of plurals, for example, young- sters may incorrectly add an -s instead of using an irregular plural—two "mans" instead of two "men." With the past tense, children may add -ed instead of us- ing an irregular past tense: "I goed home" instead of "I went home" (Mervis & Johnson, 1991).

These examples give some insight into the complexities of mastering the grammatical rules of one's language. Not only must children learn an extensive set of specific rules, but they must also absorb, on a case-by-case basis, all of the exceptions. Despite the enormity of this task, most children have mastered the basics of their native tongue by the time they enter school. How do they do it? As we see in the Forces in Action feature, biological, psychological, and so- ciocultural forces all contribute.

How Children Learn Grammar

FORCES IN ACTION

The noted linguist, Noam Chomsky (1959, 1982) claimed that grammatical rules are so complex that toddlers and preschoolers cannot infer them solely on the basis of speech that they hear. He claimed, instead, that mastery of grammar is rooted in biology: The brain must be "prewired" in some fashion for the task of learning grammar. According to this view, children are born with neural circuits that allow them to deduce the grammar of their native tongue. This idea is supported by the fact that, from very early in infancy, the brain has regions that are devoted specifically to language (see pages 85–86 in Chap- ter 3).

Of course, sociocultural influences are important, too. After all, children growing up in a home where Japanese is spoken master Japanese grammar, not Russian or English grammar! Experience provides the information that the lan- guage-acquisition device uses to infer grammatical rules. For many children, parents' speech is the prime source of information about language. Parents fine- tune their speech so that it includes examples of the forms their children are attempting to master (Hoff-Ginsberg, 1990). For example, at about 2 or 3 years of age, children first begin to experiment with pronouns like *you, I, she,* and *he.* Parents provide many examples of pronouns during the early phases when children are first attempting to understand how to use them correctly. In much the same way, as 2- and 3-year-olds begin to use auxiliary verbs such as *should, could, may,* and *well,* their parents' speech is especially rich in these verbs (Sokolov, 1993). By providing extra instances of the parts of speech that chil- dren are mastering, parents make it easier for children to unearth new gram- matical rules.

Psychological forces are also fundamental. As we have seen, children do not master grammar by simply repeating what they hear. Instead, children ac- tively try to make sense out of language. They seem to formulate grammatical rules tentatively, then look for evidence that would confirm or reject the tenta- tive rule. Fortunately, parents provide enough feedback that children can eval- uate their proposed rules. Most of the feedback is indirect. When a child's speech is incorrect or incomplete, parents don't say, "That's wrong!" or "How ungrammatical!" Instead, they will rephrase or elaborate the child's remark. If a child were to say, "Sara eat a cookie," a parent might reply "Yes, Sara is eating a cookie." "That be monkey" could lead to "Yes, that is a monkey." A parent's reply captures the meaning of the child's remark while demonstrating correct grammatical forms (Bohannon, MacWhinney, & Snow, 1990). At the same time, when a child's remark is well formed, a parent will often simply repeat it or continue the conversation. Thus, when parents rephrase their children's speech, this means that some aspect of the remark was ungrammatical; if they continue the conversation, this means that the remark was grammatical. This gives children enough information to confirm or disconfirm their tentative rules.

Thus the key players in grammatical development are a specialized brain, a rich language environment, and a child actively seeking to identify rules in speech. Combined, they keep children on the trail that leads to the mastery of grammar. Of course, as children's speech becomes more grammatical, others can understand it more readily, which means that children are increasingly able to use language to communicate with others. Let's look at the emergence and growth of these communication skills.   ❧

Communicating with Others

Imagining these two preschoolers arguing is an excellent way to learn what is needed for effective communication. Both youngsters probably try to speak at the same time; their remarks may be rambling or incoherent; and they neglect

to listen to each other altogether. These actions reveal three key elements in effective oral communication with others:

- People should take turns, alternating as speaker and listener.
- When speaking, remarks should be clear to the listener, from his or her own perspective.
- When listening, pay attention and let the speaker know if his or her remarks don't make sense.

Complete mastery of these elements is a lifelong pursuit. After all, even adults often miscommunicate with one another, violating each of these prescriptions in the process. However, youngsters grasp many of the basics of communication early in life.

TAKING TURNS

Many parents begin to encourage turn-taking long before infants have said their first words (Field & Widmayer, 1982):

> *Parent:* Can you see the bird?
> *Infant:* (cooing) Ooooh.
> *Parent:* It *is* a pretty bird.
> *Infant:* Ooooh.
> *Parent:* You're right, it's a cardinal.

Soon after 1-year-olds begin to speak, parents encourage their youngsters to participate in conversational turn-taking. To help their children along, parents often carry both sides of conversation to show how the roles of speaker and listener are alternated (Ervin-Tripp, 1970):

> *Parent:* (initiating conversation) What's Kendra eating?
> *Parent:* (illustrating reply for child) She's eating a cookie.

Help of this sort is needed less often by age 2, when spontaneous turn-taking is common in conversations between youngsters and adults (Barton & Tomasello, 1991). By 3 years of age, children have progressed to the point that if a listener fails to reply promptly, the child will often repeat his or her remarks to elicit a response and keep the conversation moving (Garvey & Berninger, 1981).

EFFECTIVE SPEAKING

The meaning of a message should be clear. However, clarity can only be judged with regard to the listener's age, the topic of conversation, and the setting of the conversation. For example, think about the simple request, "Please hand me the Phillips screwdriver." This message may be clear to older listeners who are familiar with variants of screwdrivers, but it is vague to younger listeners, to whom all screwdrivers come from the same mold. Of course, if the tool box is filled with Phillips screwdrivers of assorted sizes, the message is ambiguous even to a knowledgeable listener.

Consistently constructing clear messages is a fine art, which we would hardly expect young children to have mastered. By the preschool years, however, youngsters have made their initial attempts to calibrate messages, adjusting them to match the listener and the context. For example, 4-year-olds use simpler grammar and avoid complex topics when talking to 2-year-olds (Shatz & Gelman, 1977). When asked to describe an object, 5-year-olds describe it in more detail when the listener cannot see the object than when the listener can (Pratt, Scribner, & Cole, 1977). These findings show that preschoolers are already sensitive to the importance of the listener's skill and the conversational setting in formulating a clear message.

Parent-child "conversations" begin long before infants can talk. Early on, parents promote the idea of taking turns by alternating roles of speaker and listener.

LISTENING WELL

Sometimes, messages are vague or confusing; in such situations, a listener needs to ask the speaker to clarify the message. Preschoolers do not always realize when a message is ambiguous. Told to find "the red toy," they may promptly select the red ball from a pile that includes a red toy car, a red block, and a red toy hammer. Instead of asking the speaker to refer to a specific red toy, preschool listeners often assume that they know which toy the speaker had in mind (Beal & Belgrad, 1990). During the elementary school years, youngsters gradually master the many elements involved in determining whether another person's message is consistent and clear (Ackerman, 1993).

These improvements in communication skill complete our catalog of children's many astonishing accomplishments in communication and language during the first five years of life. By the time children are ready to enter kindergarten, they use language with remarkable proficiency and are able to communicate with growing skill.

TEST YOURSELF

1. _____ are fundamental sounds that are used to create words.
2. Infants' mastery of language sounds may be fostered by _____, in which adults speak slowly and exaggerate changes in pitch and loudness.
3. Older infants' babbling often includes _____, a pattern of rising and falling pitch that distinguishes statements from questions.
4. Youngsters whose early vocabularies are dominated by words that are names, and for whom language is primarily an intellectual tool, use a _____ style.
5. In _____, a young child's meaning of a word is broader than an adult's meaning.
6. Noam Chomsky, a noted linguist, emphasized the role of _____ in children's acquisition of grammar.
7. When talking to 2-year-olds, 4-year-olds _____.
8. According to Piaget's theory, preschoolers are egocentric. How should this egocentrism influence their ability to communicate? Are the findings that we have described on children's communication skills consistent with Piaget's view?

Putting It All Together

The preschool years mark the transition from an infant who routinely depends on others to an independent 5-year-old ready to begin the long process of schooling. Piaget explained this transition in terms of a progression through qualitatively different stages. The first two years form the sensorimotor period, which has as its climax the ability to use symbols. The years 2 to 7 form the preoperational period, when children begin to explore the power of symbolic thought. Their thinking has limits, however, including the egocentrism that explains Jamila's head-nodding during phone conversations.

We also looked at the information-processing approach, in which cognitive development is described in terms of both general and task-specific processes. We saw that the basic skills of attention and memory improve considerably during the preschool years. However, there are imperfections in children's memory, so preschoolers like Cheryl (the child involved in an alleged case of abuse) do not always provide reliable testimony.

Next, we examined Vygotsky's view of cognitive development: that is, an apprenticeship in which children progress when collaborating with others who are more knowledgeable than they. We learned that children like Victoria talk to themselves during a transition period in which the control of cognitive processes is transferred from others to self.

In the last section, we saw that infants and preschoolers master the sounds, meanings, and grammar of their native language early in life. For example, infants like Nabina often can understand words long before they have spoken. However, effective use of language to communicate is much slower to develop, continuing throughout the life span.

As a result of this growing intellectual and linguistic power, children are able to have more elaborate interactions and relationships with others, as we'll see in Chapter 5.

Thinking about Development

1. Generate a list of the basic elements of Piaget's, Vygotsky's, and the information-processing approaches to intellectual development. Then compare the approaches in their emphasis on the role of language in intellectual development.

2. How do information-processing and Vygotsky's theory address some of the shortcomings of Piaget's theory mentioned on pages 117–120?

3. What is the relation between the perceptual skills described in Chapter 3 and the attentional processes described on page 122?

4. In Chapter 2, we described how children with low birth weight often have delayed intellectual development. According to the differing perspectives of Piaget, Vygotsky, and information-processing, what forms might the delay take?

Summary

The Onset of Thinking: Piaget's Account

Basic Principles of Cognitive Development

■ According to Piaget, thought is always adaptive and organized. Adaptation includes assimilation, in which experiences are readily incorporated into existing schemes, and accommodation, in which experiences cause schemes to be modified. Piaget proposed that the child's cognitive structures periodically undergo massive change. The result is four different periods of mental development from infancy through adulthood. All individuals go through all four periods, but not necessarily at the same rate.

Sensorimotor Thinking

■ The first two years of life constitute Piaget's sensorimotor period, which is divided into six stages. As infants progress through the stages, schemes become more sophisticated. By 8–12 months, one scheme is used in the service of another; by 12–18 months, infants experiment with schemes; and by 18–24 months, infants engage in symbolic processing.

Preoperational Thinking

■ From 2 to 7 years of age, children are in Piaget's preoperational period. Although now capable of using symbols, their thinking is limited by egocentrism, the inability to see the world from another's point of view. Preoperational children are also unable to reverse mental operations and sometimes confuse appearance with reality.

Some Faults of the Theory

■ Piaget's theory has been criticized because children's performance on tasks is sometimes better explained by ideas that are not part of his theory. Another shortcoming is that children's performance from one task to the next is not as consistent as the theory predicts it to be. Yet another criticism is that Piaget's account of thinking underemphasizes sociocultural influences.

Information Processing during Infancy and Early Childhood

■ According to the information-processing view, mental development involves changes in mental hardware and in mental software.

Attention

■ Compared to older children, preschoolers are less able to pay attention to task-relevant information. Their attention can be improved by making irrelevant stimuli less noticeable.

Memory

■ Infants can remember and can be reminded of events that they seem to have forgotten. Preschool children can remember events that they experienced more than one year previously. Common activities consisting of a sequence of events are stored in memory as a script. However, scripts may distort children's recall when the actual events do not conform exactly to the script.

■ Preschoolers are sometimes asked to testify in cases of child abuse. When they are questioned repeatedly, preschoolers often have difficulty distinguishing what they experienced from what others may suggest that they have experienced. Inaccuracies of this sort can be minimized by following certain guidelines when interviewing children, such as warning them that interviewers may try to trick them.

Quantitative Knowledge

■ Infants are able to distinguish small quantities, such as "twoness" from "threeness." By 3 years of age, youngsters can count small sets of objects and in so doing adhere to the one-to-one, stable-order, and cardinality principles.

■ Learning to count to larger numbers involves learning rules about unit and decade names. This learning is more difficult for English-speaking children compared to children from Asian countries, because names for numbers are irregular in English.

Mind and Culture: Vygotsky's Theory

The Zone of Proximal Development

■ Vygotsky believed that cognition develops first in a social setting and only gradually comes under the child's independent control. The difference between what children can do with assistance and what they can do alone constitutes the zone of proximal development.

Scaffolding

■ Control of cognitive skills is most readily transferred to the child through scaffolding, a teaching style in which teachers let children take on more and more of a task as they master its different components.

Private Speech

■ Children often talk to themselves, particularly when the task is difficult or after they have made a mistake. Such private speech is one way in which children help to regulate their own behavior. It represents an intermediate step in the transfer of control of thinking from others to the self.

Language

The Road to Speech

■ Phonemes are the basic units of sound from which words are constructed. Infants can hear phonemes soon after birth. They can even hear phonemes that are not used in their native language. This ability diminishes after the first birthday.

■ Caregiver speech is adults' speech to infants that is slower and has greater variation in pitch and loudness. Infants prefer caregiver speech, perhaps because it gives them additional language clues.

■ Newborns' communication is limited to crying, but at about 3 months of age, babies coo. Babbling soon follows, consisting of a single syllable; over several months, infants' babbling comes to include longer syllables and intonation.

First Words and Many More

■ After a brief period in which children appear to understand other's speech but do not speak themselves, most infants begin to speak around the first birthday. The first use of words is triggered by the realization that words are symbols. Soon after, the child's vocabulary expands rapidly. Some youngsters use a referential style that emphasizes words as names and that views language

as an intellectual tool. Other children use an expressive style that emphasizes phrases and that views language as a social tool.

■ Most children learn the meanings of words much too rapidly for them to consider all plausible meanings systematically. Instead, children use certain rules to determine the probable meanings of new words. The rules do not always yield the correct meaning. An underextension is a child's meaning that is narrower than an adult's meaning; an overextension is a child's meaning that is broader.

■ Children's vocabulary is stimulated by experience. Both parents and television can foster the growth of vocabulary. The key ingredient is to actively involve children in language-related activities.

Speaking in Sentences: Grammatical Development

■ Soon after children begin to speak, they create two-word sentences that are derived from their own experiences. Moving from two-word to more complex sentences involves adding grammatical morphemes. Children first master grammatical morphemes that express simple relations, then those that denote complex relations. Mastery of grammatical morphemes involves learning rules as well as the exceptions to the rules.

■ Some linguists claim that grammar is too complex for children to learn solely from their experience; instead, the brain must be prewired for the task. However, language experience is important. Parents' speech is a model for their children. Children try to infer grammatical rules from speech that they hear; parents give children feedback concerning these tentative rules.

Communicating with Others

■ Parents encourage turn-taking even before infants begin to talk and, later, demonstrate both the speaker and listener roles for their children. By 3 years of age, children spontaneously take turns and prompt one another to take their turn.

■ Preschool children adjust their speech in a rudimentary fashion to fit the listener's needs. However, preschoolers are unlikely to identify ambiguities in another's speech; instead, they are likely to assume that they knew what the speaker meant.

Key Terms

accommodation   *(111)*
animism   *(115)*
attentional processes   *(122)*
assimilation   *(111)*
babbling   *(132)*
cardinality principle   *(126)*
caregiver speech   *(131)*
cooing   *(132)*
egocentrism   *(114)*
expressive style   *(133)*
fast mapping   *(134)*
grammatical morpheme   *(136)*

habituation   *(131)*
information-processing view   *(121)*
intonation   *(132)*
one-to-one principle   *(125)*
organization   *(111)*
overextension   *(135)*
phonemes   *(130)*
primary circular reaction   *(113)*
private speech   *(129)*
referential style   *(133)*

scaffolding   *(128)*
scheme   *(111)*
script   *(123)*
secondary circular reaction   *(113)*
sensorimotor period   *(112)*
stable-order principle   *(126)*
telegraphic speech   *(136)*
tertiary circular reaction   *(113)*
underextension   *(135)*
zone of proximal development   *(127)*

If You'd Like to Learn More

FLAVELL, J. H., MILLER, P. H., & MILLER, S. A. (1993). *Cognitive development* (3rd ed.). Englewood Cliffs, NJ: Prentice-Hall. This book, written by a trio of leading researchers, describes cognitive development during infancy and the preschool years. Piaget's and Vygotsky's theories are presented, as is the information-processing perspective. This is probably the best general-purpose reference book on cognitive development for undergraduates.

GARVEY, C. (1984). *Children's talk.* Cambridge, MA: Harvard University Press. This engaging book shows how children use language socially and also as an intellectual tool. It is filled with many entertaining examples of children's talk.

KAIL, R. (1990). *The development of memory in children* (3rd ed.). New York: Freeman. This book describes memory in infants and toddlers, as well as in older children and adolescents. Much research is discussed, but in a straightforward, easy-to-read style.

SIEGLER, R. S. (1991). *Children's thinking* (2nd ed.). Englewood Cliffs, NJ: Prentice-Hall. The author is a leading proponent of the information-processing approach to cognitive development, and this book reflects that orientation. He discusses Piaget's theory and language, but the best coverage is given to information-processing topics such as memory, problem-solving, and academic skills.

❧ Kendra's son Roosevelt was a happy, affectionate 18-month-old. Kendra so loved spending time with him that she kept avoiding the decision. She wanted to return to her job as a loan officer at the local bank. Kendra knew a woman in the neighborhood who had cared for some of her friends' children, and they all thought she was a fantastic babysitter. But Kendra still had a nagging feeling that going back to work wasn't a "motherly" thing to do—that being away during the day might hamper Roosevelt's development.

❧ Six-year-old Juan got his finger trapped in the VCR when he tried to remove a tape. While he cried and cried, his 3-year-old brother, Antonio, and his 2-year-old sister, Carla, watched but did not help. Later, when their mother had soothed Juan and concluded that his finger was not injured, she worried about her younger children's reactions. In the face of their brother's obvious distress, why had Antonio and Carla done nothing?

❧ Meda and Frank are in their early 50s. Though not married, they have lived together since the early 1970s, when both were active in protests against the war in Viet Nam. Their daughter, Hope, is now 6 years old. True to their countercultural roots, both Meda and Frank want their daughter to pick activities, friends, and, ultimately, a career based on her interests and abilities, not on her gender. Both are now astonished that Hope seems to be totally indistinguishable from other 6-year-olds reared by parents with conventional outlooks. Hope's close friends are all girls, and they often play "house" or play with dolls. What seems to be going wrong with Meda and Frank's plans for a "gender-neutral" girl?

Entering
the Social World

 Will Rogers, a famous American humorist in the 1920s and 1930s, once claimed, "I never met a man I didn't like." It certainly is true that humans enjoy one another's company. Social relationships of all sorts—friends, lovers, co-workers, teammates—make life both interesting and satisfying.

In this chapter, we trace the origins of these social relationships. We begin with the first social relationship—between an infant and a parent. We'll also see how this relationship is affected by the separation that comes when parents like Kendra, the mother in the first vignette, work full-time.

In the next section, we'll see how children's social horizons expand beyond parents to include peers. Then we'll look at some of the factors that determine whether children like Antonio and Carla, the younger siblings of the boy who trapped his finger in the VCR, help others in distress.

As children's interactions with others become more wide-ranging, they begin to learn about the social roles they are expected to play. Among the first social roles that children learn are those associated with gender—how society expects boys and girls to behave. We'll examine the development of children's awareness of gender roles. In the process, we'll learn why Hope, the 6-year-old in the vignette, seems to have such traditional interests despite her parents' efforts at gender-neutral childrearing.

Beginnings: Trust and Attachment

LEARNING OBJECTIVES

✥ *What are the crises that determine Erikson's three stages of psychosocial development in infancy and early childhood?*

✥ *How do infants form an emotional attachment to mother, father, and other significant people in their lives?*

✥ *What are the different varieties of attachment relationships, how do they arise, and what are their consequences?*

✥ *Is attachment jeopardized when parents of infants and young children are employed outside of the home?*

Suppose that, as a young child, you were well fed and clothed and that you had frequent contact with other children and adults. Instead of being reared by parents, however, you were cared for by a steady stream of responsive adults, perhaps as many as 50 different people by the time you were 4 years old. How might you have developed? We can answer this question with a fair degree of certainty. These were the actual conditions for many children who grew up in institutions in Europe following World War II because their parents had died during the war. Although these children's intellectual development was fairly normal, their social development was not. Typically, these youngsters craved the attention of others; their extreme need for social contact often made them unpopular with their peers and disobedient with their teachers (Tizard & Hodges, 1978).

Findings like these underscore the importance of an extended relationship with a warm, caring adult for a young child's development. Some of our keenest insights into the nature of psychosocial development come from a theory

Perspective	Examples of Theories	Main Ideas	Emphases in Biopsychosocial Framework	Positions on Developmental Issues
Psychodynamic	Erikson's psycho-social theory	Personality develops through a sequence of stages	Sociocultural and life-cycle forces crucial; less emphasis on psychological	Nature–nurture interaction, discontinuity, universal sequence but individual differences in rate

proposed by Erik Erikson. We first encountered Erikson's theory in Chapter 1; it is summarized in the chart on page 146. Erikson described development as a series of eight stages, each with a unique crisis for psychosocial growth. When a crisis is resolved successfully, an area of psychosocial strength is established. When the crisis is not resolved, that aspect of psychosocial development is stunted, which may limit the individual's ability to resolve future crises.

In the first part of this chapter, we'll examine Erikson's views of development during infancy and early childhood.

Erikson's Stages of Early Psychosocial Development

In Erikson's theory, infancy and the preschool years are represented by three stages, shown in the chart. Let's take a closer look at each stage.

BASIC TRUST VERSUS MISTRUST

Erikson argues that a sense of trust in oneself and others is the foundation of human development. Newborns leave the warmth and security of the uterus for an unfamiliar world. If parents respond to their infant's needs consistently, the

Erikson's First Three Stages		
Ages	*Crisis*	*Strength*
Infancy	Basic trust vs. mistrust	Hope
1 to 3 years	Autonomy vs. shame and doubt	Will
3 to 5 years	Initiative vs. guilt	Purpose

infant comes to trust and feel secure in the world. Of course, the world is not always pleasant and can sometimes be dangerous. Parents may not always reach a falling baby in time, or they may accidentally feed an infant food that is too hot. Erikson sees value in these experiences, because infants learn mistrust. **With a proper balance of trust and mistrust, infants can acquire *hope,* which is an openness to new experience tempered by wariness that discomfort or danger may arise.**

AUTONOMY VERSUS SHAME AND DOUBT

Between 1 and 3 years of age, children gradually come to understand that they can control their own actions. With this understanding, children strive for autonomy, for independence from others. However, autonomy is counteracted by doubt that the child can handle demanding situations and by shame that may result from failure. **A blend of autonomy, shame, and doubt gives rise to *will,* the knowledge that, within limits, youngsters can act on their world intentionally.**

INITIATIVE VERSUS GUILT

Most parents have their 3- and 4-year-olds take some responsibility for themselves (by dressing themselves, for example). Youngsters also begin to identify with adults and their parents; they begin to understand the opportunities that are available in their culture. Play begins to have purpose as children explore adult roles, such as mother, father, teacher, athlete, or psychology editor. Youngsters start to explore the environment on their own, ask many questions about the world, and imagine possibilities for themselves.

This initiative is moderated by guilt as children realize that their initiative may place them in conflict with others; they cannot pursue their ambitions with abandon. **Purpose is achieved with a balance between individual initiative and a willingness to cooperate with others.**

One of the strengths of Erikson's theory is its ability to tie together important psychosocial developments across the entire life span. We will return to the remaining stages in later chapters. For now, let's concentrate on the first of Erikson's crises—the establishment of trust in the world—and look at the formation of bonds between infants and parents.

The Growth of Attachment

Sigmund Freud was the first modern theorist to emphasize the importance for psychological development of the infant's emotional ties to the mother. Today, however, the dominant view of early human relationships is that of John Bowlby (1969). **His work originated in *ethology,* a branch of biology concerned with the adaptive behaviors of different species. Bowlby believed that children who form an *attachment* to an adult—that is, an enduring social-emotional relationship—are more likely to survive.** This person was usually the mother but need not be; the key was a strong emotional relationship with a responsive, caring person. Attachments could form with fathers, grandparents, or others.

Bowlby argued that evolutionary pressure favored behaviors likely to elicit caregiving from an adult, such as clinging, sucking, crying, and smiling. That is, over the course of human evolution, these behaviors have become a standard part of the human infant's biological heritage. Together with adults' responses, they create an interactive system that leads to the formation of attachment relationships.

Let's look at some of the steps in the formation of an attachment relationship.

STEPS TOWARD ATTACHMENT

The attachment relationship develops gradually over the first several months after birth, reflecting the baby's growing cognitive skill (described in Chapter 4). The first step is for the infant to learn the difference between people and other objects. Typically, in the first few months, babies begin to respond differently to people and to objects—for example, smiling more and vocalizing more to people. This suggests that they have begun to identify members of the social world.

During these months, mother and infant begin to synchronize their interactions. Remember from Chapter 2 that young babies' behavior goes through cycles. Infants move from a state in which they are alert and attentive to a state in which they are distressed and inattentive. Caregivers begin to recognize these states of behavior and adjust their own behavior accordingly. A mother who notices that her baby is awake and alert begins to smile at her baby and talk to it. These interactions often continue until the baby's state changes, which prompts the mother to stop. By 3 months of age, if the baby is alert but the mother does not interact but just stares silently, the baby becomes at least moderately distressed, looking away from her and sometimes crying (Toda & Fogel, 1993).

Thus, mothers and infants gradually calibrate their behaviors so that they are both "on" at the same time (Gable & Isabella, 1992). These interactions provide the foundation for more sophisticated communication and foster the infant's trust that the mother will respond predictably and reassuringly.

By approximately 6 or 7 months, most infants have singled out the attachment figure—usually the mother—as a special individual. An infant smiles at the mother and clings to her mother more than to other people. The attachment figure has emerged as the infant's stable social-emotional base. For example, a 7-month-old like the one in the photograph may explore a novel environment but periodically look toward the mother, as if seeking reassurance that all is well. Such behavior suggests that the infant trusts and has confidence in the mother. It indicates that the attachment relationship has been established.

After infants become attached to their mothers, they rapidly develop attachment relationships with other people, including fathers, siblings, and grandparents (Schaffer & Emerson, 1964). Let's take a glimpse at the nature of infants' relationships with their fathers.

FATHER–INFANT RELATIONSHIPS

In North America, attachment typically first develops between infants and their mothers, because mothers are still the primary caregivers. However, most babies soon become attached to their fathers, too.

Although infants usually become attached to both parents, they interact with them differently. Fathers spend much more time playing with their babies than they do taking care of them. In countries around the world—Australia, India, Israel, Italy, Japan, and the United States—"playmate" is the customary role for fathers (Roopnarine, 1992). Fathers even play with infants differently than mothers do. Rough-and-tumble, physical play is the norm for fathers, whereas mothers spend more time reading and talking to babies, showing them toys, and playing games like pat-a-cake (Parke, 1990). These differences in interactional style remain even when fathers care for their infants full-time while mothers are employed full-time outside of the home (Lamb & Oppenheim, 1989).

Given the opportunity to play with mothers or fathers, infants more often choose their fathers. However, when the infants are distressed, mothers are preferred (Field, 1990). Thus, although most infants become attached to both parents, mothers and fathers typically have distinctive roles in their children's early social development.

FORMS OF ATTACHMENT

Although most infants have become attached to an adult by 8 or 9 months of age, the type of attachment relationship varies. Mary Ainsworth (1978, 1993) pioneered the study of different forms of attachment, using a procedure that has come to be known as the Strange Situation. As the chart shows, the Strange Situation involves a series of episodes—each about 3 minutes long—during which the infant remains in an unfamiliar room that is filled with interesting toys. Over the course of the episodes, the baby is separated briefly from the mother and experimenters observe the baby's response when he or she is reunited with the mother.

Sequence of Events in the Strange Situation

1. Observer shows the experimental room to mother and infant, and then leaves the room.
2. Infant is allowed to explore the playroom for 3 minutes; mother watches but does not participate.
3. A stranger enters the room and remains silent for 1 minute, then talks to the baby for a minute, and then approaches the baby. Mother leaves unobtrusively.
4. The stranger does not play with the baby but attempts to comfort it if necessary.
5. After 3 minutes, the mother returns, greets and consoles the baby.
6. When the baby has returned to play, the mother leaves again, this time saying "bye-bye" as she leaves.
7. Stranger attempts to calm and play with the baby.
8. After 3 minutes, the mother returns, and the stranger leaves.

Ainsworth and other scientists have discovered four primary types of attachment relationships (Ainsworth, 1993; Main & Cassidy, 1988). **In the most common form, a** *secure attachment relationship,* **when infants are reunited with their mothers after a brief separation, they want to be near the mother and usually want to be held by her.** Eventually, these babies will return to play. These babies seem to be saying, "I missed you terribly, I'm delighted to see you, but now that all is well, I'll get back to what I was doing."

Some infants form *insecure attachment relationships* **in which, as the name implies, they act as if they do not perceive the attachment relationship to be stable and dependable.** For example, about 20% of North American infants who are reunited with their mothers actually avoid them. If the mother picks them up, these babies respond like the one in the photograph.

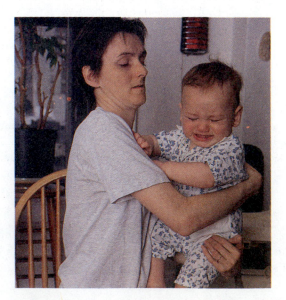

Infants in these *avoidant attachment relationships* **actually look away or turn away from the mother.** If she leaves them on the floor, they may crawl away or otherwise ignore her. Infants with an avoidant attachment look as if they're saying, "You left me *again*. I guess I'll just have to take care of myself!"

A third group of infants—about 10–15% of North American babies—apparently have mixed feelings toward the mother. **Infants with a *resistant attachment relationship* often want to be held when they are reunited with the mother, but they are very difficult to console.** These babies seem to be telling the mother, "Why do you do this to me? I need you desperately and yet you just leave me without warning. I want to hold you as hard as I can so that you won't leave me, but I'd also like to hit you to show you how much it hurts me when you leave."

The last group of infants seems to be confused by the entire Strange Situation. **Typically, about 5–10% of North American babies form *disorganized or disoriented attachment relationships,* in which they remain motionless when the mother leaves, as if unable to understand what has happened to them.** When the mother returns, they may have a dazed look. These babies seem to be wondering, "What's going on here? I want you to be here, but you left and now you're back. I don't know whether to laugh or cry!"

Secure attachments and the different forms of insecure attachments are observed worldwide. As you can see in the graph, secure attachments are the most common throughout the world (van IJzendoorn & Kroonenberg, 1988). This is fortunate because, as we'll see, a secure attachment provides a solid basis for subsequent social development.

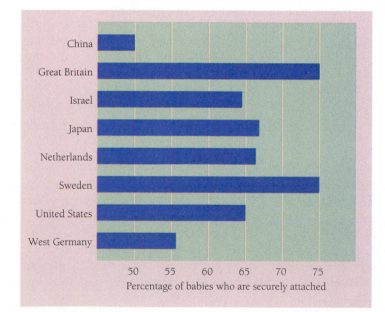

Percentage of babies who are securely attached

CONSEQUENCES OF ATTACHMENT

Erikson and other theorists (e.g., Sroufe & Fleeson, 1986) believe that infant–parent attachment, the first social relationship, lays the foundation for all of the infant's later social relationships. If this view is correct, infants who experience the trust and compassion of a secure attachment should develop into preschool children who interact confidently and successfully with their peers. Unfortunately, the predicted outcome is less positive for infants who have avoidant, resistant, or disorganized attachments. These children, like the youngsters described on page 146 who grew up in institutions after World War II, have not experienced a successful, satisfying first relationship as infants. Consequently, they should be more prone to problems in their social interactions as preschoolers.

Both of these predictions are supported by research. In general, children with secure attachment relationships interact more capably with their peers than do children with insecure attachment. Here are some findings that support this conclusion.

- Among 3- and 4-year-olds who are best friends, interactions were relatively tranquil and satisfying when both friends had been securely attached as infants. In contrast, disagreements were common and not resolved readily when one of the youngsters had been attached insecurely as an infant (Park & Waters, 1989).
- Among 4- and 5-year-olds attending a preschool, children whose behavior to others was marked by abnormal levels of hostility were six times more likely to have had a disorganized attachment as infants than a secure attachment (Lyons-Ruth, Alpern, & Repacholi, 1993).
- Among 11-year-olds attending a summer camp, children who had had secure attachment relationships as infants interacted more skillfully with their peers and had more close friends than did 11-year-olds who had had insecure attachment relationships (Elicker, Englund, & Sroufe, 1992).

The conclusion seems inescapable: Secure attachment serves as the prototype for later successful social interactions. That is, a secure attachment evidently promotes trust and confidence in other humans, which leads to more skilled social interactions later in childhood.

Of course, attachment is only the first of many steps along the long road of social development. Infants with insecure attachments are not forever damned, but this initial misstep *can* interfere with their social development. Consequently, we need to look at the conditions that determine the quality of attachment, which is the topic of the Forces in Action feature.

**FORCES
IN ACTION**

What Determines Quality of Attachment?

The answer to this question begins with biological forces. Remember infants' biological heritage includes behaviors such as clinging and smiling that are designed to elicit caregiving from adults. Along with their appearance, such behaviors make it clear that babies are dependent on others, which prods adults to care for them.

Once caregiving is underway, the quality of attachment reflects the quality of interaction between parents and their babies (van IJzendoorn et al., 1992). A secure attachment is most likely when parents respond to their infants predictably and appropriately. For example, Fabio always notices when his son, Sasha, smiles or talks. When Sasha cries, gestures, or tries to communicate in other ways, Fabio attempts to understand Sasha's intent and tries to respond appropriately. Behaviors like Fabio's evidently help to convey to babies that social interactions are predictable and satisfying. Apparently, they instill in infants the trust and confidence that is the hallmark of secure attachment.

Of course, not all caregivers react to babies in a reliable and proper manner. Some respond intermittently or only after the infant has cried long and hard. When these caregivers finally do respond, they are sometimes annoyed by the infant's demands and may misinterpret the baby's intent. Over time, these babies tend to see social relationships as erratic and often frustrating. Such conditions do little to foster trust and confidence.

Longitudinal studies attest to how important a caregiver's sensitivity is for the quality of attachment. In a study by Cox and her colleagues (1992), mothers and fathers were observed at home as they interacted with their 3-month-olds. Then, when the infants were 12 or 13 months old, they were tested in the Strange Situation twice, once with each parent.

Several aspects of parents' behaviors with their 3-month-olds predicted the security of the infants' attachment at 1 year. For both mothers and fathers, babies were more likely to form secure attachments when their parents

- were sensitive, responding quickly and appropriately to their infant's signals;
- expressed much positive emotion toward the baby;
- enjoyed playing with the infant, especially play in which parent and infant both participated actively; and,
- were frequently physically affectionate with the infant.

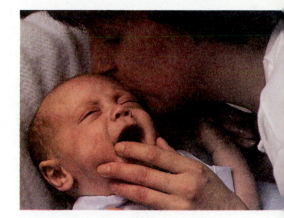

When parents respond predictably and sensitively to their infants, as this mother is doing, secure attachments are the likely result.

How does predictable and responsive parenting promote secure attachment relationships? To answer this question, we need to consider psychological factors. Think for a moment about your own friendships or romantic relationships. Such relationships are most satisfying when we believe that we can trust others—that we can depend upon them in times of need. Much the same formula seems to hold for infants. An infant needs to learn that a caregiver is concerned about his or her needs and will try to meet them. When parents are dependable and caring, babies come to trust them and to know that they can be relied on for comfort in times of stress. **This expectation is called an *internal working model*; it is thought to affect close relationships throughout the person's life (Bretherton, 1992).**

The formation of attachment well illustrates the combined influence of the different components of the biopsychosocial framework. Many infant behaviors that elicit caregiving in adults—smiling and crying, for example—are biological in origin. When the caregiver is responsive to the infant (a sociocultural force), then a secure attachment forms in which the infant trusts caregivers and knows that they can be relied upon in stressful situations (psychological force). ❧

Attachment, Work, and Alternate Caregiving

Each day, millions of U.S. preschool children attend day care or nursery school programs. This phenomenon is linked to the increase of both two-earner couples and single-parent households in the United States in the 1990s. Many parents, particularly women who have traditionally been sole caregivers, have misgivings about their children spending so much time in the care of others. Should parents worry? Can this care disrupt the development of parent–child relationships? The answer depends, in part, on the child's age.

When children begin full-time day care after their first birthday, day care actually has a number of beneficial effects on children and relatively few harmful ones. Overall, children who attend day care are more mature intellectually and socially than their counterparts who stay at home full-time with a parent. Research indicates that children who attend early childhood programs are more self-confident, outgoing, and self-sufficient (Clarke-Stewart & Fein, 1983). Sometimes these youngsters are less agreeable and less compliant, but this difference can be traced to greater maturity. Assertive, self-confident day-care youngsters may be more insistent in pursuing their own interests and thus less inclined to go along with parental requests.

In general, working parents like Kendra, the mother in the vignette at the beginning of the chapter, can enroll their preschoolers in high-quality day care programs with no fear of harmful consequences. The key, of course, is the quality of the day care. Some factors to look for in a first-rate program would be (a) a low ratio of children to caregivers, (b) infrequent staff turnover, (c) ample opportunities for educational and social stimulation, and (d) effective communication between parents and day care workers concerning the general aims and routine functioning of the day care program.

INFANCY—A SPECIAL CASE

For children less than a year old, guidelines are not as straightforward. The chief concern is that secure attachment might be disrupted by extended separation from a parent who works full-time outside of the home. When infants receive full-time parental care until their first birthday, about 70% typically form secure attachments to their parents. However, when parents work full-time and babies spend roughly 40 hours each week with alternative caregivers, approximately 60–65% form secure attachments (Lamb, Sternberg, & Prodromidis, 1992). Thus, although secure attachments are the norm for both working and nonworking parents, the odds of secure attachment are somewhat less for infants placed in full-time day care before their first birthday (Clarke-Stewart, 1989).

Several factors are known to increase the odds of an insecure attachment for infants of working parents (Jaeger & Weinraub, 1990; Lamb, Sternberg, & Prodromidis, 1992):

- *Hours the infant spends in alternative care.* Insecure attachments are more likely when infants spend more than 20 hours per week with an alternate caregiver.
- *Gender.* Boys' attachment relationships are more affected by alternative caregiving than are girls'.
- *Birth order.* First-born children's attachment is more affected by alternative caregiving than is later-born children's attachment.
- *Quality of parenting.* Employment can cause the quality of a parent's interactions with an infant to deteriorate. Stress, fatigue, guilt, or marital conflict may all contribute to less responsive caregiving. These conditions can easily lead to the formation of insecure attachment.

Based on these factors, here are some general guidelines for working parents of infants. First, try to limit the amount of time the baby spends in alternate care to no more than 20 hours weekly until the first birthday. Second, be sure that work does not reduce the quality of parenting. If parents experience too much stress, they should seek a counselor who can help them cope more effectively. If parents are constantly tired, they should see if work schedules can be rearranged to accommodate both work and parenting.

Of course, in many instances, this may be easier said than done. Fortunately, employers, too, have begun to do their part, realizing that convenient, high-quality child care makes for a better employee. In Flint, Michigan, for example, child care was an element of the contract between the United Auto Workers and General Motors. Many cities, such as Pittsburgh, have modified their zoning codes so that new shopping complexes and office buildings must include child care facilities, like those in the photograph. Businesses are realiz-

ing that the availability of excellent child care helps attract and retain a skilled labor force. Mayor Sophie Masloff, when Pittsburgh revised its zoning code, said, "With more women in the work force, more so than ever before, we just knew [providing workers with adequate child care] was a necessity."

With effort, organization, and help from the community and business, full-time employment and high-quality caregiving *can* be compatible. We will return to this issue in Chapter 11, from the perspective of the parents. For now, the Real People feature provides one example of a father who stays at home to care for his daughter while the mother works full-time.

Lois, Bill, and Sarah

Lois, 46, and Bill, 61, had been married nearly four years when Lois gave birth to Sarah. Lois, a kindergarten teacher, returned to work full-time four months after Sarah was born. Bill, who had been half-heartedly pursuing a Ph.D. in education, became a full-time househusband. Bill does the cooking and takes care of Sarah during the day. Lois comes home from school at noon so that the family can eat lunch together, and she is home from work by 4. Once a week, Bill takes Sarah to a parent–infant play program. The other parents, all mothers in their 20s or 30s, first assumed that Bill was Sarah's grandfather and had trouble relating to him as an older father. Soon, however, he was an accepted member of the group. On the weekends, Lois's and Bill's grown children from pre-

REAL PEOPLE

vious marriages often visit and enjoy their turns caring for and playing with Sarah. By all accounts, Sarah looks to be a healthy, happy, outgoing 9-month-old. Is this arrangement nontraditional? Clearly. Is it effective, for Sarah, Lois, and Bill? Definitely. Sarah receives the nurturing care that she needs, Lois goes to work assured that Sarah is in Bill's knowing and caring hands, and Bill relishes being the primary caregiver.   ❧

TEST YOURSELF

1. _____ proposes that maturational and social factors come together to pose eight unique challenges for psychosocial growth during the life span.
2. Infants must balance trust and mistrust to achieve _____, an openness to new experience that is coupled with awareness of possible danger.
3. By approximately _____ months of age, most infants have identified a special individual—usually but not always the mother—as the attachment figure.
4. Joan, a 12-month-old, was separated from her mother for about 15 minutes. When they were reunited, Joan would not let her mother pick her up. When her mother approached, Joan would look the other way or toddle to another part of the room. This behavior suggests that Joan has a(n) _____ attachment relationship.
5. The single most important factor in fostering a secure attachment relationship is _____.
6. Tim and Douglas, both 3-year-olds, rarely argue; when they disagree, one goes along with the other's ideas. The odds are good that both boys have _____ attachment relationships with their parents.
7. Several factors influence the formation of insecure attachment relationships among infants who spend much time in alternate care, including the amount of time spent in alternate care, the infant's gender and position in the birth order, and _____.
8. Explain how life-cycle factors in the biopsychosocial framework are illustrated by the impact of alternate caregivers on infants and on older children.

Interacting with Others

LEARNING OBJECTIVES

❧ ***When do youngsters first begin to play with each other? How does play change during infancy and the preschool years?***

❧ ***What determines whether preschool children cooperate with one another?***

❧ ***What determines whether children help one another? What experiences make children more inclined to help?***

Stephanie and Ben, both 8-month-olds, get together on Saturday when their fathers bring them to a neighborhood park for a picnic lunch. This "tradition"

Answers: (1) Erik Erikson, (2) hope, (3) 6 or 7, (4) avoidant insecure, (5) responding consistently and appropriately, (6) secure, (7) the quality of caregiving

began when the babies were 3 months old and is enjoyed by all. Both fathers were surprised at how interested the babies have been in each other, even as 3-month-olds. Now each baby enjoys watching the other. Sometimes Stephanie will babble, and Ben will smile in reply. These exchanges, although simple because of the babies' limited mental, linguistic, and motor skills, represent their first interactions with peers. Such interactions will become more complex during childhood and adolescence. As we shall see in Chapters 10 and 14, they remain an important fixture throughout adulthood.

The Joys of Play

Soon after the first birthday, children begin *parallel play,* **in which each youngster plays alone but maintains a keen interest in what another is doing.** For example, each of the toddlers in the photograph has his own toys, but

each is watching the other play, too. Exchanges between youngsters become more common. When one toddler talks or smiles, the other usually responds (Howes, Unger, & Seidner, 1990).

Beginning at roughly 15 to 18 months, toddlers no longer simply watch one another at play. **Instead, they engage in similar activities and talk or smile at one another, illustrating** *simple social play.* Play has now become truly interactive. For example, youngsters now offer toys to one another (Howes & Matheson, 1992).

Toward the second birthday, *cooperative play* **is observed: Now a distinct theme organizes the children's play, and they take on special roles based on the theme.** Like the children in the photograph, they may play "hide-and-seek" and alternate the roles of hider and finder, or they may have a tea party and take turns being the host and the guest (Parten, 1932).

By looking at the pie charts, you can see how the nature of young children's play changes dramatically in a few years. These charts were derived from observing 1-to-5-year-olds at a day care center as they interacted with peers (Howes & Matheson, 1992). Notice that 1½-year-olds spend the vast majority of their time in parallel play; other forms of play are relatively rare. By the time

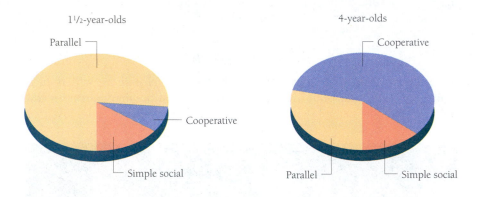

children are 3½ to 4 years old, parallel play is much less common, and cooperative play has become the norm.

A variation of cooperative play that is the trademark of play during the preschool years is make-believe. As children grow older, they often drink pretend coffee from toy cups or have telephone conversations with imaginary partners. For example, Harris and Kavanaugh (1993) examined how easily children use props in make-believe, such as pretending that a popsicle stick is a spoon or a toothbrush. They asked youngsters to pretend to brush a toy bear's teeth with the popsicle stick or to use it to stir the bear's tea. Most 28-month-olds did so readily. In contrast, 21-month-olds typically played with the bear or with the stick; only a few of these children complied with the request to use the stick in make-believe play.

This pattern of developmental change fits with Piaget's account of the sensorimotor period (see pages 112–114). Remember, the ability to use symbols emerges in the last sensorimotor stage, which spans the ages of 18 to 24 months. The younger children in the Harris and Kavanaugh (1993) study were in the earliest phases of symbolic development, which explains why make-believe was uncommon in this group. The older children have graduated to preoperational thought, so make-believe is well within their grasp.

Make-believe play is not only entertaining; it also allows children to explore topics that frighten them. A child who is afraid of the dark may reassure a doll who is also afraid of the dark. By explaining to the doll why she need not be afraid, the child comes to understand and regulate her own fear of darkness. With make-believe, children explore other emotions as well, including anger, joy, and affection (Gottman, 1986). As we see in the Spotlight on Research, many children invent imaginary companions.

Pretend play is common during the preschool years. This advance reflects children's growing abilities to use symbols.

My Friend "Archer"

Archer is a 5-year-old boy with black hair and orange eyes, who usually wears a T-shirt. Archer is imaginary, a make-believe companion for a preschool child. Imaginary companions were once thought to be fairly rare and a sign of possible developmental problems. More recent research casts doubt on both of these conclusions (Taylor, Cartwright, & Carlson, 1993). First, nearly two-thirds of all preschoolers report imaginary companions. Second, the presence of an imaginary companion is actually associated with many positive social characteristics: Preschoolers with imaginary companions tend to be more sociable and have more real friends than preschoolers who do not have imaginary companions.

Recent research by Marjorie Taylor and her colleagues at the University of Oregon (1993) helps to shed light on the nature of imaginary companions and the preschoolers who invent them. They interviewed children who, according to their parents, had imaginary companions, along with children who had no such companions. The children were asked several questions about their imaginary friends. They were first asked the imaginary friend's name. Then they were asked about the friend's age, size, hair color, eye color. Later, children were tested on a task like the one described on page 158 to assess their ability to make-believe. They were also tested on tasks that showed their ability to distinguish reality from fantasy.

Taylor and her co-workers found that children easily described their imaginary companions. All of the imaginary friends had names (for example, Bla-Bla, Mr. Ghost, Bazooie, and Thunder, as well as Sara, Tina, and Jacob). Most imaginary friends were about the child's own age or younger and they were about the same size or smaller. When asked to use the telephone to call the imaginary friend, most youngsters readily engaged in this bit of make-believe. In contrast, children with no imaginary companions were much more reluctant to pretend that they were using the phone to call a real friend. When asked to pretend that they were performing specific actions, such as brushing their teeth, children with imaginary companions were more likely to use imaginary objects. For example, they would brush their teeth with an imaginary toothbrush, whereas children without imaginary companions more often used a finger as the toothbrush. Thus, children with imaginary companions seem to engage in make-believe of all sorts more often and more willingly than children without imaginary companions.

Children's vivid fantasy play with their imaginary companions does not mean that the distinction between fantasy and reality has become blurred. Taylor and her colleagues administered several tasks designed to assess children's ability to distinguish fantasy from reality. In every case, children with imaginary companions answered these questions just as accurately as youngsters who did not have imaginary companions. For example, shown pictures of one boy with a cookie and another boy pretending to have a cookie, children with imaginary companions understood that the boy pretending to have a cookie could not see, touch, or eat the cookie.

Clearly, having imaginary companions is not a sign of a disturbed child who has invented a fantasy world because reality has become too threatening. Instead, children with imaginary companions are skilled at and enjoy fantasy play. Their imaginary companions are simply one particularly interesting manifestation of the richness of their fantasy play.   ❧

In most cultures, boys and girls play separately because their styles of play differ: Girls are more supportive of one another, whereas boys often try to dominate each other.

ELEANOR E. MACCOBY

"Why do we see such pronounced attraction to same-sex peers and avoidance of opposite-sex peers in childhood? . . . My hypothesis is that girls find it aversive to try to interact with someone who is unresponsive and they begin to avoid such partners."

SEX DIFFERENCES IN PLAY

Between 2 and 3 years of age, most youngsters begin to prefer playing with peers of their own sex. This preference increases gradually during the preschool years; by age 6, youngsters pick same-sex peers as playmates about two-thirds of the time (LaFreniere, Strayer, & Gauthier, 1984).

Is this pairing of boy with boy and girl with girl unique to Western cultures at the end of the 20th century? Apparently not. Whenever children around the world choose playmates, girls prefer playing with girls and boys with boys. Parental encouragement is not necessary for youngsters to segregate by sex. Should parents push their children into playing with peers of the other sex, most youngsters resist (Maccoby, 1990). Why? Boys and girls differ in how they play. When girls interact, their actions and remarks tend to support one another; conflicts that arise are resolved through discussion and compromise (McCloskey & Coleman, 1992). In contrast, boys' play is rougher. When boys interact, intimidation, threats, and exaggeration are common as one boy tries to dominate the others. When boys and girls are together, girls find that their supportive, compromising style has no impact on boys, who are more likely to respond to assertive overtures (Smith & Inder, 1993).

Whatever the exact cause, the preference to play with same-sex peers that emerges in the preschool years is a constant throughout the life span (Moller, Hymel, & Rubin, 1992). As we shall see in Chapters 7, 10 and 11, time spent at leisure (and later, at work) is commonly segregated by sex during adolescence and adulthood.

Learning to Cooperate

Cooperative play is built on the implicit and sometimes explicit agreement that all players will adhere to certain rules for the common benefit. Hide-and-seek, for example, is no fun when one child only wants to hide and refuses to take a turn as the seeker. Of course, although cooperation may be the ideal, children do not always play together well. Conflicts and arguments are common when youngsters play.

What are some of the factors that determine whether children cooperate or conflict? Age is certainly one. Remember that older children are less egocentric (pp. 114–115). Simply knowing that others view things differently helps to reduce conflicts. Also, preschoolers' growing communicative and social skills make it easier for them to cooperate (Lourenco, 1993).

Cooperation is influenced by other factors. Children are more likely to cooperate if they see peers who are cooperative and can observe, firsthand, that cooperation works. Children who observe successful cooperation are much more likely to cooperate themselves when given the opportunity (Liebert, Sprafkin, & Poulos, 1975).

Children's eagerness to cooperate is strongly influenced by the response to their cooperative overtures. When children try to cooperate but their peers do not go along, the incentive to cooperate vanishes rapidly; instead, youngsters look after their own interests. In contrast, when one child's cooperative gesture leads to another youngster's cooperative response, cooperation flourishes as children see for themselves the beauty of working together (Brady, Newcomb, & Hartup, 1983).

Piecing these findings together, we see why long-lasting cooperation is so fragile. Cooperation only works when all participants agree to cooperate; a few people—or perhaps even just one person—who fails to go along can undermine all of the benefits of cooperation. Young children in particular need to be directed by their parents into practical cooperative relationships, so that they may directly experience the benefits associated with greater cooperation (Parke & Bahvnagri, 1989).

Some cultures go to greater lengths than others to encourage cooperation. Historically, many ethnic groups within the United States have emphasized the individual and encouraged self-reliance. Other cultures, such as China, place a premium on what is good for all; people are seen as being strongly interdependent. Reflecting these cultural differences, Chinese children tend to be substantially more cooperative than North American children (Domino, 1992). For example, in one study (Orlick, Zhou, & Partington, 1990), investigators recorded the frequency of cooperation among kindergartners in Beijing, China, and in Ottawa, Canada. In the Canadian kindergartens, 22% of the interactions were cooperative, which meant that children supported or helped a peer. In the Chinese kindergartens, 85% of the interactions were cooperative.

What should we make of this difference? Evidently, young children *can* be cooperative if they view such behavior as mutually beneficial and if their culture expects them to cooperate. The See for Yourself feature describes how you can determine whether youngsters living near you are cooperative.

Children are more likely to cooperate when they observe others cooperating and when their cooperative gestures are reciprocated.

Children Cooperating and Competing

SEE FOR YOURSELF

You may not be convinced that youngsters growing up in the United States and Canada are especially competitive. To see for yourself, arrange to spend an hour observing young children. You could go to a neighborhood playground, but parents are often present to regulate youngsters' behavior. A better choice would be a nursery school or day care center. Your college may have a facility where you could, with permission, observe children from behind a one-way mirror. You should record all occurrences of cooperative behavior, defined as sharing, helping, or being physically affectionate with another child. Also record each instance of conflict behavior, defined as inconsiderate, aggressive, or destructive behavior.

If the facility where you make your observations is typical of those in North America, you can expect to see about 5 to 7 instances of cooperative behavior in one hour, but 15 to 30 cases of conflict behavior! If you should have the good fortune to travel to China and repeat your observations, you would observe 35 to 40 instances of cooperative behavior in that same hour, compared to perhaps 5 to 10 cases of conflict behavior. At least compared to their Chinese counterparts, North American preschoolers are much less considerate of their peers!   ❧

Helping Others

Prosocial behavior **is any behavior that benefits another person.** Cooperation is one form of prosocial behavior. Of course, cooperation often "works" because individuals gain more than they would by not cooperating. **In contrast, altruism is behavior that is driven by feelings of responsibility toward other people, such as helping and sharing, in which individuals do not benefit directly from their actions.** If two youngsters pool their funds to buy a candy bar to share, this is cooperative behavior. If one youngster gives half of her lunch to a peer who forgot his own, this is altruism.

Rudimentary acts of altruism can be seen by 18 months of age. When toddlers see other people who are obviously hurt or upset, they will, like the tod-

dler in the photograph, appear concerned, try to comfort the person who is in pain (by hugging or patting), and try to determine why the person is upset (Zahn-Waxler et al., 1992). Apparently, at this early age, they recognize some of the qualities of states of distress. During the preschool years, children gradually begin to understand others' needs and learn appropriate altruistic responses (Farver & Branstetter, 1994). Let's look at some of the specific skills that set the stage for altruistic behaviors.

SKILLS UNDERLYING ALTRUISTIC BEHAVIOR

Remember from Chapter 4 that preschool children are often egocentric, so they may not see the need for altruistic behavior. For example, young children might not share candy with a younger sibling, because they cannot imagine how unhappy the sibling is without the candy. In contrast, school-age children, who can more easily take another person's perspective, would perceive the unhappiness and would be more inclined to share. In fact, research consistently indicates that altruistic behavior is related to perspective-taking skill. Youngsters who understand others' thoughts and feelings better share with others and help them more often (Bengtsson & Johnson, 1992).

Related to perspective-taking is *empathy,* **which is the actual experiencing of another's feelings.** Presumably, a child who deeply feels another individual's fear, disappointment, sorrow, or loneliness should be more likely to help that individual than a child who does not feel those emotions. In fact, this link between empathy and altruistic behavior is found by most investigators (Eisenberg & Miller, 1987).

The findings of a study by Lennon, Eisenberg, and Carroll (1986) are typical. Preschoolers watched a videotape in which a child falls on a playground and, in obvious distress, cries for help. Experimenters recorded children's emotional reactions (for example, their facial expressions) as they watched the videotape. Later, the preschool subjects were told that they could help to make a game for the child injured in the videotape. The amount of empathic responding to the videotape was positively correlated with the time spent working on the game. That is, youngsters who empathized most with the injured child in the videotape worked the hardest to help cheer up that child. Thus, amount of empathy predicted amount of altruism—in this case, creating a game.

Of course, responding empathically does not guarantee that children will act altruistically. Some caring children who would like to help others may not be able to do so. An older brother might want to share candy with a younger sibling but will not because a parent forbids it. Sometimes children may not help because they lack the time or believe that others will help. It is necessary to consider the context in which behavior occurs, as this helps determine whether a child will act altruistically. A number of contextual features are known to influence children's altruism.

- *Feelings of responsibility.* Children act altruistically when they feel responsible for the person in need. Children may help siblings and friends, for example, more often than strangers, simply because they feel a direct responsibility for people that they know well (Costin & Jones, 1992).

- *Feelings of competence.* Children act altruistically when they feel that they have the skills necessary to help the person in need. Suppose, for example, that a preschooler is growing more and more upset because she can't figure out how to work a computer game; a peer who knows little about computer games is not likely to come to the young girl's aid, because the peer doesn't know what to do to help. If the peer tries to help, he or she could end up looking foolish (Peterson, 1983).

- *Mood.* Children act altruistically when they are happy or feeling successful but not when they are sad or feeling as if they have failed. A preschool child who has just spent an exciting morning as the "leader" in nursery school is more inclined to share treats with siblings than is a preschooler who was punished by the teacher (Moore, Underwood, & Rosenhan, 1973).

- *Costs of altruism.* Children act altruistically when such actions entail few or modest sacrifices. A preschool child who has received a snack that she doesn't particularly like is more inclined to share it with others than one who has received her very favorite food (Eisenberg & Shell, 1986).

So when are children most likely to help? When they feel responsible for the person in need, have the skills that are needed, are happy, and believe that they will need to give up little by helping. When are children least likely to help? When they feel neither responsible nor capable of helping, are in a bad mood, and believe that helping will entail a large personal sacrifice.

With these guidelines in mind, see if you can explain why Antonio and Carla, the children in the second chapter-opening vignette, watched idly as their older brother cried. The last two factors—mood and costs—are not likely to be involved. However, the first two factors may explain the failure of Antonio and Carla to help their older brother. Our explanation appears on page 164, just before Test Yourself.

SOCIALIZATION OF ALTRUISM

Contextual factors clearly play an important role in children's altruism. However, children also differ from one another in their feelings of obligation to other humans. Some youngsters are more inclined to help regardless of the setting. For example, in one study in which children were led to believe that a peer had been hurt by a machine, about 10% of the children came to the aid of the injured child (Peterson, 1983). Why did these youngsters come to the aid of the apparent victim when the remaining 90% did not? Why did these children feel a stronger obligation to help than did the rest?

One factor that has been linked to children's altruism is parents' disciplinary style. Altruistic children typically have parents who emphasize reasoning when disciplining their children. This approach often emphasizes the rights and needs of others as well as the impact of a child's misbehavior on others. For example, in the following dialogue, the father tries to make his daughter see how her actions upset her friend.

Father: Why did you take the crayons away from Annie?
Daughter: Because I wanted them.
Father: How do you think that made her feel? Do you think she was happy or sad?
Daughter: I dunno.
Father: I think you know.
Daughter: Okay. She was sad.

When parents regularly include reasoning as part of their discipline, their children are often more altruistic. This sort of discipline may increase children's feelings of responsibility to others.

NANCY EISENBERG

". . . children who engage in prosocial action come to think of themselves as altruistic, and, consequently, may engage in more future prosocial behavior in order to be consistent with their self image . . ."

Father: Would you like it if I took the crayons away from you? How would *you* feel?

Daughter: I'd be mad. And sad, too.

Father: Well, that's how Annie felt, and that's why you shouldn't just grab things away from someone. It makes them angry and unhappy. Ask first, and if they say "no," then you mustn't take them.

Repeated exposure to reasoning during discipline apparently strengthens children's general feelings of responsibility toward other people (Hoffman, 1988).

Parents also influence their children's altruism by their own altruistic behavior. When parents express warmth and concern for other people, this increases their children's feelings of empathy (Eisenberg et al., 1991). Parents who behave altruistically—by being helpful to others and being responsive to them—have children who help, share, and are less critical of others (Bryant & Crockenberg, 1980). Thus, by serving as good models of altruistic behavior, parents can foster their children's altruism.

A third way to influence children's altruism is by praising them for it. By frequently making remarks such as, "It really makes me happy that you helped Matt tie his shoes," parents can encourage their children's altruism. **Particularly effective is** *dispositional praise,* **in which parents link the child's altruistic behavior to an underlying altruistic disposition.** For example, a parent might say "Thanks for helping me to make breakfast; I knew that I could count on you because you are such a helpful person." When children hear remarks like this repeatedly, their self-concept apparently changes to include these characteristics. Children begin to believe that they really are helpful (or nice or friendly). With these characteristics as important elements of their self-concept, children are more likely to behave altruistically when others are in need (Mills & Grusec, 1989).

Thus, parents can foster altruism in their youngsters by using reasoning to discipline them, behaving altruistically themselves, and praising the children's altruistic acts. Also, contextual factors play a role, and altruism requires perspective-taking and empathy. Combining all of these ingredients, we can give a general account of children's altruistic behavior. As children get older, their perspective-taking and empathic skills develop, which enables them to see and feel another's needs. Nonetheless, children are never invariably altruistic (or, fortunately, invariably nonaltruistic), because particular contexts affect altruistic behavior, too.

POSTSCRIPT: WHY DON'T ANTONIO AND CARLA HELP?

Here are our explanations. First, neither Antonio nor Carla may have felt sufficiently responsible to help, because (a) with two children who could help, each child's feeling of individual responsibility is reduced, and (b) younger children are less likely to feel responsible for an older brother. Second, it's our guess that neither child has had many opportunities to use the VCR. In fact, it's likely that they both have been strongly discouraged from venturing near it. Consequently, they don't feel very competent to help, because neither knows how it works or what they should do to help Juan remove his finger.

TEST YOURSELF

1. Toddlers who are 12 to 15 months old often engage in _____ play, in which they play separately but look at one another and sometimes communicate verbally.

2. One of the advantages of _____ play is that children can use play to explore topics that frighten them.

3. When girls interact, conflicts are typically resolved through _____; boys more often resort to intimidation.

4. Compared to young children in North America, youngsters in China are _____ cooperative.

5. _____ is the ability to understand and feel another person's emotions.

6. Contextual influences on prosocial behavior include feelings of responsibility, feelings of competence, _____, and the costs associated with behaving prosocially.

7. Parents can foster altruism in their children by using reasoning to discipline them, behaving altruistically themselves, and _____.

8. How might children's temperament, which we discussed in Chapter 2, influence the development of their play with peers?

Gender Roles and Gender Identity

LEARNING OBJECTIVES

❧ *What are our stereotypes about males and females? How well do they correspond to actual differences between boys and girls?*

❧ *When do young children understand that gender is fixed? How does this understanding influence their learning about roles for girls and boys?*

❧ *How are gender roles changing? What further changes might the future hold?*

Family and well-wishers are always eager to know the sex of a newborn. Why are people so interested in a baby's sex? The answer is that being a "boy" or "girl" is not simply a biological distinction. Instead, these terms are associated with distinct social roles. **Like a role in a play, a *social role* is a set of cultural guidelines as to how a person should behave, particularly with other people.** The roles associated with gender are among the first that children learn, starting in infancy. Youngsters rapidly learn about the behaviors that are assigned to males and females in their culture. At the same time, they begin to identify with one of these groups. As they do, they take on an identity as a boy or girl.

What makes up the "female role" and the "male role" in North America today? Let's see.

Images of Men and Women: Facts and Fantasy

All cultures have *gender stereotypes*—beliefs and images about males and females that may or may not be true. For example, many men and women believe that males are rational, active, independent, competitive, and aggressive. At the same time, many men and women claim that females are emotional, passive, dependent, sensitive, and gentle (Ruble, 1983).

Based on gender stereotypes, we expect males and females to act and feel in particular ways, and we respond to their behavior differently, depending on their gender. For example, if you saw this toddler, you would probably assume that it was a girl, based on her taste in toys. Furthermore, your assumption

would lead you to believe (a) that she plays more quietly and (b) that she is more readily frightened than if you had assumed the child to be a boy (Stern & Karraker, 1989). Once it is assumed that the child is a girl, gender stereotypes lead to a whole host of inferences about behavior and personality.

Many of these inferences are false. Research reveals that males and females often *do not* differ in the ways specified by cultural stereotypes. What are the bona fide differences between males and females? Of course, in addition to the obvious anatomical differences, males are typically larger and stronger than females throughout most of the lifespan. Beginning in infancy, boys are more active than girls (Eaton & Enns, 1986). In contrast, girls have a lower mortality rate and are less susceptible to stress and disease (Zaslow & Hayes, 1986).

When it comes to social roles, activities for males tend to be more strenuous, involve more cooperation with others, and often require travel. Activities for females are usually less demanding physically, more solitary, and take place closer to home. This division of roles is much the same worldwide (Whiting & Edwards, 1988).

The extent of gender differences in the intellectual and psychosocial arenas remains uncertain. Research suggests differences between males and females in several areas:

- *Verbal ability.* Females typically excel on standardized tests of general language development and in the quality of their speech production (Hyde & Linn, 1988). Furthermore, girls are less likely to have language-related problems such as reading disability or stuttering (Halpern, 1986).
- *Mathematics.* Throughout the elementary school years, girls receive higher grades in math and obtain higher scores on standard achievement tests (Hyde, Fennema, & Lamon, 1990). However, during the high school and college years, boys achieve high scores on standardized tests but girls sometimes receive better grades in math courses (Kimball, 1989).
- *Spatial ability.* On problems like these, which measure the ability to manipulate visual information mentally, you must decide which figures are rotated variants of the standard shown at the left. Males typically respond more rapidly and accurately than females (Linn & Peterson, 1985).

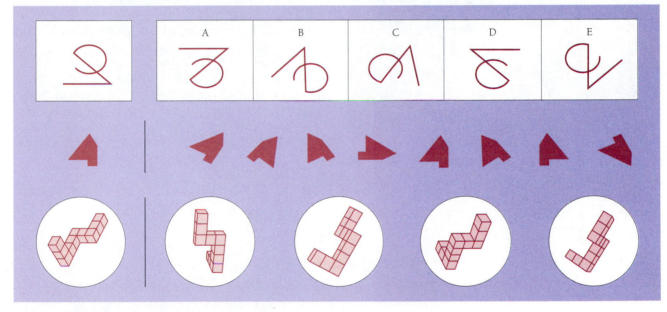

Pellegrino and Kail, 1982.

- *Social influence.* Girls are more likely than boys to comply with the directions of adults (Maccoby & Jacklin, 1974). Girls and women are also more readily influenced by others in a variety of situations, particularly when they are under group pressure (Becker, 1986).
- *Aggression.* In virtually all cultures that have been studied, males are more aggressive. This difference begins as early as the preschool years and remains throughout the life span (Sanson et al., 1993).

In most other intellectual and social domains, boys and girls are similar. When thinking about areas in which sex differences have been found, keep in mind that sex differences often depend on a person's experiences and social class (Serbin, Powlishta, & Gulko, 1993). Also, sex differences may fluctuate over time, reflecting historical change in the contexts of childhood for boys and girls. Finally, each result just described refers to a difference in the *average* performance of boys and girls. These differences tend to be small, which means that they do not apply to all boys and girls. Many girls have greater spatial ability than many boys; many boys are more susceptible to social influence than are some girls.

Sex Typing

Folklore holds that parents and other adults—teachers and television characters, for example—directly shape children's behavior in the direction of the roles associated with their sex. Boys are rewarded for boyish behavior and punished for girlish behavior. Actually, parents treat their sons and daughters similarly in many respects. Parents are equally affectionate and caring toward sons and daughters; parents encourage both sons and daughters to achieve and to be independent. Where parents treat boys and girls differently is in sex-typed activities. Daughters are encouraged when they play with dolls, "dress up," or help others; sons are praised for rough-and-tumble play or for playing with blocks (Lytton & Romney, 1991).

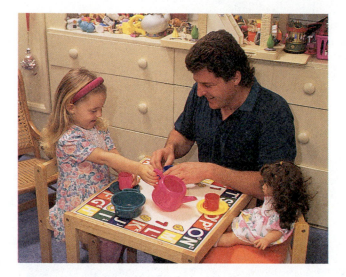

Fathers are more likely than mothers to engage in sex-typed play with children, and, consequently, do more to teach youngsters about sex roles.

Fathers may be especially influential in teaching youngsters about gender roles. Fathers are more likely than mothers to treat sons and daughters differently. For example, fathers often encourage gender-related play, and they are more likely to accept dependence in their daughters (Snow, Jacklin, & Maccoby, 1983).

Thus, through encouraging words, critical looks, and other forms of praise and punishment, adults influence boys and girls to behave differently (Jacobs & Eccles, 1992). However, children learn more than simply the specific behaviors associated with their gender. **A child gradually begins to identify with one group and to develop a** *gender identity*—**a sense of the self as a male or a female.**

GENDER IDENTITY

If you were to listen to a typical conversation between two 4-year-olds, you might hear something like this:

> *Maria:* When I grow up, I'm going to be a singer.
> *Juanita:* When I grow up, I'm going to be a papa.
> *Maria:* No, you can't be a papa—you'll be a mama.
> *Juanita:* No, I wanna be a papa.
> *Maria:* You can't be a papa. Only boys can be papas and you're a girl!

From parents and peers, children quickly learn whether they are boys or girls. Most 3-year-olds, for example, know this information and can accurately classify photographs of children and adults as male or female. Between 4 and 5 years of age, most youngsters also learn that gender is ordinarily fixed—boys become men and girls become women (Fagot, 1985). In the conversation between the 4-year-old girls, Maria understands that gender is stable, but Juanita does not.

Children's understanding that they will be a particular gender for a lifetime helps them interpret others' behaviors and actions. Once a boy has identified himself as a male, for example, he can become interested in the activities and characteristics of older boys and men and begin to value those activities. Thus, a child's gender identity can influence his or her perception of others' behavior and regulate his or her own behavior (Fivush, 1993).

How does gender identity accomplish these tasks? According to a theory proposed by Martin and Halverson (1987), children first decide whether behaviors, activities, or objects are female or male. The 4-year-old boy in the pho-

tograph, watching a group of older girls playing in sand, will decide that sand is for girls and, because he is a boy, sand is not for him. Seeing a group of older boys playing football, he will decide that football is for boys and, because he is a boy, football is acceptable and he should learn more about it.

The diagram illustrates this sort of decision making. According to this viewpoint, only children who understand gender stability should have extensive knowledge of sex-stereotyped activities. That is, not until children understand that gender is stable do they begin to divide the world into activities that are appropriate for their gender and those that are not.

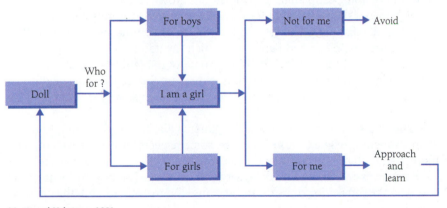

Martin and Halverson, 1981.

Martin and Little (1990) found that gender stability does, indeed, precede knowledge of sex-typed activities. They measured preschool children's understanding of gender and their knowledge of sex-typed activities (for example, that girls play with dolls and boys play with airplanes). The youngest children in their study—3½-to-4-year-olds—did not understand gender stability and knew little of sex-typed activities. By age 4, children understood gender stability but still knew little of sex-typed activities. By 4½ years, many children understood gender stability *and* knew gender-appropriate and gender-inappropriate activities. Importantly, there were no children who lacked gender stability but knew about sex-typed activities, a combination that is impossible according to the decision-making scheme shown in the diagram.

Knowledge of gender roles becomes more elaborate over the preschool and early elementary school years. Typically, 4- and 5-year-olds have stereotypic views of occupations; youngsters assume that males become doctors and athletes, whereas females become nurses and teachers. By age 7, children have quite sophisticated knowledge of gender-appropriate clothing, interests, and activities (Serbin, Powlishta, & Gulko, 1993). By age 8, children understand gender-related psychological attributes. Asked such questions as "Who cries a lot?," "Who always says, 'Thank you'?," and "Who gets into fights?," most 8-year-olds' answers conform to cultural stereotypes about men and women (Best et al., 1977).

Gender stereotypes tend to be self-perpetuating: Boys will learn about carpentry but not child care; girls will do the reverse. Furthermore, information that is inconsistent with gender schemas is typically either forgotten or distorted to make it conform to the cultural stereotype (Liben & Signorella, 1993). A youngster who is shown a picture of a child in an activity that violates gender stereotypes—a boy playing with dolls or a girl sawing wood—will probably remember the picture as showing a girl playing with dolls or a boy sawing wood. In remembering the picture, the sex of the depicted child is changed to be consistent with the cultural stereotype (Levy, 1989).

Evolving Gender Roles

Gender roles are not etched in stone; they change with the times. Today, for example, more women in the United States are employed outside of the home than ever before, and the numbers continue to grow. Working outside of the home has become an accepted role for women in the United States, and the range of possible occupations for women has grown, too.

What does the future hold for gender roles? Some insights come from the results of the Family Lifestyles Project (Weisner & Wilson-Mitchell, 1990). This research has examined families in which the adults were members of the counterculture of the 1960s and 1970s. Some of the families are deeply committed to living their own lives and to rearing their children without traditional gender stereotypes. In these families, men and women share the household, financial, and child care tasks.

The results of this project show that parents like Meda and Frank, from the chapter-opening vignette, can influence some aspects of gender stereotyping more readily than others. On the one hand, children in these families tend to have same-sex friends and to like sex-typed activities: The boys enjoy physical play, and the girls enjoy drawing and reading. On the other hand, the children have few stereotypes concerning occupations: They agree that girls could be president of the United States and drive trucks and that boys could be nurses and secretaries. They also have fewer sex-typed attitudes about the use of objects. They claim that boys and girls are equally likely to use an iron, a shovel, a hammer and nails, and a needle and thread.

Apparently, some features of gender roles and identities are more readily influenced by experience than others. This is as it should be. For most of their history as a species, homo sapiens have existed in small groups of families, hunting animals and gathering vegetation. Women have given birth to the children and cared for them. Over the course of human history, it has been adaptive for women to be caring and nurturing, because this increases the odds of a secure attachment and, ultimately, the survival of the infant. Men's responsibilities have included protecting the family unit from predators and hunting with other males, roles for which physical strength and aggressiveness are crucial.

Circumstances of life at the end of the 20th century are, of course, substantially different. Men can rear children, and women can generate income to purchase food for the family. The range of acceptable roles for girls and boys and women and men has never been wider. At the same time, the cultural changes of the past few decades cannot erase hundreds of thousands of years of evolutionary history (Kenrick, 1987). Consequently, we should not be surprised to find that boys and girls often differ in their styles of play, that girls tend to be more supportive of one another in their interactions, and that boys are usually more aggressive. As indicated in the You May Be Wondering feature, children whose parents are lesbian or gay also tend to grow up with conventional sex-role identity and interests.

Today, males and females occupy a wider range of roles than ever before. For example, many fathers are primary caregivers for their children.

Children of Gay and Lesbian Parents

More than a million youngsters in the United States have a gay or lesbian parent. In most of these situations, the children were born in a heterosexual marriage that ended in divorce when one parent revealed his or her homosexuality. Rarer, but becoming more common, are children born to single lesbians or to lesbian couples.

You may be wondering what happens to these youngsters. Is their development like that of children whose parents are heterosexual? Or does it differ, particularly when it comes to gender-related issues? Our answers to these questions must be tentative, because research on this topic is scarce. The number of studies is small, and almost all have examined children who were born to a heterosexual marriage that ended in divorce when the mother came out as a lesbian. Most of the lesbian mothers have been European American and well-educated.

Bearing these limits in mind, the general pattern is one of normal psychosocial development in children of lesbian mothers (Patterson, 1992). Preschool boys and girls apparently identify with their own gender and acquire the usual gender-based preferences, interests, activities, and friends. As adolescents and young adults, the vast majority are heterosexual (Bailey et al., 1995). In other dimensions, such as self-concept, social skill, moral reasoning, and intelligence, the development of children of lesbian mothers resembles that of the children of heterosexual parents. For example, in one study of 15 lesbian couples and 15 heterosexual couples, the children were comparably intelligent and comparably well adjusted psychologically (Flaks et al., 1995).

These conclusions, if substantiated by further research, have important implications. First, psychological theories have traditionally considered that the two-parent family, with both mother and father present, provides the best circumstances for development. Findings like these challenge the conventional wisdom in suggesting that it is what a parent provides for children that matters, not the parent's sexual orientation. Second, in many U.S. states, gay and lesbian adults are automatically deemed unfit as parents, a judgment that is totally unsupported by the research. (For more on this issue, read the Current Controversies feature on pages 367–368 of Chapter 10.) ❧

YOU MAY BE WONDERING ?

TEST YOURSELF

1. _____ are beliefs and images about males and females that may or may not be true.
2. Research on intellectual functioning and social behavior has revealed sex differences in verbal ability, mathematics, _____, social influence, and aggression.
3. _____ may be particularly influential in teaching gender roles, because they more often treat sons and daughters differently.
4. According to Martin and Halverson's theory, children must understand gender _____ in order to have extensive knowledge of sex-stereotyped activities.
5. When children are asked to remember information that is inconsistent with their gender stereotypes, they often _____.
6. Children studied in the Family Lifestyles Project, whose parents were members of the counterculture of the 1960s and 1970s, had traditional gender-related views toward friends and _____.
7. How do the different forces in the biopsychosocial framework contribute to the development of gender roles?

Putting It All Together

Though the cartoon is funny, you probably wouldn't care to consider the alternative—living alone—because interactions with other people are so important throughout life. Having completed this chapter, you now know that these interactions start early in life. In the first part of this chapter, we saw that responsive caregiving often leads to the formation of a secure attachment between infant and parent. When infants who have had secure attachments grow up, they tend to interact more successfully with other people. Infants who spend much time with an alternate caregiver are somewhat less likely to form secure attachments. However, in older children like Roosevelt, the 18-month-old in the chapter-opening vignette, time spent in day care is often beneficial.

In the second part of the chapter, children's social relations expanded from parents to peers. Even babies play with others, and play rapidly becomes more complex over the preschool years. Toddlers also show concern for others. However, as children grow older, whether they actually help others depends upon perspective-taking and empathic skills, the context in which help is required, and styles of parental discipline. For example, in the second chapter-opening vignette, Antonio and Carla did not help their older brother because they did not feel great responsibility to help and because they did not feel capable of helping.

As children's social horizons continue to expand, they soon learn that they are expected to play certain roles in society, based on their gender. By the end of the

Answers: (1) *gender stereotypes,* (2) *spatial ability,* (3) *fathers,* (4) *identity,* (5) *forget the information or distort it to make it consistent with the stereotype,* (6) *preferred activities*

preschool years, most children know that gender is fixed, and they begin to use this knowledge to select activities and objects that are appropriate for them. These choices are influenced by parents' values and expectations, but some aspects of gender roles are easier to change than others. For example, Meda and Frank, the parents in the third chapter-opening vignette, will probably find it easier to modify their daughter's career goals than to modify her style of play.

Of course, despite the rapid and sometimes dramatic change that we've witnessed in this chapter, social and interpersonal development is far from complete by the end of the preschool years. Much additional change takes place in school-age children and adolescents, as we'll see in Chapter 7.

Thinking about Development

1. Chapter 4 included Piaget's description of the growth of cognitive skill during infancy. What cognitive changes during infancy might be important prerequisites for the formation of an attachment relationship?

2. Suppose some kindergarten children want to raise money for a gift for one of their classmates who is in the hospital. Based on what you know about the factors that influence children to be altruistic, what specific advice can you give the kindergartners as they plan their fund raising?

3. The women's liberation movement became a powerful social force in North America during the 1960s. Describe how you might do research to determine whether the movement has changed the sex roles that young children learn.

Summary

Beginnings: Trust and Attachment

Erikson's Stages of Early Psychosocial Development

■ In Erikson's theory of psychosocial development, individuals face certain psychosocial crises at different phases in development. The crisis of infancy is to establish a balance between trust and mistrust of the world, producing hope; between 1 and 3 years of age, youngsters must blend autonomy and shame to produce will; and between 3 and 5 years of age, initiative and guilt must be balanced to produce purpose.

The Growth of Attachment

■ Attachment is an enduring social-emotional relationship between infant and parent. For both adults and infants, many of the behaviors that contribute to the formation of attachment are biologically programmed. Attachment develops gradually over the first year of life; by about 6 or 7 months, infants have identified an attachment figure, typically the mother. In the ensuing months, infants often become attached to other family members.

■ Research with the Strange Situation, in which infant and mother are separated briefly, reveals four primary

forms of attachment. Most common is a secure attachment, in which infants have complete trust in the mother. Less common are three types of attachment relationships in which this trust is lacking. In avoidant relationships, infants deal with the lack of trust by ignoring the mother; in resistant relationships, infants often seem angry with her; in disorganized relationship, infants seem to not understand the mother's absence.

■ Children who have had secure attachment relationships during infancy often interact with their peers more readily and more skillfully. Secure attachment is most likely to occur when mothers respond sensitively and consistently to their infant's needs.

Attachment, Work, and Alternate Caregiving

■ The impact of parental employment on children depends on the child's age. Children who are 1 year or older actually benefit from exposure to other children and caregivers in day care; they often become more advanced socially. For younger children, insecure attachments are slightly more likely when both parents work outside of the home. This depends, however, on the amount of time spent with alternative caregivers and the quality of caregiving provided, as well as the child's gender and position in the birth order.

Interacting with Others

The Joys of Play

■ Even infants notice and respond to one another, but the first real interactions, at about 12 to 15 months, take the form of parallel play, in which toddlers play alone while watching each other. A few months later, simple social play emerges, in which infants engage in similar activities and interact with one another. At about 2 years of age, cooperative play organized around a theme becomes common. Make-believe play is also common; in addition to being fun, it is one way in which children can examine frightening topics.

Learning to Cooperate

■ Cooperation becomes more common as children get older. Children cooperate more readily if they are shown that cooperation is effective and if peers respond to their cooperation with further cooperation. Cooperation is also influenced by societal values; it is more common in cultures that prize cooperation more highly than competition.

Helping Others

■ Prosocial behaviors, such as helping or sharing, are more common in children who understand (perspective-taking) and experience (empathy) another's feelings.

■ Prosocial behavior is more likely when children feel responsible for the person in distress. Also, children more often help when they believe that they have the skills needed, when they are feeling happy or successful, and when the perceived costs of helping are small.

■ Parents can foster prosocial behavior in their children by using reasoning during discipline, by serving as good models of prosocial behavior, and by praising their children for prosocial acts.

Gender Roles and Gender Identity

Images of Men and Women: Facts and Fantasy

■ Gender stereotypes are beliefs about males and females that are often used to make inferences about a person, simply based on his or her gender. Studies of sex differences reveal that girls have greater verbal and mathematical skill, but boys have greater spatial skill. Girls are more prone to social influence, but boys are more aggressive. These differences can vary on the basis of a number of factors, including historical time.

Sex Typing

■ Parents treat sons and daughters similarly, except in sex-typed activities. Fathers may be particularly important in sex typing, because they are more likely to treat sons and daughters differently.

■ Three-year-olds know whether they are boys or girls. By 5 years of age, children understand that they will grow up to become men or women. Once gender identity is established, children look to others of their sex for information about activities, behaviors, and interests that are appropriate for them.

Evolving Gender Roles

■ Gender roles are changing. However, studies of nontraditional families indicate that some components of gender stereotypes are more readily changed than others.

Key Terms

If You'd Like to Learn More

BERNDT, T. J., & LADD, G. W. (Eds.). (1989). *Peer relationships in child development*. New York: Wiley. This edited book contains chapters by many of the leading investigators of children's peer relations. Most chapters are fairly technical, but they provide a good overview of work in this area.

BOWLBY, J. (1988). *A secure base: Parent–child attachment and healthy human development*. New York: Basic Books. The foremost modern attachment theorist describes his theory. The book is based on a series of lectures and is highly readable.

ERIKSON, E. H. (1982). *The life cycle completed: A review*. New York: Norton. This book contains Erikson's summary of the eight stages of psychosocial development.

SCARR, S. (1984). *Mother care, other care*. New York: Basic Books. One of the leading investigators of the effects of day care on children reviews the research, describes the elements of high-quality care, and tells how to obtain such care. Written in a straightforward style.

PART II

School-Age Children and Adolescents

❧ Adrian, a sixth-grader who is starting middle school, just took his first social studies test—and failed. He was shocked because he'd always had A's and B's in elementary school. Adrian realizes that glancing through the textbook chapter once before a test is probably not going to work in middle school, but he's not sure what else he should be doing.

❧ Christine's cousins always teased her about going to a "hick" junior high school. Her school, which served a small town in a rural area, did have far fewer students than her cousins' school in a wealthy suburb. Yet Christine was able to play on the softball, basketball, and track teams, sang in the choir, and was vice-president of Student Council. Her cousins were always cut from sports teams and were never elected to student government. Frankly, she never understood why they bragged so much about their school.

❧ Charlene, an African American third-grader, received a score of 75 on an intelligence test administered by a school psychologist. Based on the test score, the psychologist believes that Charlene is mildly mentally retarded and should receive special education. Charlene's parents are indignant; they believe that the tests are biased against African Americans, so the score is meaningless.

❧ Sanjit, a second-grader, has taken two separate intelligence tests, and both times he had above-average scores. His parents took him to an ophthalmologist, who determined that his vision was 20-30—nothing wrong with his eyes. Nevertheless, Sanjit absolutely cannot read. Letters and words are as mysterious to him as Metallica's music would be to Mozart. What is wrong?

❧ Tomoko moved to the United States when her father was transferred to a new job managing a Subaru plant. Tomoko likes her fourth-grade teacher and her classmates, but many aspects of school puzzle her. Why does the class spend so much time grading each other's papers? Why does everyone in the class know so little math? Why is there so little homework? Tomoko's parents have many of the same questions and are troubled by them, fearing that Tomoko may fall behind her peers in Japan.

Off to School

Every fall, American 5- and 6-year-olds trot off to kindergarten, marking the start of an educational journey that will last 13 or more years. We begin this chapter by describing the cognitive development that makes school learning possible. Along the way, we'll discover some skills that Adrian, the sixth-grader in the first vignette, must master to succeed in middle school.

Next, we'll look at the smorgasbord of educational experiences that are available in the United States. Some students, like Christine in the second vignette, attend small schools; others go to schools with an enrollment larger than many universities. Schools also differ in philosophies of teaching, organization, and kinds of teachers. How do these variations influence students? We answer this question in the second part of the chapter.

In many schools, students take intelligence tests. In the third section of this chapter, we'll look at tests to see what they measure and to understand the issue of bias that was raised by Charlene's parents in the third vignette.

Tests are often used to help identify children with atypical or special needs, like Sanjit in the fourth vignette. These children are the focus of the fourth part of the chapter.

We end the chapter by asking, "How good are U.S. schools?" We answer this question many ways, including the comparison of U.S. and Japanese schools that so concerns Tomoko's parents in the fifth vignette.

Cognitive Development

LEARNING OBJECTIVES

🌿 *What are the distinguishing characteristics of thought during Piaget's concrete-operational and formal-operational stages?*

🌿 *What are some of the limitations of Piaget's account of thinking during the formal-operational stage?*

🌿 *How do children use strategies to improve learning and remembering?*

🌿 *What is the role of monitoring in successful learning and remembering?*

More Sophisticated Thinking: Piaget's Version

You probably remember Jean Piaget, from Chapters 1 and 4. As you can see in the chart, Piaget believed that thought develops in a sequence of stages. The first two stages, sensorimotor and preoperational thinking, characterize infancy

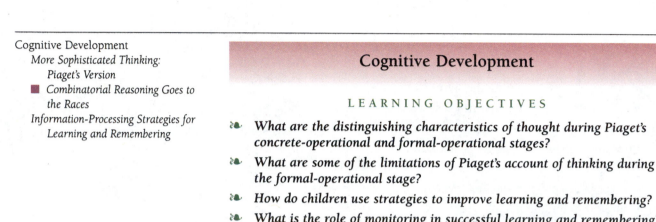

Perspective	Examples of Theories	Main Ideas	Emphases in Biopsychosocial Framework	Positions on Developmental Issues
Cognitive	Piaget's theory	Thinking develops in sequence of stages	Main emphasis on biological and social forces, less on psychological, little on life cycle	Strongly nature, discontinuity, and universal sequence of stages

and the preschool years. In the next few pages, we describe the remaining two stages, the concrete-operational and formal-operational, which apply to school-age children and adolescents.

THE CONCRETE-OPERATIONAL PERIOD

You're about one-third of the way through the book and deserve a break. Try this joke.

> Mr. Jones went into a restaurant and ordered a whole pizza for dinner. When the waiter asked if he wanted it cut into six or eight pieces, Mr. Jones said: "Oh, you'd better make it six! I could never eat eight!" (McGhee, 1976, p. 422)

Okay, this is not such a great joke (to put it mildly). However, many 6-to-8-year-olds think it's hilarious. To understand why youngsters find it so funny, let's review what we learned in Chapter 4 about some of the limits of preoperational thinking. We mentioned three:

- Preschoolers are egocentric, believing that others see the world as they do.
- Preschoolers sometimes confuse appearances with reality.
- Preschoolers are unable to reverse their thinking.

None of these limits applies to children in the concrete-operational stage, which extends from approximately 7 to 11 years. Egocentrism wanes gradually. Why? As youngsters have more experiences with friends and siblings who assert their own perspectives on the world, children realize that theirs is not the only view (LeMare & Rubin, 1987). The understanding that events can be interpreted in different ways leads to the realization that appearances can be deceiving. **Also, thought can be reversed, because school-age children have acquired *mental operations,* which are actions that can be performed on objects or ideas and that consistently yield a result.** Recall from Chapter 4 that on the conservation task, concrete-operational children realize that the amount of water is the same after it has been poured into a different beaker, pointing out that the pouring can always be reversed.

Now we can understand why 7-year-olds laugh at the joke about cutting a pizza into six pieces instead of eight. Think of a joke as a puzzle in which the aim is to determine why a particular remark is funny or incongruous. Generally, people like jokes that are neither too simple nor too complex to figure out. Jokes are best when understanding the punch line involves an intermediate level of difficulty (Brodzinsky & Rightmyer, 1980). For children just entering the concrete-operational stage, knowing that the amount of pizza is the same whether it is cut into six or eight pieces taps their newly acquired understanding of conservation, so they laugh (McGhee, 1976).

In discussing the concrete-operational period, we have emphasized the advantages to children of mental operations. At the same time, as the name implies, concrete-operational thinking is limited to the tangible and real, to the here and now. The concrete-operational youngster takes "an earthbound, concrete, practical-minded sort of problem-solving approach, one that persistently fixates on the perceptible and inferable reality right there in front of him" (Flavell, 1985, p. 98). Thinking abstractly and hypothetically is beyond the ability of concrete-operational children; these skills are acquired in the formal-operational period, as we'll see in the next section.

THE FORMAL-OPERATIONAL PERIOD

With the onset of the formal-operational period, which extends from roughly age 11 into adulthood, children and adolescents expand beyond thinking about only the concrete and the real. Instead, they can apply psychological operations to abstract entities, too; they are able to think hypothetically and reason abstractly.

To illustrate these differences, let's look at problem solving, where formal-operational adolescents often take a very different approach from concrete-operational children. In one of Piaget's experiments (Inhelder & Piaget, 1958), subjects were presented with several flasks, each containing what appeared to be the same clear liquid. Subjects were told that one combination of the clear liquids will produce a blue liquid; they were asked to determine the necessary combination.

A typical concrete-operational youngster, like the one in the photograph, plunges right in, mixing liquids from different flasks in a haphazard way. In contrast, formal-operational adolescents understand that setting up the problem in abstract terms is the key. The problem is not really about pouring liquids but about combining different elements until all possible combinations have been tested. So a teenager might mix liquid from the first flask with liquids from each of the other flasks. If none of those combinations produced a blue liquid, an adolescent would conclude that the liquid in the first flask is not an essential part of the mixture. The next step would be to mix the liquid in the second flask with each of the remaining liquids. A formal-operational thinker would continue in this manner until he or she finds the critical pair that produces the blue liquid. For adolescents, the problem is not one of concrete acts of pouring and mixing. Instead, they understand that it involves identifying possible combinations and then evaluating each one. This sort of adolescent combinatorial reasoning is illustrated in the Real People feature.

Combinatorial Reasoning Goes to the Races

REAL PEOPLE

As a 15-year-old, one of the authors (RK) delivered the Indianapolis *Star.* In the spring of 1965, the newspaper announced a contest for all newspaper carriers. The task was to list the most words that could be created from the letters contained in the words "SAFE RACE." Whoever listed the most words would win two tickets to the Indianapolis 500 auto race.

Kail realized that this was a problem in combinatorial reasoning. All he needed to do was create all possible combinations of letters, then look them up. Following this procedure, he had to win (or, at worst, tie). So he created exhaustive lists of possible words, beginning with each of the letters individually, then all possible combinations of two letters, and working his way up to all possible combinations of all eight letters (e.g., SCAREEFA, SCAREEAF). This was monotonous enough, but no more so than the next step: looking up all of those possible words in a dictionary. (Remember, this was in the days before computerized spell-checkers.) Weeks later, he had generated a list of 126 words. As predicted, a few months later, he learned that he had won the contest. Combinatorial reasoning has its payoffs!   ❧

Adolescents' more sophisticated thinking is also shown in their ability to make appropriate conclusions from facts, what is known as *deductive reasoning.* Suppose we tell a person the following two statements:

1. If you hit a glass with a hammer, the glass will break.
2. You hit the glass with a hammer.

The correct conclusion, of course, is "The glass will break,"—a conclusion that formal-operational adolescents do reach. Concrete-operational youngsters sometimes reach this conclusion, too—but based on their experience, not because the conclusion is logically necessary. To see the difference, imagine that the two statements are now:

1. If you hit a glass with a feather, the glass will break.
2. You hit a glass with a feather.

The conclusion "the glass will break" follows from these two statements just as logically as it did from the first pair. In this instance, however, the conclusion is contrary to fact—it goes against what experience tells us is really true. Concrete-operational 10-year-olds resist reaching conclusions that are contrary to known facts, whereas formal-operational 15-year-olds reach them much of the time (Markovits & Vachon, 1989). Formal-operational teenagers understand that these problems are about abstractions that need not correspond to real-world relations. In contrast, concrete-operational youngsters reach conclusions based on their knowledge of the world.

COMMENTS ON PIAGET'S VIEW

As mentioned in Chapter 4, although Piaget provides our single most comprehensive theory of cognitive development, his account of mental development during the early years has some shortcomings. The same is true of his description of formal-operational thinking. Let's look at two questionable aspects.

1. *Formal-operational thinking as a capability.* Simply because adolescents have attained the formal-operational stage does not mean that they always reason at this level. Adolescents (and adults) often fail to reason logically, even when they are capable of doing so and when it would be beneficial to them. For example, adolescents typically show more sophisticated reasoning when the problems are relevant to them personally than when they are not (Ward & Overton, 1990). Consequently, Piaget's account of formal operations is really a description of how adolescents can think, not how they always or even usually think.

2. *Formal operations as an endpoint.* Cognitive development is complete by age 12 or 13 in Piaget's theory. After adolescents have attained the formal-operation level, their thinking is said to remain the same qualitatively. Of course, people continue to acquire more knowledge and skills, but the fundamental processes of thinking do not change, according to Piaget. Many theorists (e.g., Fischer, 1983) have criticized this aspect of the theory and have proposed further developmental changes in thinking during late adolescence and adulthood, which we'll discuss in Chapter 9.

Because of these limits to Piaget's theory, we need to look at other approaches to complete our account of mental development during childhood and adolescence. In the next few pages, we'll focus on the information-processing approach that we examined in Chapter 4.

Information-Processing Strategies for Learning and Remembering

Last week, one of the authors had just written four pages of text for this book that would have made Hemingway green with envy, when the unthinkable happened: A power failure knocked out the computer, and all those wonderful words were lost. If only the text had been saved to the hard drive . . . but it hadn't.

This tale of woe sets the stage for a main issue of the information-processing approach. As the chart reminds us, information-processing psychologists believe that cognitive development proceeds by increases in the efficiency with which children process information. One of the key issues in this approach is the means by which children store information in permanent memory and retrieve it when needed later. **That is, according to information-processing psychologists, most human thought takes place in** *working memory,* **where a relatively small number of thoughts and ideas can be stored briefly.** As you read these sentences, for example, the information is stored in working memory. However, as you read additional sentences, they displace the contents of sentences that you read earlier. **For you to learn this information, it must be transferred to** *long-term memory,* **a permanent storehouse of knowledge that has unlimited capacity.** If information that you read is not transferred to long-term memory, it is lost, just as our words vanished from the computer's memory when the power failed.

Perspective	Examples of Theories	Main Ideas	Emphases in Biopsychosocial Framework	Positions on Developmental Issues
Cognitive	Information-processing theory	Thought develops by increase in efficiency at handling information	Emphasis on biological and psychological, less on social and life cycle	Nature–nurture interaction, continuity, individual differences in universal structures

MEMORY STRATEGIES

How do you try to learn the information in this or your other textbooks? If you're like most college students, you probably use some combination of highlighting key sentences, outlining chapters, taking notes, writing summaries, and testing yourself. These are all effective learning strategies that can make it easier for you to store text information in long-term memory.

Children begin to use simple strategies fairly early. For example, 7- or 8-year-olds use rehearsal, a strategy of repetitively naming information that is to be remembered. As they get older, children learn other memory strategies, and they also learn when it is best to use them. That is, children and adolescents begin to identify the unique characteristics of different memory problems and figure out which memory strategies are most appropriate. For example, when reading a textbook or watching a television newscast, the aim is to remember the main points, not the individual words or sentences. Rehearsal is ineffective here. However, outlining or writing a summary works well in these instances, because such strategies identify the main points *and* group them (Kail, 1990).

Thus, successful learning and remembering involves identifying the goals of memory problems and choosing suitable strategies. As you might expect, younger children sometimes misjudge the objectives of a memory task and therefore choose an inappropriate strategy (McGilly & Siegler, 1990). Or they may understand the memory task but not pick the best strategy. These skills improve gradually during childhood and adolescence, but even high school students do not always use effective learning strategies when they should (Slate, Jones, & Dawson, 1993).

These developmental changes can be seen in research in which children and adolescents are taught two memory strategies. One is effective for the material to be learned, but the other is not. The children then have an opportunity to use each strategy. Later, when asked to learn more of the same material, 11- and 12-year-olds usually opt for the more effective strategy. Younger children, in contrast, use either strategy indiscriminately, apparently not understanding that only one is well suited for the material (McGivern et al., 1990).

Highlighting and outlining are effective strategies for learning material from a textbook because they help to identify the main points and to organize them.

MONITORING

Learning is most likely to occur when students evaluate their progress toward the goal of the memory task. That is, they need to monitor the effectiveness of the strategy they have chosen. Is the strategy working? If not, students should begin anew, reanalyzing the memory task to select a better approach. If the strategy *is* working, they should determine the portion of the material that they have not yet mastered and concentrate their efforts there.

Monitoring skills improve gradually with age. For example, elementary school children can accurately identify material that they have not yet learned, but they do not consistently focus their study efforts on this material (Kail, 1990).

The diagram summarizes all of these events and the sequence in which they should occur. Beginning by analyzing a memory task to determine the goals, people select an appropriate strategy, then monitor its usefulness until the task is completed. Throughout childhood and adolescence, individuals gradually become more competent in each of these skills, as well as more adept at coordinating them.

Perhaps this has a familiar ring to it. It should, for the chart simply summarizes an important set of study skills. Analyzing, strategizing, and monitoring are key elements of productive studying. The study goals change when you move from this book to your math text to a novel that you are reading for English, but the basic sequence still holds. Studying should always begin

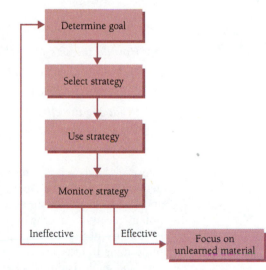

with a clear understanding of what goal you are trying to achieve, because this sets the stage for all of the events that follow. Too often, we see students like Adrian—the student in the vignette at the beginning of the chapter—who just read text material, without any clear idea of what they should be getting out of it. Always plan a study session with a well-defined goal, such as "Become familiar with the basic contents of Chapter 6 in my human development book." With this goal in mind, your strategy would be to read the introduction and outline carefully. Then skim the rest of the chapter, paying attention to headings and learning objectives. Finally, read the chapter summary in detail. When you've finished, see if you can write an outline of only the main topics of the chapter. If you can, then you know that you are familiar with the basic contents of the chapter; you've met the goal. If not, you need to do more. Perhaps you skimmed the contents too rapidly. Another way to check your learning is to try answering these questions!

TEST YOURSELF

1. During Piaget's _____ stage, children are first able to represent objects mentally in different ways and to perform mental operations.
2. Hypothetical and deductive reasoning are characteristic of children in Piaget's _____ stage.
3. Piaget's account of formal operations has been criticized because adolescents' reasoning is often less sophisticated than the theory predicts and because _____.
4. Children and adolescents often select a memory strategy after they have _____.
5. The term _____ refers to periodic evaluation of a strategy to determine whether it is working.
6. Formal-operational adolescents are able to reason abstractly. How might this ability help them to use the study skills in the chart on page 185 more effectively?

Effective Schools and Effective Teachers
Size of School and Size of Classes
Classroom Organization and
*   Atmosphere*
■ *Traditional and Open Classrooms*
The Transition to Secondary School
Ability Grouping
Teachers

Effective Schools and Effective Teachers

LEARNING OBJECTIVES

🌿 *How do the size of a school and the size of classes affect students?*

🌿 *How do traditional and open classrooms compare?*

🌿 *What are the benefits of attending a junior high or middle school?*

🌿 *What are the effects of grouping students by ability?*

🌿 *What are some of the hallmarks of effective teaching?*

Roosevelt High School, in the center of Detroit, has an enrollment of 3500 students in grades 9–12. Opened in 1936, the building shows its age. The rooms are drafty, the desks are decorated with generations of graffiti, and new technology means an overhead projector. Monroe County High School, in an affluent suburb of Seattle, has an enrollment of 1800 students in grades 10–12. The building is brand-new and contains elaborate computer facilities, an observatory, and a television in every classroom. Plainview School, in Plainview, South Dakota (population 8752) has 42 students enrolled in grades 1–12. The school consists of one large room, where all students are taught by the same teacher.

As these hypothetical examples illustrate, American schools are as heterogeneous as the students in them. Schools can be old and plain or modern and

Answers: (1) concrete-operational, (2) formal-operational, (3) the formal-operational stage is portrayed as the final stage of intellectual development, (4) determined the goal of the memory task, (5) monitoring

high-tech; they can be small and intimate or large and impersonal. Do these variations affect what children can accomplish in school? Sometimes they do, as we shall see.

Size of School and Size of Classes

Historically, American schools have had far fewer pupils than they do today. However, just as local department stores have given way to Wal-Mart, K-Mart, and the like, many small, local elementary and secondary schools have been replaced by much larger, consolidated schools like the one in the photograph.

Consolidation is often motivated by economic reasons, but it is also claimed on educational grounds that a larger school can offer more to students than its smaller counterpart. In fact, students apparently do not learn more in larger schools. Research indicates that students in smaller and larger schools do equally well on measures of scholastic achievement (Rutter et al., 1979).

School size does have an impact on social behavior, but the edge goes to smaller schools, not larger ones. Smaller schools have many of the same extracurricular activities—sports, music, student government—that are found in larger schools. But because of the smaller enrollment, students like Christine in the second vignette have more opportunity to participate. A substantially greater percentage of students are involved in extracurricular activities in smaller schools than in larger schools (Lindsay, 1984).

In smaller schools, there are greater opportunities to take the responsibilities that come with group membership and the special challenges associated with leadership. These opportunities are less common in larger schools, where students may feel anonymous—like a student with a number, not a name. This helps explain why antisocial behavior is more common in larger schools (Rutter et al., 1979).

The same conclusion—smaller is better—applies to class size, but with a catch. Being in a class of fewer than 20 students has clear benefits. Reading and math achievement improve in classes of this size (Finn & Achilles, 1990). When classes are this small, teachers spend less time on discipline and more on instruction. Also, in small classes, teachers are better able to individualize instruction, matching their teaching to the specific needs of each student (Cahan et al., 1983).

When classes swell to more than 20 or 25 students, the impact of class size largely disappears. That is, students in classes of 30, for example, do not learn noticeably more than students in classes of 35 or 40. Beyond some magic number—about 15 or 20—teachers can no longer tailor their teaching to individuals; predictably, achievement suffers (Hedges & Stock, 1983).

Classroom Organization and Atmosphere

When schools were designed in the early 1900s, they invariably had rectangular classrooms like the one in the photograph. With the desks organized in rows, the large windows provided adequate light and ventilation for all (Sommer, 1969). Today, of course, many classrooms are lighted and ventilated artificially; nevertheless, straight rows of desks remain common in American schools. When classrooms are organized this way, teachers direct more of their attention to children seated in the front and middle of the room (Adams, 1969). Arranging desks in a circle leads to more student participation in class (Rosenfield, Lambert, & Black, 1985).

The arrangement of a classroom often reflects a teacher's philosophy or approach to education. More often than not, teachers who organize their rooms in traditional rows adhere to a traditional philosophy of education. Teachers who place desks in a circle or in clusters are more likely to support an open-classroom philosophy. These philosophies differ on a number of key points (Minuchin & Shapiro, 1983), as shown in the table on page 189.

When traditional and open classrooms are compared, students from traditional classrooms typically have somewhat better scores on achievement tests (Giaconia & Hedges, 1982). However, open classrooms have their assets, too. Students in open classrooms tend to be more independent, more cooperative, and better accepted by their peers, and they generally like school more (Walberg, 1986).

Findings like these indicate that both approaches have their merits. An open classroom promotes social development and personal growth, whereas a traditional classroom tends to result in greater scholastic achievement. To foster both achievement and social development, teachers draw on elements of both philosophies. This explains why many of today's classrooms fall somewhere between the purely traditional and the purely open approach (Aitken, Bennett, & Hesketh, 1981).

Features of Traditional and Open Classroom Philosophies

	Traditional Classroom	*Open Classroom*
Aim of instruction	Acquiring knowledge	Acquiring knowledge, learning to work with others, personal growth
Role of teacher	Leads the students through the learning process	Structures an environment so that students can learn on their own
Daily schedule	Teacher organizes the day	Students choose from different activities
Individual versus collaborative learning	Students work alone	Students work together
Evaluation	Based on absolute standards or in relation to other students	Based on each student's improvement

Traditional and Open Classrooms

The best way to understand differences in classroom organization and atmosphere is to visit some actual elementary school classrooms. Try to visit three or four rooms in at least two different schools. (You can usually arrange this by speaking with the school's principal.) Take along the table at the top of the page that lists the characteristics of traditional and open classrooms. Start by watching how the teachers and children interact. Then, for each of the five distinguishing characteristics listed in the table, decide if the room is primarily traditional, primarily open, or in between. If possible, ask the teacher about traditional and open classroom philosophies, and ask him or her to describe the classroom. Later, you can examine your results to decide whether the classroom is consistently traditional or open with regard to all of the characteristics. Also, you can determine if the teacher's description of the room matches your evaluation. See for yourself! ❧

SEE FOR YOURSELF

The Transition to Secondary School

The 42 students at Plainview School are unusual; today, few American students complete their primary and secondary education in a single school building. You probably attended an elementary school, a junior high or middle school, and a high school. A junior high arrangement is known as a 6-3-3 organization and a middle school arrangement is a 5-3-4, for the number of years that students spend in each school. These have been common in the United States since the 1920s. Junior highs developed first, as a way to adapt to growing enrollments and to deal with the special needs of young adolescents. Middle schools emerged later, in the 1960s, as young people began to reach puberty earlier.

Research does not indicate a decided advantage for either the 6-3-3 or the 5-3-4 arrangement. Surprisingly, both suffer by comparison with a much older arrangement, 8-4. Simmons and Blyth (1987) conducted a five-year longitudinal study of nearly 1000 students in Milwaukee. Some attended elementary school until eighth-grade, then went directly to a high school. Others went to elementary school through sixth grade, then went to junior high and high schools. Compared to seventh-grade students in the 8-4 system, seventh-graders in the 6-3-3 systems viewed school less positively, had lower grades and achievement scores, and participated in fewer extracurricular activities. Among girls, seventh-graders in the 6-3-3 system had lower self-esteem and were less likely to be leaders in extracurricular activities than were seventh-graders in the 8-4 system.

How can we understand these unexpected results? The key is that the transition to a new school is stressful for students. In the 6-3-3 and 5-3-4 arrangements, students make this transition first as they are just entering adolescence. At this age, young people are already trying to adjust to their changing bodies, to changing responsibilities, and to changing expectations. The shift from an intimate, friendly elementary school to an impersonal, bureaucratic junior high or middle school is yet another adjustment during a time that is already trying. For students in the 8-4 arrangement, the shift to high school is challenging, but it comes later in adolescence, when most youths are better able to meet the challenge. The shift may be particularly trying for girls, who are more troubled than boys by the bodily changes brought about by puberty.

Modern junior high and senior high schools are often quite large, which sometimes creates an impersonal environment in which students feel lost in the masses, as if no one truly cares about them.

Reverting to 8-4 schools nationwide is not practical. But can we make the transitions in 6-3-3 or 5-3-4 systems less abrupt? Yes. The key is for junior high and middle schools to create a warmer, more personal, more intimate atmosphere, so that students don't feel lost among the masses. One approach is to create "teams" within schools. A junior high school with 300 seventh-graders, for example, might be divided into three groups of 100 students. A group of teachers would work exclusively with each group of 100, who would have all of their classes together. In this arrangement, teachers and students would come to know each other well. Three school units would have the supportive atmosphere of an elementary school under a common roof—an arrangement that would ease the transition to junior high or middle school (Felner & Adan, 1988).

Ability Grouping

"Bluebirds," "rabbits," and "sea shells." Such innocent-sounding names are typical of those assigned to groups of students who differ in ability. Based on scores on standardized tests of achievement, students are often divided into groups of above-average, average, and below-average ability. Grouping by ability, often known as *tracking,* is common in U.S. schools, particularly when classes are too large for teachers to individualize instruction. The basic idea is that if teachers cannot gear their teaching to individual children, tracking creates groups of youngsters of comparable ability, who can be instructed accordingly.

The usual outcomes of this practice are not encouraging. As you might expect, bluebirds, rabbits, and sea shells are poor disguises for the real identities of these groups, which, as the cartoon shows, children quickly discover. When they do, the self-esteem of

children in the low-ability group drops. In addition, despite the specialized instruction that low-ability children receive, they do not catch up; instead, they fall further behind children in the other groups. These results, when combined with the fact that more talented youngsters progress well in classes with less talented students, suggests that ability grouping has relatively little merit in elementary schools (Oakes, Gamoran, & Page, 1992).

Teachers

Take a moment to recall your teachers in elementary school, junior high, and high school. Some you probably remember fondly, for they were enthusiastic and innovative, and they made learning fun. You may remember others with bitterness. They seemed to have lost their love of teaching and children, making class a living hell. Your experiences tell you that some teachers are better than others, but what is it that makes an effective teacher? Personality and enthusiasm are *not* the key elements. Although you may enjoy warm and eager teachers, classroom management skills matter most when it comes to students' achievement. Students learn the most when teachers can devote most of their time to instruction. When teachers must spend a lot of time disciplining students, or when students do not move smoothly from one class activity to the next, instructional time is wasted, and students are apt to learn less (Brophy & Good, 1986).

How can teachers manage classrooms well? Reinforcing appropriate behavior—through praise or token rewards—is an effective technique (Kazdin, 1982). Tokens can be exchanged for toys or food. Or an entire class may be rewarded with a party or field trip when a specified number of tokens is earned. This technique has the advantage that peers urge one another to behave properly for the common good.

When teachers frequently use class time to discipline their students, they have less time to devote to teaching, so their class often learns less.

TEACHERS' EXPECTATIONS

We all form impressions when we first meet others. Are teachers able to keep such impressions from interfering with their objectivity? Not always. Teachers often treat high- and low-ability children differently (Minuchin & Shapiro, 1983). Compared to low-ability children, high-ability children

- receive more attention and instruction from teachers
- get more opportunities and more time to respond
- get more praise when they answer correctly and less criticism when they err

When teachers behave this way, it only serves to confirm the expectations they have formed about their students. A less skilled reader, for example, receives less instruction, gets less time to answer in class, and receives less praise if he or she happens to answer correctly. These conditions are hardly encouraging for such a student. Different expectations for success thus result in different teaching, which leads to the expected outcome—a self-fulfilling prophecy (Raudenbusch, 1984).

Of course, teachers will continue to form impressions of their students' abilities and talents. The key is to avoid having "David as he is now" turn into the expectation that "David will always be this way."

PEERS AS TUTORS

Children often help one another. In many schools, this happens informally, when a youngster is stuck on a problem and seeks a friend's help. Some schools, however, have formal peer tutoring programs, in which older or more capable students tutor others who are younger or less capable. Children who are tutored in this fashion *do* learn. What may surprise you is that tutors often improve as much or even more than the tutees, evidently because teaching helps tutors to organize their knowledge (Topping & Whiteley, 1993). The benefits of tutoring are not limited to learning: Tutors and tutees often have more motivation for schoolwork and more positive attitudes toward school.

The effectiveness of peer tutoring also bears on the issue of ability grouping, which we mentioned on pages 190–191. Proponents of tracking often charge that high-ability students lose out when placed in a classroom that includes students from all ability levels. In fact, in such a classroom, the most capable students can tutor the less capable ones, and everyone benefits!

When children tutor one another, both children benefit: The tutee benefits from the extra teaching, and the act of teaching helps a tutor to master the material as well.

COMPUTERS IN THE CLASSROOM

New technologies—TV, videotape, or pocket calculator—soon find themselves in the classroom. Microcomputers are no exception; virtually all American public schools now use computers to aid instruction. As one computer advocate put it, "We are moving rapidly toward a future when computers will comprise the dominant delivery system in education. . . . Not since the invention of the printing press has a technological device borne such implications for the learning process" (Bork, 1985, p. 1).

A primary function of computers in the schools is tutoring (Lepper & Gurtner, 1989). Computers allow instruction to be individualized and interactive. Students proceed at their own pace, receiving feedback and help when necessary.

Computers are also valuable as a medium for experiential learning (Lepper & Gurtner, 1989). Simulation programs allow students to explore the world in ways that would be impossible or dangerous otherwise. Students can change the law of gravity or see what happens to a city when no taxes are imposed (Republicans think they are in heaven; Democrats are apoplectic).

Finally, the computer is a multipurpose tool that can help students achieve traditional academic goals more readily (Kleiman, 1984). A word-processing program can relieve much of the drudgery associated with revising a document, thereby encouraging better writing. A graphics program can allow even people who lack artistic talent to produce beautiful illustrations.

Some critics fear that computers eliminate an important human element in learning. To some, "a classroom in which children spend the day plugged into their own individual desktop computers seems a chilling spectacle" (Lepper & Gurtner, 1989, p. 172). Many worry that when computers are introduced into classrooms, students will become more isolated from each other and from the teacher; learning will become a solitary activity. In reality, students interact with each other more when computers are introduced, not less (Hawkins et al.,

1982). As the photograph shows, students often cluster around a colleague as he or she works, and they often consult the class "expert" on a particular program. Teachers, freed from many of the drill-type tasks that now occupy the school day, can turn their attention to more creative elements of instruction.

TEST YOURSELF

1. Students at smaller schools have _____.
2. Ideally, a class should have no more than _____ students, as this usually allows teachers to individualize instruction.
3. Among the advantages of an open classroom are that students tend to be more independent and more cooperative. The primary disadvantage is that _____.
4. Girls who attend junior high or middle schools may have lower self-esteem because _____.
5. One way to reduce the stress associated with the transition from elementary school to junior high or middle school is _____.
6. When students are grouped by ability, those in the low-ability group lose self-esteem and _____.
7. Students are most likely to achieve when their teacher is _____.
8. A computer is used in the classroom as a tutor, _____, and to help students achieve traditional academic goals more readily.
9. Suppose that a candidate for your local school board contends that (a) open classrooms are harmful, (b) tracking should be implemented in grades K–12, and (c) computers in classrooms are a waste of money. How might you respond to some of the candidate's claims?

Answers: (1) *more opportunities to participate in school activities,* (2) *15–20,* (3) *they have lower scores on achievement tests,* (4) *the stress associated with entering a new school occurs at a trying time in their lives,* (5) *by creating "teams" within junior high schools,* (6) *fall further behind students in higher-ability groups,* (7) *skilled in organizing and managing a classroom,* (8) *as a medium for experiential learning*

Aptitudes for School

LEARNING OBJECTIVES

- *Why were intelligence tests first developed? What were their features?*
- *How well do intelligence tests work?*
- *How do heredity and environment influence intelligence?*
- *What is the nature of intelligence?*
- *How and why do test scores vary for different racial and ethnic groups?*

American schools faced a crisis at the beginning of the 20th century. Between 1890 and 1915, school enrollment nearly doubled nationally, because of an influx of immigrants and because reforms restricted child labor and emphasized education (Chapman, 1988). With the increased enrollment, teachers were confronted by ever greater numbers of students who did not learn as readily as the "select few" students who had populated their classes previously. How to deal with "feebleminded" children was one of the pressing issues of the day for U.S. educators.

Binet and the Development of Intelligence Testing

These problems were not unique to the United States. In 1904, the Minister of Public Instruction in France asked two noted psychologists of the day, Alfred Binet and Theophile Simon, to formulate a way to recognize children who would be unable to learn in school without special instruction. Binet and Simon's approach was to select simple tasks that French children of different ages ought to be able to do, such as naming colors, counting backward, and remembering numbers in order. Based on preliminary testing, Binet and Simon identified problems that normal 3-year-olds could pass, that normal 4-year-olds could pass, and so on. **Children's *mental age* or *MA* referred to the difficulty of the problems they could solve correctly.** A child who passed problems that the average 7-year-old could pass would have an MA of 7.

Binet and Simon used mental age to distinguish "bright" from "dull" children. A "bright" child would have the MA of an older child—for example, a 6-year-old with an MA of 9. A "dull" child would have the MA of a younger child—for example, a 6-year-old with an MA of 4. Binet and Simon confirmed that "bright" children identified using their test did better in school than "dull" children. Voila—the first objective measure of intelligence!

THE STANFORD-BINET

Lewis Terman, of Stanford University, revised Binet and Simon's test substantially and published a version known as the Stanford-Binet in 1916. **Terman described performance as an *intelligence quotient,* or *IQ,* which was simply the ratio of mental age to chronological age, multiplied by 100:**

$$IQ = MA/CA \times 100$$

At any age, children who are perfectly average have an IQ of 100, because their mental age equals their chronological age. Furthermore, roughly two-thirds of children taking a test will have IQ scores between 85 and 115. The IQ score can also be used to compare intelligence in children of different ages. A 4-year-old girl with an MA of 5 has an IQ of 125 (5/4 × 100), just like that of an 8-year-old boy with an MA of 10 (10/8 × 100). Although IQ scores are no longer computed in this way, the concept of intelligence as the ratio of MA to CA helped to popularize the Stanford-Binet test.

By the 1920s, the Stanford-Binet had been joined by many other intelligence tests. Educators greeted these new devices enthusiastically, for they seemed to offer an efficient and objective way to assess a student's chances of succeeding in school (Chapman, 1988).

At this point, you're probably wondering why we've spent so much time discussing a test that is more than 75 years old. The reason is that the Stanford-Binet has more than historical value; it remains a popular test. The Stanford-Binet, last revised in 1986, along with the Wechsler Intelligence Scale for Children-III (WISC-III) and the Kaufman Assessment Battery for Children (K-ABC), are the primary individualized tests of intelligence in use today.

Lewis Terman (1877–1956), a pioneer of intelligence testing in America who devised the Stanford-Binet test.

Do Tests Work?

To answer this question, we need to consider two separate issues. **First, we need to know if a test is *reliable*, which means that it yields scores that are consistent.** Reliability is often measured by administering similar forms of a test on two occasions. On a reliable test, a person will have similar scores on both occasions. In fact, modern intelligence tests are quite reliable. If a child takes an intelligence test and then retakes it days or a few weeks later, the two scores are usually quite similar (Wechsler, 1991).

What do these scores *mean*? Are they really measuring intelligence? **These questions raise the issue of *validity*, which refers to the extent that a test really measures what it claims to measure.** Validity is usually assessed by determining the relation between test scores and other, independent measures of the construct that the test is thought to measure. For example, to measure the validity of a test of extroversion, we would first have children take the test. Then we would observe these same youngsters in some social setting, such as during a school recess, and record who is outgoing and who is shy. The test would be valid if scores correlated highly with our independent observations of extroverted behavior.

How would we extend this approach to intelligence tests? Ideally, we would administer the intelligence tests and then correlate the scores with other, independent estimates of intelligence. Therein lies the problem. There are no other independent ways to estimate intelligence; the only way to measure intelligence is with tests. Consequently, many follow Binet's lead and obtain measures of performance in school, such as grades or teachers' ratings of their students. The correlations between these measures and scores on intelligence tests typically fall somewhere between .4 and .6 (Brody, 1992). For example, the correlation between scores on the WISC-III and grade-point average is .47 (Wechsler, 1991). This correlation is positive but far from 1. Obviously, some youngsters with high test scores do not excel in school, whereas others with low scores get good grades. In general, however, tests do a reasonable job of predicting school success.

Does this mean that intelligence tests are synonymous with intelligence? Probably not. Tests measure intellectual skills, such as verbal ability and abstract reasoning, that are important for success in school. However, tests ignore those aspects of intelligence that are not crucial for scholastic achievement, such as practical problem-solving skills. Consequently, it is fair to conclude that current intelligence tests are reasonably valid measures of *only* the components of intelligence that are required for achievement in school.

Can you think of other elements of intelligence that are not included in traditional tests? Let's see if they're included in newer theories of intelligence.

The Elements of Intelligence

If verbal ability and abstract reasoning are only some of the elements of intelligence, what are the others? According to Howard Gardner's (1983) *theory of multiple intelligences,* intelligence includes six distinct components:

- *Linguistic intelligence* includes knowing the meaning of words, the ability to use words to understand new ideas, and using language to convey ideas to others.
- *Logical-mathematical intelligence* includes understanding relations that can exist among objects, actions, or ideas and logical or mathematical operations that can be performed on these.
- *Spatial intelligence* is the ability to imagine the appearance of an object (for example, a poodle) and to transform the appearance of an object mentally (for example, the poodle acquires pink polka dots and stands on its nose).
- *Musical intelligence* is the ability to comprehend or produce sounds varying in pitch, rhythm, and emotional tone.
- *Bodily-kinesthetic intelligence* is the ability to use one's body (or parts of it) in highly differentiated ways, as do dancers, craftspeople, and athletes.
- *Personal intelligence* is the ability to identify different feelings, moods, motivations, and intentions in others and in oneself.

In Howard Gardner's theory, musical intelligence is one of six distinct components of intelligence.

You probably recognize the first three elements because they are similar to intelligence as it has been assessed on tests for nearly a century. But the last three elements stretch traditional, school-based definitions of intelligence. By including both old and new, Gardner has produced a much broader approach to intelligence.

Another groundbreaking view of intelligence is Robert Sternberg's (1985) *triarchic theory,* which includes three subtheories:

- According to the *contextual* subtheory, intelligent behavior must always be considered in the context of the individual's culture. Intelligence involves adapting to that culture in order to achieve one's goals.
- According to the *experiential* subtheory, intelligence is revealed in different ways, depending on the familiarity of the task. For a novel task, intelligence is associated with the ability to apply one's existing knowledge to a new situation; for familiar tasks, intelligence is associated with being able to finish the task with little mental effort.
- According to the *componential* subtheory, intelligent behavior involves organizing basic cognitive processes into an efficient strategy for completing a task.

In contrast to most approaches to intelligence, Sternberg's does not concentrate on identifying specific domains of intelligence. Instead, the triarchic theory emphasizes that intelligence depends on the strategies that people use to complete tasks (the componential subtheory), the familiarity of those tasks (the experiential subtheory), and the relevance of the tasks to personal and cultural goals (the contextual subtheory).

The triarchic theory also pinpoints a profound problem. Look around you. Do you share the same experiences and cultural background with every one of your classmates? If you don't, should you compare your score on an intelligence test with others' scores? Comparing test scores for different cultural groups is a controversial practice, as we see in the next section.

The Impact of Race, Ethnicity, and Social Class

The results in this graph have been the source of controversy for decades. On many intelligence tests, the average score of African Americans is about 15 points lower than that of European Americans (Brody, 1992). This difference in

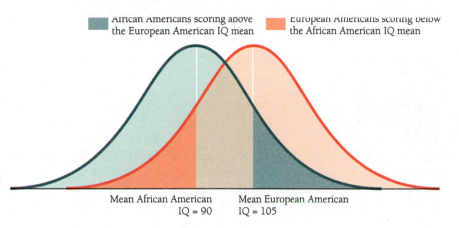

African Americans scoring above the European American IQ mean

European Americans scoring below the African American IQ mean

Mean African American   Mean European American
IQ = 90   IQ = 105

test scores has been linked to the fact that children in some racial and ethnic groups are evaluated on test items requiring experiences that are not part of their own culture. Look at a simple problem like this one:

A conductor is to an orchestra as a teacher is to what?
book   school   class   eraser

Children whose background includes exposure to orchestras are more likely to answer this question correctly than children who lack such exposure.

The problem of bias has led to the development of *culture-fair intelligence tests,* which include test items based on experiences that are common to many cultures. An example is Raven's Progressive Matrices, which consists solely of items like the one shown here. Examinees are asked to select the piece that would complete the design correctly (6, in this case). Performance on culture-fair tests does predict achievement in school, but these tests are not entirely free of cultural influence, as their creators had hoped (Anastasi, 1988). Why? Culture can influence a child's familiarity with the entire testing situation, not simply familiarity with particular items. A culture-fair test will underestimate a child's intelligence if, for example, the child's culture encourages children to solve problems in collaboration with others and discourages them from excelling as individuals.

If all test scores reflect cultural influences, at

least to some degree, how should we interpret test scores? Remember that tests assess successful adaptation to a particular cultural context; they have little validity beyond that context. Most intelligence tests predict success in a school environment that often encompasses middle-class values. Tests do so for African American and Hispanic American students as well as for European American students. Regardless of their racial or ethnic group, children with low test scores are usually not destined for success in school. The low score reported for Charlene, in the third chapter-opening vignette, means that at this time she probably lacks the skills to succeed in school—nothing more and nothing less.

Outside of school, test scores are almost meaningless; intelligence tests measure "school smarts," not "street smarts." Consequently, when one group has higher average scores than another, this means that one group has more of the specific skills that are critical for success in the middle-class school environment, not that they have more of some pervasive general-purpose ability called intelligence.

By focusing, as we have, on groups of people, it's easy to lose sight of the fact that individuals *within* these groups differ in intelligence. Look again at the graph on page 197; you'll see that the average difference in IQ scores between European Americans and African Americans is small compared to the entire range of scores for these groups. What causes individuals within groups to differ? We'll see in the next section.

Hereditary and Environmental Factors

Joanna, a 5-year-old European American girl, was administered the WISC-III and obtained a score of 112. Ted, a 5-year-old boy, took the same test and received a score of 92. What can account for the 20-point difference in scores? Heredity and experience both matter. Some of the evidence for hereditary factors is shown in the graph. If genes influence intelligence, then siblings' test

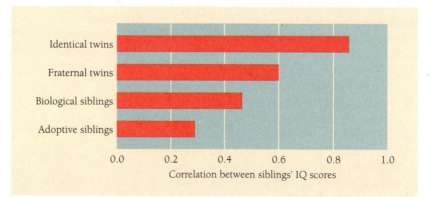

scores should become more alike as siblings become more similar genetically (Bouchard & McGue, 1981). Identical twins are identical genetically, and they typically have virtually identical test scores, which would be a correlation of 1.0. Fraternal twins have about 50 percent of their genes in common, just like nontwins who have the same biological parents. Consequently, their test scores should (a) be less similar than scores for identical twins, (b) as similar as other siblings who have the same biological parents, and (c) more similar than those of children and their adopted siblings. You can see in the graph that each of these predictions is supported.

Environment also counts. Children with high test scores typically have parents who are stimulating, responsive, and involved (Bradley, Caldwell, &

Rock, 1988). In addition, among European American children, an environment that includes plenty of variety and appropriate play materials is linked to high test scores; among African American children, a well-organized home environment is associated with higher scores (Bradley et al., 1989).

The importance of a stimulating environment is also demonstrated by intervention projects designed to prepare poor children for school. Intervention programs for preschool youngsters typically include an elaborate, structured curriculum for both children and their parents (Ramey & Ramey, 1990). When children participate in these enrichment programs, their test scores increase by about 10 points (Clarke & Clarke, 1989). In the Spotlight on Research feature, we look at one of these "success stories" in detail.

The Carolina Abecedarian Project

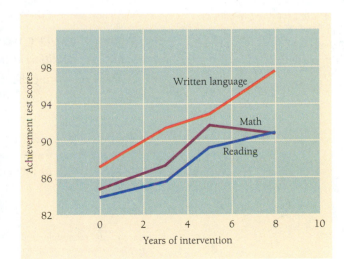

SPOTLIGHT ON RESEARCH

When children grow up in never-ending poverty, the cycle is predictable and tragic. Youngsters have few of the intellectual skills to succeed in school, so they fail. Lacking an education, they find minimal jobs (if they can work at all). Thus, their children, too, are destined to grow up in poverty.

Since Project Head Start was begun in 1965 by President Lyndon Johnson as part of the War on Poverty, massive educational intervention has been an important tool in the effort to break this cycle of poverty. Intervention programs can work, if the intervention is massive and is sustained over several years (Ramey & Ramey, 1990).

Perhaps the best known intervention project is the Carolina Abecedarian Project, directed by Craig Ramey and Frances Campbell (Campbell & Ramey, 1994; Ramey & Campbell, 1991). Children in this project were born to mothers who had less than a high school education, had an average IQ score of 85, and had no income in most cases. Some of the children attended a special day care facility daily from 4 months until 5 years of age. The center had a curriculum that emphasized mental, linguistic, and social development for infants and prereading skills for preschoolers.

Some children also participated in another intervention program during the first three years of elementary school. During this phase, a teacher would visit the home a few times each month, bringing materials designed to improve reading and math. The teachers taught the parents how to use the materials with their children and also acted as facilitators between home and school.

Children who participated in both the preschool and school-age programs had approximately eight years of intensive intervention. Children who participated in only one program had either three (school-age) or five (preschool) years of intervention. Some children, of course, did not participate in either program. Thus, this study is longitudinal, because children were tested repeatedly over a period of eight years, and experimental, because children were assigned randomly to different groups.

Campbell and Ramey (1994) measured the impact of intervention in several ways, including scores on intelligence tests, scores on achievement tests, and the children's need for special services in school. The graph shows some of their results—children's performance on three achievement tests. These scores are

Based on data from Campbell and Ramey, 1994.

from tests that children took as 12-year-olds, four years after the school-age intervention had ended. Nevertheless, in all three domains, performance clearly depends on the amount of intervention. Youngsters who had a full eight years of intervention generally have the highest scores; those with no intervention always have the lowest scores.

An improvement of 7–10 points may not strike you as very much, but it is a substantial improvement from a practical standpoint. For example, the Written Language scores of the youngsters with eight years of intervention place them at the 44th percentile; in contrast, children with no intervention have scores at the 20th percentile.

Of course, massive intervention over eight years is expensive. But so are the economic consequences of poverty, unemployment, and their byproducts. Programs like the Abecedarian Project show that the repetitive cycle of school failure and education can be broken. In the process, they also show that intelligence is fostered by an environment that is stimulating and responsive.   ❧

TEST YOURSELF

1. Binet devised his tests to identify children _____.
2. IQ was first defined as the ratio of _____ × 100.
3. A test is _____ if it yields consistent scores.
4. The validity of intelligence tests is often documented by showing that test scores are correlated with _____.
5. Sternberg's triarchic theory includes contextual, _____, and componential subtheories.
6. Children from various racial and ethnic groups sometimes receive lower scores on intelligence tests because items on the test _____.
7. When children participate in intervention programs, their scores on intelligence tests _____.
8. How do the subtheories of Sternberg's triarchic theory illustrate the different forces in the biopsychosocial framework?

Special Children, Special Needs

LEARNING OBJECTIVES

❧ **What are the characteristics of gifted and creative children?**

❧ **What are the different forms of mental retardation?**

❧ **What is a learning disability?**

❧ **What are the distinguishing features of hyperactivity?**

Throughout history, societies have recognized children with limited mental abilities as well as those with extraordinary talents. Today, we know much about the extremes of human talents. Let's begin with a glimpse at gifted and creative children.

Answers: (1) who would have difficulty learning in school, (2) mental age to chronological age (MA/CA), (3) reliable, (4) success in school, (5) experiential, (6) assess experiences that are not part of their culture, (7) often increase, by about 10 points

Gifted and Creative Children

In many respects, Bridgette is an ordinary middle-class 12-year-old: She is the goalie on her soccer team, takes piano lessons on Saturday mornings, sings in her church youth choir, and likes to go roller skating. However, when it comes to intelligence and academic prowess, Bridgette leaves the ranks of the ordinary. She received a score of 175 on an intelligence test and is taking a college calculus course. **Bridgette is _gifted,_ which traditionally has referred to individuals with scores of 130 or greater on intelligence tests (Horowitz & O'Brien, 1986).**

Bridgette doesn't fit the stereotype of gifted children, who are often thought to be emotionally troubled and unable to get along with their peers (Halpern & Luria, 1989). In fact, research discredits the stereotype of gifted people as distressed and socially inept. Actually, gifted youngsters tend to be more mature than their peers and to have fewer emotional problems (Luthar, Zigler, & Goldstein, 1992). Also, gifted children's thinking seems to develop in the same sequence as nongifted children's thinking, just more rapidly. Gifted children simply think like older nongifted children (Jackson & Butterfield, 1986).

With the traditional definition of giftedness in terms of IQ scores, exceptional ability is associated exclusively with the scholastic skills that are central to intelligence tests. Modern definitions of giftedness are broader and include exceptional talent in an assortment of areas, such as art, music, creative writing, and dance (Ramos-Ford & Gardner, 1991).

Whether the domain is music or math, exceptional talent seems to have several prerequisites (Feldman & Goldsmith, 1991; Rathunde & Csikszentmihalyi, 1993):

- The child's love for the subject and overwhelming desire to master it
- Instruction, beginning at an early age, with inspiring and talented teachers
- Support and help from parents, who are committed to promoting their child's talent

The message here is that exceptional talent must be nurtured. Without encouragement and support from stimulating and challenging mentors, a youngster's talents will wither, not flourish.

Contrary to stereotypes, gifted children are emotionally stable and get along with their peers. Their thinking resembles that of older adolescents who are their mental peers.

CREATIVITY

If you've seen the movie _Amadeus,_ you know the difference between being talented and being creative. Mozart and Salieri were rival composers in Europe during the 18th century. Both were talented, ambitious musicians. Yet, more than 200 years later, Mozart's work is revered but Salieri's is all but forgotten. Why? Then and now, Mozart's work was recognized as creative, but Salieri's was not.

What is creativity and how does it differ from intelligence? **Intelligence is often associated with _convergent thinking,_ which means using information that is provided to determine a standard, correct answer. In contrast, creativity is often linked to _divergent thinking,_ in which the aim is not a single correct answer (often there isn't one) but instead to think in novel and unusual directions (Guilford, 1967).**

Divergent thinking is often measured by asking children to produce a large number of ideas in response to some specific stimulus (Kogan, 1983). Children might be asked to name different uses for a common object, such as a coat hanger. Or they might be shown a page filled with circles and asked to draw as

NATHAN KOGAN
". . . divergent thinking performance in children can be enhanced by a variety of procedures—for example, direct instruction, incentives, role playing, and modeling."

many different pictures as they can, using the circles. Both the number of responses and their originality are used to measure creativity.

Creativity, like giftedness, must be cultivated. Youngsters are more likely to be creative when their home and school environments value nonconformity and encourage children to be curious. When schools, for example, emphasize mastery of factual material and discourage self-expression and exploration, creativity usually suffers (Thomas & Berk, 1981). In contrast, creativity can be enhanced by experiences that stimulate children to be flexible in their thinking and to explore alternatives (Starko, 1988).

Gifted and creative children represent one extreme of human ability. Who are at the other extreme? Mentally retarded youngsters, the topic of the next section.

Mentally Retarded Children

"Little David" was the oldest of four children. He learned to sit days before his first birthday, he began to walk at 2, and said his first words as a 3-year-old. At 5 years of age, David's development was far behind that of his agemates. A century ago, David would have been called "feebleminded" or "mentally defective." In fact, David had Down syndrome, which we first described in Chapter 2 (see pages 45–46). David had an extra 21st chromosome; as a consequence of this extra gene, David experienced retarded mental development.

According to the American Association on Mental Retardation, mental retardation is "significantly subaverage general intellectual functioning existing concurrently with deficits in adaptive behavior. . ." (Grossman, 1983, p. 1). This definition emphasizes that an individual is determined to be mentally retarded only when intelligence is substantially below average *and* when the individual does not adapt well to his or her environment.

The standard definition of below-average intelligence has been a score of 70 or less on an intelligence test such as the Stanford-Binet. Adaptive behavior is usually evaluated from interviews with a parent or other caregiver. One common measure, the Vineland Adaptive Behavior Scales (Sparrow, Balla, & Cicchetti, 1984), assesses competence in four general domains:

- Motor skills: how well children use their arms and legs for movement and how well they use their hands and fingers to manipulate objects
- Communication: how well children speak and how well they understand what others say
- Socialization: how well children interact with others, showing responsibility and sensitivity
- Daily living skill: how well children (a) care for themselves, (b) perform household chores, and (c) use money

Individuals with deficits in these domains and IQ scores of 70 or less are considered to be mentally retarded.

TYPES OF MENTAL RETARDATION

Your image of a mentally retarded child may be that of a child with Down syndrome, like the one shown on page 45. In reality, mentally retarded individuals are just as varied as are nonretarded people. How should we describe this variety? One approach is to distinguish the causes of mental retardation. **Some cases of mental retardation—no more than 25%—can be traced to a spe-**

cific biological or physical problem; these are cases of *organic mental retardation.* Down syndrome is one example of an organic form of mental retardation; phenylketonuria, which we also discussed in Chapter 2, is another (see pages 48–49). The remaining cases of mental retardation apparently do not involve biological damage. **Instead, cases of** *familial mental retardation* **simply represent the lower end of the normal distribution of intelligence.**

As you might suspect, the biological damage associated with organic mental retardation usually results in substantial mental retardation. Familial mental retardation is usually less pronounced. These variations in severity are captured in several common descriptive systems. The American Association on Mental Retardation, for example, identifies four levels of retardation, which are shown in the chart along with the range of IQ scores associated with each level. The chart also shows the three levels of retardation typically used by educators in the United States (Cipani, 1991).

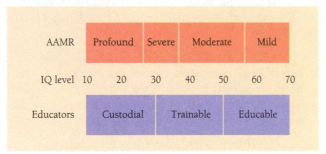

AAMR	Profound	Severe	Moderate	Mild

IQ level 10   20   30   40   50   60   70

Educators	Custodial	Trainable	Educable

The most severe forms of mental retardation are, fortunately, relatively uncommon. Approximately 10% of all cases of mental retardation fall in the categories of profound, severe, and moderate. Profoundly and severely retarded individuals usually have so few skills that they must be supervised constantly. As a consequence, they usually live in institutions for retarded persons, where they can sometimes be taught self-help skills such as dressing, feeding, or toileting (Reid, Wilson, & Faw, 1991).

Moderately retarded persons may develop the intellectual skills of a nonretarded 7- or 8-year-old. With this level of functioning, they can sometimes support themselves, typically at a sheltered workshop, where they perform simple tasks under close supervision.

The remaining 90% of individuals with mental retardation are classified as mildly or educably mentally retarded. These individuals go to school and can master many academic skills, but at an older age than a nonretarded child. Individuals with mild mental retardation often lead independent lives. Like the man in the photograph, many mildly retarded people work. Some marry. Comprehensive training programs that focus on vocational and social skills can be effective, helping individuals with mild mental retardation to become productive citizens and satisfied human beings (Ellis & Rusch, 1991).

REAL PEOPLE

Little David—the Rest of the Story

Little David—so named because his father was also David—was the oldest of four children; none of his siblings was mentally retarded. As the children grew up, they interacted the way most siblings do; they'd laugh and play together and sometimes fight and argue. Every day, beginning as a teenager and continuing into adulthood, David rode a city bus from home to his job at a sheltered workshop. He worked six hours daily, performing tasks such as making bows for packages and stuffing envelopes. He saved his earnings regularly and used them to buy what became his prized possessions—a camera, a color TV, and a VCR. As David's siblings entered adulthood, they began their own families. David relished his new role as "Uncle David" and looked forward to frequent visits from his nieces and nephews. As David entered his 40s, he began to suffer memory loss and was often confused. (These symptoms are common to Down syndrome adults during middle age; we'll discuss them in more detail in Chapter 13.) When he died, at age 47, family and friends grieved over their loss. Yet they all marveled at the richness of David's life; by any standards, David had led a full and satisfying life.   &.

Little David's mental retardation represents one end of the intelligence spectrum; Bridgette's precocity represents the other. Falling between these two extremes are other special children: those who have learning disability.

Children with Learning Disability

For some children with normal intelligence, learning is a struggle. **These youngsters suffer from** *learning disability,* **a term that refers to a child who (a) has difficulty in mastering one or more academic subjects, (b) has normal intelligence, and (c) is not suffering from other conditions that could explain poor performance, such as sensory impairment or inadequate instruction (Hammill, 1990).**

In the United States, about 5% of school-age children are classified as learning disabled, which translates into roughly 2 million affected youngsters (Moats & Lyon, 1993). The number of distinct disabilities and the degree of overlap among them is still hotly contested (Stanovich, 1993). However, one common classification scheme distinguishes disability in language (including listening, speaking, and writing), in reading, and in arithmetic (Dockrell & McShane, 1993).

Children with reading disability often have difficulty mastering the sounds associated with different letters.

The great number of learning disabilities complicates the task for teachers and researchers. It suggests that each type of learning disability may have its own cause and treatment. Take reading as an example. **Many children with reading disability have problems in** *phonological processing*—**understanding and using the sounds in written and oral language.** For a reading-disabled child like Sanjit, in the fourth chapter-opening vignette, all vowels sound alike. These youngsters benefit from explicit, extensive instruction on the connections between letters and their sounds (Lovett et al., 1994). In the case of arithmetic disability, children often have difficulty in recognizing what operations are needed and how to perform them. Here, instruction emphasizes determining the goal of arithmetic problems, using the goals to select correct arithmetic

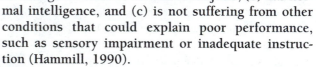

operations, and using the operations accurately (Goldman, 1989).

The key to helping these children is to move beyond the generic label *learning disability* to pinpoint the specific cognitive and academic deficits that hamper an individual child's performance in school. With a precise account of these deficits, instruction can be planned to improve the child's skills (Moats & Lyon, 1993).

This is much easier said than done, because diagnosing learning disability remains so difficult. Some children have both reading and language disabilities; others have reading and arithmetic disabilities; still others have a learning disability and another problem, attention-deficit hyperactivity disorder, which we discuss next.

Attention-Deficit Hyperactivity Disorder

Let's begin with a case study of Stuart, an 8-year-old.

> [His] mother reported that Stuart was overly active as an infant and toddler. His teachers found him difficult to control once he started school. He is described as extremely impulsive and distractible, moving tirelessly from one activity to the next. . . . His teacher reports that he is immature and restless, responds best in a structured, one-on-one situation, but is considered the class pest because he is continually annoying the other children and is disobedient. (Rapaport & Ismond, 1990, p. 120).

Stuart suffers from attention-deficit hyperactivity disorder (ADHD), a common childhood problem in the United States. Roughly 3–15% of all school-age children are diagnosed with ADHD; boys outnumber girls by a 3:1 ratio (Wicks-Nelson & Israel, 1991).

Three symptoms are at the heart of ADHD (American Psychiatric Association, 1987):

- *Overactivity.* Children with ADHD are unusually energetic, fidgety, and unable to keep still, especially in situations where they need to limit their activity, such as school classrooms.
- *Inattention.* Youngsters with ADHD do not pay attention in class and seem unable to concentrate on schoolwork; instead, they skip from one task to another.
- *Impulsivity.* Children with ADHD often act before thinking; they may run into a street before looking for traffic or interrupt others who are already speaking.

Not all children with ADHD show all of these symptoms to the same degree. Some, like the boy in the photograph, may be primarily hyperactive. Others may be primarily impulsive and show no signs of hyperactivity; their disorder is often described simply as attention-deficit disorder (Barkley, 1990).

Children with ADHD often have problems in conduct and in their academic performance. Like Stuart, many hyperactive children are aggressive and therefore are not liked by their peers (Barkley, 1990; McGee, Williams, & Feehan, 1992). Although youngsters with ADHD usually have normal intelligence, their scores on reading, spelling, and arithmetic achievement tests are often below average; they are often considered to be learning disabled (Pennington, Groisser, & Welsh, 1993).

CAUSES

Many parents believe that too much sugar or food additives cause their children to become "hyper." In fact, except for a few children who are allergic to food dyes or overly sensitive to sugar, research provides no support for a connection between children's diet and ADHD (McGee, Stanton, & Sears, 1993; Wolraich et al., 1994).

The primary causes of ADHD lie elsewhere. Heredity contributes; identical twins more often both have ADHD than do fraternal twins (Gillis et al., 1992). A stressful home environment also contributes; youngsters with ADHD often come from families in which parents are in conflict or are experiencing stress themselves (Anastopoulous et al., 1992). The Forces in Action feature shows how all of these factors must be considered in treating ADHD.

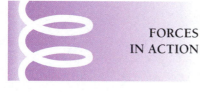

**FORCES
IN ACTION**

Treating ADHD

The key to treating ADHD is to remember that the disorder has its roots in the biological, psychological, and social forces of the biopsychosocial framework. Some children seemingly inherit a predisposition for the disorder (biological force). Stress at home (sociocultural force) can trigger the disorder, in which children have difficulty regulating their attention (psychological force). Responding to the biological bases, many physicians prescribe stimulant drugs, such as Ritalin, for children with ADHD. You may be surprised that stimulants are given to children who are already overactive, but stimulants actually have a calming influence for many of these youngsters, allowing them to focus their attention (Barkley, 1990).

Medication does not, by itself, improve children's performance in school, because it doesn't affect psychological and social influences. Consequently, children with ADHD need to learn to regulate their behavior and attention more effectively. For example, they can be encouraged to remind themselves to read instructions before starting assignments (Kendall, 1987).

Another approach is to teach parents techniques for encouraging attention and goal-oriented behavior at home. This approach is illustrated in work by Anastopoulos and his colleagues (1993). Parents of children with ADHD attended nine training sessions in which they learned how to use positive reinforcement to foster their children's attention and compliance. The parents also learned effective ways to punish their children for being inattentive. Following training, their children showed fewer symptoms of ADHD. Equally important, parents who had received the training felt a greater sense of competence in their parenting. They also reported that they experienced significantly less parental stress than before the training.

Thus, parent-training techniques combined with medication and instruction to regulate behavior target each of the causes of ADHD. Consequently, it's not surprising that such comprehensive treatment leads children with ADHD to become more attentive and less disruptive and to improve their schoolwork (Carlson et al., 1992).   ❧

TEST YOURSELF

1. A problem with defining giftedness solely in terms of IQ scores is that _____.
2. Creativity is associated with _____ thinking, in which the goal is to think in novel and unusual directions.
3. Cases of _____ mental retardation can be linked to specific biological or physical problems.
4. Individuals who are _____ mentally retarded often go to school, have jobs, and marry.
5. The most common forms of learning disability are _____.
6. Key symptoms of attention-deficit hyperactivity disorder are overactivity, _____, and impulsivity.
7. ADHD can be treated effectively by administering stimulant drugs, teaching children how to regulate their attention, and _____.
8. How might Jean Piaget have explained differences between retarded and nonretarded children's intellectual functioning? How might an information-processing psychologist explain these differences?

Grading U.S. Schools

LEARNING OBJECTIVES

- *Are today's students learning less than students of previous generations?*
- *Are today's high school graduates adequately prepared to enter the work force?*
- *How do U.S. students compare to students in other countries?*

"U.S. Students Trail Industrial World in Math Skills"
"Weak Reading Slows 90 Million"

You've probably read headlines like these in your local newspaper. They're hard to miss—seemingly, they appear almost weekly. The headlines imply that American schools are in bad shape and that American students are lousy. Are they really? To answer this question, we need criteria to evaluate U.S. schools and the students who attend them. One way to rate schools is to compare today's students with those of previous decades; another is to determine whether U.S. students leave school well prepared to enter the work force; a third is to compare them with students from other countries. In this section, we'll examine each of these criteria.

Answers: (1) it excludes talent in areas such as art, music, and dance, (2) divergent, (3) organic, (4) mildly or educably, (5) reading- and other language-related disabilities, (6) inattentiveness, (7) teaching parents how to encourage their children

Historical Trends in Achievement

For more than a quarter century, the National Assessment of Educational Progress has tracked scholastic achievement in a nationally representative sample of American students. Some typical results are shown in the graphs, which

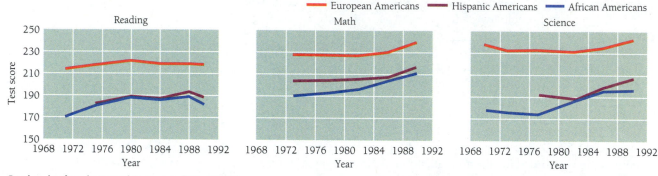

Based on data from the National Assessment of Educational Progress.

depict elementary school students' performance on tests that measure achievement in reading, math, and science (Owen, 1991). In reading, African American and Hispanic American students' scores have gone up slightly since the 1970s, while European American students' scores have remained the same. In math, all groups' scores have gone up slightly. In science, African American and Hispanic American students' scores have gone up substantially, while those of European American students have remained the same.

Overall, these trends indicate that today's elementary school students are certainly doing no worse than their predecessors; in fact, African American and Hispanic American students are achieving at higher levels. Trends for junior high and high school students point to the same conclusion. But are these levels of achievement adequate? One way to answer this question is to look at the skills of the typical U.S. high school graduate.

Skills of U.S. High School Graduates

How well educated are graduates of U.S. high schools? That depends, because standards have changed over the years. During the 19th century, you were literate if you could write or print your own name; by World War II, you were literate if you had a fourth-grade education. These definitions are inadequate for today's world. A modern definition of literacy is "using printed and written information to function in society, to achieve one's goals, and to develop one's knowledge and potential" (Kirsch et al., 1993, p. 2). Literacy includes understanding prose that appears in newspapers and magazines as well as comprehending documents such as tables, schedules, and applications, and quantitative material such as bank statements and pay stubs.

Using this modern definition of literacy, how do North Americans fare? The best answer comes from the *National Adult Literacy Survey* (Kirsch et al., 1993), which included a nationally representative sample of 13,000 U.S. adults. Each was administered a series of problems designed to assess prose, document, and quantitative literacy. Performance was scored on a scale that ranged from 0 to 500, with larger numbers indicating greater literacy.

The graph at the top of page 209 shows average literacy levels for African American, Hispanic American, and European American high school graduates. Although European Americans tend to score about 15% higher than African

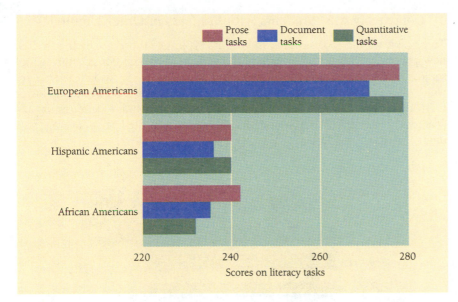

Americans and Hispanic Americans, all groups have average scores in the middle 200s. To understand the approximate level of skill represented by this number, let's look at specific items from the different scales.

- On the *prose* tasks, the average high school graduate can underline a sentence that explains the action in a short article but cannot write a brief letter that adequately explains an error on a credit-card statement.
- On the *document* tasks, the average high school graduate can locate an intersection on a map but cannot look at a bar graph to determine relative quantities.
- On the *quantitative* tasks, the average high school graduate can complete a bank deposit statement but cannot use a bus schedule to calculate the time to travel from one stop to another.

By conventional standards, the vast majority of all three groups *are* literate; only 15% of each group are in the lowest category of literacy. Yet many critics contend that by modern standards, although high school graduates in the United States are not illiterate, they need to be more literate. The modern world requires an ever more sophisticated work force, and the evidence suggests that today's workers often fall short. For example, U.S. businesses report spending more than $25 billion annually in remedial training for new employees (Kearns, 1989). More direct evidence comes from analyses of the literacy requirements of specific jobs. Some analyses suggest that literacy scores of 300 or greater are needed for professional, technical, managerial, clerical, and sales positions (Barton & Kirsch, 1990). Jobs of this sort are vital to the economy—and will probably become more so—yet only about one-third of U.S. high school graduates achieve this level of literacy (Kirsch et al., 1993).

How can U.S. students achieve greater literacy? Comparisons with students from other countries suggest some answers.

Technological change requires a more literate work force. Today's clerical workers, for example, must know much more than how to type: They must work with a variety of software—word processing and spreadsheets, for example—that continuously becomes more sophisticated.

Comparing U.S. Students with Students in Other Countries

This graph should look familiar to you; it's typical of those appearing in U.S. newspapers. The graph shows math achievement of college-bound high school seniors in countries worldwide (Salganik et al., 1993). U.S. students don't fare well—they're near the bottom of the list, with a score that is substantially lower than those of students in the leading nations. We can phrase these results another way: The very best U.S. students only perform at the level of average students in Taiwan and Korea.

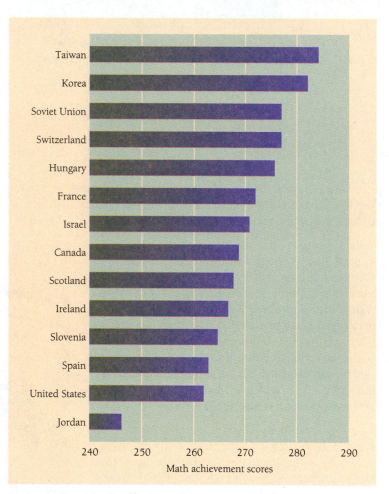

Based on data from Salganik et al., 1993.

Perhaps you're skeptical of these findings. Maybe you believe that these comparisons are flawed because U.S. high schools educate all students, not just a select few as in some other countries. U.S. scores just *look* lower because they are based on a student population with a much wider range of ability than is the case in other countries.

If you're right, comparisons among elementary school children should be revealing, because elementary schools are not selective. In all industrialized countries, nearly all young children attend elementary school. In reality, however, the results are virtually the same: U.S. students trail students in other countries. The most comprehensive evidence comes from studies conducted by Stevenson and Lee (1990) of first- and fifth-graders in the United States, Japan, and Taiwan. Their findings, shown in the graphs at the top of page 211, are

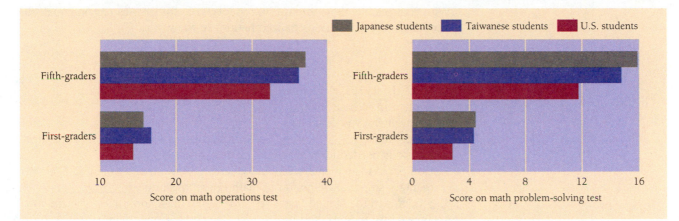

Japanese students   Taiwanese students   U.S. students

Fifth-graders

First-graders

10   20   30   40

Score on math operations test

Fifth-graders

First-graders

0   4   8   12   16

Score on math problem-solving test

Based on data from Stevenson and Lee, 1990.

sobering and substantiate the concerns expressed about American schools by the parents of Tomoko, the fourth-grader in the last chapter-opening vignette. You can see that U.S. first- and fifth-graders lag behind their counterparts in Taiwan and Japan, in both math operations and math problem solving.

Why do U.S. students manage so poorly? Stevenson and Lee (1990) point to a number of relevant factors.

1. *Time in school and how it is used.* By fifth grade, students in Japan and Taiwan spend 50% more time than U.S. students in school, and more of that time is devoted to academic activities in Japan and Taiwan than in the U.S.
2. *Time spent on homework and attitudes toward it.* Students in Taiwan and Japan spend more time on homework and value homework more than U.S. students do.
3. *Parents' attitudes.* U.S. parents are more often satisfied with their children's performance in school; in contrast, Japanese and Taiwanese parents set much higher standards for their children.
4. *Parents' beliefs about effort and ability.* Japanese and Taiwanese parents believe more strongly than U.S. parents that effort is the key factor in school success, not native ability.

When these factors are combined, we start to see why students in Japan and Taiwan excel. They spend more time in and out of school on academic tasks. Furthermore, their parents (and teachers) set loftier scholastic goals and believe that students can attain these goals with hard work. Japanese classrooms even include a written description of ideal students—*gambaru kodomo*—they who strive the hardest (Stevenson & Lee, 1990).

From their experiences with Japanese students, teachers, and schools, Stevenson and Stigler (1992) have suggested several ways in which U.S. schools could be improved:

- Give teachers more free time to prepare lessons and correct students' work.
- Improve teachers' training by allowing them to work closely with older, more experienced teachers.
- Organize instruction around sound principles of learning such as providing multiple examples of concepts and giving students adequate opportunity to practice newly acquired skills.
- Set higher standards for children, who need to spend more time and effort in school-related activities in order to achieve those standards.

HAROLD W. STEVENSON
"Belief in the importance of hard work, coupled with the belief that this should occur in elementary school, appears to be one of the most important bases for the rapid cognitive development of Chinese and Japanese children during the elementary school years."

With changes like these to improve schools, U.S. students can again equal students from the other industrialized nations in the world.

TEST YOURSELF

1. Since the 1970s, elementary school students' performance in reading, math, and science has _____.
2. Today, literacy is defined as _____.
3. Approximately _____ of U.S. high school graduates have the literacy skills needed for managerial, clerical, and sales positions.
4. Compared to elementary school students in Taiwan and Japan, U.S. elementary students are poorer in math operations and _____.
5. Students in the United States spend less time in school than Japanese and Taiwanese students, and U.S. students spend less time doing _____.

6. What forces in the biopsychosocial framework are illustrated by historical changes in literacy?

Putting It All Together

At approximately 6 years of age, children enter Piaget's period of concrete operations; at roughly the same time, they begin school. As they grow, their thinking moves beyond the concrete to the abstract. Like Adrian in the first chapter-opening vignette, they gradually pick up the study strategies that are essential for school achievement.

We saw that schools differ in size, organization, and philosophy and that these variations influence the outcome of schooling. For example, although most modern schools have larger enrollments than their predecessors, smaller schools allow students to participate more extensively in school activities (as was true of Christine in the second chapter-opening vignette), which fosters social development.

We traced the origins of intelligence testing in the schools and examined how tests are used today. We saw that test scores predict school achievement because they tap the knowledge and skills that are prerequisites for school success. Low test scores, like the one reported for Charlene in the third vignette, indicate that a student probably lacks the skills needed for school success.

We also examined one of the reasons why educating U.S. children is such a challenge: Contemporary schools serve a wide range of youngsters, including gifted children, mentally retarded children, and learning-disabled children like Sanjit in the fourth chapter-opening vignette. The aim is for all children to be educated to their fullest potential, but we still don't know how best to accommodate all students in today's schools.

We ended the chapter by grading U.S. schools. By historical standards, today's students are extraordinarily capable. Nevertheless, for the needs of a technologically sophisticated society, American students are undereducated. Tomoko's parents, in the fifth vignette, are right to be worried, because U.S. students lag far behind students in Japan and other industrialized countries. However, there is reason for optimism. The same cross-cultural comparisons that reveal the gap between U.S. and Japanese students suggest ways in which American schools can be revitalized for the 21st century. Parents' attitudes and beliefs help to explain why Asian students surpass U.S. students in school achievement. This influence will be apparent in the next chapter, too, as we watch children expand their social horizons.

Thinking about Development

1. Which elements of the biopsychosocial framework are emphasized in Piaget's theory of cognitive development, as described in this chapter and in Chapter 4?

2. Explain how variations in the transition to secondary school illustrate life-cycle factors at work.

Answers: (1) stayed about the same, (2) being able to use printed and quantitative information effectively, (3) one-third, (4) math problem solving, (5) homework

3. If Jean Piaget were asked to create an intelligence test, how might it differ from the type of test that Binet created? How would a test devised by Howard Gardner, the proponent of the theory of multiple intelligences, differ from Binet's test?

4. How might our definitions of giftedness and mental retardation change if they were based on Robert Sternberg's triarchic theory?

5. How do the factors associated with effective schools and effective teaching in U.S. schools (discussed on pages 186–193) relate to the factors responsible for Japanese students' success compared to that of U.S. students?

Summary

Cognitive Development

More Sophisticated Thinking: Piaget's Version

■ In progressing to Piaget's stage of concrete operations, children become less egocentric, rarely confuse appearances with reality, and are able to reverse their thinking. They now solve perspective-taking, conservation, and class-inclusion problems correctly. Thinking at this stage is limited to the concrete and the real.

■ With the onset of formal-operational thinking, adolescents can think hypothetically and reason abstractly. In deductive reasoning, they understand that conclusions are based on logic, not on experience.

■ Critics of Piaget's account of formal-operational thinking point to two shortcomings. First, in everyday thinking, adolescents' reasoning is often less sophisticated than would be expected of formal-operational thinkers. Second, Piaget assumed that after the formal-operational stage is reached, thinking never again changes qualitatively.

Information-Processing Strategies for Learning and Remembering

■ Rehearsal and other memory strategies are used to transfer information from working memory, a temporary store of information, to long-term memory, a permanent store of knowledge. Children begin to rehearse at about 7 or 8 and take up other strategies as they get older.

■ Effective use of strategies for learning and remembering begins with an analysis of the goals of any learning task. It also includes monitoring one's performance to determine whether the strategy is working. Collectively, these processes make up an important group of study skills.

Effective Schools and Effective Teachers

Size of School and Size of Classes

■ School size does not affect achievement, but smaller schools can be beneficial for students' social development because they offer greater opportunity to participate in school activities, with less risk that a student will feel anonymous.

■ Classes that have approximately 20 or fewer students foster achievement; when classes have more than 20 students, size of class is not related to achievement.

Classroom Organization and Atmosphere

■ Traditional classrooms emphasize the acquisition of knowledge by students working alone under a teacher's direction. Open classrooms also emphasize learning to work with others and personal growth. In open classrooms, students may work together, and the teacher's role is to structure an environment in which students can learn on their own. Traditional classrooms seem to promote academic achievement, but open classrooms foster social and personal development.

The Transition to Secondary School

■ The transition to middle school or junior high school is often stressful. Creating "teams" within middle schools or junior high schools can create a more personal environment that reduces some of the stress associated with this transition.

Ability Grouping

■ Tracking does not help less capable students, who continue to fall behind. In fact, both talented and less talented students often fare better in classes that include students with a range of abilities.

Teachers

■ Teachers are most likely to succeed when they can organize a classroom well so that class time is devoted largely to instruction. Teachers' impressions of their students can sometimes give rise to self-fulfilling prophecies: Students succeed or fail in part because the teacher expected them to succeed or fail.

■ Students learn when being tutored and from tutoring others. Today's students also make use of the computer, as a tutor, as a medium of experiential learning, and as a multipurpose tool.

Aptitudes for School

Binet and the Development of Intelligence Testing

■ Binet created the first intelligence test in order to identify students who would have difficulty in school. Using this work, Terman created the Stanford-Binet in 1916; it remains an important intelligence test. The Stanford-Binet introduced the concept of the intelligence quotient (IQ): MA/CA × 100.

Do Tests Work?

■ Intelligence tests are reliable, which means that people usually get consistent scores on the tests. Intelligence tests are reasonably valid measures of achievement in school, but they probably do not measure aspects of intelligence that are important outside of school.

The Elements of Intelligence

■ Modern theories of intelligence include a number of discrete components of intelligence. Gardner's (1983) theory includes linguistic, logical-mathematical, spatial, musical, bodily-kinesthetic, and personal intelligences. Sternberg's (1985) triarchic theory includes contextual, experiential, and componential subtheories.

Impact of Race, Ethnicity, and Social Class

■ The average IQ score for African Americans is about 15 points lower than the average score for European Americans. This difference has been attributed to the facts that more African American children live in poverty and that most intelligence tests assess knowledge based on middle-class experiences. IQ scores are valid predictors of school success, however, because middle-class experience is often a prerequisite for success in U.S. schools.

Hereditary and Environmental Factors

■ Evidence for the impact of heredity on IQ comes from the finding that siblings' IQ scores become more alike as siblings become more similar genetically. Evidence for the impact of the environment comes from the finding that children who live in responsive, well-organized home environments tend to have higher IQ scores, as do children who participate in intervention projects.

Special Children, Special Needs

Gifted and Creative Children

■ Traditionally, gifted children have been those with high scores on IQ tests. Contrary to folklore, gifted children are socially mature and emotionally stable. Modern definitions of giftedness have been broadened to include exceptional talent in, for example, the arts.

■ Creativity is associated with divergent thinking, in which the aim is to think in novel and unusual directions. Tests of divergent thinking can predict which children are most likely to be creative. Creativity can be fostered by experiences that encourage children to think flexibly and to explore alternatives.

Mentally Retarded Children

■ Individuals with mental retardation have IQ scores of 70 or lower and deficits in adaptive behavior. Organic mental retardation, which is severe but relatively infrequent, can be linked to specific biological or physical causes; familial mental retardation, which is less severe but more common, reflects the lower end of the normal distribution of intelligence. Most retarded persons are classified as mildly or educably retarded; they attend school, work, and have families.

Children with Learning Disability

■ Children with a learning disability have normal intelligence but have difficulty mastering specific academic subjects. The most common is reading disability, which often can be traced to inadequate understanding and use of language sounds.

Attention-Deficit Hyperactivity Disorder

■ Children with ADHD are distinguished by being overactive, inattentive, and impulsive. They often have conduct problems and do poorly in school. ADHD is due to heredity and to environmental factors, particularly a stressful home environment.

■ Children with ADHD are often administered stimulants, which calm them. They can also be taught more effective ways of regulating their behavior and attention.

Grading U.S. Schools

Historical Trends in Achievement

■ Analyses of achievement in reading, math, and science indicate that today's students are not performing below the level of students of a generation ago; in fact, African American and Hispanic American students are achieving at higher levels.

Skills of U.S. High School Graduates

■ According to traditional definitions of literacy, people in the United States are highly literate. When literacy is defined in terms of understanding prose, documents, and quantitative information, however, only a minority of U.S. high school graduates have the skills necessary for success in today's increasingly sophisticated workplace.

Comparing U.S. Students with Students in Other Countries

■ Elementary and high school students in the United States do poorly in comparison with students from other industrialized countries. U.S. students spend less time in school and use that time less effectively. Also, U.S. parents and teachers have modest scholastic goals for the children.

Key Terms

convergent thinking (201)
culture-fair intelligence tests (197)
deductive reasoning (183)
divergent reasoning (201)
familial mental retardation (203)

gifted (201)
intelligence quotient (IQ) (194)
learning disability (204)
long-term memory (184)
mental age (MA) (194)
mental operations (181)

organic mental retardation (202)
phonological processing (204)
reliability (195)
validity (195)
working memory (184)

If You'd Like to Learn More

BREDEKAMP, S., & SHEPARD, L. (1989). How best to protect children from inappropriate school expectations, practices, and policies. *Young Children, 44,* 14–24. The authors describe a number of ways in which teachers can meet children's needs in classrooms where students differ markedly in their talents and abilities.

CLEMENTS, D. H., NASTASI, B. K., & SWAMINATHAN, S. (1993). Young children and computers: Crossroads and directions from research. *Young Children, 48,* 56–64. The authors document how children benefit from well-planned computer activities, particularly those involving collaboration with others.

FISKE, E. B. (1992). *Smart schools, smart kids.* New York: Touchstone. The author examines some exceptional U.S. schools in order to discover the key ingredients to a successful school.

FLAVELL, J. H., MILLER, P. H., & MILLER, S. A. (1993). *Cognitive development* (3rd ed.). Englewood Cliffs, NJ: Prentice-Hall. We recommended this book in Chapter 4 as a good source of information about cognitive development in young children, but it also covers the development of thinking in school-age children and adolescents.

GARDNER, H. (1993). *Creating minds.* New York: Basic Books. The author describes the lives of extraordinarily creative persons such as Einstein and Picasso in order to understand the conditions that foster creativity.

INGERSOLL, B. (1988). *Your hyperactive child: A parent's guide to coping with attention deficit disorder.* New York: Doubleday. The author provides a good general introduction to hyperactivity and debunks many of the myths that are associated with the disorder.

KAIL, R., & PELLEGRINO, J. W. (1985). *Human intelligence: Perspectives and prospects.* New York: Freeman. The authors consider intelligence from the traditional viewpoint of the intelligence-testing movement, then examine alternative perspectives on intelligence suggested by the theories of Piaget, Gardner, and Sternberg.

STEVENSON, H. W., & STIGLER, J. W. (1992). *The learning gap.* New York: Summit. The authors, who have done some of the most extensive cross-cultural research on schools, explore why U.S. schoolchildren do so poorly in comparison to Japanese students and suggest what we could learn from Japanese schools.

❧ Tanya and Sheila, both sixth-graders, wanted to go to a Pearl Jam concert with two boys from their school. When Tanya asked if she could go, her mom said, "No way!" Tanya replied defiantly, "Why not?" Her mother blew up: "Because I say so. That's why. Stop bugging me." Sheila wasn't allowed to go either. When she asked why, her mom said, "I just think that you're still too young to be dating. I don't mind your going to the concert. If you want to go just with Tanya, that would be fine. What do you think of that?"

❧ Only 36 hours had passed since the campers arrived at Crab Orchard Summer Camp. Nevertheless, groups had already formed spontaneously, based on the campers' main interests: arts and crafts, hiking, and swimming. Within each group, leaders and followers had already emerged. This happened every year, but the staff was always astonished at how quickly a "social network" emerged at camp.

❧ Every day, 7-year-old Roberto follows the same routine when he gets home from school: He watches one action-adventure cartoon on TV after another until it's time for dinner. Roberto's mother is disturbed by her son's constant TV-viewing, particularly because of the amount of violence in the shows that he likes. Her husband tells her to stop worrying: "Let him watch what he wants to. It won't hurt him and, besides, it keeps him out of your hair."

Expanding Social Horizons

 Although you've never had a course called "Culture 101," your knowledge of your culture is deep. Like all human beings, you have been learning, since birth, to live in your culture. **Teaching children the values, roles, and behaviors of their culture—*socialization*—is a major goal of all peoples.** In most cultures, the task of socialization falls initially to parents, who set and try to enforce standards of behavior for their children. In their effort to achieve these goals, parents resort to various styles, ranging from the brusque, almost confrontational approach of Tanya's mother to the more conversational, empathic style used by Sheila's mother.

Soon other powerful forces contribute to socialization. Peers become influential, through both individual friendships and social groups like those that formed at Crab Orchard Summer Camp. The media—particularly television—contribute to socialization as well. Children like Roberto in the third vignette are exposed to a much wider range of experiences and values than was ever possible in the pre-TV era.

All of these elements influence children's behaviors, values, and social roles. In this chapter, we look at the contribution of each to socialization.

Family Relationships

LEARNING OBJECTIVES

❧ *What are the primary dimensions of parenting? How do they affect children's development?*

❧ *What determines how siblings get along? How do first-born, later-born, and only children differ?*

❧ *How do divorce and remarriage affect children?*

❧ *What factors contribute to child abuse?*

Family. The term is as sacred to most Americans as baseball, apple pie, and Chevrolet. But what comes to mind when you think of family? Television has given us one answer. From *Leave It to Beaver* to *Family Ties* to *Married with Children*, the family in the United States has usually consisted of a mother, a father, and two or three children. In reality, of course, families are as diverse as the people in them. Some families consist of a single parent and an only child. Others include two parents, many children, and grandparents or other relatives.

All of these family configurations have a common goal: The care and socialization of children. We'll begin our study of family functioning by looking at relationships between parents and children, and then at relationships between siblings. Next, we consider how children are influenced by divorce and remarriage. Finally, we examine the forces that can cause parents to abuse their children.

Dimensions and Styles of Parenting

In his brutally frank way, Calvin is raising several questions that have long been central to the study of human development. What is the nature of the par-

CALVIN AND HOBBES © 1993 Watterson./Dist. by Universal Press Syndicate. Reprinted with permission. All rights reserved.

ent–child relationship? How does this relationship influence development throughout the life span? How do children influence parents?

We can begin to answer these questions by understanding the ways in which parents differ. Think about your own parents. When you were a child and adolescent, were they frequently physically affectionate with you, hugging or kissing you? Or were they more reserved? Did your parents often tell you exactly what to do? Or did they let you do what you wanted?

These questions focus on two key dimensions of parent–child relationships that emerge consistently in research. One dimension is the degree of warmth and responsiveness that parents show to their children. At one extreme, some parents are openly warm and affectionate with their children; they are involved with them emotionally and readily spend time and effort with them. At the other extreme are parents who are relatively uninvolved with their children and sometimes even hostile toward them. Such parents often seem more focused on their own wishes than their children's.

As you might expect, children benefit from warm and responsive parenting. When parents are warm toward them, children typically feel secure, happy, and are better behaved. In contrast, when parents are uninvolved or hostile, their children are often anxious, less controlled, and, as the cartoon indicates, low in self-esteem (Rothbaum & Weisz, 1994).

A second dimension of parental behavior has to do with the control that parents exercise over their children's behavior. At one extreme are controlling, demanding parents. Such parents sometimes seem to be running their children's lives. At the other extreme are parents who make few demands and rarely exert control; their children are free to do almost anything without fear of parental reproach.

B.C. © 1994. Reprinted by permission of Johnny Hart and Creators Syndicate, Inc.

Neither of these extremes is desirable. Parenting without any control fails, because children aren't shown the behavioral standards that their culture has for them. Overcontrol is unsatisfactory because it deprives children of the opportunity to meet behavioral standards on their own, which is the ultimate goal of socialization.

Parents need to strike a balance, maintaining adequate control while still allowing their children the freedom to make some decisions for themselves. This is easier said than done, but some important guidelines come from learning theories. These were described in Chapter 1 and are shown in the chart. The keys include using rewards effectively and modeling appropriate behavior

Perspective	Examples of Theories	Main Ideas	Emphases in Biopsychosocial Framework	Positions on Developmental Issues
Learning	Behaviorism (Watson, Skinner) Social-learning theory (Bandura)	Environment controls behavior People learn through modeling and observing	In all theories, some emphasis on biological and psychological, major focus on social, little recognition of life cycle	In all theories, strongly nurture, continuity, and universal principles of learning

for children. Parents should start by setting standards that are appropriate for the child's age, then showing the child how to meet them, and, finally, rewarding him or her for doing so (Maccoby, 1980). Suppose that a mother wants her preschool son to put away his toys at bedtime. This is a reasonable request: The child is physically capable of carrying the toys, and he knows where they're stored. The mother should show her son how to complete the task and then praise him whenever he does.

Once standards are set, they should be enforced consistently. Time and time again, research has shown that children and adolescents are more compliant when parents enforce rules regularly. The mother should insist that her son pick up his toys every night, not just occasionally. When parents enforce rules sporadically, children come to see rules as optional instead of obligatory, and they try to avoid complying with them (Lytton, 1980).

Most parents also rely on punishment as a means of controlling their children. As we explained in Chapter 1, punishment consists of the application of an aversive stimulus or the removal of attractive stimuli. Take a moment to think of some common methods that parents use to punish. Does your list include spanking or making critical comments such as "No wonder you didn't clean up your room—you never do anything around here to help!" **These illustrate *power-assertion* methods of *punishment,* all of which rely upon a parent's greater power.** Power assertion includes physical punishment, threats, or humiliation. In the short term, power assertion "works," in the limited sense that children usually perform the desired behavior or stop the offending behavior. In the long term, however, power assertion is ineffective because (1) children become fearful of their parents, (2) they are less likely to internalize social rules, and (3) as social learning theory reminds us, children often imitate their parents' aggressive behavior (Hoffman, 1970; Parke & Slaby, 1983).

Other methods of punishment are much more effective. **In *time-out,* when children misbehave, they briefly sit alone in a quiet, unstimulating location.** Some parents have children sit alone in a bathroom; others put them in an isolated corner of a room, as shown in the photograph. Time-out is punishing because it interrupts the child's ongoing activity and isolates him

or her from other family members, toys, books, and generally, all forms of rewarding stimulation. The period is sufficiently brief—usually just a few minutes—for a parent to use the method consistently. During time-out, both parent and child typically calm down. Then, when time-out is over, the parent can talk with the child, making clear why the punished behavior was objectionable and explaining what the child should do instead. "Reasoning" like this—even with preschool children—is useful because it emphasizes why the parent punished and how punishment can be avoided in the future.

CULTURAL DIFFERENCES IN DIMENSIONS OF PARENTAL BEHAVIOR

Views about the "proper" amount of control and the "proper" amount of warmth reflect parents' cultural heritage. European Americans want their children to be happy and self-reliant individuals, and they believe that these goals can best be achieved when parents are warm and exert moderate control (Goodnow, 1992; Spence, 1985). In contrast, in many countries in Asia and Latin America, individualism is less important than cooperation and collaboration (Okagaki & Sternberg, 1993). In China, for example, Confucian principles dictate that parents are always right and that emotional restraint is the key to family harmony (Chao, 1983). Based on these principles, we would expect to find that Chinese parents are not as warm toward their children but are more controlling than their North American counterparts. Lin and Fu (1990) found exactly this pattern, as shown in the charts. Compared to mothers and fathers in the United States, mothers and fathers in Taiwan were more likely to emphasize parental control and less likely to express affection.

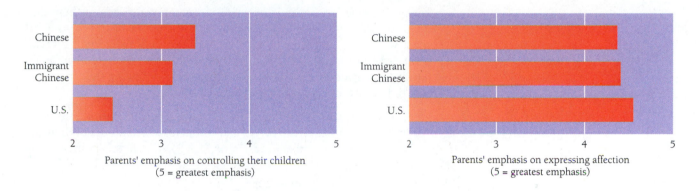

Parents' emphasis on controlling their children
(5 = greatest emphasis)

Parents' emphasis on expressing affection
(5 = greatest emphasis)

Also shown in the charts are the results for a third group studied by Lin and Fu. Parents in this group emigrated from Taiwan and were living in the United States, where their children were born. The findings for this group were between the other groups in terms of both warmth and control. That is, immigrant Chinese parents were less controlling than Taiwanese parents but more controlling than U.S. parents. Likewise, they were warmer toward their children than Taiwanese parents, but not as warm as U.S. parents. Both results suggest that the immigrant group was gradually becoming assimilated into U.S. culture.

Thus, Chinese parents' behavior is consistent with the Confucian principles that are central to traditional Chinese culture. Among European Americans, parents' behavior often reflects longstanding cultural beliefs in the importance of individualism and self-reliance. In these and all societies, cultural values help to specify appropriate ways for parents to interact with their offspring.

PARENTAL STYLES

When the dimensions of warmth and control are combined, four prototypic styles of parenting emerge (Baumrind, 1975, 1991b).

- ***Authoritarian parenting* combines high control with little warmth.** These parents lay down the rules and expect them to be followed without discussion or argument. Hard work, respect, and obedience are what authoritarian parents wish to cultivate in their children. There is little give and take between parent and child, because authoritarian parents do not balance their demands with consideration for children's needs or wishes. This style was illustrated by Tanya's mother in the first chapter-opening vignette. The mother felt no obligation whatsoever to explain why she would not allow Tanya to attend the concert.

- **Authoritative parenting** **combines a fair degree of parental control with warmth and responsiveness to the children.** Authoritative parents favor giving explanations for rules and encouraging discussion. This style is exemplified by Sheila's mother in the chapter-opening vignette. She explained why she did not want Sheila going to the concert with the boys and encouraged her daughter to discuss the issue with her.
- **Indulgent-permissive parents** **are warm and caring but exert little control over their children.** They tend to accept much of their children's behavior and punish them infrequently. A parent using this style would readily agree to the girls' request to go to the concert, simply because it is something that they want to do.
- **Indifferent-uninvolved parents** **are neither warm nor controlling.** These parents provide for the basic physical and emotional needs of their children but little else. They try to minimize the amount of time and effort spent with their children and avoid becoming emotionally involved with them. Had Tanya and Sheila had mothers who used this style, they might have simply gone to the concert without asking, knowing that their parents didn't care and would rather not be bothered.

Parental style is fairly stable over time. Parents who are authoritative with their school-age children tend to be authoritative when their children are adolescents (McNally, Eisenberg, & Harris, 1991). Given this stability, you shouldn't be surprised to learn that parental style influences children's development (Baumrind, 1991a; Maccoby & Martin, 1983):

- Children with authoritarian parents typically have lower grades in school, have lower self-esteem, and are less skilled socially.
- Children with authoritative parents tend to have higher grades and are often responsible, self-reliant, and friendly.
- Children with indulgent-permissive parents have lower grades and are often impulsive and easily frustrated.
- Children with indifferent-uninvolved parents usually have low self-esteem and are impulsive, aggressive, and moody.

Many of these outcomes can be seen in a study by Lamborn and her colleagues (1991), examining the influence of parental style on high school students' psychosocial development and performance in school. The results depicted in the graphs are complex but show a very consistent pattern. Adolescents with au-

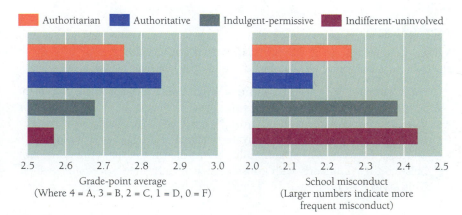

Authoritarian   Authoritative   Indulgent-permissive   Indifferent-uninvolved

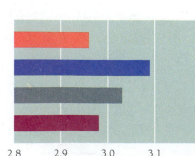

2.8   2.9   3.0   3.1   3.2

Self-reliance
(Larger numbers indicate more self-reliance)

2.5   2.6   2.7   2.8   2.9   3.0

Grade-point average
(Where 4 = A, 3 = B, 2 = C, 1 = D, 0 = F)

2.0   2.1   2.2   2.3   2.4   2.5

School misconduct
(Larger numbers indicate more
frequent misconduct)

thoritative parents have the best scores on all measures: They are the most self-reliant, have the best grades, and misbehave the least in school. Adolescents with indifferent-uninvolved parents tend to be at the other extreme: They are lower in self-reliance, have lower grades, and are the most likely to be involved in school misconduct.

Adolescents with either authoritarian or indulgent-permissive parents are in between the other groups on most measures. Adolescents with authoritarian parents were the least self-reliant of all four groups, but in grades and school misconduct they ranked behind adolescents with authoritative parents. Adolescents with indulgent-permissive parents were nearly as self-reliant as those with authoritative parents, but their grades were lower, and they were more likely to misbehave in school.

We can summarize these results by noting that authoritative parenting is consistently associated with positive outcomes in the three domains studied. A parental style that combines control, warmth, and affection seems to be best for children. Importantly, this conclusion apparently holds for children and parents from several different ethnic groups in the United States, including people of African, Asian, and Hispanic descent (Lamborn et al., 1991; Steinberg et al., 1992).

CHILDREN'S CONTRIBUTIONS: RECIPROCAL INFLUENCE

From what we've said thus far, it may seem that parent–child relations are a one-way street: Parents influence their children's behavior but not vice versa. Actually, nothing could be further from the truth. Beginning at birth and throughout the life span, children influence the way parents treat them. The family is really a dynamic, interactive system in which parents and children influence each other.

To illustrate this process, let's imagine two children responding to a parent's authoritative style. The first child readily complies with parental requests and responds well to family discussions concerning parental expectations. These parent–child relations are a textbook example of successful authoritative parenting.

The second child behaves differently. Although the parent attempts to use the same authoritative style that was so successful with the first child, the second child often complies reluctantly and sometimes defies requests altogether. Over time, the parent becomes more controlling and less affectionate. This leads the child to become even less likely to comply in the future, producing even more authoritarian parental behavior.

These examples illustrate that parental styles often evolve as a consequence of children's behavior in general. A child's temperament can be a particularly strong influence on parents' disciplinary styles (Anderson, Lytton, & Romney, 1986). Remember from Chapter 2 (pages 72–73) that temperament consists of biologically based differences in children's emotionality, activity, and sociability. Now think about young children who, by temperament, are eager to please adults and who are less active. A parent may discover that a modest amount of control is adequate for these youngsters. Now imagine youngsters who, by temperament, are not as sociable but are more active. With them, a parent may need to be more controlling and directive. Thus, influence is reciprocal. Children's behavior helps to determine how parents treat them. The resulting parental behavior can influence children's behavior, which in turn causes parents to change their behavior. These cycles of reciprocal influence from child to parent to child to parent go on throughout the life of the parent–child relationship. As you will see in Chapters 10 and 12, they continue even when both parent and child are adults.

A reciprocal parent–child relationship is central to human development, but other relationships within the family are also influential. For many children, relationships with siblings are very important, as we'll see in the next few pages.

Siblings

For most of a year, every first-born child is an only child. Some remain "onlies" forever, but most children have brothers and sisters. Some first-borns are joined by many siblings in rapid succession. Others have a single younger brother or sister. As the family gains new members, parent–child relationships become more complex. Parents can no longer focus on a single child but must adjust to the needs of multiple children. Just as important, siblings also influence each other's development. By the preschool years, siblings spend more time together than with parents, which suggests just how influential sibling relationships can be (Dunn, 1983).

The birth of a sibling is often distressing for older children. They may become withdrawn or return to more childish behavior. Distress of this sort is more common in first-born youngsters who are less than 3 years old when a sibling is born. Their distress can be linked to the many changes that occur in their lives with a sibling's birth, particularly the need to share parental attention and affection (Gottlieb & Mendelson, 1990). However, distress can be avoided if parents remain responsive to their older children's needs (Howe & Ross, 1990). In fact, one of the benefits of a sibling's birth is that fathers become more involved with their older children (Stewart et al., 1987).

With newborns, many older siblings are like the one in the photograph, taking on parental tasks such as feeding or changing diapers (Wagner, Schubert, & Schubert, 1985). As the infant grows, interactions between siblings become more common and more complicated. For example, toddlers tend to talk more to parents than to older siblings. However, by the time preschoolers are 4 years old, the situation is reversed: Now younger siblings talk more to older siblings than to their mother (Brown & Dunn, 1992). Older siblings also become a source of care and comfort for younger siblings when they are distressed or upset (Garner, Jones, & Palmer, 1994).

As time goes by, some siblings grow close, becoming best friends in ways that nonsiblings can never be. Other siblings constantly argue, compete, and, overall, simply do not get along with each other. These patterns of sibling interaction seem to be established early in development and remain fairly stable. Dunn, Slomkowski, and Beardsall (1994), for example, interviewed mothers twice about their children's interaction. The first time was when the children were 3- and 5-year-olds; the second time was 7 years later, when the children were 10- and 12-year-olds. Dunn and her colleagues found that siblings who got along as preschoolers often continued to do so as young adolescents, whereas siblings who quarreled as preschoolers often quarreled as young adolescents.

What factors contribute to the quality of sibling relationships? The Forces in Action feature has the answer.

When Do Siblings Get Along?

FORCES IN ACTION

Biological, psychological, and sociocultural forces all help determine whether siblings get along well. Among the biological forces are the child's sex and temperament. Sibling relations are more likely to be warm and harmonious between siblings of the same sex than between siblings of the opposite sex (Dunn & Kendrick, 1981). Also, relations are smoother when neither sibling is temperamentally emotional (Brody, Stoneman, & McCoy, 1994). Psychological forces contribute, too. Siblings' perceptions of each other and their parents' treatment of them is important. Siblings more often get along when they believe that parents have no "favorites" but treat all siblings similarly (Stocker & McHale, 1992). Also, relationships generally improve as the younger sibling approaches adolescence, because siblings begin to perceive one another as equals (Buhrmester & Furman, 1990). Finally, sociocultural forces also come into play. A warm, harmonious relationship between parents often makes for positive sibling relationships; in contrast, when conflict is common in the parents' relationship, conflict between siblings is much more common, too (Volling & Belsky, 1992).

These factors are not independent; they influence each other. You can see this interaction in a study by Brody, Stoneman, and McCoy (1994), who assessed children's temperament as well as the quality of parent–child relationships, mother–father relationships, and sibling relationships. They found that temperament affected sibling relationships directly: Children with "difficult" temperamental characteristics (for example, overly emotional) were more likely to have conflicts with siblings. Brody and his colleagues found that parental conflict affected sibling relationships indirectly. When parental conflict was common, parents no longer treated all their children the same, which led to conflict among siblings.

A biopsychosocial perspective on sibling relationships makes it clear that, in their pursuit of family harmony (otherwise known as peace and quiet), parents can influence some of the factors affecting sibling relationships but not others. Parents *can* help to reduce friction between siblings by being equally affectionate, responsive, and caring to all of their children, and by caring for one another. At the same time, parents (and prospective parents!) must realize that some dissension is natural in families, especially those with young boys and girls. Children's different interests lead to conflicts that youngsters cannot resolve because their social skills are limited.   ❧

IMPACT OF BIRTH ORDER

First-born children are often "guinea pigs" for most parents, who have lots of enthusiasm but little practical experience rearing children. Parents typically have high expectations for their first-borns. They are both more affectionate and more punitive toward them. As more children arrive, most parents become more adept at their roles, having learned "the tricks of the trade" from earlier children. With later-born children, parents have more realistic expectations and are more relaxed in their discipline (Baskett, 1985).

The different approaches that parents use with their first- and later-born children help explain differences that are commonly observed between these children. First-born children generally have higher scores on intelligence tests and are more likely to go to college. They are also more willing to conform to parents' and adults' requests. In contrast, perhaps because later-born children are less concerned about pleasing parents and adults, they are more popular with their peers and more innovative (Eaton, Chipperfield, & Singbeil, 1989).

What about only children? According to conventional wisdom, parents like the ones in the photograph dote on "onlies," who therefore become selfish and egotistical. Is the folklore correct? In a comprehensive analysis of more than 100 studies, only children were not worse off than other children on any measure. In fact, only children were found to succeed more in school and to have higher levels of intelligence, leadership, autonomy, and maturity (Falbo & Polit, 1986).

This general pattern is not limited to North American only children. In China, only children are common because of governmental efforts to limit population growth. There, too, comparisons between only and non-only children often find no differences; when differences are found, the advantage usually goes to the only child (Falbo & Poston, 1993). Thus, contrary to the popular stereotype, only children are not "spoiled brats" (nor, in China, are they "little emperors" who boss around parents, peers, and teachers). Instead, only children are, for the most part, much like children who grow up with siblings.

Whether U.S. children grow up with siblings or as onlies, they are more likely than children in other countries to have their family relationships disrupted by divorce. What is the impact of divorce on children and adolescents?

Divorce and Remarriage

In the 1990s, nearly half of all North American children will experience their parents' divorce (Chase-Lansdale & Hetherington, 1990). Divorce is clearly a stressful experience that affects many aspects of children's lives. Some of the consequences are shown in the graph, which is based on the results of 92 separate studies involving a total of more than 13,000 preschool through college-

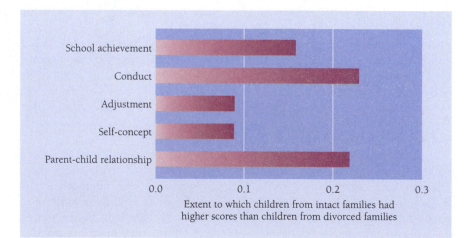

Extent to which children from intact families had higher scores than children from divorced families

age children (Amato & Keith, 1991). On measures ranging from school achievement to adjustment to parent–child relations, children whose parents had divorced fared poorly when compared to children from intact families.

The impact of divorce is much the same for boys and girls, but it is more pronounced on school-age children and adolescents. In addition, in the United States, the harm associated with divorce has dropped in the 1980s and 1990s (Amato & Keith, 1991). Apparently, as divorce has become more frequent— and therefore familiar—it has become, if not less painful, at least less harmful.

How does divorce influence development? Several factors have been identified (Amato & Keith, 1991). First, the absence of one parent means that children are supervised less closely and may not have a parent available when they need help. Second, single-parent families experience economic hardship, which creates stress and often means that opportunities once taken for granted are no longer available. Third, the conflict between parents that is common to divorcing adults is extremely distressing to children. In fact, many of the problems that are ascribed to divorce are really caused by marital conflict occurring before the divorce (Cherlin et al., 1991).

Life for children after divorce is not all gloom and doom. Children do adjust to their new life circumstances (Chase-Lansdale & Hetherington, 1990). Certain factors can ease the transition for children. For example, children adjust to divorce more readily if their divorced parents get along, especially on disciplinary matters (Hetherington, 1989). **This helps explain why some investigators find that children benefit from *joint custody,* an arrangement in which both parents retain legal custody of the children (Maccoby et al., 1993).**

Of course, many parents do not get along after a divorce, which eliminates joint custody as an option. Traditionally, mothers have been awarded custody, but in recent years the percentage of fathers given custody has increased, especially for sons. This practice coincides with findings that children often adjust better when they live with same-sex parents: Boys fare better with fathers, and girls fare better with mothers (Camara & Resnick, 1988).

Divorced people usually remarry, creating a new family that includes a parent, stepparent, biological children, and stepchildren. Interactions in these blended families are usually complicated and, despite the high hopes of the husband and wife, problems are common.

BLENDED FAMILIES

Following divorce, most children live in a single-parent household for about five years. However, more than two-thirds of divorced men and women eventually remarry (Glick, 1989; Glick & Lin, 1986). **The resulting unit, consisting of a biological parent, a stepparent, and children of one or both, is known as a *blended family.*** Because mothers are more often granted custody, the most common form of blended family is a mother, her children, and a stepfather. Preadolescent boys typically benefit from the presence of a stepfather, particularly when he is warm and involved. In contrast, preadolescent girls do not adjust readily to their mother's remarriage, apparently because it disrupts the intimate relationship they have established with her. However, as boys and girls enter adolescence, both benefit from the presence of a caring stepfather (Hetherington, 1993).

The best strategy for stepfathers is to become interested in their new stepchildren but to avoid encroaching on established relationships. Newly remarried single mothers must be certain that their enthusiasm for their new spouse does not come at the expense of time and affection for their children. Both parents and children need to have realistic expectations about the blended family. They *can* be successful, but much effort is required, because of the many complicated relationships, conflicting loyalties, and jealousies that usually exist.

Much less is known about blended families consisting of a father, his children, and a stepmother. Several factors converge to make a father's remarriage difficult for his children (Brand, Clingempeel, & Bowen-Woodward, 1988). First, one reason fathers are awarded custody may be that judges believe the children are unruly and will profit from a father's "firm hand." Consequently, many children in this type of family do not adjust well to many of life's challenges, such as a father's remarriage. Second, fathers are sometimes granted custody because they have a particularly close relationship with their children, especially their sons. As is the case with a mother's remarriage, the children sometimes fear that their father's remarriage will disturb this relationship. Finally, noncustodial mothers are more likely than noncustodial fathers to maintain close and frequent contact with their children (Maccoby et al., 1993). The constant presence of the noncustodial mother may interfere with a stepmother's efforts to establish close relationships with her stepchildren, particularly with her stepdaughters.

Over time, children adjust to the blended family. If the marriage is happy, most children clearly profit from the presence of two caring adults. Unfortunately, second marriages are slightly more likely than first marriages to end in divorce, so many children relive the trauma of divorce. As you can imagine, such recurring episodes of conflict severely disrupt children's development, accentuating the problems observed in youngsters following an initial divorce (Capaldi & Patterson, 1991).

Regrettably, divorce is not the only way that parents can disturb their children's development. As we'll see in the next few pages, some parents harm their children more directly, by abusing them.

Parent–Child Relationships Gone Awry: Child Abuse

The first time that 7-year-old Max came to school with bruises on his face, he explained to his teacher that he had fallen down the basement steps. When Max had similar bruises a few weeks later, his teacher spoke with the school principal, who contacted local authorities. It turned out that Max's mother thrashed him with a paddle for even minor misconduct; for serious transgressions, she beat Max and made him sleep alone in a dark, unheated basement.

Unfortunately, cases like Max's occur far too often. Maltreatment comes in many forms (Zuraivin, 1991):

- *Physical abuse,* involving assault that leads to injuries including cuts, welts, bruises, and broken bones
- *Sexual abuse,* involving fondling, intercourse or other sexual behaviors
- *Psychological abuse,* involving ridicule, rejection, or humiliation
- *Neglect,* in which children do not receive adequate food, clothing, or medical care

The frequency of child maltreatment is difficult to estimate, because so many cases go unreported. However, most experts agree that somewhere between 500,000 and 2.5 million U.S. children are maltreated annually (Widom, 1989).

The prognosis for these youngsters is not favorable. More than 2000 children die annually from abuse and neglect; more than 150,000 are seriously injured (U.S. Advisory Board on Child Abuse and Neglect, 1995). Even when there is no lasting physical damage, abused children have delayed cognitive development and often perform poorly in school. They may be aggressive toward their peers and remain distant from teachers and other adults. Their world seems to be hostile and frightening (Haskett & Kistner, 1991; Kurtz et al., 1993). Adults who were abused as children often experience emotional problems such as depression or anxiety, are more prone to thinking about or attempting suicide, and are more likely to be violent toward spouses and their own children (Malinosky-Rummell & Hansen, 1993).

Parents who abuse their children were once thought to be severely disturbed or deranged. Today, we know that the vast majority of abusing parents cannot be distinguished from other parents in terms of standard psychiatric criteria (Wolfe, 1985). In fact, modern accounts of child abuse no longer look to a single or even a small number of causes. Instead, a host of factors combine to place some children at risk for abuse and to protect others; the number and combination of factors determine if the child is a likely target for abuse (Belsky, 1993). Let's look at three of the most important factors: those associated with the cultural context, those associated with parents, and those associated with children themselves.

One reason that child abuse is so prevalent in the United States is that the culture generally condones physical punishment: Americans believe that, under some circumstances, parents can strike their children.

The most general category of contributing factors are those dealing with culture. Abuse is more common:

- in countries such as the United States, where physical punishment of children is accepted, than in countries like Sweden, where it is not (Zigler & Hall, 1989);
- among families living in poverty, in part because lack of money increases the stress of daily life (Straus & Kantor, 1987); and,
- in families that are socially isolated from relatives or neighbors, because isolation deprives the children of adults who could protect them (Garbarino & Kostelny, 1992).

These factors contribute to child abuse, but they are only part of the puzzle. Abuse is more common in isolated U.S. families living in poverty, but it does not occur in a majority of those families, and it does occur in middle-class families, too. Consequently, we need to look for explanations why abuse occurs in some families but not others. Today, we know that parents who abuse their children

- were, as children, sometimes maltreated themselves (Simons et al., 1991);
- have high expectations for their children but do little to help them achieve those goals (Trickett et al., 1991); and
- rely on physical punishment to control their children (Trickett & Kuczynski, 1986).

Overall, then, the typical abusing parent is often an unhappy individual whose social skills are limited, making it difficult to interact with other people pleasantly and, in the case of the children, humanely.

To place the last few pieces in the puzzle, we must look at the abused children themselves. Our discussion of reciprocal influence between parents and children (pages 223–224) reminds us that children may inadvertently, through their behavior or physical characteristics, contribute to their own abuse. In fact, younger children are more often abused than older ones, probably because they are less able to regulate aversive behaviors that may elicit abuse (Belsky, 1993). Also, unhealthy children are more often abused, perhaps because they are more likely to behave in ways that parents find aversive, such as crying and whining excessively. Another explanation is that sickness increases the level of stress in a family, setting the stage for abuse (Sherrod et al., 1984).

This long list of contributing factors dashes any hope for a simple solution to the puzzle of child abuse. Because abuse is more apt to occur when many of the contributing factors are present, eradicating child abuse would entail a massive effort. Part of this effort would involve changing U.S. attitudes toward "acceptable" levels of punishment and poverty. Another would involve dealing with parents, providing counseling and training in social skills.

It would be naive to expect all of these changes to occur soon, if ever. But by focusing on some of the more manageable factors, the risk of maltreatment can be reduced, if not eliminated entirely. For example, families can be taught more effective ways of coping with situations that might otherwise trigger abuse (Wicks-Nelson & Israel, 1991). Social support also helps. When parents know that they can turn to helpful adults for advice and reassurance, they can more readily manage the stresses of child-rearing that might otherwise lead to abuse. Finally, we must remember that most parents who have abused their children deserve care and compassion, not censure. In most families in which abuse takes place, parents and children are attached to each other; maltreatment is a consequence of ignorance and stress, not malice.

TEST YOURSELF

1. A(n) _____ parental style combines high control with low involvement.
2. Children who have low self-esteem and are impulsive, aggressive, and moody often have parents who rely on a(n) _____ style.
3. Typically, the birth of a sibling is less traumatic when children are older and when parents _____.
4. With later-born children, parents often have more realistic expectations and are _____.
5. Among the effects of divorce on children are inadequate supervision of children, conflict between parents, and _____.
6. When mothers remarry, daughters do not adjust as readily as sons because _____.
7. Child abuse is more common in countries that _____.
8. Children are more likely to be abused when they are younger and when they are _____.
9. How can child abuse be explained in terms of the biological, psychological, and sociocultural forces in the biopsychosocial framework?

Answers: (1) authoritarian, (2) indifferent-uninvolved, (3) remain responsive to the older child's needs, (4) more relaxed in their discipline, (5) economic hardship, (6) the remarriage disrupts an intimate mother-daughter relationship, (7) condone physical punishment, (8) unhealthy

Peers

LEARNING OBJECTIVES

❧ *Why do children become friends? What are the benefits of friendship?*

❧ *What are the important features of groups of children and adolescents? How do these groups influence individuals?*

❧ *Why are some children more popular than others? What are the causes and consequences of being rejected?*

Children's social relationships rapidly expand beyond the family and begin to include peers. As we saw in Chapter 4, peer interactions begin in late infancy; they grow in significance during the school-age years. To understand the nature and influence of peer relationships, let's examine children's friendships, their behavior in groups, and the nature of popularity.

Friendships

Most 4- and 5-year-olds claim to have a "best friend." If you ask them how they can tell that a child is their best friend, their comments will probably resemble those of 5-year-old Kara.

> *Interviewer:* Why is Laura your best friend?
> *Kara:* Because she plays with me. And she's nice to me.
> *Interviewer:* Are there any other reasons?
> *Kara:* Yeah, she lets me play with her dolls.

Of course, older children and adolescents also have best friends, but they describe them differently. Comments by 13-year-old Shauna are typical:

> *Interviewer:* Why is Leah your best friend?
> *Shauna:* She helps me. And we think alike. My mom says that we're like twins!
> *Interviewer:* What else tells you that she's your best friend?
> *Shauna:* Because I can tell her stuff—special stuff, like secrets—and I know that she won't tell anybody else.
> *Interviewer:* Anything else?
> *Shauna:* Yeah. If we fight, later we always tell each other that we're sorry.

For both Kara and Shauna, best friends have common interests, and they get along. However, Shauna's friendship with Leah has other dimensions as well. She is typical of older children and adolescents in believing that loyalty, trust, and intimacy are important ingredients of friendship.

These changes in friendships follow three developmental stages, according to William Damon (1988). In the first phase, spanning the ages of 4 to 7, friends are playmates—children who enjoy playing together. Friendships are often brief; they may dissolve when conflict erupts. In the next phase, from ages 8 to 10, trust and assistance emerge as themes. Friendship is more than mutual liking and joint play; now, children believe that friends can count on each other for help and support. Finally, beginning at about 11 years, intimacy and loyalty enter the picture. Adolescents believe, much more than younger children do, that friends should defend one another. They also believe, just as strongly, that friends should not deceive or abandon one another.

WILLARD W. HARTUP
"To become friends, children must discover their similarities and their differences, exploiting the former and resolving the latter."

The emphasis on loyalty in adolescent friendships apparently goes hand in hand with the emphasis on intimacy. If a friend is disloyal, adolescents are afraid that they may be humiliated because their intimate thoughts and feelings will become known to a much broader circle of people (Berndt & Perry, 1990). Intimacy is more common in friendships among girls, who are more likely than boys to have one exclusive "best friend." Because intimacy is at the core of their friendships, girls are also more likely to be concerned about the faithfulness of their friends and to worry about possible rejection by them (Buhrmester & Furman, 1987).

The emergence of intimacy in adolescent friendships means that friends also come to be seen as important sources of social support. This change is shown in a study by Levitt, Guacci-Franco, and Levitt (1993a) in which African American, European American, and Hispanic American 7-, 10-, and 14-year-olds were asked to whom they turn when they need help, are bothered by something, or want to have fun. For all ethnic groups, both 7- and 10-year-olds relied on close family members—parents, siblings, and grandparents—as primary sources of support, but not friends. However, 14-year-olds relied on close family members less often and said they would turn to friends instead. Turning to friends for help is part of the process of becoming independent of parents, which is one of the tasks of adolescence (as we'll see in Chapter 8).

WHO BECOMES FRIENDS?

Like the children shown in the photograph, most friends are alike in age, sex, and race (Hartup, 1992b). Because friends are supposed to treat each other as

equals, friendships are rare between an older, more experienced child and a younger, less experienced child. Because children typically play with same-sex peers, boys and girls rarely become friends.

Friendships are more common between children from the same race or ethnic group than between children from different groups. This reflects the racial segregation of U.S. society. Friendships among children of different groups are more common in schools where classes are smaller (Hallinan & Teixeira, 1987). Evidently, when classes are large, children select friends from the large number of available same-race peers. In contrast, fewer same-race peers are available in smaller classes, so children more often become friends with children of other races. Interracial friendships are usually confined to school, unless children come from integrated neighborhoods. That is, when children live in different, segregated neighborhoods, their friendship will not extend to out-of-school settings (DuBois & Hirsch, 1990).

Of course, friends are not only alike in age, sex, and race. Children and adolescents are usually drawn together because they have similar attitudes toward school, recreation, and the future (Hartup, 1992b; Tolson & Urberg, 1993). Tom, who enjoys school, likes to read books, and plans to go to Harvard, will probably not befriend Barry, who thinks that school is stupid, listens to his disc player constantly, and plans to quit high school to become a rock star. As time passes, friends becomes more similar in their attitudes and values (Kandel, 1978).

CONSEQUENCES OF FRIENDSHIPS

Friends are good for you. Researchers consistently find that children benefit from having a friend. For example, children with friends more often act prosocially—sharing and cooperating with others (Hartup, 1992a). Children with friends tend to be better adjusted as well. For example, students with high-quality friendships in elementary school often adjust more readily to junior high or middle school. As seventh-graders, they are better liked and cause fewer problems at school (Berndt & Perry, 1990).

Thus, friends are not simply special playmates and companions; instead, they are important resources. Children learn from their friends and can turn to them for support in times of stress. Friendships are one important way in which peers influence children's development. Peers also influence development through groups, the topic of the next section.

Groups

At the summer camp in the second chapter-opening vignette, new campers always formed groups based on common interests. Groups are just as prevalent in American schools. "Jocks," "preps," "burnouts," "nerds," and "brains"—you may remember these or similar terms referring to groups of older children and adolescents. During late childhood and adolescence, the peer group becomes the focal point of social relationships for youth. **The starting point is often a *clique*—a small group of children or adolescents who are friends and tend to be similar in age, sex, race, and attitudes.** Members of a clique spend time together and often dress, talk, and act alike. **Several cliques that have similar values and attitudes sometimes become part of a larger group called a *crowd*, known by a label such as "jocks" or "nerds."**

Some crowds have more status than others. For example, students in many junior and senior high schools say that the "jocks" are the most prestigious crowd, whereas the "burnouts" are among the least prestigious. Self-esteem in older children and adolescents often reflects the status of their crowd. During the school years, young people from high-status crowds tend to have greater self-esteem than those from low-status crowds (Brown & Lohr, 1987).

Identifying School Crowds

Most junior high and high school students know the different crowds in their school and the status of each. The number of crowds varies, as do their names, but the existence of crowds seems to be a basic fact of social life in late childhood and early adolescence.

SEE FOR YOURSELF

To learn more about crowds, try to talk individually to four or five students from the same junior high or high school. You could begin by describing one of the crowds from your own high school days. Then ask each student to name the different crowds in his or her school. Ask each student to describe the defining characteristics of people in each crowd. Finally, ask each student which crowd has the highest status in school and which has the lowest.

When you've interviewed all of the students, compare their answers. Do the students agree about the number and types of crowds in their school? Do they agree on the status of each? Next, compare your results with those of other students in your class. Are the results similar in different schools? Can you find any relation between the types of crowds and characteristics of the school (for example, rural versus urban)? See for yourself!   ❧

Why do some students become nerds but others join the burnouts? Parenting is part of the answer. The parental styles that we discussed in the first part of the chapter (pages 221–223) are related to the crowds that students join. This is shown in a study by Brown and his colleagues (1993), who examined the impact of parental practices on students' membership in particular crowds. The investigators measured the extent to which parents emphasized academic achievement, how much parents monitored their children's out-of-school activities, and how much parents involved their children in joint decision making.

Whenever children and adolescents form groups, some individuals soon step forward to occupy leadership roles.

Each of these parental practices influenced children's membership in school crowds. When parents emphasized achievement, their children were more likely to be in the popular, jock, and normal crowds but less likely to be in the druggie crowd. When parents monitored their children's out-of-school behavior, their children were more likely to be in the brain crowd and less likely to be in the druggie crowd. Finally, when parents included their children in joint decision making, their children were more likely to be in the brain and normal crowds but less likely to be in the druggie crowd. These relations were true regardless of the racial heritage of the family.

What seems to happen is that when parents use the practices associated with authoritative parenting—control coupled with warmth—their children become involved with crowds that endorse adult standards of behavior (for example, normals, jocks, brains). However, when parents' style is uninvolved or indulgent, their children are less likely to identify with adult standards of behavior. In fact, they become involved with crowds like druggies, who disavow these standards.

GROUP STRUCTURE

Groups—be they in school, at a summer camp as in the second-chapter opening vignette, or elsewhere—typically have a well-defined structure. **Often groups have a *dominance hierarchy,* headed by a leader to whom all other members of the group defer.** Other members know their position in the hierarchy. They yield to members who are above them in the hierarchy and assert themselves over members who are below them. A dominance hierarchy is useful in reducing conflict within groups, because every member knows his or her place.

What determines where members stand in the hierarchy? In children, especially boys, physical power is often the basis for the dominance hierarchy. The leader is usually the member who is the most intimidating physically (Pettit et al., 1990). Among girls and older boys, hierarchies are often based on individual traits that relate to the group's main function. At Crab Orchard Summer Camp, for example, the leaders are most often the children with the greatest camping experience. Among Girl Scouts, girls chosen to be patrol leaders tend to be bright and goal-oriented and to have new ideas (Edwards, 1994). These characteristics are appropriate, because the primary function of patrols is to help plan activities for an entire troop of Girl Scouts. Thus, this type of group structure is effective; the people with skills that are most useful have the greatest influence (Hartup, 1983).

PEER PRESSURE

Groups establish norms—standards of behavior that apply to all group members—and may pressure members to conform to these norms. Popular accounts usually characterize such "peer pressure" as an irresistible, harmful force. In reality, peer pressure is neither all-powerful nor always evil. For example, most junior high and high school students resist peer pressure to behave in ways that are clearly antisocial, such as stealing (Brown, Lohr, & McClenahan, 1986).

However, peer pressure can be powerful when the standards for appropriate behavior are not clear-cut. Tastes in music and clothing, for example, are completely subjective, so young people conform to peer group guidelines. As one 14-year-old girl put it, "Like, you're not going to go to school and say you listen to Lite Rock 97" (Aamidor, 1993).

Similarly, standards concerning smoking, drinking, and using drugs are often fuzzy. Drinking is a good case in point. Parents and groups like SADD (Students Against Driving Drunk) may discourage teens from drinking. Yet American culture is filled with youthful models who drink, seem to enjoy it, and suffer no apparent ill effects—actually, they seem to enjoy life even more. With such contradictory counsel, it is not surprising that youth look to their peers for answers (Chassin et al., 1986). Consequently, some youth do drink (or smoke, use drugs, have sex) to conform to their group's norms; others abstain, again reflecting their group's norms.

Who's Hot and Who's Not: Popularity and Rejection

Eileen is, without question, the most popular child in her fourth-grade class. Most of the other youngsters like to play with her and want to sit near her at lunch or on the school bus. Whenever the class must vote to pick a child for something special—to be class representative to the student council, to recite the class poem on Martin Luther King Day, or to lead the classroom to the lunch room—Eileen invariably wins.

Jay is not as fortunate as Eileen. In fact, he is the least popular child in the class. His presence is obviously unwanted in any situation. When he sits down at the lunch table, other kids move away. When he tries to join a game of four-square, the others quit. Students in the class detest Jay as much as they like Eileen.

Peer pressure is most powerful when standards for appropriate behavior are subjective, as is the case with styles of dress.

Popular and rejected children like Eileen and Jay are common. In fact, studies of popularity (Newcomb, Bukowski, & Pattee, 1993) reveal that most children can be placed in one of five categories:

- *Popular children* **are liked by many classmates.**
- *Rejected children* **are disliked by many classmates.**
- *Controversial children* **are both liked and disliked by classmates.**
- *Average children* **are liked and disliked by some classmates, but without the intensity found for popular, rejected, or controversial children.**
- *Neglected children* **are ignored by classmates.**

What determines whether a child will be popular, rejected, controversial, or neglected? Bright and physically attractive children are more often popular (Johnstone, Frame, & Bouman, 1992). However, the most important ingredient in becoming popular is social skill. Popular children are friendly and cooperative. They know how to get along with others (Crick & Dodge, 1994). For example, they fit in with groups instead of trying to make groups adjust to them. When conflicts arise with peers, they try to understand the root of the problem and often provide useful solutions (Hartup, 1992b). The Spotlight on Research highlights some of the social skills that are associated with being popular.

SPOTLIGHT ON RESEARCH

Keys to Popularity

Popularity is based, in large part, on children's social skills. Popular youngsters are more often skilled socially, whereas unpopular children are not. Evidence for this conclusion comes from a study by Wentzel and Erdley (1993). The subjects in this study—440 sixth- and seventh-grade boys and girls—evaluated their peers on a number of dimensions:

- *Prosocial behavior.* Children were asked to name classmates who were likely to share, to cooperate, or to help others when they have a problem.
- *Antisocial behavior.* Children were asked to name classmates who start fights or break rules.
- *Popularity.* Children were asked to indicate how much they would like to participate in school activities with their classmates.

To measure prosocial and antisocial behavior, children were given the names of 25 classmates and asked to circle the names of children who fit these behavioral descriptions: shares, helps other children, starts fights, breaks rules. The number of times that a child's name was circled on the first two lists (shares, helps other children) was a measure of that child's prosocial behavior; the number of times that a child's name was circled on the last two lists (starts fights, breaks rules) was a measure of the child's antisocial behavior. Finally, popularity was measured by providing a list of names and asking children to rate, on a scale from 1 to 5, how much they would like to be in school activities with each child whose name appeared on the list.

Influences on popularity can be seen in the table at the top of page 237, which includes correlations between ratings of popularity and (a) prosocial behavior and (b) antisocial behavior. You can see that, for both boys and girls, prosocial behaviors were related positively to popularity: Popular youngsters typically share, cooperate, and help; unpopular youngsters do not. Antisocial behaviors were also related to popularity, although not as strongly as prosocial behaviors. Popular boys and girls were less likely to start fights and to break rules than were unpopular boys and girls.

Findings like these appear to indicate that being well liked is straightfor-

Correlations between Boys' and Girls' Popularity and Their Prosocial and Antisocial Behavior		
Sex	*Type of Behavior*	*r*
Boys	Prosocial	.62
	Antisocial	−.24
Girls	Prosocial	.59
	Antisocial	−.19

Wentzel and Erdley, 1993.

ward: Be nice, not obnoxious. Share, cooperate, and help instead of being disruptive. Despite this apparent simplicity, not all children have these keys to popularity, as we shall soon see. ❧

Why do some children fail in their efforts to be popular and end up in one of the other categories? We know the most about rejected children. As you might suspect, the common denominator among rejected children is that they are socially unskilled. Many rejected children are aggressive, attacking their peers without provocation (Dodge, Bates, & Petit, 1990). Other rejected youngsters have poor self-control and are often disruptive in school (French, 1988, 1990). When conflicts arise, rejected children often become angry and retaliate (Bryant, 1992).

CONSEQUENCES OF REJECTION

No one enjoys being rejected. For children, repeated rejection by one's peers can have serious long-term consequences (Parker & Asher, 1987). Compared to children in the other categories, rejected youngsters are more likely:

- to drop out of school
- to commit juvenile offenses
- to suffer from psychopathology

For example, Morison and Masten (1991) first identified popular and rejected elementary school children. They did so by asking third- and sixth-grade children to nominate their classmates for roles in an imaginary school play. Popular children were defined as those who were frequently nominated for roles like "a good leader," "everyone likes to be with," and "has many friends." Rejected children were those frequently nominated for roles like "picks on other kids," "too bossy," and "teases other children too much."

Seven years later, the children and their parents completed a range of questionnaires measuring academic achievement, social skill, and personality. The popular children tended to be doing well in school and were seen as socially competent. However, the rejected children were less likely to be doing well in school, had lower self-esteem, and had more frequent behavioral problems. Popularity clearly pays long-term dividends; unfortunately, rejection has a price as well.

CAUSES OF REJECTION

Peer rejection can be traced, at least in part, to the influences of parents (Hartup & Moore, 1990). Children see how their parents respond to different social situations and may imitate these responses later. Parents who are friendly and cooperative with others are demonstrating effective social skills for their youngsters. Parents who are belligerent and combative are demonstrating tactics that are much less effective. In particular, when parents typically respond to interpersonal conflict like the father in the photo—with intimidation or aggression—their children may imitate them, hampering the development of their social skills and making them less popular in the long run (Keane, Brown, & Crenshaw, 1990).

Parents also contribute to their children's social skill and popularity through their disciplinary practices. Inconsistent discipline—punishing a child for misbehaving one day and ignoring the same behavior the next—is associated with antisocial, aggressive behavior, paving the way for rejection (Dishion, 1990). Consistent punishment that is tied to parental love and affection is more likely to promote social skill and, in the process, popularity (Dekovic & Janssens, 1992).

Thus, the origins of rejection are clear: Socially awkward, aggressive children are often rejected because they rely upon an aggressive interpersonal style, which can be traced to parenting. The implication is that by teaching youngsters (and their parents) more effective ways of interacting with others, we can make rejection less likely. With improved social skills, rejected children would not need to resort to antisocial behaviors that peers deplore. Training of this sort *does* work. Rejected children can learn skills that lead to peer acceptance and thereby avoid the long-term harm associated with being rejected (Mize & Ladd, 1990).

TEST YOURSELF

1. Friends are usually similar in age, sex, race, and _____.
2. Children with friends more often act prosocially and are _____ than children without friends.
3. As a group forms, a _____ typically emerges, with the leader at the top.
4. Peer pressure is most powerful when _____.
5. Popular children often share, cooperate, and _____.
6. Rejected youngsters are more likely to drop out of school, to commit juvenile offenses, and _____.
7. How could developmental change in the nature of friendship be explained in terms of Piaget's stages of intellectual development, discussed in Chapters 4 and 6?

Answers: (1) attitudes, (2) better adjusted, (3) dominance hierarchy, (4) standards for appropriate behavior are vague, (5) help others, (6) to suffer psychopathology

Television: Boob Tube or Window on the World?

LEARNING OBJECTIVES

🐾 *What is the impact of watching television on children's attitudes and behavior?*

🐾 *How does TV viewing influence children's creativity and cognitive development?*

The cartoon exaggerates TV's impact on North American children, but only somewhat. After all, think about how much time you spent in front of a TV while you were growing up. If you were a typical U.S. child and adolescent, you spent much more time watching TV than you did interacting with your parents or in school. The numbers tell an incredible story. School-age children spend about 25 hours each week watching TV (Nielson, 1990). Extrapolated through adolescence, the typical U.S. high school graduate has watched 20,000 hours of TV—the equivalent of 2 full years of watching TV 24 hours daily! No wonder social scientists and lay people alike have come to see TV as an important contributor to the socialization of North American children.

Of course, not all children watch the same amount of TV. A very small number of children, like Chris in the Real People feature, watch virtually no TV. For most youngsters, however, viewing time increases gradually during the preschool and elementary school years, reaching a peak at about 11 or 12 years of age. Boys watch more TV than girls. Also, children with lower IQs watch more than those with higher IQs; children from lower-income families watch more TV than children from higher-income families (Huston, Watkins, & Kunkel, 1989).

MRS. HORTON, COULD YOU STOP BY SCHOOL TODAY?"

©1995 Martha F. Campbell. Reprinted with permission.

Is There Life without TV?

Chris, a 12-year-old boy, is among the 1% of North American youngsters who do not have a TV at home. Long before Chris was born, his parents decided that they could do without TV, and they have since remained steadfast in their commitment to be TV-less.

What does Chris do to fill the 25 hours per week that most kids his age spend watching TV? He reads, plays with friends, listens to music, and draws. There is nothing particularly odd in this list of activities; Chris simply does them more often than his peers. Here is how Chris spent one "typical" afternoon:

3:30—home from school and ate a snack

REAL PEOPLE

3:45—walked to the drug store with his friend, Scott, to buy baseball cards, then went to Scott's house, where they organized and traded cards

5:30—back at home; played his guitar until dinner

6:00—dinner

6:30—homework

7:00—listened to music while drawing futuristic cars

8:30—played cards with his dad until bedtime

We asked Chris' mom, Terri, about his TV-less life.

Us: Does Chris ever watch TV?

Terri: Sure. All of his friends have TVs, so he'll watch with them sometimes.

Us: Does that bother you?

Terri: Not really. It's not as if he feels TV-deprived and deliberately goes there to watch TV. He enjoys watching TV with friends, but that's just one thing that he likes to do. By not watching TV at home, all of us have learned to do other things with our time, things that are more productive.   🍂

It is hard to imagine that massive viewing of TV would have no effect on children's behavior. After all, 30-second TV ads are designed to influence children's preferences in toys, cereals, and hamburgers, so the programs themselves ought to have even more impact.

Influence on Attitudes and Social Behavior

Back in 1954, the Chairman of the U.S. Senate Subcommittee on Juvenile Delinquency, Estes Kefauver, was concerned about the amount of violence in television programming. At that time, only about half of the households in the United States had television sets, yet the public was already aware of the frequent portrayal of violence in TV programs and worried about its effects on viewers, especially young ones. Anecdotes suggesting a link were common: A 6-year-old fan of Hopalong Cassidy (a TV cowboy of the 1950s) asked his father for real bullets for his toy gun, because his toy bullets didn't kill people the way Hopalong's did (Schramm, Lyle, & Parker, 1961).

More than 40 years later, citizens remain concerned about violence on TV—with good reason. Children's cartoons, like the one shown in this photograph, typically have one violent act every three minutes. (The term *violence* here refers to use of physical force against another person.) The average North American youngster will see several thousand murders on TV before reaching adolescence (Waters, 1993).

What is the impact of this steady diet of televised mayhem and violence? According to Bandura's (1986) social learning theory, which we first described in Chapter 1, children learn by observing others; they watch others and often imitate what they see. Applied to TV, this theory predicts more aggressive behavior from children who watch violent TV. This prediction was supported by laboratory studies conducted in the 1960s (Bandura, Ross, & Ross, 1963). Children watched specially created TV programs in which an adult behaved violently toward a plastic "Bobo" doll; the adult kicked and hit the doll with a plastic hammer. When children were given the opportunity to play with the doll, those who had seen the TV program were much more likely to behave aggressively toward the doll than were children who had not seen the program.

Critics noted many limitations in this and other early studies and doubted that viewing TV violence in more realistic settings would have such pronounced effects on children (Klapper, 1968). Today, however, we know that viewing TV violence "hardens" children, making them more accepting of interpersonal violence. Suppose, for example, a child is baby-sitting two youngsters who begin to argue and then fight. Baby-sitters who are frequent viewers of TV violence are more inclined to let them "slug it out," because they see this as a normal, acceptable way of resolving conflicts (Drabman & Thomas, 1976).

Is this increased tolerance for aggression reflected in children's behavior? Will Roberto, the avid cartoon-watcher in the chapter-opening vignette, become more aggressive? Or, as his father believes, is this TV watching simply "fun" without consequence? The answer from research is clear: Roberto's father is wrong. Frequent exposure to TV violence causes children to be more aggressive. One of the most compelling studies examined the impact of children's TV viewing at age 8 on criminal activity at age 30 (Huesmann, 1986). The graph shows quite clearly that 8-year-olds exposed to large doses of TV vio-

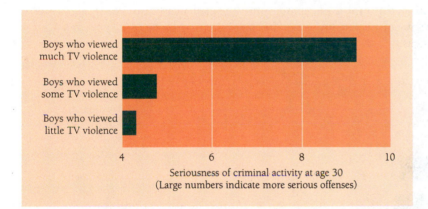

Seriousness of criminal activity at age 30
(Large numbers indicate more serious offenses)

lence had the most extensive criminal records as 30-year-olds. The link was found for both males and females, although females' level of criminal activity was much lower overall. Thus, children who are frequent viewers of TV violence learn to resort to aggression in their interactions with others. For many, their aggression eventually puts them behind bars.

Of course, violence is only one part of what children see on TV. Let's examine other ways in which TV is an important influence on children as they develop.

STEREOTYPES

TV is said to provide a "window on the world." Unfortunately, the view is distorted, particularly when it comes to minorities, women, and the elderly. In the early days of TV, African Americans almost never appeared in programs. When

Television programs often present a distorted view of the world, one that is based on stereotypes of women, minorities, and the elderly, not on reality.

they did appear, they were limited to minor roles such as the gentle buffoon. Today, African American actors account for 10–15% of TV casts, which approximates the percentage of African Americans in the U.S. population. However, other minorities—including Asian Americans, Hispanic Americans, and Native Americans—appear very infrequently (Liebert & Sprafkin, 1988).

The situation is much the same for women and the elderly. Their portrayal on TV bears little resemblance to reality. No more than one-third of all TV roles are for women. When women are shown on TV, they are often passive and emotional. Most are not employed; those who have jobs are often in stereotypical female careers such as teachers or secretaries (Liebert & Sprafkin, 1988). Also, the land of television evidently has a fountain of youth, because older Americans are grossly underrepresented. Although nearly 20% of the U.S. population is 60 or older, less than 5% of the characters in prime-time TV are that age. Ironically, older adults on TV are usually men, despite the fact that women far outnumber men at this point in the life span (Gerbner, 1993).

Surprisingly, we know relatively little about the effects of these stereotyped portrayals on children's attitudes toward minorities or the elderly. However, the impact of the stereotyped presentation of females is clear. As you can imagine, children who watch TV frequently end up with more stereotyped views of males and females. For example, Kimball (1986) studied sex-role stereotypes in a small Canadian town that was located in a valley and could not receive TV programs until a transmitter was installed nearby in 1974. Two years later, views of personality traits, behaviors, occupations, and peer relations were measured in the town's children. The graphs show that boys' and girls' views

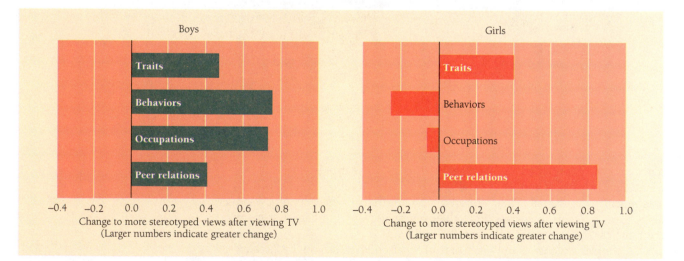

on these issues became more stereotyped after TV was introduced. For example, girls had more stereotyped views of peer relations. Now they believed that boasting and swearing were characteristic of boys but that sharing and helping were characteristic of girls. The boys in the town had acquired more stereotyped views of occupations, now believing that girls could be teachers and cooks, whereas boys could be physicians and judges.

Findings like these indicate that TV viewing causes children to adopt many of the stereotypes that dominate television programming (Signorielli & Lears, 1992). For many children and adolescents, TV's slanted depiction of the world *becomes* reality.

CONSUMER BEHAVIOR

Sugary cereals, hamburgers and french fries, snack foods, toys, clothing . . . . These products are the focus of a phenomenal amount of TV advertising that is directed toward children. A typical youngster may see more than 50 commercials a day! As early as 3 years of age, children distinguish commercials from programs. However, preschool children often believe that commercials are simply a different form of entertainment—one designed to inform viewers. Not until 8 or 9 years of age do most children understand the persuasive intent of commercials. At the same time that children grasp the aim of commercials, they begin to realize that commercials are not always truthful (Liebert & Sprafkin, 1988).

Commercials are effective sales tools with children. Children grow to like many of the products advertised on TV. Like the youngster in the photograph, they may urge parents to buy products that they have seen on television. In one study (Greenberg, Fazel, & Weber, 1986), more than 75% of the children reported that they had asked their parents to buy a product they had seen advertised on TV. More often than not, parents had purchased the product for them!

This selling power of TV commercials has long concerned advocates for children, because so many ads focus on children's foods that have little nutritional value and that are associated with problems such as obesity and tooth decay. The U.S. government once regulated the amount and type of advertising on children's TV programs (Huston, Watkins, & Kunkel, 1989), but today the responsibility falls largely to parents. In the You May Be Wondering Feature, we recommend some ways for parents to regulate their children's TV viewing.

No More Child Couch Potatoes!

YOU MAY
BE WONDERING
?

If you know a child who sits glued to the TV screen from after school until bedtime, has his or her own remote control, and reads *TV Guide* from cover to cover, it's time to take action. Here are some suggestions:

1. Children need absolute rules concerning the amount of TV and the types of programs that they can watch. These rules must be enforced consistently!

2. Children shouldn't fall into the trap of "I'm bored, so I'll watch TV." Children should be encouraged to know what they want to watch *before* they turn on the TV set.

3. Adults can watch TV with children and discuss the programs. Parents can, for example, express their disapproval of a character's use of aggression and suggest other means of resolving conflicts. Parents can also point to the stereotypes that are depicted. The aim is for the children to learn that TV's account of the world is often inaccurate and to encourage the children to watch TV critically. (What may happen, of course, is that they can't stand the parent's constant chatter and stop watching altogether!)

4. Parents need to be good TV viewers themselves. The first two tips listed here apply to viewers of all ages! When a child is present, parents shouldn't watch violent programs or others that are inappropriate for the young. And parents should throw away the remote control so that they, too, will watch TV deliberately and selectively, instead of mindlessly flipping between channels.   ❧

PROSOCIAL BEHAVIOR

TV is clearly a potent influence on children's aggression and on the stereotypes they form. Can this power be put to more prosocial goals? Can TV viewing help children learn to be more generous, to be more cooperative, and to have greater self-control? Yes, according to early laboratory studies. In these experiments, children were more likely to act prosocially after they watched brief films in which a peer acted prosocially. For example, children were more likely to share or more likely to resist the temptation to take from others when they had seen a filmed peer sharing or resisting temptation (Liebert & Sprafkin, 1988).

An early study by Bryan and Walbek (1970) typifies this sort of experimentation. Third- and fourth-grade children received a prize for playing a game, then watched a film about another child who had received the same prize and was asked to donate some of the prize to charity. In one version of the film, the child donated part of the prize; in another version, the child did not. The children in the study were then given the opportunity to donate a portion of their winnings to the same charity shown in the film. Children were much more likely to donate when they had seen the film about the generous child than when they had seen the film about the stingy one. Thus, from watching others who were generous, children themselves learned to be generous.

Research with actual TV programs leads to the same conclusion. Youngsters who watch TV shows that emphasize prosocial behavior, such as *Mister Rogers' Neighborhood,* are more likely to behave prosocially. In fact, a comprehensive analysis revealed that the impact of viewing prosocial TV programs is much greater than the impact of viewing televised violence (Hearold, 1986). Boys, in particular, benefit from viewing prosocial TV, perhaps because they are usually much less skilled prosocially than girls are.

Although research indicates that prosocial behavior *can* be influenced by TV watching, two important factors restrict the actual prosocial impact of TV viewing. First, prosocial behaviors are portrayed on TV programs far less frequently than aggressive behaviors; opportunities to learn prosocial behaviors from television are limited. Second, in the real world of TV watching, the relatively small number of prosocial programs must compete with other kinds of television programs, as well as other activities, for children's time. Children simply may not watch the few prosocial programs that are televised. Clearly, we are far from harnessing the power of television for prosocial uses.

ALETHA C. HUSTON
". . . television can be a positive force in family life as well as a negative influence. Well-designed programs for children can be selected for their children's benefit just as books and toys are selected."

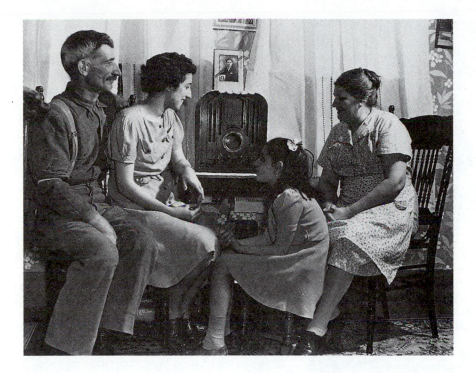

Influences on Creativity

The photograph shows a common pastime in the 1930s and 1940s: children listening to the radio instead of watching television. During those years, radio included adventure, comedy, music, sports, and news programs. When TV was introduced, many of these programs were transported (with minor changes) into the new medium. Some early critics noted that radio programs required listeners to generate their own mental images of the activity depicted in the program, but TV provided viewers with ready-made images. Would this difference stifle viewers' creativity? Years later, we know the answer is yes. Although some studies find no link between the amount of TV viewing and creativity, about half find a negative relation. As children watch more TV, the tendency is for them to be less creative on measures of divergent thinking like those described on page 201 of Chapter 6 (Valkenburg & van der Voort, 1994).

What explains this negative relation? Perhaps, as the early critics observed, frequent TV viewers do not develop skill in creating their own images because TV provides ready-made images. Another possibility is that children who watch TV frequently have less time for other activities that do stimulate creative thinking, such as reading (Valkenburg & van der Voort, 1994). Whatever the explanation, it is clear that creativity can be added to the list of developmental phenomena that can be harmed by excessive TV viewing.

Influences on Cognition

1969 was a watershed in the history of children's television. That year marked the appearance of a program produced by Children's Television Workshop that was designed to use the power of video and animation to foster such skills as recognizing letters and numbers, counting, and vocabulary in preschool children. Evaluations conducted in the early years of the program showed that it

achieved its goals: Preschoolers who watched the show regularly were more proficient at the targeted academic skills than were children who watched less often. Frequent viewers also adjusted to school more readily, according to teachers' ratings (Bogatz & Ball, 1972).

By now, of course, you know that we're talking about Big Bird, Bert, Ernie, and other members of the cast of *Sesame Street* shown in the photo. Since appearing in 1969, *Sesame Street* has become one of the longest-running shows in TV history. Today, mothers and fathers who watched *Sesame Street* as preschoolers are watching with their own youngsters.

More recent studies have confirmed these benefits. Rice and her colleagues (1990), for example, found that 3-year-olds who watched *Sesame Street* frequently had larger vocabularies as 5-year-olds than did 3-year-olds who watched infrequently.

Building on the success of *Sesame Street*, Children's Television Workshop has developed a number of other successful programs. *Electric Company* was designed to teach reading skills, *3-2-1 Contact* focused on science and technology, and *Square One TV* aimed at mathematics (Liebert & Sprafkin, 1988). More recent programs have included *Reading Rainbow, Where in the World Is Carmen Sandiego?*, and *Bill Nuy Science Guy*. Programs like these leave little doubt that TV's socializing influence need not be limited to the learning of aggression and stereotypes. Children *can* learn academic skills and useful social skills, if parents insist that their youngsters be good viewers, and if they insist that TV improve the quality and variety of programs available for children and adolescents.

TEST YOURSELF

1. When children watch a lot of TV violence, they become more aggressive and _____.
2. Preschool children believe that commercials _____.
3. Youngsters who watch *Sesame Street* frequently improve their academic skills and, according to their teachers, _____.
4. Use the difference between divergent and convergent thinking, explained in Chapter 6, to describe the impact of TV viewing on children's creativity and cognitive development.

Answers: (1) *more accepting of violence,* (2) *represent a different, informative type of program but do not understand the intent to persuade,* (3) *adjust to school more readily*

Putting It All Together

In this chapter, we've examined some of the many forces that contribute to socialization. Parents, peers, and TV emerged as mighty shapers of children's development. We learned that parental style influences both cognitive and social development. Children reared by parents with the authoritarian style favored by Tanya's mother often have low self-esteem and low social skill; children reared by parents with the authoritative style used by Sheila's mother tend to be self-reliant and friendly and to do well in school. We saw that groups like those at Crab Orchard Summer Camp are an important element of social life among older children and adolescents and that their influence is greatest when behavioral standards are not clear. Finally, we saw that TV's influence is tremendous. It can cause children like Roberto to rely on aggression to resolve interpersonal conflict, and it can give them a stereotyped view of the world.

Thus, parents, siblings, peers, and television define much of the sociocultural context of development for American children, and their impact is considerable. Through the combined power of parents, siblings, peers, and television, children acquire the beliefs and behaviors of their culture. Full, adult membership in their culture is not far away. Only adolescence remains, and that topic will be examined in Chapter 8.

Thinking about Development

1. Effective parents and popular children seem to have many characteristics in common. What are they?

2. How are the life-cycle factors of the biopsychosocial framework illustrated by the impact of a woman's remarriage on her daughter?

3. In Chapter 5, we described some important differences in the ways that boys and girls interact with same-sex peers. How might these differences help explain differences between boys and girls in the basis for dominance hierarchies (described on pages 234–235)?

4. Some skeptics remark that television programming is simply a reflection of society at large, so children learn nothing—good or bad—that they wouldn't learn from their culture sooner or later anyway. Defend or refute this statement.

Summary

Family Relationships

Dimensions and Styles of Parenting

■ One key factor in parent–child relationships is the degree of warmth that parents express: Children clearly benefit from warm, caring parents. A second factor is control, which is complicated because neither too much nor too little control is desirable. Effective parental control involves setting appropriate standards, enforcing them, and trying to anticipate conflicts.

■ Power assertion is an ineffective and sometimes harmful form of punishment. Time-out, in which children are isolated briefly, is a much more effective way of punishing children.

■ Taking into account both warmth and control, four prototypic parental styles emerge. (a) Authoritarian parents are controlling but uninvolved. (b) Authoritative par-

ents are fairly controlling but are also responsive to their children. (c) Indulgent-permissive parents are loving but exert little control. (d) Indifferent-uninvolved parents are neither warm nor controlling. Authoritative parenting seems best for children, in terms of both cognitive and social development. However, parental styles are also determined by characteristics of the children themselves, such as their temperament.

Siblings

■ The birth of a sibling can be stressful for children, particularly when the children are still young and when parents ignore their needs. Siblings get along better when they are of the same sex, believe that parents treat them similarly, enter adolescence, and have parents who get along well.

■ Parents have higher expectations for first-born children, which explains why such children are more intelligent and more likely to go to college. Later-born children are more popular and more innovative. Contradicting the folklore, only children are almost never worse off than children with siblings. In some respects (such as intelligence, achievement, and autonomy), they are often better off.

Divorce and Remarriage

■ A divorce can harm children in a number of areas, ranging from school achievement to adjustment. The impact of divorce stems from less supervision of children following divorce, economic hardship, and conflict between parents. Children often benefit when parents have joint custody following divorce, or when they live with the same-sex parent.

■ When a mother remarries, daughters sometimes have difficulty adjusting because the new stepfather encroaches on an intimate mother–daughter relationship. A father's remarriage can cause problems because children fear that the stepmother will disturb intimate father–child relationships and because of tension between the stepmother and the noncustodial mother.

Parent–Child Relationships Gone Awry: Child Abuse

■ Children who are abused often lag behind in cognitive and social development. Cultural factors contributing to child abuse include a culture's views on violence, poverty, and social isolation. Parents who abuse their children were often neglected or abused themselves and tend to be unhappy, socially unskilled individuals. Younger or unhealthy children are more likely to be targets of abuse.

Peers

Friendships

■ Friendships among preschoolers are based on common interests and getting along well. As children grow, loyalty, trust, and intimacy become more important features in their friendships. Friends are usually similar in age, sex, race, and attitudes. Children with friends are more skilled socially and better adjusted.

Groups

■ Older children and adolescents often form cliques—small groups of like-minded individuals—that become part of a crowd. Some crowds have higher status than others, and members of higher-status crowds often have higher self-esteem than members of lower-status crowds.

■ Common to most groups is a dominance hierarchy, a well-defined structure with a leader at the top. Physical power often determines the dominance hierarchy, particularly among boys. However, with older children and adolescents, dominance hierarchies are more often based on skills that are important to the group.

■ Peer pressure is neither totally powerful nor totally evil. In fact, groups influence individuals primarily in areas where standards of behavior are unclear, such as tastes in music or clothing, or concerning drinking, drug use, and sex.

Who's Hot and Who's Not: Popularity and Rejection

■ Popular children are socially skilled. They often share, cooperate, and help others. They are unlikely to behave in antisocial ways, such as starting a fight.

■ Some children are rejected by their peers, often because they are too aggressive. Such children are often unsuccessful in school and have behavioral problems. Their aggressive style of interacting can be linked to parents who are belligerent or combative and who are inconsistent in their discipline.

Television: Boob Tube or Window on the World?

Influence on Attitudes and Social Behavior

■ Children's social behaviors and attitudes are influenced by what they see on TV. Youngsters who frequently watch televised violence become more aggressive, whereas those who watch prosocial TV become more socially skilled. Children who watch TV frequently may adopt TV's distorted view of women, minorities, and older people.

Influences on Creativity

■ Children who watch TV frequently tend to be less creative, perhaps because they rely on ready-made images provided by TV and do not develop skill in creating their own imagery.

Influences on Cognition

■ Preschool children who watch *Sesame Street* frequently improve their academic skills and adjust more readily to school.

Key Terms

authoritarian parenting (221)
authoritative parenting (222)
average children (236)
blended family (227)
clique (233)
controversial children (236)
crowd (233)

dominance hierarchy (234)
indifferent-uninvolved
   parenting (222)
indulgent-permissive
   parenting (222)
joint custody (227)
neglected children (236)

popular children (236)
power assertion (220)
punishment (220)
rejected children (236)
socialization (217)
time-out (220)

If You'd Like to Learn More

BERNDT, T. J., & LADD, G. W. (Eds.), (1990). *Peer relationships in child development.* New York: Wiley. This collection of chapters, written by experts in the field, provides a comprehensive account of theory and research on peer relationships.

BRAZLETON, T. B. (1984) *To listen to a child.* Reading, MA: Addison-Wesley. Writing for parents, the author describes many of the common problems of childhood and ways that parents can deal with them.

KALTER, N. (1990). *Growing up with divorce.* New York: Free Press. The author's goal is to show parents how they can help their children cope with divorce.

LIEBERT, R. M., & SPRAFKIN, J. (1988). *The early window: Effects of television on children and youth* (3rd ed.). New York: Pergamon. The authors of this book, themselves leading researchers on the impact of TV, describe this research and provide valuable insights into the nature of the television industry.

Linda just celebrated her 12th birthday and is eagerly looking forward to the greater independence of adolescence. At the same time, Linda is concerned that she has gained weight and that her body is no longer as lean as it was during her childhood years. Linda is thinking about going on a diet, an idea that seems reasonable to her because her mother diets constantly to remain a size 4.

Dea was born in Seoul of Korean parents but was adopted by a Dutch couple in Michigan when she was 3 months old. Growing up, she considered herself a red-blooded American. In college, however, Dea realized that others saw her as an Asian American, an identity she had never given much thought. She began to wonder, "Who am I really? American? Dutch American? Asian American?"

When 15-year-old Aaron announced that he wanted an after-school job at the local supermarket, his mother was delighted, believing that he would learn much from the experience. Five months later, she had her doubts. Aaron had lost interest in school, and they argued constantly about how he spent his money.

For six months, 15-year-old Jenny had been dating Todd, a 17-year-old. She thought that she was truly in love for the first time and she often imagined being married to Todd. They had had sex a few times, each time without contraception. It sometimes crossed Jenny's mind that if she got pregnant, she could move into her own apartment and begin a family.

Until 4 months ago, Jalen had been an excellent student and a starter on the basketball team. Then Jalen's father had died unexpectedly of a heart attack at age 48. Jalen had to take a job at the local plant to supplement the family income. Working left him too tired to study and forced him to quit the basketball team. He had planned to go to college, but now he doubted that he could afford it. Besides, he had probably inherited the heart disease that killed his father. Jalen kept wondering, "Why me?"

Rites of Passage
to Young Adulthood

You probably have graphic memories of your own adolescence. You can probably recall moments that were exhilarating—graduating from high school, your first paycheck from a part-time job, and your first feelings of love and sex. Of course, painful times were common too—the first day on a job when you couldn't do anything right, not knowing what to say on a date with a person you desperately wanted to impress, and countless arguments with your parents. Feelings of pride and accomplishment accompanied by feelings of embarrassment and bewilderment are common to individuals who are on the threshold of adulthood.

You may be surprised to know that adolescence is a recent cultural invention. For much of recorded history, children moved directly into adulthood; when they attained puberty, they were considered to be young adults. In today's industrialized societies, the transition from childhood to adulthood is more gradual, spanning the teenage years that we know as adolescence. During these years, individuals like Linda try to adjust to the changes taking place in their bodies; others, like Dea, grapple with their identities; still others, like Aaron, first enter the world of work; and, many, like Jenny and Todd, have their first experiences with love and sex. These topics are the focus of the first four sections of this chapter; they can be challenging developmental issues. Adolescents like Jalen sometimes encounter special obstacles that make adolescence difficult to handle; these are the focus of the last section.

251

Farewell to Childhood: Puberty

LEARNING OBJECTIVES

❧ *What changes define puberty? When do they occur?*

❧ *What are the effects of maturing early or late? Are they the same for boys and girls?*

❧ *What are some of the causes of eating-related disorders, such as obesity and anorexia nervosa?*

Clearasil, Oxy 10, Stridex, Phisoderm, and Sea Breeze. These and similar products represent a multimillion-dollar industry in the United States, devoted to the sole purpose of preventing and eliminating pimples. Like the appearance of body hair, the emergence of breasts, and the enlargement of the penis and testicles, pimples and blemishes are a sign that the child is gone, replaced by an adolescent. Let's begin this chapter by looking at the biological signs of adolescence.

Physical Growth

During the elementary school years, children steadily gain weight and grow taller. In a year, the average 6-to-10-year-old girl or boy gains about 5 to 7 pounds and grows 2 to 3 inches. Growth in these years represents the calm before the storm. During the adolescent growth spurt, which begins at about age 11 in girls and at about age 13 in boys, growth is more rapid than at any other point in the life span except for the prenatal and infant periods. This period of rapid growth lasts a few years; girls have typically achieved most of their mature stature by age 15 and boys by age 17. At the peak of the growth spurt, a girl may gain 20 pounds in a year and a boy, 25 (Tanner, 1970).

The growth spurt is but one of a collection of physical changes occurring in early adolescence known as *puberty.* These changes are shown in the charts on page 253. In girls, puberty begins with growth of the breasts and the start of the growth spurt. **Later, pubic hair emerges, followed by the onset of menstruation,** *menarche,* **typically at about age 13.** Early menstrual cycles can be irregular and often happen without ovulation.

For boys, puberty usually commences with the growth of the testes and scrotum, followed by the appearance of pubic hair, the start of the growth spurt, and growth of the penis. Approximately one year later, at about age 13, most boys have the first spontaneous ejaculation, a discharge of fluid contain-

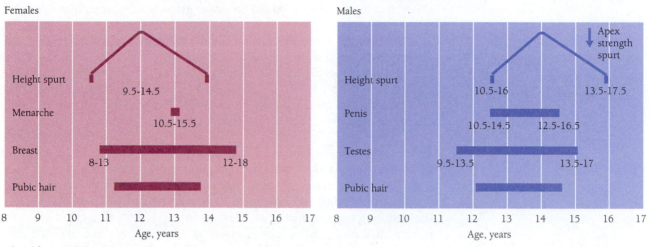

Adapted from Marshall and Tanner, 1970.

ing sperm. Initial ejaculations often contain relatively few sperm; only months or sometimes years later are there sufficient sperm to fertilize an egg (Chilman, 1983).

Today's children enter puberty earlier and are, as adults, taller and heavier than previous generations. **These changes in physical development from one generation to the next are known as** *secular growth trends,* **and they have been quite large.** For example, the average height of a U.S. sailor in the War of 1812 was 5 feet, 2 inches. The graph shows that the age at which American girls experience menarche has dropped more than 1½ years since the start of the 20th century.

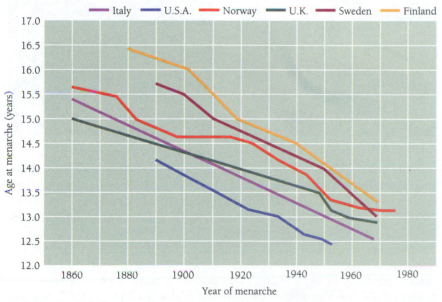

Marshall and Tanner, 1986.

This accelerated development has occurred primarily in industrialized societies where health care and diet have improved substantially. In many Third World countries, where children's living conditions have not improved, adult stature has remained the same (Martorell, Mendoza, & Castillo, 1988). Also, there is a limit to the impact of improved living conditions on growth. In countries that provide adequate nutrition and health care for most of their young, children of recent generations are no longer growing bigger than previous generations (Roche, 1979).

These findings seem to demonstrate the combined power of heredity and experience on physical growth. Genetics apparently determines a target stature. Historically, few people received enough nutrition and health care throughout childhood to reach this target. Only in the past century have industrialized nations provided adequate food and health care, which explains why adult stature has increased so much and is now leveling off in those countries.

RATE OF MATURATION

Of course, puberty does not always begin at age 11 for girls and age 13 for boys. For many children, puberty begins months or years before or after these norms. An early-maturing boy might begin puberty at age 11 or 12, whereas a late-maturing boy might start at 15 or 16. An early-maturing girl might start puberty at 9 or 10, a late-maturing girl, at 14 or 15. For example, the girls shown in the photographs are the same age, but only one has reached puberty.

The timing of maturity is regulated, in part, by genetics. However, experience also influences the onset of puberty. For example, puberty occurs earlier in girls who experience much family conflict (Belsky, Steinberg, & Draper, 1991). The exact mechanism is unknown, but stress apparently influences the levels of hormones that trigger puberty.

Whether children mature early or late does not predict their physical stature as adults. However, maturing early or late has differing psychological consequences for boys and girls. For boys, early maturation is beneficial. In some of the pioneering studies conducted in California (Jones, 1965; Jones & Bayley, 1950), boys who matured early were more likely to be elected to positions in student government and more often excelled in athletics. The late-maturing boys were judged to be more childish, less relaxed, less confident, and more likely to seek attention. By contrast, early-maturing girls were often less confident and less sociable than later-maturing girls.

Of course, some of these pioneering findings are more than 50 years old. Is the impact of early and late maturation much the same today? Yes. An extensive longitudinal study of adolescents growing up in Milwaukee during the 1970s confirmed that early maturation has benefits for boys and, more often than not, costs for girls (Simmons & Blyth, 1987). Some of the specific effects in this study included the following:

Early-maturing boys

- dated more often
- had more positive feelings about their physical development and athletic abilities

Early-maturing girls

- had more negative feelings about their physical development
- had poorer grades and were more often in trouble in school

Early maturation may benefit boys because others, perceiving them to be more mature, may be more willing to give them adultlike responsibilities. Early maturation may hamper girls' development by leading them to associate with older adolescents who apparently encourage them to engage in age-inappropriate activities, such as drinking, smoking, and sex, for which they are ill prepared (Brooks-Gunn, 1988).

By young adulthood, most of the effects associated with rate of maturation have vanished. That is, early-maturing, on-time, and late-maturing adolescents cannot be distinguished as adults (Simmons & Blyth, 1987). Thus, rate of maturation seemingly influences the path through adolescence but not the path that development follows through the rest of life.

Eating Disorders

Growth requires enormous reserves of energy, and many parents worry that their children may not be getting enough to eat. At the same time, however, some youngsters *do* become fat, and some adolescents become irrationally preoccupied with their weight. Let's look at each of these problems.

OBESITY

Ricardo, 12, has been overweight for most of his life. He dislikes the playground games that entertain most of his classmates during recess, preferring to stay in the classroom. He has relatively few friends and is not particularly happy with his lot in life. In many ways, Ricardo is typical of the 5–10% of U.S. children and adolescents who are obese (at least 20% over the ideal body weight for their age and height). These individuals are often unpopular and have low self-esteem. Furthermore, they are at risk for many medical problems, including high blood pressure and diabetes, which are made all the more likely because the vast majority of overweight children and adolescents become overweight adults (Epstein & Wing, 1987).

Heredity plays an important role in juvenile obesity. For example, adopted children's and adolescents' weight is related to the weight of their biological parents, not to the weight of their adoptive parents (Stunkard et al., 1986). Genes may influence obesity by helping to determine a person's activity level. Some young people may be genetically more prone to be inactive, making it more difficult for them to burn off calories and easier to gain weight. **Heredity may also help to set a youth's *basal metabolic rate*, which is the speed with which the body consumes calories.** Children and adolescents with a slower basal metabolic rate burn off calories less rapidly, making it easier for them to gain weight (Epstein & Cluss, 1986).

JEANNE BROOKS-GUNN
"*. . . social events are experienced differently as a function of pubertal development. Puberty acts as a social stimulus for others, altering how adults and peers respond to the girl as her body develops.*"

Obesity can harm physical and psychological development. Obesity has its roots in heredity and the environment.

The environment is also influential. Television advertising, for example, encourages people to eat tasty but fattening goods. Parents play a role, too. They may inadvertently encourage obesity by shifting control of eating from internal to external signals. Infants eat primarily because of internal signals: They eat when they experience hunger and stop eating as they begin to feel full. During the preschool years, this internal control of eating is replaced gradually by a reliance on external signals. After school or while watching television, children and adolescents may have a candy bar out of habit, not because they are hungry. Parents who urge their children to "clean their plates" even when they are no longer hungry are encouraging them to ignore internal cues to eating. Obese children and adolescents may overeat because they rely on such external cues, disregarding internal cues to stop (Birch, 1991).

Obese youth *can* lose weight. The most effective procedures are those that involve the entire family. In one successful program, children and parents first set goals concerning caloric intake and exercise. They might agree to daily goals of 2000 calories of food and of 20 minutes of exercise. Both children and parents monitor eating and exercise. Children earn rewards from parents when they meet the goals; parents earn a refund from the program when they and their children meet the goals (Epstein et al., 1990).

The graphs show typical results obtained more than four years after completion of such a program (Epstein & Wing, 1987). Notice the results for

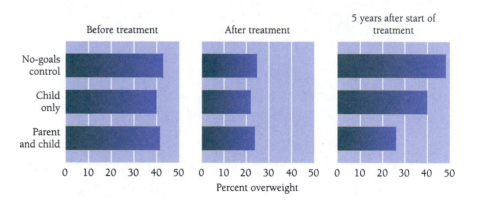

young people who participate alone and those who participate with their parents but in a program that does not link rewards to eating and exercise goals. Children and adolescents lose weight while they are participating in the program, but they regain almost all of it in the ensuing years. In contrast, when youth and their parents participate together, the children and adolescents maintain their weight at lower levels. Apparently, parental involvement results in long-lasting change in the young people's lifestyle—particularly their eating and their exercising—which allows them to sustain their initial weight loss. Of course, many remain overweight. It is best to establish good eating and exercise habits so as to avoid obesity in the first place.

ANOREXIA NERVOSA

Wendy was hospitalized despite her strong objections when she was 16 years old. She said there was nothing wrong with her, but she weighed only 68 pounds and she had lost 42 pounds in the past 2 years. Because of the weight loss, she had stopped having menstrual periods. Even so, she refused to quit dieting. She said she felt good knowing she had enough self-control to stay on her diet even though she was hungry. . . .

As a child, Wendy had been a good student, but she did not do as well at school as her older brothers did. Thus her parents praised her brothers more than they praised her. But as her weight dropped, her schoolwork suffered and she became more isolated from her classmates.

Wendy's parents said she had been a pleasant, obedient child. When they set limits on her activities, she complied willingly. Therefore, they were surprised and upset when they could not get her to abandon her diet and resume eating normally. Because they and her doctor feared for her life, they finally placed her in the hospital for treatment (Leon & Dinklage, 1989).

This persistent refusal to eat, accompanied by an irrational fear of being overweight, typifies a condition known as *anorexia nervosa*. As was the case with Wendy and the girl in the photograph, anorexia primarily affects females and usually begins with the onset of adolescence (Attie, Brooks-Gunn, & Petersen, 1990). Adolescents with anorexia tend to be well-behaved, conscien-

tious, good students from middle-class families. Their body image is grossly distorted: Despite being painfully thin, they claim to be overweight (Attie, Brooks-Gunn, & Petersen, 1990). The disorder is quite serious: Damage to the heart is common, and without treatment, as many as 15% of adolescents with anorexia die (Wicks-Nelson & Israel, 1991).

FORCES IN ACTION

Who Becomes Anorexic?

How would you answer this question? It probably won't surprise you that biological, psychological, and sociocultural influences are all important. We can start with our cultural ideal of the female body. In many industrialized cultures—and certainly in the United States—the ideal female body is tall and slender. As girls enter adolescence, these cultural norms become particularly salient and important. At the same time, girls experience a "fat spurt" in which they gain about 25 pounds, most of it fat. After this pattern of normal growth, some girls unfortunately perceive themselves as overweight and begin to diet. This is especially common if, like Linda in the first chapter-opening vignette the mother is preoccupied with her own weight (Attie, Brooks-Gunn, & Petersen, 1990). Faced with a culture that values being thin (sociocultural influence) and a change in her body (biological influence), the adolescent girl believes she is fat (psychological force) and tries to lose weight.

The elements of the biopsychosocial framework can foster anorexia in other ways. Family dynamics—including psychological and sociocultural forces—are also important. Adolescent girls are more prone to anorexia if their parents are autocratic, leaving their adolescent daughters with little sense of self-control. As girls enter adolescence and seek greater autonomy, they discover that their weight is something they can control by limiting their intake of food. In dieting, they are able to assert their autonomy and begin to achieve individual identity (Graber et al., 1994).

The cultural emphasis on thinness, combined with a regimented home life, can explain many cases of anorexia. Of course, most teenage daughters growing up in regimented homes in the United States do not become anorexic. There is a biological factor. Monozygotic twins are more likely to both be anorexic than are dizygotic twins (Fisher & Brone, 1991). This result points to an inherited predisposition for anorexia.

Summarizing all of these influences, who is most susceptible to anorexia? The disorder is most likely to develop in girls who inherit the predisposition, who internalize cultural ideals of thinness, and whose parents grant them little independence. Of course, the desire to achieve independence from parents and a unique identity is not unique to adolescents with anorexia. All adolescents struggle with these issues, as we'll see in the next section.   🐦

TEST YOURSELF

1. The adolescent growth spurt typically begins at about 11 years of age in girls and at _____ years of age in boys.
2. The onset of puberty in girls is marked by the growth of the breasts and in boys is marked by _____.
3. Maturing early tends to be beneficial, at least temporarily, for

   _____.
4. Parents may inadvertently contribute to obesity by _____.
5. Girls are more likely to become anorexic when their mothers

   _____.

6. Compare the effects of early maturation on boys and on girls.

Who Am I? The Search for Identity

LEARNING OBJECTIVES

- *How do adolescents achieve a unique identity?*
- *How do adolescents achieve an ethnic identity?*
- *Is adolescence always a time of storm and stress?*

Every day I ask myself why I am not the person that I would like to be. My relationship with myself is a very unhappy one. I am temperamental, a person of many moods. I pretend, so people cannot discern it. This is what I hate most about my life. I always act not like my true self. (Ginott, 1969, p. 30)

I'm sensitive, friendly, outgoing, popular, and tolerant, though I can also be shy, self-conscious, and even obnoxious! I'd like to be friendly and tolerant all of the time. That's the kind of person I want to be, and I'm disappointed when I'm not. I'm responsible, even studious now and then, but on the other hand, I'm a goof-off, too, because if you're too studious, you won't be popular. (Harter, 1990, p. 352)

I'm 5 feet, 10 inches tall and I weigh 125 pounds. I'm fat and ugly.

Jeesh, does my mom get upset when she hears me say that! But that's what I see when I look in the mirror. She says I don't see straight, but she's the one who wears glasses. . . .

I want to express my individuality and wear sweaters like the ones Gina has and slacks like Leah's. And I want the same running shoes that everyone's got now. (Turpin, 1993, pp. 41–42)

These remarks—all from teenagers—help to convey the complexity of the typical adolescent's sense of self or identity. As we learned in Chapter 6, when children enter the teenage years, their thinking is no longer limited to the concrete, here-and-now. Instead, formal operations afford them the power of abstract and hypothetical reasoning. Because of these advances, how would you expect young adolescents to describe themselves? If you said, "in increasingly abstract psychological and social terms," you're right. Self-reflection becomes common: Adolescents look for an identity that helps integrate the many different and sometimes conflicting elements of the self (Marcia, 1991).

Identity versus Role Confusion

Erik Erikson's (1968) account of identity formation has been particularly influential in our understanding of adolescence. By now, Erikson's theory should have a familiar ring to it, because we've discussed it in Chapters 1 and 5. You can see in the chart that Erikson proposed stages of development, each consti-

Perspective	Examples of Theories	Main Ideas	Emphases in Biopsychosocial Framework	Positions on Developmental Issues
Psychodynamic	Erikson's psycho-social theory	Personality develops through a sequence of stages	Sociocultural and life-cycle forces crucial; less emphasis on psychological	Nature–nurture interaction, discontinuity, universal sequence but individual differences in rate

tuting a unique developmental challenge. For adolescents, the crisis is between identity and role confusion. As adolescents near entry into the adult world, they struggle to achieve an identity that will allow them to become a part of that world. The crisis involves balancing the desire to try out many possible selves and the need to select a single self.

Adolescents who achieve a sense of identity are well prepared to face the next developmental challenge—establishing intimate, sharing relationships with others. However, Erikson believed that teenagers who are confused about their identity can never experience intimacy in any human relationship. Instead, throughout their lives, they remain isolated and respond to others stereotypically.

How do adolescents achieve an identity? Erikson believes that they deliberately experiment with different selves to learn more about possible identities. Much of this testing is career-oriented. Some adolescents, like the ones shown here, may envision themselves as rock stars; others may imagine being profes-

sional athletes, Peace Corps workers, or bestselling novelists. Other testing is romantically oriented. Teens may fall in love and imagine living independently with the loved one. Still other exploration involves religious and political beliefs.

We'll concentrate on the career and romantic aspects of identity later in this chapter. For now the important point is that teens commonly give different identities a trial run, just as you might test-drive different cars before selecting one. By fantasizing about their future, adolescents begin to discover who they will be.

The self-absorption that marks the teenage search for identity is often called *adolescent egocentrism* **(Elkind, 1978).** Unlike preschoolers, adolescents know that others have different perspectives on the world. However, many adolescents believe, wrongly, that they are the usual focus of others' thinking. A teen who spills catsup on herself while eating lunch may imagine that all of her friends are thinking only about the stain on her blouse. **The feeling of many adolescents is that they are, in effect, actors whose performance is watched constantly by their peers—a phenomenon that is called the** *imaginary audience.*

A related feature of adolescent self-absorption is the *personal fable,* **which is the tendency for teenagers to believe that their experiences and feelings are unique, that no one has ever felt or thought as they do.** Whether it is the excitement of first love, the despair of broken relationships, or the confusion of planning for the future, adolescents often believe that they are the first to experience these feelings and that no one else could possibly understand the power of their emotions (Elkind & Bowen, 1979).

For most youth, adolescent egocentrism, imaginary audiences, and personal fables become less important as they move through adolescence, reflecting their progress toward achieving an identity. Let's look at this progress more carefully.

Resolving the Identity Crisis

As adolescents try to achieve an identity, they progress through different phases or statuses. Four different identity statuses are common (Marcia, 1980, 1991):

- *Achievement:* Individuals who have explored alternatives and have deliberately chosen a specific identity.
- *Moratorium:* Individuals who are still examining different alternatives and have yet to find a satisfactory identity.
- *Foreclosure:* Individuals whose identity was determined largely by adults, rather than from personal exploration of alternatives.
- *Diffusion:* Individuals who are confused or often overwhelmed by the task of achieving an identity and are doing little to achieve one.

In early adolescence, diffusion and foreclosure are the most common statuses. The common element in these statuses is that teens are not exploring alternative identities. They are avoiding the crisis altogether or have resolved it by taking on an identity based on suggestions from parents or other adults. However, as individuals move further into adolescence and into young adulthood, they have more opportunity to explore alternative identities, so diffusion and foreclosure become less common. At the same time, the pie charts show that achievement and moratorium become more common (Meilman, 1979).

During adulthood, some individuals may seek different identities, creating cycles in which they alternate between moratorium and achievement statuses.

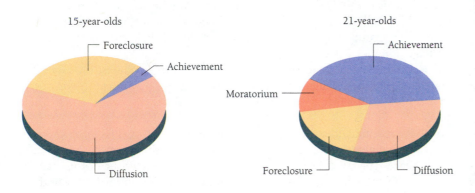

15-year-olds   21-year-olds

Sometimes young people reach the achievement status for some aspects of identity but not others. Dellas and Jernigan (1990), for example, found that 39% of the college students in their sample were in the achievement status for careers, but only 22% were in this status for religion and 13% for politics. Furthermore, only 3% of students in their sample were in the same status for all three content areas. Evidently, adolescents and young adults do not achieve a sense of identity all at once; instead, the crisis of identity is first resolved in some areas and then in others.

When the achievement status is attained, the period of active experimentation ends, and individuals have a well-defined sense of self. However, over a lifetime, an individual's identity is sometimes reworked, in response to new life challenges and circumstances. Consequently, individuals may return to the moratorium status for a period, only to reemerge later with a changed identity. In fact, individuals may go through these changes several times, creating "MAMA" cycles in which they alternate between the *moratorium* and *achievement* statuses as they explore new alternatives in response to personal and family crises (Marcia, 1991). For example, a middle-aged manager who has placed career above all else but finds himself unemployed may decide to reorganize his life around his family and service work.

What circumstances help adolescents to achieve identity? The parenting styles described in Chapter 7 play an important role (Marcia, 1980). Authoritative parenting, in which parents encourage discussion and recognize their children's autonomy, is associated with the achievement status. This style of parenting apparently encourages adolescents to undertake the personal experimentation that leads to the attainment of an identity. In contrast, authoritarian parenting, in which parents set rules with little justification and enforce them without explanation, is associated with the foreclosure status. These teens are discouraged from personal experimentation; instead, their parents simply tell them what identity to adopt. Finally, an indulgent-permissive parental style, in which parents make few demands on their children, is associated with the diffuse status. This result fits the general pattern: Children of indulgent-permissive parents tend to be less mature socially than their peers. Overall, adolescents are most likely to establish a well-defined identity in a family atmosphere where the parents encourage the children to explore alternatives on their own but do not pressure or provide explicit direction (Harter, 1990).

Ethnic Identity

Roughly one-third of the adolescents and young adults living in the United States are members of ethnic minority groups, including African Americans, Asian Americans, Italian Americans, Hispanic Americans, and Native Americans. These individuals typically develop an ethnic identity: They feel a part of their ethnic group and learn the unique elements of their group's culture and heritage (Phinney, 1990).

Achieving an ethnic identity seems to occur in three phases. Initially, adolescents have not examined their ethnic roots. A teenage African American girl in this phase remarked, "Why do I need to learn about who was the first Black woman to do this or that? I'm just not too interested." (Phinney, 1989, p. 44). For this girl, ethnic identity is not yet an important personal issue. In the second phase, adolescents have begun to explore the personal impact of their ethnic heritage. The curiosity and questioning that is characteristic of this stage is captured in the comments of a teenage Mexican American girl who said, "I want to know what we do and how our culture is different from others. Going to festivals and cultural events helps me to learn more about my own culture and about myself." (Phinney, 1989, p. 44). In the third phase, individuals achieve a distinct ethnic self-concept. One Asian American adolescent explained his ethnic identification like this: "I have been born Filipino and am born to be Filipino . . . I'm here in America, and people of many different cultures are here, too. So I don't consider myself only Filipino, but also American" (Phinney, 1989, p. 44).

To see if you understand the differences between these stages of ethnic identity, reread the vignette about Dea, the Dutch-Asian-American college student. Then decide which stage applies to her. The answer appears on page 263.

Older adolescents are more likely than younger ones to have achieved an ethnic identity, because they are more likely to have had opportunities to explore their cultural heritage (Phinney & Chavira, 1992). The pie charts show the percentage of 16- and 19-year-olds in each of three phases of ethnic identity. Not until age 19 have most adolescents attained an ethnic identity. Such individuals tend to have higher self-esteem and find that their interactions with

Part of establishing an ethnic identity is learning cultural traditions, such as cooking special meals.

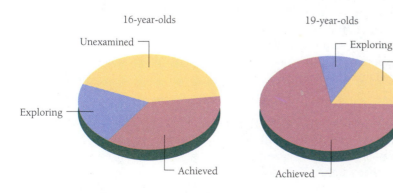

16-year-olds

Unexamined

Exploring

Achieved

19-year-olds

Exploring

Unexamined

Achieved

family and friends are more satisfying (Phinney, 1989). What contributes to the achievement of an ethnic identity? As was the case with overall identity, adolescents are most likely to achieve an ethnic self-concept when their parents use an authoritative style (Rosenthal & Feldman, 1992).

Some individuals achieve a well-defined ethnic self-concept and, at the same time, identify strongly with the mainstream culture. In the United States, for example, many Chinese Americans embrace both Chinese and American culture; in England, many Indians identify with both the Indian and British cultures. For other individuals, the cost of strong ethnic identification is a weakened tie to mainstream culture. Some investigators report that, for Hispanic Americans, strong identification with American culture is associated with a weaker ethnic self-concept (Phinney, 1990).

These differences emphasize an important point. Racial and ethnic groups living in the United States are diverse. African American, Asian American, Hispanic American, and Native American cultures and heritages differ, so we should expect the nature and consequences of a strong ethnic self-concept to differ in these and other ethnic groups. Even within any particular group, the nature and consequences of ethnic identity may change over successive generations (Montgomery, 1992).

JEAN S. PHINNEY
". . . [ethnic] adolescents' comments reveal a developmental trend from concrete, dualistic thinking about multiple group identities with minimal conflict, through a period of discomfort because of awareness of conflict, toward a more abstract, integrated view."

DEA'S ETHNIC IDENTITY

Dea, the Dutch-Asian-American college student, doesn't know how to integrate the Korean heritage of her biological parents with the Dutch American culture in which she was reared. This would put her in the second stage: On the one hand, she has begun to examine her ethnic roots, which means that she's progressed beyond the first stage. On the other hand, she has not yet integrated her Asian and European roots, as would be characteristic of adolescents in the third stage.

The Myth of Storm and Stress

The belief that adolescence is inherently a time of storm and stress has been with us for nearly a century. For many early theorists, personal tumult was an essential and often positive component of development during the adolescent years. For example, G. Stanley Hall, an influential American developmental psychologist at the beginning of the 20th century, wrote that adolescence was ". . . strewn with wreckage of mind, body, and morals" (1904, p. xiv). Of course, the combative teen has been a favorite character of U.S. novelists and filmmakers for the past 50 years.

Today, we know that the rebellious teen is largely a myth. Consider the following conclusions derived from research findings (Steinberg, 1990). Most adolescents

- admire and love their parents
- rely upon their parents for advice
- embrace many of their parents' values
- feel loved by their parents

Not exactly the image of the rebel, is it? These results undermine the view that adolescence is necessarily a time of turmoil and conflict.

Some particularly convincing evidence comes from a study (Offer et al., 1988) of adolescents from ten different countries: the United States, Australia, Germany, Italy, Israel, Hungary, Turkey, Japan, Taiwan, and Bangladesh. Repeatedly, these investigators found most adolescents moving confidently and

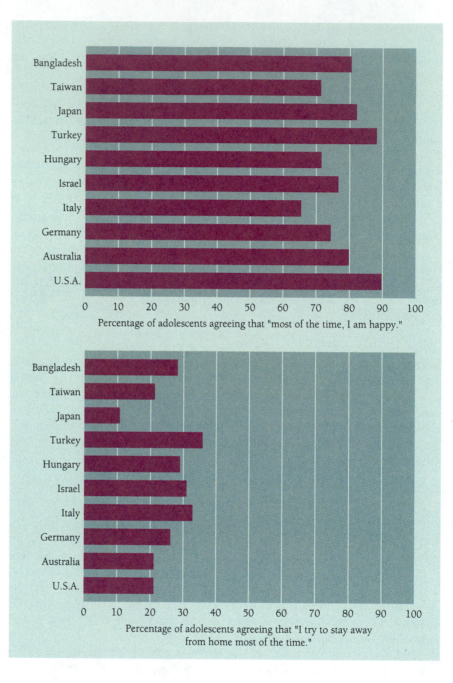

happily toward adulthood. For example, as the graphs show, most adolescents around the world reported that they were usually happy, and few avoided their homes.

Of course, parent–child relations do change during adolescence. As teens become more independent, their relationships with their parents become more egalitarian. Parents must adjust to their children's growing sense of autonomy by beginning to treat them more like equals (Laursen & Collins, 1994). As a consequence, teens tend to spend less time with their parents, to be less affectionate toward them, and to argue more often with them about matters of style, taste, and freedom. However, these changes are not a matter of storm and stress; they are natural by-products of a changing parent–child relationship, in which the "child" is nearly a fully independent young adult (Steinberg, 1990). Adolescence is an interesting and challenging time for youth and their parents, but not inherently tempestuous as the myth would lead us to believe.

TEST YOURSELF

1. For Erikson, the crisis of adolescence is between identity and _____.

2. The _____ status would describe an adolescent who has attained an identity largely based on her parents' advice and urging.

3. Adolescents are more likely to achieve an ethnic identity when their parents use a(n) _____ style of parenting.

4. When teenagers identify strongly with their own ethnic group, this means that their identification with mainstream American culture is _____.

5. In ten countries around the world, most adolescents report that they are happy and that _____.

6. Children's relations with their parents change in adolescence, reflecting adolescents' growing independence and a _____ parent–child relationship.

7. Your local newspaper has just printed a feature article describing all of the "storm and stress" that typifies adolescence. Write a letter to the editor in which you set the record straight.

Looks can be deceiving. Although teenagers often differ from their parents in preferences for clothes and music, most teens report that they love and respect their parents and turn to them for advice.

<table>
<tr><td>

Flipping Burgers and Waiting Tables: Entering the World of Work

</td><td>

Flipping Burgers and Waiting Tables: Entering the World of Work
   Part-Time Work
   Career Development
   ■ *The Life of Lynne, a Drama in Three Acts*

</td></tr>
</table>

LEARNING OBJECTIVES

❧ *What is the impact of part-time employment on adolescent development?*

❧ *How do adolescents choose a specific career?*

"What do you want to be when you grow up?" Children are often asked this question in fun. Beginning in adolescence, however, it takes on special significance because work is such an important component of a person's identity. A job—be it as bricklayer, reporter, or child care worker—helps to define who we are.

Many U.S. teens have their first exposure to the world of work in part-time employment after school or on weekends, so let's begin with this topic.

Answers: (1) role confusion, (2) foreclosure, (3) authoritative, (4) sometimes strong and sometimes weak, depending on the individual circumstances, (5) they do not avoid being home, (6) more egalitarian

Part-Time Work

The teen photographed here is engaged in an American adolescent ritual—the part-time job. Today, a substantial majority of high school seniors work part-time. Out of every five adolescent part-time workers, one works at a fast-food

restaurant like McDonald's or Burger King, and another works in a retail store as a cashier or salesperson. Boys are more likely to be manual laborers, busboys, or newspaper carriers. Girls are more often baby sitters, maids, or restaurant workers, and they are usually paid less than boys (Greenberger & Steinberg, 1983; Mortimer, 1991).

Part-time work is a new aspect of adolescence. Prior to World War II, fewer than 10% of U.S. tenth-graders worked part-time while attending high school. That figure jumped to more than 25% during the 1970s and to 75% in the 1980s. This development is unique to the United States. In other industrialized countries in Western Europe and Asia, high school students who also hold part-time jobs are a clear minority. Compared to high-school students in these countries, U.S. students have a shorter school day and much less homework, which means that they have time to work (Reubens, Harrison, & Kupp, 1981).

Adults often praise these emerging work habits, believing that through early exposure to the workplace, adolescents will learn self-discipline, become self-confident, and acquire important job skills (Snedeker, 1982). For most adolescents, however, the reality is very different. Part-time work can actually be harmful, particularly for adolescents who work more than approximately 15 hours per week. Several specific problems are common.

1. *School performance suffers.* When students work extensively, they devote less time to homework and are more apt to cut classes. Not surprisingly, their grades are lower than those of their peers who work less or not at all (Steinberg, Fegley, & Dornbusch, 1993). Why should 15 hours of work be so detrimental to school performance? A 15-hour work schedule might involve four 3-hour shifts after school and another 3-hour shift on the weekend. This would seem to leave ample opportunity to study, but only if students use their time effectively. In fact, many high school students apparently do not have the foresight and discipline necessary to consistently meet the combined demands of work and school.

2. *Mental health and behavioral problems.* Adolescents who work long hours are more likely to experience anxiety and depression, and their self-esteem often suffers. Many adolescents find themselves in jobs that are repetitive and boring but stressful. Conditions like these undermine self-esteem and breed anxiety.

Extensive part-time work also leads to more frequent substance abuse and interpersonal problems with peers or parents. Bachman and Schulenberg (1993) examined these factors in a representative sample of more than 50,000 U.S. high school seniors. They found that extensive work was associated with a cluster of negative outcomes:

- Increased substance abuse, including cigarettes, alcohol, marijuana, and cocaine
- More frequent problem behavior, including violence towards others, trouble with police, and arguments with parents

Why employment is associated with all of these problems is not clear. Perhaps employed adolescents turn to drugs to help them cope with the anxiety and depression brought on by work. Arguments with parents may become more common because anxious, depressed adolescents are more prone to argue or because wage-earning adolescents may believe that their freedom should match their income. Regardless of the exact mechanism involved, extensive part-time work is clearly detrimental to the mental health of most adolescents.

3. Misleading affluence. Adults sometimes argue that work is good for teenagers because it teaches them "the value of a dollar." Here, too, reality is at odds with the adage. Few working teens set aside much of their income for future goals, such as a college education, or use it to contribute to their family's expenses. The typical teenage pattern is to "earn and spend." Working adolescents spend most of their earnings on themselves—to buy clothing, snack food, or cosmetics and to pay for entertainment. Because parents customarily pay for many of the essential expenses associated with truly independent living—rent, utilities, and groceries, for example—working adolescents often have a vastly higher percentage of their income available for discretionary spending than do working adults. Thus, for many teens, the part-time work experience provides unrealistic expectations about how income can be allocated (Bachman, 1983).

Adolescents who work extensively at part-time jobs during the school year often do poorly in school. Part of the problem is the difficulty in balancing time to work, study, and sleep.

The message that emerges repeatedly from research on part-time employment is hardly encouraging. Like Aaron, the teenage boy in the chapter-opening vignette, adolescents who work long hours at part-time jobs do not benefit from the experience. To the contrary, they do worse in school, are more likely to have behavioral problems, and learn how to spend money rather than how to manage it. These effects are similar for adolescents from different ethnic groups (Steinberg & Dornbusch, 1991) and are comparable for boys and girls (Bachman & Schulenberg, 1993).

Does this mean that teenagers who are still in school should never work part-time? Not necessarily. Part-time employment can be successful, depending on the circumstances. One key is the number of hours of work. Although the exact number of hours varies, of course, from one student to the next, most students could easily work 5 hours weekly without harm, and many could work 10 hours weekly. Another key is the type of job. When adolescents have jobs that allow them to use their skills (for example, bookkeeping, computing, or typing) and to acquire new ones, self-esteem can be enhanced, and they can learn from their experiences. By these criteria, a teen who spends 30 hours each week bagging groceries is bound to show some of the harmful effects that we have described; a teen who likes to tinker with cars and spends Saturdays working in a repair shop will not.

Finally, summer jobs typically do not involve conflict between work and school. Consequently, many of the harmful effects associated with part-time employment during the school year do not hold for summer employment. In fact, such employment sometimes enhances adolescents' self-esteem, especially when they save part of their income for future plans (Marsh, 1991).

Career Development

Faced with the challenge of selecting a career, many adolescents may be attracted to the approach taken by the teenage boy in the cartoon. Choosing a career is difficult, in part because it involves determining the kinds of jobs that will be available in the future. Predicting the future is risky, but the U.S. Bureau of Labor Statistics projects that by the year 2000, more than 75% of all jobs will be in service industries, such as education, health care, and banking. The remaining jobs—fewer than 25%—will be associated with the production of goods. In the future, there will be fewer jobs in agriculture, forestry, and manufacturing (Bureau of Labor Statistics, 1992).

"Your son has made a career choice, Mildred. He's going to win the lottery and travel a lot."

LAUGH PARADE, © 1985. Reprinted courtesy of Bunny Hoest and Parade Magazine.

Knowing the types of jobs that experts predict will be plentiful, how do adolescents begin the long process of selecting a career that will bring them happiness and fortune? Theories of vocational choice describe this process. According to the theory proposed by Donald Super (1976, 1980), identity is a primary force in an adolescent's choice of a career. **Beginning at the age of 13 or 14, adolescents use their emerging identities as an initial source of ideas about careers, a process called** *crystallization*. During those years, teenagers start to use their ideas about their own talents and interests to narrow down potential career prospects. A teenage boy who is extroverted and sociable may decide that working with people should be part of his career. Such initial decisions are provisional; many adolescents experiment with different hypothetical careers and try to envision what each might be like.

The next phase often begins at about 18 years of age; it is an extension of the activities associated with crystallization. **During** *specification*, **adolescents further limit their career possibilities by learning more about specific lines of work and starting to obtain the training that is required for a specific job.** Our hypothetical extroverted teenage boy who wants to work with people may decide that a career in sales would be a good match for his abilities and interests. Some, like the teen shown in the photo, may begin an apprenticeship as a way to learn a trade.

The end of the teenage years or the early 20s marks the beginning of the third phase. **During** *implementation*, **individuals enter the work force and learn firsthand about jobs.** This is a time of learning about responsibility and productivity, learning to get along with co-workers, and altering one's lifestyle to accommodate work. This period is often unstable. Individuals sometimes change positions frequently, as they adjust to the reality of life in the workplace.

In the Real People feature, you can see these three phases in one person's career development.

"The Life of Lynne," A Drama in Three Acts

REAL PEOPLE

Act 1: Crystallization   Throughout high school, Lynne was active in a number of organizations. She enjoyed being busy and liked the constant contact with people. Lynne was often nominated for office, and more often than not, she asked to be treasurer. Not that she was greedy or had her hand in the till; she simply found it satisfying to keep the financial records in order. By the end of her junior year, Lynne decided that she wanted to study business in college, a decision that fit with her good grades in English and math.

Act 2: Specification   Lynne was accepted into the business school of a large state university. She decided that accounting fit her skills and temperament, so this became her major. During the summers, she worked as a cashier at J. C. Penney's. This helped to pay for college and gave her experience in the world of retail sales.

Act 3: Implementation   A few months after graduation, Lynne was offered a junior accounting position with Wal-Mart. Her job required that she work Tuesday through Friday, auditing Wal-Mart stores in several nearby cities. Lynne liked the pay, the company car, the pay, the feeling of independence, and the pay. However, having to hit the road every morning by 7:30 A.M. was a jolt to someone used to rising casually at 10 A.M. Also, Lynne often found it awkward to deal with store managers, many of whom were twice her age and very intimidating. She was coming to the conclusion that there was much more to a successful career as an accountant than simply having the numbers add up correctly.   ❧

The "Life of Lynne" illustrates the continuous give and take between an individual's self-concept and his or her career development. A person's self-concept makes some careers more attractive than others; occupational experiences further refine and shape a person's self-concept.

One other aspect of Lynne's life sheds more light on Super's theory. After 18 months on the job, Lynne's accounting group was merged with another; this would have required Lynne to move to another state, so she quit. After six months looking for another accounting job, Lynne gave up and began to study to become a real estate agent. The moral? Economic conditions and opportunities also shape career development. Changing times can force individuals to take new, often unexpected career paths.

PERSONALITY-TYPE THEORY

Super's (1976, 1980) work helps to explain how self-concept and career aspirations develop hand in hand, but it does not explain why particular individuals are attracted to one line of work rather than another. Explaining the match between people and occupations has been the aim of a theory devised by John Holland (1985, 1987). **According to Holland's *personality-type theory*, people find work fulfilling when the important features of a job or profession fit the worker's personality.** People are satisfied with their work when it complements their personality and dissatisfied when it does not.

Holland identified six prototypic personalities that are relevant to the world of work. Each one is best suited to a specific set of occupations, as indicated in

Personality Types in Holland's Theory		
Personality Type	*Description*	*Careers*
Realistic	Individuals enjoy physical labor and working with their hands, and they like to solve concrete problems.	mechanic, truck driver, construction worker
Investigative	Individuals are task-oriented and enjoy thinking about abstract relations.	scientist, technical writer
Social	Individuals are skilled verbally and interpersonally, and they enjoy solving problems using these skills.	teacher, counselor, social worker
Conventional	Individuals have verbal and quantitative skills that they like to apply to structured, well-defined tasks assigned to them by others.	bank teller, payroll clerk, traffic manager
Enterprising	Individuals enjoy using their verbal skills in positions of power, status, and leadership.	business executive, television producer, real estate agent
Artistic	Individuals enjoy expressing themselves through unstructured tasks.	poet, musician, actor

Holland, 1985, 1987.

According to Holland's personality-type theory, enterprising individuals often are successful in business because they enjoy powerful positions where they can use their verbal skills.

the right-hand column of the table above. Remember, these are merely prototypes. Most people do not match any one personality type exactly. Instead, their work-related personalities are a blend of the six.

Combining Holland's work-related personality types with Super's theory of career development gives us a very comprehensive picture of vocational growth. On the one hand, Super's theory explains the developmental progression by which individuals translate general interests into a specific career; on the other hand, Holland's theory explains what makes a good match between specific interests and specific careers.

Of course, trying to match interests to occupations can be difficult. Fortunately, several tests can be used to describe a person's work-related personality and the jobs for which he or she is best suited. In the Strong Interest Inventory (SII), for example, people express their liking of different occupations, school subjects, activities, and types of people (for example, very old people, people who live dangerously). These answers are compared to the responses obtained from a normative sample of individuals from different occupations. The result is a profile, a portion of which is shown on page 271.

You can see that each of Holland's types—called "general occupational themes" on the SII—is listed. Under each heading are black and shaded bars that show typical responses of women and men. The dot shows where the person's responses fall compared to other people of the person's own gender. Looking in the left column, you can see that this woman has less interest than the average female on the realistic and investigative themes but has more interest than the average female on the artistic theme. In the right column, this woman has average interest on the social and conventional themes, but less than average interest on the enterprising theme. Of the six general occupational themes, this person's interests seem to correspond best with the artistic personality in Holland's theory.

By looking at the basic interest scales that are listed under the artistic occupational theme, we can get an even more precise idea of this woman's interests. Compared to the average female, this woman shows high interest in art, writing, and culinary arts (cooking). Her interest in music and applied arts is only average. Evidently, her ideal job would be as a writer for either an art magazine or a cooking magazine!

Looking at the remaining occupational themes will serve as a reminder that the match between interests and occupations is often far from perfect. Although this woman's interest in the realistic and social occupational themes is only average overall, she has high interest in agriculture and in religious activities.

If you are still undecided about a career, we encourage you to visit your college's counseling center and arrange to take a test like the SII. The results will help you to focus on careers that would match your interests and help you to choose a college major that would lead to those careers.

Even if you are fairly certain of your vocational plans, you might take one of these tests anyway. As we saw with Lynne (and will discuss more in Chapters 11 and 14), career development does not end with the first job. People continuously refine their career aspirations over the life span, and these test results might be useful later in your life.

Consulting Psychologists Press, Inc., 1994.

TEST YOURSELF

1. Adolescents who work extensively at part-time jobs during the school year often get lower grades, have behavior problems, and _____.
2. Part-time employment during the school year can be beneficial if adolescents limit the number of hours that they work and _____.
3. During the _____ phase of vocational choice, adolescents learn more about specific lines of work and begin training.
4. Individuals with a(n) _____ personality type are best suited for a career as a teacher or counselor.
5. For each of the six personality types in Holland's theory, think of a person you know who fits the personality. (The chart on page 270 will be helpful as you do this.) Do you think that the person's occupation represents a good match for his or her personality?

"How Do I Love Thee?": Romantic Relationships

LEARNING OBJECTIVES

❧ *What are the functions of dating?*

❧ *At what age do adolescents become sexually active? What factors influence them to do so?*

❧ *Why do sexually active adolescents use contraceptives so infrequently?*

❧ *What are some of the behaviors that make adolescents particularly vulnerable to AIDS?*

❧ *What circumstances can make date rape especially likely?*

❧ *What determines an adolescent's sexual preference?*

As the photographs below reveal, the fires of romantic relationships have long warmed the hearts of American adolescents. Though the circumstances surrounding romantic relationships have changed over the years, romance has remained a central component of adolescence.

Dating

At about 14 or 15 years of age, the typical American boy begins to date. American girls begin to date about a year earlier, reflecting the fact that they reach puberty earlier than boys do. The first experiences with dating often occur when same-sex groups go places knowing that a mixed-sex crowd will be attending. Examples are going to a mall with friends or going to a dance in seventh grade. A somewhat more advanced form of dating involves several boys and several girls going out together as a group. Ultimately, dates involve well-defined couples. By the high school years, most students will have had at least one steady girlfriend or boyfriend (Sorenson, 1973).

As you might suspect, cultural factors strongly influence dating patterns. For example, European American parents tend to encourage independence in their teenagers more than traditional Hispanic American and Asian American parents, who emphasize family ties and loyalty to parents. Dating is a sign of independence and usually results in less time spent with family, which explains why Hispanic American and Asian American adolescents often begin to date at an older age and date less frequently (Xiaohe & Whyte, 1990).

Originally, the primary function of dating was to select a mate, but today dating serves a variety of functions for adolescents (Padgham & Blyth, 1991). Dating

- is a pleasant form of recreation and entertainment
- helps to teach adult standards of interpersonal behavior
- is a means to establish status among peers
- provides an outlet for sexual experimentation
- provides companionship like that experienced between best friends
- leads to intimacy, in which teens share innermost feelings with their partners

The functions of dating change during adolescence, as these pie charts on high school and college students' views indicate (Roscoe, Diana, & Brooks, 1987). For high school students, recreation is clearly the dominant reason for dating.

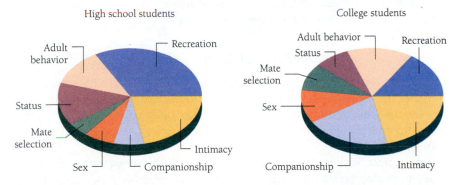

Among college students, dating begins to serve some longer-term goals: Intimacy, companionship, and learning adult standards of behavior are now the most frequently reported reasons for dating.

SEXUAL ORIENTATION

For most adolescents, dating and romance involve members of the opposite sex. However, as part of the search to establish an identity, many adolescents wonder, at least in passing, if they are homosexual. In fact, roughly 10–15% of adolescent boys and girls report at least one instance of sexual activity with a member of their own sex (Hass, 1979). For most adolescents, these experiences are simply a part of the larger process of role experimentation common to adolescence. However, the adolescent search for self-definition leads roughly 5% of teenage boys and girls to identify themselves as gay in their sexual orientation. This identification usually occurs in mid-adolescence, but not until young adulthood do most gay individuals express their sexual orientation publicly (Bell, Weinberg, & Hammersmith, 1981).

Why do gay adolescents wait so long—three to five years—before declaring their sexual orientation? Many believe, correctly, that their peers are not likely to support them (Newman & Muzzonigro, 1993). For example, in one national survey, only 40% of 15-to-19-year-old boys agreed that they could befriend a gay person (Marsiglio, 1993). Adolescents who said that they could not befriend a gay peer were most often younger, identified themselves as religious fundamentalists, and had parents who were less educated.

The roots of sexual orientation remain poorly understood. Scientists have discredited several ideas concerning the roots of sexual orientation. Research (Bell, Weinberg, & Hammersmith, 1981; Patterson, 1992) has shown each of the following to be false:

• Sons become gay when reared by a domineering mother and a weak father.
• Girls become lesbians when their father is their primary role model.
• Children reared by gay and lesbian parents usually end up adopting their parents' sexual orientation.
• Gay and lesbian adults were, as children, seduced by an older person of their sex.

What, then, does determine a person's sexual orientation? The exact factors probably differ from one person to the next, but many scientists today share the view that biology plays an important role (Money, 1987). The exact nature of this role remains a mystery, but some recent evidence points to an inherited component. A gene on the X chromosome that is passed from mothers to sons appears to be a contributing factor of homosexuality in males (Hamer et al., 1993).

In romantic relationships of all sorts, sexuality is very often an important element. Let's look now at the onset of sexual behavior during adolescence.

Awakening of Sexual Interests

Part of the experimentation and exploration that we associate with adolescence involves sex. Sexuality is a central issue for adolescents because of their growing involvement in romantic relationships. Sex is also conspicuous because it is emphasized on television and in movies and because it is seen as a way to establish adult status.

For most adolescents, sex progresses from kissing to petting above the waist to petting below the waist to intercourse (Rodgers & Rowe, 1993). One glimpse at the extent of adolescent sexuality comes from the percentage of adolescents at different ages who have experienced sexual intercourse (National Research Council, 1987), shown in the chart. Notice that by the end of adolescence, most American boys and girls have had intercourse at least once.

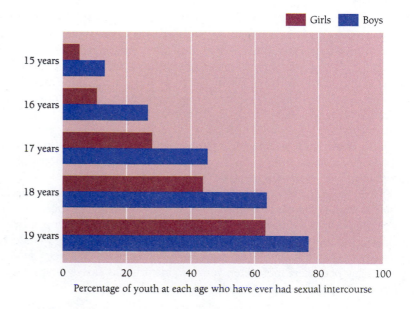

Percentage of youth at each age who have ever had sexual intercourse

Why are some adolescents sexually active whereas others are not? Parents' and peers' attitudes toward sex play a key role. In one study of high school students (Treboux & Busch-Rossnagel, 1990), positive attitudes toward sex by parents and friends were associated with students' positive attitudes, which, in turn, were associated with more frequent and more intense sexual behavior. That is, when parents and friends had positive attitudes toward sexuality in general, students had more open attitudes and were more likely to have sexual intercourse. In another study of junior high and high school students (DiBlasio & Benda, 1990), sexually active adolescents

- believed that their friends were also sexually active
- judged that the rewards of sex (for example, emotional and physical closeness) outweighed the costs (for example, guilt and fear of pregnancy or disease)
- were lower in their religious commitment

Thus, sexual activity reflects the influence of parents and peers as well as the individual's own beliefs and values.

Adolescents' sexual behavior is a cause for concern because it can have life-lasting consequences. In the next few pages, let's ponder some of these problems.

TEENAGE PREGNANCY

Roughly one in ten adolescent girls in the U.S. becomes pregnant. About 60% of pregnant teenagers give birth; the remaining 40% abort the pregnancy (Henshaw, 1993). The result is that roughly 500,000 babies are born to U.S. teenagers annually. For most, the future for baby and mother is not promising. The babies face medical problems, largely because most teenage mothers receive little or no prenatal care. As they grow, babies of teenage mothers generally do less well in school and more often have behavioral problems (Dryfoos, 1990). For the mothers, incomplete education, poverty, and marital problems are common (Furstenberg, Brooks-Gunn, & Morgan, 1987). Of course, not all teenage mothers and their infants follow this dismal life course. Some teenage mothers finish school, find good jobs, and have happy marriages; their children do well in school, academically and socially. However, we need to emphasize that teenage pregnancies with "happy endings" are clearly the exception; for most teenage mothers and their children, life is a struggle.

The solution to teen pregnancies seems simple enough—abstinence from sex, or contraception—but as we'll see in a few pages, the problem is more complicated. First, let's look at another problem associated with adolescent sex.

SEXUALLY TRANSMITTED DISEASES

A number of diseases are transmitted from one person to another through sexual intercourse. Some, like syphilis and gonorrhea, are caused by bacteria. Although these diseases can have serious complications if they are not treated, both are usually cured readily with penicillin. In contrast, the prognosis is bleak for individuals who contract the human immunodeficiency virus (HIV), which typically leads to acquired immunodeficiency syndrome (AIDS). In persons with AIDS, the immune system is no longer able to protect the body from infections and, sooner or later, they die from one of these infections.

Young adults—those in their 20s—account for roughly 25% of all AIDS cases in the United States. Most of these people contracted the disease during adolescence. Many factors make adolescents especially susceptible to AIDS. Teenagers and young adults are more likely than older adults to engage in un-

Ads like this one are designed to make adolescents realize that they are not invulnerable to AIDS; if they engage in high-risk behaviors frequently, eventually they will contract the disease.

protected sex and to use intravenous drugs—common pathways for the transmission of AIDS. Also, adolescents often have sex with many partners, increasing their risk of exposure to the disease.

SAFE SEX? NO SEX?

Teens would reduce the risk of becoming pregnant and contracting sexually transmitted diseases if they used contraceptives or avoided sexual intercourse altogether. Let's talk first about contraception. Only a minority of sexually active teenagers use birth control. Those who do often use ineffective methods, such as withdrawal, or use them inconsistently (National Research Council, 1987).

Adolescents' infrequent use of contraceptives can be traced to several factors (Adler, 1994).

- *Ignorance.* Many adolescents are seriously misinformed about the facts of conception. For example, many do not know when during the menstrual cycle conception is most likely to occur.
- *Illusion of invulnerability.* Too many adolescents deny reality. They believe that they are invincible—"It couldn't happen to me"—only others become pregnant or contract AIDS.
- *Lack of motivation.* For some adolescent girls, becoming pregnant is appealing. Like Jenny in the vignette at the beginning of the chapter, they picture having a child as a way to break away from their parents, to gain status as independent-living adults, and to have "someone to love them."
- *Access to contraceptives.* Some teenagers do not know where to obtain contraceptives. Others may find it awkward to do so. Still others don't know how to use contraceptives.

One attack on teen pregnancy and teen cases of AIDS involves making contraceptives more readily available. This approach is highlighted in the Current Controversies feature.

CURRENT CONTROVERSIES

Condoms in the Classroom

In middle schools and high schools throughout the United States, students can obtain contraceptives, usually by visiting a health clinic located in the school. Many programs require parents' permission for students to obtain contraceptives, but some do not.

These programs have prompted considerable debate, much of it bitter. On one side, many educators, parents, health officials and students argue that they are addressing the reality of today's adolescents. Peter Beilenson, city health commissioner in Baltimore, remarked, "Both the health department and the school system strongly stress abstinence as the best avenue for young people. But we have to deal with the reality that in the Baltimore school system three-quarters or more of the students are sexually active" (*New York Times*, 1992, December 4, p. A28). On the other side, many parents and religious leaders echo the sentiments of Baltimore minister Melvin Tuggle, who argued that school-based distribution of contraceptives "sends a message that it is O.K. to have sex as long as you don't get pregnant" (*New York Times*, 1993, February 16, p. B16).

What do you think? Should contraceptives be available to students in their schools? Should a student need parental permission to obtain contraceptives? What messages do we send to youth by making contraceptives readily available? What messages do we send by withholding them? ❧

Regardless of their opinion about contraceptives in schools, no professionals believe that simply making contraceptives more available will solve these problems. Broader educational programs that present the truth about sex, teenage pregnancy, AIDS, and contraception can be effective for adolescents, who too often rely on peers for information about health and sexuality (Boyer & Hein, 1991). Such programs not only teach the relevant biology but also include a focus on responsible sexual behavior or abstention from premarital sex altogether (Dreyfoos, 1990).

One effective program is called "Postponing Sexual Involvement" (Howard & McCabe, 1990). Under the direction of trained, older adolescents, students discuss the pressures to become involved sexually, common "lines" that teens use to induce others to have sex, and strategies for responding to those lines. Accompanying the discussions are opportunities for students to practice the strategies in role-playing sessions. Students who participate in these programs are less likely to have intercourse; when they do have intercourse, they are more likely to use contraceptives (Howard & McCabe, 1990).

The conclusion is that adolescents need more than catchy aphorisms like "True love waits." Love and sex are enormously complicated and emotionally charged issues, even for adults; effective programs recognize this complexity and try to provide adolescents with useful skills for dealing with the many issues involved in their emerging sexuality.

These interpersonal skills are also critical in understanding another problem associated with sexual behavior among adolescents and young adults.

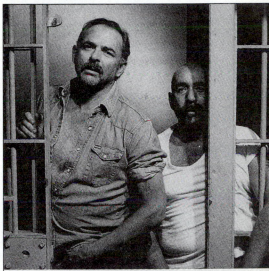

If you don't take no for an answer, these could be your new roommates.

If she says, "No, stop!" and you don't listen, you're committing rape. A felony. And you could go to jail. Where it may take you a while to get used to the guys in your new dorm.

Against her will is against the law.
This tagline is used with permission from Pi Kappa Phi.

This ad is part of a campaign designed to encourage explicit communication between males and females about sexual matters.

SEXUAL COERCION

Cindy reported that her date "lifted up my skirt and took off my panties when I was drunk. Then he laid down on top of me and went to work." **Like Cindy, many adolescent and young women are forced to have sexual intercourse by males they know, a situation known as** *date rape* or *acquaintance rape* (Ogletree, 1993). Traditional sex-role socialization helps to set the stage for sexual coercion. Males learn that an intense sexual drive is a sign of masculinity. Females learn that being sexually attractive is one way to gain a male's attention. However, "good girls" are expected to be uninterested in sex and to resist attempts for sex. Both males and females learn these expectations; consequently, males often assume that a female says "no" because she is supposed to say "no," not because she really means it (Muehlenhard, 1988). Unless, and sometimes even if, a woman's communications are crystal clear—"*STOP!!* I *don't* want to do this!"—an adolescent or young adult male will often assume, incorrectly and egocentrically, that her interest in sex matches his own (Kowalski, 1992).

A number of circumstances increase the possibility that adolescent and young adult males will misinterpret or ignore a woman's verbal or nonverbal communications regarding sexual intent. For example, heavy drinking usually impairs a woman's ability to send a clear message and makes men less able and less inclined to interpret such messages (Abbey, 1991). Another factor is a couple's sexual history. If a couple has had sex previously, the male may tend to dismiss his partner's protests, interpreting them as fleeting feelings that can be overcome easily (Shotland & Goodstein, 1992).

Date-rape workshops represent one approach to the problem (Feltey, Ainslie, & Geib, 1991). Most emphasize the importance of communication between females and males. Females need to be clear and consistent in expressing their intent. Before engaging in sex, men need to understand a woman's intentions, not simply assume that they know. Here are some guidelines that are often presented at such workshops; you may find them useful (Allgeier & Allgeier, 1995):

1. Know your own sexual policies. Decide when sexual intimacy is acceptable for *you*.
2. Communicate these policies openly and clearly.
3. Avoid being alone with a person until you have communicated these policies and believe that you can trust the person.
4. Avoid using alcohol or other drugs when you are with a person with whom you do not wish to become sexually intimate.
5. If someone tries to force you to have sex, make your objections known: Talk first, but struggle and scream if necessary.

TEST YOURSELF

1. For college students, three primary functions of dating are learning adult standards of behavior, intimacy, and _____.
2. Not until _____ do most gay individuals express their sexual orientation publicly.
3. _____ apparently plays a key role in determining sexual orientation.
4. When parents approve of sex, their adolescent children are _____.
5. Babies born to teenage mothers usually face medical problems, do less well in school, and often have _____.
6. Adolescents are particularly vulnerable to AIDS because they often engage in unprotected sex and because they _____.
7. Adolescents often fail to use contraception, due to ignorance, the illusion of invulnerability, lack of access to contraception, and _____.
8. Date rape is more likely if either partner has been drinking and if the couple _____.
9. First look at the functions of dating, listed on page 273, then look back to Chapter 5, where we discussed differences in boys' and girls' ways of interacting with peers. How well do these styles of interaction prepare boys and girls for romantic relationships?

A Look at the Dark Side: Problems of Adolescent Development

LEARNING OBJECTIVES

🍂 **Why do teenagers drink?**

🍂 **What leads some adolescents to become depressed? How can depression be treated?**

🍂 **What are the causes of juvenile delinquency?**

Some young people do not adapt well to the new demands and responsibilities of adolescence and respond in ways that are unhealthy. In this last section of

Answers: (1) *companionship,* (2) *young adulthood,* (3) *biology,* (4) *more likely to be sexually active,* (5) *behavioral problems,* (6) *sometimes experiment with intravenous drugs,* (7) *because the girl may see becoming pregnant as a sign of adult independence,* (8) *has had sex previously*

Chapter 8, we look at three problems, often interrelated, that create the three D's of adolescent development: drugs, depression, and delinquency.

Use of Drugs

Throughout history, people have used substances that alter their behavior, thoughts, or emotions. Today, drugs used commonly in America include alcohol, marijuana, hallucinogens (like LSD), heroin, cocaine, cigarettes (because of the nicotine they contain), barbiturates, and amphetamines. The graph pro-

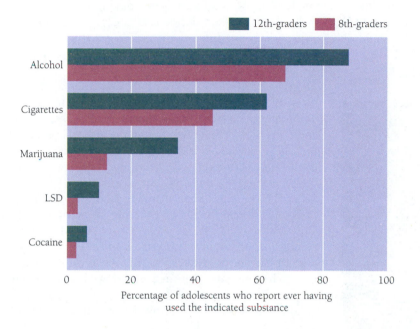

Percentage of adolescents who report ever having used the indicated substance

vides a picture of the use of these drugs by U.S. adolescents. The vast majority of adolescents avoid drugs, with one glaring exception—alcohol. A majority of high school seniors have drunk alcohol within the past month (Johnston, O'Malley, & Bachman, 1993). These figures have changed in recent years, as discussed in the See for Yourself feature.

Trends in Drinking and Drug Use

Every spring since 1975, approximately 16,000 high school seniors across the United States have been surveyed concerning their lifestyles and values. Since 1991, eighth- and tenth-graders have been included as well. The results are published annually in a volume entitled *National Survey Results on Drug Abuse,* published by the U.S. Public Health Service. The survey is conducted annually because adolescents' use of drugs changes—often dramatically—from one year to the next. For example, in 1975, 55% of high school seniors reported that they had ever used an illicit drug. This figure reached a peak of 66% in 1982 but has declined every year since; only 41% of the class of 1992 reported ever using illicit drugs.

See if your library has the most recent volume in the series; it will probably be in the section containing U.S. government documents. Find the results for any of the drugs discussed here and examine trends over the past five years. Is use by high school students continuing to decline? Are the results similar for eighth- and tenth-graders? For boys and girls? See for yourself! ❧

SEE FOR YOURSELF

TEENAGE DRINKING

Why do most adolescents avoid cigarettes, marijuana, LSD, and cocaine but readily consume alcohol? There are a number of reasons (Fields, 1992):

- *Experimentation.* Something new to try
- *Relaxation.* A means to reduce tension
- *Escape.* To avoid a harsh or unpleasant real world
- *Feelings of exhilaration.* To increase one's self-confidence, usually by reducing one's inhibitions

Of course, these reasons don't apply to all teenagers. Some never drink. Others experiment briefly with drinking, then decide it is not for them. Still others, however, drink heavily: Nearly one-third of high school seniors report having had five or more drinks within the previous two weeks (Johnston et al., 1993).

Adolescents often drink because of encouragement from their peers.

What determines whether an adolescent joins the majority who drink? Not surprisingly, peers are influential: Many adolescents drink because their peers do so and exert pressure on them to join the group (Dielman et al., 1992). The family is also instrumental in determining adolescents' drinking. When family problems are frequent, teenagers often drink to reduce stress (Rhodes & Jason, 1990). Also, when drinking is an important part of parents' social lives—for example, stopping at a bar after work or inviting friends over for a drink—adolescents apparently learn that drinking is a pleasant activity and are more likely themselves to drink. In contrast, when parents limit their drinking to small quantities of alcohol to complement meals, their adolescent children are less likely to drink (Kline, Canter, & Robin, 1987).

Another contributing factor is adolescents' misunderstanding of the impact of alcohol on behavior. Many teenage drinkers believe that alcohol actually improves their intellectual, motor, and sexual prowess, when the truth is that the effects are just the opposite (Christiansen & Goldman, 1983).

Finally, heredity also contributes. Tolerance for alcohol is at least partially inherited. Many individuals of Asian descent, for example, feel nauseated after drinking small amounts of alcohol, which may explain why alcoholism is relatively rare among Asian Americans. Other individuals evidently find it easy to drink because they inherit the ability to consume large quantities of alcohol before they experience some of the unpleasant side effects (Schucket, 1987).

Because teenage drinking has so many causes, no single approach is likely to eliminate alcohol abuse. Adolescents who drink to reduce their tension can profit from therapy designed to teach them more effective means of coping with stress. School-based programs that feature student-led discussion can be effective in teaching the facts about drinking and strategies for resisting peer pressure to drink (Baker, 1988).

Depression

Sometime in your life, you have probably had the blues—days when you had little energy or enthusiasm for activities that you usually enjoy. You wanted to be alone, and you may have doubted your abilities. These feelings are perfectly normal, can usually be explained as reactions to specific events, and vanish in a matter of hours or days. For example, after an exciting vacation with family and friends, you may be depressed at the thought of returning to school to start new and difficult courses. Yet your mood improves as you renew friendships and become involved in activities on campus.

Now imagine experiencing these same symptoms continuously for weeks or months. Also suppose that you lost your appetite, slept poorly, and were unable to concentrate. **Pervasive feelings of sadness, irritability, and low self-esteem characterize an individual with** *depression.* About 3–10% of adolescents are depressed; adolescent girls are more often affected than boys (Nolen-Hoeksema & Girgus, 1994).

Research reveals that unhappiness, anger, and irritation often dominate the lives of depressed adolescents. They believe that family members, friends, and classmates are not friendly to them. Depressed adolescents wish to be left alone much more often than do nondepressed adolescents (Larson et al., 1990). Rather than being satisfying and rewarding, life is empty and joyless for depressed adolescents.

For some adolescents, depression is triggered by a life event that results in fewer positive reinforcements. The loss of a friend, for example, would deprive a teenager of many rewarding experiences and interactions, making the teen feel sad. Feeling lethargic and melancholy, the adolescent withdraws from social interaction and thereby misses further opportunities for rewarding experiences. This situation can degenerate rapidly into a vicious circle in which the depressed adolescent becomes progressively more depressed and more likely to avoid interactions that might be rewarding (Lewinsohn, 1974).

Depression often begins with a situation in which an adolescent feels helpless to control the outcome. Think back to Jalen, the adolescent in the last vignette at the beginning of the chapter. His life circumstances changed dramatically due to the unexpected death of his father. Similarly, a teen romance may end because a family moves to a distant city; a junior high athlete may play poorly in the championship game because of illness; or, a high school senior may get a lower score on the SAT exam due to a family crisis the night before taking the test. In each case, the adolescent could do nothing to avoid an undesirable result. Most teens recognize that such feelings of helplessness are specific to the particular situation. **In** *learned helplessness,* **however, adolescents and adults generalize these feelings of helplessness and believe that they are always at the mercy of external events, with no ability to control their own destinies.** Such feelings of learned helplessness often give rise to depression (Seligman, 1989).

Experiences like these do not lead all adolescents to become depressed. Some adolescents seem more vulnerable to depression than others, which has led scientists to look for biological factors. Studies of twins and adopted children indicate that heredity definitely has a part in depression. The exact biochemical mechanism seems to involve neurotransmitters (McNeal & Cimbolic, 1986). **Some depressed adolescents have reduced levels of** *norepinephrine,* **a neurotransmitter that helps to regulate arousal.**

TREATING DEPRESSION

It is essential to treat depression; otherwise, depressed adolescents are prone to more serious problems (including suicide, which is examined in the You May

Adolescents may become depressed when they feel that they cannot control events around them.

Be Wondering feature). Two general approaches are commonly used in treating depression (Kazdin, 1990). One is to administer antidepressant drugs designed to correct the imbalance in neurotransmitters; the other is psychotherapy. The aims of therapy vary, but typically adolescents learn to develop social skills—so that they can have rewarding social interactions—and to restructure their interpretation of events—so that they can recognize situations where they can exert control over their lives.

YOU MAY BE WONDERING

Preventing Teen Suicides

Suicide is the third most frequent cause of death (after accidents and homicide) among U.S. adolescents (National Center for Health Statistics, 1993). Roughly 10 adolescents in 100 report having attempted suicide at least once, but only 1 in 10,000 actually commits suicide. Suicide is more common among boys than girls and more common among European American adolescents than among African American adolescents. However, Native American adolescents have the highest rate of suicide of any ethnic group in the United States (Garland & Zigler, 1993).

Depression is one frequent precursor of suicide; substance abuse is another (Rich, Sherman, & Fowler, 1990). Few suicides are truly spontaneous; in most cases, there are warning signals (Atwater, 1992). Here are some common signs:

- Threats of suicide
- Preoccupation with death
- Change in eating or sleeping habits
- Loss of interest in activities that were once important
- Marked changes in personality
- Persistent feelings of gloom and helplessness
- Giving away valued possessions

If someone you know shows these signs, *don't ignore them,* hoping that they aren't for real. Instead, ask the person if he or she is planning on hurting himself or herself. Be calm and supportive and, if the person appears to have made preparations to commit suicide, don't leave him or her alone. Stay with the person until other friends or relatives can come. More important: *Insist* that the adolescent seek professional help. Therapy is essential to treat the feelings of depression and hopelessness that give rise to thoughts of suicide (Garland & Zigler, 1993).   ❧

Delinquency

Skipping school. Shoplifting. Selling cocaine. Murder. **When adolescents commit acts like these, which are illegal as well as destructive toward themselves or others, this represents *juvenile delinquency*.** Because delinquency applies to such a broad range of activities, it is useful to identify different forms of delinquent behavior. ***Status offenses* are acts that are not crimes if committed by an adult, such as truancy, sexual promiscuity, and running away from home.** (An adult is someone older than 16, 17, 18, or 19, depending on the state.) ***Index offenses* are acts such as robbery, rape, and arson, which are crimes regardless of the age of the perpetrator.**

Adolescents are responsible for many of the index offenses committed in the United States. The graph, based on information presented in the FBI's *Uniform Crime Reports* (1992), shows the percentage of cases of motor vehicle

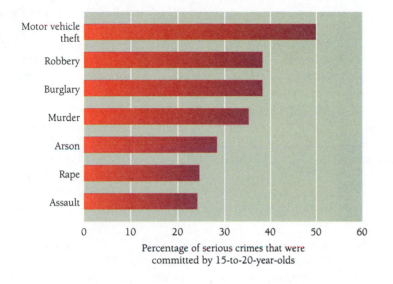

Percentage of serious crimes that were
committed by 15-to-20-year-olds

theft, burglary, robbery, murder, arson, rape, and assault that were committed by 15-to-20-year-olds. Adolescents are responsible for nearly half of the cars stolen in the United States and for more than one-fourth of the murders. Of course, most of this mayhem can be linked to the acts of a few: Less than 5% of American adolescents are arrested for serious crimes (Dryfoos, 1990).

Violent crimes committed by teens have increased in the 1990s, in part because of the growth of teen gangs. For most adolescents, membership in a gang is fleeting. In one study of adolescent gangs over a two-year period, fewer than 25% of the adolescents in the sample belonged to a gang throughout. However, while they *are* gang members, these adolescents are much more likely to become involved in criminal activity and drug use than are delinquent youth who do not belong to gangs (Thornberry et al., 1993).

CAUSES OF DELINQUENCY

In the 1957 musical *West Side Story*, members of the Jets gang explain to a policeman why they are delinquent:

Dear kindly Sergeant Krupke,
You gotta understand.
It's just our bringing upkee,
That gets us out of hand.

Although the Jets seem incredibly old-fashioned (almost quaint) by the standards of today's teenage gangs, they correctly recognize the developmental roots of delinquency and gangs. Today, psychologists and sociologists have identified several developmental forces that contribute to delinquency. Many of these combine to make youth particularly vulnerable to delinquency.

1. *Social class*. Adolescent crime occurs in all social strata but is more frequent among adolescents from lower social classes. This relationship may reflect a number of factors. First, crime is more common in lower-class neigh-

borhoods, so adult criminal models are readily available to children. Second, lower-class adolescents often experience little success in school and usually have little invested in the outcome of their academic efforts; criminal activity is an arena in which they can excel and gain the recognition of their peers. According to Katie Buckland, a prosecutor in Los Angeles, youth who join gangs are "the ambitious kids . . . trying to climb up their own corporate ladder. And the only corporate ladder they see has to do with gangs and drugs" (Kantrowitz, 1993, p. 44). Third, the constant stress of life on the brink of economic disaster can reduce the effectiveness of parenting in lower-class homes (Patterson, DeVaryshe, & Ramsey, 1989).

2. *Family processes.* Delinquent behavior is often related to inadequate parental supervision. Adolescents who are unsupervised (because, for example, their parents are at work) are much more likely to become involved in delinquent acts (Patterson et al., 1989). Parents may also contribute to delinquent behavior if their discipline is inconsistent and if their marital relationship is marked by constant conflict. When family life is riddled with arguments, threats, and the like, the gang represents an appealing makeshift family for some adolescents.

3. *Self-control.* As most children develop, they become more capable of regulating their own behavior. They become better able to inhibit impulsive tendencies, to delay gratification, and to consider the impact of their behavior on others (Rotenberg & Mayer, 1990). That is, they learn to rise above the immediate pressures of a situation, to avoid giving in to impulses, and to think about the consequences of their actions. Delinquent youth do not follow the usual developmental pattern. Instead, they are much more inclined to act impulsively, and they often are unable or unwilling to postpone pleasure (Rutter & Giller, 1984). Seeing a fancy new CD player or a car, delinquent youth are tempted to steal it, simply so that they can have it *right now.* When others inadvertently get in their way, delinquent adolescents often respond without regard to the nature of the other person's acts or intentions.

TREATMENT AND PREVENTION

Given the wide-ranging causes of delinquency, it would be naive to expect a single or simple cure. Instead, delinquency must be attacked along several fronts simultaneously:

- Delinquent adolescents can be taught effective techniques for self-control.
- Parents of delinquent youth can be taught the importance of supervising and monitoring their children's behavior and the necessity for consistent discipline.
- Families of delinquents can learn to function more effectively as a unit, with special emphasis on better means of resolving conflict.
- Schools can develop programs that motivate delinquent youth to become invested in their school performance.
- Communities can improve economic conditions in neighborhoods where delinquency reigns.

Programs that include many of these strategies have met with success; adolescents who participate are less likely to be arrested again. The programs thereby address a major problem affecting not only adolescent development but all of North American society (Alexander et al., 1989; Dryfoos, 1990). The Spotlight on Research feature illustrates one such approach.

Teaching Social Skills to Aggressive Adolescents

One of the characteristics of delinquent adolescents is that they often interpret others' actions as reflecting aggression. In addition, delinquent adolescents often do not know how to resolve conflicts nonviolently (Slaby & Guerra, 1988). Consequently, many programs to help delinquent adolescents include training in social skills. A study by Guerra and Slaby (1990) illustrates the features of this approach. In this study, 120 adolescents who were incarcerated for having committed violent acts were randomly assigned to one of three groups. The 40 adolescents assigned to a training condition attended 12 one-hour sessions, in which they were taught ways of dealing with social problems more effectively. Over the course of training, adolescents were taught a model of social problem solving that included the following elements:

> (a) Is there a problem? (b) stop and think, (c) why is there a conflict? (d) what do I want? (e) think of solutions, (f) look at consequences, (g) choose what to do and do it, and (h) evaluate the results. (Guerra & Slaby, 1990, p. 272)

Thus, training emphasized identifying the specific nature of the problem, not simply assuming that others were acting in a hostile manner, as well as thinking of alternatives to aggression as a means of resolving real conflicts. For example, they were taught to pay attention to cues that would signal that a person's intent is not aggressive or violent and to think of nonviolent ways of responding in social interactions.

The remaining adolescents were assigned to one of two control groups. In one, adolescents simply participated in testing but received no training. In the other, adolescents attended 12 one-hour sessions designed to improve academic skills (like reading and math) but not social skills. This group was included to control for the possibility that mere repeated contact with and attention from an interested adult might improve adolescents' social skills.

Guerra and Slaby (1990) evaluated the effectiveness of training in several ways: (1) by examining adolescents' ability to solve hypothetical social problems before and after training, (2) by examining adolescents' attitudes toward aggression, and (3) by examining supervisors' ratings of adolescents' behavior. By all three measures, adolescents in the training condition improved compared to those in the two control conditions. After training, adolescents were able to solve hypothetical social problems more effectively, were less likely to endorse aggression as a means of solving interpersonal conflict, and were rated by their supervisors as being less aggressive, less impulsive, and more flexible in their social interactions.

Thus, it is possible to teach social skills to delinquent adolescents, and their behavior improves as a result. Of course, alone, this will not "cure" juvenile delinquency, but social-skill training is emerging as one essential element of an overall solution to the problem of delinquency.   ❧

TEST YOURSELF

1. The reasons that teenagers drink include relaxation, escape, a desire for feelings of exhilaration, and _____.
2. Teens are less likely to drink when their parents drink _____.
3. Depression has been linked to life events that produce fewer positive reinforcements, situations in which teenagers feel helpless, and _____.
4. Treatments for depression include drugs that correct imbalances in neurotransmitters and therapy that emphasizes _____.

5. Acts like truancy and running away from home, which are not crimes when committed by adults, are known as _____.

6. The factors that contribute to juvenile delinquency include social class, _____, and inadequate self-control.

7. Are the causes of teenage drinking, depression, and delinquency much the same, or is each problem of adolescent development caused by a unique set of factors?

Putting It All Together

In the voyage from the land of childhood to the land of adulthood, the choppy waters of adolescence must be navigated. Most teens do complete the journey successfully, becoming adults who will someday watch their own children make the same trip. As one writer noted:

> It is easy to forget that a personality unfurling itself can be glorious as well as inconvenient. No doubt Jesus was considered a pain by his elders, as was Gandhi. The young need to check out their wingspreads, and adults need to be adult enough to withstand the onslaught of beautiful hair, terrible noise and challenge to every sensible norm. . . . (Pacy, 1993, p. 35)

The spreading of wings that characterizes adolescence was evident in all its splendor in the five sections of this chapter.

We began with the physical changes associated with puberty. These outward signs of looming adulthood are often confusing and can cause some adolescents, like Linda in the first chapter-opening vignette, to become overly concerned with their weight.

Next, we looked at the struggle to achieve an identity. Adolescents and young adults often experiment with different roles in their efforts to realize an identity. When parents support this experimentation, the search for identity is more likely to succeed. For example, Dea, the teen in the second vignette, realized that she was uniquely blessed with roots in three different cultures; she came to love elements of each and forge a novel Dutch-Asian-American identity.

Our next stop was the world of work. Aaron's experiences in part-time work, described in the third chapter-opening vignette, are typical. Adolescents rarely balance school and heavy part-time work effectively. We also saw that selecting a career involves matching interests and aptitudes with specific occupations, then determining the skills and education needed for the chosen line of work.

From work we moved to romance and sex. Interest in sex mounts in the teenage years, and many adolescents become sexually active. Like Jenny, the 15-year-old in the fourth vignette, many teenagers have unprotected sex, which can lead to pregnancy and sexually transmitted diseases.

We ended the chapter by looking at the dark side of adolescence. Some young people do not handle adolescent difficulties well, leading to drugs, depression (like Jalen, the basketball player in the fifth vignette), and delinquency.

Thinking about Development

1. Describe how obesity and anorexia nervosa exemplify nonnormative influences on development, as defined in Chapter 1. Can you make a case that anorexia also illustrates a history-graded influence?

2. Although Piaget's theory was not concerned with identity formation, how might his theory explain why identity is a central issue during adolescence?

3. Suppose you have been hired by your state government to help officials formulate laws that would regulate part-time work for juveniles. What recommendations would you make?

4. According to the "storm and stress" view of adolescence, sexual behavior would be one way for adolescents to rebel against their parents. Does research on adolescent sexuality support this prediction?

5. Explain how depression illustrates the interaction of biological, psychological, and sociocultural forces on development.

Answers: (1) *experimentation,* (2) *in small amounts, to complement meals,* (3) *an imbalance in neurotransmitters,* (4) *the development of social skills,* (5) *status offenses,* (6) *disrupted family processes*

Summary

Farewell to Childhood: Puberty

Physical Growth

■ Puberty consists of a series of bodily changes occurring in early adolescence, including a period of rapid growth. Today, children enter puberty earlier and are bigger at maturity than in previous generations.

■ Early maturation tends to be beneficial to boys, apparently because others perceive them to be more mature and are more likely to treat them as adults. Early maturation is sometimes harmful to girls, both in terms of their success in school and their interactions with other boys and girls.

Eating Disorders

■ Many obese children and adolescents are unpopular, have low self-esteem, and are at risk for medical disorders. Obesity reflects both heredity and acquired eating habits. The most effective programs for treating obesity in adolescents are those in which children and their parents set eating and exercise goals, and both are rewarded for their performance.

■ Anorexia nervosa is a disorder that typically affects adolescent girls. It is characterized by an irrational fear of being overweight. Several factors contribute to anorexia, including cultural standards for thinness, a need for independence within autocratic families, and heredity.

Who Am I?—The Search for Identity

Identity versus Role Confusion

■ Erikson claimed that the crisis of adolescence is to achieve an identity. Experimentation with different possible selves is an integral part of the quest for identity.

Resolving the Identity Crisis

■ Associated with the search for identity are four statuses: Diffusion and foreclosure are more common in early adolescence; moratorium and achievement tend to emerge in late adolescence and young adulthood.

■ Authoritative parenting is most conducive to the achievement of identity. Authoritarian parenting is associated with foreclosure, whereas indulgent-permissive parenting is associated with diffusion.

Ethnic Identity

■ Adolescents from ethnic groups often progress through three phases in acquiring an ethnic identity: ini-

tial disinterest, exploration, and identity achievement. Achieving an ethnic identity usually results in higher self-esteem. It is more likely with authoritative parents, and it is not consistently related to the strength of the child's identification with mainstream culture.

The Myth of Storm and Stress

■ Contrary to myth, adolescence is not usually a period of storm and stress. Most adolescents love their parents, rely on them for advice, and adopt their values. The parent–child relationship becomes more egalitarian during the adolescent years, reflecting adolescents' growing independence.

Flipping Burgers and Waiting Tables: Entering the World of Work

Part-Time Work

■ Most adolescents in the United States have part-time jobs. This phenomenon, which gathered steam in the 1980s, is unique to the United States. Adolescents who are employed more than 15 hours per week during the school year typically do poorly in school, often have lowered self-esteem and increased anxiety, and have problems interacting with others. Employed adolescents save relatively little of their income. Instead, they spend most of it on themselves, which can give them misleading expectations about how to allocate income.

■ Part-time employment can be beneficial if adolescents work relatively few hours and if the work allows them to use existing skills or to acquire new ones. Summer employment, because it does not conflict with the demands of school, can also be beneficial.

Career Development

■ Super's theory of vocational choice proposes that an adolescent's identity and career aspirations develop in parallel. He proposes three phases of vocational development during adolescence and young adulthood: crystallization, in which basic interests are identified; specification, in which jobs associated with interests are identified; and implementation, which marks entry into the work force.

■ Holland proposed six different work-related personality types: realistic, investigative, social, conventional, enterprising, and artistic. Each is uniquely suited to certain jobs. People are happy when their personality fits their job and unhappy when it does not.

"How Do I Love Thee?": Romantic Relationships

Dating

■ Boys and girls begin to date in early adolescence. Dating often begins with the meeting of same-sex groups and progresses to well-defined couples. For high school students, dating is recreation; for college students, it is a source of intimacy and companionship, as well as a means to learn adult standards of behavior.

■ Adolescents often wonder about their sexual orientation, but only a small percentage report engaging in homosexual experiences. Research has discredited many explanations of the origins of a homosexual orientation. Current theorizing emphasizes the contributions of biology.

Awakening of Sexual Interests

■ By age 18, most North American adolescents have had sexual intercourse. Adolescents are more likely to be sexually active if they believe that their parents and peers approve of sex. Pregnancy and sexually transmitted diseases are two common consequences of adolescent sexual behavior, because sexually active adolescents use contraceptives infrequently.

■ Another common problem is that adolescent and young adult females are forced into sex against their will, typically because males misinterpret or disregard females' intentions. Sexual coercion is particularly likely when either partner has been drinking or when the couple has had sex previously. Date-rape workshops work to improve communication between males and females.

A Look at the Dark Side: Problems of Adolescent Development

Use of Drugs

■ Today, the only drug that many adolescents use regularly is alcohol. Adolescents are attracted to alcohol and other drugs by their need for experimentation, for relaxation, for escape, and for feelings of exhilaration.

■ The factors that influence whether adolescents drink are encouragement from parents and peers, ignorance concerning the effects of alcohol, and heredity.

Depression

■ Depressed adolescents have little enthusiasm for life, believe that others are unfriendly, and wish to be left alone. Depression can be triggered by an event that deprives them of rewarding experiences, by an event in which they felt unable to control their own destiny, or by an imbalance in neurotransmitters.

■ Treatment of depression relies on medications that correct the levels of neurotransmitters and therapy designed to improve social skills and restructure adolescents' interpretation of events.

Delinquency

■ A relatively small percentage of adolescents are involved in one-fourth to one-half of the serious crimes committed in the United States. Adolescent criminal activity has been linked to social class, family processes, and lack of self-control. Efforts to reduce adolescent criminal activity must take aim at all of these variables.

Key Terms

achievement status   (261)
adolescent egocentrism   (260)
anorexia nervosa   (257)
basal metabolic rate   (255)
crystallization   (268)
date (acquaintance) rape   (277)
depression   (281)
diffusion status   (261)

foreclosure status   (261)
imaginary audience   (260)
implementation   (268)
index offense   (282)
juvenile delinquency   (281)
learned helplessness   (281)
menarche   (253)
moratorium status   (261)

norepinephrine   (281)
personal fable   (260)
personality-type theory   (269)
puberty   (253)
secular growth trends   (253)
specification   (268)
status offense   (282)

If You'd Like to Learn More

BANCROFT, J., & REINISCH, J. M. (Eds.). (1990). *Adolescence and puberty.* New York: Oxford University Press. An excellent collection of articles that cover all of the issues relating to adolescent sexual behavior.

DRYFOOS, J. G. (1990). *Adolescents at risk: Prevalence and prevention.* New York: Oxford University Press. This author describes some of the most effective ways of approaching common adolescent problems.

GREENBERGER, E., & STEINBERG, L. (1986). *When teenagers work: The psychological and social costs of adolescent employment.* New York: Basic Books. Two of the leading researchers on the impact of adolescent employment describe their own findings as well as others' results.

HARTER, S. (1990). Self and identity development. In S. S. Feldman & G. R. Elliott (Eds.), *At the threshold: The developing adolescent.* Cambridge, MA: Harvard University Press. This chapter provides an excellent overview of identity achievement during adolescence, written by a leading researcher.

HOLLAND, J. L. (1985). *Making vocational choices: A theory of vocational personalities and work environments* (2nd. ed.). Englewood Cliffs, NJ: Prentice-Hall. In this book, Holland provides a comprehensive account of his theory of work-related personality types.

PHINNEY, J. S., & ROTHERAM, M. J. (Eds.). (1987). *Children's ethnic socialization: Pluralism and development.* Newbury Park, CA: Sage. This collection of papers is an ideal place to start reading about modern research on ethnic identity.

STEINBERG, L. D., & LEVINE, A. (1990). *You and your adolescent.* New York: Harper Perennial. This outstanding book has a number of useful guidelines helping parents to know when their teenager has a problem that may require professional help.

TANNER, J. M. (1978). *Fetus into man.* Cambridge, MA: Harvard University Press. We recommended this book in Chapter 3 because of its description of early physical growth. It also has a good account of physical changes associated with puberty.

Early and Middle Adulthood

❧ Marcus woke up with the worst headache he ever remembered having in his life. "If this is what adulthood is like, they can keep it," he muttered to himself. Like many young adults in the United States, Marcus had spent his 21st birthday celebrating at a nightclub. But the phone call from his mother that woke him in the first place reminded him that he wasn't an adult in every way; she had called to see if he needed any money.

❧ Juan is a 25-year-old who started smoking cigarettes in high school, to be part of the "in crowd." Juan has decided he would like to quit, but he's worried that quitting smoking will be too difficult. He has also heard that it doesn't really matter if he quits or not, because his health will never recover. Juan wonders if it will be worthwhile to quit.

❧ Mary Ann is an energetic 22-year-old who just graduated from college and plans to begin a doctoral program in biology in the fall. During a recent get-together, some high school friends she hadn't seen in a couple years remarked that Mary Ann had changed a lot. She used to be quick to make a decision, but now she ponders many different viewpoints before making up her mind. Things just don't seem as clear-cut to her as they used to.

❧ Manuel, 33 years old, is manager of the men's department at a major store in a large shopping mall. He recently discovered that one of his employees was taking money from the cash register. The employee told Manuel that the money was needed to pay for medical bills for a child who was very ill. He pleaded with Manuel not to disclose what was going on, arguing that the company had so much money that the amount that was taken would not be missed. Manuel wondered what he should do.

❧ Felicia is a 19-year-old sophomore at a community college. She expects her study of early childhood education to be difficult but rewarding. She figures that along the way she will meet a great guy, whom she will marry soon after graduation. They will have two children before she turns 30. Felicia sees herself getting a good job teaching preschool children and some day owning her own day care center.

Becoming
an Adult

 There comes a time in life when you stop feeling like a child and want to be an adult. In some societies, the transition to adulthood is abrupt and dramatic, marked by clear rites of passage. In Western society, it is fuzzier; the only apparent marker may be a birthday ritual like the one Marcus experienced. We may even ask adults what it's like to be one. We'll explore different answers as we go.

Without question, young adulthood is the peak of physical processes and health. It is also a time when people like Juan, who acquired unhealthy habits earlier in life, may decide to adopt a better lifestyle. Young adulthood also marks the peak of some cognitive abilities, and the continued development of others. The changes that Mary Ann's friends observed reflect the continued growth of thinking.

On a more personal level, young adulthood is a time of making plans and dreaming of what lies ahead. Felicia's ideas of what her future holds reflect a desire to see herself as a productive and successful adult. This brings us to the lead-off question in the chapter.

When Does Adulthood Begin?

LEARNING OBJECTIVES

❧ *What role transitions have been used to mark entry into adulthood in Western societies? How do non-Western cultures mark the transition to adulthood?*

❧ *How does going to college fit in the transition to adulthood?*

❧ *What psychological criteria mark the transition to adulthood?*

Take a moment to try the following exercise. Think for a minute about the first time you felt like an adult. When was it? What was the context? Who were you with? How did you feel? Now think about yourself between the ages of 18 and 22. Is this the period when the transition to adulthood is completed? Why or why not?

Even though it is arguably one of the most important life transitions that we ever experience, it is difficult to pin down exactly when we cross the boundary from adolescence or youth to adulthood in Western industrialized societies. Celebrations marking the achievement of a certain age, like the one in the photograph, are helpful but do not signal a clean break with youth and full accep-

tance as an adult. Certainly, Marcus, the 21-year-old in the first vignette, may feel like an adult with regard to purchasing alcohol legally, but he may not feel that way in other respects, such as supporting himself financially.

In this section, we will examine some of the ways in which societies mark the transition to adulthood. We will see that the criteria vary widely from culture to culture, as well as within a single culture.

Role Transitions As a General Framework

One cool spring evening, a group of former high school classmates got together to catch up on what had been going on in their lives lately. It was getting late, and all but three of the group had gone. Gradually, the conversation turned to the topic of growing up and becoming adults, as each of them would be turning 21 in the next few months. Joyce looked older than her 20 years. Her 5-year-old son was playing quietly on the floor. Next to Joyce sat Sheree, an art major. She wore extremely cool clothes, purchased at the store where she works part-time. The third young woman, Marcia, looked a bit tired from her long day as an intern at Arthur Andersen, one of the Big Six accounting firms. Joyce spoke first. "I had Jimmy when I was 15. I thought it would make me grown up and give me someone who would love me. But it gave me grownup bills and no job. I still can't afford my own place, so I live with my mom."

Sheree declared, "It's like, sure I'm an adult. I can do whatever I want, whenever I want. It's like, I don't have to answer to anybody, OK?" Marcia had a different view: "As for me, I don't think I'll *really* be an adult until I complete my education, can support myself, and get married."

Are these young people adults? Yes and no. As we will see, it depends on how you define adulthood.

ROLE TRANSITIONS IN WESTERN SOCIETIES

The most widely used criteria for deciding whether a person has reached adulthood are *role transitions,* which involve assuming new responsibilities and duties. Social scientists have noted that several role transitions serve as markers of attaining adulthood: completing education, beginning full-time employment, establishing an independent household, marriage, and becoming a parent (Hogan & Astone, 1986).

Interestingly, the age at which people tend to experience these marker events varies over time. For example, during the 20th century, the average age for completing school rose steadily, as the proportion of people going to college increased from roughly 10% in the early part of the century to over 50% today. On the other hand, the average age of first marriage and parenthood dropped steadily from 1900 to around 1960, before rising sharply from 1960 to the late 1980s (Modell, 1989). Such complexities make it difficult to use any one event as the marker of becoming an adult. Like the three women we encountered at the beginning of this section, people can experience some marker events but not others, further complicating the issue.

Although people tend to celebrate the marker events associated with role transitions (for example, giving baby showers or graduation parties), the connection between these events and attaining adulthood is unclear in Western industrialized societies. Such is not the case in all cultures, however.

CROSS-CULTURAL EVIDENCE OF ROLE TRANSITIONS

In contrast to Western societies, other cultures tend to be clearer about when a person becomes an adult. Anthropological studies indicate that most non-

In most non-Western cultures, getting married is the major role transition that marks the point when a person becomes an adult. The couple being married will most likely be viewed by their society as adults once the ceremony is over.

Western cultures consider marriage to be the most important determinant of adult status (Schlegel & Barry, 1991).

Many non-Western cultures also have a well-defined set of requirements that boys must meet in order to become men (Gilmore, 1990). Around the world, these requirements tend to focus on three key features: In order to be a man, it is necessary to prove that one can provide, protect, and impregnate.

Young men must demonstrate that they can provide for their future family by becoming capable of adult work, such as hunting. They must show that they can protect a family and their village by being physically fit to engage in warfare if necessary. To do so, they typically undergo initiation rituals in which they are subjected to tests of physical endurance, such as long marches with little to eat or drink. Finally, they must also show that they are capable of impregnating a future wife. This may be done through premarital sexual encounters or, in some cultures, by fathering children prior to marriage.

In contrast to the requirements for boys to be regarded as men, most cultures do not have tests of accomplishment for girls to become women (Gilmore, 1990). Instead, most cultures rely on menarche as the primary, and usually the only, marker. The onset of menstruation is thus viewed as an indicator that a girl has become a woman and is now capable of having children.

Rituals marking initiation into adulthood, often among the most important ones in a culture, are termed *rites of passage*. Since about 1900, researchers have described rites of passage as including three phases (van Gennep, 1909): physical separation from the main group of residents, the temporary granting of a transition status, and reincorporation into the group as a person having a new status. These phases may involve highly elaborate steps that take days or weeks, or they may be compressed into a few minutes. Initiates are usually dressed in apparel reserved for the ritual, to denote their special position. (This is true in many Western transitions as well; consider the ritual attire for graduations or weddings, for example.) Rituals may also include the use of mind-altering drugs or other trance-inducing behaviors (such as sleep deprivation, drumming, dancing, and pain). In general, these rites are much different than those experienced by Western young adults.

Rites of passage in non-Western societies also provide an important role for older adults: serving as the ritual leader or guide through the transition (Keith, 1990). Because rituals change little over the years, they provide continuity through the life span. Older adults lead young people through the same rituals they themselves experienced years earlier. A Western counterpart is the family holiday tradition, such as a New Year's dinner, in which certain foods are prepared and customs observed. Through rituals, cultures the world over maintain contact and social continuity across the generations.

JENNIE KEITH
"Kinship, reproduction, and domestic living arrangements [are] sources of significant thresholds in the life course everywhere."

Going to College

One of the most common rites of passage to adulthood in the United States is completing one's education. For more than half of the people 18–22 years of age, this means going to college (National Center for Educational Statistics, 1993). Colleges themselves vary considerably, from two-year community colleges and technical schools to large research universities with extensive graduate programs. Therefore, it is difficult to generalize about the college experience as a whole. For many students, however, going to college right after high school serves as a catalyst for intellectual and personal growth (Kitchener & King, 1989; Perry, 1970). We will examine some of these changes later in this chapter (pages 315–319).

Historically, the majority of college students were between the ages of 18 and 25. However, the face of college campuses is changing rapidly, as you can probably tell by looking around your own. By the year 2000, projections indicate that more than half of all college students will be over 25, and a significant portion will be over 35 (National Center for Educational Statistics, 1991). Additionally, an increasing number of students interrupt their college careers to pursue other personal interests for a while; many return after one or more years of being out of school.

Some people define the transition to adulthood as the point at which one's education is complete. But for people like this returning adult student, this criterion may not apply. This problem illustrates the complexity of defining exactly when adulthood begins.

Colleges usually refer to students over 25 as *returning adult students*, which implies that these individuals have already reached adulthood. Overall, returning adult students tend to be problem solvers, self-directed, and pragmatic, and to have relevant life experiences that they can integrate with their coursework (Harringer, 1994). Compared to younger college students, returning adult students are more highly motivated, more involved in studying and learning, more likely to use critical thinking in their learning, and more likely to interact with faculty (Ross, 1989). Why these differences exist is related to the kinds of changes in thinking that occur in adulthood, which we will explore in detail a bit later in this chapter (pages 309–319).

With the prospect that most U.S. college students will be over 25 in the near future, completing one's education may no longer be a useful marker of adulthood. In fact, the reverse may become the norm: A mark of adulthood may be the realization that one's education is not yet complete. Many returning adult students go to college either because they did not have the opportunity when they were younger or because changes in their job responsibilities require additional education.

One sizable group of North Americans who are going to college in increasing numbers are people with disabilities. With the enactment of the Americans with Disabilities Act in 1990, colleges and universities became accessible for these adults, and supportive services were created on campus. In part, these services serve an educational function, to correct misinformation and stereotypes about people with disabilities. For example, people with learning disabilities have long faced barriers in college and in the workplace (Rusch, Szymanski, & Chadsey-Rusch, 1992). These issues and programs designed to address them are discussed in more detail in the You May Be Wondering feature.

Individuals with Learning Disabilities and the Transition to College

Since the passage of the Rehabilitation Act of 1973, which mandated that educational programs be provided to people with disabilities, increasing numbers of U.S. students who have learning disabilities and behavior disorders have been taking advantage of the opportunity to go to college. Indeed, the number of college students with learning disabilities has increased tenfold since the late

**YOU MAY
BE WONDERING**

1970s (McGuire, Norlander, & Shaw, 1990). These opportunities help these people make the transition to adulthood.

Numerous programs have been established at two- and four-year colleges to assist students with learning disabilities (Bursuck & Rose, 1992; Gajar, 1992). These programs range from providing training and outreach services to making course materials available in alternative formats. In all cases, the goals of support programs are to help students succeed in college to the best of their abilities and deal with their subsequent transition to the world of work.

One common step for many students with learning disabilities is to enroll in a community college after high school (Bursuck & Rose, 1992). Siperstein (1988) developed a three-step model that describes the transition process. The first stage, entry into college, involves background preparation for the transition to college, through guidance counseling in high school and orientation programs in college. The second stage, management of academic and social changes during college, involves carefully selecting the most appropriate course of study and helping students make connections with other students. Finally, the stage of exit from college and entry into employment requires comprehensive services to help students find jobs and help with survival skills (such as how to create a personal budget) when appropriate.

Providing support services in the academic environment appears to work; most students with learning disabilities have successful experiences in college (Bursuck & Rose, 1992; Gajar, 1992). Support services that provide help with other parts of the transition to adulthood (such as becoming financially independent) also increase the likelihood of success.   ⚜

Psychological Views on Becoming an Adult

From a psychological perspective, becoming an adult means interacting with the world in a fundamentally different way. In general, psychological research has focused on how adults think differently, how their psychosocial issues change, and how the frequency of reckless behavior decreases.

In the cognitive domain, young adulthood is a time for applying knowledge and skills acquired in adolescence, most often through work (Schaie, 1977). As we will see later in this chapter, other researchers have described additional differences between adolescents' and adults' cognition, related to the transition from formal operational thinking to postformal thought.

Behaviorally, a major difference between adolescence and adulthood is a significant drop in the frequency of reckless behavior such as driving at high speed, having sex without contraception, or committing antisocial acts like vandalism (Arnett & Taber, 1994). From this perspective, people who have become adults maintain a higher degree of self-control and compliance with social conventions (Hart, 1992).

On the psychosocial front, young adulthood marks the transition from concern with identity (considered in Chapter 8) to concern with autonomy and intimacy, which we will explore here and in Chapter 10 (Erikson, 1982). Becoming independent from one's parents entails being able to fend for oneself, but it does not imply a complete severing of the relationship. On the contrary, adult children usually establish a rewarding relationship with their parents, as we will see in Chapter 12.

ESTABLISHING INTIMACY

According to Erikson, the major task for young adults is dealing with the psychosocial conflict of *intimacy versus isolation.* This is the sixth step in

According to Schaie, applying knowledge and skills in a job setting reflects the primary task of young adulthood in the cognitive domain. Doing so helps distinguish adolescence and adulthood.

Erikson's theory of psychosocial development, the basic tenets of which are summarized in the table. Erikson believed that once a person's identity has been established, he or she is ready to create a shared identity with another, the key ingredient for intimacy (Erikson, 1982). Without a clear sense of identity, Erikson argued, a person would be afraid of entering into a committed long-term relationship or would be likely to become overdependent on the partner as a source of identity.

Perspective	Examples of Theories	Main Ideas	Emphases in Biopsychosocial Framework	Positions on Developmental Issues
Psychodynamic	Erikson's psycho-social theory	Personality develops through sequence of stages	Biological, social, and life-cycle forces crucial; less emphasis on psychological	Nature–nurture interaction, discontinuity, universal sequence but individual differences in rate

Several studies support this view (Matula et al., 1992). For example, Whitbourne and Tesch (1985) interviewed college seniors and 24-to-27-year-old alumni to ascertain their levels of identity formation and intimacy. Interestingly, the researchers found that identity formation continues into young adulthood; more alumni than seniors were classified as being in the moratorium or achievement stages of identity formation (see Chapter 8 for discussions of these levels). Additionally, more alumni than seniors had begun developing intimate relationships. Most important, those alumni who had well-formed identities were more likely than those who did not to be capable of true intimacy, which is exactly what Erikson predicted.

It looked as if Erikson's theory was strongly supported, but investigators began wondering whether the same patterns held for men and women. The results of this research are more complicated. Apparently, most men and career-oriented women resolve identity issues before intimacy issues (Dyk & Adams, 1990; Patterson, Sochting, & Marcia, 1992). These individuals complete their educations and make initial career choices before becoming involved in a committed relationship.

In contrast, some women resolve intimacy issues before identity issues. They marry and rear children, and only after their children have grown and moved away do they deal with the question of their own identity (Schiedel & Marcia, 1985; Whitbourne & Tesch, 1985). Still other women deal with both identity and intimacy issues simultaneously—for example, by entering into relationships that allow them to develop identities based on caring for others (Dyk & Adams, 1990).

Thus, this part of Erikson's theory is most applicable in the cases of men and career-oriented women. But many women find alternative ways of confronting and resolving the issues of identity and intimacy in young adulthood.

So When Do People Become Adults?

The perspectives considered in this section do not give any definitive answers to the question of when people become adults. All we can say is that the transition depends on culture and a number of psychological factors. In cultures without clearly defined rites of passage, defining oneself as an adult rests on one's perception of whether personally relevant key criteria have been met.

TEST YOURSELF

1. The most widely used criteria for deciding whether a person has reached adulthood are _____.
2. Rituals marking initiation into adulthood are called _____.
3. Students over 25 are referred to as _____.
4. In the cognitive domain, adulthood is a time for _____.
5. Behaviorally, a major difference between adolescence and adulthood is a significant drop in the frequency of _____.
6. Why are formal rites of passage important? What has Western society lost by eliminating them?

Physical Development and Health
    Growth, Strength, and Physical Functioning
    Health Status
    ■ *Guns and Violence As a Health Problem*
    Lifestyle Factors
    Social, Gender, and Ethnic Issues in Health
    ■ *Healthy Adulthood*

Physical Development and Health

LEARNING OBJECTIVES

❧ *In what respects are young adults at their physical peak?*

❧ *How healthy are young adults in general?*

❧ *How do smoking, drinking alcohol, and nutrition affect young adults' health?*

❧ *How does young adults' health differ as a function of socioeconomic status, gender, and ethnicity?*

Young adulthood is the peak of physical functioning. As the photograph suggests, most young adults (including weekend athletes) are in the best physical

shape of their lives. Indeed, the early 20s are the best years for strenuous work, trouble-free reproduction, and peak athletic performance. We will see that these achievements are indicative of a physical system that is at its peak. But we will also see that people's physical functioning is affected by several health-related behaviors.

Growth, Strength, and Physical Functioning

As young adults, people reach their maximum height (Tanner, 1978). Height remains stable through middle adulthood, declining somewhat in old age (as described in Chapter 13). Men's and women's bodies take on their full adult form as muscle and fat tissue increase, especially during the early 20s; men achieve their full shoulder and upper-arm size, and women achieve their full breast and hip size. Because of these changes, weight increases during the 20s, generally remaining at a plateau until middle age for reasons we will explore in Chapter 12.

Although men have more muscle mass and tend to be stronger than women, physical strength in both sexes peaks during the late 20s and early 30s, declining slowly throughout the rest of life (Whitbourne, 1985). Coordination and dexterity peak around the same time (Whitbourne, 1985). Because of these trends, few professional athletes remain at the top of their sport in their mid-30s. Indeed, individuals such as Joe Montana (an NFL quarterback who retired in his late 30s) and Nolan Ryan (a baseball pitcher who remained successful until his mid-40s) are famous partly because they were exceptions. Most sports superstars, like Shaquille O'Neal shown below, are in their 20s.

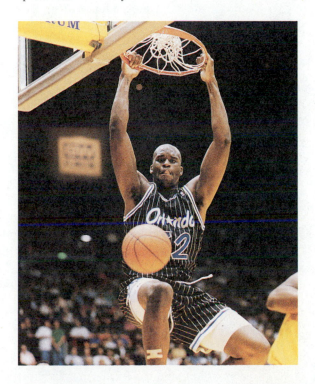

Sensory acuity also is at its peak in the early 20s (Whitbourne, 1985). Visual acuity remains high until middle age, when people tend to become far-sighted and require glasses for reading. Hearing begins to decline somewhat by the late 20s, especially for high-pitched tones. By old age, this hearing loss may affect the ability to understand speech. People's ability to smell, taste, feel pain and changes in temperature, and maintain balance largely remain unchanged until late life.

Health Status

How is your overall health? If you are a young adult, chances are better than 90% that you will say that your health is good or better (USDHHS, 1990). Relatively speaking, young adults get many fewer colds and respiratory infections than they did when they were children. Even when young adults get a cold, they are more likely to recover fairly easily. Childhood allergies have been outgrown or have gone into remission. Indeed, only about 1% of young adults are limited in their ability to function because of a health-related condition.

Because of the overall healthy status of American young adults, death from disease, especially during the early 20s, is relatively rare (U.S. Bureau of the Census, 1994). The death rate from disease and chronic conditions remains relatively low until late middle age. For example, even though cancer is the leading cause of death due to disease in young adults, the death rate is less than 1 person in 10,000. This compares with 16 per 10,000 in people 45–54, and 108 in people over age 65 (U.S. Bureau of the Census, 1994).

So what are the leading causes of death among young adults in the United States? In general, accidents (mostly automobile crashes) are the leading cause for people up to age 35, followed by cancer, cardiovascular disease, and murder (USDHHS, 1994). After age 35, disease becomes the major cause of death.

When we look more carefully at these statistics, though, we uncover important gender and ethnic differences (USDHHS, 1994). Young adult men are twice as likely to die as women of the same age; men are most likely to die in auto accidents and women from cancer. An important exception is that in some large U.S. cities (such as Philadelphia), AIDS is the leading killer of young adult males. African American young adults are more than twice as likely to die as their European American counterparts, and Hispanic Americans have more health problems than any other ethnic group, largely due to poverty and reduced access to health care (Otten et al., 1990).

As indicated earlier, murder is the fifth highest cause of death in young adults nationwide. But among African American men it is number one. As you can see in the graph, young U.S. men are murdered at a rate at least four times higher than in any other industrialized country (and over 70 times higher than in Austria!)

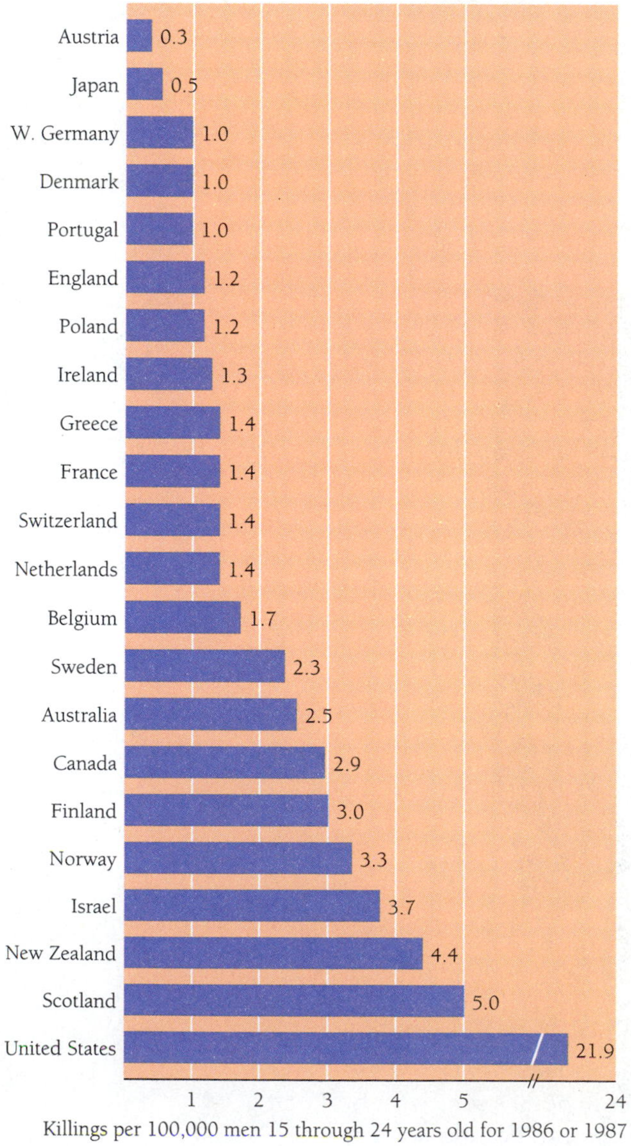

Austria   0.3
Japan   0.5
W. Germany   1.0
Denmark   1.0
Portugal   1.0
England   1.2
Poland   1.2
Ireland   1.3
Greece   1.4
France   1.4
Switzerland   1.4
Netherlands   1.4
Belgium   1.7
Sweden   2.3
Australia   2.5
Canada   2.9
Finland   3.0
Norway   3.3
Israel   3.7
New Zealand   4.4
Scotland   5.0
United States   21.9

Killings per 100,000 men 15 through 24 years old for 1986 or 1987

(Fingerhut & Kleinman, 1990). Looked at another way, U.S. males between the ages of 15 and 35 have a 1 in 40 chance of being killed violently. Some possible reasons for these high rates are explored further in the Current Controversies feature.

Guns and Violence as a Health Problem

Between 1979 and 1994, more than 40,000 U.S. children and teens were killed by violent acts (Wilmington, DE, *News-Journal*, April 25, 1994). As you could infer from the graph comparing homicide rates for young adult males around the world, this total far surpasses that of any other industrialized country.

A major factor in these staggering statistics is the availability of guns. Experts estimate that there are 60 million guns already in the hands of individuals (which translates into one gun for every household), with the number increasing by about 3 million per year (Centers for Disease Control, 1992). Despite the claims of gun-rights advocates that "Guns don't kill people, people kill people," the data reveal a much different story.

A major study of two cities similar geographically, economically, and demographically, but in different countries, clearly showed the effects of easily obtainable guns. Sloane and colleagues (1988) compared violent death statistics in Seattle, Washington and Vancouver, British Columbia (Canada). The two cities had very similar rates of violent assaults and similar rates of arrest, conviction, and jail sentences. But murder rates in Seattle were nearly double those in Vancouver. Sloane and colleagues point out that guns are readily available in Seattle, whereas they are highly regulated in Vancouver.

It is interesting that the study was published in the highly respected *New England Journal of Medicine*, making an explicit connection between violence and health. Indeed, five years later, U.S. President Bill Clinton made the connection part of his attempt to reform U.S. health care.

With murder the highest cause of death of young adults in some segments of U.S. society, and fifth overall, it is clear that violence is a significant health problem. Despite the high personal and economic costs, however, the topic of gun control remains controversial in the United States.

The evidence is clear: Where strict gun control laws are in effect, the murder rate and the related health care costs are substantially lower than in the United States. Yet the political issues are complex. What do you think should be done?   ❧

Lifestyle Factors

Take a look at the man in the photograph. He illustrates several things you should *not* do if you are trying to maintain good health. In this section, we will consider such lifestyle factors as smoking, drinking, and eating poorly, to see how they affect health. We will return to this theme in Chapter 12, when we examine additional aspects of health promotion.

SMOKING

Smoking is the single biggest contributor to health problems. The health risks of smoking have been known for decades. In this country

alone, roughly 320,000 people die each year and 10 million more suffer from smoking-related diseases (USDHHS, 1988).

The risks of smoking are many. The American Cancer Society estimates that over half of all cancers (including cancer of the lung, larynx, mouth, esophagus, bladder, kidney, pancreas, and cervix) are related to smoking. Emphysema, a disease that destroys the air sacs in the lungs, is primarily caused by smoking, and the carbon monoxide and nicotine inhaled in cigarette smoke foster the development of cardiovascular disease (Wantz & Gay, 1981). As noted in Chapter 2, smoking is a potent teratogen; smoking during pregnancy can cause stillbirth, low birth weight, or perinatal death.

Interestingly, awareness of these serious health problems have had little effect on the number of adolescents who smoke, as we saw in Chapter 8. In fact, awareness of the hazards of smoking has lowered smoking rates appreciably only in adult men since the 1960s. Among adult women, smoking rates rose to roughly 30%—now they smoke nearly as much as men. In fact, lung cancer has replaced breast cancer as the most common form of cancer in women. It was the only cause of death among women to show an increase during the 1980s (USDHHS, 1991).

Evidence continues to mount that the hazards of smoking are not limited to the smoker. Nonsmokers who breathe secondhand smoke are also at considerably higher risk for smoking-related diseases, including chronic lung disease, lung cancer, and cardiovascular disease (Garland et al., 1985; Pershagen, Hrubec, & Svensson, 1987; USDHHS, 1984). Partners of smokers are especially vulnerable; for example, wives of smokers are three times more likely to have heart attacks than wives of nonsmokers (Nachtigall & Nachtigall, 1990). Pregnant women who breathe secondhand smoke for as little as two hours per day at home or work are more likely to give birth to low-birth-weight infants (Martin & Bracken, 1986). For these reasons, many states and communities have passed stricter legislation banning smoking in public buildings, and smoking is banned entirely on airline flights within the United States and on many international flights.

Juan, the man in the second opening vignette, is typical of people who want to stop smoking. Most people who try to stop smoking begin the process in young adulthood. Although some smokers who want to quit may find formal programs helpful, over 90% of those who stop do so on their own. But as Juan suspects, quitting smoking is not easy; 70–80% of those who try to quit relapse at least once (Cohen et al., 1989). For most people, quitting occurs only after a long period of stopping and relapsing.

Regardless of how it happens, quitting smoking has enormous health benefits, despite what people may have heard. For example, women who have stopped smoking for three years have a risk of heart attack equivalent to women who have never smoked (Rosenberg, Palmer, & Shapiro, 1990). The risk of lung cancer returns to normal after a period of 10–15 years. Even people who do not quit until late life (even after age 70) show marked improvements in health (LaCroix et al., 1991).

In sum, the evidence is clear: If you don't smoke, don't start. If you do, you're never too old to stop.

DRINKING ALCOHOL

If you are over 21, chances are you drink occasionally; surveys estimate that more than 60% of U.S. adults drink alcohol once in a while (Post, 1987). These rates have not changed much over the years. This is not surprising, given the number of advertisements for alcoholic beverages, as well as the fact that drink-

People like those shown here who are exposed to secondhand smoke have higher risks of cancer and other smoking-related disorders, even if they are nonsmokers. This increased risk has resulted in much stricter rules about smoking in public.

ing is a common issue in adolescence (as we saw in Chapter 8). Offering people a drink at social events or bringing a bottle of wine to the person hosting a party is a widespread custom in many societies. Nevertheless, the amount of alcohol being consumed in the United States has been decreasing, partly in response to tougher laws regarding underage drinking and regarding drinking and driving.

For the majority of people, drinking alcohol poses no serious health problems, as long as they do not drink and drive. In fact, numerous studies have shown that for people who drink no more than two glasses of beer per day, alcohol consumption may be beneficial. For example, light drinkers (one glass of beer or wine per day) have a lower risk of stroke than either abstainers or heavy drinkers, even after controlling for hypertension, smoking, and medication (Gill et al., 1986).

But for roughly 1 in 10 drinkers and their family members, alcohol consumption does considerable harm. Around 18 million North Americans are heavy drinkers; roughly 11 million of them are alcoholics. The incidence of heavy drinking remains fairly constant at around 10% through the adult life span (Post, 1987). However, identification of individuals as alcoholics tends to peak by middle age (Scott & Mitchell, 1988).

Alcoholism is viewed by most experts as a form of *addiction,* **which means that alcoholics demonstrate physical dependence on alcohol and experience withdrawal symptoms when they do not drink.** Dependence occurs when a drug, such as alcohol, becomes so incorporated into the functioning of the body's cells that the drug becomes necessary for normal functioning (Berkow, 1987). If the drug is discontinued, the body reacts in ways that are opposite to the effects of the drug. Because alcohol is a depressant, withdrawal symptoms include restlessness, irritability, and trembling. Alcoholism results when the person becomes so dependent on the drug that it interferes with his or her personal relationships, health, occupation, and social functioning.

Drinking heavily, especially over a long period of time, has serious consequences. Consuming more than five or six drinks per day causes liver damage, which may begin as a form of hepatitis but turn into cirrhosis, a very serious liver disease that is the leading cause of death in alcoholics (Eckhardt et al., 1981). **Long-term alcoholism is an indirect cause of** *Wernicke-Korsakoff syndrome,* **a brain disease whose symptoms include severe memory loss for recent events, severe disorientation, confusion, and visual problems.** Wernicke-Korsakoff syndrome is actually caused by a thiamine vitamin deficiency, resulting from the fact that alcohol interferes with thiamine absorption. Because alcoholics tend to have poor diets, they are at increased risk for vitamin deficiencies and this syndrome (Thompson, 1978). In women, heavy drinking reduces fertility and can cause menstrual periods to stop (Greenwood, Love, & Pratt, 1983). As pointed out in Chapter 2, drinking during pregnancy is associated with serious risks to the fetus.

Several approaches have been used to help people stop drinking. Because the identification of alcoholism peaks by middle age, most people seeking treatment are young adults (Scott & Mitchell, 1988). The most widely known treatment option is Alcoholics Anonymous, founded in Akron, Ohio in 1935 by two former alcoholics. Other treatment approaches include inpatient and outpatient programs at treatment centers, behavior modification, and group therapy (Zimberg, 1985). Typically, the goal of these programs is abstinence.

Unfortunately, we know very little about the long-term success of the various programs; what data exist indicate that on average, the number of people seeking treatment who do *not* relapse within three years is not more than 30% (Wiens & Menustik, 1983). Clearly, the relapse potential is very high.

Alcohol treatment programs, like the one shown here, help address one of the most problematic and expensive health care problems in adulthood.

Eating a healthy diet may prevent many diseases across the life span.

NUTRITION

How many times did your parents tell you to eat all of your vegetables? Or perhaps they said, "You are what you eat." Most people have disagreements with parents about food while growing up, but as adults later realize that those lima beans and other despised foods really were healthful.

Experts agree that nutrition directly affects one's mental, emotional, and physical functioning (Steen, 1987). With increasing age, this relation becomes even more important, because health is determined in part by the cumulative effects of dietary habits over the years.

Nutritional requirements and eating habits change across the life span. An adolescent can eat large quantities of food and be hungry a short time later. In contrast, grandparents eat considerably less. **This change is due mainly to differences in *metabolism*, or how much energy the body needs.** Body metabolism and the digestive process slow down with age.

Requirements for some specific nutrients also change, but others remain constant (Steen, 1987). Younger adults require more carbohydrates than older adults, because they need more energy to run their higher metabolism. However, the needs for protein, vitamins, and minerals show little change during adulthood.

Three aspects of diet have health connections that become especially important in young adulthood: obesity, cardiovascular disease, and cancer. Let's look first at obesity, since being overweight is associated with several serious health problems, such as high blood pressure (hypertension), cardiovascular disease, and certain cancers. Studies indicate that people who are overweight are also more likely to die sooner than their normal-weight counterparts.

Young adulthood is the period of life associated with the highest risk of being overweight; young adults are the prime targets of weight reduction programs (Williamson et al., 1990). The plethora of weight loss clinics and books is testimony to the fact that losing weight is big business. However, the best way to do it is straightforward: eat a diet low in fat and high in the proper nutrients, and exercise more.

Even if you're not overweight, did you ever worry as you were eating a triple-dip cone of premium ice cream that you really should be eating fat-free frozen yogurt instead? If so, you are one of the people who have taken to heart (literally) the link between diet (especially fat) and cardiovascular disease. The American Heart Association (1990) makes quite clear that foods high in saturated fat (such as our beloved ice cream) should be replaced with foods low in fat (such as fat-free frozen yogurt).

The main goal of these recommendations is to lower your level of cholesterol. High cholesterol is one risk factor for cardiovascular disease. **There is an important difference between two different types of cholesterol: *low-density lipoproteins (LDLs)* and *high-density lipoproteins (HDLs)*. Lipoproteins are fatty chemicals attached to proteins carried in the blood. LDLs cause fatty deposits to accumulate in arteries, impeding blood flow, whereas HDLs help keep arteries clear and break down LDLs.**

It is not so much the overall cholesterol number, but the ratio of LDLs to HDLs that matters most in cholesterol screening. High levels of LDLs are a risk factor in cardiovascular disease, and high levels of HDLs are considered a protective factor. Lowering high LDL levels is usually accomplished through changes in diet, and occasionally by medication. Reducing LDL levels is effective in diminishing the risk of cardiovascular disease in adults of all ages (Löwik et al., 1991). HDL levels can be raised through exercise and a high-fiber diet. Weight control is also an important component.

Some researchers believe that diet plays a role in roughly one-third of all cancers. For example, high levels of fat in the diet increase the risk of breast, pancreatic, prostate, ovarian, and colon cancers. Eating a high-fiber, low-fat, low-sodium diet also lowers the risk of cancer (Petrus & Vetrosky, 1990). Evidence to support the diet–cancer link comes from a cross-cultural study of Japanese and Japanese American women. Japanese women were more likely to get stomach and esophageal cancers (associated with high nitrate levels in the meats that are common in Japanese diets), whereas Japanese American women were more likely to get breast cancer, associated with the higher fat levels in American diets. These findings clearly demonstrate that diet and health have important connections.

Social, Gender, and Ethnic Issues in Health

Which of the two individuals shown in the photographs is likely to be healthier? Why? At several points in this section, we have indicated that although most young adults are very healthy, there are important individual differences. Let's see what they are.

SOCIAL FACTORS

The two most important social influences on health are socioeconomic status and education. In the United States, income level is a major determinant of how healthy a person is likely to be, mainly because income is linked to having access to adequate health care. Regardless of ethnic group, people who live in poverty are more likely to be in poor health than people who do not.

Related to income is education. College graduates are less likely to develop chronic diseases such as hypertension and cardiovascular disease than people who do not go to college. In fact, people who have less education are not only more likely to contract a chronic disease, they are more likely to die from it. In a large, representative sample of 5652 working adults between 18 and 64, educational level was associated with good health even when the effects of age, gender, ethnicity, and smoking were accounted for (Pincus, Callahan, & Burkhauser, 1987).

Does education *cause* good health? Not exactly. Higher educational level is associated with higher income, as well as more awareness of dietary and lifestyle influences on health. Thus, more highly educated people are in a better position to afford health care and know more about the kinds of foods and lifestyle appropriate to improve health.

GENDER

Do you think men or women are healthier? This question is difficult to answer, primarily because women were not routinely included in many major studies of health until the 1990s (Kolata, 1990b). For example, most of the longitudinal data about risk factors for cardiovascular disease comes from studies of men. We do know that women live longer than men, for reasons discussed in Chapter 13. Women also use health services more often, because they tend to pay more attention to changes in their bodies (Nathanson & Lorenz, 1982).

ETHNIC GROUP DIFFERENCES

In the United States, the poorest health conditions exist in inner-city slums. Overall death rates in such communities far surpass other segments of the country. For example, African American men in New York's Harlem have a lower life expectancy than men in some Third World countries (McCord & Freeman, 1990). Why is this the case?

The main reasons are poverty and racism. As noted earlier, poverty is associated with poor nutrition and inadequate health care throughout life (Otten et al., 1990). Even when they have access to health care, African Americans are less likely than European Americans to receive coronary bypass surgery, kidney transplants, and other treatments (Council on Ethical and Judicial Affairs, 1990).

But there is another factor: stress related to racism. Unlike men in most Third World countries, African American men are the targets of racism. Research demonstrates that people who suppress their anger are at increased risk of hypertension. People who are subjected to racism may not feel able to show their anger and therefore keep it bottled up. Coupled with a physiological predisposition of many African Americans to retain sodium in their kidneys while under stress, which can result in kidney disease, this combined reaction can be fatal (Goleman, 1990).

African Americans who live in inner-city neighborhoods do not have access to the same high-quality health care as do more affluent people, and often must use expensive emergency rooms for basic care. This difference reflects social forces on health.

Of course, to the extent that other ethnic groups suffer from poverty and cannot obtain adequate health care, they also have poorer health. As noted earlier in this chapter, inner-city Hispanic Americans are also less likely to have adequate medical care. Thus, until poverty and access to health care and racism are addressed, inner-city minority groups will be at a serious disadvantage in terms of health.

Healthy Adulthood

FORCES IN ACTION

In this section, we have seen that physical development in young adulthood involves a complex set of interacting influences. The biopsychosocial model introduced in Chapter 1 can help us understand these interactions. On the biological front, genetics plays a key role. We may have inherited superb athletic ability (or not), and we may have predispositions for or protection against such things as cardiovascular disease or alcoholism. Psychologically, we may have learned about the influence of lifestyle on physical health. As we will see next, we have cognitive abilities to think about what we eat and do to our bodies. We have seen that the social influence of poverty is very powerful, reducing the quality of health care to which poor people have access. The importance of life-cycle forces is critical, though they are less apparent. As we will see in Chapters 12 and 13, health and lifestyle decisions we make as young adults have profound effects later in life; for example, failure to maintain sufficient calcium intake can cause osteoporosis in later life, and eating a high-fat diet can cause cardiovascular disease years later.

It is also important to recognize how the basic forces of development interact. For example, intervention programs will not work if they fail to consider the interrelated effects of individual differences in genetics, cognitive developmental level, and access to care. Moreover, money spent on prevention at one point in the life span can yield great savings on treatment of disease later.

One way to understand how the biopsychosocial model can be useful is to think of a major health problem, identify an existing program aimed at addressing it, and analyze it to see whether all of the forces on development are being addressed. The results of your analysis may surprise you.   ❧

TEST YOURSELF

1. In young adulthood, most people reach their maximum _____.
2. Coordination and dexterity both tend to peak during the _____.
3. The most common cause of death during the early 20s is _____.
4. The primary cause of death among young African American men is

   _____.
5. Over half of all cancers are believed to be related to _____.
6. Alcoholism is viewed by most experts as a form of _____.
7. The two most important social influences on health are education and

   _____.
8. In the United States, the poorest health conditions exist for African Americans living in _____.
9. How could you design a health care system that provides strong incentives for healthy lifestyles during young adulthood?

Cognitive Development

LEARNING OBJECTIVES

❧ *What is intelligence in adulthood?*

❧ *What types of abilities have been identified? How do they change?*

❧ *What is postformal thought? How does it differ from formal operations?*

Susan, a 33-year-old woman who had recently been laid off from her job as a secretary, slid into her seat on her first day of class as a college student. She was clearly nervous. "I'm worried that I won't be able to compete with these

Cognitive Development
  How Should We View Intelligence in Adults?
  What Happens to Intelligence in Adulthood?
  ■ *The Seattle Longitudinal Study*
  Going beyond Formal Operations: Thinking in Adulthood

Answers: (1) *height,* (2) *late 20s and early 30s,* (3) *accident,* (4) *murder,* (5) *smoking,* (6) *addiction,* (7) *socioeconomic status,* (8) *inner-city slums*

younger students, that I may not be smart enough," she sighed. "Guess we'll find out soon enough, though, huh?"

Many returning adult students like Susan and the people in the photograph worry that they may not be "smart enough" to keep up with 18- or 19-year-olds. Are these fears realistic? In this section, we will examine the evidence concerning intellectual performance in adulthood. We will see how the answer to this question depends on the types of intellectual skills being used.

How Should We View Intelligence in Adults?

We interrupt this section for a brief exercise. Take a sheet of paper and write down all the abilities you can think of that reflect intelligence in adults. When you have finished, you may rejoin this section, which will still be in progress.

It's a safe bet that you listed more than one ability as reflecting intelligence in adults. You are not alone. **Most theories of intelligence are *multidimensional*—that is, they identify several domains of intellectual abilities.** As discussed in Chapter 6 (pp. 195–197), there is disagreement about the number and types of abilities, but virtually everyone agrees that no single generic type of intelligence is responsible for all the different kinds of mental activities we perform.

Sternberg (1985) captured the essence of multidimensionality in his triarchic theory of intelligence (discussed in Chapter 6). In addition to multidimensionality, three other concepts have been advanced as vital to intellectual development in adults: multidirectionality, interindividual variability, and plasticity (Baltes, 1993; Baltes, Dittmann-Kohli, & Dixon, 1984; Dittmann-Kohli & Baltes, 1990). Let's look at each of these concepts in turn.

Over time, the various abilities underlying adults' intelligence show *multidirectionality*: Some aspects of intelligence improve whereas other aspects decline during adulthood. Closely related to this is *interindividual variability*: These patterns of change also vary from one person to another. In the next two sections, we will see evidence for both multidirectionality and interindividual variability when we examine developmental trends for specific sets of intellectual abilities.

Finally, people's abilities reflect *plasticity*: They are not fixed, but can be modified under the right conditions at just about any point in adulthood. Because most research on plasticity has focused on older adults, we will return to this topic in Chapter 13.

The theories of intelligence in adulthood espoused by Baltes and colleagues emphasize that intelligence has many components, which show varying development in different abilities and different people. This view is closely related to the life-span perspective we discussed in Chapter 1, which is summarized in the table at the top of page 311. Recall Riley's (1979) theory that development occurs because of the integration of biological, psychological, sociocultural, and life-cycle forces—a view incorporated in Baltes' ideas about how intelligence develops during adulthood. Let's turn our attention now to the evidence that supports this theoretical view.

Perspective	Examples of Theories	Main Ideas	Emphases in Biopsychosocial Framework	Positions on Developmental Issues
Life span and life cycle	Riley's life-span perspective	Development is multiply determined	Strong emphasis on the interaction of all four forces; cannot consider any in isolation	Nature–nurture interaction, continuity and discontinuity, context-specific

What Happens to Intelligences in Adulthood?

Given that intelligence in adults is a complex, multifaceted construct, how might we proceed to study the intelligences of adults? For a sneak preview, look carefully at the situations depicted in the photographs. The formal testing session and the practical problem depicted are two common ways to examine

adult intelligence. Formal testing typically assesses primary or secondary abilities and involves tests from which we can compute overall IQ scores like those discussed in Chapter 6. Tests involving practical problems try to assess people's ability to use intelligence in everyday situations. Let's find out what happens in each.

PRIMARY ABILITIES

From our previous discussion, we know that intelligence consists of many different skills and abilities. **Since the 1930s, researchers have agreed that intellectual abilities can be studied as groups of related skills (such as memory or spatial ability) called** *primary mental abilities.* Roughly 25 primary mental abilities have been identified. Because it is difficult to study all of the primary mental abilities, researchers have focused on five representative ones:

- *Number:* the basic skills underlying your mathematical reasoning
- *Word fluency:* how easily you can produce verbal descriptions of things
- *Verbal meaning:* your vocabulary ability
- *Inductive reasoning:* your ability to extrapolate from particular facts to general concepts
- *Spatial orientation:* your ability to reason in the three-dimensional world in which we live

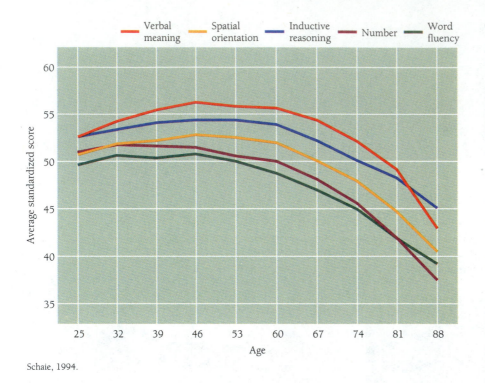

Schaie, 1994.

Do these primary abilities show change in adulthood? To answer this question, Schaie (1994) undertook one of the most comprehensive studies of any phenomenon in human development. Details of this study can be found in the Spotlight on Research feature a little later in this section. Beginning in 1956, Schaie began testing residents of Seattle every seven years. By using a sequential research design (described in Chapter 1), he has been able to provide very detailed descriptions of the development of primary mental abilities.

As you can see in the graph on the left, scores on tests of primary mental abilities improve gradually until the late 30s or early 40s. Small declines begin in the 50s, increase as people age into their 60s, and become increasingly large in the 70s (Schaie, 1994).

Cohort differences were also found. As you can see in the graph below, more recently born younger and middle-aged cohorts performed better than older cohorts on some skills, such as inductive reasoning ability, but not others. An example of the latter is that older cohorts outperformed younger ones on number skills (Schaie, 1994). These cohort effects probably reflect differences in educational experiences; younger groups' education emphasized fig-

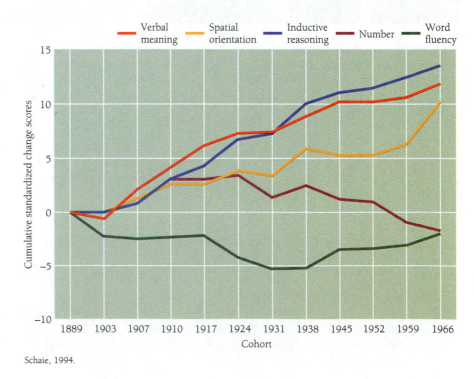

Schaie, 1994.

uring things out on one's own, whereas older groups' education emphasized rote learning. Additionally, older groups did not have calculators or computers, so they had to do mathematical problems by hand.

What can we conclude from Schaie's pioneering research? Two points are clear. First, intellectual development during adulthood is marked by a gradual leveling off of gains, followed by a period of relative stability, and then a time of gradual decline in most abilities. Second, these trends vary from one cohort to another.

The Seattle Longitudinal Study

SPOTLIGHT ON RESEARCH

One of the most important research projects on adult intellectual development is the longitudinal study, conducted by K. Warner Schaie in Seattle, Washington, since 1956. Not only has this study uncovered most of what we know about how intellectual abilities change across adulthood; it has also been the basis for creating new research methodology (the sequential design, discussed in Chapter 1). Over the course of the study, more than 5000 individuals have been tested at six testing cycles (1956, 1963, 1970, 1977, 1984, and 1991). All of the participants were recruited through a very large health maintenance organization in Seattle that is representative of the upper 75% of the socioeconomic spectrum. Like most longitudinal studies, Schaie's has encountered selectivity effects—that is, people who return over the years for retesting tend to do better initially than those who fail to return. However, an advantage of Schaie's sequential design is that by bringing in new groups of participants, he has been able to estimate the importance of selection effects, a major improvement over previous research.

Among the many important findings from the study are the differential changes in abilities over time and the cohort effects summarized in the text. But Schaie uncovered many individual differences as well; some people showed developmental patterns closely approximating the overall trends, but others showed unusual patterns. For example, some individuals showed steady declines in most abilities beginning in their 40s and 50s, others showed declines in some abilities but not others, but some people showed little change in most abilities over a 14-year period. Such individual variation in developmental patterns means that average trends, like those depicted on page 312, must be interpreted cautiously; they reflect group averages and do not represent the patterns shown by each person in the group.

Additionally, Schaie (1994) identified several variables that appear to reduce the risk of cognitive decline in old age:

- Absence of cardiovascular and other chronic diseases
- Living in favorable environmental conditions (such as good housing)
- Remaining cognitively active through reading and lifelong learning
- Having a flexible personality style in middle age
- Being married to a person with high cognitive status
- Being satisfied with one's life achievements in middle age

Schaie's findings indicate that intellectual development in adulthood is influenced by a wide variety of health, environmental, personality, and relationship factors. By attending to these influences throughout adulthood, we can at least stack the deck in favor of maintaining good intellectual functioning in late life.   ❧

SECONDARY MENTAL ABILITIES

Rather than focusing separately on specific primary abilities, some researchers argue that it makes more sense to study a half dozen or so broader skills, termed *secondary mental abilities,* that subsume the primary abilities. Two of these secondary mental abilities have received a great deal of attention in adult developmental research: fluid intelligence and crystallized intelligence.

Fluid intelligence **consists of the abilities that make you a flexible and adaptive thinker, that allow you to make inferences, and that enable you to understand the relations among concepts.** It includes the abilities you need to understand and respond to any situation, but especially new ones: inductive reasoning, integration, abstract thinking, and the like (Horn, 1982). An example of a question that taps fluid abilities is:

What letter comes next in the series $d\,f\,i\,m\,r\,x\,e$?*

Other typical ways of testing fluid intelligence include mazes, puzzles, and relations among shapes. Most of the time, these tests are timed, and higher scores are associated with faster solutions.

Crystallized intelligence **reflects knowledge that you have acquired through life experience and education in a particular culture.** Crystallized intelligence includes your breadth of knowledge, comprehension of communication, judgment, and sophistication with information (Horn, 1982). Your ability to remember historical facts, definitions of words, knowledge of literature, and sports trivia information are some examples. Many popular television game shows (such as *Jeopardy* and *Wheel of Fortune*) are based on contestants' accumulated crystallized intelligence.

Even though crystallized intelligence involves cultural knowledge, it is based partly on the quality of a person's underlying fluid intelligence (Horn, 1982). For example, the breadth of your vocabulary depends to some extent on how quickly you are able to make connections between new words you read and information already known, which is a component of fluid intelligence.

Developmentally, fluid and crystallized intelligence follow two very different paths, as you can see in the graph. Notice that fluid intelligence declines throughout adulthood, whereas crystallized intelligence improves. Although we do not yet fully understand why fluid intelligence declines, it may be related to underlying changes in the brain from the accumulated effects of disease, injury, and aging (Horn & Hofer, 1992). In contrast, the increase in crystallized intelligence (at least until late life) indicates that people continue adding knowledge every day.

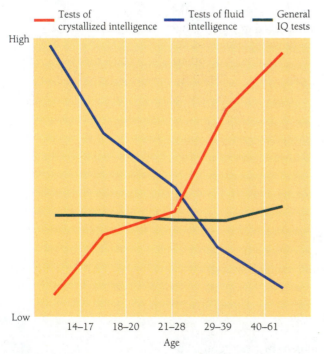

Tests of crystallized intelligence — Tests of fluid intelligence — General IQ tests

High / Low

Age: 14–17   18–20   21–28   29–39   40–61

Horn, 1970.

*The next letter is *m*. The rule is to increase the difference between adjacent letters in the series by one each time. Thus, *f* is two letters from *d*, *i* is three letters away from *f*, and so on.

What do these different developmental trends imply? First, they indicate that although learning continues through adulthood, it becomes more difficult the older one gets. Consider what happens when Michael, age 17, and Marguerite, age 50, try to learn a second language. Although Marguerite's verbal skills in her native language (a component of crystallized intelligence) are probably better than Michael's, his probable superiority in the fluid abilities necessary to learn another language will usually make it easier for him to do so.

Second, these developmental trends point out once again that intellectual development varies a great deal from one set of skills to another. Beyond the differences in overall trends, differences in individuals' fluid and crystallized intelligence also vary. Whereas individual differences in fluid intelligence remain relatively uniform over time, individual differences in crystallized intelligence increase with age, largely because maintaining crystallized intelligence depends on being in situations that require its use (Horn & Hofer, 1992). For example, few adults get much practice in solving complex letter series tasks like the one on page 314. But because people can improve their vocabulary skills by reading, and because people differ considerably in how much they read, differences are likely to emerge. In short, crystallized intelligence provides a rich knowledge base to draw upon when material is somewhat familiar, whereas fluid intelligence provides the power to deal with learning in novel situations.

Going beyond Formal Operations: Thinking in Adulthood

Suppose you were given the following problem to solve.

> Michael has a reputation for flirting with women, especially when he's at a party. Clare, his wife, gets very upset when he flirts. In fact, she warns him that if he does it one more time, she will leave him. Tonight, Michael and Clare are at a party and he begins to flirt. What does Clare do?

When this and similar problems are presented to adolescents and adults, interesting differences emerge. Adolescents tend to point out that Clare gave Michael a clear ultimatum, which Michael ignored, and conclude that Clare will leave him. These individuals tend to approach the problem in formal operational terms, as discussed in Chapter 6. They reason deductively from the information given in order to come to a single solution grounded in their own experience. Formal operational thinkers are certain that such solutions are right because they are based in their own experience and are logically driven.

But many adults are reluctant to draw any conclusions based on the limited information in the problem. They point out that there is much about Clare and Michael that is unknown: How long have they been married? Did Clare know about Michael's flirting before marrying him? Could Clare support herself financially if she left? Are there children involved? From this perspective, the problem is much more ambiguous. Adults may eventually decide that Clare leaves (or stays), but they do so only after considering aspects of the situation that go well beyond the information given in the problem. Such thinking

How couples like the one shown here resolve conflict is a good reflection of their individual levels of cognitive development. Indeed, hypothetical situations involving conflict resolution are often used in research on postformal thought.

shows a recognition that other people's experiences may be quite different from one's own.

Clearly, the thought process these adults use is different than formal operations (Cavanaugh et al., 1985). Unlike formal-operational thinking, this approach involves considering situational constraints and circumstances, realizing that reality sometimes constrains solutions, and knowing that feelings matter.

Researchers in the 1960s began wondering whether there might be development of thinking beyond adolescence. This work was grounded primarily in Piaget's theory, the basic points of which are summarized in the table. Researchers assumed that Piaget's description of cognitive development was adequate up to adolescence but suspected that there might be stages of thinking beyond formal operations.

Perspective	Examples of Theories	Main Ideas	Emphases in Biopsychosocial Framework	Positions on Developmental Issues
Cognitive	Piaget's theory (and extensions)	Thinking develops in sequence of stages	Main emphasis on biological and social forces, less emphasis on psychological, little on life cycle	Strongly nature, discontinuity, and universal sequence of stages

In one of the first systematic investigations of cognitive growth beyond adolescence, Perry (1970) traced the development of thinking during the undergraduate years. He found that 18-year-old first-year students tended to rely heavily on the expertise of authority figures to determine which ways of thinking were right and which were wrong. For these students, thinking is tightly tied to logic, as Piaget had argued, and the only legitimate answers were ones that were logically derived.

But by the time these students were seniors, things had changed. In the meantime, the students had gone through a phase in which they were much less sure of what answers were right—or if there were any right answers at all. However, when they were ready to graduate, they were fairly adept at examining different sides of an issue and had developed commitments to particular viewpoints. They recognized that they were the source of their own authority, that they must take a position on an issue, and that other people may hold different positions from theirs but be equally committed. During the college years, then, individuals become able to understand many perspectives on an issue, choose one, and still allow others the right to hold differing views. Perry concluded that this kind of thinking is very different from formal operations and represents another level of cognitive development.

Based on several additional longitudinal studies and numerous cross-sectional investigations, researchers came to the conclusion that this type of thinking represents a qualitative change beyond formal operations (Commons et al., 1989; Kitchener & King, 1989; Kramer et al., 1991). **Postformal thought is characterized by a recognition that truth (the correct answer) may vary from situation to situation, that solutions must be realistic in order to be reasonable, that ambiguity and contradiction are the rule rather than the exception, and that emotion and subjective factors usually play a role in**

thinking. In general, the research evidence indicates that postformal thinking has its origins in young adulthood (Commons et al., 1989).

Several research-based descriptions of the development of thinking in adulthood have been offered. **One of the best is the description of the development of *reflective judgment*, a way in which adults reason through dilemmas involving current affairs, religion, science, personal relationships, and the like.** Based on more than a decade of longitudinal and cross-sectional research, Kitchener and King (1989) refined descriptions and identified a systematic progression of reflective judgment in young adulthood. The stages represent age-related progressions in thinking. However, the rate of development is highly variable, making it difficult to tie specific ages to particular stages.

- *Stage 1.* Knowledge is assumed to exist absolutely and concretely and can be obtained through direct observation. There is an absolute correspondence between belief and truth. There is a correct answer to every question.
- *Stage 2.* Knowledge is absolutely certain, but may not be available right now. Knowledge can be obtained either from direct observation or from authorities. Beliefs are justified by an authority.
- *Stage 3.* Knowledge is assumed to be certain or only temporarily uncertain. When uncertain, one can only know through intuition or bias until certainty is obtained. When knowledge is certain, beliefs are justified by an authority; when uncertain, they are justified intuitively.
- *Stage 4.* Knowledge is uncertain and idiosyncratic, because situational variables dictate that we can never know anything with certainty. Beliefs are justified by appealing to evidence, but they are based on idiosyncratic reasons, such as choosing evidence that fits an established belief.
- *Stage 5.* Knowledge is sensitive to the situation and is subjective. We know only our own interpretations of the world. Beliefs are justified within a certain context or situation; they are balanced against other beliefs, which may interfere with drawing conclusions.
- *Stage 6.* Knowledge is personally constructed by evaluating evidence, others' opinions, and so forth in different situations. Thus, we can know both our own and others' personal constructions of issues. Beliefs are justified by comparing evidence and opinions on different sides of an issue and by using our own values.
- *Stage 7.* Knowledge is constructed by reasonable inquiry into conjectures about the world, or reasonable solutions to problems at hand, based on pragmatic factors. Beliefs are justified probabilistically on the basis of evidence and argument, or as the most complete understanding of an issue available.

As you can see from these descriptions, adults move from a firm belief in an absolute correspondence between personal perception and reality to the recognition that the search for truth is an ongoing, never-ending process. Other researchers find similar trends. For example, Kramer (1989; Kramer et al., 1991) reported a developmental trend involving three stages: absolutist, relativistic, and dialectical. Absolutist thinking involves firmly believing that there is only one correct solution to a problem and that personal experience is the basis for all truth. Adolescents and adults in their early 20s tend to think this way. Relativistic thinking involves realizing that there are many sides to an issue and that correct actions or solutions depend on circumstances. Adults in their late 20s through early middle age use this style most. One potential danger with relativistic thinking is that it can lead to a cynical approach to life: "I'll do my thing and you do yours." Because relativistic thinkers tend to reason things out on a case-by-case basis, they are unlikely to be committed to any one position for long. The final stage, dialectical thinking, solves this problem. Dialectical thinkers see the merits in different viewpoints, but are able to synthesize them into a workable solution to which they are strongly committed.

As you can see, although the various approaches to postformal thinking differ in some details, they all agree that adults progress from believing in one and only one right way of thinking and acting to accepting the fact that there are multiple solutions, each potentially equally acceptable (or equally flawed). This progression is important; it allows for the integration of emotion with thought in dealing with practical, everyday problems, as we will see next.

INTEGRATING EMOTION AND LOGIC IN LIFE PROBLEMS

A theme in descriptions of postformal thinking is movement from thinking "I'm right because I've experienced it" to thinking "I'm not so sure who's right because your experience is different from mine." Mary Ann, the recent college graduate in the third opening vignette, is a typical example of this shift. Problem situations used to seem pretty straightforward, but they now appear much more complicated; the "right thing to do" is much tougher to figure out for her these days.

Differences in thinking styles have major implications for dealing with life problems. For example, couples who are able to understand and synthesize each other's point of view are much more likely to resolve conflicts; couples not able to do so are more likely to feel resentful, drift apart, or even break up (Kramer, 1989; Kramer et al., 1991).

Besides an increasing understanding that there is more than one "right" answer, adult thinking is characterized by the integration of emotion with logic (Labouvie-Vief, 1985). Adults tend to make decisions and analyze problems not so much on logical grounds, but rather on pragmatic and emotional grounds. Mature thinkers realize that thinking is an inherently social enterprise that demands making compromises with other people and tolerating contradiction and ambiguity.

A good example of the difference between formal and postformal thought from this perspective can be seen in decisions regarding sexual behavior. As we saw in Chapter 8, sexually active adolescents rarely use condoms; in contrast, condom use increases in adulthood. Labouvie-Vief might argue that this is because sexuality is too emotionally charged for adolescents to deal with intellectually, whereas adults are better able to incorporate emotion into their thinking. But is this interpretation reasonable?

It appears to be. In one study, high school students, college students, and middle-aged adults were given three dilemmas to resolve (Blanchard-Fields, 1986). One dilemma had low emotional involvement, involving conflicting accounts of a war between two fictitious countries, North and South Livia, written by a partisan from each of the countries. The other two dilemmas had high emotional involvement. In one, parents and their adolescent son disagreed about going to visit the grandparents (the son did not want to go). In the other, a man and a woman had to resolve an unintentional pregnancy (the man was anti-abortion, the woman was pro-choice).

The results are shown in the graph on page 319. You should note two important findings. First, there were clear developmental trends in reasoning level, with the middle-aged adults best able to integrate emotion into thinking. Second, the high school and college students were equivalent on the fictitious war dilemma, but the young adult students more readily integrated emotion and thought on the visit and pregnancy dilemmas. These results support the kinds of developmental shifts suggested by Labouvie-Vief.

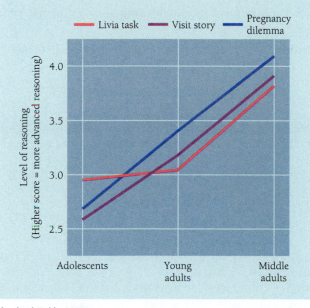

Blanchard-Fields, 1986.

The mounting evidence of continued cognitive development in adulthood paints a more positive view of adulthood than that of Piaget, who focused only on logical thinking. The integration of emotion with logic that happens in adulthood provides the basis for decision making in the very personal and sometimes difficult arenas of love and work, which we will examine in detail in Chapters 10 and 11, respectively. In the present context, it sets the stage for envisioning one's future life, a topic we take up in the next section.

TEST YOURSELF

1. Most modern theories of intelligence are _____ because they identify many domains of intellectual abilities.
2. Number, verbal fluency, and spatial orientation are some of the _____ abilities.
3. _____ reflects knowledge that you have acquired through life experience and education in a particular culture.
4. Kitchener and King describe a kind of postformal thinking called _____.
5. Adult thinking is marked by the integration of _____ and logic.
6. Many young adult college students seemingly get more confused about what they want to major in and how certain they are about what they know as they progress through college. From a cognitive developmental approach, why does this happen?

Answers: (1) multidimensional, (2) primary, (3) crystallized intelligence, (4) reflective judgment, (5) emotion

Moral Reasoning

LEARNING OBJECTIVES

❧ *How does reasoning about moral issues change through the life span?*

❧ *How does concern for justice and caring for other people contribute to moral reasoning?*

❧ *What cultural differences have been found in moral reasoning?*

Imagine that you were asked to solve the following problem:

> In Europe, a woman was near death from cancer. One drug might save her, a form of radium that a druggist in the same town had recently discovered. The druggist was charging $2000, ten times what the drug cost him to make. The sick woman's husband, Heinz, went to everyone he knew to borrow the money, but he could only get together about half of what it cost. He told the druggist that his wife was dying and asked him to sell it cheaper or let him pay later. But the druggist said, "No." The husband got desperate and broke into the man's store to steal the drug for his wife. Should the husband have done that? Why? (Kohlberg, 1969, p. 379)

Problems like this one present a moral dilemma. One can think of many reasons why Heinz should or should not steal the drug. Lawrence Kohlberg created this story and others like it to study how people reason about moral dilemmas. The situations in these stories were deliberately created to complicate decision making; choosing the "correct" thing to do is hard, because any decision involves some undesirable consequences. These situations resemble those found in real life, such as the one faced by Manuel, the men's department manager we met in the fourth opening vignette, who had an employee taking money to pay for medical bills.

Kohlberg analyzed children's, adolescents', and adults' responses to a large number of dilemmas like those involving Heinz and his wife. He was not interested in an individual's decision but in the reasoning that the individual used to justify the decision. **Moral reasoning involves the rules of ethical conduct people bring to bear on a problem to explain what they think is the right thing to do.** It should be emphasized that reasoning about hypothetical situations, such as whether or not Heinz should steal the drug, may not correspond to what a person would actually do if faced with a real situation. Indeed, the connection between moral reasoning and moral behavior is far from perfect.

In this section, we will consider Kohlberg's theory of the development of moral reasoning. Kohlberg believed that moral reasoning develops according to a specific sequence. We will see that his ideas have sparked some very interesting debates.

Kohlberg's Theory

Kohlberg (1984, 1987) believed very strongly that moral reasoning develops over the life span in a sequence of discrete stages. He based his theory on Piaget's theory; for example, Kohlberg believed in a universal, invariable sequence of stages that show qualitative changes in reasoning. The table on page 321 presents a quick overview of Kohlberg's perspective.

Perspective	Examples of Theories	Main Ideas	Emphases in Biopsychosocial Framework	Positions on Developmental Issues
Cognitive	Kohlberg's moral reasoning theory	Thinking develops in sequence of stages	Main emphasis on biological and social forces, less emphasis on psychological, little on life cycle	Strongly nature, discontinuity, and universal sequence of stages

A person's level and stage of moral reasoning is measured by having the individual respond to the question "Why?"—not by classifying what the person says the individual in the story should do. Thus, Kohlberg emphasized the rules that people use over the decisions they make. At the earliest stages, moral reasoning is based on external forces, such as the promise of reward or the threat of punishment. However, at the most advanced levels, moral reasoning is based on a personal, internal moral code that is unaffected by others' views or society's expectations. Let's take a closer look.

Kohlberg identified three levels of moral reasoning: preconventional, conventional, and postconventional. Each level is further subdivided into two substages. **At the *preconventional level*, moral reasoning is based on external forces.** For most children, many adolescents, and some adults, moral reasoning is controlled almost exclusively by rewards and punishments. **Individuals in Stage 1 moral reasoning assume an *obedience orientation*, which means believing that authority figures know what is right and wrong.** Consequently, a person should do what authorities say is right to avoid being punished. At this stage, a person might argue that Heinz should not steal the drug because an authority figure (e.g., parent, police officer) said that he should not do it.

In Stage 2 of the preconventional level, people adopt an *instrumental orientation*, in which they look out for their own needs. Individuals are usually nice to others because they expect the favor to be returned in the future. Someone at this stage could justify stealing the drug because Heinz's wife might do something nice for Heinz in return.

At the *conventional level*, adolescents and adults look to society's norms for moral guidance. In other words, people's moral reasoning is largely determined by others' expectations of them. **In Stage 3, adolescents' and adults' moral reasoning is based on *interpersonal norms*.** The aim is to win the approval of other people by behaving as "good boys" and "good girls" would. An adolescent or adult at this stage might argue that Heinz should not steal the drug because he must keep his reputation as an honest man.

Stage 4 of the conventional level focuses on *social system morality*. Here, adolescents and adults believe that social roles, expectations, and laws exist to maintain order within society and to promote the good of all people. An adolescent or adult in this stage might reason that Heinz should not steal the drug, even though his wife might die, because it is illegal and no one is above the law.

At the *postconventional level*, moral reasoning is based on a personal moral code. The emphasis is no longer on external forces like punishment, reward, or social roles. **In Stage 5, people base their moral reasoning on a *social contract*.** Adults agree that members of social groups adhere to a social contract because a common set of expectations and laws benefits all group members. However, if these expectations and laws no longer promote the welfare of individuals, they become invalid. Consequently, an adult in this stage might reason that Heinz should steal the drug because social rules about property rights no longer benefit individuals' welfare. (Indeed, the Declaration of Independence, written by Thomas Jefferson in 1776, made a similar argument about the laws of England.)

Finally, in Stage 6 of the postconventional level, *universal ethical principles* **dominate moral reasoning.** Abstract principles such as justice, compassion, and equality form the basis of a personal code that may sometimes conflict with society's expectations and laws. An adult might argue that Heinz should steal the drug because saving a life is a principle that takes precedence over everything, including the law.

Putting all of the stages together, the entire sequence of moral development looks like this:

*   *Preconventional Level: Punishment and Reward*

    Stage 1: Obedience to authority
    Stage 2: Nice behavior in exchange for future favors

    Conventional Level: Social Norms

    Stage 3: Live up to others' expectations
    Stage 4: Follow rules to maintain social order

    Postconventional Level: Moral Codes

    Stage 5: Adhere to a social contract when it is valid
    Stage 6: Personal moral system based on abstract principles

EVIDENCE FOR THE THEORY

Kohlberg proposed that his stages formed an invariant sequence. That is, individuals should move through the six stages in the order listed and in only that order. In reality, however, most individuals do not progress to the final stages; adults' reasoning usually remains at the conventional level.

In such a stage theory, the level of moral reasoning should be strongly associated with a person's age and level of cognitive development: Older and more advanced thinkers should, on the average, be more advanced in their moral development. Indeed, they usually are (Stewart & Pascual-Leone, 1992).

Support for Kohlberg's sequence of stages also comes from longitudinal studies in which individuals' level of reasoning is traced over several years. According to the theory, individuals should progress through each stage in sequence, never skipping stages. In fact, virtually no individuals skip any of the stages in Kohlberg's sequence (Colby et al., 1983). A related prediction is that, over time, individuals should either become more advanced in their level of moral reasoning or remain at the same level. They should *not* regress to a lower level of moral reasoning. Longitudinal studies find that only a small percentage of individuals regress to a lower stage. As predicted, the vast majority remain at the same level or progress to a more advanced level (Walker & Taylor, 1991).

A final and particularly controversial aspect of the theory is Kohlberg's claim that the sequence of stages is universal: All people in all cultures should progress through the six-stage sequence. Here, the evidence is mixed. On the one hand, when children and adolescents in cultures worldwide are asked to reason about moral dilemmas, their responses typically fall in Stages 2 or 3, just like answers from North American children and adolescents. On the other hand, moral reasoning by adults in other cultures is often not described well by Kohlberg's stages (Snarey, 1985). In many non-Western cultures, adults reason according to moral principles but do not emphasize justice as Kohlberg does in Stages 5 and 6. This suggests that Kohlberg's theory may be most applicable to moral reasoning in cultures with philosophical and religious traditions like those of Western nations. However, we'll see in the next section that even within Western cultures, justice is not the sole basis for moral thinking. We will return to the issue of cultural differences in moral reasoning a bit later.

The developmental sequence described by Kohlberg usually takes many years to unfold. But on occasion, we may be able to watch the process occur much more dramatically, such as when individuals seemingly undergo a major transformation in their motivation for doing certain things. One noteworthy example of such a transformation was depicted in Steven Spielberg's Oscar-winning movie *Schindler's List*, as described in the Real People feature.

REAL PEOPLE

Schindler's List

The outbreak of war typically provides shrewd business people the chance to profit from the increased demand for manufactured goods relating to military needs. The outbreak of World War II in Europe in 1939 was no exception. Oskar Schindler was an entrepreneur who saw an opportunity to make a great deal of money by working for the Germans in Poland after they had taken over the country. His flamboyant demeanor brought him to the attention of the local German commanders, for whom Schindler did favors. Motivated by the potential for personal profit at the expense of others, he opened a factory in which he employed Jews.

Schindler's company was quite successful. But as the war continued, official German policy toward Jews changed to one of extermination. Jewish citizens in Poland and other countries were rounded up and shipped to concentration camps, or were sometimes executed immediately. Schindler's attitudes began to change. He was approached by some of his employees, who asked him to give the Germans a list of names of people who were essential employees in the factory. The list provided protection, as the plant's products were used in the war effort. Gradually, Schindler's motivation changed. Rather than being driven by profit, he followed the higher principle of preserving life, to the point that he would create cover stories for the Germans to support the claim that certain employees were essential. He even went to Auschwitz to rescue some of his employees who had been sent there by mistake.

Oskar Schindler's list saved many lives. He still wanted to make a profit, but the primary reason he employed Jews in his factory had undergone a fundamental shift due to a change of heart. At least in terms of his reasoning toward his employees, it appears that Schindler began in Kohlberg's preconventional level—where he was motivated solely by personal profit—but moved to the postconventional level—where he was motivated by the higher principle of saving lives. For his courage, he is considered by many to be a hero.   ❧

Alternatives to Justice

Carol Gilligan (1982, 1985) has sharply criticized Kohlberg's theory. She claims that care and responsibility in interpersonal relationships also play a critical role in moral development, especially for women:

> The moral imperative that emerges repeatedly in interviews with women is an injunction to care, a responsibility to discern and alleviate the "real and recognizable trouble" of this world. For men, the moral imperative appears rather as an injunction to respect the rights of others and thus to protect from interference the rights to life and self-fulfillment. (1982, p. 100)

In place of Kohlberg's preconventional, conventional, and postconventional levels, Gilligan identified a developmental progression in which individuals gain greater understanding of caring and responsibility. In the first stage, children are preoccupied with their own needs. In the second stage, people care for others, particularly those who are less able to care for themselves, like infants and the aged. The third stage unites caring for others and for oneself in an emphasis on caring in all human relationships.

Notice that Gilligan shares Kohlberg's view that moral reasoning becomes qualitatively more sophisticated as individuals develop, progressing through a number of distinct stages. However, Gilligan emphasizes care, helping people in need, instead of justice, treating people fairly.

What does research tell us about the importance of justice and care in moral reasoning? Gilligan's claim that females and males differ in the bases of their moral reasoning might be wrong. The common outcome is that girls and boys as well as men and women reason about moral issues similarly (Walker, 1989). However, it turns out that females and males often think about moral issues in terms of both justice and care in interpersonal relationships. The exact characteristics of the moral problem at hand help to determine whether justice, care, or both will be the basis for moral reasoning.

Cultural Differences in Moral Reasoning

We have seen that U.S. children, adolescents, and adults include both justice and care in their moral reasoning, weighing them differently depending on the situation. Overall, North American children and adults use justice-based reasoning more often than care-based reasoning, but this is not true of all cultures.

Indeed, many critics have noted that Kohlberg's emphasis on the rights of individuals and on justice reflects the tradition within both Western culture and Judeo-Christian theology. But not all cultures and religions share this emphasis, so moral reasoning might be based on different values in other cultures. The Hindu religion, for example, emphasizes duties and responsibilities to others as the starting point for society (Simpson, 1974). Accordingly, children and adults reared with traditional Hindu beliefs might emphasize care in their moral reasoning more than would individuals brought up within the Judeo-Christian tradition.

Miller and Bersoff (1992) tested this hypothesis by constructing moral dilemmas that included two solutions: one based on justice and one based on care. For example, in one dilemma,

> Ben planned to travel to San Francisco in order to attend the wedding of his best friend. He needed to catch the very next train if he was to be on time for the ceremony, as he had to deliver the wedding rings. However, Ben's wallet was stolen in the train station. He lost all of his money as well as his ticket to San Francisco.
>
> Ben approached several officials as well as passengers . . . and asked them to loan him money to buy a new ticket. But, because he was a stranger, no one was willing to lend him the money he needed.
>
> While Ben . . . was trying to decide what to do next, a well-dressed man sitting next to him walked away for a minute. . . . Ben noticed that the man had left his coat unattended. Sticking out of the man's coat pocket was a train ticket to San Francisco. . . . He also saw that the man had more than enough money in his coat pocket to buy another train ticket. (p. 545)

One course of action, which emphasizes individual rights and justice, was the following:

Ben should not take the ticket from the man's coat pocket—even though it means not getting to San Francisco in time to deliver the wedding rings to his best friend. (p. 545)

Another course of action, this one placing a priority on caring for others, was as follows:

Ben should go to San Francisco to deliver the wedding rings to his best friend—even if it means taking the train ticket from the other man's coat pocket. (p. 545)

Children and adults living in the United States and others living in India read dilemmas like these and indicated the alternative that they preferred. The results revealed substantial cultural differences. The graph shows that a slight

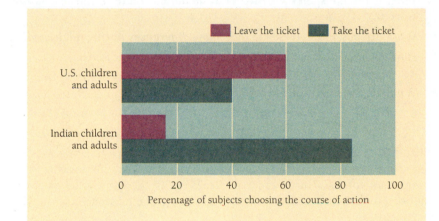

majority of U.S. children and adults selected the justice-based alternative. In contrast, the overwhelming majority of Indian children and adults selected the care-based alternative.

Clearly, one's moral reasoning reflects the emphases of the culture in which one is reared. Consistent with the predictions of Kohlberg's theory, judgments by U.S. children and adults reflect their culture's priority on individual rights and justice. In contrast, judgments by Indian children and adults reflect their culture's priority on caring for other people.

The net result of this and other work is to provide a broader view of moral reasoning. As Kohlberg claimed, moral reasoning becomes progressively more sophisticated as children develop, shifting from external rewards and punishments to social norms and personal moral codes. However, contrary to Kohlberg's original claims, those codes are not always based on justice and rights. Instead, caring for others sometimes serves the basis for moral reasoning, depending on the exact nature of the moral dilemma and the cultural context in which a person develops.

TEST YOURSELF

1. For children at the preconventional level, moral reasoning is strongly influenced by the presence of _____.
2. Gilligan criticized Kohlberg's theory on the grounds that it was based exclusively on using _____ as the basis for moral reasoning.

3. In India, moral judgments are often based on _____ , whereas in the United States, they tend to be based on _____ .
4. What parallels are there between cognitive development and Kohlberg's theory of moral reasoning?

Who Do You Want to Be?: Personality in Young Adulthood

LEARNING OBJECTIVES

❧ *What is the life-span construct? How do adults create scenarios and life stories?*

❧ *What are possible selves? Do they show differences during adulthood?*

❧ *How does self-concept come to take adult form? What is its developmental course through adulthood?*

❧ *What are personal control beliefs?*

In Chapter 8, we saw how children and adolescents deal with the question "What do you want to be when you grow up?" As a young adult, you have arrived at the "grown up" part, but you may not yet be ready to answer "What do you want to be?" This is especially true during the early years of young adulthood, when the search for identity that marked adolescence is just coming to a close.

In this section, we will examine how the search for identity in adolescence meets the cognitive, social, and personal reality of adulthood. In particular, we will see how people create life scenarios and life stories, possible selves, self-concept, and personal control beliefs. Let's begin by considering how people construct images of their adult lives.

Creating Scenarios and Life Stories

Trying to figure out what (and who) you want to be as an adult takes lots of thought, hard work, and time. These efforts pay off. **Based on information incorporated from personal experience, as well as input from other people, young adults create a *life-span construct* that represents a unified sense of the past, present, and future.** Several factors influence the development of a life-span construct; identity, values, and society are only a few. Together, they not only shape the creation of the life-span construct but also influence the way it is played out (Whitbourne, 1987). The life-span construct represents a link between Erikson's notion of identity, which was a major focus during adolescence, and the adult view of the self.

The first way in which the life-span construct is manifested is through the *scenario*, which consists of expectations about the future. The scenario takes aspects of a person's identity that are particularly important now and projects them into a plan for the future. For example, you may find yourself think-

SUSAN KRAUSS WHITBOURNE
"The starting point for the theory of adult identity processes is the assumption that the normal adult strives to feel loving, competent, and good."

ing about the day you will graduate and be able to apply all of the information you have learned. In short, a scenario is a game plan for how life is to go in the future.

Felicia, the sophomore human development student in the fifth opening vignette, has a fairly typical scenario. You'll remember that she planned on completing a degree in early childhood education, marrying after graduation, and having two children by age 30. **Tagging future events with a particular time or age by which they are to be completed creates a** *social clock.* This personal timetable gives the person a way to keep track of progress through adulthood. It can use biological markers of time (such as menopause), social aspects of time (such as getting married), and historical time (such as the turn of the century) (Hagestad & Neugarten, 1985).

Felicia will use her scenario to evaluate her progress toward her personal goals. With each new event, she will check where she is against where her scenario says she should be. If she is ahead of her plan, she may be proud of having made it. If she is lagging behind, she may chastise herself for being slow. But if she criticizes herself too much, she may change her scenario altogether. For example, if she does not go to college, she may decide to change her career goals entirely: Instead of owning her own day care center, she may aim to be a manager in a department store.

As a way to understand how people create scenarios, and to appreciate the similarities and differences among them, take the time to complete the exercises in the See for Yourself feature.

When I Was 35, It Was a Very Good Year

SEE FOR YOURSELF

To experience how people think through the future and create scenarios, try the following exercises. First, take a few days to write your own scenario. Imagine what your future will be like. Will you get married? When? To what kind of person? Will you have children? A career? How far will you advance? What will you be known for? Will you coach your child's soccer team? Run for the school board?

When you've finished your scenario, talk to your friends and ask them the same kinds of questions. Notice any similarities and differences between their responses and your own. Ask them where they got their ideas about the future.

Bring the results of your explorations into class for discussion and comparison. Have you and your classmates identified common themes that people see in their future? See for yourself.   ❧

As people start achieving some of the things in their scenarios, they create the second aspect of the life-span construct, the *life story,* **which is a personal narrative that organizes past events into a coherent sequence.** Our life story becomes our autobiography as we move through adulthood.

According to research, what we remember about the events that make up our life story changes over time (Neisser & Winograd, 1988). These distortions come in part because subsequent events change the meaning of earlier events, and in part because we want to present ourselves in a positive and favorable light. Such distortions may enable us to believe that we accomplished something on time (when we were actually late) and to feel better about our plans and goals that do not materialize.

Scenarios and life stories provide the bases for the continuing process of identity formation during adulthood (Whitbourne, 1986). Whitbourne believes that based on assimilation and accommodation, we create our own identities in much the same way that Piaget said we create our knowledge. As the figure shows, there is continuous feedback between identity and experience; this explains why we may reevaluate ourselves at one point in time, yet appear defensive and self-protective at another. Chapter 12 will discuss how this process results in changes in middle age, and Chapter 14 how it relates to integrity in late life.

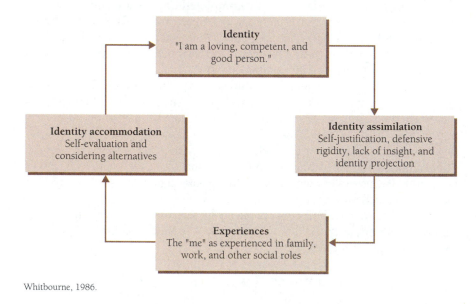

Whitbourne, 1986.

Possible Selves

Creating a scenario presupposes that adults have the ability to project themselves into the future and speculate about what they might be like (Markus & Nurius, 1986). How do we do this? **Projecting ourselves into the future involves creating *possible selves* that represent what we could become, what we would like to become, and what we are afraid of becoming.**

What you could or would like to become reflects personal goals or values; you may envision yourself as a good parent, as rich and famous with thousands of adoring fans, or as in good physical condition. What you are afraid of becoming is usually reflected in specific fears—of being alone, of your life being meaningless, or of being a certifiable couch potato. Possible selves are very powerful motivators. In fact, much of adult behavior can be interpreted as efforts to achieve or avoid these possible selves and to protect the current view of the self (Markus & Nurius, 1986).

Whether age differences appear in possible selves is a complicated issue, depending on how the investigators examine the data. In one approach, researchers asked people to describe their hoped-for and feared possible selves (Cross & Markus, 1991). The subjects were mostly middle-class men and women, ranging in age from 18 to 86. Their responses were grouped into categories (such as family, personal, material). Age differences depended on the type of possible self examined. In terms of hoped-for selves, 18-to-24-year-olds listed family concerns most often (such as marrying the right person). In contrast, 25-to-39-year-olds listed family concerns last; their main concerns were personal issues such as being a more caring or loving person. By age 40–59,

One of the tasks of young adulthood is to think about the kind of adult one would like to become. Seeking out information about different occupations is one way to accomplish this.

family issues reemerged as primary, but the focus was on different issues (such as being the kind of parent who can "let go" of the children). For 60-to-86-year-olds, personal issues were again the most important, involving such things as remaining active and healthy.

All age groups listed physical issues as part of their most feared selves. For the younger groups, the fears most often involved being overweight and, for women, getting wrinkles and becoming unattractive. Middle-aged and older subjects often mentioned fear of getting Alzheimer's disease or being unable to care for themselves.

Overall, young adults were far more likely to have multiple possible selves and to believe that they could actually become the hoped-for self and successfully avoid the feared self. By old age, both the number of possible selves and strength of belief had decreased. Older adults were more likely to believe that neither the hoped-for nor the feared self was under their personal control.

Other researchers have examined possible selves in a different way by asking adults to describe their present, past, future, and ideal self (Ryff, 1991). Instead of examining categories of possible selves, this approach focuses on people's perceptions of change over time. The data indicate that young and middle-aged adults see themselves as improving with age (like Linus in the cartoon) and expecting to continue getting better in the future. In contrast,

PEANUTS, © 1989. Reprinted with permission of UFS, Inc.

older adults see themselves as having remained stable over time, but they foresee decline in their future.

These findings may indicate that the older group has internalized negative stereotypes about aging, especially in view of the fact that they were currently healthy and well-educated. To the extent that this explanation is true, the data provide strong support for an approach to personality development based on people's perceptions of reality. We will consider such a view in Chapter 12.

Taken together, the research on possible selves offers a way to examine the creation of scenarios and life stories systematically. It also provides a foundation for understanding how adults organize their self-perceptions into a coherent whole.

Self-Concept

In addition to looking into the future, adulthood brings with it a reexamination of the self-perceptions first formed in adolescence (see Chapter 8). The changes that occur in self-concept during young adulthood can best be understood as the outcome of a developmental process integrating self-concept with thinking (Kegan, 1982). Does the self-concept created through this interactive process undergo further change with age? The answer is, apparently not. In one of the few longitudinal studies of self-concept, researchers first surveyed a group of men about their self-concept when they were first-year college students, and then followed them for 14 years (Mortimer, Finch, & Kumka, 1982). The results raised important issues concerning the stability of self-concept and the importance of self-perceptions and life events.

Over the 14-year period, the men showed little change in self-concept as a group. The basic components of self-concept remained stable, despite some fluctuations in specific variables. For example, well-being and competence declined during college, but increased after graduation.

The data also revealed intriguing relations between perceptions of competence and life events. The course of a man's career, his satisfaction with his marriage, his relationship with his parents, and his overall life satisfaction could be predicted by his perceived level of competence. For example, men like those in the photo, whose competence scores remained above the group average, reported fewer job problems and higher marital and life satisfaction than men whose competence scores were below the group average.

Even more interesting was that a man's degree of confidence as a college senior was related to his later evaluation of life events—this may even have been a self-fulfilling prophecy. The researchers suggested that these men may have actively sought and created experiences that fit their perceptions of competence. This explanation is supported by longitudinal research on gifted women, whose high self-confidence in early adulthood was mirrored as high life satisfaction during their 60s (Sears & Barbee, 1978). These findings also provide additional support for Whitbourne's (1986) model (see pages 326–328), as they demonstrate that identity colors the way people interpret and experience events, which in turn shapes the future directions of their identity.

Personal Control Beliefs

At several points in this section, we have encountered the notion of personal control. **Personal control beliefs reflect the degree to which you believe that**

your performance in a situation depends on something that you do. For example, suppose you don't get a job that you think you should have. Was it your own fault? Or was it because the company was too shortsighted to recognize your true talent? Which of these options you select provides insight into a general tendency. Do you generally believe that outcomes depend on the things you do? Or are they due to factors outside of yourself, such as luck or the power of others?

Personal control is a very important concept that can be applied broadly (Baltes & Baltes, 1986). For example, personal control beliefs are not only important in personality development, but also (as we will see in Chapter 13) in memory performance in late life. Despite its importance, we do not have a clear picture of the developmental course of personal control beliefs. Evidence from both cross-sectional studies (Gatz & Siegler, 1981) and longitudinal studies (Lachman, 1985) is contradictory. Some data indicate that younger adults are less likely to hold internal control beliefs (that is, believe that they are in control of outcomes) than are older adults. Other research finds the opposite.

The contradiction may be due to the complex nature of personal control beliefs (Lachman, 1985). People's control beliefs vary depending on which domain, such as intelligence or health, is being assessed. Indeed, other research shows that perceived control over one's development shows an overall age-related decline, whereas perceived control over marital happiness increases (Brandtstädter, 1989). Additionally, younger adults are less likely than older adults to acknowledge the influence of outside influences on their behavior.

The sense of personal control is a complex, multidimensional aspect of personality that has broad implications for other aspects of adult development. Thus, it is possible that no overall age trends can be identified. Instead, changes in personal control beliefs may well depend on one's experiences in different domains and may differ widely from one domain to another.

TEST YOURSELF

1. A _____ is a unified sense of a person's past, present, and future.
2. A personal narrative that organizes past events into a coherent sequence is a _____.
3. Representations of what we could become, what we would like to be, and what we are afraid of becoming are _____.
4. The organized, coherent, integrated pattern of self-perceptions that includes the notions of self-esteem and self-image is called the

   _____.
5. _____ reflect the degree to which a person's performance in a situation is believed to be under his or her control.
6. How might people's scenarios, life stories, and other aspects of personality vary as a function of cognitive developmental level and self-definition as an adult?

Answers: (1) life-span construct, (2) life story, (3) possible selves, (4) self-concept, (5) personal control beliefs

Putting It All Together

In this chapter, we have seen how people make the transition from adolescence to adulthood. For many people, like Marcus, the transition is fuzzy, having more to do with arbitrary legal issues than anything else. In some cultures, though, there are clear, formalized rites of passage that make it much easier to pinpoint the beginning of adulthood. Young adults are fine physical specimens, reaching their peak in most areas of functioning. It is a time when people like Juan think about abandoning unhealthy habits acquired earlier in life, in favor of healthier lifestyles. Like Mary Ann, most young adults continue their cognitive growth by thinking in new ways. Young adulthood is a time when intellectual growth continues in some areas, but decline begins in others. Although people have been making moral decisions since early childhood, it becomes harder for young adults like Manuel to know what is right when faced with the dilemmas of real-world pressures. Young adults also tend to dream about their future like Felicia does, mapping out their lives in detail.

All in all, young adulthood is an exciting time of life. In many respects, life will never be this good, at least physically, ever again. New avenues are opened, and adult responsibilities are undertaken. The most important of these responsibilities are the topics for the next two chapters: love and work.

Thinking about Development

1. Given the patterns of cognitive and personality development described in the chapter, what differences would you expect to observe between 18-year-old and 35-year-old first-year college students? How would these differences be apparent in the classroom?

2. Recall that one of the forces in the biopsychosocial model is the social environment in which a person lives. What effect would living in an urban ghetto rather than a middle-class suburb have on moral reasoning? Why?

3. Describe the biological, psychological, social, and life-cycle forces influencing the possible selves people envision for themselves.

4. What connections do you see between crystallized intelligence, postformal thinking, and moral reasoning?

Summary

When Does Adulthood Begin?

Role Transitions As a General Framework

■ The most widely used criteria for deciding whether a person has reached adulthood are role transitions, which involve assuming new responsibilities and duties. Some societies use rituals, called rites of passage, to mark this transition clearly. These rituals tend to focus mainly on men. However, such rituals are largely absent in Western culture.

Going to College

■ By the turn of the century, half of all college students will be over 25. These students tend to be more moti-

vated and have many other positive characteristics. College also serves as a catalyst for cognitive development.

Psychological Views on Becoming an Adult

■ According to Schaie, a difference between adolescence and adulthood is the distinction between acquiring knowledge and applying knowledge and skills. A second major difference is a drop in the rate of participation in reckless behavior.

So When Do People Become Adults?

■ In cultures without clearly defined rites of passage, people become adults when they fully feel like adults.

Physical Development and Health

Growth, Strength, and Physical Functioning

■ Young adulthood is the time when several physical abilities peak: height, strength, muscle development, coordination, dexterity, and sensory acuity. Most of these abilities begin to decline in middle age.

Health Status

■ Young adults are also at the peak of health. Death from disease is relatively rare, especially during the 20s. Accidents are the leading cause of death. However, homicide and violence are major factors in some ethnic groups, and AIDS is a rapidly growing cause of death. Ethnic minorities have less access to good health care, and poverty is also a major barrier to good health.

Lifestyle Factors

■ Smoking is the single biggest contributor to health problems. It is related to half of all cancers and is a primary cause of respiratory and cardiovascular disease. Although it is difficult, quitting smoking has many health benefits.

■ For most people, drinking alcohol poses few health risks. For alcoholics, though, the consequences can be serious: withdrawal symptoms, liver disease, Wernicke-Korsakoff syndrome, and fertility problems. Several treatment approaches have been used for problem drinkers.

■ Nutritional needs change somewhat during adulthood, mostly due to changes in metabolism. Some nutrient needs, such as carbohydrates, change. The ratio of LDLs to HDLs in serum cholesterol, which can be controlled through diet in most people, is an important risk factor in cardiovascular disease.

Social, Gender, and Ethnic Issues in Health

■ The two most important social factors in health are socioeconomic status and education. The poorest health conditions exist for African Americans living in poor, inner-city slums. Other ethnic groups who have limited access to health care also suffer. Whether women or men are healthier is difficult to answer, because women have been excluded from much health research. Higher education is associated with better health, due to better access to health care and more knowledge about proper diet and lifestyle.

Cognitive Development

How Should We View Intelligence in Adulthood?

■ Most modern theories of intelligence are multidimensional. According to Baltes' research, its components show varying development in different abilities and different individuals.

What Happens to Intelligence in Adulthood?

■ Intellectual abilities can be studied as groups of related skills called *primary mental abilities*. These abilities develop differently and change in succeeding cohorts. More recent cohorts perform better on some skills, such as inductive reasoning, but older cohorts perform better on number skills.

■ Fluid intelligence consists of abilities that make people flexible and adaptive thinkers. Fluid abilities generally decline during adulthood. Crystallized intelligence reflects knowledge that people acquire through life experience and education in a particular culture. Crystallized abilities improve until late life.

Going beyond Formal Operations: Thinking in Adulthood

■ Postformal thought is characterized by a recognition that truth may vary from one situation to another, that solutions must be realistic, that ambiguity and contradiction are the rule, and that emotion and subjectivity play a role in thinking. One example of postformal thought is reflective judgment.

Moral Reasoning

Kohlberg's Theory

■ Kohlberg developed a theory of moral reasoning based on how people think about moral dilemmas. The theory proposes three levels (preconventional, conventional, postconventional), each containing two stages, resulting in a universal sequence. Stage 1 is obedience to authority; Stage 2 involves nice behavior in exchange for future favors; in Stage 3, live up to others' expectations; in Stage 4, follow rules to maintain social order; in Stage 5, adhere to a social contract when it is valid; Stage 6 involves personal morals based on abstract principles. There is strong evidence that the stages always occur in sequence, but there is less evidence for the universality of the theory.

Alternatives to Justice

■ Gilligan criticizes Kohlberg's theory on the grounds that it gives too much importance to justice in moral reasoning. Gilligan claimed that women based their reasoning more on an ethic of care and responsibility in interpersonal relationships. Research evidence suggests that males and females use both the justice approach and the care/responsibility approach, depending on the circumstances.

Cultural Differences in Moral Reasoning

■ Research evidence suggests that people in Western cultures tend to use a justice-based approach to moral reasoning more often than individuals in other cultures.

Who Do You Want to Be?: Personality in Young Adulthood

Creating Scenarios and Life Stories

■ Young adults create a life-span construct that represents a unified sense of the past, present, and future. This is manifested in two ways: through a scenario that maps out the future based on a social clock, and in the life story, which creates an autobiography.

Possible Selves

■ People create possible selves by projecting themselves into the future and thinking about what they would like to become, what they could become, and what they are afraid of becoming. Age differences in these projections depend on the dimension examined. In hoped-for selves, 18–24-year-olds and 40–59-year-olds report family issues as most important, whereas 25–39-year-olds and older adults consider personal issues to be most important. However, all groups include physical aspects as part of their most feared selves.

Self-Concept

■ Self-concept in adulthood is believed to develop in stages that integrate Piagetian and postformal thinking with emotional development. Self-concept appears to be relatively stable during adulthood.

Personal Control Beliefs

■ Personal control is an important concept with broad applicability. However, the developmental trends are complex, because personal control beliefs vary considerably from one domain to another.

Key Terms

addiction   (305)
conventional level   (321)
crystallized intelligence   (314)
fluid intelligence   (314)
high-density lipoproteins
    (HDLs)   (306)
instrumental orientation   (321)
interindividual variability   (310)
interpersonal norms   (321)
intimacy versus isolation   (298)
life story   (327)
life-span construct   (326)
low-density lipoproteins
    (LDLs)   (306)

metabolism   (306)
moral reasoning   (320)
multidimensional   (310)
multidirectionality   (310)
obedience orientation   (321)
personal control beliefs   (330)
plasticity   (310)
possible selves   (328)
postconventional level   (321)
postformal thought   (316)
preconventional level   (321)
primary mental abilities   (311)
reflective judgment   (317)
returning adult students   (297)

rites of passage   (296)
role transitions   (295)
scenario   (326)
secondary mental abilities   (314)
social clock   (327)
social contract   (321)
social system morality   (321)
universal ethical principles   (322)
Wernicke-Korsakoff
    syndrome   (305)

If You'd Like to Learn More

BELENKY, M. F., CLINCHY, B. M., GOLDBERGER, N. R., & TARULE, J. M. (1986). *Women's ways of knowing: The development of self, voice, and mind.* New York: Basic Books. The authors build a case that women think differently than men; they present data from interviews with 135 women, documenting five modes of thinking. The writing style is engaging.

BENNETT, W. I., GOLDFINGER, S. E., & JOHNSON, G. T. (Eds.). (1987). *Your good health: How to stay well and what to do when you're not.* Cambridge, MA: Harvard University Press. This good collection of articles blends scientific evidence with practical advice on a wide variety of health-related topics.

COMMONS, M., SINNOTT, J., RICHARDS, F., & ARMON, C. (Eds.). (1989). *Beyond formal operations,* Vols. I & II. New York: Praeger. This excellent collection of theory and research describes postformal thinking during adulthood.

KEGAN, R. (1982). *The evolving self: Problem and process in human development.* Cambridge, MA: Harvard University Press. This is a very intriguing, sometimes poetic, thought-provoking integration of cognitive and personality development.

WHITBOURNE, S. K. (1986). *The me I know: A study of adult identity.* New York: Springer-Verlag. This is the definitive study on the search for identity. It is based on extensive interviews and shows how adults integrate personal, family, and work issues.

❧ Jamal and Deb, both 25, have been madly in love since they met at a party about a month ago. They spend as much time together as possible and pledge that they will stay together forever. Deb finds herself daydreaming about Jamal at work and can't wait to go over to his apartment. She wants to move in, but her co-workers tell her to slow down.

❧ Kevin and Beth are on cloud nine. They got married one month ago and have recently returned from their honeymoon. Everyone who sees them can tell that they love each other a lot. They are highly compatible and have much in common, sharing most of their leisure activities. Kevin and Beth wonder what lies ahead in their marriage.

❧ Frank and Marilyn, both in their late 40s, weren't so lucky; they just got divorced. Although two of their children are married, their youngest daughter is still in college. The financial pressures Marilyn feels are beginning to take their toll. She wonders if her financial situation is similar to that of other recently divorced women.

❧ Bob, 32, and Denise, 33, just had their first child, Matthew, after several years of trying. They've heard that having children in their 30s can have advantages, but Bob and Denise wonder if people are just saying that to be nice to them. They are also concerned about the financial obligations they are likely to face.

Relationships in Adulthood

 Imagine yourself years from now. Your children are all grown and have children and grandchildren of their own. In honor of your 80th birthday, they have all gathered, along with your friends. As a present to you, they have assembled hundreds of photographs and dozens of videos from your life. As you begin looking at them, you realize how lucky you have been to have so many wonderful people in your life. Your relationships have made your adult life fun and worthwhile. As you watch the videos and look at the pictures, you wonder what it must be like to go through life totally alone. You think of all the wonderful experiences you would have missed in early and middle adulthood—never knowing what friendship is all about, never being in love, never dreaming about children and becoming a parent, never wishing on a star that you and someone special could be together. That is what we'll explore in this chapter: the ways in which we share our lives with others. First, we will consider what makes good friendships and love relationships. Because these relationships form the basis of our lifestyles, we will examine these next. In the third section, we will see what happens when marriages end. Finally, we will consider what it is like to be a parent. Throughout this chapter, the emphasis will be on aspects of relationships that are experienced by nearly everyone during young adulthood and middle age. In Chapter 12, we will examine aspects of relationships specific to middle-aged adults; in Chapter 14 we will do the same for relationships in later life.

Relationships

LEARNING OBJECTIVES

🥢 *What types of friendships do adults have? How do adult friendships develop?*

🥢 *What is love? How does it begin? How does it develop through adulthood?*

🥢 *What is the nature of violence in some relationships?*

What would your life be like if you had no one to share it with? There would be no one to go shopping or cruising with, no one to talk to on the phone, no one to cuddle close to while watching the sunset at a mountain lake. Although there are times when we really want to be alone, for the most part we are social creatures. We need people. Without friends and lovers, life would be pretty lonely.

In the next few sections, we take a look at several important kinds of relationships we have with others. First, we'll consider friendships. Next, we'll see what happens when love enters the picture, and we'll consider how people find mates. Unfortunately, some relationships turn violent; we'll examine the factors underlying aggressive behaviors between partners in the last section.

Friendships

What is an adult friend? Someone who is there when you need to share? Someone not afraid to tell you the truth? Someone to have fun with? Friends, of course, are all of these and more.

People tend to have more friends and acquaintances during young adulthood than at any subsequent period (Antonucci, 1985). Friendships are important throughout adulthood, in part because a person's life satisfaction is strongly related to the quantity and quality of contacts with friends (Antonucci, 1985). The importance of maintaining contacts with friends cuts across ethnic lines as well. For example, African Americans who have many friends are happier than those with only a few friends (Ellison, 1990). Thus, regardless of one's background, friendships play a major role in determining how much we enjoy life.

GENDER DIFFERENCES IN FRIENDSHIPS

Men's and women's friendships tend to differ in adulthood, continuing the patterns we first encountered in adolescence in Chapter 7 (Rawlins, 1992; Tannen,

1990). Women tend to base their friendships on more intimate and emotional sharing and use friendship as a means to confide in others. For women, getting together with friends often takes the form of asking them over for coffee to discuss personal matters. In contrast, men tend to base friendships on shared activities or interests. They are more likely to go bowling or fishing or to talk sports with their friends. For men, confiding in others is inconsistent with the need to compete; this may be one reason men are reluctant to do so (Huyck, 1982). Indeed, competition is often a part of men's friendships, as evidenced in pickup basketball games. However, the competition is usually set up so that the social interaction is the most important element, not who wins or who loses (Rawlins, 1992). Interestingly, the act of confiding, which is essential for intimacy (as we will see later), is a basis of the female approach to friendship. Compared to men, women have much more experience with such intimate sharing from early childhood, and they are more comfortable with vulnerability. Social pressure on men to be brave and strong may actually inhibit their ability to form close friendships (Rawlins, 1992).

MALE–FEMALE FRIENDSHIPS

Such differences in friendship formation create interesting opportunities and difficulties when men and women want to be friends with each other. Cross-gender friendships offer an opportunity to explore tasks or skills that are more commonly associated with the other gender, such as mowing the lawn, sewing, home repair, and cooking. But women may not understand why men want to set up mini-competitions all the time, and men may be baffled at why women keep wanting to talk about their problems (Tannen, 1990). Men also have a tendency to sexualize cross-gender friendships more often than women, who may be offended at such overtures and would prefer to remain just friends (Rawlins, 1992). Still, many men and women enjoy close friendships with each other and find their respective perspectives enjoyable.

Love Relationships

Love is one of those things that everybody feels but nobody can define completely. (Test yourself: Can you explain fully what you mean when you look at someone special and say, "I love you"?) One way researchers have tried to understand love is to think about what components are essential. In an interesting series of studies, Sternberg (1986) found that love has three basic components: (1) *passion*, an intense physiological desire for someone; (2) *intimacy*, the feeling that one can share all one's thoughts and actions with another; and (3) *commitment*, the willingness to stay with a person through good and bad times. Based on different combinations of these three components, Sternberg identified seven forms of love:

1. *Liking.* Intimacy is present, as are closeness, understanding, support, and affection, but there is no commitment or passion. This form describes most of our friendships.
2. *Infatuation.* As in the case of Jamal and Deb, the couple we met in the first vignette, there is lots of passion here, based on strong physical attraction. This is what people call "love at first sight." But infatuation can end just as quickly as it starts, as there is no intimacy or commitment.
3. *Empty love.* Sometimes, relationships lose their passion and intimacy, and are based only on commitment. An example is couples who no longer "love" each other but do not divorce because they have children.

Friendships among adults are a major source of their social network. Women base friendships on intimate and emotional sharing; men tend to base theirs on shared activities.

Love comes in many sizes, shapes, and styles. As described in the text, the seven types of love can be combined in many ways to characterize the various types of relationships adults have.

4. *Romantic love.* When couples connect both intimately and passionately, romance is born. But there is no commitment to complement their physical and emotional bonds.

5. *Fatuous love.* Once in a while, couples are "swept off their feet" into a rapid courtship and marriage. Their commitment is based on passion, because they have not given themselves time to let intimacy develop. Such relationships often fail as a result.

6. *Companionate love.* In this case, intimacy and commitment are both present. This type characterizes long-term friendships, as well as long-term marriages in which passion has diminished.

7. *Consummate love.* The goal of all love relationships is to have commitment, intimacy, and passion all present. Such complete love is very difficult to maintain without devoting a great deal of energy to working at it.

Ideally, a true love relationship has all three components. As we will see next, the balance among these components may shift as time passes.

LOVE THROUGH ADULTHOOD

The different combinations of love can be used to understand how relationships develop. Early in any relationship, passion is usually high, but intimacy and commitment tend to be low. This results in infatuation: an intense, physically based relationship in which the two people have a high risk of misunderstanding and jealousy. The desire for physical intimacy is high; emotional intimacy and commitment are low.

But infatuation is short-lived. Whereas even the smallest touch is enough to drive each partner into wild, lustful ecstasy in the beginning, with time it takes more and more to get the same feeling. As passion fades, a relationship either acquires emotional intimacy or it ends. Trust, honesty, openness, and acceptance must be a part of any strong relationship; when they are present, romantic love develops.

Given more time, people become committed to each other. They spend much of their time together, make decisions together, care for each other, share possessions, and develop ways to settle conflicts. Couples usually show outward signs of commitment, such as wearing a lover's ring, having children together, or simply sharing the mundane details of daily life, from making toast at breakfast to before-bed rituals.

Although the styles of love appear to differ with age, some important aspects of love relationships maintain their same relative importance over time. In one study, researchers examined communication, sexual intimacy, respect, help and play behaviors, emotional security, and loyalty. As can be seen in the graph, the importance of some aspects of love differ as a function of age. But the relative rankings of the different components of love are the same for all age groups.

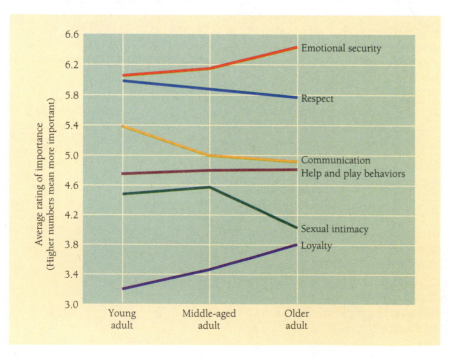

Thus, although the particular weightings may vary, there are remarkable similarities across age groups in the nature of love relationships (Reedy, Birren, & Schaie, 1981). These results make intuitive sense. For example, young couples may focus more on communication, because they are still in the process of getting to know each other, but communication is important in any relationship.

FALLING IN LOVE

Everybody wants to be loved by somebody, but actually having it happen is fraught with difficulties. In his book *The Prophet,* Kahlil Gibran points out that love is two-sided: just as it can give you the greatest ecstasy, so can it cause you the greatest pain. Yet, like the couple in the photograph above, most of us are willing to take the risk.

As you may have experienced, taking the risk is fun (at times) and difficult (at other times). Making a connection can be ritualized, as when people use pickup lines in a bar, or it can happen almost by accident, as when two people literally run into each other in a crowded corridor. The dating scene may even bring us into contact with people who have high opinions of themselves, as in the Far Side cartoon. The question that confronts us is "How do men and women fall in love?"

The answer is that they do it quite differently. Men tend to be more romantic: believing in love at first sight, feeling that there is only one true love destined for them, regarding love as magical and impossible to understand, and believing rather quickly that they are compatible with their partner. Women tend to be cautious pragmatists who believe that financial security is as important as passion in a relationship, that there are many people whom a person could learn to love, and that love does not conquer all differences (Peplau & Gordon, 1985). These

"Well, look who's here . . . God's gift to warthogs."

THE FAR SIDE, © 1983 Gary Larson. Reprinted with permission of Chronicle Features. All rights reserved.

Dissatisfaction in relationships has different meanings for men and women. For men, but not for women, it is a good prediction of the demise of the relationship.

SPOTLIGHT ON RESEARCH

DAVID M. BUSS

"Few domains of human activity generate as much discussion, as many laws, or such elaborate rituals in all cultures [as mating]."

differences even carry over into views about the best way to make up after a fight: Most men believe that the best way for a woman to apologize is through passionate sex, whereas most women believe the best way for a man to apologize is through a personal, heartfelt discussion (Peplau & Gordon, 1985). Finally, a man's dissatisfaction with a heterosexual relationship is a much better predictor of the relationship's demise than a woman's dissatisfaction, in part because women's approach to love includes a stronger desire to try to make the relationship work (Cowan & Cowan, 1992).

How do these behaviors compare cross-culturally? In an extraordinary study, Buss and a large team of researchers (1990) identified the effects of culture and gender on heterosexual mate preferences in 37 cultures worldwide, as described in the Spotlight on Research feature. Chastity proved to be the characteristic showing the most variability across cultures, being highly desired in some cultures but mattering little in others. Interestingly, in their respective search for mates, men around the world valued physical attractiveness in women, whereas women around the world looked for men capable of being good providers. But men and women around the world agreed that love and mutual attraction were most important, and nearly all cultures rated dependability, emotional stability, kindness, and understanding as important factors. Attraction, it seems, has some characteristics that transcend culture.

The Mating Game around the World

If you were a woman living in India, how would the man of your dreams differ from the ideal man of a woman living in Finland? Likewise, how do the desired men differ for women living in Nigeria and Great Britain? Buss and his colleagues decided to find out. They specifically examined the effects of culture and gender on mate preferences, using a truly worldwide sample. A total of 9474 participants from 33 countries, on six continents and five islands, took part in the study.

The researchers asked participants to complete questionnaires concerning important factors in choosing a mate, such as rating desired characteristics of potential mates, and preferences concerning potential mates, such as ranking characteristics of potential mates from highest to lowest. Data were gathered by research teams in each country. In some cases, the survey items had to be modified to reflect the local culture. For example, many couples in Sweden, Finland, and Norway never get married, opting instead simply to live together. In Nigeria, items had to reflect the possibility of many wives due to the practice of polygyny. Data collection in South Africa was described as "a rather frightening experience," due to the difficulty in collecting data from both white and Zulu samples in the midst of civil unrest. Finally, in some cases data were never received, because of government interference or the lack of official approval to conduct the study. Such problems highlight the difficulty in doing cross-cultural research and the need to take local culture into account in designing research instruments.

Each culture displayed a unique ordering of preferences concerning ideal characteristics. Nevertheless, two main dimensions emerged, as shown in the figure on page 343. The closer countries are in the figure, the more similar men and women in them were in ranking desirable qualities in a mate.

First, cultures varied as to whether they represented more traditional values or modern industrial values in mate selection (represented in the figure by the horizontal dimension). In traditional cultures, men placed a high value on a mate's chastity, desire for home and children, and being a good cook and

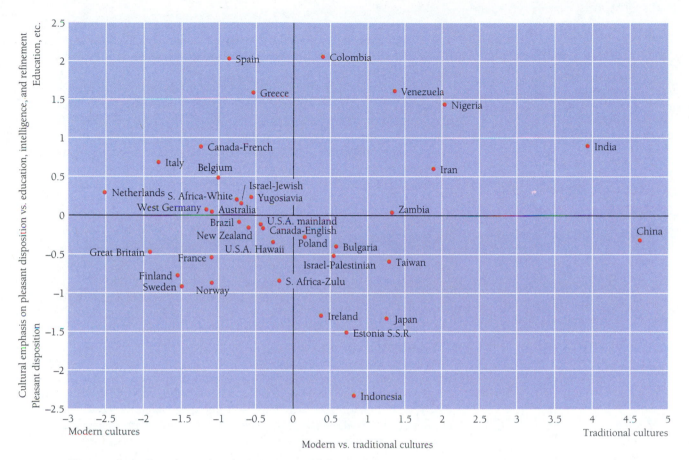

(Note: numbers refer to the number of rating points away from average.)

housekeeper; women placed a high value on a mate's ambition and industry, being a good financial prospect, and holding favorable social status. People in modern industrial cultures still valued these qualities, but to a lesser extent. Countries such as China, India, Iran, and Nigeria represent the traditional end, whereas the Netherlands, Great Britain, Finland, and Sweden represent the modern end.

The vertical dimension reflects the relative importance of education, intelligence, and social refinement, as opposed to a pleasing disposition in choosing a mate. As you can see in the figure, people in Spain, Colombia, and Greece highly valued education, intelligence, and social refinement; in contrast, people in Indonesia placed a greater emphasis on having a pleasing disposition.

Overall, Buss and his colleagues' results clearly demonstrate that mate selection is a complex process no matter where you live. The study also shows that socialization plays a key role in attractiveness; characteristics that are highly desirable in one culture may not be so desirable in another.   🖋

Violence in Relationships

Up to this point, we have been considering relationships that are relatively healthy and positive. Sadly, this is not always the case. **Sometimes relationships become violent; one person becomes aggressive toward the partner, creating an *abusive relationship*.** Such relationships have received increasing attention over the past few decades. Indeed, some authors believe, as does the U.S. criminal justice system under some circumstances, that abusive relationships can be used as an explanation for antisocial or criminal behavior (Walker, 1984). **For example, in the case of** *battered woman syndrome,* **a woman believes that she cannot leave the abusive situation, and she may even go so far as to kill her abuser.**

What kind of aggressive behaviors occur in abusive relationships? What causes such abuse? Researchers are beginning to find answers to these and related questions. Based on a decade of research on abusive partners, O'Leary (1993) argues that there is a continuum of aggressive behaviors toward a spouse, which progresses as follows: verbally aggressive behaviors, physically aggressive behaviors, severe physically aggressive behaviors, and murder of the partner. Examples of each are listed in the chart below.

Verbal aggression ⟶	*Physical aggression* ⟶	*Severe aggression* ⟶	*Murder*
Insults	Pushing	Beating	
Yelling	Slapping	Punching	
Name-calling	Shoving	Hitting with object	

Two points are interesting concerning this continuum. First, there may be fundamental differences in the types of aggression, beyond the level of severity. Lower levels of physically aggressive behavior, such as pushing or slapping, are relatively common; 25–40% of men and women who are in committed relationships display such behaviors on occasion (Riggs & O'Leary, 1992; Straus, Gelles, & Steinmetz, 1980). In contrast, some men are extremely abusive from the outset of the relationship; they are thought to make up the subset of batterers who cause serious physical injury to their partners and create coercive control over their lives (Stark, 1992).

The second interesting point, depicted in the next chart, is that the suspected underlying causes of aggressive behaviors differ as the type of aggressive

Verbal aggression ⟶	*Physical aggression* ⟶	*Severe aggression* ⟶	*Murder*
Insults	Pushing	Beating	
Yelling	Slapping	Punching	
Name-calling	Shoving	Hitting with object	

Causes
Need to control[a] ⟶
Misuse of power[a] ⟶
Jealousy[a] ⟶
Marital discord ⟶

Accept violence as a means of control ⟶
Modeling of physical aggression ⟶
Abused as a child ⟶
Aggressive personality styles ⟶
Alcohol abuse ⟶

Personality disorders ⟶
Emotional lability ⟶
Poor self-esteem ⟶

Contributing factors: job stressors and unemployment

Note: Need to control and variables on the left are associated with all forms of aggression; acceptance of violence and variables in the middle are associated with physical aggression, severe aggression, and murder. Personality disorders and the variables on the right are associated with severe aggression and murder.

[a.] More relevant for males than for females

behaviors changes (O'Leary, 1993). As you can see, the number of suspected causes of aggressive behavior increases as the level of aggression increases. Thus, the causes of aggressive behavior become more complex as the level of aggression worsens. Such differences in cause imply that the approaches to treating abusers should vary with the nature of the aggressive behavior (O'Leary, 1993). Situational factors that contribute to all levels of aggression are alcoholism, job stress, and unemployment; the presence of these factors increases the likelihood that violence will occur in the relationship (O'Leary, 1993).

Gender differences have been reported in some of the underlying causes of aggressive behavior in relationships (O'Leary, 1993). Most important, the triad of need to control, misuse of power, and jealousy are more pertinent causes for men than for women. For example, men are more likely than women to act aggressively because they want to make sure their partner knows "who the boss is" and who makes the rules.

Two additional, and controversial, causes of aggressive or abusive behaviors have been widely discussed: attitudes held by a patriarchal society and having been abused as a child. Feminist critiques of the causes of family violence argue that male aggression toward the female partner results in part from the inequality of women in a patriarchal society (Dobash & Dobash, 1992; Yllö, 1993). From this perspective, abuse is considered to be a "normal" result of male socialization, in which domination of women is strongly reinforced in society. Indeed, the pattern of gender differences discussed above supports this view, in that men are more likely than women to act aggressively out of a need to exert control or power. Also, there is some cross-cultural evidence showing that when women and men are treated more equally, men are unlikely to abuse women (Levinson, 1988). Thus, male violence against women is thought to be one of the means for men to dominate women (Yllö, 1993).

The second controversial cause of aggressive behavior in relationships concerns the widely held belief that people who are abusers were probably abused themselves as children (O'Leary, 1993). But is there evidence to support this view? It certainly looks that way when people who are in therapy for abusing their partners are examined. In this case, 60% of men had been victims of child abuse themselves, and 44% had witnessed violence between parents (O'Leary, 1993). Because few women are in therapy as abusers, similar statistics for them are unavailable.

But if abusive individuals in the general population are examined, including those who are not in therapy, the picture changes dramatically. In general community samples, 13% of men and 12% of women who were physically aggressive toward their partners had been exposed to violence in their families of origin, either by being abused themselves or witnessing their parents be violent toward each other (O'Leary, 1993).

These statistics underscore the complexity of the causes of aggressive behaviors toward one's partner. At least in community samples, the majority of aggressive partners were not victims of abuse themselves as children. Having experienced or witnessed violence as a child may be more predictive of which people may end up in therapy for abusive behavior than of who is likely to become abusive in the first place.

Researchers are also beginning to document differences in how aggressive behaviors are viewed by the men and women who display them. For example, partners in relatively new relationships who display lower levels of physical aggression (pushing, shoving) tend not to view them as abusive, and they claim not to have done them in self-defense (Cascardi, Vivian, & Meyer, 1991; O'Leary et al., 1989). However, women in longer-term relationships view their

Violence in relationships is a serious problem and usually involves men who abuse women. Organizations such as this one provide much-needed safe havens for victims of abuse.

aggressive acts as self-defense; men still tend not to see them as either abusive or self-defense (Cascardi et al., 1991). And the reasons why men and women kill their partners also differ (Browne & Williams, 1993; Cascardi & O'Leary, 1992). Men tend to murder their partners on the basis of jealousy and need for control. In contrast, women usually have contacted law enforcement agencies repeatedly to ask for protection prior to murdering their partners, indicating that women kill mainly in self-defense.

You may wonder why people stay in abusive relationships. One reason is that many abused individuals have low self-esteem and do not believe that there is anything they can do about their situation; indeed, many believe that they deserve their abuse (Walker, 1984). Fear also plays a major role, especially with abused women, as some who leave the relationship are tracked down and killed by (ex-)boyfriends and (ex-)husbands. Other victims may minimize the abuse, saying that it only happens when their lover is drunk or high, or when stressed, or even that it is a sign of love for them. Surprisingly, some abused women who are beaten regularly do not consider their relationships unhappy (O'Leary et al., 1989).

Many communities have realized the seriousness of abuse and have established shelters for battered women and their children. Programs have also been established to treat abusive men. However, the legal system in many localities is not set up to deal with domestic violence; women in some locations cannot sue their husbands for assault, and restraining orders may offer little real protection from additional violence. Much remains to be done to protect women and their children from the fear and the reality of continued abuse.

FORCES IN ACTION

Influences on Relationships in Adulthood

Adult relationships are complex. Who chooses whom, and whether the feelings will be mutual, results from the interaction of developmental forces described in the biopsychosocial model presented in Chapter 1. Biologically, it turns out that there are two distinct stages: attraction and attachment (Liebowitz, 1983). These two stages reflect fundamentally different neurochemical processes (Fisher, 1994). Attraction is associated with neurochemicals related to the amphetamines, which account for the exhilaration of falling in love. Attachment, which some people might call long-term commitment and tranquility, is reflected neurochemically in substances related to morphine, a powerful narcotic. (Love really does do a number on your brain!)

Psychologically, we saw in Chapter 9 that an important developmental issue is intimacy; according to Erikson, mature relationships are impossible without it. Additionally, the kinds of relationships you saw and experienced as a child (and whether they involved violence) affect how you define and act in relationships you develop as an adult. The social forces of culture shape the characteristics you find desirable in a mate and determine whether you are likely to encounter resistance from your family when you have made your choice. Life-cycle forces matter, too; different aspects of love are more or less important, depending on your stage in life.

In short, to understand adult relationships, one must take the forces of the biopsychosocial model into account. Relying too heavily on one or two of the forces provides an incomplete description of why people are successful (or not) in finding a partner or a friend. Using the biopsychosocial model also keeps us aware that people's needs in relationships differ as they move through adulthood.   ❧

TEST YOURSELF

1. Friendships based on intimacy and emotional sharing are more characteristic of _____.
2. Competition is a major part of most friendships among _____.
3. Love relationships in which intimacy and passion are present but commitment is not are termed _____.
4. Chastity is an important quality that men look for in a potential female mate in _____ cultures.
5. Aggressive behavior that is based on abuse of power, jealousy, or need to control is more likely to be displayed by _____.
6. Why is intimacy (discussed in Chapter 9) a necessary prerequisite for adult relationships, according to Erikson? What aspects of relationships discussed here support (and refute) this view?

Lifestyles

LEARNING OBJECTIVES

❧ *Why do some people decide not to marry, and what are these people like?*

❧ *What are the characteristics of cohabiting people?*

❧ *What are gay male and lesbian relationships like?*

❧ *What is marriage like through the course of adulthood?*

Developing relationships is only part of the picture in understanding how adults live their lives with other people. Putting relationships in context is the goal of the following sections, as we explore adults' lifestyles: singlehood, cohabitation, gay male and lesbian couples, and marriage.

Singlehood

During the early years of adulthood, most people are single. Current estimates are that approximately 75% of men and 60% of women between the ages of 20 and 25 are unmarried, with increasing numbers deciding to stay that way. These percentages have been rising over the past few decades, and they are fairly similar in all industrialized countries (Burns, 1992).

DECIDING NOT TO MARRY

Men and women typically decide whether to remain single between 25 and 30 (Phillis & Stein, 1983). Why do some people decide to remain single? Various explanations have been offered, including changes in sexual standards, increased financial independence of women, liberation movements, and changes in views about marriage (Safilios-Rothschild, 1977; Stein, 1978). Some adults may simply postpone the decision about whether to marry indefinitely and slide into singlehood.

Because they spend a lifetime without a spouse, single adults develop long-standing alternative social patterns based on friendships. Never-married women may become highly involved with relatives—caring for an aged parent, living with a sibling, or actively helping nieces and nephews. Loneliness is typically not a major problem (Essex & Nam, 1987; Rubinstein, 1987). Unfortunately, little is known about whether never-married men develop similar patterns.

WHAT ARE NEVER-MARRIED PEOPLE LIKE?

Many never-married adults have more androgynous gender identities, have high achievement needs, are more autonomous, and want to maintain close relationships with others (Phillis & Stein, 1983). Many singles are acutely aware of their ambivalent feelings: desires to have a successful career, and equally strong desires for intimacy. For many, this ambivalence is the reason they choose not to risk marriage.

A difficult issue for single people is others' expectations that they should marry. People often assume that everyone should get married, and sometimes force a single person to defend his or her status. This pressure to marry is especially strong for women; frequent questions like "Any good prospects yet?" may leave women feeling conspicuous or left out as many of their friends marry.

Although attitudes are changing, Western society remains highly couple-oriented. As their friends marry, single people's friendship networks shrink. Still, most never-married people report that they are quite happy; the satisfaction derived from careers and friendships is sufficient (Alwin, Converse, & Martin, 1985).

The United States, like most Western countries, is a very couple-oriented society. Single adults may feel like the "odd person out" when all of their friends are in relationships.

Cohabitation

Being unmarried does not necessarily mean living alone. **People in committed relationships may decide that living together, or** *cohabitation*, **provides a way to share daily life.** Cohabitation is becoming an increasingly popular lifestyle choice in the United States as well as in Canada, Europe, Australia, and elsewhere. Although cohabitants come from all socioeconomic backgrounds and represent all ages, most tend to be from lower socioeconomic groups. For instance, some younger and older couples alike cohabit for financial reasons (Glick & Norton, 1979).

Young adults view cohabitation more as a step toward marriage than as a permanent alternative to it (Bumpass, Sweet, & Cherlin, 1991). This is especially true of women, who are much more eager to marry their partners than are men. Men are more open to cohabiting and do not feel the need for as strong an emotional commitment before living together. Women generally expect a deeper commitment and may feel exploited if it is absent (Macklin, 1988).

Most cohabiting couples either marry or end the relationship within two to three years (Macklin, 1988). Interestingly, having cohabited does not seem to make marriages any better; in fact, it may do more harm than good, resulting in marriages that are less happy (Booth & Johnson, 1988). Why is this the case? Part of the answer may be that cohabiting couples tend to be less conventional, less religious, and come from lower socioeconomic backgrounds, which may put them at higher risk for divorce (DeMaris & Rao, 1992). Part of the reason may also be that marrying after already having lived with someone represents much less of a change in the relationship than when a couple marry who have not been cohabiting; such couples lack the newly wedded bliss seen in couples who have not cohabited (Thompson & Colella, 1992). Although there are many good reasons for cohabiting, preparing a couple for marriage apparently is not one of them.

Gay Male and Lesbian Couples

What is it like to be in a gay male or lesbian relationship? One woman shares her experience in the Real People feature.

REAL PEOPLE

Maggie O'Carroll's Story

I am a 35-year-old woman who believes that each person is here with a purpose to fulfill in his or her lifetime. "Add your light to the sum of light" are words I live by in my teaching career, my personal life with friends and family, and living in general. I do not believe that our creator makes mistakes, although at times I am very discouraged by the level of hatred that is evident in the world against many groups, but against homosexuals in particular.

For me, being a lesbian is the most natural state of being. I do not think of it as a mishap of genetics, a result of an unhappy or traumatic childhood, or an unnatural tendency. From the time I was a child I had a definite and strong sense of my sexual identity. However, I am aware of the homophobia that is present at all levels of my own life and in the community. That is where my sense of self and living in the world collide.

Society does not value diversity. We, as a people, do not look to people who are different and acknowledge the strength it takes to live in this society. Being gay in a homophobic, heterosexist society is a burden that manifests itself in many forms, such as through alcohol and drug abuse rates that are much higher than in the heterosexual community. The lack of acknowledgment of gay people's partners by family members, co-workers, and society at large is a stamp of nonexistence and invisibility. How can we build a life with a partner and then not share that person with society?

I consider myself a fortunate gay person in that I have a supportive family. Of the five children in my family, two of us are gay. My parents are supportive and love our partners. My siblings vary in their attitudes. One sister invited me and my partner to her wedding. Nine years later, my other sister refused to do that. Her discomfort over my sexual orientation meant that I spent a special event without my partner at my side. However, my straight brother was allowed to bring a date. It was very hurtful and hard to forgive.

In the larger community, I have been surprised by the blatant hatred I have experienced. I have demeaning comments aimed at me. The home I live in has been defaced with obscenities. But on a more positive note, I have never been more strongly certain of who I am. I am indebted to those who have supported me over the years with love and enlightenment, knowing that who I am is not a mistake. As I age, it becomes clearer to me that I am meant to share the message that our differences are to be appreciated and respected.   ❧

Less is known about the developmental course of gay male and lesbian relationships than heterosexual relationships, largely because they were almost never the focus of research. To date, two primary aspects of gay male and lesbian relationships have been examined, usually in comparison to married heterosexual couples: sexual expression and interpersonal relations.

Sexual expression is one difference between heterosexual couples and gay male or lesbian couples. On average, gay men have sex with each other early in the relationship more than any other type of couple, but frequency declines rapidly as the relationship continues (Blumstein & Schwartz, 1983). In contrast, lesbian couples are more likely to have intense, intimate, monogamous relationships than are gay men, and they tend to have sex far less frequently than any other group (Blumstein & Schwartz, 1983). Lesbian couples are also more likely to stay together than are gay men.

Gay male and lesbian relationships are similar to marriages in many ways; financial problems and decisions, household chores, and deciding who has the most decision-making power are issues for all couples. Moreover, gay male and lesbian parents do not differ substantially from heterosexual parents in terms of style (Harris & Turner, 1986). Like all couples, decisions are made about the style of the relationship, whether the roles of nurturer and provider are clearly defined, and whether the relationship will be sexually open (Blumstein & Schwartz, 1983). Gay male and lesbian couples overall are more egalitarian than heterosexual couples, with lesbian couples most egalitarian of all (Peplau, 1991). Overall, there appear to be few differences and many similarities between heterosexual, gay male, and lesbian couples.

The characteristics of gay male and lesbian couples are much the same as those of heterosexual couples. On most dimensions, this couple would be essentially the same as a married heterosexual couple.

Marriage

Most adults want their love relationships to result in marriage. However, U.S. residents are in less of a hurry to achieve this goal; the median age at first marriage for adults in the United States has been rising for several decades. As you can see in the graph, between 1970 and the late 1980s, the median age for men rose about 3 years, from roughly 23 to 26, and the age for women rose nearly 4 years, from roughly 20 to 24 (U.S. Bureau of the Census, 1991). This trend is not bad; brides under age 20 at the time they are first married are three

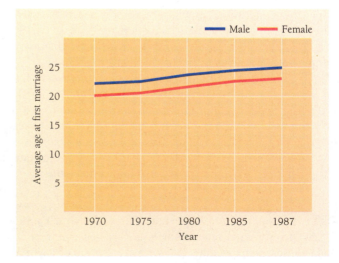

times more likely to end up divorced than first brides in their 20s, and six times more likely than first-time brides in their 30s (U.S. Bureau of the Census, 1991). Let's explore age and other factors that keep marriages going strong over time.

WHAT FACTORS HELP MARRIAGES SUCCEED?

One reason that age is important has to do with the couple's level of psychosocial development. Erikson (1982) points out that intimacy, the task of young adulthood, is difficult to achieve unless one has developed a strong sense of identity, the task of adolescence (see Chapter 8). Because many adolescents are still trying to decide who they are, teenage newlyweds may initially find themselves compatible but soon grow apart as they mature. Additional complicating factors, such as pregnancy and unemployment, can also stack the deck against successful teenage marriages.

A second important predictor of successful marriage is *homogamy*, or similarity of values and interests. To the extent that the partners share similar values, goals, attitudes, socioeconomic status, and ethnic background, their relationship is more likely to succeed (Diamond, 1986). Homogamy is an important factor in a wide variety of cultures and societies, as diverse as suburbanites in Michigan and Africans in Chad (Diamond, 1986).

A third factor in predicting marital success is a feeling that the relationship is equal. **According to *exchange theory*, marriage is based on each partner contributing something to the relationship that the other would be hard-pressed to provide.** Satisfying and happy marriages result when both partners perceive that there is a fair exchange in all the dimensions of the relationship. Problems achieving such equity can arise because of the competing demands of work and family, an issue we will take up again in Chapter 11.

What do couples give as their own reasons for staying together? The lists below show the top ten reasons (in order of frequency) given by women and men who have been married at least 15 years (Lauer & Lauer, 1985).

Men	Women
My spouse is my best friend.	My spouse is my best friend.
I like my spouse as a person.	I like my spouse as a person.
Marriage is a long-term commitment.	Marriage is a long-term commitment.
Marriage is sacred.	Marriage is sacred.
We agree on aims and goals.	We agree on aims and goals.
My spouse has grown more interesting.	My spouse has grown more interesting.
I want the relationship to succeed.	I want the relationship to succeed.
An enduring marriage is important to social stability.	We laugh together.
We laugh together.	We agree on a philosophy of life.
I am proud of my spouse's achievements.	We agree on how and how often to show affection.

The lists are striking for their high degree of similarity in the reasons and their rankings. But does similarity in reasons for staying together translate inevitably into happy marriages?

DO MARRIED COUPLES STAY HAPPY?

Few sights are happier than a couple on their wedding day. Newlyweds like Kevin and Beth, in the second opening vignette, are at the peak of marital bliss.

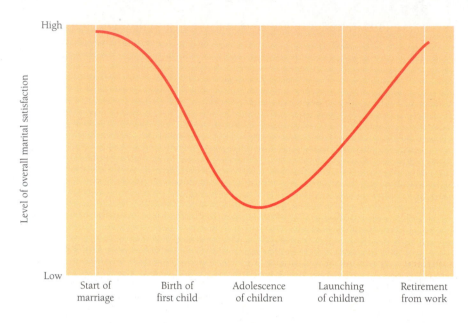

As you might suspect, though, couples' feelings do change over time. Like any relationship, marriage has its peaks and valleys. As shown in the graph, over-all marital satisfaction tends to be highest at the beginning of the marriage, falls until the children begin leaving home, and rises again in later life (Berry & Williams, 1987).

Marriages are most intense in their early days. The couple spends considerable time talking, going out, establishing their marital roles, arguing, making up, and making love. When husbands and wives share many activities and are open to new experiences together, bliss results (Olson & McCubbin, 1983). When the marriage is troubled, the intensity of the early phase creates considerable unhappiness (Swenson, Eskew, & Kohlhepp, 1981).

Early in a marriage, the couple must learn to adjust to the different perceptions and expectations each person has for the other. Many wives tend to be more concerned than their husbands with keeping close ties with their friends. Women are also more likely to identify problems in the marriage and want to talk about them (Peplau & Gordon, 1985). The couple must also learn to handle confrontation. Indeed, learning effective strategies for resolving conflict is an essential component of a strong marriage, as these strategies provide ways for couples to discuss their problems maturely.

Less-educated couples experience greater dissatisfaction with their marriages, as do couples who do not pool their financial resources (Kurdek, 1991a). This occurs because less-educated couples face many additional stressors (e.g., higher rates of unemployment, lower financial security), and the failure to pool resources may reflect a lack of trust in the partner.

As newlywedded bliss fades, marital satisfaction tends to decline (Glenn & McLanahan, 1981, 1982). The most common reason for this drop is the birth of children. For most couples, having children means having substantially less time to devote to the marriage. Taking care of children is hard work, requiring energy that used to be spent on keeping the marriage alive and well (Glenn & Weaver, 1978). Most couples are ecstatic over having their first child, a tangible product of their love for each other. But soon the reality of child care sets in, with 2:00 A.M. feedings, diaper changing, and the like, not to mention the long-term financial obligations that will continue at least until the child becomes an adult.

The early period of a relationship requires adjustment. As this couple is demonstrating, there needs to be considerable discussion of issues such as finances in order for individual styles to mesh more easily.

Childless couples may also experience a decline in marital satisfaction. Specifically, couples who are childless because of infertility face the stress associated with the inability to have children, which lowers their marital satisfaction (Matthews & Matthews, 1986).

By midlife, marital satisfaction hits its lowest point, but there are differences in how husbands and wives view the relationship (Turner, 1982). Husbands at all stages of the marriage tend to describe it in positive terms, whereas middle-aged wives tend to be more critical. For example, one study found that 80% of husbands but only 40% of wives rated their marriages favorably in midlife (Lowenthal, Thurnher, & Chiriboga, 1975). Wives' chief complaint about their husbands was that they were too dependent and clingy; interestingly, newlyweds also differ in this regard, but at that point husbands describe their wives as being too dependent.

For most couples, marital satisfaction improves after the children begin to leave (Rhyne, 1981). The upward shift is especially apparent in wives, and it stems from the increased financial security after children leave, the relief from the day-to-day duties of parenting, and the additional time that wives have with their husbands.

For some middle-aged couples, however, marital satisfaction continues to be low. They may have grown apart but continue to live together (exhibiting empty love in Sternberg's theory). In essence, they have become emotionally divorced; for these couples, spending more time together is not a welcome change (Fitzpatrick, 1984). Because the physical appearance of one's partner is a contributor to marital satisfaction, particularly for men, age-related changes in appearance may contribute to further deterioration of the relationship (Margolin & White, 1987).

Marital satisfaction is fairly high in older couples (Lee, 1988). However, satisfaction in long-term marriages—that is, marriages of 40 years or more—is a complex issue. One study found that 80% of couples married at least 50 years recollected their marriages as being happy from their wedding day to the present (Sporakowski & Axelson, 1984). In general, however, marital satisfaction among older couples increases shortly after retirement but then decreases with health problems and advancing age (Gilford, 1984). The level of satisfaction in these marriages appears to be unrelated to the amount of past or present sexual interest or sexual activity, but it is positively related to the degree of interaction with friends (Bullock & Dunn, 1988; Lee, 1988). Surprisingly, though, only approximately 25% of these couples named their spouse as being one of their closest friends (Sporakowski & Axelson, 1984). Indeed, many older couples have simply developed detached, contented styles (Norton & Moorman, 1987).

Although no two marriages are exactly the same, couples must be flexible and adaptable. Couples (like the one shown in the photograph) who have been happily married for many years show an ability to roll with the punches and to adapt to changing circumstances in the relationship. For example, a serious illness of one spouse may not be detrimental to the relationship and may even make the bond stronger. Likewise, couples' expectations about marriage change over time, gradually becoming more congruent (Weishaus & Field, 1988). It takes a great deal of love, humor, and perseverance to stay happily married a long time. But it *can* be done.

TEST YOURSELF

1. A difficulty for many single people is that _____.
2. Young adults view cohabitation as a _____ marriage.
3. Gay male and lesbian relationships are similar to _____.
4. According to _____, marriage is based on each partner contributing something to the relationship that the other would be hard-pressed to provide.
5. For most couples, marital satisfaction _____ after the birth of the first child.
6. Given that the research literature indicates some advantage to having one's first child after the age of 30, would there be even more advantages in waiting until 40 or later? What issues are important to consider?

Divorce and Remarriage

LEARNING OBJECTIVES

❧ *Who gets divorced? How does divorce affect relationships with children?*

❧ *What are remarriages like? How are they similar to and different from first marriages?*

Despite what couples pledge on their wedding day, some marriages do not last until death parts the couple; rather, they are dissolved through divorce. But even though divorce is stressful and difficult, thousands of people each year also choose to try again and remarry. Most enter their second (or third or fourth) marriage with renewed expectations of success. Are these new dreams realistic? As we'll see, it depends on many things; among the most important is whether children are involved.

Divorce

Most couples enter marriage with the idea that their relationship will be permanent. Unfortunately, fewer and fewer couples experience this permanence. Rather than growing together, couples grow apart.

WHO GETS DIVORCED AND WHY?

Compared to other countries, divorce in the United States is common; as you can see in the graph on page 355, couples have roughly a 50-50 chance of remaining married for life (Fisher, 1987). In contrast, the divorce rates in Canada, Great Britain, Australia, and Sweden are about one in three, and only one in ten in Japan, Italy, Israel, and Spain (U.S. Bureau of the Census, 1991). Statistics worldwide and from different historical periods indicate that if marriages fail, they do so on average within 3 or 4 years (Fisher, 1987).

Answers: (1) others expect that they should marry, (2) step toward (3) marriages, (4) exchange theory, (5) decreases

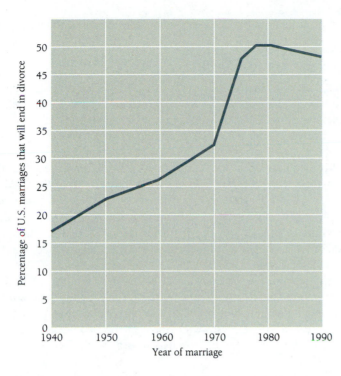

One factor consistently related to divorce rates in the United States is ethnicity. African Americans are more likely than European Americans to divorce or separate (Glenn & Supancic, 1984). Hispanic groups show considerable variability; Mexican Americans and Cuban Americans have divorce rates similar to European Americans, whereas the rate for Puerto Ricans is much higher (Bean & Tienda, 1987).

Another major factor is change in laws and social norms, which is reflected in the reasons people give for divorcing. In 1948, divorced women cited cruelty, excessive drinking, and nonsupport as the most common reasons (Goode, 1956). By 1985, the reasons had shifted to communication problems, unhappiness, and incompatibility (Cleek & Pearson, 1985). Men and women typically agree on the reasons for divorce, listed below from most frequently cited to least (Cleek & Pearson, 1985):

Reasons Men Give	*Reasons Women Give*
Communication problems	Communication problems
Basic unhappiness	Basic unhappiness
Incompatibility	Incompatibility
Sexual problems	Emotional abuse
Financial problems	Financial problems
Emotional abuse	Sexual problems
Women's liberation	Alcohol abuse by spouse
In-laws	Infidelity by spouse
Infidelity by spouse	Physical abuse
Alcohol abuse by self	In-laws

Additionally, increases in the U.S. divorce rate reflect higher expectations of marriage. Couples now expect to find partners who will help them grow personally and provide much more than just financial support, a sexual partner, and children. In many other cultures, such expectations are rare or contrary to traditional values.

EFFECTS OF DIVORCE ON THE COUPLE

Although the changes in attitudes toward divorce have eased the social trauma associated with it, divorce still takes a high toll on the psyche of the couple. A nationwide survey revealed that divorce could impair individuals' well-being for at least five years after the event, producing a greater variety of long-lasting negative effects than even the death of a spouse (Nock, 1981). A longitudinal study of divorced people showed that they were more depressed than they had been when they were married (Menaghan & Lieberman, 1986). Indeed, divorced people of all ages are less likely than married, never-married, and widowed people to say that they are "very happy" with their lives (Kurdek, 1991b; Lee, Seccombe, & Shehan, 1991). Even ten years afterward, many divorced people still report feeling angry, lonely, disappointed, abandoned, and betrayed (Wallerstein & Blakeslee, 1989).

Even though the psychological cost of divorce is high, divorced people generally do not wish they were still married. One longitudinal study found that five years after the divorce, only 20% of former partners thought that the divorce had been a mistake. However, most of the people said that they had underestimated the pain that the divorce would cause (Wallerstein & Kelly, 1980).

The effects of divorce change over time. Shortly after the breakup, ex-partners often become even angrier and more bitter toward each other than they were beforehand. Additionally, many people underestimate their attachment to each other and may be overly sensitive to criticism from the ex-spouse. Increased hostility is often accompanied by periods of depression and disequilibrium (Kelly, 1982).

Gender differences are also found. Men report being shocked by the breakup, especially if the wife filed for divorce (Kelly, 1982). Men are more likely to be blamed for the problems that led to the divorce, to accept the blame, to move out, and thereby to find their social life disrupted (Kitson & Sussman, 1982). Women are affected differently. Socially, they have fewer prospects for potential remarriage, and they find it more difficult to establish new relationships if they have custody of the children (Maccoby, Depner, & Mnookin, 1991; Masheter, 1991). Women are at a serious financial disadvantage, largely because they usually have custody of the children and are typically paid less than men. Marilyn, the recently divorced middle-aged woman we met in the third chapter-opening vignette, may have a difficult road ahead as she tries to meet her own expenses as well as pay her daughter's college tuition.

Divorce in middle age or late life has some special characteristics. In general, the trauma is greater for these individuals, because of the long period of investment in each other's emotional and practical lives (Uhlenberg, Cooney, & Boyd, 1990). Longtime friends may turn away or take sides, causing additional disruption to the social network. Middle-aged and elderly women are at a significant disadvantage for remarriage—an especially traumatic situation for women who obtained much of their identity from their roles as wife and mother. Even if the divorce occurred many years earlier, children may still blame their parents for breaking the family apart (Hennon, 1983).

RELATIONSHIPS WITH YOUNG CHILDREN

The difficulty in adjusting to divorce often depends on whether young children are involved. Trouble typically begins during the custody battle. Over 90% of

The effects of divorce differ for men and women. Women typically experience a significant decline in their financial situation, whereas men tend to experience more difficulties with domestic tasks.

the time, the mother receives custody, and the father becomes an occasional parent. Like the woman in the photo, most divorced mothers of young children end up being the primary custodial parent. For many of them, the price the mother pays for custody is very high; at the same time as her parental responsibilities are increasing, her financial resources are decreasing. On average, divorced mothers experience roughly a 70% decline in their standard of living within the first year following divorce. In contrast, their ex-husbands typically enjoy approximately a 40% rise (Weitzman, 1985). Child care is expensive, and most divorced fathers contribute less than before the separation. Furthermore, in the United States, only about one-third of all child support payments are actually made; to address this problem, most states have passed laws to enforce child support payments.

Divorced fathers pay a psychological price (Furstenberg & Nord, 1985). Although many would like to remain active in their children's lives, few actually are. One reason is that children's needs change; anticipating these changes requires frequent contact, which is hard for many men. Additionally, even when child support payments are made, noncustodial fathers find it difficult to develop good relationships with their children, often because their ex-wives express their anger by limiting contact with the children. The fact that about one-quarter of divorced couples end up as bitter enemies only makes matters worse for all concerned (Ahrons & Wallisch, 1986). The unfortunate result is that many divorced fathers become peripheral in their children's lives, often through no fault of their own (Seltzer, 1991). As you can see in the graphs, within three years after the divorce, fewer than half of the fathers are involved in decisions regarding their child, and less than 60% of the children see their fathers even once a month.

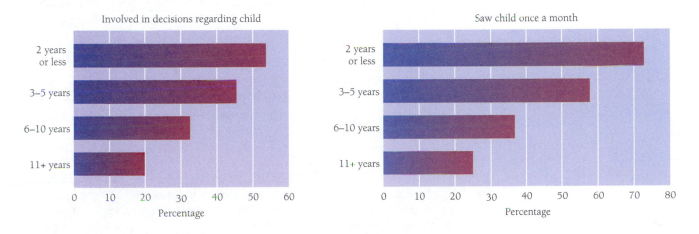

It is possible to overcome the problems between divorced people who have young children. Some former couples are able to get over their anger and cooperate with each other (Masheter, 1991). Adjustment is easier if both remarry or neither does. Interestingly, it is easier for a new husband to accept his wife's friendly relationship with her former husband than it is for a new wife to accept her husband's friendly relationship with his ex-wife (Masheter, 1991).

RELATIONSHIPS WITH ADULT CHILDREN

We saw in Chapter 5 that young children can be seriously affected by their parents' divorce. But what about when the parents of adult children divorce? Are they affected too? It certainly looks that way. Young adults whose parents divorce experience a great deal of emotional vulnerability and stress (Cooney, Smyer, Hagestad, & Klock, 1986; Cooney & Uhlenberg, 1990). One young man put it this way:

> . . . the difficult thing was that it was a time where, you know [you're] making the transition from high school to college . . . your high school friends are dispersed . . . they're all over the place. . . . It's normally a very difficult transition [college], new atmosphere, new work load, meeting new people. You've got to start deciding what you want to do, you've got to sort of start getting more independent and so forth. And then, at the same time you find out about a divorce. You know, it's just that much more adjustment you have to make. (Cooney et al., 1986)

Anger, conflicting loyalties, and worry about the parents' future are common reactions. Relationships with parents may be irreparably harmed. Even many years later, divorced fathers are less likely than mothers to experience positive relationships with their adult children. Fathers also do not believe that they will be able to rely on their children for support in times of need (Cooney & Uhlenberg, 1990). In contrast, adult daughters' relationships with their mothers are much more resilient; they may even intensify after the divorce (Cooney et al., 1986).

SEE FOR YOURSELF

The Effects of Divorce on Adult Children

One of the most overlooked effects of divorce is how it changes the relationships between parents and their adult children. Indeed, most of the research conducted on the effects of divorce on children focuses on school-age children and ignores those over the age of 18. This emphasis ignores the importance of life-cycle forces in the biopsychosocial model (see Chapter 1). Being an adult child of divorced parents creates problems that are different from those experienced by young children of divorce.

Among adult children of divorced parents are two subgroups: those whose parents divorced when they were young, and those whose parents divorced when they were 18 or older. An interesting question is whether these subgroups differ in their experiences. You be the judge and find out. While you're at it you will gain important insights into developmental research and the importance of life-cycle influences in the biopsychosocial model.

Ask around among your classmates, friends, co-workers, and family members. Locate one person from each of the two subgroups, and interview them about their experiences. Find out what they thought (and still think) about their parents' divorce, what their relationships with them are like now, and how having divorced parents influences their own love relationships. Collate and tabulate your results, then compare them to those in the book. Do they agree? See for yourself. ❧

We must not overlook the financial problems faced by middle-aged divorced women. Like Marilyn, whom we met in the chapter opening vignette, many have children in college, which creates serious financial burdens. These problems are especially keen for the middle-aged divorcee who may have spent years as a homemaker and has few marketable job skills. For her, divorce presents an especially difficult financial hardship.

Remarriage

As was true for Roseanne and Ben Thomas, shown in the photograph, the trauma of divorce does not deter people from beginning new relationships, which often lead to another marriage. Nearly 80% of divorced people remarry within the first three years (Glick & Lin, 1986). However, rates vary somewhat across ethnic groups. African Americans remarry a bit more slowly than European Americans, and Hispanics remarry more slowly than either of these other two groups (Coleman & Ganong, 1990). Remarriage is much more likely if the divorced people are young, mainly because more partners are available. Partner availability favors men at all ages, because men tend to marry women younger than themselves. For this reason, the probability that a divorced woman will remarry declines with increasing age.

Remarried people report that they experience their second marriage differently from their first. They claim to enjoy much better communication, to resolve disagreements with greater goodwill, to arrive at decisions more equitably, and to divide chores more fairly (Furstenberg, 1982). Indeed, most couples believe that they will be more likely to succeed the second time around (Furstenberg, 1982). For African Americans, this appears to be true; divorce rates for remarriages are lower than for first marriages (Teachman, 1986). However, second marriages for most other groups have about a 25% higher risk of dissolution than first marriages, and the divorce rate for remarriages involving stepchildren is about three times higher than the rate for first marriages (Glenn, 1991).

Adapting to new relationships in remarriage is different for men and women (Hobart, 1988). For remarried men, the preeminent relationship is with his new wife; other relationships, especially those with his children from his first marriage, take a back seat. For remarried women, the relationship with a new husband remains more marginal than the relationship with the children from the first marriage.

Remarriage late in life tends to be happier than remarriage in young adulthood, especially if the couple are widowed rather than divorced (Campbell, 1981). The biggest problem faced by older remarried individuals is resistance from adult children, who may think that the new spouse is an intruder and who may be concerned about their inheritance.

In sum, the most serious issue confronting people who remarry is the difficulty in adapting to stepchildren from the partner's previous marriage. When this is not part of the equation, settling into a happy relationship is easier and less complicated.

TEST YOURSELF

1. Following divorce, most women suffer disproportionately in the _____ domain compared to most men.
2. On average, within two years after a divorce, _____ fathers remain central in their children's lives.
3. For African American couples, divorce rates for remarried couples are _____ than for first marriages.
4. The most difficult part about remarriage for many middle-aged and older couples is _____.
5. Despite greatly increased divorce rates over the past few decades, the rate of marriage has not changed very much. Why do you think this is?

The Family Life Cycle

LEARNING OBJECTIVES

🐚 *What are family life stages?*

🐚 *Why do people have children?*

🐚 *What is it like to be a parent? What differences are there in different types of parenting?*

"When are you going to start a family?" is a question young couples are asked frequently. Most couples are like the one shown in the photograph; they want children because they believe that they will bring great joy, which they often do. But once the child is born, adults may feel inadequate, because children don't come with instructions. Young adults may be surprised when the reality

of being totally responsible for another person hits them. Experienced middle-aged parents often smile knowingly to themselves.

Frightening as it might be, the birth of a child transforms a couple (or a single parent) into a family. **Although the most common form of family in Western societies is the *nuclear family*, consisting of parent(s) and child(ren), the most common form around the world is the *extended family*, in which grandparents and other relatives live with parents and children.** Because we have discussed families from the child's perspective in earlier chapters, here we will focus on families from the parents' point of view.

Family Life-Cycle Stages

From a developmental perspective, families experience a series of relatively predictable changes, which constitute the *family life cycle*. One example of the family life cycle is shown in the figure. This model describes eight sequential stages, based on the age of the oldest child and the kinds of tasks

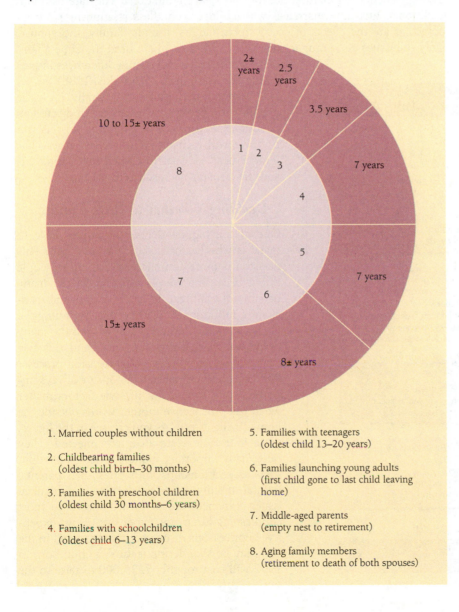

1. Married couples without children

2. Childbearing families
   (oldest child birth–30 months)

3. Families with preschool children
   (oldest child 30 months–6 years)

4. Families with schoolchildren
   (oldest child 6–13 years)

5. Families with teenagers
   (oldest child 13–20 years)

6. Families launching young adults
   (first child gone to last child leaving home)

7. Middle-aged parents
   (empty nest to retirement)

8. Aging family members
   (retirement to death of both spouses)

families confront (Duvall, 1977). As we saw in Chapter 1, this theory is conceptually related to life-span and life-course theories; an overview of the basic tenets of these theories is presented in the table.

Perspective	Examples of Theories	Main Ideas	Emphases in Biopsychosocial Framework	Positions on Developmental Issues
Life Span and Life Cycle	Duvall's family life-cycle theory	Families go through series of stages	Strong emphasis on all except biological	Nature–nurture interaction, continuity and discontinuity, universal series of stages

Family life-cycle models help us understand the changes families go through as children mature, but they also have limitations. They are based on traditional, first-time marriages with children; childless relationships are ignored, as are the effects of occupational factors, friends, family, and spouse. Only the issues pertaining to raising the oldest child are used to define a family's current stage, and ethnic differences in parenting are overlooked (Vinovskis, 1988).

Despite their limitations, family life-cycle models provide a way to organize our discussion of couples' experience of parenting. In this section, we will focus on the first six stages. The "empty nest" stage is discussed in Chapter 12, and the last stage is discussed in Chapter 14.

Deciding Whether to Have Children

One of the biggest decisions couples have to make is whether or not to have children. This decision is more complicated than most people think, because a couple must weigh the many benefits of childrearing, such as personal satisfaction, fulfilling personal needs, continuing the family line, and companionship, with the many drawbacks, including expense and lifestyle changes. What influences the decision process? Psychological and marital factors are always important, and career and lifestyle factors matter when the prospective mother works outside the home (Wilk, 1986). As you can see in the figure, these four factors are all interconnected. They raise many important matters for consideration, such as relationships with one's own parents, marital stability, career satisfaction, and financial issues. Finances are of great concern to most couples; children are expensive. How expensive? For reasons discussed in more detail in the You May Be Wondering feature, a child born in 1992 will cost roughly $225,000 to raise to the

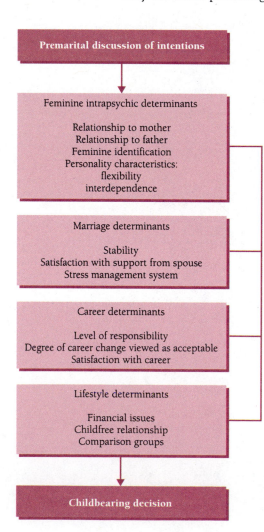

age of 18. Want to send them to a public college for four years? Add about another $130,000. No wonder couples are concerned.

The Cost of Raising a Child

You've just discovered that you're going to be a parent! Once the cheering and excitement begin to die down, you realize that you need to start putting some money aside for the child. Never having had children before, you may be wondering just how much will be enough. "I can almost guarantee you anybody having their first child will be surprised," says F. Stephen Wershing, Jr., a certified financial planner and father of a 1-year-old son (Johnston, 1993). Why, you ask?

Well, it turns out that for children born in 1992, middle-income families will spend a total of $224,800 per child by the time the child graduates from high school. Lower-income families will spend $161,620, and upper-income families will spend $314,550. That's for *each* child, and it assumes a two-parent household. It's 5% higher in single-parent families, where household expenses average more per person, especially for child care. What about college, you say? Well, that's estimated to be at least another $139,000 if you send your child to a public college or university for four years, and $293,000 for a private college. The grand total for middle-income families to raise one child born in 1992 through four years at a public college: $363,800.

Suppose you don't have medical insurance to cover the baby's delivery, or you're going through fertility treatment, or you are adopting. The average normal delivery costs around $5000, with Caesarean deliveries averaging $8000. Fertility treatments typically cost $10,000 to $15,000 for each attempt at high-tech conception (e.g., *in vitro* fertilization); multiple attempts are usually necessary, and few expenses are covered by medical insurance. Adoptions range from $5000 to $11,000 for domestic adoptions and $8000 to $20,000 for international adoptions.

Now that you've experienced "sticker shock" of a sort, here's what the experts suggest about expenses and strategies to soften the blow:

1. Drastically limit expenses as soon as you find out you're going to have a baby. You need to save money and get used to a much tighter budget. Keep in mind that you may need a bigger house, putting additional strain on your already stretched resources.
2. It's essential to keep a budget in order to know where your money is going. Comparison shopping is a must. Teach these skills to your child.
3. Take advantage of payroll savings plans at work that let you set aside pretax earnings to pay child care expenses. If you hire someone to care for your child in your home, don't forget about withholding and Social Security taxes.
4. Make out a will, and acquire adequate disability and life insurance to provide for your children if something should happen to you.

In sum, having children is an extremely expensive proposition. But knowing what lies ahead, you can plan appropriately.   ❧

For many reasons, such as personal choice, financial instability, and infertility, an increasing number of couples are remaining childfree. These couples have several advantages over those who choose to have children (Van Hoose & Worth, 1982): happier marriages, more freedom, and higher standards of living. But they must also face social criticism from the larger child-oriented society and may run the risk of feeling more lonely in old age (Van Hoose & Worth, 1982).

The Parental Role

Today, couples have fewer children and have their first child later than in the past. Indeed, until 1993 couples like the one in the photograph, in which mothers were over 30 when they had their first child, had been increasing. The slight decline since then is due mainly to smaller numbers of women of child-

bearing age in cohorts following the Baby Boomers. Delaying the first child has important benefits. Traditionally, the relationship with the mother has been thought to be crucial for the normal development of the child (Field & Widmayer, 1982). Older mothers, like Denise in the last vignette at the beginning of the chapter, are more at ease being parents, spend more time with their babies, and are more affectionate and sensitive to them (Ragozin et al., 1982).

On the other hand, the trend for young, unmarried women to have children is still increasing. As we saw in Chapter 8, adolescent mothers are especially at risk for many problems and have none of the benefits older mothers do.

The age of the father also makes a difference in how fathers interact with their children. Remember Bob, the 32-year-old first-time father in the last vignette at the beginning of the chapter? Compared to men who become fathers in their 20s, men like Bob who become fathers in their 30s are generally more invested in their paternal role and spend up to three times as much time in caring for their preschool children as younger fathers do (Cooney et al., 1993).

However, men who become fathers in their 30s are also more likely to feel ambivalent and resentful about time lost to their careers (Cooney et al., 1993).

Parenting is full of rewards, but it also takes a great deal of work. Caring for young children is demanding. It may create disagreements over division of labor, especially if both parents are employed outside the home (see Chapters 4 and 11). Mothers appear equally divided among those who love taking care of their children and working, those who don't, and those who are neutral about it (Thompson & Walker, 1989). Fathers largely report that they like taking care of their children, but they are also less involved in direct child care (LaRossa, 1988).

Being a middle-aged parent with adolescent and adult children involves special issues. As we will see in Chapter 12, the nature of parent–child relationships changes during this period, going from clearly hierarchical to more egalitarian, as both children and parents mature. As you have experienced yourself, as well as studied in Chapter 8, adolescence is a particularly trying time for all.

In general, parents manage to deal with the many challenges of childrearing reasonably well. They learn how to compromise when necessary, and when to apply firm but fair discipline. Given the choice, most parents do not regret their decision to have children.

SINGLE PARENTS

The number of single parents, most of whom are women, is increasing rapidly. Among the causes are high divorce rates, the decision to keep children born out of wedlock, and the desire of many single adults to have or adopt children. Being a single parent raises important questions. How are children affected when only one adult is responsible for child care? How do single parents meet their own needs for emotional support and intimacy?

Many divorced single parents report feelings of frustration, failure, guilt, and ambivalence about the parent–child relationship (Van Hoose & Worth, 1982). Frustration usually results from a lack of companionship and from loneliness, as many social activities are typically reserved for couples. Feelings of guilt may lead to attempts to make up for the child's lack of a father or mother. The parent may experience ambivalence toward the children, who are sometimes seen as hindrances to developing new relationships. These feelings may also arise if the children serve as a reminder of a failed marriage.

Single parents, regardless of gender, face considerable obstacles. Financially, they are usually much less well-off than their married counterparts. Integrating the roles of work and parenthood are difficult enough for two persons; for the single parent, the hardships are compounded. Financially, single mothers are hardest hit. Emotionally, single fathers may have the worst of it; according to some research, their sleep, eating, play, work, and peer relations are badly affected, and they are more depressed than any other group of men (Pearlin & Johnson, 1977). Moreover, because most men are not socialized for child-rearing, the lack of basic skills necessary to care for children may compound these problems.

One particular concern is dating (Phillis & Stein, 1983). Indeed, the three most popular questions asked by single parents involve dating: "How do I become available again?" "How will my children react?" "How do I cope with my own sexuality?" Initiating a new relationship is difficult for many single parents, especially those with older children. They may be hesitant to express this side of themselves in front of their children. The children may ask discomforting questions about their dates or express resentment toward them.

ALTERNATIVE FORMS OF PARENTING

Not all parents raise their own biological children. In fact, roughly one-third of North American couples become stepparents, like the couple shown in the photograph, or become foster or adoptive parents sometime during their lives.

To be sure, the parenting issues we have discussed thus far are just as important in these situations as when people raise their own biological children. However, some special problems arise as well.

A big issue for foster parents, adoptive parents, and stepparents is how strongly the child will bond with them. Although infants less than 1 year old will probably bond well, children who are old enough to have formed attachments with their biological parents may have competing loyalties. For example, some stepchildren remain strongly attached to the noncustodial parent and actively resist attempts to integrate them into a new family ("My real mother wouldn't make me do that"). Or they may exhibit behavioral problems such as drinking or continually invading the stepparent's privacy (Pasley & Ihinger-Tallman, 1987). Additionally, stepparents must often deal with continued visitation by the noncustodial parent, which may exacerbate any difficulties. These problems are a major reason why second marriages are at high risk for dissolution, as discussed earlier in this chapter.

Still, many stepparents and stepchildren ultimately develop good relationships with each other. Stepparents must be sensitive to the relationship between the stepchild and his or her biological, noncustodial parent. Allowing stepchildren to develop the relationship with the stepparent at their own pace also helps.

Adoptive parents also contend with attachment to birth parents, but in different ways. Even if they don't remember them, adopted children may wish to locate and meet their birth parents. Wanting to know one's origins is understandable, but such searches can strain the relationships between these children and their adoptive parents, who may interpret these actions as a form of rejection (Rosenberg, 1992). In general, though, recent research indicates that, compared to nonadopted children, adopted children are more confident, have a more positive view of the world, feel more in control of their lives, and view their adoptive parents as more nurturing (Marquis & Detweiler, 1985).

Foster parents tend to have the most tenuous relationship with their children, because the bond can be broken for any of a number of reasons having nothing to do with the quality of the care being provided. For example, a court may award custody back to the birth parents, or another couple may legally adopt the child. Dealing with attachment is difficult; foster parents want to provide secure homes, but they may not have the children long enough to establish continuity. Furthermore, because many children in foster care have been unable to form attachments at all, they are less likely to form ones that will inevitably be broken. Thus, foster parents must be willing to tolerate considerable ambiguity in the relationship and have few expectations about the future.

Gay male or lesbian couples typically make excellent parents. Children raised by such couples do not develop sexual identity problems and in some cases have advantages over children raised by heterosexual parents.

Finally, many gay male and lesbian women also desire to be parents. Some have biological children themselves, whereas others choose adoption or foster parenting. Although gay men and lesbian women make good parents, they often experience resistance from other people to the idea of their having children. As discussed in the Current Controversies feature, there are religious and legal barriers. Actually, research indicates that children reared by gay male or lesbian parents do not experience any more problems than children reared by heterosexual parents.

Gay Male and Lesbian Parents

CURRENT CONTROVERSIES

Few issues create greater controversy than the topic of gay and lesbian rights. In the early 1990s, there were heated political debates as to whether openly gay and lesbian individuals could be members of the military, and whether gay couples should be afforded the same rights as married couples. But perhaps no issue was more sensitive or sparked more heated discussion than gay males and lesbians as parents.

One position, supported most vocally by religious conservatives, held that it is unnatural and inherently deviant for gay men and lesbians to be parents (Marciano, 1985). According to this argument, gay men and lesbians are not fit parents and will raise their children to be just like them. Some courts uphold this position. In a celebrated case in 1993, a court in Virginia awarded custody of a child to her grandmother solely because the child's mother (the grandmother's own daughter) was a lesbian. In this case, the court ruled that simply being a lesbian necessarily made the child's mother an unfit parent.

Despite the popularity of these and related claims, no credible scientific evidence exists to support them. On the contrary, substantial evidence exists that children raised by gay male or lesbian parents do not develop problems of sexual identity or any other problems any more than children raised by heterosexual parents (Bozett, 1988; Parrot & Ellis, 1985). In fact, there is some evidence that children raised by gay men may even have some advantages over children raised by heterosexual men. Gay men are often especially concerned about being good and nurturing fathers, and they try hard to raise their children with nonsexist, egalitarian attitudes (Bozett, 1988).

In view of this evidence, courts in many states uphold gay male and lesbian parents' rights. For example, in 1993, a Massachusetts court allowed a lesbian physician to adopt her partner's biological child so that the child would have two parents. The fact that both parents were lesbians was considered irrelevant.

These data will not make the controversy go away, as much of it is based on long-held beliefs and prejudices. Admittedly, the data comparing children raised by different types of parents is inadequate; for example, there is very little information about children raised by lesbian women. Only when societal attitudes toward gay men and lesbians become more accepting will there be greater acceptance of their right to be parents like anyone else.   ❧

TEST YOURSELF

1. The series of relatively predictable changes that families experience is called _____.
2. Four factors that influence the decision to have children are _____.
3. A new father who is invested in his parental role, but who may also feel ambivalent about time lost to his career is probably over age _____.
4. A major issue for foster parents, adoptive parents, and stepparents is _____.
5. What difference do you think it would make to view children as a financial asset (i.e., a source of income) as opposed to a financial burden (i.e., mainly an expense)? Which of these do you think characterizes most Western societies? Can you think of an example of the other type?

Putting It All Together

In this chapter, we have seen how people find and develop adult relationships. We considered the important role that friendships play in adulthood. We saw how some relationships, like Jamal and Deb's, turn into love. Although the romantic love they feel won't last forever, we discovered other directions that love can take so that the relationship can last. Although Jamal and Deb's love gets played out the world over, what people look for in a mate varies in different cultures. Turning a love relationship into newlywedded bliss, as Kevin and Beth did, is very common; it's still true that the vast majority of people get married at some point in their lives. If Kevin and Beth have children, we can expect their newfound happiness to fade a bit, but as long as they maintain their commitment to each other, their marriage will probably last. Frank and Marilyn's divorce had fairly typical re-

Answers: (1) the family life cycle, (2) psychological factors, marital factors, career factors, and lifestyle factors, (3) 30, (4) how strongly the child will bond with them

sults: Marilyn is having trouble making the financial ends meet. Because Bob and Denise were in their 30s when their first child was born, they will likely be better suited and better prepared for parenthood than many younger parents.

Throughout the chapter, we saw that human relationships are complex. Although there are similarities around the world in how people find mates, culture plays a large part in helping people find the person who will say, "I am for you." Maintaining a strong relationship takes work, and there are many pressures that may divert partners' attention from each other. But, as the song says, people who need people are the luckiest people in the world.

Thinking about Development

1. What aspects of the research on mate selection around the world support the notion of universal patterns of development (as discussed in Chapter 1)? What aspects support diversity of experience?

2. How do the different styles of love reflect life-cycle factors in the biopsychosocial framework?

3. If marital satisfaction typically declines significantly after couples have children, but stays relatively constant for couples who do not, why do couples have children, and what keeps them together?

4. How are the life-span construct (described in Chapter 9) and the decision to become a parent related?

Summary

Relationships

Friendships

■ People tend to have more friendships during young adulthood than during any other period. Friendships are especially important for maintaining life satisfaction throughout adulthood. Men tend to have fewer close friendships and to base them on shared activities, such as sports. Women tend to have more close friendships, and to base them on intimate and emotional sharing. Gender differences in same-gender friendship patterns may explain the difficulties men and women have forming cross-gender friendships.

Love Relationships

■ Passion, intimacy, and commitment are the key components of love. These combine to form seven types of love relationships: liking, infatuation, empty love, romantic love, fatuous love, companionate love, and consummate love. Although styles of love change with age, the priorities within relationships do not. Men tend to be more romantic earlier in relationships than women, who tend to be cautious pragmatists. Selecting a mate works best when there are shared values, goals, and interests. There are cross-cultural differences with regard to the specific aspects of these that are considered most important.

Violence in Relationships

■ Levels of aggressive behavior range from verbal aggression, to physical aggression, to murdering one's partner. The causes of aggressive behaviors become more complex as the level of aggression increases. People remain in abusive relationships for many reasons, including low self-esteem and the belief that they cannot leave.

Lifestyles

Singlehood

■ Most adults decide by age 30 whether they plan on getting married. Never-married adults often develop a strong network of close friends. Dealing with other people's expectations that they should marry is often difficult for single people.

Cohabitation

■ Young adults usually cohabit as a step toward marriage, and adults of all ages may also cohabit for financial reasons. Cohabitation is only rarely seen as an alternative to marriage. Overall, more similarities than differences exist between cohabiting and married couples.

Gay Male and Lesbian Couples

■ Gay male and lesbian relationships are similar to marriages in terms of relationship issues. Lesbian couples tend to be more egalitarian and are more likely to remain together than gay male couples. Frequency of sexual expression differs in gay male, lesbian, and heterosexual couples.

Marriage

■ The most important factors in creating stable marriages are creating a stable sense of identity as a foundation for intimacy, similarity of values and interests, and the contribution of unique skills by each partner. For couples with children, marital satisfaction tends to decline until the children leave home, although individual differences are apparent, especially in long-term marriages. Most long-term marriages are happy.

Divorce and Remarriage

Divorce

■ Currently, odds are about 50-50 that a new marriage will end in divorce. Recovery from divorce is different for men and women. Men tend to have a tougher time in the short run, but women clearly have a harder time in the long run, often for financial reasons. Difficulties between divorced partners usually involve visitation and child support. Disruptions also occur in divorced parents' relationships with their children, whether the children are young or are adults themselves.

Remarriage

■ Most divorced couples remarry. Second marriages are especially vulnerable to stress if spouses must adjust

to having stepchildren. Remarriage in middle age and beyond tends to be happy, but couples may face resistance from their adult children.

The Family Life Cycle

Family Life-Cycle Stages

■ Although the nuclear family is the most common form of family in Western societies, the most common form around the world is the extended family. Families experience a series of relatively predictable changes called the *family life cycle*. This cycle provides a framework for understanding the changes families go through as children mature.

Deciding Whether to Have Children

■ Although having children is stressful and very expensive, most people do it anyway. However, the number of childfree couples is increasing.

The Parental Role

■ The timing of parenthood is important in how involved parents are in their families as opposed to their careers. Single parents are faced with many problems, especially if they are women and are divorced. The main problem is significantly reduced financial resources. A major issue for adoptive parents, foster parents, and stepparents is how strongly the child will bond with them. Each of these relationships has some special characteristics. Gay male and lesbian parents also face numerous obstacles, but they usually prove to be good parents.

Key Terms

abusive relationship (343)	*exchange theory* (351)	*homogamy* (351)
battered woman syndrome (344)	*extended family* (361)	*nuclear family* (361)
cohabitation (348)	*family life cycle* (361)	

If You'd Like to Learn More

BOSS, P. G., DOHERTY, W. J., LAROSSA, R., SCHUMM, W. R., & STEINMETZ, S. K. (Eds.). (1993). *Sourcebook of family theories and methods.* New York: Plenum. This is a superb resource book that covers all major theories and methods used in family and relationship research. This first-rate book involves easy to moderate reading on the average.

BURR, W., DAY, R., AND DAHL, K. (1992). *Family science.* Pacific Grove, CA: Brooks/Cole. This is a very readable introduction to the issues introduced in this chapter.

JANOSIK, E., & GREEN, E. (1992). *Family life: Processes and practices.* Boston: Jones and Bartlett. This is a good mid-level survey of issues pertaining to families and their development.

PRATHER, H., & PRATHER, G. (1990). *Notes to each other.* New York: Bantam. This collection of reflections on making relationships work, staying happy, and parenting makes easy reading.

SETTLES, B. H., HANKS, R. S., & SUSSMAN, M. B. (1993). *American families and the future: Analyses of possible destinies.* New York: Haworth Press. This highly readable yet scholarly discussion of the future of the North American family takes a life-span and interdisciplinary perspective.

TANNEN, D. (1990). *You just don't understand.* New York: Morrow. This highly readable and interesting book discusses the different communication styles men and women use.

🔊 Monica, a 22-year-old senior communications major, wonders about careers. Should she enter the broadcast field as a behind-the-scenes producer, or would she be better suited as a public relations spokesperson? She thinks that her outgoing personality is a factor she should consider. Would the field of broadcasting be a good match for her?

🔊 Janice, a 35-year-old African American manager at a business consulting firm, is concerned because her career is not progressing as rapidly as she had hoped. Janice works hard and has received excellent performance ratings every year. But she has noticed that there are very few women in upper management positions in her company. Janice wonders whether she will ever be promoted.

🔊 Fred has 32 years of service for an automobile manufacturer. Over the years, more and more assembly-line jobs have been eliminated by robots and other technology. Although Fred has been assured by his boss that his job is safe, he isn't so sure. He worries that he could be laid off at any time.

🔊 Jennifer, a 38-year-old sales clerk at a department store, feels that her husband doesn't do his share of the housework or child care. Her husband says that real men don't do housework, and that he's really tired when he comes home from work. Jennifer thinks that this isn't fair, especially because she works as many hours as her husband.

🔊 Claude is a 55-year-old electrician who has enjoyed outdoor activities his whole life. From the time he was a boy, he has fished and water-skied in the calm inlets of coastal Florida. Although he doesn't compete in slalom races any more, Claude still skis regularly. He still participates in fishing competitions every chance he gets.

Work
and Leisure

Work—it seems as though that's all we do sometimes. From the small chores children do to putting in 12-hour days at the office, we are taught throughout our lives that working is a natural part of life. For some people, working *is* life. In this chapter, we will explore the world of work. We will begin by considering how people choose occupations and develop in them. After that, we will examine how women and minorities contend with barriers to their occupational selection and development. Dealing with occupational transitions is considered in the third section. How to balance work and family obligations is a difficult issue for many people; it will be discussed in the fourth section. Finally, we will see how people spend their time away from work in leisure activities.

As in Chapter 10, we will focus in this chapter on issues faced by both young and middle-aged adults. It is becoming increasingly common for middle-aged people to face the issues of occupational selection once again, as they change occupations. Even in the world of work, it is no longer easy to figure out how much experience a person has simply by knowing how old he or she is.

Occupational Selection and Development

LEARNING OBJECTIVES

❧ *How do people view work? How do occupational priorities vary with age?*

❧ *How do people choose their occupations?*

❧ *What factors influence occupational development?*

❧ *What is the relation between job satisfaction and age?*

Work is such a pervasive aspect of our lives that we seldom step back and think about it. Indeed, there are few things adults do that have no connection with work. You may be taking this course as part of your preparation for work. People time personal activities around work schedules. Parents sometimes choose child care centers on the basis of their proximity to their place of employment.

In this section, we will explore what work means to adults. We will also revisit issues pertaining to occupational selection, first introduced in Chapter 8, as well as examine occupational development. Finally, we will see how satisfaction with one's job changes during adulthood.

The Meaning of Work

Did you ever stop to think about why we fight the commuting crowds like the people in the photograph are doing? Studs Terkel, the author of the fascinating book *Working* (1974), writes that work is "a search for daily meaning as well as daily bread, for recognition as well as cash, for astonishment rather than torpor; in short, for a sort of life rather than a Monday through Friday sort of dying" (p. xiii). Kahlil Gibran (1923), in his mystical book *The Prophet*, put it this way: "Work is love made visible."

For some of us, work is a source of prestige, social recognition, and a sense of worth. For others, the excitement of creativity and the opportunity to give something of themselves make work meaningful. But for most, the main purpose of work is to earn a living. This is not to imply, of course, that money is the only reward in a job; friendships, the chance to exercise power, and feeling useful are also important. The meaning most of us derive from working includes both the money that can be exchanged for life's necessities (and maybe a few luxuries, too) and the possibility of personal growth. **These *occupational priorities,* or what people want from their employment, reflect the culture and the times in which people live.**

An excellent example of these influences is the longitudinal study conducted by American Telephone and Telegraph (AT&T), begun in the mid-1950s (Howard & Bray, 1980). Look carefully at the graph. Three key things are depicted. First, the vertical axis represents the rating of the importance of

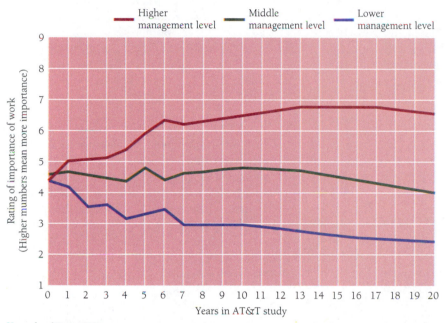

Howard and Bray, 1990.

work in employees' lives. The horizontal axis reflects two things: length of time in the study at AT&T (which gives an idea of the length of employment), and relative age (in general, the less time in the study, the younger the employee).

Notice how the importance of work changed dramatically over time. The longer employees were in the study, the more differentiated the various levels of managers became in terms of the importance of work. Underlying these changes are key differences in motivation for upward mobility, leadership, and desire for emotional support, depending on the age of the managers. For higher management levels, those who had been in the AT&T study briefly had expectations of rewards from work that were much lower than those who had been in the study ten years or more; they did not see most of their major rewards or life satisfaction coming from work. Interestingly, the picture was reversed for lower-level managers; those who had been in the study longer gave a lower rating of the importance of work.

The findings at AT&T are not unique. Other research has also documented that younger workers in upper management are less interested in materialism, power seeking, upward mobility, and competition; instead, they emphasize individual freedom, personal growth, and cooperation (Jones, 1980; Yankelovich, 1981).

Regardless of what occupational priorities people have, they view their oc-

ANN HOWARD
"The highly work involved who also put their families in the forefront [pay] a price in terms of advancement in management."

cupation as a key element in their sense of identity. This can be readily observed when adults introduce themselves socially. You've probably noticed that when asked to tell something about themselves, people usually provide information about what they do for a living. Occupation affects your life in a host of ways, often influencing where you live, what friends you make, and even what clothes you wear. In short, the impact of work cuts across all aspects of life. Work, then, is a major social role and influence of adult life. Occupation is an important anchor that complements the other major role of adulthood—love relationships.

As we will see, occupation is part of human development. Young children, in their pretend play, are in the midst of the social preparation for work. Adults are always asking them, "What do you want to be when you grow up?" School curricula, especially in high school and college, are geared toward preparing people for particular occupations. People develop interests in various occupations over time, and changes in occupation are among the most important events in the life cycle. Let us turn our attention to one of the theories explaining how and why people choose the occupations they do.

Holland's Theory of Occupational Choice Revisited

In Chapter 8, we saw that early decisions about what people want to do in the world of work are related to their personalities. Holland's (1973, 1985) theory makes explicit an intuitively appealing idea: that people choose occupations to optimize the fit between their individual traits (such as personality, intelligence, skills, and abilities) and their occupational interests. Recall from the table in Chapter 8 (see page 270) that Holland categorizes occupations in two ways: by the interpersonal settings in which people must function and by their associated lifestyles. From this perspective, he identifies six personality types that combine these factors: investigative, social, realistic, artistic, conventional, and enterprising.

How does Holland's theory help us understand the continued development of occupational interests in adulthood? Monica's situation helps illustrate this point. Monica, the college senior in the first chapter-opening vignette, found a good match between her outgoing nature and her major, communications. Indeed, most college students, regardless of age, tend to like courses and majors best when they provide a good fit with their personalities. Thus, the early occupational choices in adolescence continue to be modified and fine-tuned in adulthood.

Although the relations between personality and occupational choice are important, we must also recognize the limits of the theory as it relates to adults' occupational choices. Adult men and women are represented differently in Holland's types (Costa, McCrae, & Holland, 1984). Regardless of age, women are more likely than men to have the social, artistic, and conventional personality types. In part, these gender differences reflect different experiences in growing up (e.g., hearing that girls grow up to be nurses whereas boys grow up to be firefighters), differences in personality (e.g., gender role identity), and differences in socialization (e.g., women being expected to be more outgoing and people-oriented than men).

We also know very little about how Holland's types vary in different ethnic groups, mostly because such groups have not been included in the studies investigating the links between personality and occupation. Additionally, Holland's theory ignores the context in which occupational decisions are made. For

Holland's theory describes relations between personality and occupation. However, the theory does not apply well to situations involving minority workers.

example, he overlooks the fact that many people have little choice in the kind of job they can get, because of external factors such as family, financial pressures, or ethnicity.

Holland's theory also ignores evidence that the match between personality type and occupation changes during adulthood (Adler & Aranya, 1984). Holland takes a static view of both personality and occupations, but it must be recognized that what occupation we choose is not dictated solely by what we are like. Equally important is the dynamic interplay between us and the sociocultural context we find ourselves in—just as one would suspect, given the biopsychosocial model presented in Chapter 1. Occupational selection is a complex interaction among personal, ethnic, gender, and economic factors.

Occupational Development

For most of us, getting a job is not enough; we would also like to move up the ladder. Promotion is a measure of how well one is doing in one's career. How quickly occupational advancement occurs (or does not) may lead to such labels as "fast-tracker" or "dead-ender" (Kanter, 1976). Bill Clinton, shown here being inaugurated as the president at age 46, is an example of a fast-tracker. People who want to advance learn quickly how long to stay at one level and how to seize opportunities as they occur; others soon learn the frustration of remaining in the same job, with no chance for promotion.

How a person advances in a career seems to depend on professional socialization, which includes several factors besides those that are important in choosing an occupation. Among these are expectations, support from co-workers, priorities, and job satisfaction. Before we consider these aspects, we will look at a general scheme of occupational development.

SUPER'S THEORY

Over four decades, Super (1957, 1980) developed a theory of occupational development based on self-concept, first introduced in Chapter 8. He proposed a progression through five distinct stages during adulthood, resulting from changes in individuals' self-concept and adaptation to an occupational role: implementation, establishment, maintenance, deceleration, and retirement. **People are**

Implementation ⟶ Establishment ⟶ Maintenance ⟶ Deceleration ⟶ Retirement

located along a continuum of *vocational maturity* through their working years; the more congruent their occupational behaviors are with what is expected of them at different ages, the more vocationally mature they are. We saw in Chapter 8 that the initial two phases of Super's theory, crystallization and specification, occur primarily during adolescence, and that the first adulthood phase has its origins then as well. Each of the stages in adulthood has distinctive characteristics:

- The *implementation* stage begins in late adolescence or the early 20s, when people take a series of temporary jobs to learn firsthand about work roles and to try out some possible career choices.
- The *establishment* stage begins with selecting a specific occupation during young adulthood. It continues as the person advances up the career ladder in the same occupation.
- The *maintenance* stage is a transition phase during middle age, as workers begin to reduce the amount of time they spend fulfilling work roles.
- The *deceleration* stage begins as workers begin planning in earnest for their upcoming retirement and separating themselves from their work.
- The *retirement* stage begins when people stop working full-time.

In Super's framework, people's occupations evolve in response to changes in their self-concept. Consequently, this is a developmental process that reflects and explains important life changes. This developmental process complements Holland's ideas. Investigative and enterprising types are likely to come from more affluent families, in which the parents tended not to be in investigative or enterprising occupations. Interestingly, initial occupational goals were not as important for social types as for the other two; social types appeared more flexible in eventual occupational choice.

However, a shortcoming of Super's theory is that it assumes that once people choose an occupation, they stay in it for the rest of their working lives. Although this may have been true for some employees in the past, it is not the case for most North American workers today. The downsizing of public and private organizations since the late 1980s has all but eliminated the notion of lifetime job security with a particular employer. It remains to be seen whether new developmental stages will be found to underlie the new occupational reality.

OCCUPATIONAL EXPECTATIONS

As we saw in Chapter 8, individuals form opinions about what work in a particular occupation will be like based on what they learn in school and from their parents, peers, other adults, and the media. People have expectations regarding what they want to become and when they hope to get there. Levinson and his colleagues (1978) built these expectations into their theory of adult male development. Based on findings from a longitudinal study begun in the 1940s on men attending an elite private college, Levinson and his colleagues found considerable similarity among the participants in terms of major life tasks during adulthood. **Forming a *dream*, with one's career playing a prominent role, is one of the young adult's chief tasks.**

Throughout adulthood, people continue to refine and update their occupational expectations. This usually involves trying to achieve the dream, monitoring progress toward it, and changing or even abandoning it as necessary. For some, modifying the dream comes as a result of realizing that interests have changed or that the dream was not a good fit. In other cases, failure leads to changing the dream—for example, dropping a business major because one is failing economics courses. Other causes are age, racial, or sexual discrimination, lack of opportunity, obsolescence of skills, and changing interests. In some cases, one's initial occupational choice may simply have been unrealistic. For example, nearly half of all young adults would like to become professionals (such as lawyers or physicians), but only one person in seven actually makes it (Cosby, 1974). Some goal modification is essential from time to time, but it usually surprises us to realize that we could have been wrong about what seemed to be a logical choice in the past. As Marie, a 38-year-old advertising manager, put it, "I really thought I wanted to be a pilot; the travel sounded really interesting. But it just wasn't what I expected."

Perhaps the rudest jolt for most of us first comes during the transition from school to the real world. Reality shock sets in, and things never seem to happen the way we expect. Reality shock befalls everyone, from the young worker in the photo to the accountant who learns that the financial forecast that took days to prepare may simply end up in a file cabinet (or, worse yet, in the wastebasket) (Van Maanen & Schein, 1977). The visionary aspects of the dream may

not disappear altogether, but a good dose of reality goes a long way toward bringing a person down to earth. Such feedback comes to play an increasingly important role in a person's occupational development and self-concept. For example, the woman who thought that she would receive the same rewards as her male counterparts for comparable work is likely to become increasingly angry and disillusioned when her successes result in smaller raises and fewer promotions.

THE ROLE OF MENTORS

Imagine how hard it would be to figure out everything you needed to know in a new job with no support from the people around you. Entering an occupation involves more than the relatively short formal training a person receives. Indeed, much of the most critical information is not taught in training seminars. Instead, most people are shown the ropes by co-workers. In many cases, an older, more experienced person makes a specific effort to do this, taking on the role of a *mentor*. Although mentors by no means provide the only source of guidance in the workplace, they have been studied fairly closely.

A mentor is part teacher, part sponsor, part model, and part counselor. The mentor helps a young worker avoid trouble ("Be careful what you say around Harry"). He or she also provides invaluable information about the unwritten rules that govern day-to-day activities in the workplace (not working too fast on the assembly line, wearing the right clothes, and so on) (Levinson et al., 1978). As part of the relationship, a mentor makes sure that his or her protégé is noticed and receives credit for good work from supervisors. Thus, occupational success often depends on the quality of the mentor-protégé relationship.

The mentor fulfills two main functions: improving the protégé's chances for advancement and promoting his or her psychological and social well-being (Kram, 1980, 1985).

In Chapter 1, we saw that the ideas in Erikson's theory (1982), summarized in the table, included important aspects of adulthood related to work. Playing the role of a mentor is also a developmental phase in one's occupation.

Perspective	Examples of Theories	Main Ideas	Emphases in Biopsychosocial Framework	Positions on Developmental Issues
Psychodynamic	Erikson's psycho-social theory	Personality develops through sequence of stages	Biological, social and life-cycle forces crucial; less emphasis on psychological	Nature-nurture interaction, discontinuity, universal sequence but individual differences in rate

Helping a younger employee learn the job is one way to fulfill aspects of Erikson's phase of generativity. As we will see in more detail in Chapter 12, generativity reflects middle-aged adults' need to ensure the continuity of society through activities such as socialization or having children. In work settings, generativity is most often expressed through mentoring. In particular, the mentor ensures that there is some continuity in the corporation or profession by passing on the knowledge and experience he or she has gained over the years. Being a mentor helps middle-aged people fulfill their need to ensure the continuity of society and accomplish or produce something worthwhile (Erikson, 1982).

Some authors suggest that women have a greater need for mentors than men because they receive less socialization in the skills necessary to do well

in the workplace (Busch, 1985). However, women seem to have a more difficult time finding adequate mentors. One reason is that there are few female role models, such as the one shown in the photo, who could serve a mentoring function, especially in upper-level management. This is unfortunate, especially in view of evidence that women who have female mentors are significantly more productive than women with male mentors (Goldstein, 1979). Although many young women report that they would feel comfortable with a male mentor (Olian et al., 1988), researchers note that male mentor–female protégé relationships may involve conflict and tension resulting from possible sexual overtones, even when there has been no overtly sexual behavior on anyone's part (Kram, 1985).

Job Satisfaction

Job satisfaction is the positive feeling that results from an appraisal of one's work. In general, job satisfaction tends to increase gradually with age (James & Jones, 1980). The increased satisfaction has been linked to several factors.

(a) Older workers have had more time to find a job in which they are reasonably happy. (b) Older workers are more satisfied with the intrinsic, personal aspects of their jobs than they are with the extrinsic aspects, such as pay (Morrow & McElroy, 1987). (c) Older workers may have resigned themselves to the fact that things are unlikely to improve, resulting in a better congruence between worker desires and job attributes (White & Spector, 1987). (d) Work becomes less of a focus in people's lives as they age and achieve occupational success (Bray & Howard, 1983), so that it takes less to keep them satisfied.

However, job satisfaction does not simply increase over a lifetime, but rather follows a cyclical pattern. That is, satisfaction may fluctuate periodically based on changes that people intentionally make in their occupations (Shirom & Mazeh, 1988). Job satisfaction increases over time because people change jobs or responsibilities on a regular basis, thereby keeping their occupation interesting and challenging. How did Shirom and Mazeh figure out that job satisfaction can be cyclical? For the answer, read the Spotlight on Research feature.

Periodicity and Job Satisfaction

SPOTLIGHT
ON RESEARCH

Job satisfaction tends to increase with age. Why this is true has been the subject of much debate. One hypothesis is that job satisfaction has a complex, curvilinear relationship to the length of time one has been in a job. Satisfaction tends to be high in the beginning of a job, to stabilize or drop during the middle phase, and to rise again later. Each time a person changes jobs, the cycle repeats.

Shirom and Mazeh (1988) studied the cyclical nature of job satisfaction using a cross-sectional research design (see Chapter 1). They administered questionnaires to a representative sample of 900 Israeli junior high school teachers with varying seniority. The questionnaire contained items concerning teachers' satisfaction with salary, working hours, social status, contacts with pupils, autonomy, opportunities for professional growth, and opportunities for carrying out educational goals. By using a sophisticated data analysis technique called *spectral analysis,* they were able to identify year-to-year changes in job satisfaction.

Shirom and Mazeh found that teachers' job satisfaction followed systematic five-year cycles that were strongly related to seniority but unrelated to age. That is, the cycles begin when the person starts a job, and the level of satisfaction is then linked to how long the person has been on the job. Because the age at which people start new teaching jobs can vary a great deal, Shirom and Mazeh were able to show that the cycles had nothing to do with how old the teachers were; all ages showed the same basic pattern.

Most interestingly, Shirom and Mazeh noted that a major work-related change, a sabbatical leave, or a change in school assignment seemed to occur approximately every five years. They concluded that such changes reinitiated the cycle with high job satisfaction. When tracked over long periods, the cycle appears to show a steady increase in overall job satisfaction. This long-term gradual increase in job satisfaction is consistent with the general finding of gradual increases in job satisfaction with age, even though the fundamental cyclic nature of job satisfaction is unrelated to age.

An important implication of Shirom and Mazeh's data is that change may be necessary for long-term job satisfaction. Although the teaching profession has change built into it (such as sabbatical leaves), many occupations do not

(Latack, 1984). The option of periodic changes in job structure would have benefits for other occupations as well.   🐦

ALIENATION AND BURNOUT

No job is perfect; there is always something about it that is not as good as it could be. Perhaps the hours are not optimal, the pay is lower than one would like, or the boss does not have a pleasant personality. For most workers, such negatives are merely annoyances. But for others, they create extremely stressful situations that result in deeply rooted unhappiness with work: alienation and burnout.

When workers feel that what they are doing is meaningless and that their efforts are devalued, or when they do not see the connection between what they do and the final product, a sense of *alienation* is likely to result. Studs Terkel (1974) interviewed several alienated workers and found that all of them expressed the feeling that they were merely nameless, faceless cogs in a large machine.

Employees are most likely to feel alienated when they perform routine, repetitive actions such as those on an assembly line (Terkel, 1974). (Interestingly, many of these functions are being automated and performed by robots.) But other workers can become alienated, too. Especially since the beginning of corporate downsizing in the 1980s, many middle-level managers do not have the same level of job security that they once had. Consequently, their feelings toward their employers have become more negative in many cases (Roth, 1991).

How can employers avoid alienating workers? Research indicates that it is helpful to involve employees in the decision-making process, create flexible work schedules, and institute employee development and enhancement programs (Roth, 1991). Indeed, many organizations have instituted new practices such as total quality management (TQM), partly as a way to address worker alienation. TQM and related approaches make a concerted effort to get employees involved in the operation and administration of their plant or office. Such programs work; absenteeism drops and the quality of work improves in organizations that implement them (Offermann & Growing, 1990).

Sometimes the pace and pressure of the occupation becomes more than a person can bear, resulting in *burnout*, a depletion of a person's energy and motivation, the loss of occupational idealism, and the feeling that one is being exploited. Burnout is a stress syndrome, characterized by emotional exhaustion, depersonalization, and diminished personal accomplishment (Cordes & Dougherty, 1993). Burnout is most common among people in the helping professions, such as teaching, social work, and health care (Cordes & Dougherty, 1993). People in these professions must constantly deal with other people's complex problems, usually under difficult time constraints. Dealing with these pressures every day, along with bureaucratic paperwork, may become too much for the worker to bear. Ideals are abandoned, frustration builds, and disillusionment and exhaustion set in. In short, the worker is burned out.

The best defenses against burnout appear to be getting workers to lower their expectations of themselves and enhancing communication within organizations. No one in the helping professions can resolve all problems perfectly; lowering expectations of what can be realistically accomplished will help workers deal with real-world constraints. Similarly, improving communication among different sections of organizations, to keep workers informed of the outcome of their efforts, will help give them a sense that what they do matters in the long run. Finally, research also suggests that lack of support from one's co-workers may cause depersonalization; improving such support through teamwork can be an effective intervention (Corrigan et al., 1994).

In short, making workers feel that they are important to the organization by involving them in decisions, keeping expectations realistic, ensuring good communication, and promoting teamwork may help employees avoid alienation and burnout. As organizations adopt different management styles, perhaps these goals can be achieved.

TEST YOURSELF

1. Compared with workers a few decades ago, workers today are more concerned with individual freedom, personal growth, and _____.
2. Holland's theory deals with the relationship between occupation and _____.
3. Super believes that through their working years, people are located along a continuum of _____.
4. The role of a mentor is part teacher, part sponsor, part model, and part _____.
5. Recent research has shown that job satisfaction does not increase consistently as a person ages; rather, satisfaction may be _____.
6. Two negative aspects of job satisfaction are alienation and _____.
7. What do you think would be the relation between Holland's theory, occupational development, and job satisfaction? Would these relations be different in the case of a person with a good match between personality and occupation rather than a poor match?

Gender, Ethnicity, and Discrimination Issues

LEARNING OBJECTIVES

❧ *What are the differences between women's and men's occupational expectations? How are people viewed if they enter occupations that are not traditional for their gender?*

❧ *What factors are related to women's occupational development?*

❧ *What factors affect ethnic minority workers' occupational experiences and occupational development?*

❧ *What types of bias and discrimination hinder the occupational development of women and ethnic minority workers?*

People differ considerably in many respects when it comes to occupational choice and development. Although they're in similar occupations, the men and

Answers: (1) *cooperation,* (2) *personality,* (3) *vocational maturity,* (4) *counselor,* (5) *cyclical,* (6) *burnout.*

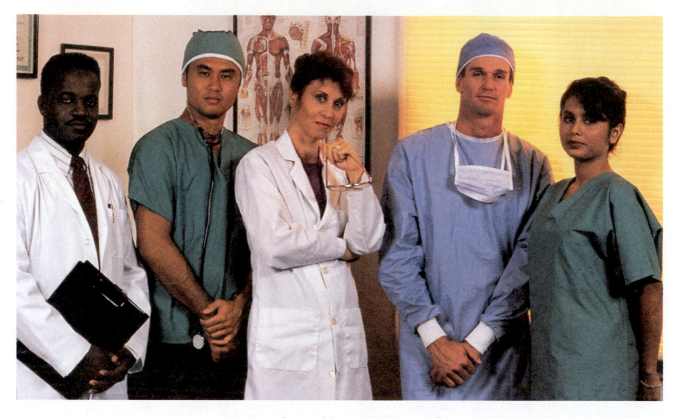

women depicted here each have different backgrounds and experiences regarding the role of work in their lives. The differences are related to gender factors, ethnicity, and age. Women, members of ethnic minorities, and middle-aged and older adults often face barriers to achieving their occupational goals.

The differing experiences of people as a function of gender, ethnicity, and age are important components for any comprehensive view of occupational choice and development. Unfortunately, they have not received the attention they deserve. What snippets of information we have clearly indicate that these demographic factors cannot be ignored.

Gender Differences in Occupational Selection

Traditionally, men have been groomed from childbirth for future employment. Boys learn at an early age that men are known by the work they do, and they are strongly encouraged to think about what occupation they would like to have. Occupational achievement is stressed as a core element of masculinity. Important social skills are taught through team games, in which they learn how to play by the rules, to accept setbacks without taking defeat personally, to follow the guidance of a leader, and to move up the leadership hierarchy by demonstrating qualities that are valued by others.

Traditionally, women have not been trained in this manner. The skills that they have learned have been quite different: how to be accommodating, deferential, quiet, and supportive (Shainess, 1984). However, an increasing emphasis has been placed on the importance of providing girls with the necessary skills for occupations outside the home. The growth of women's athletic programs is giving more women the opportunity to learn key skills as well. Given that more than half of women are now employed outside the home, and that this trend will probably continue, it is especially important that women be exposed to the same occupational socialization opportunities as men. However, major structural barriers to women's occupational selection remain (Schwartz, 1992). It is still the case that many occupational opportunities are more available to men than to women.

TRADITIONAL AND NONTRADITIONAL OCCUPATIONS

As more women enter the work force, a growing number of them work in occupations that have traditionally been male-dominated, such as construction and engineering. Research in this area has focused on three issues (Swanson, 1992): selection of nontraditional occupations, characteristics of women in nontraditional occupations, and perceptions of nontraditional occupations.

Why some women end up in nontraditional occupations appears to be related to personal feelings and experiences as well as expectations about the occupation (Brooks & Betz, 1990). Concerning personal experiences, women who attend single-sex high schools and who have both brothers and sisters end up in the least traditional occupations, apparently because they have been exposed to more options and fewer gender-role stereotypes (Rubenfeld & Gilroy, 1991). Personal feelings are important; a study of Japanese students found that women had significantly lower confidence in their ability to perform in male-dominated occupations than in female-dominated occupations (Matsui, Ikeda, & Ohnishi, 1989).

The characteristics of women in nontraditional occupations have been studied as well. Betz, Heesacker, and Shuttleworth (1990) found that women who scored high on femininity, as defined by endorsing traditional feminine gender roles, and those in female-dominated occupations had the poorest match between their abilities and their occupational choices. These findings mean that women who score high on traditional measures of femininity have difficulty finding occupations that allow them to take advantage of their abilities. Additionally, women in female-dominated occupations generally find that their jobs do not allow them to use their abilities to the fullest. In sum, it appears that many women have difficulty finding occupations that match their skills.

Despite the efforts to counteract gender stereotyping of occupations, women who choose nontraditional occupations are still viewed with disapproval by their peers of either sex, even though they have high job satisfaction themselves (Brabeck & Weisgerber, 1989; Pfost & Fiore, 1990). This finding holds up in cross-cultural research as well. In a study conducted in India, both women and men gave higher "respectability" ratings to males than to females in the same occupation, such as the example shown in the photograph (Kanekar, Kolsawalla, & Nazareth, 1989). People even make inferences about working conditions based on their perception of an occupation as traditionally masculine or feminine. Scozzaro and Subich (1990) report that female-dominated occupations were perceived as offering nice working conditions, whereas male-dominated occupations were perceived as offering good pay and promotion potential.

Taken together, these studies show that we still have a long way to go before people can

As more women enter the workforce, more are choosing occupations that were traditionally male. Women who select nontraditional occupations have high job satisfaction but are often viewed negatively by their peers.

NANCY BETZ

"Women's intellectual capacities and talents are not reflected in their educational and occupational achievements."

choose any occupation they want without having to contend with gender-related stereotypes. Although differences in opportunities for women in traditional and nontraditional occupations are narrowing, key differences remain. Finally, virtually no research has examined differences between males in traditional and nontraditional occupations (Swanson, 1992). This lack of data is troubling, for it prevents our answering important questions such as why men choose traditional or nontraditional occupations, and why some men still perpetuate gender stereotypes about particular occupations.

Women and Occupational Development

If you were to guess what a young woman who has just graduated from college will be doing occupationally ten years from now, what would you say? Would you guess that she will be strongly committed to her occupation? Would she have abandoned it for other things? Betz (1984) wanted to know the answers, so she examined the occupational histories of 500 college women ten years after graduation. Two-thirds of these women were highly committed to their occupations, which for 70% were traditionally female ones. Most had worked continuously since graduation. Only 1% had been full-time homemakers during the entire ten-year period; 79% reported that they had successfully combined occupations with homemaking. Women in traditional female occupations changed jobs less often. If they did change, the move was more likely to be to a job with a lower rank and pay compared to the changes made by women in nontraditional occupations.

Women who leave professional-level occupations such as law do not tend to do so because of child care issues. Rather, it is unsupportive or insensitive work environments, organizational politics, and the lack of professional development opportunities that lead then to quit.

An intriguing question is why highly educated women leave what appear to be well-paid occupations. Studies of women MBAs with children have identified a number of family and workplace issues (Rosin & Korabik, 1990, 1991). Family obligations, such as child care, appear to be most important for mothers working part-time. For these women, adequate child care arrangements or having the flexibility to be at home when children get out of school often make the difference between being able to accept a job or remaining at home. In contrast, mothers who have made the decision to work full-time have resolved the problem of child care. The most important workplace issues for these women are gender-related. Unsupportive or insensitive work environments, organizational politics, and the lack of occupational development opportunities appear most important for women working full-time (Schwartz, 1992). In this case, women are focusing on issues that could create barriers to their occupational development and are looking for ways around the barriers.

Ethnicity and Occupational Development

What factors are related to occupational selection and development for people from ethnic minorities? Unfortunately, not much research has been conducted from a developmental perspective. Rather, most researchers have focused on the limited opportunities ethnic minorities have and the structural barriers, such as discrimination, that they face. Most of the developmental research to date focuses on occupational selection issues and variables that foster occupational development.

With regard to occupational selection, three topics examined in recent studies are nontraditional occupations, vocational identity (the degree to which one views one's occupation as a key element of identity), and issues pertaining to occupational aspirations.

African American women and European American women do not differ in terms of plans to enter nontraditional occupations (Murrell, Frieze, & Frost, 1991). However, African American women who choose nontraditional occupations tend to plan for more formal education than necessary to achieve their goal. This may actually make them overqualified for the jobs they get; for example, a woman with a college degree may be working in a job that does not require that level of education.

Vocational identity varies with both ethnicity and gender. Compared to European American women and Hispanic men, African American and European American men have higher vocational identity when they graduate from college (Steward & Krieshok, 1991). Lower vocational identity means that people define themselves primarily in terms of things in life other than work.

A person's occupational aspiration is the kind of occupation he or she would like to have. On the other hand, occupational expectation is the occupation the person believes he or she will actually get. Hispanics differ from European Americans in several ways with regard to these variables. They have high occupational aspirations but low expectations, and they differ in their educational attainment as a function of national origin, generational status, and social class (Arbona, 1990). However, Hispanics are similar to European Americans in occupational development and work values.

If this African American woman works in a corporate setting that is responsive and sensitive to her needs, she is more likely to have higher job satisfaction.

Research on occupational development of ethnic minority workers is clear on one point: Whether an organization is responsive to the needs of ethnic minorities makes a big difference for employees. Both European American and ethnic minority managers who perceive their organizations as responsive and positive for ethnic minority employees are more satisfied with and committed to the organizations (Burke, 1991a, 1991b). But much still remains to be accomplished. African American managers report less choice of jobs, less acceptance, more career dissatisfaction, lower performance evaluations and promotability ratings, and more rapid attainment of plateaus in their careers than European American managers (Greenhaus, Parasuraman, & Wormley, 1990). Over 60% of African American protégés have European American mentors, which is problematic because same-ethnicity mentors provide more psychosocial support than cross-ethnicity mentors (Thomas, 1990).

Bias and Discrimination

Since the 1960s, organizations in the United States have been sensitized to the issues of bias and discrimination in the workplace. Hiring, promotion, and termination procedures have come under close scrutiny in numerous court cases, resulting in judicial rulings governing these processes.

GENDER BIAS AND THE GLASS CEILING

Even though the majority of women work outside the home, women in high-status jobs are unusual (Morrison et al., 1992). Not until 1981 was a woman,

Sandra Day O'Connor, appointed to the U.S. Supreme Court; it took another 12 years before a second woman, Ruth Bader Ginsburg, was appointed. As Janice noticed in the second chapter-opening vignette, few women serve in the highest ranks of major corporations, and women are substantially outnumbered at the senior faculty level of most universities and colleges.

One intuitively appealing reason for the scarcity of women in top-level jobs is work overload, insofar as women with occupations outside the home are also expected to perform most of the day-to-day housekeeping chores and child care. Contrary to intuition, however, work overload is usually not a factor; we will come back to this topic later in this chapter. **Far more important is *sex discrimination*, denying a job to someone solely on the basis of whether the person is a man or a woman.**

Baron and Bielby (1985) pull no punches in discussing sex discrimination. "Our analyses portray [sex] discrimination as pervasive, almost omnipresent, sustained by diverse organizational structures and processes. Moreover, this segregation drastically restricts women's career opportunities, by blocking access to internal labor markets and their benefits" (Baron & Bielby, 1985, p. 245). Women are being kept out of high-status jobs by the men at the top.

Women themselves refer to a *glass ceiling*, the level to which they may rise in a company but beyond which they may not go. This problem is most obvious in companies that classify jobs at various levels (as does the Civil Service). The greatest barrier facing women seems to stand at the boundary between lower-tier and upper-tier job grades (Morrison et al., 1992). Women like Janice tend to move to the top of the lower tier and remain there, whereas men are more readily promoted to the upper tier, even when other factors, such as personal attributes and qualifications, are controlled (DiPrete & Soule, 1988). Indeed, a longitudinal study of women in the high school class of 1972 showed that despite better academic records, women's achievement in the workplace is limited by structural barriers (Adelman, 1991). The U.S. Department of Labor (1991) admitted that the glass ceiling pervades the workplace. Some surveys indicate that over 90% of women believe that there is a glass ceiling in the workplace. Indeed, estimates are that if the present rate of advancement continues, it will take until the late 25th century for women to achieve equality with men in the executive suite (Feminist Majority Foundation, 1991).

Besides discrimination in hiring and promotion, women are also subject to pay discrimination. According to the U.S. Department of Labor, in many occupations men are paid substantially more than women in the same positions; indeed, on the average, women are paid only three-fourths or less of what men are paid. Although the pay gap had widened to 35% in the early 1980s, in the early 1990s it began to close because men's salaries are declining (U.S. Department of Labor, 1995).

Several solutions to this problem have been promoted. **One of these is *comparable worth*: equalizing pay in occupations that are determined to be equivalent in importance but differ in the gender distribution of the peo-**

ple doing the jobs. Determining which male-dominated occupations should be considered equivalent to which female-dominated occupations for pay purposes can be difficult and controversial.

SEXUAL HARASSMENT

Although sexual harassment of women in the workplace has been documented for centuries, only recently has it received much attention from researchers (Fitzgerald & Shullman, 1993). Interest among U.S. researchers increased dramatically after the 1991 Senate hearings involving Supreme Court nominee Clarence Thomas and Anita Hill, who accused him of sexual harassment, and the Tailhook scandal involving the mistreatment of women by U.S. Navy personnel with the knowledge of their commanders.

How many people have been sexually harassed, and what do people think sexual harassment entails? These are two areas researchers are investigating, but neither topic is straightforward. Reliable statistics on the number of victims are extremely difficult to obtain, in part due to the unwillingness of many victims to report harassment and to differences in reporting procedures. Indeed, estimates are that less than 5% of victims ever report their experiences to anyone in authority (Fitzgerald et al., 1988). Even given these difficulties, several studies document that over 40% of women report having been sexually harassed in the workplace at least once (Fitzgerald & Shullman, 1993).

Of course, the crux of the matter is what constitutes harassment. What would have to be going on in the situation depicted in the photograph for you to say that it was harassment? Using ambiguous situations like this is a technique that many researchers use. In fact, research on perceptions of what constitutes harassing behavior usually requires people to read vignettes of hypothetical incidents involving sexually suggestive touching, sexual remarks, and the like, and then decide whether it was harassment. In general, women are more likely to view such behaviors as offensive than are men (Fitzgerald & Ormerod, 1991). **Because of this gender gap in perceptions, a federal court, in the case of *Ellison v. Brady*, instituted the *"reasonable woman" standard* as the appropriate legal criterion for determining whether sexual harassment has occurred.** If a reasonable woman would view a behavior as offensive, the court held, then it is offensive even if the man did not consider it to be so.

Besides the gender of the perceiver, several other factors influence whether a behavior is considered offensive (Fitzgerald & Ormerod, 1991). These include the degree to which the behavior is explicit or extreme (for example, rape as against a friendly kiss), victim behavior (whether the victim was at all responsible for what happened), supervisory status (whether the perpetrator was a direct supervisor of the victim), harasser's intentions (whether the perpetrator knew that the victim found the behavior offensive), and frequency of occurrence (for example, a one-time occurrence as opposed to a regular event). Unfortunately, little research has been done to identify what aspects of organizations foster harassment or to determine the impact of educational programs aimed at addressing the problem.

What can be done to provide people with a safe work environment, free from sexual harassment? The Current Controversies feature discusses one approach that grew from the Tailhook scandal. Take a minute to read it, and ask yourself whether this helps to clarify the issue. Why?

CURRENT CONTROVERSIES

Sexual Harassment in the Workplace

No topic captured the public's attention faster in the early 1990s than sexual harassment. The watershed event was the 1991 Senate Judiciary Committee confirmation hearings concerning Clarence Thomas's nomination as an Associate Justice of the U.S. Supreme Court. Thomas was accused of sexual harassment by a former employee, Anita Hill. In dramatic testimony, broadcast live, charges and countercharges were debated for days. Even though Thomas was eventually confirmed, the event sparked a widespread political and social consciousness raising. In the 1992 elections, several people, primarily women, were elected after campaigns based on the perceived unfairness and inequality of the system toward women.

The main problem confronting society in the wake of these hearings was how to define sexual harassment. As noted in the text, the courts adopted the "reasonable woman" standard. But how does this standard get translated into specific behavioral guidelines? How do people know ahead of time whether what they plan to do or say is or is not harassment?

Of course, it is relatively easy to define what is clearly not harassment (such as normal social interactions, polite compliments, or friendly conversation) and what clearly is (such as rape, asking for sex in return for a good job evaluation, or sending hate mail of a sexual nature). What is extraordinarily difficult to spell out is the in-between area, the "gray zone," of all the behaviors in the middle. Is telling someone that they look "great" in a particular outfit harassment? How about yelling "babe" or "hunk" at someone? What about asking someone out on a date?

Answers to these questions are complicated because they depend on where they occur (at work or at home) and whether or not one person has a supervisory position over the other. Increasingly, behaviors that used to be written off as "boys will be boys" are now being ruled as harassing, because the victims interpret them as such. For example, several cases of name-calling in high schools (such as "slut") have been ruled to constitute harassment; the victims have successfully argued that they suffered psychological harm.

You should take a minute or two and think about what your definition of sexual harassment is. Have you ever experienced harassment? How did you feel? How has that experience affected your views? You might then talk it over with other people of both genders to see how your definition and experiences are similar or different. One thing is certain. It is likely that the issue of sexual harassment will remain controversial for years to come. 🐾

AGE DISCRIMINATION

Another structural barrier to occupational development is *age discrimination*, which involves denying a job or promotion to someone solely on the

basis of age. The U.S. Age Discrimination in Employment Act of 1986 protects workers over age 40. This law stipulates that people must be hired based on their ability, not their age. Under this law, employers are banned from refusing to hire and from discharging workers solely on the basis of age. Additionally, employers cannot segregate or classify workers or otherwise denote their status on the basis of age.

Age discrimination occurs in several ways (Snyder & Barrett, 1988). For example, employers can make certain types of physical or mental performance a job requirement and argue that older workers cannot meet the standard. Or they can attempt to get rid of older workers by using retirement. Supervisors sometimes use age as a factor in performance evaluations for raises or promotions or in decisions about which employees are eligible for additional training.

Perceptions of age discrimination are widespread; nearly 1600 suits were filed in 1993 alone, up from roughly 1100 in 1990 (Cornish, 1994). Many of these cases stem from the corporate downsizing that began in the late 1980s. Winning an age discrimination case is difficult, however (Snyder & Barrett, 1988). Job performance information is crucial. However, most companies tend to report this information in terms of general differences between younger and older adults (such as differences in recent memory ability) rather than in specific terms of older and younger workers in a particular occupation (which rarely show any differences in productivity or performance). Surprisingly, many courts do not question inaccurate information or stereotypic views of aging presented by employers, despite the lack of scientific data documenting age differences in actual job performance.

Many individuals over age 40 have lost their jobs due to corporate downsizing. Like this woman, such workers are protected by age discrimination laws; companies must not lay them off solely because of their age.

Occupational Success Is More Than Just Hard Work

FORCES IN ACTION

At some point in your life, you probably were told (and maybe believed) that choosing an occupation and enjoying occupational success were both simply a matter of working hard and performing well. As you've gotten older and experienced the world of work, you have probably seen firsthand that there is more to it than that. The biopsychosocial model provides a good framework for understanding how people choose their occupations and develop in them.

Biological forces help shape job-related abilities and skills to the extent that the skills have a genetic component (some people are clearly "natural" athletes or chemists; others are not). Whether a person actually develops these innate abilities depends in part on psychological forces such as personality and behavior. These forces find expression in what people "like" to do, the choices they make about which courses to take, or the kinds of extracurricular activities they try. Holland's theory stresses the importance of psychological forces. But whether people actually have the opportunity to make these choices reflects the social forces that either create or limit options. The powerful social forces of socioeconomic class, prejudice, and discrimination, among others, open doors for some and close off choices for others. These social forces are a major factor in antidiscrimination, affirmative action, and related legislation in the United States. But reality also tells us that a person's position in the life cycle confers a relative advantage (or disadvantage) in a competitive job market. Two individuals with identical skills and experience may not be viewed as equivalent by an organization if one is 25 and the other 55. So it matters a great deal *when* in our lives opportunity comes knocking.

The biological, psychological, social, and life-cycle forces interact in the domain of occupational selection and development. Combined with the understanding from Chapter 10 of how the biopsychosocial model helps explain the relationships people have, the present discussion will provide a good interpretive framework for our discussion of work–family issues later in this chapter.   ❧

TEST YOURSELF

1. Women who choose nontraditional occupations are viewed _____ by their peers.
2. Among reasons why women in well-paid occupations leave, _____ are most important for part-time workers.
3. Ethnic minority workers are more satisfied with and committed to organizations that are responsive and provide _____.
4. Three barriers to women's occupational development are sex discrimination, the glass ceiling, and _____.
5. What steps need to be taken in order to eliminate gender, ethnic, and age bias in the workplace?

Occupational Transitions
■ *Earl's Back in School and Changing Occupations (Again)*
Retraining Workers
Occupational Insecurity
Coping with Unemployment

Occupational Transitions

LEARNING OBJECTIVES

❧ *Why do people change occupations?*

❧ *Is worrying about potential job loss a major source of stress?*

❧ *How does the timing of job loss affect the amount of stress experienced?*

In the past, people commonly chose an occupation during young adulthood and stayed in it throughout their working years. Today, however, not many people take a job with the expectation that it will last a lifetime. Changing jobs is almost taken for granted; the average North American will change jobs between five and ten times during adulthood (Toffler, 1970). Some authors view occupational changes as positive; Havighurst (1982), for example, strongly advocates such flexibility. According to his view, building change into the occupational life cycle may help to avoid disillusionment with one's initial choice. Changing occupations may be one way to guarantee challenging and satisfying work, and it may be the best option for those in a position to exercise it (Shirom & Mazeh, 1988). The case of Earl, told in the Real People feature, exemplifies many of these aspects of occupational change.

Earl's Back in School and Changing Occupations (Again)

REAL PEOPLE

One of these days, you may be fortunate enough to meet someone like Earl. Earl was not a typical student. He was obviously older than the average undergraduate (52 years old, in fact), but that's not why he stood out. What made Earl different was that he was preparing to embark on his third occupation. For 24 years he was in the Air Force, first as a pilot and later as a staff officer. His military experiences were often exciting but scary, especially when bullets ripped through his cockpit as he flew missions over Vietnam. On returning to the United States, he taught some members of Congress how to fly. He transferred to the staff of NATO, working primarily at the Pentagon. But dealing with politicians concerning military appropriations and other matters became so frustrating that he retired. At age 44, he began his second occupation, selling insurance. Although he was promoted and did well, he became disenchanted with trying to sell insurance to people who sometimes really did not need it. Earl resigned after five years; at age 50, he went back to college to prepare for a third occupation, this time in physical therapy.

Earl's experiences may appear somewhat unusual, but in fact many people now have two or more careers during their lives. Some change careers for personal reasons; Earl's decision to enter physical therapy is an excellent example. For others, though, the changes are forced on them. For example, many middle-level executives who lost their jobs in the late 1980s and early 1990s made dramatic changes in occupation just to get a paycheck. Even Earl experienced some involuntary changes, such as his transfers during his military career. What Earl's experience tells us is that personal principles are important, and it is never too late in one's life to retool and change occupations.   ❧

Several factors have been identified as important in determining who will remain in an occupation and who will change. Some factors—such as whether the person likes the occupation—lead to self-initiated occupation changes. For example, people who really like their occupation may seek additional training or accept overtime assignments in hopes of acquiring new skills that will enable them to get better jobs. However, other factors, such as obsolete skills and economic trends, cause forced occupational changes. For example, continued improvement of robots caused some auto industry workers to lose their jobs, and economic recessions usually result in large-scale layoffs. But even forced occupational changes can have benefits. As we will see in Chapter 12, for instance, many adults go to college. Some are taking advantage of educational benefits offered as part of a separation package. Others, like Earl, are pursuing educational opportunities in order to obtain new skills; still others are looking to advance in their careers.

In this section, we will explore the positive and negative aspects of occupational transitions. First we will examine the retraining of mid-career and older workers. The increased use of technology, corporate downsizing, and an aging work force have focused attention on the need to keep older workers' skills current. Later, we will examine occupational insecurity and the effects of job loss.

Retraining Workers

When you are hired into a specific job, you are selected because your employer believes you offer the best fit between abilities you already have and those needed to perform the job. As most people can attest, though, the skills needed to perform a job usually change over time. Such changes may be due to the introduction of new technology, additional responsibilities, or promotion.

Unless a person's skills are kept up to date, the outcome is likely to be either job loss or career plateauing (Froman, 1994). **Career plateauing occurs when there is a lack of promotional opportunity in the organization or when a person decides not to seek advancement.** In cases of job loss or career plateauing, retraining may be an appropriate response. One objective might be to improve technical skills, such as new computer skills. For mid-career or older employees, retraining might focus on how to find new career opportunities—for example, through résumé preparation and career counseling.

JAN D. SINNOTT
"In the future, we as a culture may want to maximize the potential of mature adults to learn in many ways."

Many corporations, as well as community and technical colleges, offer retraining programs in a variety of fields. Organizations that promote employee development typically promote in-house courses to improve employee skills. Or they may offer tuition reimbursement programs for individuals who successfully complete courses at colleges or universities.

The retraining of mid-career and older workers highlights the need for lifelong learning (Sinnott, 1994). If corporations are to meet the challenges of a global economy, it will be imperative that they include retraining in their employee development programs. Such programs will help improve people's chances of advancement in their chosen occupations, and they will also assist people in making successful transitions from one occupation to another.

Occupational Insecurity

Changing economic conditions in the United States over the past few decades (such as the move toward a global economy), as well as changing demographics, have forced many people out of their jobs. Heavy manufacturing and support businesses (such as the steel, oil, and automotive industries) and farming were the hardest hit during the 1970s and 1980s. But no one is immune. Indeed, the corporate takeover frenzy of the 1980s and the recession of the early 1990s put many middle- and upper-level corporate executives out of work in all kinds of businesses.

As a result of these trends, many people feel insecure about their jobs. Like Fred, the auto worker in the third chapter-opening vignette, many worried workers have numerous years of dedicated service to a corporation. Unfortunately, people who worry about their jobs tend to have poorer mental health (Roskies & Louis-Guerin, 1990). For example, anxiety about one's job may result in negative attitudes about one's employer or even work in general, which in turn may result in diminished desire to be successful. Whether there is any actual basis for people's feelings of job insecurity may not matter; sometimes, what people think is true about their work situation is more important than what is actually the case. If people believe that they are at risk of losing their jobs, their mental health and behavior are often affected negatively even when the actual risk of losing their jobs is very low (Roskies & Louis-Guerin, 1990).

Coping with Unemployment

What does it feel like to lose one's job after many years of dedicated service? One man put it this way.

> After becoming used to living like a decent human being, then losing your job, working six days a week just to make the house payment for two years before selling it at a loss, then losing your wife because of all the hardships that were not your fault, then looking endlessly for a decent job only to find jobs for $4 or $5 an hour [so that I] can't afford an apartment or any place to live so having to live out of a van for the past two-and-one-half years, *how should one feel?* Please, I'm a hard worker and did a good job. I always go to work—check my record! I want to be normal again, like a real human being with a house instead of a van. (Leana & Feldman, 1992, p. 51)

As this man states so poignantly, losing one's job can have enormous personal impact (DeFrank & Ivancevich, 1986). Declines in physical health and self-esteem, depression, anxiety, and suicide are common (Lajer, 1982). Men and women seem to experience the same amount of distress following the loss of a job (Leana & Feldman, 1991). However, these effects vary with age. Middle-aged men are more vulnerable to negative effects than older or younger men, largely because they have greater financial responsibilities than the other two groups (De-Frank & Ivancevich, 1986).

Besides the degree of financial strain, the extent of the distress from losing a job is related to the timing of the loss in the adult life cycle (Estes & Wilensky, 1978). Lajer (1982) reports that admission to a psychiatric unit following job loss is more likely for people who are over age 45 or have been unemployed for a long period. However, Leana and Feldman (1992) write that workers in their 50s who lose their jobs are not always highly distressed. Some may have been planning to retire in the near future, others may be hired back as consultants, and still others see it as an opportunity to try something new.

Because unemployment rates for many ethnic minority groups are substantially higher than for European Americans, the effects of unemployment are experienced by a greater proportion of people in these groups. As far as is known, however, the nature of the distress resulting from job loss is the same regardless of ethnicity. Compared to European Americans, however, it usually takes minority workers longer to find another job. Unfortunately, we have very little data on the long-term effects of unemployment, especially from a developmental perspective.

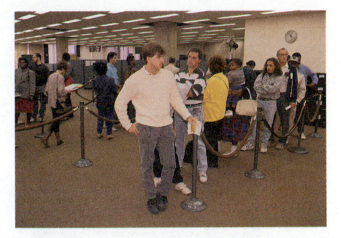

Many people's images of the type of people who collect unemployment were changed when white-collar workers were laid off in large numbers beginning in the 1980s. Losing one's job can have serious emotional effects on workers.

TEST YOURSELF

1. One response to the pressures of a global economy and an aging work force is to provide _____.

2. Two factors that could cause involuntary occupational change are economic trends and _____.

3. Fear of job loss is often a more important determinant of stress than _____.

4. The age group that is most at risk for negative effects of job loss is _____.

5. It is likely that the trend toward multiple careers will continue and become the norm. What implications will this have for theories of career development in the future?

Work and Family

LEARNING OBJECTIVES

❧ *What determines whether mothers return to work?*

❧ *How do husbands and wives view the division of household chores?*

❧ *What is role conflict? How does it affect couples' lives?*

One of the most difficult challenges facing adults is trying to balance the demands of occupation with the demands of family. Over the past few decades, the

Work and Family
  The Child Care Dilemma
  Handling Multiple Roles
  Role Conflict
  ■ *How Do Dual-Earner Couples Handle Division of Labor and Role Conflict?*

Answers: (1) *worker retraining,* (2) *obsolete skills,* (3) *actual likelihood of job loss,* (4) *middle-aged adults*

rapid increase in the number of families in which both parents are employed has fundamentally changed how we view the relation between work and family. As the photograph shows, this can even mean taking a young child to work as a way to deal with the pushes and pulls of being an employed parent. In the majority of two-parent households today, both adults work outside the home, largely because families need the dual income in order to pay the bills and maintain a moderate standard of living. As we will see, dual-earner couples with children experience both benefits and costs from this arrangement.

The Child Care Dilemma

EMPLOYED MOTHERS REVISITED

Many mothers have no option but to return to work after the birth of a child. Some, though, must grapple with the decision of whether they want to return. Surveys of mothers with preschool children reveal that the motivation for returning to work tends to be related to how attached mothers are to their work. For example, in one survey of Australian mothers, those with high work attachment were more likely to cite intrinsic personal achievement reasons for returning. Those with low work attachment cited pressing financial needs. Those with moderate work attachment were divided between intrinsic and financial reasons (Cotton, Anthill, & Cunningham, 1989). Apparently, the reasons women return (or do not return) to work following the birth of a child are complex.

CHILD CARE AND WORKER BEHAVIOR

Employed parents with small children are confronted with the difficult act of leaving their children in the care of others. In response to pressure from parents, most industrialized countries (but not the United States) provide government-supported child care centers for employees as one way to help ease this burden. Does providing a center make a difference in terms of an employee's feelings about work, absenteeism, or productivity?

The answer is that it's not as simple as opening a center. Just making a child care center available to employees does not necessarily reduce parents' work–family conflict or their absenteeism (Goff, Mount, & Jamison, 1990). The key is how the supervisor acts. Irrespective of where the child care center is located, when supervisors are sympathetic and supportive regarding family issues and child care, parents report less work–family conflict and have lower absenteeism.

It will be interesting to watch how these issues play out in the U.S. over the next several years. With the passage of the Parental Leave Act in 1993, for the first time new parents will be able to take unpaid time off to care for their children, having the right to return to their jobs. Experience from other countries indicates that parental leave has different effects on each parent. For example, a large-scale study in Sweden showed that fathers who took parental leave were more likely to continue their involvement in child care and to reduce their work involvement. Regardless of fathers' participation, mothers still retained primary responsibility for child care and stayed less involved in and received fewer rewards in the labor market (Haas, 1990; Schwartz, 1992).

Handling Multiple Roles

When both members of a heterosexual couple are employed, who cleans the house, cooks the meals, and takes care of the children when they are ill? Despite much media attention and claims of increased sharing in the duties, women still perform the lion's share of housework, regardless of employment status. Working mothers spend about twice as many hours per week as men in family work and bear the greatest responsibility for household and child care tasks (Benin & Agostinelli, 1988). This unequal division of labor causes the most arguments and the most unhappiness for dual-earner couples. This is the case with Jennifer and Bill, the couple in the fourth chapter-opening vignette; Jennifer does most of the housework.

A great deal of evidence indicates that women have reduced the amount of time they spend on housework since the 1970s, especially when they are employed, and that men have increased the amount of time they spend on such tasks (Swanson, 1992). The increased participation of men in these tasks is not all that it seems, however. Most of the increase is on weekends, with specific tasks that they agree to perform, and it is largely unrelated to women's employment status (Zick & McCullough, 1991). In short, the increase in men's participation has not done much to lower women's burdens around the house.

Men and women view the division of labor in very different terms. Men are often most satisfied with an equitable division of labor based on the number of hours spent, especially if the amount of time needed to perform household tasks is relatively small. Women are often most satisfied when men are willing to perform women's traditional chores (Benin & Agostinelli, 1988). Much the same is true concerning satisfaction for African American dual-earner couples. However, African American women were twice as likely as men to feel overburdened with housework and to be dissatisfied with their family life (Broman, 1988).

Ethnic differences in the division of household labor are also apparent. In a study of European American, African American, and Hispanic American men, several interesting patterns emerged (Shelton & John, 1993). African American and Hispanic American men tend to spend more time doing household tasks than do European American men. In the case of African American men, this finding supports the view that such households are more egalitarian than European American households. Moreover, the increased participation of African American men was primarily true of employed (as opposed to unemployed) men. There was greater participation in traditionally female tasks, such as washing dishes and cooking. Similarly, Hispanic American men also tended to participate more in these tasks. Overall, European American men spent the least time helping with traditionally female tasks. Clearly, the degree to which men and women divide household tasks varies not only with gender, but with ethnicity as well.

In sum, the available evidence from heterosexual couples indicates that women still perform more household tasks than men, but that the difference varies with ethnic groups. The discrepancy is greatest when the male endorses traditional masculine gender roles and is less when the male endorses more feminine or androgynous gender roles (Gunter & Gunter, 1990).

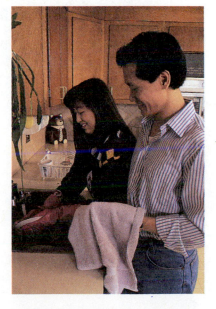

Dividing the household chores is one of the biggest challenges faced by dual-earner couples. It is still the case that women end up doing more than half of the household and child care tasks.

Role Conflict

When people have both occupations and children, they must figure out how to balance the demands of each. People agonize over how to be at their daughter's ballgame at the same time they have to be at an important business meeting. **These competing demands cause *role conflict*, which is the feeling of being pulled in multiple directions by incompatible demands.**

Role conflict regarding parenting issues is a problem expressed by many single adults and dual-earner couples. Figuring out how to balance time at work and time with family is difficult. Most employed women and men manage to resolve the tension between work and parenting, but it can be done better. How this might be accomplished is explored in the You May Be Wondering feature.

How Do Dual-Earner Couples Handle Division of Labor and Role Conflict?

YOU MAY BE WONDERING

In the 1990s, dual-earner couples must find a balance between their occupational and family roles. With the majority of couples now consisting of two wage earners, how to divide the household chores and how to care for the children have become increasingly important.

Many people believe that work and family roles influence each other: When things go badly at work, family suffers, and when there are troubles at home, work suffers. However, this appears not to be the case. Instead, the street is one-way. For the most part, problems at home have little effect on job performance, whereas trouble at work can easily spill over to home life.

Of course, it is important that the partners negotiate agreeable arrangements of household and child care tasks, but (as noted in the text), truly equitable divisions of labor are clearly the exception. Most American households with heterosexual dual-worker couples still operate under a gender-segregated system: There are traditional chores for men and women. All of these tasks are important and must be performed to keep homes safe, clean, and sanitary. All of these tasks also take time. The important point for women is not how much time is spent in performing household chores, but which tasks are performed. What bothers wives the most is not that their husbands are lazy but that they will not perform some "women's work." Men may mow the lawn, wash the car, and even cook, but they rarely vacuum, scrub the toilet, or change the baby's diaper.

The division of labor apparently occurs the way it does because that's how people saw their parents do it, and that's what they are comfortable with. John Cavanaugh had an interesting experience in this regard. While doing some volunteer maintenance work at a battered women's shelter in Appalachia, he had to use the vacuum cleaner as one of the steps in cleaning the carpet. He soon became aware that several women were following him around, pointing at him and talking excitedly. A little later, he asked why they did that. He was told that it was the first time in these adult women's lives that they had ever seen a man use a vacuum cleaner.

There is an ironic twist to all of this. Men's reluctance to do certain tasks has a price. Apparently, women would view them more positively if they performed more of the traditionally female tasks, so marital satisfaction would be likely to improve as a result. Moreover, children in such households would have role models of more equitable gender roles.

So how and when will things change? An important step would be to talk about these issues with your partner. Keep communication lines open all the time, and let your partner know if something is bothering you. Teaching your children that men and women are equally responsible for household chores will also help end the problem. Only by creating true gender equality, without differentiating among household tasks, will the unfair division of labor be ended.   ❧

Research provides some evidence of success. Women in one study were clear in their commitment to their careers, marriage, and children, and they successfully combined them without high levels of distress (Guelzow, Bird, & Koball, 1991). How did they do it? Contrary to popular belief, the age of the children was not a factor in stress level. However, the *number* of children was important, as stress increases greatly with each additional child, irrespective of their ages. Guilt was also not an issue for these women. In the same study, men reported sharing more of the child care tasks as a way of dealing with multiple role pressures. Additionally, stress is lower for men who have a flexible work schedule that allows them to care for sick children and other family matters. Together, these findings are encouraging; they indicate that more heterosexual dual-earner couples are learning how to balance work and family adaptively.

Dual-earner couples often have difficulty finding time for each other, especially if both work long hours. The amount of time together is not necessarily the most important issue; as long as the time is spent in shared activities such as eating, playing, and conversing, couples tend to be happy (Kingston & Nock, 1987). Unfortunately, many couples find themselves in the same position as Hi and Lois; by the time they have an opportunity to be alone together, they are too tired to make the most of it.

HI AND LOIS, © 1993. Reprinted with special permission of King Features Syndicate.

So exactly what effects do family matters have on work performance and vice versa? Recent evidence suggests that our work and family lives do not influence one another equally. Work stress has a far bigger impact on family life than family stress has on work performance. In general, women feel the work-to-family spillover to a greater extent than men, but both men and women feel the pressure (Gutek, Searle, & Klepa, 1991). Single mothers have an especially hard time if they have more than one child (Polit, 1984). Also, cross-cultural data from a study of dual-earner couples in Singapore showed that wives are more likely to suffer from burnout than husbands; wives' burnout resulted from both work and nonwork stress, whereas husbands' burnout resulted only from work stress (Aryee, 1993).

TEST YOURSELF

1. Parents report lower work–family conflict and have lower absenteeism when supervisors are sympathetic and supportive regarding _____.

2. Men are satisfied with an equitable division of labor based on _____, whereas women are satisfied _____.

3. Among European American, African American, and Hispanic American men, the group least likely to do traditionally female household tasks is _____.

4. If both partners in a dual-earner couple work long hours, an additional role conflict issue is _____.

5. What should organizations do to help ease workers' conflicts with multiple roles?

Time To Relax: Leisure Activities

LEARNING OBJECTIVES

❧ **What activities are leisure activities? How do people choose among them?**

❧ **What changes in leisure activities occur with age?**

❧ **What do people derive from leisure activities?**

Adults do not work every waking moment of their lives. As each of us knows, we need to relax sometimes and engage in leisure activities. Intuitively, leisure consists of activities not associated with work. More formally, researchers define *leisure* as "personally expressive discretionary activity, varying in intensity of involvement from relaxation and diversion . . . through personal development and creativity . . . up to sensual transcendence" (Gordon, Gaitz, & Scott, 1976). However, men and women differ in their views of leisure, as do people in different ethnic groups (Henderson, 1990). For example, one study of African American women revealed that they view leisure as both freedom from the constraint of needing to work and as a form of self-expression (Allen & Chin-Sang, 1990).

You can preview much of what we will learn about leisure activities by completing the exercise in the See for Yourself feature. You will have the opportunity to develop lists of favorite leisure activities for people of different ages, which you should compare to the discussion in the text.

Varieties of Leisure Activity in Adulthood

SEE FOR YOURSELF

Before reading about the research findings on the types of things people do for fun, try to find out as much about them as possible on your own. Here's an easy way. Ask several of your friends, as well as adults of different ages, what their current favorite leisure activities are. Try asking your parents, their friends, your grandparents, your adult children if you have any, and so on, in order to get a good cross-section of ages. Once you have a list of current favorites, ask them what their favorites were ten years ago. Now compare the lists and see for yourself which activities changed and which did not. Compare your results to the research described in the text, and discuss the similarities and differences in class.   ❧

Types of Leisure Activities

Leisure can include virtually any activity. To help organize the options, researchers have classified leisure activities into four categories: cultural—such as attending sporting events, concerts, church services, and meetings; physical—such as basketball, hiking, aerobics, and gardening; social—such as visiting friends and going to parties; and solitary—including reading, listening to music, and watching television (Bossé & Ekerdt, 1981; Glamser & Hayslip, 1985). Leisure activities can also be considered in terms of the degree of cognitive, emotional, or physical involvement.

An alternative approach to classifying leisure activities involves the distinction between preoccupations and interests (Rapoport & Rapoport, 1975). Preoccupations are conscious mental absorptions, much like daydreaming. Sometimes, preoccupations become more focused and are converted to interests. Interests are ideas and feelings about things one would like to do, is curious about, or is attracted to. Expression of interests occurs through various activities, such as jogging, watching television, painting, and so on.

Rapoport and Rapoport's distinction draws attention to a key truth about leisure: Any specific activity has different meaning and value, depending on the individual involved. For example, cooking a gourmet meal is an interest, or a leisure activity, for many people. For professional chefs, however, it is work and thus is not leisure at all.

Given the wide range of options, how do people pick their leisure activities? Apparently, each of us has a leisure repertoire, a personal library of intrinsically motivated activities that we do regularly (Mobily, Lemke, & Gisin, 1991). The activities in our repertoire are determined by two things: perceived competence (how good we think we are at the activity compared to other people our age) and psychological comfort (how well we meet our personal goals for performance). Other factors are important as well: income, interest, health, abilities, transportation, education, and social characteristics. For example, some leisure activities, such as downhill skiing, are relatively expensive and require transportation and reasonably good health and physical coordination for maximum enjoyment. In contrast, reading requires minimal finances (if one uses a public library) and is far less physically demanding. It is probable that how these factors influence leisure activities changes through adulthood (e.g., physical prowess typically declines somewhat). However, exactly how these factors result in changes in leisure activities is currently unknown (Burrus-Bammel & Bammel, 1985).

Developmental Changes in Leisure

As people head into later middle age, they spend less of their leisure time in strenuous physical activities and more in sedentary activities such as reading and watching television.

Cross-sectional studies have also reported age differences in the variety of leisure activities (Bray & Howard, 1983). Young adults participate in a greater range of activities than middle-aged adults. Furthermore, young adults tend to prefer intense leisure activities, such as scuba diving and hang gliding. In contrast, middle-aged adults focus more on home- and family-oriented activities. Older adults narrow the range of activities and lower their intensity even further (Gordon et al., 1976).

Longitudinal studies of changes in individuals' leisure activities over time show considerable stability over reasonably long periods (Cutler & Hendricks, 1990). Claude, the 55-year-old in the last chapter-opening vignette who likes to fish and ski, is a good example of this overall trend. As Claude demonstrates, frequent participation in leisure activities during childhood tends to continue into adulthood. Similar findings hold for the pre- and postretirement years. Apparently, one's preferences for certain types of leisure activities are established early in life; they tend to change over the life span primarily in terms of how physically intense they are.

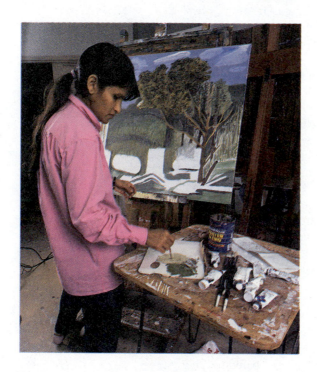

Consequences of Leisure Activities

What does the person in the photograph, or anyone else for that matter, gain from participating in leisure activities?

Researchers agree that involvement in leisure activities is related to well-being (Kelly, Steinkamp, & Kelly, 1987). The key aspect of this relation is not the level of participation. Instead, how much satisfaction you derive from your leisure activities is important in promoting well-being (Lawton, Moss, & Fulcomer, 1986–1987). Indeed, an Israeli study showed that satisfaction with leisure activities is the crucial variable (Lomranz et al., 1988). Whether leisure enhances one's well-being appears to depend on whether you like what you do for fun.

TEST YOURSELF

1. Preoccupations are conscious mental absorptions, whereas interests are _____.

2. Compared to younger adults, middle-aged and older adults prefer leisure activities that are more family- and home-centered and _____.

3. Being involved in leisure activities is related to _____.

4. How are choices of leisure activities related to physical, cognitive, and social development?

Putting It All Together

Sigmund Freud once said that the two most important aspects of adulthood are love and work. In this chapter, we have seen how pervasive work is in our lives, and how it is affected by many things. The occupation Mon-

ica ultimately chooses is partly influenced by talents or skills she may have inherited from her parents, the kind of environment in which she grew up, and the match between her personality style and her occupational skills.

Answers: (1) focused preoccupations, (2) less physically intense, (3) well-being

We saw that occupational development is not an inevitable outcome of hard work. Unfortunately, the world of work also reflects the biases, prejudices, and discrimination people face in the world at large. Janice found that being a woman and a member of an ethnic minority may make it difficult to achieve the levels of advancement in her career that she truly deserves.

Work spills over into our personal lives, too. Fred and others like him worry about job security, and this sometimes affects home life. Although retraining may be an option, it may not alleviate all the concerns. Dual-earner couples are forced to think about how to divide household tasks in order to maintain balance. Jennifer and her husband are struggling with this issue; too often, women perform most of the chores at home.

But a life that is all work and no play is dull. Just as children need a certain amount of play for their development, adults like Claude find playful outlets through leisure activities. Such activities may be as quiet as reading a book or as daring as skydiving, but being able to do something besides work gives these activities value.

Thinking about Development

1. As noted in Chapter 8, serious thinking about one's future occupation begins in adolescence. What effects do the cognitive developmental changes and life-span construct experiences during young adulthood have in refining these initial choices during adulthood?

2. What biological, psychological, social, and life-cycle factors influence occupational selection?

3. What cognitive developmental factors (discussed in Chapter 9) need to be taken into account in designing training programs for adult workers?

4. How are the multiple roles and role conflict that couples face related to marital satisfaction (discussed in Chapter 10)?

5. What biological, psychological, social, and life-cycle forces shape leisure activities?

Summary

Occupational Selection and Development

The Meaning of Work

■ Although most people work for money, other reasons are highly variable. Occupational priorities have changed over time; younger workers' expectations from their occupations are now lower, and their emphasis on personal growth potential is higher.

Holland's Theory of Occupational Choice Revisited

■ Holland's theory is based on the idea that people choose occupations to optimize the fit between their individual traits and their occupational interests. Six personality types, representing different combinations of these, have been identified. Support for these types has been found in several studies.

Occupational Development

■ Super's developmental view of occupations is based on self-concept and adaptation to an occupational role. Super describes five stages in adulthood: implementa-

tion, establishment, maintenance, deceleration, and retirement.

■ Reality shock is the realization that one's expectations about an occupation are different from the reality one experiences. Reality shock is common among young workers.

■ A mentor is a co-worker who teaches a new employee the unwritten rules and fosters occupational development. Mentor–protégé relationships develop over time, through stages, like other relationships.

Job Satisfaction

■ Older workers report higher job satisfaction than younger workers, but this may be partly due to self-selection; unhappy workers may quit. Other reasons include intrinsic satisfaction, good fit, lower importance of work, finding nonwork diversions, and life-cycle factors. Alienation and burnout are important considerations in understanding job satisfaction. Both involve significant stress for workers.

Gender, Ethnicity, and Discrimination Issues

Gender Differences in Occupational Selection

■ Boys and girls are socialized differently for work, and their occupational choices are affected as a result. Women choose nontraditional occupations for many reasons, including expectations and personal feelings. Women in such occupations are still viewed more negatively than men in the same occupations.

Women and Occupational Development

■ Women leave well-paid occupations for many reasons, including family obligations and workplace environment. Women who continue to work full-time have adequate child care and look for ways to further their occupational development.

Ethnicity and Occupational Development

■ Vocational identity and vocational goals vary in different ethnic groups. Whether an organization is sensitive to ethnicity issues is a strong predictor of satisfaction among ethnic minority employees.

Bias and Discrimination

■ Sex discrimination remains the chief barrier to women's occupational development. In many cases, this operates as a glass ceiling. Pay inequity is also a problem; women are paid a fraction of what men in similar jobs earn. Sexual harassment is a problem in the workplace. Current criteria for judging harassment are based on the "reasonable woman" standard. Denying employment to anyone over 40 because of age is age discrimination.

Occupational Transitions

Retraining Workers

■ To adapt to the effects of a global economy and an aging work force, many corporations are providing retraining opportunities for workers. Retraining is especially important in cases of outdated skills and career plateauing.

Occupational Insecurity

■ Important reasons why people change occupations include personality, obsolescence, and economic trends. Occupational insecurity is a growing problem. Fear that one may lose one's job is a better predictor of anxiety than the actual likelihood of job loss.

Coping with Unemployment

■ Job loss is a traumatic event that can affect every aspect of a person's life. Degree of financial distress and the extent of attachment to the job are the best predictors of distress.

Work and Family

The Child Care Dilemma

■ Whether a woman returns to work after having a child depends largely on how attached she is to her work. Simply providing child care on-site does not always result in higher job satisfaction. The more important factor is the degree to which supervisors are sympathetic.

Handling Multiple Roles

■ Although women have reduced the amount of time they spend on household tasks over the past two decades, they still do most of the work. European American men are less likely than either African American or Hispanic American men to help with traditionally female household tasks.

Role Conflict

■ Flexible work schedules and number of children are important factors in role conflict. Recent evidence shows that work stress has a much bigger impact on family life than family stress has on work performance. Some women pay a high personal price for having careers.

Time to Relax: Leisure Activities

Types of Leisure Activities

■ Preoccupations can become more focused as interests, which can lead to the selection of particular leisure activities. People develop a repertoire of preferred leisure activities.

Developmental Changes in Leisure

■ As people grow older, they tend to engage in leisure activities that are less strenuous and more family-oriented. Leisure preferences in adulthood reflect those earlier in life.

Consequences of Leisure Activities

■ Leisure activities enhance well-being and can benefit all aspects of people's lives.

Key Terms

age discrimination (390)	*dream* (378)	*"reasonable woman"*
alienation (382)	*glass ceiling* (388)	*standard* (389)
burnout (382)	*job satisfaction* (380)	*role conflict* (398)
career plateauing (393)	*occupational priorities* (375)	*sex discrimination* (388)
comparable worth (388)		*vocational maturity* (377)

If You'd Like to Learn More

BOLLES, R. N. (1991). *What color is your parachute?* Berkeley, CA: Ten Speed Press. This popular reference is excellent for people in search of careers. It is regularly updated.

CROSBY, F. (1991). *Juggling: The unexpected advantages of balancing career and home for women, their families and society.* New York: Free Press. Although it is moderately difficult, this makes for eye-opening reading on the topic of balancing work and family.

FEATHER, N. T. (1990). *The psychological impact of unemployment.* New York: Springer-Verlag. Feather presents a thorough, scholarly treatment of the topic, one of the best available. The reading level is moderately difficult.

GERSON, K. (1993). *No man's land: Men's changing commitments to family and work.* New York: Basic Books. This very readable book about modern men's roles is based on a series of life history interviews.

MCDANIELS, C., & GYSBERS, N. C. (1992). *Counseling for career development.* San Francisco: Jossey-Bass. This is a good introduction to topics relating to career counseling and occupational development.

CHAPTER 72

🔖 By all accounts, Dean was extremely successful. He had become controller of a moderate-sized manufacturing firm by the time he was 43. Sure, he seemed driven to succeed, and he tended to get very angry and frustrated over what others might consider minor impediments, such as when other drivers on the road did not go fast enough. But overall, he appeared to have everything going for him. So imagine Dean's surprise when, at age 46, he had a serious heart attack. It scared him, and he wondered what the chances were of having another one.

🔖 Kesha, a 54-year-old social worker, was widely regarded as the resident expert when it came to working the system of human services. Her co-workers looked up to her for her ability to get several agencies to cooperate, which they did not do normally, and to keep clients coming in for routine matters and follow-up visits. Kesha claimed that there was nothing magical about it—it was just her experience that made the difference.

🔖 Jim showed all the signs. He divorced his wife of nearly 20 years to have a relationship with a woman 15 years younger, sold his ordinary-looking mid-sized sedan for a little red sports car, and began working out regularly at the health club after years of being a couch potato. Jim claimed he hadn't felt this good in years; he was happy to be making this change in middle age. All of Jim's friends agreed: This was a clear case of midlife crisis. Or was it?

🔖 Esther faced a major milestone: Her youngest child, Megan, was about ready to head off to college. But instead of feeling depressed, as she thought she should, Esther felt almost elated at the prospect. She and Bill would finally be free of the day-to-day parenting duties of the past 30 years. Esther was looking forward to getting to know her husband again. She wondered if there was something wrong with her for being excited that her daughter was moving away.

Middle Adulthood

 There's an old saying that life begins at 40. That's good news for middle-aged adults. As we will see, they face many stressful events, but they also become liberated from many of the pressures of young adulthood. In many respects, middle age is the prime of life: A person's health tends to be relatively good and earnings to be at their peak.

Of course, middle age is when people typically get wrinkles, gray hair, and a bulging waistline. But middle-aged adults also achieve new heights in cognitive development, change their behavior if they choose, develop adult relationships with their children, and ease into grandparenthood. Along the way, they must deal with stress, changes in the way they learn, and the challenges of dealing with their aging parents. The people in the opening vignettes reflect some of the major issues middle-aged adults face. Dean appears to be paying a price for his determination to succeed. Kesha shows that expertise comes with experience. Jim makes us wonder if middle age is a time of disruption. Esther reminds us that middle age is a time of family milestones, too.

Some of these issues are based more on stereotypes than on hard evidence. Which is which? You will know by the end of the chapter.

Physical Changes and Health
   Changes in Appearance
   ■ *Dealing with Physical Aging*
   Reproductive Changes
   ■ *Having Babies in Late Middle Age*
   Stress and Health
   Exercise

Physical Changes and Health

LEARNING OBJECTIVES

❧ *How does appearance change in middle age?*

❧ *What reproductive changes occur in men and women in middle age?*

❧ *What is stress? How does it affect physical and psychological health?*

❧ *What benefits are there to exercise?*

The reality of middle age generally strikes early one morning in the bathroom mirror. Standing there, staring through half-awake eyes, you see *it*. One solitary gray hair, or one tiny wrinkle at the corner of your eye, and you worry that your youth is gone, your life is over, and you will soon be acting the way your parents did when they totally embarrassed you in your younger days. Like the worried woodchuck in the cartoon, middle-aged people become concerned that they are over the hill, sometimes going to great lengths to prove that they are still vibrant.

BLOOM COUNTY, © 1983, Washington Post Writers Group. Reprinted with permission.

Crossing the boundary to middle age in the United States is typically associated with turning 40 (or the big four-oh, as many people term it). This event is often marked with a special party (with the accompanying "over the hill" motif), society's attempt at creating a rite of passage between youth and maturity.

As people move into middle age, they begin experiencing some of the physical changes associated with aging. In this chapter, we will focus on the ones most obvious in middle-aged adults: appearance, reproductive capacity, and stress and coping. In Chapter 13, we will consider changes that may begin in middle age but are usually not apparent until later in life, such as slower reaction time and sensory changes.

Changes in Appearance

On that fateful day when the hard truth stares at you in the bathroom mirror (as for the person in the photograph), it probably doesn't matter to you that getting wrinkles and gray hair are universal and inevitable. Wrinkles are caused

by changes in the structure of the skin and its connective and supporting tissues, as well as the cumulative effects of damage from exposure to sunlight and smoking cigarettes (Kligman, Grove, & Balin, 1985). It may not make you feel better to know that gray hair is perfectly natural and caused by a cessation of pigment production in hair follicles (Kenney, 1982). What matters is that these changes are affecting *you*.

To make matters worse, you may have also noticed that your clothes aren't fitting properly, even though you watch what you eat. You remember a time not very long ago when you could eat whatever you wanted; now it seems that as soon as you look at food you put on weight. Your perceptions are correct; most people gain weight between their early 30s and mid-50s, producing the infamous "middle-aged bulge" as metabolism slows down (Shephard, 1978).

People's reactions to these changes in appearance vary. Some people are extremely upset and rush out to purchase hair coloring and wrinkle cream. Others just take it as another stage in life. To get a sense of the range of responses, try the exercise in the See for Yourself feature.

Dealing with Physical Aging

How do people deal with the signs of physical aging? Find out for yourself by doing the following exercises.

1. Look through popular fashion magazines such as *Vogue, Cosmopolitan, GQ,* and *Elle,* and watch television programs. Pay attention to advertisements and articles dealing with wrinkles, hair, and weight. How many can you find that give the message that these natural signs of aging are acceptable? Do you detect a difference between messages aimed at men and women?

SEE FOR YOURSELF

2. Talk to men and women you know who are over 40. Ask them how they feel about the physical changes that have happened to them. Do you detect any gender differences?

3. Talk to someone from a culture other than your own. Find out how people in another culture view the physical changes associated with aging. Are the changes that accompany aging looked upon in the same way around the world?

These exercises should provide you with some insights into how people and corporations (through their advertisements) view the physical changes that occur in middle age. Compare your findings with other students' results and discuss any gender differences you uncovered. Do people ignore these changes? See for yourself.   ❧

Another physical change is loss of bone mass. Especially in women, loss of bone mass is a potentially serious problem. The changes shown in the diagram begin in the 30s and accelerate in the 50s; the result can be a dramatic reduc-

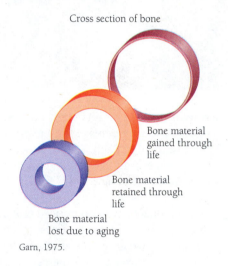

Cross section of bone

Bone material gained through life

Bone material retained through life

Bone material lost due to aging

Garn, 1975.

tion in the amount of bone mass. These changes make bones weaker and more brittle, thereby making them easier to break. Also, bones take longer to heal in middle-aged and older adults.

If these bone changes are severe, the disease *osteoporosis* results; bones become porous like honeycombs and extremely easy to break. In severe cases, osteoporosis can cause spinal vertebrae to collapse, causing the person to stoop and to become shorter (Meier, 1988). Although the severe effects of osteoporosis typically are not observed until later life, this disease does occur in women in their 50s. Osteoporosis is more common in women than men, largely because women have less bone mass in general, because some girls and women do not consume enough calcium to build strong bones from childhood to young adulthood, and because the physiological changes following menopause (such as a decrease in estrogen) accelerate bone loss (Heaney et al., 1982). To reduce the risk of osteoporosis, researchers recommend that women eat foods high in calcium (such as milk and broccoli), reduce alcohol intake, and take calcium supplements if necessary. Exercise also helps reduce the risk of osteoporosis if undertaken while the ovaries are still producing estrogen.

Reproductive Changes

Besides changes in the way we look, middle age brings transitions in internal biological processes as well. These changes differ dramatically for women and men. Some people, like the teenagers in the cartoon, view the changes in women as the flip side of puberty, and to some extent the analogy is appropriate.

THE CLIMACTERIC AND MENOPAUSE

For women, middle age brings a major biological change: the loss of the ability to bear children through natural means (Rykken, 1987). **This process, termed the *climacteric*, usually begins in the 40s and is usually complete by age 50 or 55.** The length of time it takes for all of the reproductive changes to occur differs considerably from woman to woman; for some it takes only a year or two, but others may experience more gradual changes for a decade.

The most important change during the climacteric is a dramatic drop in the production of estrogen, the primary female hormone (Mayo Clinic, 1992). This is responsible for the physical and psychological symptoms such as hot flashes, chills, headaches, and depression that accompany the climacteric. **Additionally, menstruation becomes irregular and eventually stops; this specific change is termed *menopause*.** Although some women stop menstruating around age 40, and others may still be having regular periods in their mid-50s, most women have their last period around age 50 or 51. However, as ovulation may continue for a year or two after the last period, women should continue to use contraceptives for this length of time if they do not want to become pregnant. Finally, women also experience gradual changes in the vagina during the climacteric, including thinning of the vaginal wall and diminished lubrication, which may make intercourse painful. The use of a non-petroleum–based lubricating jelly usually solves this problem.

Some physicians believe that the symptoms accompanying the climacteric may be lessened by *hormone replacement therapy*, in which women take low doses of estrogen and progesterone. In addition to relieving hot flashes, hormone replacement therapy affords some protection against osteoporosis and cardiovascular disease. Strongly recommended for women who experienced the climacteric before age 40, hormone replacement therapy is often continued for many years into later life. Research evidence is mixed as to whether hormone replacement therapy may be linked to increases in breast cancer and other forms of cancer. Given the lack of definitive evidence either way, most physicians believe that the benefits outweigh possible risks (Mayo Clinic, 1992).

Even without hormone replacement therapy, most women report that the symptoms accompanying the climacteric are not very severe (Matthews et al., 1990), although ethnic differences in symptoms have been reported. In one study, for example, European American women reported a decrease in the physical symptoms (such as headaches) after the climacteric, but African American women reported more symptoms afterward (Jackson, Taylor, & Pyngolil, 1991). In all the cultures studied, few women express regret at the loss of fertility; rather, they feel more powerful and free (Sheehy, 1992).

Recent advances in reproductive technology have enabled women who have undergone the climacteric to have children. As is discussed in the Current Controversies segment, such births force us to rethink the meaning of the climacteric, as well as raising ethical questions.

CURRENT CONTROVERSIES

Having Babies in Late Middle Age

Reproductive technology such as *in vitro* fertilization (see Chapter 2) using donated eggs has made it possible for postmenopausal women to have children. Scientists have thus fundamentally changed the rules of reproduction. Even though a woman has gone through the climacteric, she can have children. Technology can make her pregnant, if she so chooses and has access to the proper medical centers.

What does this do to our understanding of human reproduction? On the one hand, it changes the whole notion of the so-called biological clock, a woman's urge to have children before menopause. Some women who have given birth in this way have done so because their daughters were not able to have children; they consider this act another way to show their parental love. Others view it as a way to equalize reproductive potential in middle age between men and women, as men remain fertile throughout adulthood.

Clearly, these are complicated issues. But as reproductive technology continues to advance faster than our ability to think through the issues, we will be confronted with increasingly complex ethical questions. Should children be born to older parents? Might not there be some advantage, considering the life experience such parents would have, compared to young parents? Are such births merely selfish acts, or could they provide an alternative way for younger adults to have a family? What dangers are there to older pregnant women? How do you feel about it?   🐚

During middle age, women experience the end of their ability to bear children without medical intervention. However, as this middle-aged man can attest, men remain capable of fathering children.

REPRODUCTIVE CHANGES IN MEN

Reproductive changes in men are far less dramatic. Sperm production declines gradually by approximately 30% between the ages of 25 and 60 (Solnick & Corby, 1983). But even a man of 80 is still half as fertile as he was at age 25 and remains potentially capable of fathering a child. Sexual functioning does change as men age. Most men need more time to achieve an erection and orgasm, feel less need to ejaculate, and experience a longer resolution phase during which erection is impossible (Rykken, 1987). The important point is that unlike women, men do not normally experience a loss of fertility in adulthood.

Many men experience problems due to changes in the prostate gland, which is located beneath the bladder and surrounds the urethra. The gland produces fluids in semen that help sperm survive in the acidic environment of the vagina (Mayo Clinic, 1992). With increasing age, a man's prostate gland enlarges and stiffens, which may make it more difficult to urinate. Unless there is an accompanying infection, an enlarged prostate is not serious. However, prostate cancer becomes a serious threat during middle age, with incidence peaking between the ages of 60 and 80 (Mayo Clinic, 1992). Although prostate cancer is not caused by enlargement (indeed, the cause is unknown), enlargement may be misdiagnosed as cancer unless more careful diagnostic tests are performed.

Stress and Health

There's no doubt about it—life is full of stress. Look at the woman in the photo, and think for a moment about all the things that bother you, such as exams, jobs, relationships, and finances. For most people, this list gets long quickly. But, you may wonder, isn't this true for people of all ages? Is stress more important in middle age?

Although stress affects people of all ages, it is during middle age that the effects of both short- and long-term stress become most apparent. In part, this is because it takes time for stress disorders to manifest themselves, and in part it is due to the gradual loss of physical capacity, as the normal changes accompanying aging begin to take their toll. As we will see, psychological factors play a major role as well.

You may think that stress affects health mainly in people who hold certain types of jobs, such as air traffic controllers, high-level business executives, and textbook authors. In fact, business executives actually have *fewer* stress-related health problems than waitresses, construction workers, secretaries, laboratory technicians, machine operators, farm workers, and painters (Smith et al., 1978). What do all of these truly high-stress jobs have in common? These workers have little direct control over their jobs.

Although we understand some important workplace factors related to stress, our knowledge is largely based on research examining middle-aged men. Unfortunately, the relation of stress to age, gender, and ethnic status remains to be researched. For example, in all age groups, women are more likely than men to report that stress has a significant effect on their health (U.S. Department of Health and Human Services, 1988). Middle-aged people report the highest levels of stress, whereas people over age 65 reported the lowest. Why? As we will see in the next section, part of the reason may be due to the number of pressures middle-aged people feel: Children are in college, the job has high demands, the mortgage payment and other bills always need paying, the marriage needs some attention, the in-laws would like to visit, and on it goes.

WHAT IS STRESS?

Think about the last time you felt stressed. What was it about the situation that made you feel stressed? How did you feel? **The answers to questions like these provide a way to understand the dominant framework used to study stress, the *stress and coping paradigm*.** Because the stress and coping paradigm emphasizes the interaction between a person and the environment, it fits well with the biopsychosocial framework.

In the stress and coping paradigm, whether you feel stressed depends on how you interpret a situation or event (Lazarus & Folkman, 1984). What the situation or event is, or what you do to deal with it, does not matter. **Stress results when you** *appraise* **a situation or event as taxing or exceeding your personal, social, or other resources and endangering your well-being. It is the day-to-day** *hassles,* **or the things that upset and annoy us, that prove to be stressful for the most part.**

Coping **is any attempt to deal with stress.** People cope in several different ways. Sometimes people cope by trying to solve the problem at hand; for example, you may cope with a messy roommate by moving out. At other times, people focus on how they feel about the situation and deal with things on an emotional level; feeling sad after breaking up with your partner would be one way of coping with the stress of being alone. Sometimes people cope by simply redefining the event as not stressful—saying that it was no big deal that you failed to get the job you wanted would be an example of this approach.

An important point to keep in mind is that people appraise different types of situations or events as stressful at different times during adulthood. For example, the pressures from work and raising a family are typically greater for younger and middle-aged adults than for older adults. However, stressers due to chronic disease are often more important to older adults than to their younger counterparts. From a biopsychosocial perspective, such life-cycle factors must be taken into account when considering what kinds of stress adults of different ages are experiencing.

HOW DOES STRESS AFFECT PHYSICAL HEALTH?

A great deal of research has been conducted over the years examining links between stress and physical health. Several links have been discovered and some are relatively widely known. You may already know that stress has been linked to tension headaches (Holyroad, Appel, & Andrasik, 1983) and ulcers (Smith et al., 1978). Probably the most well-known connection between stress and health involves the link with cardiovascular disease. Due mostly to the pioneering work of Friedman and Rosenman (1974), we know that two behavior patterns differ dramatically in terms of risk of cardiovascular disease. Type A behavior pattern is associated with high rates of cardiovascular disease, whereas Type B behavior pattern is not associated with cardiovascular disease.

People who demonstrate *Type A behavior pattern* **(like Dean in the first chapter-opening vignette) tend to be intensely competitive, angry, hostile, restless, aggressive, and impatient. In contrast, people who show** *Type B behavior pattern* **tend to be just the opposite.** Type A individuals are at least twice as likely as Type B people to develop cardiovascular disease, even when other risk factors such as smoking and hypertension are taken into account. Indeed, cardiovascular disease is rare in people under age 70 except among Type A people (Eisdorfer & Wilkie, 1977).

The connection between Type A behavior pattern and developing cardiovascular disease is well established. But how do these behavior types relate to *recovery* from a heart attack? Although it is relatively rare, Type B people sometimes do have heart attacks. Who recovers better, Type A people or Type B people?

The answer, based on a 22-year longitudinal follow-up from the original Friedman and Rosenman study, may surprise you. Ragland and Brand (1988) discovered that Type A people recover from a heart attack better than Type B people. Why? Some of the characteristics of being Type A may help motivate people like the man shown in the photograph to stick to diet and exercise regimens after heart attacks and have a more positive attitude toward recovery (Ivancevich & Matteson, 1988). Indeed, although the anger and hostility components of Type A behavior create the increased risk for cardiovascular disease, the other components appear to aid the recovery process (Ivancevich & Matteson, 1988). Thus, if Dean learns how to control his hostility, his other Type A characteristics could benefit his recovery. In contrast, the laid-back approach to life of Type B people may actually work against them during recovery.

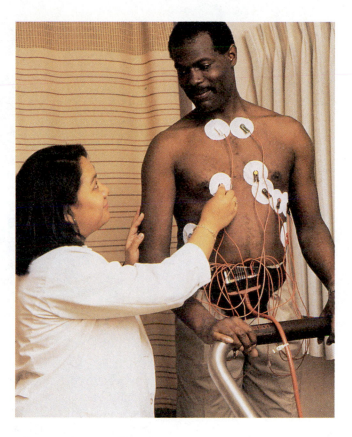

HOW DOES STRESS AFFECT PSYCHOLOGICAL HEALTH?

Many people still believe that stress causes psychological disorders. Actually, researchers have known for many years that even an accumulation of stress does not directly cause depression, schizophrenia, or anxiety disorders (Dohrenwend, 1979). Although stress is not directly related to psychopathology, it is associated with other psychological processes. For example, chronic stress related to financial pressures and fear of crime promotes social isolation and distrust of others in some adults (Krause, 1991). Although stress does not directly cause psychopathology, it does influence how people behave.

Exercise

Ever since the time of Hippocrates, physicians and researchers have known that exercise significantly slows the aging process. Indeed, evidence suggests that a program of regular exercise can slow the physiological aging process by as much as a decade (Thomas & Rutledge, 1986).

Adults benefit from *aerobic exercise*, which places moderate stress on the heart by maintaining a pulse rate between 60% and 90% of the person's maximum heart rate. You can calculate your maximum heart rate by subtracting your age from 220. Thus, if you are 40 years old, your target range would be 108 to 162 beats per minute. The minimum time necessary for aerobic exercise to be of benefit depends on its intensity; at low heart rates, sessions may need to last an hour, whereas at high heart rates, 15 minutes may suffice. Examples of aerobic exercise include jogging, step aerobics, swimming, and cross-country skiing.

What happens when a person exercises aerobically (besides becoming tired and sweaty)? Physiologically, adults of all ages show improved cardiovascular functioning and maximum oxygen consumption, lower blood pressure, and better strength, endurance, flexibility, and coordination (Posner et al., 1990; Smith & Serfass, 1981). Psychologically, people who exercise aerobically report lower levels of stress, better moods, and better cognitive functioning. However, there is conflicting scientific evidence regarding these benefits (Blumenthal et al., 1988).

The best way to gain the benefits of aerobic exercise is to maintain physical fitness through the life span, beginning at least in middle age like the people in the photograph. In planning an exercise program, three points should be remembered. First, check with a physician before beginning an aerobic exercise program. Second, bear in mind that moderation is important. A study of nearly 17,000 middle-aged and older men found that those who exercised moderately (walked 9 miles per week or cycled for 6 to 8 hours per week) had a 21% to 50% lower risk of dying than men who did not exercise, whereas men who exercised strenuously (walked 20 miles per week or cycled more than 15 hours per week) had a significantly higher risk of dying than men who exercised moderately. Third, the reasons why people exercise change during adulthood. Younger adults tend to exercise to improve their physical appearance, whereas middle-aged and older adults are more concerned with physical and psychological health (Trujillo, Walsh, & Brougham, 1991).

TEST YOURSELF

1. Two universal changes in appearance in middle age are gray hair and
   _____.
2. Severe bone loss may result in the disease _____.
3. The cessation of menstruation is termed _____.
4. Reduction of fertility in men occurs _____.
5. The stress and _____ paradigm defines stress on the basis of the person's appraisal of a situation as taxing his or her well-being.
6. Research indicates that Type _____ individuals have a better chance of recovering from a heart attack than Type _____ individuals.
7. The media are full of advertisements for anti-aging creams, diets, and exercise plans. Based on what you have read in this section, how would you evaluate these ads?

Answers: (1) *wrinkles,* (2) *osteoporosis,* (3) *menopause,* (4) *gradually,* (5) *coping,* (6) *A, B*

Cognitive Development

LEARNING OBJECTIVES

❧ *How does practical intelligence develop in adulthood? What are the developmental trends of exercised and unexercised abilities?*

❧ *How does a person become an expert?*

❧ *What is meant by lifelong learning? What differences are there between adults and young people in how they learn?*

Compared to the rapid cognitive growth of childhood, or the controversies about cognition in young adulthood, cognitive development in middle age is relatively quiet. For the most part, the trends seen in young adulthood (discussed in Chapter 9) are continued and solidified. Cognitive development in middle age involves developing expertise and flexibility in solving practical problems, such as dealing with complex forms like the tax form on the right. We will also see how important it is to continue learning throughout adulthood.

Practical Intelligence

Take a moment to think about the following problems (Denney, 1989, 1990; Denney, Pearce, & Palmer, 1982).

- Let's say that a middle-aged woman is frying chicken in her home when, all of a sudden, a grease fire breaks out on top of the stove. Flames begin to shoot up. What should she do?

- Let's say that a man finds that the heater in his apartment is not working. He asks his landlord to send someone out to fix it, and the landlord agrees. But, after a week of cold weather and several calls to the landlord, the heater is still not fixed. What should the man do?

Form **1040** — U.S. Individual Income Tax Return 1994

Middle-aged adults are faced with many practical problems in everyday life. You may not think of cooking as complex, but making certain all the various dishes are done at the same time requires planning.

These practical problems are certainly different from the examples of measures of fluid and crystallized intelligence in Chapter 9. The most obvious difference is that these problems are more realistic; they reflect real-world problems that people might actually face. One criticism of traditional measures of intelligence is that they do not assess the kinds of skills adults actually use in everyday life (Labouvie-Vief, 1985). Most people spend more time at tasks such as managing their personal finances, dealing with uncooperative people, and juggling busy schedules than they do solving esoteric mazes.

In reaction to the shortcomings of traditional approaches to testing adults' intelligence, different ways of viewing intelligence have emerged (Cavanaugh, 1991; Ceci, 1990; Dixon, 1992). **These alternative views focus on the skills and knowledge necessary for people to function in everyday life, termed** *practical intelligence.* The examples at the beginning of this section illustrate how practical intelligence is measured. Such real-life problems differ in three main ways from traditional tests (Wagner & Sternberg, 1986): people are more motivated to solve them; personal experience is more relevant; and they have more than one correct answer.

Denney (1982) postulated that performance on tests of practical intelligence depends on two different components, whose developmental trends are shown in the graph. **The bottom dashed line represents** *unexercised ability,*

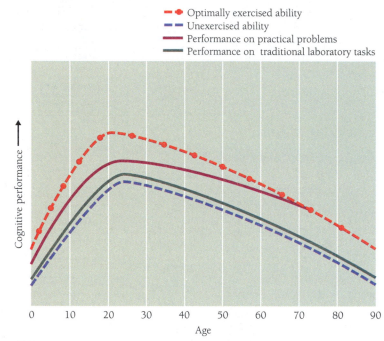

Denney, 1982.

the level of performance a person would exhibit without practice or training. Unexercised abilities are those that are not used very often, are not well developed, or are called upon to handle new situations. For example, when you are presented with a problem you have never seen before, the cognitive skills you bring to bear would be unexercised abilities. Unexercised abilities reflect the lower limit to your ability to perform cognitive problems.

The upper dashed line represents *optimally exercised ability,* **the level of performance a normal, healthy adult would demonstrate under the best conditions of training or practice.** Optimally exercised abilities are those that you use the most, or the ones that you have practiced the most. Problems that tap these abilities are typically performed accurately and more quickly than those that test unexercised abilities, as you can see by comparing the solid line with the dotted line in the figure. Optimally exercised abilities, then, reflect areas in which you have greater cognitive expertise.

Whether a specific ability is unexercised or optimally exercised varies from individual to individual; for example, one person may have little training in mathematical reasoning, whereas a faculty member in the mathematics department would be highly skilled. Thus, how an ability is classified depends on the person's experience; it is not a property of the skill in question.

The overall developmental course of both abilities is the same: They increase until young adulthood, plateau through middle age, and decline thereafter. As shown in the graph, the difference between performance on practical problems and optimally exercised ability is hypothesized to close rapidly during middle age. But do the data support Denney's speculations?

When people's answers to practical problems are evaluated in terms of how likely the answers are to be effective, practical intelligence does not appear to decline appreciably until late life (Denney, 1989, 1990). Successful solutions depend on prior experience, so it is not surprising that maturity brings effective approaches to problems. This pattern is similar to the one we encountered for crystallized intelligence (see page 314).

However, the number of solutions generated tends to peak in middle age and decline somewhat thereafter (Denney & Pearce, 1989). The ability to generate many approaches in novel situations appears to diminish. This pattern is reminiscent of the one for fluid intelligence (see page 314). Thus, adults of all ages can figure out one effective way to deal with an uncooperative landlord, but the *number* of ways a person figures out tends to decrease with age.

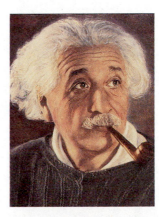

Becoming an Expert

One day, John Cavanaugh was driving along when his car suddenly began coughing and sputtering. As deftly as possible, he pulled over to the side of the road, turned off the engine, opened the hood, and proceeded to look inside. It was hopeless; to him, it looked like a jumble of unknown parts. When the car had been towed to a garage, a middle-aged mechanic decided to try his hand at fixing it. Within a few minutes, the car was running like new. How?

We saw in Chapter 9 that aspects of intelligence grounded in experience (crystallized intelligence) tend to improve throughout most of adulthood. Some developmentalists have gone so far as to claim that each of us becomes an expert at something that is important to us, such as our work, interpersonal relationships, cooking, sports, or auto repair (Dixon, Kramer, & Baltes, 1985). In this sense, an expert (like the mechanic or Kesha, the social worker in the second opening vignette) is someone who is much better at a task than people who have not put much effort into it (such as Cavanaugh, in terms of auto repair). We tend to become selective experts in some areas, while remaining rank amateurs or novices at others.

What makes experts better than novices? Most important, experts have built up a wealth of knowledge about alternative ways of solving problems or making decisions. These enable them to bypass steps needed by novices (Ericsson & Smith, 1991). Experts don't always follow the rules as novices do, are more flexible, creative, and curious, and have superior strategies for accomplishing a task (Charness & Bosman, 1990). Even though they may be slower in terms of raw speed, experts' ability to skip steps puts them at a decided advantage. In a way, this represents "the triumph of knowledge over reasoning" (Charness & Bosman, 1990).

Research evidence suggests that expert performance tends to peak in mid-

What makes people such as Albert Einstein and Stephen Hawking clearly experts is that they have a great deal of knowledge that they could access very quickly. Each of us develops expertise in some area during adulthood.

dle age and drop off slightly after that (Charness & Bosman, 1990). However, the declines in expert performance are not nearly as great as they are for the abilities of information processing, memory, and fluid intelligence that underlie expertise. Thus, it appears that knowledge based on experience is an important component of expertise.

But why are expertise and information processing, memory, and fluid intelligence not strongly related? After all, we saw in Chapter 9 that the latter abilities underlie good cognitive performance. Rybash, Hoyer, and Roodin (1986) proposed a process called *encapsulation* as the answer. **Their notion is that the *processes of thinking* (information processing, memory, fluid intelligence) become connected or *encapsulated* to the *products of thinking* (expertise).** This process of encapsulation allows expertise to compensate for declines in underlying abilities, perhaps by making thinking more efficient.

Let's consider how encapsulation might work with the example of auto mechanics. As a rule, people learning auto mechanics are taught to think as if they were playing a game of Twenty Questions, in which the optimal strategy is to ask a question such that the answer eliminates half of the remaining possibilities. In the beginning, a repairperson learns the thinking strategy and the content knowledge about automobiles separately. But as the person's experience with repairing automobiles increases, the thinking strategy and content knowledge merge; instead of having to go through a Twenty Questions approach, they just "know" how to proceed to diagnose the trouble.

One of the outcomes of encapsulation appears to be a decrease in the ability to explain how one arrives at a particular answer. It appears that the increased efficiency that comes through merging the process with the product of thinking comes at the cost of being able to explain to others what one is doing. This could be why some instructors have a difficult time explaining the various steps involved in solving a problem to novice students.

We will return to the topic of expertise in Chapter 13 when we discuss wisdom, which some believe to be the outcome of becoming an expert in living.

Lifelong Learning

What do all of the people in the photographs below and at the top of page 421 have in common? They work in occupations in which information and technology change rapidly. To keep up with these changes, many organizations and professions now emphasize the importance of learning how to learn, rather than learning specific content that may become outdated in a couple of years.

 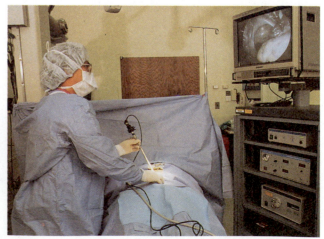

For most people, a college education should probably not be the last educational experience they have in their careers. Workers in many professions, such as medicine, nursing, social work, psychology, and teaching, are now required to obtain continuing education credits in order to stay current in their fields.

The need for lifelong learning is obvious on most college campuses. You have probably seen middle-aged adults in your classes (or you may be one yourself). The story of one middle-aged student is presented in the Real People feature. Many college instructors are including experiential elements in courses, as a reaction to the need for real-world connections.

College at Midlife

Patrice had worked for a savings and loan for 15 years, rising to the level of Vice President for Savings and Investment. Her achievement was even more remarkable because she had only a high school education. But when she wanted to change jobs, she ran into a cruel reality: Without a college degree, she had little chance to get another executive-level position, even though she had years of experience. So, at age 37, Patrice decided to quit her job and get her degree.

Overcoming her fear that she couldn't compete was the hard part at first. Her reasons for being in school were much different from those of her younger classmates; Patrice was there for her self-esteem more than to please someone else. She found that her life experience was an advantage; many students eventually looked up to her for her insights. Her study skills were different. She found it hard to learn information by rote memorization; instead, she emphasized how information fit together. Although grades were somewhat important, learning was her primary goal. She enjoyed seeing how she could apply knowledge learned in one class to another one. Even the professors expressed delight at having her in class.

After five and one-half years, Patrice graduated with a degree in accounting. She had distinguished herself by being on the dean's list every semester she was in college, which really made her feel good about herself.   ✿

REAL PEOPLE

Lifelong learning takes place in settings other than college campuses, too. Many organizations offer workshops for their employees on a wide range of topics, from specific job-related topics to leisure-time activities. Additionally, many channels on cable television offer primarily educational programming, and computer networks and bulletin boards are available for educational exchanges. Only a few generations ago, a high school education was the ticket to a lifetime of secure employment, but now lifelong learning is rapidly becoming the norm.

Lifelong learning is gaining acceptance as the best way to approach the need for continuing education and for retraining displaced workers. But should lifelong learning be approached as merely an extension of earlier educational experiences? Knowles (1984) argues that teaching aimed at children and youth differs from teaching aimed at adults. Adult learners differ from their younger counterparts in several ways:

- Adults have a higher need to know why they should learn something before undertaking it.
- Adults enter a learning situation with more and different experience on which to build.
- Adults are most willing to learn those things they believe are necessary to deal with real-world problems rather than abstract, hypothetical situations.
- Most adults are more motivated to learn by internal factors (such as self-esteem or personal satisfaction) than by external factors (such as a job promotion or pay raise).

Lifelong learning is becoming increasingly important, but educators need to keep in mind that learning styles change as people age.

TEST YOURSELF

1. The skills and knowledge necessary for people to function in everyday life make up _____.
2. The difference between performance on practical problems and optimally exercised ability is hypothesized to _____ during middle age.
3. Even though they may be slower in terms of raw speed, experts are at a distinct advantage over novices because they _____.
4. The way in which the process of thinking becomes connected to the products of thinking is termed _____.
5. Due to rapidly changing technology and information, many educators now support the concept of _____.
6. Based on the cognitive developmental changes described in this section, what types of jobs would be done best by middle-aged adults?

Personality

LEARNING OBJECTIVES

🐦 **What are the major dimensions of personality traits in adulthood? How stable are they through adulthood? What happens to gender-role identity?**

🐦 **What is generativity? Do people pass through predictable transitions in adulthood?**

🐦 **What is the role of personal perceptions in personality development?**

The topic of personality development in middle age gets us into one of the hottest debates in theory and research in adult development and aging. Unlike

most of the other topics we have covered in this chapter, research on personality in middle-aged adults, like those in the photograph above, is grounded in several competing theories, such as the psychoanalytic approach we encountered in Chapter 1. Most of this work relies on longitudinal research, which we also discussed in Chapter 1. First, we will examine the evidence that personality traits remain fairly stable in adulthood. This position makes the claim that what you are like in young adulthood predicts pretty well what you will be like the rest of your life. But there is also considerable evidence that certain key issues confronting adults change throughout adulthood, requiring adults to change with them. This alternative position claims that change is the rule during adulthood. Some researchers claim that these personality changes bring with them a midlife crisis.

At no other point in the life span is this debate about stability versus change in personality as heated as it is concerning middle age. In this section, we will consider the evidence for both stability and change, as well as an alternative view that may account for both.

Stability Is the Rule: Costa and McCrae's Model of Personality

One of the most important advances in research on adult development and aging in the past few decades was the emergence of a personality theory aimed specifically at describing adults. Due mostly to the efforts of Costa and McCrae, we are able to describe adults' personality traits by using five dimensions (Costa & McCrae, 1988): neuroticism, extraversion, openness to experience, agreeableness, and conscientiousness. These dimensions are strongly grounded in cross-sectional, longitudinal, and sequential research, with some studies examining the same people over several decades of their lives, as we will see. First, though, let's take a closer look at each dimension.

- *Neuroticism.* **People who are high on the *neuroticism* dimension tend to be anxious, hostile, self-conscious, depressed, impulsive, and vulnerable.** They may show violent or negative emotions that interfere with their ability to get along with others or to handle problems in everyday life.
- *Extraversion.* **Individuals who are high on the *extraversion* dimension thrive on social interaction, like to talk, take charge easily, readily express their opinions and feelings, like to keep busy, have boundless**

energy, and prefer stimulating and challenging environments. Such people tend to enjoy people-oriented jobs, such as social work and sales, and they often have humanitarian goals.

- *Openness to experience.* **Being high on the *openness to experience* dimension tends to mean a vivid imagination and dream life, appreciation of art, and a strong desire to try anything once.** These individuals tend to be naturally curious about things and to make decisions based on situational factors rather than absolute rules. People who are readily open to new experiences place a relatively low emphasis on personal economic gain. They tend to choose jobs such as ministry or counseling that offer diversity of experience rather than high pay.
- *Agreeableness.* **Scoring high on the *agreeableness* dimension is associated with being accepting, willingness to work with others, and caring.** Interestingly, persons who score low on this dimension (that is, demonstrate high levels of *antagonism*) show many of the characteristics of the Type A behavior pattern discussed earlier in this chapter.
- *Conscientiousness.* **People who show high levels of *conscientiousness* tend to be hard-working, ambitious, energetic, scrupulous, and persevering.** Such people have a strong desire to make something of themselves.

WHAT'S THE EVIDENCE FOR TRAIT STABILITY?

Costa and McCrae, as well as other researchers, have examined whether their dimensions of personality remain stable through adulthood. In one study (Costa, McCrae, & Arenberg, 1980), more than 100 men were tested three times, with each of the follow-up testings about 6 years apart. Even over a 12-year span, the dimensions examined remained very stable.

Was this finding a fluke? Apparently not. Other researchers find similar stability over 8-year spans (Siegler, George, & Okun, 1979) and even 30-year spans (Leon et al., 1979). Even spouses' ratings of their partner's personality traits showed no systematic changes over a 6-year period (Costa & McCrae, 1988). Thus, it looks like people's personality traits change little over very long periods of time.

Stability in personality traits through adulthood is a very important finding, especially considering the many life situations that do change (e.g., getting married, changing jobs, having children leave home). One way to view this evidence is that the traits described by Costa and McCrae provide the building blocks of personality. In this view, the raw material on which personality is built remains relatively constant. But, as we will see next and again in Chapter 14, what a person chooses to do with these building blocks, and the behaviors based on them, may not be as consistent.

DOES GENDER ROLE IDENTITY CONVERGE?

Costa and McCrae make a strong case for the stability of personality traits through adulthood. For the most part, though, this work focuses on traits that are equally likely to occur in both men and women. Would stability also apply to gender-related characteristics?

What we consider to be appropriate personality traits for men and women reflects shared cultural beliefs and stereotypes of what constitutes masculinity and femininity (Williams & Best, 1990). Across a wide age range in U.S. society, women are traditionally described as weaker, less active, more concerned with affiliation, and more nurturing and deferential. Men are regarded as stronger, more active, and higher in autonomy, achievement, and aggression (Huyck, 1990).

PAUL T. COSTA

ROBERT R. MCCRAE

"Do we imagine that the Five Factor Model . . . is the last word in personality assessment? Of course we do not. It is, we hope and believe, a serviceable model, a taxonomy adequate for the needs of a young science."

Gender role identity stereotypes vary with age (Gutmann, 1987). Older men are less likely to be viewed as aggressive, but rather as powerful men striving for peace. Older women are viewed either as matriarchs overseeing extended families or as evil people who use power malevolently. In some cultures, older adults are even viewed as genderless, as there is no need for well-defined gender roles once a person can no longer have children (Gailey, 1987).

But these findings deal with stereotyped beliefs that gender role identity changes during midlife. Empirical evidence that it actually does is another matter altogether. Overall, the data are mixed. Some studies find a tendency for middle-aged and older adults to endorse similar self-descriptions concerning gender role identity. For example, some research indicates that both men and women describe themselves as more nurturing, intimate, and tender with increasing age (Gutmann, 1987; Sinnott, 1986). Collectively, data from these studies indicate that men and women are most different in their gender role identities in late adolescence and young adulthood but become increasingly similar in midlife and old age (Huyck, 1990).

Increasing similarity in self-descriptions does not guarantee increased similarity in the way men and women behave. For example, older men often indicate a willingness to develop close relationships, but few actually do, because they lack the necessary skills (Turner, 1982). Thus, the convergence may be happening more internally than behaviorally (Troll & Bengtson, 1982). Does gender role identity converge? At this point, the statistical evidence appears to indicate that it does, but the behavioral evidence appears to indicate it does not.

Change Is the Rule: Changing Priorities in Midlife

Joyce, a 52-year-old preschool teacher, thought carefully about the question. "I definitely feel differently about what I want to accomplish. When I was younger, I wanted to advance and be a great teacher. I still want to be good, but I'm more concerned now with providing help to the new teachers around here. I've got lots of on-the-job experience that I can pass along."

Joyce is not alone. Despite the evidence that personality traits change little during adulthood, many middle-aged people like the man in the photograph report that they are increasingly concerned with helping younger people achieve

rather than with getting ahead themselves. **In his psychosocial theory, Erikson argued that this shift in priorities reflects *generativity,* or being productive by helping others in order to ensure the continuation of society by guiding the next generation.**

Achieving generativity can be very enriching. It is grounded in the successful resolution of the previous six phases of Erikson's theory. The basic idea, summarized in the table, is that generativity is the next stage of psychosocial development, which has proceeded in sequence since birth. There are many avenues for generativity, such as through mentoring (see Chapter 11), volunteering, foster grandparent programs, and many other activities.

Perspective	Examples of Theories	Main Ideas	Emphases in Biopsychosocial Framework	Positions on Developmental Issues
Psychodynamic	Erikson's psychosocial theory	Personality develops through sequence of stages	Biological, social, and life-cycle forces crucial; less emphasis on psychological	Nature–nurture interaction, discontinuity, universal sequence but individual differences in rate

Some adults do not achieve generativity. Instead, they become bored, self-indulgent, and unable to contribute to the continuation of society. **Erikson referred to this state as *stagnation,* in which people are not able to deal with the needs of their children or are unable to provide mentoring to younger adults.**

Some theorists question whether Erikson's description of generativity is adequate to describe adulthood. For example, Kotre (1984) contends that adults experience many opportunities to express generativity that differ in importance, and that most adults do not show generativity all the time. Rather, he believes that generativity is more like a set of impulses felt at different times in different settings, such as at work or in grandparenting. Only rarely is generativity continuous in adulthood.

LIFE TRANSITION THEORIES

Although Erikson's notion of generativity provided much insight into adulthood, many theorists believe that middle adulthood includes other important changes. Indeed, Carl Jung, one of the founders of psychoanalytic theory, believed that adults may experience a midlife crisis. **In general, a *midlife crisis* is considered to be a time of psychological upheaval, during which people reevaluate their lives.**

Some theorists, such as Levinson and colleagues (1978), Gould (1978), and Vaillant (1977) have developed more precise stage theories. They account for personality change in adulthood by studying fairly exclusive and nonrepresentative groups of adults (in some cases only men) over several decades. All of these theories postulate that adults go through a series of predictable stages of growth and transition (including some version of a midlife crisis) in a universal sequence. Much of the data was gathered through interviews and personal reflections of the study participants.

Despite the popularity of these theories, some of which were turned into best-selling books, the evidence for universal age-related stages is based on far fewer and much more selective samples (such as men who went to Harvard) than are the data from the personality trait research. As the You May Be Wondering feature indicates, the bulk of the evidence does not support the view of a universal stage such as a midlife crisis.

Evidence suggesting that adults go through predictable stages that are tied to specific periods of adulthood tends to be based on small, selective samples. Although many adults do undergo significant change, it does not appear to be associated with a specific age.

Does Everyone Have a Midlife Crisis?

Ask people to give an example of what they think a midlife crisis is, and chances are they will relate a story like that of Jim, the recently divorced guy with the red sports car in the chapter-opening vignette. Indeed, few people in the United States would have difficulty providing an example, as most people believe that a midlife crisis is inevitable. In part, this belief is fostered by descriptions of personality development in adulthood that have appeared in the popular press.

We have seen that theorists such as Erikson believe that adults face several important challenges and that by struggling with these issues people develop new aspects of themselves. But does this mean that everyone necessarily has a midlife crisis? Some researchers say it does, at least for men: In some studies, men report intense inner struggles that were much like depression (Levinson et al., 1978).

However, by far the bulk of the research evidence fails to support the idea that most adults experience difficulty in midlife. Research involving women and men, using a variety of methods such as interviews and personality tests, shows that unexpected events (such as divorce or job transfers) are much more likely to create stress than are normative midlife events (such as menopause or becoming a grandparent) (Baruch, 1984; Haan, Milsap, & Hartka, 1986; Roberts & Newton, 1987). Reanalysis of Costa and McCrae's data, specifically looking for evidence of a midlife crisis, revealed only a handful of men who fit the classic profile, and even then the crisis came anywhere between the ages of 30 and 60 (Costa & McCrae, 1978; Farrell & Rosenberg, 1981). There may be universal stresses during midlife, but there is no set way of dealing with them (Farrell & Rosenberg, 1981).

Is there a midlife crisis? The evidence indicates that for most people, midlife is no more or no less traumatic than any other period. Even investigators who believed strongly in the existence of a midlife crisis when they began their research admitted that they could find no support for it despite extensive testing and interviewing (Farrell & Rosenberg, 1981). Thus, Jim's behavior may have an explanation, but it's not because he's going through a universal midlife crisis. ❧

Seeking the Middle Ground:
A Cognitive Theory of Personality

Thus far, we have considered two approaches to personality development that leave you with little control—either you remain largely unchanged or you inevitably face certain issues. But elsewhere we have seen the importance of a person's perception of things. Earlier in this chapter, for example, we discussed the model of stress and coping, and Chapter 9 included Whitbourne's life story approach to identity. Could perception be important in personality as well?

Hans Thomae's (1980) cognitive theory of personality points out that perceptions, especially about one's own aging, are important for understanding whether change occurs through adulthood. Thomae lists three key postulates:

- *Perception of change, rather than objective change, is related to behavior change.* If we believe that we have changed over time or are likely to change in the future, then we will act differently, regardless of what other people think about us.
- *People perceive and evaluate change in their life situation in terms of their dominant concerns and expectations at the time.* People view the same problem differently, depending on what stage of the life cycle they are in, as explained in the biopsychosocial model (see Chapter 1). For example, how you deal with the need to work overtime depends on whether you are a young parent or a middle-aged adult whose children have moved out.
- *Adjustment to aging is determined by the balance between people's cognitive and motivational structures.* You adjust to your own aging better when you perceive your life situation positively, believe that growth has occurred, and perceive the changes you have experienced as being in harmony with where you want to be heading in your life.

From Thomae's perspective, personality development in adulthood is much more complex than trait theories or Eriksonian theories imply. Each of us has the potential for change, but we tend not to do so unless we have a good reason and desire it.

This point was demonstrated by the Bonn Longitudinal Study of Aging, in which researchers identified the most important components of successful aging (Thomae, 1976). Unlike many other longitudinal studies of personality in adulthood, the Bonn study included measures of physical/biological functioning in addition to many aspects of personality and social development. The results pointed to many different pathways of successful aging, depending on specific interactions among social, biological, motivational, and life-cycle factors. In short, there are many ways to age successfully.

Thomae's cognitive theory proposes that people change during adulthood to the extent that they believe they should change, that they feel they may need to in the future, or that they think they have already and must continue to do so. This may help explain why there is some evidence even in trait research for change, and why research on the midlife crisis has failed to find evidence for a universal period of stress that is tied to a specific age. It also points once again to the fact that people's perceptions of reality are potent predictors of behavior.

The idea that people change across adulthood is supported by our observation of people we know or people in the news. Tom Hayden was one of the leaders of the student protest movement of the 1960s but later became a respected state legislator in California.

TEST YOURSELF

1. The _____ dimension in Costa and McCrae's theory includes anxiety, hostility, and impulsiveness.
2. Behavioral research indicates that gender role identity _____ in middle age.

3. According to Erikson, an increasing concern with helping younger people achieve is termed _____.

4. Research indicates that all middle-aged adults experience stress, and that most _____ experience a midlife crisis.

5. According to the cognitive theory of personality, _____ change is the most important consideration.

6. According to the cognitive theory of personality, people change because _____.

7. How can you reconcile the data from trait research, which indicates little change, with the data from other research, which shows substantial change in personality in adulthood?

Family Dynamics and Middle Age

LEARNING OBJECTIVES

❧ *How does the relationship between middle-aged parents and their young adult children change?*

❧ *How do middle-aged adults deal with their aging parents?*

❧ *What styles of grandparenthood do middle-aged adults experience? How do grandchildren and grandparents interact?*

Family Dynamics and Middle Age
Letting Go: Middle-Aged Adults and Their Children
■ *How Do You Think Your Children Turned Out?*
Giving Back: Middle-Aged Adults and Their Aging Parents
■ *Caring for Parents*
Grandparenthood

Take a look at the family in the photograph. What do you see? Did you notice the many generations in the family? Family ties across the generations provide the context for socialization and for continuity in the family's identity. At the center are members of the middle-aged generation, who serve as the links between their aging parents and their maturing children.

Think about the major issues confronting a typical middle-aged couple: maintaining a good marriage, parenting responsibilities, children who are becoming adults themselves, job pressures, and concern about aging parents, just to name a few. Middle-aged adults are truly involved with life in a large way; they clearly have quite a lot to deal with every day. **Indeed, middle-aged adults are sometimes referred to as the** *sandwich generation* **to reflect their position between two generations (their parents and their children) that put demands and pressures on them.**

In this section, we will examine the dynamics of middle-aged parents and their maturing children, as well as those of middle-aged adults and their aging parents. Later, we will consider what happens when people become grandparents.

Letting Go: Middle-Aged Adults and Their Children

Being a parent has a rather strange side, when you think about it. After creating children out of love, parents spend considerable time, effort, and money preparing them to become independent and leave. For most parents, this happens during middle age.

BECOMING FRIENDS AND THE EMPTY NEST

Sometime during middle age, most parents experience two positive developments with regard to their children. Suddenly their children see them in a new light, and the children leave home.

After the strain of raising adolescents, parents appreciate the transformation that occurs when their children head into young adulthood. In general, parent–child relationships improve considerably when children become young adults (Troll & Bengtson, 1982). The difference can be dramatic, as in the case of Deb, a middle-aged mother. "When Sacha was 15, she acted as if I was the dumbest person on the planet. But now that she's 21, she acts as if I got smart all of a sudden. I like being around her. She's a great kid, and we're really becoming friends."

A key factor in making this transition as smoothly as possible is the extent to which parents foster and approve of their children's attempts at being independent. Most parents manage the transition to an empty nest successfully. Indeed, research has shown that the vast majority of parents are like Esther, the mother in the last chapter-opening vignette: happy (some describe it as "joyful" and "liberating") to see their children leave. Only people who derive a major part of their identity from being a parent have difficulties.

Even though their children leave home, middle-aged parents do not abandon them. Parents still provide considerable financial help (such as paying college tuition) when possible. Most help in other ways ranging from the mundane (making the washer and dryer available to their college-age children) to the extraordinary (providing the down payment for their child's house). Young adults and their middle-aged parents generally believe that they have strong, positive relationships and that they can count on each other for help when necessary (Troll & Bengtson, 1982).

Of course, all this help doesn't mean that everything is perfect. Conflicts still arise. One study found that about one-third of middle-class fathers surveyed complained about their sons' lack of achievement or about their daughters' poor choice of husbands (Nydegger, 1986).

Once children have gone, parents may take stock and ask themselves what kind of job they did as parents. As discussed in the Spotlight on Research feature, the question of how one's children "turned out" is rather complex.

SPOTLIGHT ON RESEARCH

How Do You Think Your Children Turned Out?

As parents gaze lovingly on their newborn child, they have visions of what their son or daughter will grow up to be. A few decades later, parents get to see how close their child came to matching their dreams. When the child becomes a young adult, parents begin to evaluate their child's accomplishments, personal qualities, and interpersonal skills. In short, parents begin to assess how their child turned out.

Ryff and colleagues (1994) argue that this assessment is an important part of the parents' midlife evaluation of themselves. Moreover, because parents are the major influence on children (see Chapters 4 and 7), the stakes for this self-evaluation are high; how one's child turns out is a powerful statement about one's success or failure as a parent (Ryff et al., 1994).

To test this idea, Ryff and colleagues (1994) assessed a random sample of 114 middle-aged mothers and 101 middle-aged fathers, all from different middle-class families in the Midwest, who had at least one child of age 21 or over. The researchers asked the parents to rate their child's adjustment and educational and occupational attainment, to compare the child to others of that age, and to rate their psychological well-being.

Overall, results showed that the parents' views of their children's personal and social adjustment correlated closely with measures of parents' own well-being. Parents' sense of self-acceptance, purpose in life, and environmental mastery were strongly related to how well they thought their children were adjusted. Similar, but somewhat weaker, relations were found between children's accomplishments and parental well-being. No differences between mothers and fathers were found.

Parents were also asked how well they thought their children were doing compared to themselves when they were the same age. These data were intriguing. Parents who thought their children were better adjusted (that is, more self-confident, happy, and interpersonally skilled) than they themselves were in early adulthood had low levels of well-being. Why? Shouldn't parents be pleased that their children are well adjusted? Ryff and colleagues suggest that this finding, though seemingly counterintuitive, is really understandable in terms of social comparison. That is, people suffer negative consequences (such as having lower self-esteem) when they perceive other people as doing better than they are (Suls & Wills, 1991). Even though parents by and large want their children to be happy, they may have difficulty accepting it if they turn out to be *too* happy.

In contrast, parents who rated their children as having attained better educational and occupational levels felt more positive about themselves compared to parents who rated their children lower on these dimensions. In this case, parents may feel that they have fulfilled the American dream, helping the next generation do better than they did.

Ryff and colleagues showed that midlife parents' self-evaluations are clearly influenced by their perceptions of how their children turned out. Perhaps this is one way that parents can justify the time and energy they have devoted to their children.   🙢

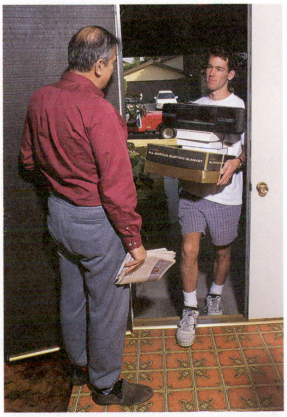

WHEN CHILDREN COME BACK

Parents' satisfaction with the empty nest is sometimes short-lived. Like the father in the photograph, roughly half of all middle-aged parents who have adult children have at least one (typically unmarried) child living with them. Interestingly, this living arrangement is more common if the parents are in good health, and parents continue to do most of the housework (Ward, Logan, & Spitze, 1992). Adult children do not move back home primarily to help their parents, but rather for financial reasons or help with child care, when the young adult is a single parent.

Although middle-aged parents rarely turn their backs on their children, most had not planned on children returning home to live once they had moved out. Neither generation is thrilled with living together again. Both tend to handle the situation better if the returning children are in their early 20s and if the situation is clearly temporary (Clemons & Axelson, 1985). Still, conflict can arise. About 4 in 10 parents report serious conflicts, and arguments over lifestyle, friends, and personal care habits are common (Clemons & Axelson, 1985). Parents' marriages are negatively affected when such conflicts arise, except when parents and adult children get along harmoniously and when both choose to live together. When times are hard, though, adult children may not have much choice but to live with their parents. Fortunately, parents never stop being parents; most willingly extend their hearts, hands, and homes to their children whenever they are needed.

TRYING ON NEW ROLES

Being a middle-aged parent affords the opportunity to assume new roles (Green & Boxer, 1986). **Mothers (more than fathers) tend to take on the role of** *kinkeepers,* **the people who gather the family together for celebrations and keep family members in touch with each other.** Studies of African American families, for example, have shown that kinship ties provide a wide variety of support, from financial aid and role models for young parents to caregiving for the older generation (Stanford & Lockery, 1984). Kinkeeping becomes especially important once grandchildren arrive, as discussed in more detail later in this chapter. Middle-aged mothers may also go to college or begin new careers because their children encourage them. Unfortunately, much less is known about new roles for middle-aged fathers.

Giving Back: Middle-Aged Adults and Their Aging Parents

So far in this section, you have probably had little trouble seeing yourself in the role of adult child. Try now to imagine your middle-aged parents in the same role in relation to their parents (your grandparents). Of course, if you are already

middle-aged, this exercise is a lot easier! As is the case in the photo, being someone's child is a role that people still play well into adulthood, and sometimes, into their 60s and 70s.

How do middle-aged adults relate to their parents? What happens when their parents become frail? We will consider these issues in this section.

KEEPING IN TOUCH

According to a widespread myth, older parents are largely neglected by their middle-aged children. The myth is sustained by the belief that at some time in the past (the "good old days"), middle-aged children were more devoted to their parents than they are today—that today's children just don't care for their parents as they used to (Lee, 1985).

These beliefs are wrong. True, proportionately fewer older adults live with their children today than a century ago, but this is mainly because older adults today are far more financially independent (Lee, 1985). A century ago, Social Security did not exist, and there were no other pension plans, so older adults had to live with other family members in order to make ends meet, not necessarily because they wanted to. Today, most older adults live within a 30-minute drive of one of their children. (Of course, their other children may be scattered across the country.)

Middle-aged children and their parents contact each other fairly frequently. Roughly 80% of older parents have seen one of their children in the past two weeks, a rate that does not differ between urban and rural dwellers (Krout, 1988). Middle-aged children report that they enjoy visiting their parents. Some use these visits to reevaluate the meaning of the relationship as their parents approach death (Helson & Moane, 1987).

CARING FOR AGING PARENTS

Most middle-aged adults have parents who are in reasonably good health. For a growing number of people, however, being a middle-aged child of aging parents involves providing some level of care. As is the case in the photograph, the job of caring for older parents usually falls to a daughter or a daughter-in-law.

This gender difference is striking. Even after ruling out all other demographic characteristics of adult child caregivers and their care recipients, daughters are more than three times as likely to provide care as sons (Dwyer & Coward, 1991). This gender difference is also found in other cultures. In Japanese culture, for example, even though the oldest son is responsible for parental care, it is his wife who actually does the day-to-day caregiving.

In some situations, older parents must move in with one of their children. Such moves usually occur after decades of both generations living independently. This history of independent living sets the stage for adjustment difficulties following the move; both lifestyles must be accommodated. Most of the time, adult children provide care for their mothers, who may in turn have provided care for their husbands before they died. (Spousal caregiving is discussed in Chapter 14.)

Caring for one's parent presents a dilemma (Wolfson et al, 1993). **Most adult children feel a sense of responsibility, termed *filial obligation*, to care for their parent if necessary.** For example, adult child caregivers sometimes express the feeling that they "owe it to mom or dad" to care for them; after all, their parent provided for them for many years, and now the shoe is on the other foot.

But caring for an older parent is not without its price. It usually doesn't happen by choice; each party would just as soon live apart. The potential for conflict over daily routines and lifestyles is high. Overall, stress in adult caregiving results primarily from two sources (Robinson & Thurnher, 1979):

• Adult children may have trouble coping with declines in their parents' functioning, especially those involving cognitive abilities. If caregivers do not know why their parents are declining, they may feel ambivalent and antagonistic toward their parents.

- When the caregiving situation is perceived as confining, or seriously infringes on the adult child's other responsibilities (spouse, parent, employee, and so forth), the situation is likely to be perceived negatively, which may lead to feelings of anger and guilt.

Research indicates that middle-aged adults expend a great deal of energy, time, and money helping their older parents (Brody, 1990). In fact, nearly 90% of the daily help older people receive comes from adult children and other relatives (Morris & Sherwood, 1984). These efforts pay off. Family care helps prevent or at least delay institutionalization (Brody, 1981).

Caring for a parent comes at some psychological cost. Even the most devoted adult child caregiver feels depressed, resentful, angry, and guilty at times (Halpern, 1987). Many middle-aged caregivers are pressed financially, as they may still be paying child care or college tuition expenses, and they may not be able to save adequately for their own retirement. Financial pressures are especially serious for those caring for parents with chronic conditions, such as Alzheimer's disease, that require services that are not covered by medical insurance. In some cases, adult children may even need to quit their jobs in order to provide care if adequate alternatives, such as adult day care, are unavailable.

From the parent's perspective, things aren't always rosy either. Independence and autonomy are important traditional values in North American culture, and their loss is not taken lightly. Older adults are more likely than their children to express the desire to pay a professional for assistance rather than ask a family member for help; they may find it demeaning to live with their children (Brody et al., 1983; Hamon & Blieszner, 1990). Most move in only as a last resort. Frank, a 79-year old retired steelworker, said it more bluntly: "Getting help from my kid and living in her house were the *last* things I wanted to do. I don't need her telling me what to do and messing up my life. I'm her *father*. I'd rather have help from a stranger. I just didn't have the money."

It is difficult to determine whether older parents are satisfied with the help their children provide (Thomas, 1988). Those who are satisfied tend to be in somewhat better health, do not mind living with relatives, and believe that families should help. In contrast, those who are frail, who have little desire to live with relatives, and who prefer help from sources outside the family are least satisfied.

Caring for an older parent is becoming increasingly common. It is often difficult for caregiver and care recipient alike, but in the absence of appropriate alternatives, many families have little choice.

Caring for Parents

FORCES IN ACTION

Perhaps no other event in a person's life seems as fraught with meaning as beginning to care for a parent. Viewing this event from the perspective of the biopsychosocial framework helps provide insight into why this event stands out. The biological forces operating include all of the changes occurring due to aging, which we will consider in Chapters 13 and 14. These changes vary from person to person, but the result for some individuals is that they need help in order to live independently. Meanwhile, middle-aged children are undergoing physiological changes themselves, discussed earlier in this chapter. Although these changes normally do not interfere with everyday life, they represent the beginnings of noticeable aging.

Psychological forces are also operating. Beyond the cognitive and personality issues discussed earlier in this chapter, simply being confronted with children who are becoming independent and parents who may be less independent places additional psychological demands on people. On the social front, middle age usually represents a relatively good period, as occupational stress tends to drop while earnings are at their peak.

The life-cycle forces are considerable. More than anything, it is the timing of events that creates the potential for stress in midlife. If the "generational sandwich" does not form simultaneously with the personal transitions middle-aged adults face, their ability to deal with all of the issues is enhanced. If a person is faced with the prospect of caring for aging parents at the same time as children are moving out, the likelihood of stress is greater than if parental caregiving begins after the children have already gone.

We will return to some of these same themes in Chapter 14 when we examine the balance between competence and environmental press. There, we will consider this topic from the perspective of the biopsychosocial framework.

Grandparenthood

Middle age often brings with it the transition to grandparenthood, which is an exciting time for most adults (Robertson, 1977). Most people become grandparents for the first time during middle age. However, some do not reach this milestone until they are older, and some teenage mothers whose children also become parents during their teens may achieve grandparenthood before they reach age 30 (Kivnick, 1982).

For many, grandparenthood involves adopting new roles. For example, many middle-class grandmothers see themselves as providing pleasure and gratification to their grandchildren without being responsible for raising them (Robertson, 1977). Increasingly, though, grandparents find themselves in the position of caring for grandchildren when the middle generation cannot afford adequate child care.

HOW DO GRANDPARENTS INTERACT WITH GRANDCHILDREN?

Keisha, an 8-year-old girl, smiled brightly when asked to describe her grandparents. "Nana Mary gives me chocolate ice cream, and that's my favorite! Poppy Bill sometimes takes care of me when momma and daddy go out, and plays ball with me." **Keisha's grandparents, like roughly one-third of all grandparents, use the *formal style* of interacting with grandchildren.** These grandparents see their role in relatively traditional terms, occasionally indulging the grandchild (for example, giving chocolate ice cream), occasionally babysitting, and expressing a strong interest in the grandchild, but maintaining a hands-off attitude toward child-rearing (which is left to the parents).

Besides formal, four other interaction styles have been identified (Neugarten & Weinstein, 1964). **Another fairly common style is *fun-seeking*, which is characterized by informal playfulness.** These grandparents see themselves as a primary source of fun for their grandchildren, and they avoid more serious interactions. **The *distant* grandparent appears mainly on holidays, birthdays, or other family celebrations with gifts for the grandchildren but otherwise has little contact.** A distant style is common when grandparents and grandchildren live far apart, but it may also come about by choice, even if they live close by. **Some grandparents, usually grandmothers, serve as *surrogate parents*, assuming all of the normal roles of a parent.** This may be because the parent works and cannot afford child care, or because the parents are incapable of providing care (e.g., are incarcerated, are drug or alcohol abusers, or have abdicated their parental responsibilities). **Finally, some grandparents serve as *dispensers of family wisdom,* assuming an authoritarian position and giving information and advice.**

Grandparenting style tends to vary with the age of the grandchild (Kalish, 1975). Grandparents tend to be playful with very young grandchildren and develop more formal relationships as the grandchildren grow up. Such changes parallel those in the relationship between parents and children.

Also relevant are the social and personal dimensions of grandparenthood (Robertson, 1977). The social dimension includes societal needs and expectations of what grandparents are to do, such as passing on family history to grandchildren. The personal dimension includes the personal satisfaction and individual needs that are fulfilled by being a grandparent. Many of the functions grandparents serve can be understood as reflecting different levels of the social and personal dimensions (Cherlin & Furstenberg, 1986). Like the grandfather in the photo, many grandparents pass on skills, as well as religious, social, and vocational values (social dimension) through storytelling and advice, and they may feel great pride and satisfaction (personal dimension) from working with grandchildren on joint projects.

Grandchildren today give grandparents a great deal in return. For example, grandchildren keep grandparents in touch with youth and the latest trends. In addition, grandchildren today can save many grandparents from the embarrassment of still thinking that "to rap" means to have a conversation with someone (a meaning of the term from the 1960s).

BEING A GRANDPARENT IS MEANINGFUL

Does it matter to people to be a grandparent? You bet it does, at least to the vast majority of grandparents (Kivnick, 1982). For some, grandparenting is the most important thing in their lives. For others, meaning comes from being seen as wise, from spoiling grandchildren, from recalling the relationship they had with their own grandparents, or from taking pride in the fact that they will be followed by not one but two generations.

Do grandparents derive a specific kind of meaning, depending on what relationship style they adopt? Apparently, there is no connection (Miller & Cavanaugh, 1990). Most grandparents derive several different meanings, regardless of the style of their relationship with the grandchildren. Similar findings are reported when overall satisfaction with being a grandparent is examined; no matter what their style is, grandparents can be satisfied with their role (Thomas, Bence, & Meyer, 1988).

Clearly, grandparents are a diverse group. We cannot develop standardized patterns of interaction styles and meanings. This may merely be a function of different positions in the life span: How a 52-year-old grandfather interacts with his 3-year-old granddaughter is bound to differ from the way a 93-year-old grandmother interacts with her 12-year-old grandson. Grandparent–grandchildren relationships may be too idiosyncratic to be described adequately in general terms (Bengtson & Robertson, 1985).

GRANDPARENTS AND GRANDCHILDREN

Perhaps you are fortunate enough to have a grandparent still alive. If so, think a minute about how your relationship has changed over the years. Like most people, you may have had a closer relationship when you were under age 10 than during adolescence (Kahana & Kahana, 1970). By young adulthood, most people report that their grandparents represent a special resource, and they feel that they have a close relationship. Additionally, most young adults think that they have a responsibility to help their grandparents when necessary, without expecting anything in return (Robertson, 1976). Grandmothers and granddaughters report feeling closer than do grandfathers and grandsons (Hagestad, 1978).

We noted in Chapter 10 that the divorce rate in the United States is roughly 50% for recent marriages. Many grandparents face the possibility that contact with their grandchildren will be limited as a result of the divorce (Johnson, 1988). Many states do not have specific protections for grandparents' rights following their child's divorce (Edelstein, 1990). In general, contact is best with maternal grandmothers whose daughters have custody of the grandchildren. In contrast, paternal grandfathers are least likely to maintain contact if their sons do not have custody of the grandchildren (Cherlin & Furstenberg, 1986). Because grandparenthood is an important and meaningful role, diminished contact with grandchildren due to divorce is an especially difficult ordeal for everyone concerned.

ETHNIC DIFFERENCES

How grandparents and grandchildren interact varies in different ethnic groups. For example, African American grandmothers under age 40 report feeling pressured to provide care for grandchildren they were not eager to have; in contrast, those over age 60 tend to feel that they are fulfilling an important role. In general, African American grandfathers tend to perceive grandparenthood as a central role to a greater degree than European American grandfathers (Kivett, 1991).

Grandparenting style also varies with ethnicity, which may sometimes create tension within families. Kornhaber (1985) relates the case of an 18-month-old girl who had one pair of Latino grandparents and one pair of Nordic grandparents. Her Latino grandparents tickled her, frolicked with her, and doted over her. Her Nordic grandparents loved her just as much but tended to just let her be. Her Latina mother thought that the Nordic grandparents were "cold and hard," and her Nordic father accused the Latino grandparents of "driving him crazy" with their displays of affection. The child, though, was flexible enough to adapt to both styles.

Native American grandparents like those in the photograph appear to have some interactive styles different than other groups (Weibel-Orlando, 1990).

Fictive grandparenting **is a style that allows adults to fill in for missing or deceased biological grandparents, functionally creating the role of surrogate grandparent. In the** *cultural conservator* **style, grandparents request that their grandchildren be allowed to live with them in order to ensure that the grandchildren learn the native ways.** In general, Native American grandmothers take a more active role in these styles than grandfathers.

THE CHANGING ROLE OF GRANDPARENTS

Grandparenthood today is tougher than it used to be. For many reasons, detachment rather than close involvement characterizes an increasing number of grandparent–grandchild relationships, in contrast to the more involved styles of a few decades ago (Rodeheaver & Thomas, 1986). Families are more mobile, which means that grandparents are more often separated from their grandchildren by geographical distance. Grandparents are more likely to have independent lives, apart from their children and grandchildren. As mentioned earlier, many grandparents rarely see their grandchildren who are living with former daughters-in-law or sons-in-law. Also, grandparents are no longer revered dispensers of child-rearing advice, so they are likely to take a back seat for the sake of family harmony. In short, we may need to reexamine the roles of grandparents in their grandchildren's lives, as well as the traditional styles of grandparenting that have guided research up until now.

Despite the obstacles, most grandparents are comfortable with their role. Most report that they have little desire (and no responsibility) for rearing their grandchildren. In fact, grandparents who feel responsible for advising their grandchildren tend to be less satisfied with their role than those who feel that their role is mainly to enjoy their grandchildren (Thomas, 1986). Thus, for maximum satisfaction, the role should be grandparental rather than parental.

TEST YOURSELF

1. The vast majority of parents are _____ to see the last child leave home.
2. The people who gather the family together for celebrations and keep family members in touch are called _____.
3. Most caregiving for aging parents is provided by _____.
4. For aging parents, the loss of _____ makes it difficult to live with their children.
5. The most common style of grandparenting is _____, in which grandparents see their role in relatively traditional terms.
6. _____ grandparents have a style called cultural conservator.
7. If you were to create a guide to families for middle-aged adults, what would the most important pieces of advice be? Why did you select these?

Putting It All Together

Is it any wonder why middle age gets bad press? There's a lot to face: signs of biological aging, children leaving, cognitive abilities changing, and parents dying. But middle age also has much going for it, from many people's perspective: generally good relationships with children, grandparenthood, and accumulated experience. We saw how middle age is partly a continuation of previous developmental trends (for example, in aspects of cognitive development and personality) and partly a time of new challenges (such as getting used to physical changes and dealing with different generations in the family).

We learned that Dean, the Type A individual, is well positioned to recover from his heart attack if he reduces his anger and hostility. Kesha's expertise in social work is typical of middle-aged adults, many of whom become experts in one area or another. We saw that Jim's behav-

ior is not a reflection of a universal midlife crisis. Esther's joy and relief when her youngest daughter moved out is the reaction of most middle-aged parents who acquire an empty nest (at least until their adult children decide to move back).

Judging from the information in this chapter and in Chapters 10 and 11, middle age has many positive aspects—relatively good health, the best financial security most people ever have, stable relationships with partners, good relations with children, expertise in some area, and the prospect of rewarding relationships with grandchildren. It has its challenges, too. Getting used to physical aging can be hard, as is caring for an aging parent. But for many people, on balance these are the best years of their lives.

Thinking about Development

1. The experience of undergoing the physical changes related to aging, such as gray hair, reflects the interaction of biological, psychological, social, and life-cycle factors. How so?

2. How are the cognitive developmental changes discussed in this chapter related to those discussed in Chapter 9, with regard to primary and secondary mental abilities and postformal thought?

3. How does personality development in middle age relate to the continuity–discontinuity issue discussed in Chapter 1?

4. As noted in Chapter 10 (p. 353), marital satisfaction improves as children leave home. Based on the discussion in this chapter, why does this happen?

5. How do family relationships in middle age fit into Duvall's model, discussed in Chapter 10 (pp. 361-362)?

Summary

Physical Changes and Health

Changes in Appearance

■ Some of the signs of aging appearing in middle age include wrinkles, gray hair, and weight gain. An important change, especially in women, is loss of bone mass, which in severe form may result in the disease osteoporosis.

Reproductive Changes

■ The climacteric (loss of the ability to bear children by natural means) and menopause (cessation of menstruation) occur in the 40s and 50s and constitute a major change in reproductive ability in women. Most women do not have severe physical symptoms associated with the hormonal changes.

■ Reproductive changes in men are much less dramatic; even older men are usually still fertile. Physical changes do affect sexual response.

Stress and Health

■ In the stress and coping paradigm, stress results from a person's appraisal of an event as taxing his or her resources. Daily hassles are viewed as the primary source of stress.

■ The types of situations people appraise as stressful change through adulthood. Family and career issues are more important for young and middle-aged adults; health issues are more important for older adults.

■ Type A behavior pattern is characterized by intense competitiveness, anger, hostility, restlessness, aggression, and impatience. It is linked with a person's first heart attack and with cardiovascular disease. Type B behavior pattern is the opposite of Type A; it is associated with lower risk of first heart attack, but poorer prognosis afterward if an attack should occur. Following an initial heart attack, Type A behavior pattern individuals have a higher recovery rate.

■ Whereas stress is unrelated to serious psychopathology, it is related to social isolation and distrust.

Exercise

■ Aerobic exercise has numerous benefits, especially to cardiovascular health and fitness. The best results are obtained through a moderate exercise program maintained throughout adulthood.

Cognitive Development

Practical Intelligence

■ Research on practical intelligence reveals differences between optimally exercised ability and unexercised ability. This gap closes during middle adulthood. Practical intelligence appears not to decline appreciably until late life.

Becoming an Expert

■ People tend to become experts in some areas and not in others. Experts tend to think in more flexible ways than novices and to be able to skip steps in solving problems. Expert performance tends to peak in middle age.

Lifelong Learning

■ One must teach adults differently than children and youth. Older students learn differently and are motivated differently.

Personality

Stability Is the Rule: Costa and McCrae's Model of Personality

■ Costa and McCrae postulate five dimensions of personality: neuroticism, extraversion, openness to experience, agreeableness, and conscientiousness. Several longitudinal studies indicate that personality traits show long-term stability.

■ There is some evidence that gender role identity converges in middle age, to the extent that men and women are more likely to endorse similar self-descriptions. However, these similar descriptions do not necessarily translate into similar behavior.

Change Is the Rule: Changing Priorities at Midlife

■ Erikson believed that middle-aged adults become more concerned with doing for others and passing social values and skills to the next generation—a set of behaviors and beliefs he labeled *generativity*. Those who do not achieve generativity are thought to experience stagnation.

■ For the most part, there is little support for theories based on the premise that all adults go through predictable life stages at specific points in time. Individuals may face similar stresses, but transitions may occur at any time in adulthood. Research indicates that not everyone experiences a crisis at midlife.

Seeking the Middle Ground: A Cognitive Theory of Personality

■ A cognitive theory of personality is based on the view that what people perceive is more important for understanding behavior than what is objectively true. This means that people's behavior will change to the extent that they believe it should, it needs to, or it already has.

Family Dynamics and Middle Age

■ Middle age is sometimes referred to as the sandwich generation, due to its position between children and older parents.

Letting Go: Middle-Aged Adults and Their Children

■ Parent–child relations improve dramatically when children emerge from adolescence. Most parents look forward to having an empty nest. Difficulties emerge to the extent that raising children has been a primary source of personal identity for parents. However, once children have left home, parents still provide considerable support.

■ Children move back home primarily for financial or child-rearing reasons. Neither parents nor children generally like the situation.

■ Middle-aged mothers tend to adopt the role of kinkeepers in order to keep family traditions alive and as a way to link generations.

Giving Back: Middle-Aged Adults and Their Aging Parents

■ Middle-aged children contact their parents fairly

frequently. The vast majority of help older adults receive comes from their children. Caring for aging parents usually falls to a daughter or daughter-in-law. When parents move in with their children, it generally creates a stressful situation due to conflicting feelings and roles. The potential for conflict is high, as is financial pressure. Older parents are often dissatisfied with the situation as well.

Grandparenthood

■ Becoming a grandparent means assuming new roles. Five styles of interaction between grandparents and grandchildren have been identified: formal, fun-seeking, distant, surrogate parent, and dispenser of family wisdom. The style tends to vary with the age of the grandchild. Also relevant are the social and personal dimensions of grandparenting.

■ Grandparents derive a great deal of meaning from the role, regardless of their grandparenting style. Most children and young adults report positive relationships with grandparents, and young adults feel a responsibility to care for them if necessary. An important concern for some grandparents is their ability to maintain contact with grandchildren following the divorce of the grandchildren's parents.

■ Ethnic differences have been reported in the extent to which grandparents take an active role in their grandchildren's lives.

■ In an increasingly mobile society, grandparents are more frequently assuming a distant relationship with their grandchildren.

Key Terms

aerobic exercise   (415)
agreeableness   (424)
appraise   (414)
climacteric   (411)
conscientiousness   (424)
coping   (414)
cultural conservator   (438)
dispenser of family wisdom   (436)
distant style   (435)
encapsulated   (420)
extraversion   (423)
fictive grandparents   (438)

filial obligation   (433)
formal style   (435)
fun-seeking style   (435)
generativity   (426)
hassles   (414)
hormone replacement therapy   (411)
kinkeepers   (432)
menopause   (411)
midlife crisis   (426)
neuroticism   (423)
openness to experience   (424)
optimally exercised ability   (418)

osteoporosis   (410)
practical intelligence   (418)
processes of thinking   (420)
products of thinking   (420)
sandwich generation   (429)
stagnation   (426)
stress and coping paradigm   (413)
surrogate parents   (435)
Type A behavior pattern   (414)
Type B behavior pattern   (414)
unexercised ability   (418)

If You'd Like to Learn More

BRODY, E. M. (1990). *Women in the middle: Their parent-care years*. New York: Springer. This description of the experiences of women who provide care for their parents is research-based but contains many good examples.

CHERLIN, A. J., & FURSTENBERG, F. F. (1986). *The new American grandparent*. New York: Basic Books. This is a very readable overview of research on the meanings and styles of grandparenthood.

ESTES, C. P. (1992). *Women who run with the wolves*. New York: Ballantine Books. Femininity is discussed from a Jungian point of view, as revealed through story and myth.

KEEN, S. (1991). *Fire in the belly: On being a man*. New York: Bantam Books. This very readable book presents a new model of masculinity in contemporary society.

TAN, A. (1989). *The Joy Luck Club*. New York: Putnam. This novel explores the bond among four Chinese American women and their adult daughters.

WHITBOURNE, S. K. (1985). *The aging body*. New York: Springer. This excellent resource covers the biological and physiological changes that occur in adulthood, with the psychological implications of these changes discussed in detail.

Later Adulthood

❧ Sarah is an 87-year-old African American woman who comes from a family of long-lived individuals. She has never been to a physician in her entire life, and she has never really been seriously ill. Sarah figures it's just as well that she has never needed a physician, because for most of her life she had no health insurance. Because she feels healthy and has more living that she wants to do, Sarah figures that she'll live for several more years.

❧ Frank is an 80-year-old man who has been physically active his whole life. He still enjoys sailing, long-distance biking, and cross-country skiing. Although he considers himself to be in excellent shape, he has noticed that his endurance has decreased, and his hearing isn't quite as sharp as it used to be. Frank wonders: Is there something he can do to stop these declines, or are they an inevitable part of growing older?

❧ Maria is a 75-year-old widow who is widely recognized for her keen insight into life's challenges. People of all ages seek her advice on everything from love relationships to career choices to secret family recipes. Maria is regarded as a very wise woman. Younger people consider her to be proof that wisdom comes with age, but some older people believe that Maria's insights come from her wide and varied life experience.

❧ Robert is a 67-year-old former lawyer. For the past three years, he has been having increasing difficulty remembering information. This was one of the main reasons why he retired. During the past few months, things have gotten worse. He gets hostile for no reason, wanders away from home, and once even failed to recognize his 10-year-old granddaughter. Robert's family is worried that he may have Alzheimer's disease.

The Personal Context
of Later Life

STOP! Before you read this chapter, do the following exercise. Take out a piece of paper and write down all the adjectives you can think of that describe aging and older adults, as well as all of the "facts" about aging that you know.

Now that you have your list, look over it carefully. Are most of your descriptors positive or negative? Do you have lots of "facts" written down, or just a few? Most people's lists contain at least some words and phrases that reflect images of older adults as portrayed by the media. Many of the media's images are stereotypes of aging that may only be loosely based on reality. For example, people over age 60 are almost never pictured in ads for perfume (Elizabeth Taylor is a notable exception), but they are shown in ads for wrinkle removers.

In this chapter, we begin our journey through old age. We will form a realistic picture of aging. Our emphasis in this chapter will be on physical and cognitive changes; the differences between normal and abnormal functioning in mental health will also be examined.

What Are Older Adults Like?

LEARNING OBJECTIVES

🌾 *What are the characteristics of older adults in the population?*

🌾 *How long will most people live? What factors influence this?*

What is it like to be old? Do you want your own late life to be described by the words and phrases you wrote at the beginning of the chapter? Do you look forward to becoming old, or are you afraid of what may lie ahead?

Growing old is not something we think about very much until we have to. Most of us experience the coming of old age the way Jim does in the Far Side cartoon. It's as if we go to bed one night middle-aged and wake up the next day feeling old. But we can take comfort in knowing that when that day comes, we will have plenty of company.

You never see it coming

THE FAR SIDE © 1991 Farworks, Inc./Dist. by Universal Press Syndicate. Reprinted with permission. All rights reserved.

The Demographics of Aging

Did you ever stop to think about how many older adults you see in your daily life? Did you ever wonder if your great-grandparents had the same experience? There have never been as many older adults alive as there are now. The proportion of older adults in the population of industrialized countries has increased tremendously in this century, due mainly to better health care and to lowering women's mortality rate during childbirth.

People who study population trends, called *demographers,* **use a graphic technique called a** *population pyramid* **to illustrate these changes.** Notice the shape of the population pyramid in 1900, shown in the first panel of the figure. At the turn of the century, there were so many more people un-

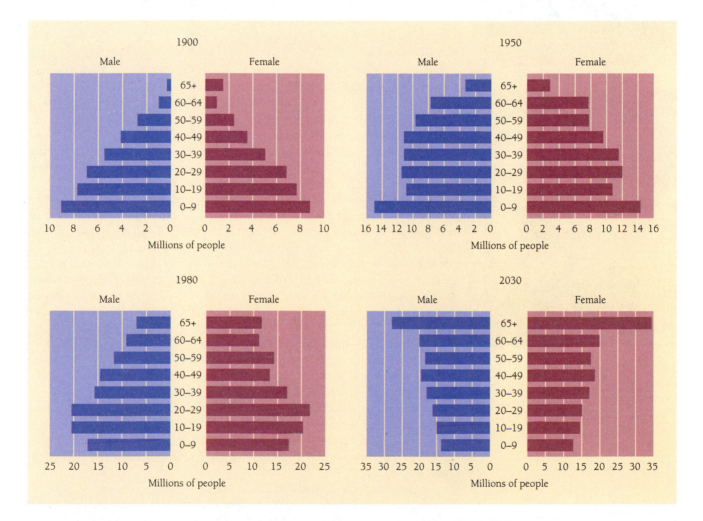

der the age of 20 than there were people over age 60 that the figure is indeed shaped like a pyramid. Projections for 2030 (when the last of the Baby Boomers have reached 65) indicate that a dramatic change will have occurred; it's almost as if the 1900 pyramid had been turned upside down! The number of people over 65 will outnumber those in any other age group.

The rapid increase in the number of older adults (individuals over age 60) will bring profound changes to everyone's lives. As we move into the 21st cen-

The U.S. and Canada are not the only countries experiencing rapid increases in the number of older adults. In fact, many countries have much greater increases.

tury, older adults will be a major marketing target, and they will wield considerable political and economic power. The sheer number of older adults will place enormous pressure on pension systems (especially Social Security), health care (including long-term care), and other human services. The costs will be borne by a relatively small number of taxpaying workers in the cohorts behind them.

The growing strain on social service systems will be intensified because the most rapidly growing segment of the U.S. population is the group of people over age 80. In fact, according to some projections, the number of such people could roughly triple between 1990 and 2030, from 1.3% of the population to 4% (American Association of Retired Persons, 1993). As we will see in this chapter and in Chapter 14, individuals over age 80 generally need more assistance with daily living than do people under 80.

THE DIVERSITY OF OLDER ADULTS

Older adults are not all alike, any more than people at other ages. Older women outnumber older men in all ethnic groups in the United States, for reasons we will explore later. The number of older adults among ethnic minority groups is increasing faster than among European Americans. For example, the number of Native American elderly has increased 65% in recent decades; Asian and Pacific Islander elderly have quadrupled; older adults are the fastest-growing segment of the African American population; and the number of Hispanic American elderly is also increasing rapidly.

Older adults in the future will be better educated, too. At present, only half of the people over age 65 have a high school diploma, and 10% have four or more years of college. By 2030, it is estimated that 85% will have a high school diploma and 75% will have a college degree. These dramatic changes will be due mainly to better educational opportunities for poorer students and greater need for formal schooling in order to find a good job. Also, better-educated people tend to live longer, mostly because they have higher incomes—which give them better access to good health care and a chance to follow healthier lifestyles.

Internationally, the number of older adults is also growing rapidly, especially among developing countries. To a large extent, these rapid increases are due to improved health care in these countries. Such increases will literally change the face of the population, as more people live to old age.

How these population changes will affect developing countries is unknown. However, even economically powerful countries such as Japan are trying to cope with increased numbers of older adults that strain the country's resources. This may mean that developing countries will need additional financial support.

Even though the financial implications of an aging population are predictable, we have done surprisingly little to prepare. For example, there is virtually no research data on the characteristics of older workers (even though mandatory retirement has been virtually eliminated for several years), on differences between the young-old (ages 65–80) and the old-old (over age 80), or on specific health care needs of older adults with regard to chronic illness (American Psychological Society, 1993). These issues will need to be addressed in the very near future, so that policymakers will have data to help prepare society for the coming changes.

How Long Will You Live?

The number of years a person can expect to live, termed *longevity*, is jointly determined by genetic and environmental factors. Researchers distinguish between three types of longevity: average life expectancy, useful life expectancy, and maximum life expectancy.

***Average life expectancy* (or median life expectancy) is the age at which half of the people born in a particular year will have died.** As you can see in the graph, average life expectancy for people in the United States has in-

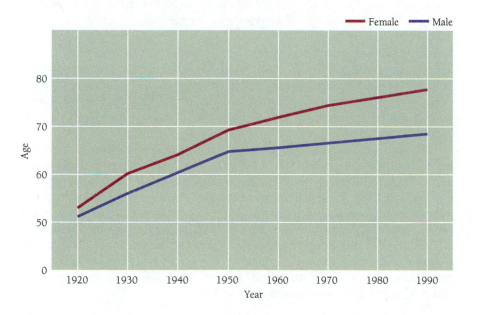

creased steadily during this century. This increase is due mainly to significant declines in infant mortality and in the number of women dying during childbirth, the elimination of major diseases such as smallpox and polio, and improvements in medical technology that prolong the lives of people with chronic disease.

***Useful life expectancy* is the number of years that a person is free from debilitating chronic disease and impairment.** Ideally, useful life expectancy exactly matches the actual length of a person's life. However, medical technology sometimes enables people to live for years even though they may not be able to perform routine daily tasks. Accordingly, people are placing greater emphasis on the quality (rather than just the quantity) of life in making medical treatment decisions.

***Maximum life expectancy* is the oldest age to which any person lives.** Currently, scientists estimate that the maximum limit for humans is around 120 years, mostly because the heart and other key organ systems are limited in how long they can last without replacement.

GENETIC FACTORS IN LIFE EXPECTANCY

Probably the best indicator of a long life is coming from a family of long-lived individuals. For example, roughly four years are added to your average life expectancy for each parent who lives to age 80 (Woodruff-Pak, 1988).

Some chronic diseases also have genetic links that shorten life expectancy, including cardiovascular disease, several forms of cancer, cystic fibrosis, and Alzheimer's disease. For example, for each parent, grandparent, or sibling who dies of cardiovascular disease before age 50, you lose four years from your average life expectancy.

ENVIRONMENTAL FACTORS IN LIFE EXPECTANCY

Many aspects of the environment affect how long you will live: acquired diseases (e.g., AIDS), toxins, and pollutants. Additionally, lifestyle factors such as stress, smoking, diet, drugs, alcohol, and exercise influence life expectancy. Being married helps extend life, but more so for men than women (Woodruff-Pak, 1988).

Environmental influences are even more important for poor people. People living in poor neighborhoods are more likely to have little money for good diets, to be more exposed to toxins such as lead, and to live in more polluted areas. The combination of environmental factors can be shocking: the American Cancer Society estimates that an unmarried smoker living alone in a large city may lose up to 22 years.

Perhaps the most controversial of environmental influences on longevity are technological improvements in health care. We now have the ability to extend life significantly, as we can keep people alive longer through medical interventions. Even when a disease is incurable, many of its victims may live longer because medical technology, such as life-support systems, keeps them alive. But many people are asking a tough question: Is extending life always beneficial? This question forces people to separate the quality of life from the quantity of life. As explained in the Current Controversies feature, there is often a high price to pay for extending life in all cases. We will also revisit this issue in Chapter 15, in connection with euthanasia.

CURRENT CONTROVERSIES

Quantity versus Quality of Life

Suppose for a moment that you are a physician. One of your patients is a 79-year-old woman who has been in good health for most of her life. She lives independently and is able to visit her friends and family regularly. Because she had been complaining of some unusual pain, you ordered several tests. The results have come back, and they indicate a very serious disease. There is a way to treat it, but the treatment has a very high probability of leaving the patient bedridden and totally dependent on others for basic care. Without treatment, the woman may have about six months to live, but she would be able to continue living independently. What would you recommend?

This dilemma is being faced increasingly often by health care professionals. Today, we have the knowledge and technology to treat many diseases, thereby extending life. Most people believe that the maximum possible use of these tools is appropriate. However, these tools sometimes bring a high price: Life may be lengthened, but the person may not be able to enjoy it.

Health care professionals and ethicists are beginning to debate the merits of extending the quantity of life without also considering the quality of life. What does "quality of life" mean? Does it mean independent functioning? Being able to get by with a little help? With a live-in nurse? Or does it vary enough from person to person that each of us must answer the question ourselves? If so, how should individuals be brought into these decision processes, and how far should physicians and other health care professionals push various treatment options? This debate is related to similar issues raised in the discussion of euthanasia in Chapter 15.

These are difficult questions. Because technological advances continue to occur more rapidly than we solve ethical questions concerning their appropriate use, society will continue to grapple with these issues. Where do you stand? ❧

ETHNIC AND GENDER DIFFERENCES IN LIFE EXPECTANCY

Ethnic differences in average life expectancy are complex. For example, African Americans' average life expectancy at birth is roughly 7 years lower for men and 5 years lower for women than that of European Americans. But if we compare these same groups at age 85, the average life expectancy for African Americans is 1 year longer than it is for European Americans (National Center for Health Statistics, 1993b). Perhaps because they do not typically have access to the same quality of care that European Americans usually do, African Americans who survive to age 85 tend to be healthier than their European American counterparts. They may well have needed little medical care throughout their lives. Sarah, the 87-year old woman in the first chapter-opening vignette, is an example.

Similarly, the roughly 7-year advantage that women have over men at birth dwindles to only 1 year by age 85 (National Center for Health Statistics, 1993). Because men are more susceptible to disease and to accidental death throughout their lives, those who survive to old age are healthier.

Average life expectancy is influenced by many factors. The complex differences across different ethnic groups reflect such things as variable access to quality health care and the likelihood that people will die of accidents earlier in life.

TEST YOURSELF

1. The fastest-growing segment of the population in the United States is people of age _____.
2. The age at which half of the people born in a particular year have died is called _____.
3. Think back to the lifestyle influences on health discussed in Chapter 12. If most people actually followed very healthy lifestyles, what do you think would happen to average life expectancy?

Physical Changes and Health

LEARNING OBJECTIVES

❧ *What are the major biological theories of aging?*

❧ *What physiological changes normally occur in later life?*

❧ *What are the principal health issues for older adults?*

Physical Changes and Health
Biological Theories of Aging
Physiological Changes
■ *Preventing Accidents Involving Older Adults*
Health Issues

If your family has kept photograph albums over many years, you are able to see how your grandparents or great grandparents changed over the years. Some of the more visible differences are changes in the color and amount of hair and the addition of wrinkles, but many other physical changes are harder to see. In this section, we will consider some of these, as well as a few things that adults can do to improve their health. As noted in Chapter 12, many aging changes

LEONARD HAYFLICK

"Knowledge of biological phenomena often extends to the molecular level, but our understanding of the basic causes of aging is nearly as primitive as it was a century ago."

Whether we like them or not, the wrinkles on this person's face are an inevitable part of aging. As noted in the text, wrinkles are due to normal physiological changes involving cross-linking processes.

begin during middle age but typically do not affect people in their daily lives until later in life. But first, we will ask a basic question: Why do people grow old in the first place?

Biological Theories of Aging

Why does everyone who lives long enough grow old and eventually die? To date, we have no definitive answer, but several complementary biological theories, taken together, provide some insights (Hayflick, 1994).

There are four major groups of biological theories of aging. **Wear-and-tear theory suggests that the body, much like any machine, gradually deteriorates and finally wears out.** This theory explains some diseases, such as osteoarthritis, rather well. Years of use of the joints causes the protective cartilage lining to deteriorate, resulting in pain and stiffness. However, wear-and-tear theory does not explain most other aspects of aging very well.

Cellular theories **explain aging by focusing on processes that occur within individual cells, leading to the buildup of harmful substances over a lifetime.** Most of these theories stress the destructive effects that certain substances have on cellular functioning. **For example, some theorists believe that** *free radicals*—**chemicals produced randomly during normal cell metabolism, which bond easily to other substances inside cells—cause cellular damage that impairs functioning.** Aging is caused by the cumulative effects of free radicals over the life span. Free radicals may play a role in some diseases, such as atherosclerosis and cancer. **Another cellular theory focuses on** *cross-linking,* **in which some proteins interact randomly with certain body tissues, such as muscles and arteries.** The result of cross-linking is that normal, elastic tissue becomes stiffer, so that muscles and arteries are less flexible over time. The results in some cases can be serious; for example, stiffening in the heart muscle forces the heart to work harder, which may increase the risk of heart attacks. Although we know that these substances accumulate, we do not fully understand how they may cause aging.

Metabolic theories **focus on aspects of the body's metabolism to explain why people age.** Two important processes in this approach are caloric intake and stress. There is some evidence that limiting the number of calories people eat in an otherwise well-balanced diet is related to longer life expectancy and lower rates of disease (Monczunski, 1991). It remains to be seen whether the type of diet (e.g., low-fat) or the number of calories per se is the secret. How readily one adapts to physical stress is also significant; younger adults can tolerate higher levels of physical exertion than can older adults. It is possible that death occurs because the body can no longer adapt to stress.

Finally, *programmed cell death theories* **suggest that aging is genetically programmed.** Although there may not be a single aging gene as such, there is evidence that there may be a genetic code, yet to be discovered, that controls cell life. We know that there is a genetic component involved in many age-related chronic diseases such as Alzheimer's disease, cardiovascular disease, and some forms of cancer. At present, though, we do not know how such programming gets activated or how it causes aging.

Despite the variety of biological theories, none is adequate by itself to explain aging fully. Indeed, much about the aging process remains to be discovered, especially in sorting out the differences between normal aging (the disease-free changes that happen to everyone) and disease-related aging. Moreover, we also need to learn how these various factors in biological aging may interact.

Physiological Changes

Growing older brings with it several inevitable physiological changes. Like Frank, whom we met in the second chapter-opening vignette, older adults find that their endurance has declined, relative to what it was 20 or 30 years earlier, and that their hearing has declined. In this section, we will consider some of the most important physiological changes that occur in the neurons, the cardiovascular and respiratory systems, and the sensory systems. We will also consider general health issues such as sleep, nutrition, and cancer.

CHANGES IN THE NEURONS

The most important normal changes involve structural changes in the neurons, the basic cells in the brain, and in communication among neurons. We encountered the basic structures of the neuron in Chapter 3. Two structures in neurons are most important for our present discussion: the dendrites, which pick up information from other neurons, and the axon, which transmits information inside a neuron from the dendrites to the terminal branches. Each of the changes we will consider impairs the neurons' ability to transmit information, which ultimately affects how well the person functions. Three structural changes are most important in normal aging: neurofibrillary tangles, dendritic changes, and neuritic plaques.

For reasons that are not understood, fibers that compose the axon sometimes become twisted together to form spiral-shaped masses called *neurofibrillary tangles.* These tangles interfere with the neuron's ability to transmit information down the axon. Some degree of tangling occurs normally with age, but large numbers of neurofibrillary tangles are associated with Alzheimer's disease (Duara, London, & Rapoport, 1985).

Changes in the dendrites are more complicated. Some dendrites shrivel up and die, making it more difficult for neurons to communicate with each other. However, some dendrites continue to grow (Curcio, Buell, & Coleman, 1982). This may help explain why older adults continue to improve in some areas, as we will discover later in this chapter. Why some dendrites degenerate and others do not is poorly understood; it may reflect the existence of two different families of neurons.

Damaged and dying neurons sometimes collect around a core of protein and produce *neuritic plaques.* It is likely that such plaques also interfere with normal functioning of healthy neurons. Normally, large numbers of plaques are not found until around age 90 (Adams, 1980). A large concentration of plaques in persons under age 90 is one of the diagnostic criteria of Alzheimer's disease.

Because neurons do not physically touch each other, they must communicate via chemicals called *neurotransmitters.* With age, the levels of these neurotransmitters decline (Rogers & Bloom, 1985). These declines are believed to be responsible for numerous age-related behavioral changes, including those in memory and sleep, and perhaps in afflictions such as Parkinson's disease.

The changes in neurons that we have described are simply a normal part of aging. These normal changes do not result in Alzheimer's or related diseases, conditions we will discuss in more detail on pages 471–476. This point is important, as it means that serious behavioral changes such as severe memory impairment are not caused by normal changes in the brain.

CARDIOVASCULAR AND RESPIRATORY SYSTEMS

Cardiovascular diseases such as heart attack, irregular heartbeat, stroke, and hypertension increase dramatically with age (USDHHS, 1993). Overall death

This African American man is at greater risk of having a heart attack because he has had poorer access to preventive health care and has not had the financial resources to have a healthy lifestyle.

rates from cardiovascular disease have been declining over recent decades, mainly because fewer adults smoke cigarettes and many people have reduced the amount of fat in their diets. However, the death rate from cardiovascular diseases for some ethnic groups (e.g., African Americans) remains much higher because of poorer preventive health care and less healthy lifestyles due to lack of financial resources.

Normal changes in the cardiovascular system begin by young adulthood. Fat deposits are found in and around the heart and in the arteries. Eventually, the amount of blood that the heart can pump per minute will decline roughly 30%. The amount of muscle tissue in the heart also declines, due to its replacement by connective tissue. There is also a general stiffening of the arteries, due to calcification. These changes appear irrespective of lifestyle, but they occur more slowly in people who exercise, eat low-fat diets, and manage to lower stress effectively (see Chapter 12).

As people grow older, their chances of having a stroke increase. **Strokes, or *cerebral vascular accidents,* are caused by interruptions in the blood flow in the brain due to a blockage or to a *hemorrhage* in a cerebral artery.** Blockages of arteries may be caused by clots or by deposits of fatty substances due to atherosclerosis. Hemorrhages are caused by ruptures of the artery. A single, large cerebral vascular accident may produce serious cognitive impairment, such as the loss of the ability to speak, or physical problems, such as the inability to move an arm. The nature and severity of the functional impairment are usually determined by which specific area of the brain is affected. Recovery from a single stroke depends on many factors, including the extent and type of the loss, the ability of other areas in the brain to assume the functions that were lost, and personal motivation.

Numerous small cerebral vascular accidents can result in a disease termed *multi-infarct dementia.* Unlike Alzheimer's disease, another form of dementia discussed later in this chapter, multi-infarct dementia can have a sudden onset and may or may not progress gradually. Moreover, individuals' symptom patterns vary a great deal, depending on which specific areas of the brain are damaged. In some cases, multi-infarct dementia has a much faster course than Alzheimer's disease, resulting in death an average of two to three years after onset; in others, the disease may progress much more slowly, with idiosyncratic symptom patterns (Blass & Barclay, 1985).

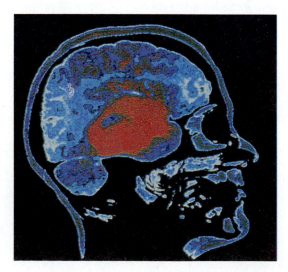

Single cerebral vascular accidents and multi-infarct dementia are diagnosed similarly. Evidence of damage is usually obtained from diagnostic imaging (e.g., computed tomography, or CT scans; magnetic resonance imaging, or MRI), which provides pictures like those shown here. Neuropsychological tests confirm the other evidence. Known risk factors for both conditions include hypertension and a family history of the disorders.

Because of the cumulative effects of breathing polluted air over a lifetime, it is hard to say which changes in the lungs are strictly age-related. Due mostly to stiffening of the rib cage and air passages with age, and destruction of the air sacs in the lungs from pollution and smoking, the maximum amount of air in one breath at age 85 compared to age 25 has dropped by 40%. This decline is the main cause of shortness of breath after physical exertion in later life. **The most common form of incapacitating respiratory disease among older adults is** *chronic obstructive pulmonary disease (COPD).* The woman in the photograph suffers from emphysema, the most common form of COPD. Asthma is another common type of COPD.

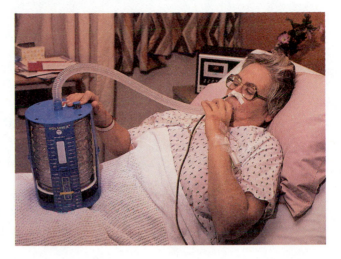

PARKINSON'S DISEASE

Parkinson's disease **is known primarily for its characteristic motor symptoms: very slow walking, difficulty getting into and out of chairs, and a slow hand tremor.** These problems are caused by a deterioration of neurons in the midbrain that produce the neurotransmitter dopamine. Symptoms are treated effectively with the drug L-dopa, which raises the functional level of dopamine in the brain.

For reasons we do not yet understand, roughly 30–50% of the time Parkinson's disease also involves severe cognitive impairment, with additional brain changes similar to Alzheimer's disease. It remains to be seen whether this form of Parkinson's disease actually represents a separate disease.

SENSORY CHANGES

Many changes occurring in the sensory system are noticeable by late life. In the eye, the lens becomes thicker and takes on a yellowish cast. Because of these structural changes, older adults are much more susceptible to glare, take longer to adapt to changes in illumination, experience trouble reading things close to them, and generally require more light to see (Kline & Schieber, 1985). As people age, it takes longer for their eyes to adapt when going from bright light to darkness, or vice versa. This is relevant in many situations, such as while driving at night and having to adjust between bright oncoming headlights and the darkness of the road.

Declines in hearing are among the best-known sensory changes. **There is substantial loss in the ability to hear high-pitched tones, a condition called** *presbycusis.* Although this condition is most severe in older adults, individuals at any age can severely damage their hearing through continued exposure to loud noise, including loud music. For example, listening to loud music through headphones while exercising is particularly harmful, because blood flow to the receptor cells for hearing is increased, making them particularly vulnerable to damage.

Few age changes in taste have been reported (Spitzer, 1988). However, substantial age declines in smell occur after age 70 in many people (Murphy, 1986). These changes can be dangerous; for example, very old adults often have difficulty detecting the substance added to natural gas to make leaks noticeable, which could prove fatal.

Changes in balance make older people increasingly likely to fall (Ochs et al., 1985). However, few systematic age differences have been found in touch, temperature, or pain sensitivity.

The sensory changes people experience have important implications for their everyday lives. Some, such as difficulty reading things close up, are minor annoyances that are easily corrected (by wearing reading glasses). Others are

These steps may not look dangerous to you, but for many older adults they may be. Older adults are much more prone to lose their balance and fall, resulting in potentially serious injuries.

more serious and less easily addressed. For example, the ability to drive a car is affected by changes in vision and in hearing. Because sensory changes may also lead to accidents around the home, it is important to design a safer environment that takes these changes into account. The You May Be Wondering feature summarizes some of these interventions.

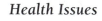

YOU MAY BE WONDERING

Preventing Accidents Involving Older Adults

Accidental injuries become more frequent and serious in later life. Changes in physical and information-processing abilities contribute to increases in accident frequency. For example, the awareness of hazards is dimmed by poor eyesight and hearing. Arthritis and impaired coordination can make older adults unsteady. Medications for many chronic diseases can cause drowsiness or distractibility. How can these problems be avoided?

Many accidents can be prevented by maintaining health through prevention and conditioning. But making some relatively simple environmental changes also helps. For example, falls are the most common cause of accidental serious injury and death among older adults. Here are some steps that can help reduce the potential for falls:

- Illuminate stairways and provide light switches at both the top and the bottom of the stairs.
- Avoid high-gloss floor finishes, due to glare and their tendency to be slippery when wet.
- Provide night lights or bedside remote-control light switches.
- Be sure that both sides of stairways have sturdy handrails.
- Tack down carpeting on stairs, or use nonskid treads.
- Remove throw or area rugs that tend to slide on the floor.
- Arrange furniture and other objects so that they are not obstacles.
- Use grab bars on bathroom walls and nonskid mats or strips in bathtubs.
- Keep outdoor steps and walkways in good repair.   ❧

Health Issues

In Chapter 12, we examined how lifestyle factors can lower the risk of many chronic diseases. The importance of health promotion does not diminish with increasing age. As we will see, lifestyle factors influence sleep, nutrition, and cancer.

SLEEP

Older adults have more trouble sleeping than do younger adults (Bootzin & Engle-Friedman, 1987). Compared to younger adults, older adults report that it takes roughly twice as long to fall asleep, that they get less sleep on an average night, and that they feel more negative effects following a night with little sleep. Some of these problems are due to physical disorders, medication side effects, and the effects of caffeine, nicotine, and stress. **A person's *circadian rhythm*, or sleep-wake cycle, can become disrupted as well.** For example, taking an afternoon nap actually disrupts sleep later that night (Hauri, 1982).

NUTRITION

Under normal circumstances, older adults do not need any vitamin or mineral supplements, as long as they are eating a well-balanced diet (Lundgren, Steen, & Isaksson, 1987). Even though body metabolism declines with age, older

Older adults often complain of difficulty sleeping at night. Sometimes, sleeping problems contribute to naps during the day, which in turn exacerbate the sleeping problems later that night.

adults need to consume the same amounts of proteins and carbohydrates as young adults, because of changes in how readily the body extracts the nutrients from these substances.

CANCER

One of the most important health promotion steps people can take is cancer screening. In many cases, screening procedures involve little more than tests performed in a physician's office (e.g., screening for colon cancer), blood tests (e.g., screening for prostate cancer), or X rays (e.g., screening for breast cancer).

Screening pays off. As you can see in the graph, the risk of getting cancer increases markedly with age. Why this happens is not fully understood. Un-

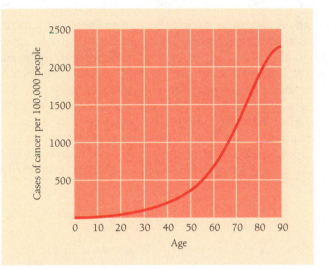

High fat diets of snack food, coupled with smoking and obesity, contribute to an unhealthy lifestyle.

healthy lifestyles (smoking and poor diet), genetics, and exposure to cancer-causing chemicals certainly are important, but they do not fully explain the age-related increase in risk. Early detection of cancer is essential in order to maximize the odds of surviving. However, some physicians are reluctant to use aggressive screening and prevention measures with older adults (List, 1988), perhaps due to the mistaken belief that older patients have lower survival rates. For their part, older adults may be reluctant to request the necessary tests, because they tend not to question their physician's judgment (List, 1988). More attention needs to be paid to such screening programs among older adults.

TEST YOURSELF

1. The biological theory of aging that includes the factors of free radicals and cross-linking is _____.
2. Damaged and dying neurons that collect around a core of protein produce _____.
3. The risk of getting cancer _____ markedly with age.
4. In this section, we have concentrated on the biological forces in development. Think about the other forces (psychological, social, and life-cycle), and list some reasons why scientists have yet to propose a purely biological theory that accounts for all aspects of aging.

Answers: (1) cellular theory, (2) neuritic plaques, (3) increases

Cognitive Processes

LEARNING OBJECTIVES

❧ *What changes occur in attention and reaction time as people age? How do these changes relate to everyday life?*

❧ *What changes occur in memory with age? What can be done to remediate these changes?*

❧ *What is wisdom, and how is it related to age?*

Many older adults need to keep track of several medication regimens. However, each drug has its own pattern; some are taken only with meals, others are taken every eight hours, and still others are taken twice daily. Imagine an older person needing to take medications for arthritis, allergies, and high blood pressure. Keeping these regimens straight is important to avoid potentially dangerous interactions and side effects. This older person faces the problem of remembering to take each medication at the proper time.

Such situations place a heavy demand on cognitive resources, such as attention and memory. In this section, we will examine age-related changes in these and other cognitive processes, such as reaction time, intelligence, and wisdom.

Information Processing

In Chapter 1, we saw that one theoretical framework for studying cognition is information-processing theory. As summarized in the table, this framework provides a way to identify and study the basic mechanisms by which people take in, store, and remember information. We have already seen in Chapters 4 and 6 that information-processing theory has guided much research on cognition in childhood and adolescence. This approach has also been important to investigators examining age-related differences in basic processes such as attention and reaction time.

Perspective	Examples of Theories	Main Ideas	Emphases in Biopsychosocial Framework	Positions on Developmental Issues
Cognitive	Information-processing theory	Thought develops by increases in efficiency at handling information	Emphasis on biological and psychological, less on social and life cycle	Nature–nurture interaction, continuity, individual differences in universal structures

ATTENTION

Imagine yourself sitting at a computer terminal. You are told to press a key as fast as you can every time you see a red X, the target. To make things more difficult, you will also see other letters and colors (green X's, green O's, red O's), which you are to ignore. You will also have no idea where on the screen the target will appear, so you must search for it. **This task is aimed at assessing in-**

dividuals' attentional *selectivity*, **or the ability to pick out important from irrelevant information in the environment.** Adults over age 60 are much slower than adults under age 25 at finding targets in visual arrays like computer screens, especially when the arrays are complex (e.g., when nontargets are similar to targets). However, if a signal is given indicating where on the display the target will appear, these age differences disappear (Plude & Doussard-Roosevelt, 1989). Thus, older adults have trouble locating targets but, once they are found, can identify them as well as younger adults.

A second way that attention has been studied is a familiar one. You have probably encountered many situations in which you had to do two things at once: writing notes while listening to a lecture, talking on the phone while driving, like the man in the photo, listening to a CD while reading a book, and so on. **These situations demand *divided attention*, or performing more than one task at a time.** As long as the two competing tasks are relatively easy, older and younger adults are equally able to perform both fairly well. However, as task difficulty increases, older adults are less able to perform both equally well; younger adults usually do better (McDowd & Craik, 1988).

The research on attention shows that older adults are slower than younger adults at finding targets; they are especially at a disadvantage as tasks become more complicated. However, providing signals or other types of support helps their performance.

REACTION TIME

You are driving home from a friend's house when all of a sudden, a car pulls out of a driveway right into your path. You must hit the brakes as fast as possible or you will have an accident. How quickly can you move your foot from the accelerator to the brake?

This real-life situation is an example of *reaction time*, the speed with which a person can make a particular response. Reaction time is one of the most studied phenomena of aging, and hundreds of studies all point to the same conclusion: People slow down as they get older. In fact, the slowing-with-age finding is so well documented that many researchers accept it as the only universal behavioral change in aging yet discovered (Kail & Salthouse, 1994). Even Garfield feels the effects.

GARFIELD, © 1994 Paws, Inc. Reprinted with permission of Universal Press Syndicate Inc. All rights reserved.

The most important reason that reaction times slow down is that it takes longer for older adults to decide that they need to respond. This is especially true when the situation involves ambiguous information, as shown in the graph. You should notice two things in the graph. First, there is an orderly slowing of responding with age, even when the information presented indicates that a response will definitely be needed (uncertainty level 0). Second, older

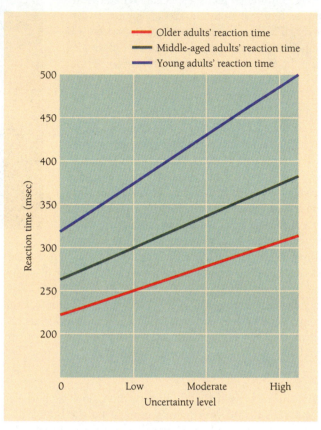

Stelmach, Goggin, and Garcia-Colera, 1987.

adults are more affected by ambiguity; the difference between them and the middle-aged adults increases as the uncertainty level increases (i.e., it is less certain that a response is needed).

Although response slowing is inevitable, the amount of the decline can be reduced if older adults are allowed to practice making quick responses or if they are experienced in the task. For example, Salthouse (1984) showed that although older secretaries' reaction times (measured by how fast they could tap their finger) were slower than those of younger secretaries, their computed typing speed was no slower than that of their younger counterparts. Why? Typing speed is calculated on the basis of words typed corrected for errors; because older typists are more accurate, their final speeds were just as good as those of younger secretaries, whose work tended to include more errors. Also, older secretaries have a greater typing span, meaning that they are better at anticipating what letters come next (Kail & Salthouse, 1994).

INFORMATION PROCESSING IN EVERYDAY LIFE: OLDER DRIVERS

Several bits of information we have considered so far coalesce around a controversial issue: whether older drivers should be screened more closely before their driver's licenses are renewed. This is a sensitive topic. For many people, the automobile is the only reliable means of transportation, and it is also a means of remaining independent. However, age-related changes in vision, hearing, attention, and reaction time do affect people's competence as drivers.

Moreover, the number of older adults is rapidly increasing. Should there be a maximum age for driving? If not, should there be a mandatory battery of sensory and information-processing tests? These questions will spark increasing debate over the next few decades.

Memory

"Memory is power" (Johnson-Laird, 1988, p. 41). Indeed it is, when you think of the importance of remembering tasks, faces, lists, instructions, and our personal past and identity. Perhaps that is why people put a premium on maintaining a good memory in old age; like Dagwood, many older adults use it to judge whether their mind is intact. But as depicted in the cartoon, poor memory is often viewed as an inevitable part of aging. Many people believe that forgetting a loaf of bread at the store when one is 25 is all right, but forgetting it

BLONDIE, © 1993. Reprinted with special permission of King Features Syndicate.

when one is 65 is cause for alarm—a sign of Alzheimer's disease or some other malady. In this section, we will sort out the myth and the reality of memory changes with age.

WHAT CHANGES?

In order to understand age differences in memory, we need to distinguish between laboratory tasks and real-world tasks. Laboratory tasks, used most often in research on memory, include such things as learning lists of words or remembering text passages. Real-world tasks include such things as remembering how to get home or remembering to purchase gasoline on the way. Almost all of the data we have on adult age differences in memory are based on laboratory tasks; we know much less about the nature of age differences in real-world situations (Verhaeghen, Marcoen, & Goosens, 1993).

On laboratory memory tasks, older adults almost always perform worse than younger adults when tested in a *free recall* paradigm in which they are simply asked to report everything they can remember about the material they learned. Older adults have shorter memory spans and recall substantially fewer items from lists and text passages (Verhaeghen et al., 1993). These age differences are large; for example, more than 80% of a sample of adults in their 20s do better than adults in their 70s. These differences are not reliably lowered by slower presentation, giving cues or reminders during recall, or providing specific strategies (such as imagery) during study.

All is not bleak, though. **Age differences diminish for tasks requiring *recognition* of the correct item from a list of correct and incorrect choices, such as a multiple-choice test.** Also, age differences are considerably smaller (and sometimes are eliminated) when older adults have graduated from college or have high verbal ability (Meyer & Rice, 1989).

Remembering when to take out the trash is an example of a real-world memory task.

As mentioned earlier, the pessimistic view of memory aging derived from laboratory studies may not apply to the real world. A good example of this is seen in research by Kirasic and Allen (1985), who examined younger and older adults' ability to find items in familiar and unfamiliar grocery stores. As you can see in the graph, older adults were actually better than younger adults in fa-

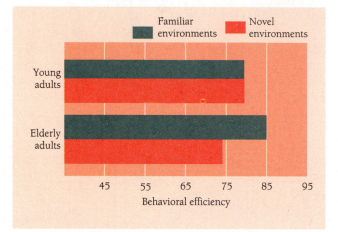

miliar stores, while the opposite was true for novel stores. Other research on real-world memory problems, such as how well people remember appointments and tasks, also shows either no age differences or better performance by older adults (West, 1986).

THE IMPACT OF BELIEFS ABOUT MEMORY AGING

Regardless of the exact findings from actual studies of memory, there is widespread belief that it inevitably declines. This is significant, because research shows that what adults believe about their memory ability is related to how well they perform (Cavanaugh, in press). This relation is seen primarily in how much effort people exert trying to remember. For example, people who believe that their memory is good work harder at remembering than people who believe their memory is poor. Moreover, these beliefs are also related to the assumptions people make about the degree to which memory (or other cognitive abilities) is "supposed" to change (Cavanaugh, Feldman, & Hertzog, 1995). For example, if you think that memory is supposed to get much worse as you get older, then your estimate of how much your memory has declined will be much greater than an estimate by someone who thinks memory should decline only a little with age.

Overall, research on memory beliefs shows that although some changes in memory are normal, people can essentially convince themselves that these changes are much worse and pervasive than they really are. It may even be the case that altering your central beliefs about memory aging may help you develop compensatory strategies that lower the magnitude of these changes, or at least help compensate for them (Cavanaugh, in press).

WHEN IS MEMORY CHANGE ABNORMAL?

Because people are concerned that memory failures may reflect disease, identifying true cases of memory-impairing disease is extremely important. Differentiating normal and abnormal memory changes is usually accomplished through a wide array of tests.

A first step is to find out whether the memory problems are interfering with everyday functioning. Normal age-related memory changes are not severe enough to cause difficulty in completing daily living tasks such as finding the way home or knowing one's spouse's name. When these kinds of problems appear, it is appropriate to suspect a serious underlying reason.

Once a serious problem is suspected, the next step is to obtain a thorough examination. This should include a complete physical and neurological examination and a complete battery of neuropsychological tests. These may help identify the nature and extent of the underlying problem and provide information about what steps, if any, can be taken to alleviate the difficulties.

The most important point to keep in mind is that there is no magic number of times that a person must forget something before it becomes a matter for concern. Indeed, many memory-impairing diseases progress slowly, and poor memory performance may only be noticed gradually over an extended period of time. The best course is to have the person examined; only with complete and thorough testing can these concerns be checked appropriately.

REMEDIATING MEMORY PROBLEMS

Remember the person at the beginning of this section who had to figure out how to remember when to take several different medications? In the face of normal age-related declines, how could this problem be solved?

Support programs can be designed for people to help them remember. Sometimes, as in the example, people experiencing normal age-related memory changes need extra help because of the high memory demands they face. At other times, people need help because the memory changes they are experiencing are greater than normal.

Camp and colleagues (1993) developed the E-I-E-I-O framework to handle both situations. The E-I-E-I-O framework combines two types of memory: explicit and implicit. **Explicit memory involves the conscious and intentional recollection of information; remembering this definition on an exam is one example. Implicit memory involves effortless and unconscious recollection of information; knowing that stop signs are red octagons is usually not something that people need to exert effort to remember when encountering one on the road.** The framework also includes two types of memory aids. **External aids are memory aids that rely on environmental resources, such as notebooks or calendars. Internal aids are memory aids that rely on mental processes, such as imagery.** The experience in the framework that comes with suddenly remembering something is the O that follows these E's and I's. As you can see in the table, the E-I-E-I-O framework allows different types of memory to be combined with different types of memory aids to provide a broad range of intervention options to help people remember.

Type of Memory	Type of Memory Aid	
	External	*Internal*
Explicit	Appointment book	Mental imagery
	Grocery list	Rote rehearsal
Implicit	Color-coded maps	Spaced retrieval
	Sandpaper letters	Conditioning

In general, explicit-external interventions are the most frequently used, probably because they are easy to use and widely available (Cavanaugh, Grady,

& Perlmutter, 1983). For example, virtually everyone owns an address book, and small notepads are sold in hundreds of stores.

But explicit-external interventions have other important applications, too. The medication problem is best solved with an explicit-external intervention: a pillbox that is divided into compartments corresponding to days of the week and different times of the day. Research shows that this type of pillbox is the easiest to load and results in the fewest errors (Park et al., 1991). Memory interventions like this can help older adults maintain their independence. Nursing homes also use explicit-external interventions, such as bulletin boards with the date and weather conditions, or activities charts like the one shown in the photograph, to help residents keep in touch with current events.

Later, we will see how the E-I-E-I-O framework provides insight into how people with Alzheimer's disease can be helped to improve their memory. At that point, we will consider spaced retrieval, an implicit-internal intervention. In the meantime, see how many different categories of memory interventions you can discover. Check the See for Yourself feature for details.

SEE FOR YOURSELF

Helping People Remember

The text lists several different ways in which people's memory can be helped. Perhaps you never thought about how many memory aids you use in your everyday life, such as notebooks, calendars, lists, setting things by the door, asking your friends, rereading things, and so forth.

This real-world exercise has two parts. First, using the E-I-E-I-O framework, analyze your own daily routine and list all of the ways you help yourself remember. (You may be surprised at how many different ways you do this!) Next, do the same for a few of your friends and relatives. Try to make sure you talk with people of different ages. Tabulate your results and share them with your classmates. Which cell in the table contains the aids that people use the most? See for yourself. 🦃

Training Intellectual Abilities

In Chapter 12, we saw that intelligence reaches its overall peak in middle age, with evidence of declines in performance thereafter. Are these declines an inevitable part of aging, or can they be slowed or even eliminated?

This question provided the basis for Willis and Schaie's (in press) important series of studies examining how much older adults' performance could be boosted through direct intervention and training. Because all of their participants came from the Seattle Longitudinal Study, described in Chapter 9, Willis and Schaie had longitudinal data on each person's past performance. To see how well training worked, two groups of people were identified. One group included people who had shown significant declines in inductive reasoning (figuring out the general concept from a list of specific examples) or spatial ability (being able to create three-dimensional images from two-dimensional representations) over a span of 14 years. The other group included people whose performance on these abilities had remained roughly constant over the same period.

Willis and her colleagues provided training in both abilities. Their results were impressive: Roughly two-thirds of the people showed significant improvements in performance. About 40% of the people who had previously declined improved so much that, after training, they performed as well as they had 14 years earlier! These training effects were maintained over time; seven years after their initial training, people were still performing well. This was especially true for people who had previously shown declining performance.

These results provide strong evidence that declines in performance on intelligence tests are reversible in at least some areas. However, much research remains; we do not know whether these impressive gains would also be found for other abilities. Still, Willis and Schaie's findings provide reason for hope that, for some abilities in some people, intellectual decline may not be inevitable.

Wisdom

For thousands of years, cultures around the world have greatly admired people who were wise. Tales of wise people, usually older adults, have been passed down from generation to generation to teach lessons about important matters of life and love (Chinen, 1989). Maria, the woman in the third vignette at the beginning of the chapter, knows these lessons and freely passes them on to others. What is it about these truths that makes someone who knows them wise?

From a psychological perspective, wisdom has been viewed as involving three cognitive processes (Kramer, 1990): practical and social intelligence, such as the ability to solve real-world problems; insight into the deeper meanings underlying a given situation; and awareness of the relative, uncertain, and paradoxical nature of human problems, reflected in postformal thinking (see Chapter 9). A growing body of research has been examining these aspects.

Based on years of research using in-depth think-aloud interviews with young, middle-aged, and older adults about normal and unusual problems that people face, Baltes and Staudinger (1993) describe four characteristics of wisdom:

- Wisdom deals with important and/or difficult matters of life and the human condition.
- Wisdom is truly "superior" knowledge, judgment, and advice.

DEIDRE A. KRAMER

"Cognition and affect work in concert to allow for effective, or wise, social action within the life course."

- Wisdom is knowledge with extraordinary scope, depth, and balance, applicable to specific situations.
- Wisdom, when used, is well intended and combines mind and virtue (character).

The researchers used this framework to discover that people who are wise are experts in the basic issues in life (Baltes & Staudinger, 1993). Wise people know a great deal about how to conduct life, how to interpret life events, and what life means.

Research shows that wisdom is not the same thing as creativity. Wisdom is the growth of expertise and insight, whereas creativity is the generation of a new solution to a problem (Simonton, 1990). Baltes and Staudinger (1993) have shown that wisdom may not be the province of older adults exclusively. For example, one study had people respond to life planning problems like the following. A 15-year-old girl wants to get married right away. What should she consider and do? Answers were then analyzed in terms of the degree to which they reflect wisdom. Contrary to what many people expect, there is no association between age and wise answers. Whether a person is wise depends on whether he or she has extensive life experience with the type of problem given (Smith & Baltes, 1990).

Research based on cognitive developmental changes in adulthood, such as those discussed in Chapter 9, has uncovered other aspects in the growth of wisdom. According to several investigators, a wise person is one who is able to integrate thinking, feeling, and acting into a coherent approach to a problem (Kramer, 1990; Orwoll & Perlmutter, 1990). This research implies that empathy or compassion is an important characteristic of wise people. They are able to overcome automatic responses so as to show concern for core human experiences and values (Pascual-Leone, 1990). Thus, wise people are able to see through situations and get to the heart of the matter, rather than being caught in the superficial aspects. Indeed, there is some evidence that, compared to young and middle-aged adults, older adults are more generous in donating their time and money to charity and express greater social concern (Haan, Milsap, & Hartka, 1986).

So what specific factors help one become wise? Baltes (1993) identifies three factors: (a) *general personal conditions,* such as mental ability; (b) *specific expertise conditions,* such as mentoring or practice; and (c) *facilitative life contexts,* such as education or leadership experience. Other researchers point to additional criteria. For example, Kramer (1990) argues that the *integration of affect and cognition* that occurs during adulthood results in the ability to act wisely. Personal growth during adulthood, reflecting Erikson's concepts of generativity and integrity, helps foster the process as well. All of these factors take time. Thus, although growing old is no guarantee of wisdom, it does provide the time that, if used well, will provide a supportive context for it.

Cognitive Changes in Later Life

FORCES IN ACTION

In this section, we have seen considerable evidence that the biopsychosocial framework is useful in understanding cognitive aging. Normal aging brings decline in several abilities, whereas other skills remain largely intact or even improve. Why is there such variation in developmental trends?

Biological forces operate to reduce the efficiency of basic information-processing abilities, primarily through normal changes in the brain. Coupled with the psychological forces of less use and the social forces of lower cognitive demands, these changes can help account for declines in some areas, such as divided attention. However, physiological changes in the brain do not affect all areas equally; psychological forces create greater practice with some skills; and social needs to maintain contact with the world mean that some skills, as in areas of expertise, continue to operate well.

Life-cycle forces are also important in understanding cognitive changes in later life. The same cognitive event often has very different meanings, depending where in life people are. For example, not being as efficient at performing two tasks at once (a typical divided-attention situation) may be only mildly annoying and easily dismissed in young adulthood, but it might be seen as a sign of cognitive slippage by an older adult. Such changes in interpretation even of apparently universal events, such as forgetting something at the grocery store, become even more common as people reach late life and worry about whether they may be getting Alzheimer's disease, a topic we will explore next.   ❧

TEST YOURSELF

1. As long as the competing tasks in a test of divided attention are easy, older adults perform _____ younger adults.
2. Compared to age differences in free recall performance, age differences in recognition memory performance are _____.
3. Two intellectual abilities that have been trained successfully in older adults are _____.
4. Three factors that help a person become wise are _____.
5. How would the view that wisdom involves life experience fit into the discussion of expertise in Chapter 12?

Mental Health and Interaction

LEARNING OBJECTIVES

❧ *How does depression in older adults differ from depression in younger adults? How is it diagnosed and treated?*

❧ *How are anxiety disorders treated in older adults?*

❧ *What is Alzheimer's disease? How is it diagnosed and managed? What causes it?*

Suppose that Mary, the woman in the Real People feature, were a relative of yours. How would you deal with the situation? How would you have figured out that the way she was behaving was not normal? What would you do to try to improve Mary's life?

What's the Matter with Mary?

Mary lived by herself for 30 years after her husband died. For all but the last 5 years or so, she managed very well. Her children, who lived in various parts of the country, visited her when they could. Friends down the street looked in on her and cooked meals for her occasionally. Little by little, family members and

REAL PEOPLE

friends began noticing that Mary wasn't behaving quite right. For example, her memory slipped, she sounded confused sometimes, and her moods changed without warning. Some people attributed these changes to the fact that Mary was in her 80s. But when they discovered that she sometimes forgot things in the refrigerator and then ate them even though they had grown moldy, and that she occasionally ate other strange things, they began to think differently. The family ultimately realized that she could no longer care for herself; help had to be found. She moved to a group home but continued to deteriorate. She started having trouble remembering things from even a few minutes before. Names of family members became mixed up at first and later forgotten entirely. She began to wander. Finally, Mary had to be placed in a nursing home. The times when she was living in the present became fewer. Her physical abilities continued to decline, until she eventually could not feed herself. Toward the end of her life, she could not eat solid food and had to be force-fed. Mary died from Alzheimer's disease after about 15 years of slow, agonizing decline.   🙠

Every day, families turn to mental health professionals for help in dealing with psychological problems their aging relatives are having. Unfortunately, myths interfere with appropriate mental health diagnoses and interventions for older adults. For example, many people mistakenly believe that nearly all older adults are either depressed, demented, or both. When they observe older adults behaving in these ways, they take no action because they believe that nothing can be done.

In this section, we will see that such beliefs are wrong. Only a minority of older adults have mental health problems, and most such problems respond to therapy. Sometimes these problems manifest themselves differently in younger and older adults, so we need to know what to look for. Accurate diagnosis is essential. Let's examine some of the most widely known disorders: depression, anxiety disorders, and Alzheimer's disease.

Depression

In Chapter 8, we saw that when adolescents complain about irritability, feel sad, and have low self-esteem, it is likely that they are depressed. We also saw that depression is sometimes triggered by a life event that leads to a decrease in positive reinforcement, creating a vicious cycle of learned helplessness. Do these same characteristics apply to depression in later life, or are there important differences?

HOW IS DEPRESSION DIAGNOSED?

Depression in later life is usually diagnosed on the basis of two clusters of symptoms. In both cases, the symptoms must have been present for at least two weeks. **As with adolescents, the most prominent symptom of depression is feeling sad or down, termed *dysphoria*.** Whereas younger people are likely to label these feelings as "feeling depressed," older adults may refer to them as "feeling pessimistic" or "feeling helpless" (Fry, 1986). Older adults are also more likely than younger people to appear apathetic and expressionless, to confine themselves to bed, to neglect themselves, and to make derogatory statements about themselves.

The second cluster of symptoms includes physical changes such as loss of appetite, insomnia, and trouble breathing (Fry, 1986). In young people, these symptoms are almost always a sign of some underlying psychological problem.

But in older adults, they may simply reflect normal, age-related changes. Thus, older adults' physical symptoms of depression must be evaluated very carefully.

An important step in diagnosis is ruling out other possible causes of the symptoms. For example, other health problems, neurological disorders, medications, metabolic conditions, and substance abuse can all cause behaviors that resemble depression. An important criterion to be established is that the symptoms interfere with daily life; clinical depression involves significant impairment of daily living.

WHAT CAUSES DEPRESSION?

There are two main groups of theories about the causes of depression. As noted in Chapter 8, one focuses on biological and physiological processes, particularly on imbalances in specific neurotransmitters. Because most neurotransmitter levels decline with age, some researchers believe that depression in later life is likely to be a biochemical problem (Thompson & Gallagher, 1986). The general view that depression has a biochemical basis underlies current approaches to drug therapies. We mentioned these briefly in Chapter 8, but they will be described in greater detail in the next section.

A second set of theories focuses on psychosocial factors, such as loss and internal belief systems. Several types of loss have been associated with depression, including loss of a spouse, a job, or good health. How a person interprets a loss, rather than the event itself, causes depression (Gaylord & Zung, 1987). **In this approach, *internal belief systems*, or what one tells oneself about why certain things are happening, are emphasized as the cause of depression.** For example, experiencing an unpredictable and uncontrollable event such as the death of a spouse may cause depression because you believe the event happened to you because you are a bad person (Beck, 1967). People who are depressed tend to believe that they are personally responsible for the bad things that happen to them, that things are unlikely to get better, and that their whole life is a shambles.

This view is related to the learned helplessness explanation of depression, discussed in Chapter 8. Older adults are likely to view themselves as under the control of external, environmental events, as discussed in Chapter 14.

Compared to rates of 3–10% in adolescents, the chance of a person ever experiencing clinical depression at some point in adulthood is around 15%. Contrary to popular belief, however, the rate of severe depression declines from young adulthood to old age (LaRue, Dessonville, & Jarvik, 1985; Nolen-Hoeksema, 1988).

HOW IS DEPRESSION TREATED?

Regardless how severe depression is, people benefit from treatment, often through a combination of medication and psychotherapy (Thompson & Gallagher, 1986).

Drug therapies work by altering the balance of neurotransmitters in the brain. **For very severe cases of depression, medications such as *heterocyclic antidepressants (HCAs), monoamine oxidase (MAO) inhibitors,* or *selective serotonin reuptake inhibitors (SSRIs)* can be administered.** For many years, HCAs were known as *tricyclic antidepressants,* because this was the only form available, but the introduction of monocyclic, bicyclic, and tetracyclic drugs led to the change in name (Berkow, 1987). Although they are widely prescribed, HCAs cannot be taken if the person is also taking medications to control hypertension or has certain metabolic conditions. MAO inhibitors cause

Although older adults may be reluctant to seek out psychotherapy, it is an effective approach for treating depression, as is the case here, as well as other mental health problems.

dangerous and potentially fatal interactions with foods containing tyramine or dopamine, such as cheddar cheese, wine, and chicken liver. Consequently, MAO inhibitors are usually used only if HCAs are ineffective or cannot be prescribed. Selective serotonin reuptake inhibitors (SSRIs) gained wide popularity beginning in the late 1980s, because they have the lowest overall side effects of any antidepressant. SSRIs work by boosting the level of serotonin, which is a neurotransmitter involved in regulating moods. One of the SSRIs, Prozac, has been the subject of controversy, as it has been linked in a small number of cases with the serious side effect of high levels of agitation. Other SSRIs, such as Zoloft and Serzone, appear to have fewer adverse reactions.

Psychotherapy is a popular approach to treating depression, based on the idea that focusing on the psychological aspects of depression is helpful. Two forms of psychotherapy have been shown to be effective with older adults. **The basic idea in *behavior therapy* is that depressed people experience too few rewards or reinforcements from their environment.** Thus, the goal of behavior therapy is to increase the good things that happen and minimize the negative things (Lewinsohn, 1975). Often, this is accomplished by having people increase their activities; simply by doing more, the likelihood that something nice will happen is increased. Additionally, behavior therapy seeks to get people to reduce the negative things that happen by learning how to avoid them. The increase in positive events and decrease in negative events comes about through practice and homework assignments during the course of therapy, such as going out more or joining a club to meet new people.

A second effective approach is *cognitive therapy*, which is based on the idea that maladaptive beliefs or cognitions about oneself are responsible for depression. From this perspective, a depressed person views the self as unworthy and inadequate, the world as insensitive and ungratifying, and the future as bleak and unpromising (Beck et al., 1979). In cognitive therapy, a person is taught how to recognize these thoughts and to reevaluate the self, the world, and the future more realistically, resulting in a change in the underlying beliefs.

The most important fact to keep in mind about depression is that it *is* treatable. Thus, if an older person behaves in ways that could indicate depression, it is a good idea to have him or her examined by a mental health professional. Even if it turns out not to be depression, another underlying and possibly treatable condition may be uncovered.

Anxiety Disorders

Imagine you are about to give a speech to an audience of several hundred people. During the last few minutes before you begin, you start to feel nervous, your heart begins to pound, and your palms get sweaty. **These feelings, common even to veteran speakers, are similar to those experienced more frequently by people with *anxiety disorders*.**

Anxiety disorders include problems such as feelings of severe anxiety for no apparent reason, phobias with regard to specific things or places, and obsessive-compulsive disorders (in which thoughts or actions are repeatedly performed). Anxiety disorders are diagnosed in as many as 10% of older women and 5% of older men (Cohen, 1990). The reasons for this gender difference are unknown.

Common to all anxiety disorders are the physical symptoms just described. They occur in adults of all ages but are particularly common in older adults, due to loss of health, relocation stress, isolation, fear of losing independence, and many other reasons (Fry, 1986).

Anxiety disorders can be treated with medication and psychotherapy. The most commonly used medications are the benzodiazepines, which include the drugs Valium and Librium. These drugs must be monitored very carefully in older adults, because the amount needed to treat the disorder is very low and the potential for side effects is great. For older adults, the treatment of choice is psychotherapy, especially relaxation therapy. Such therapy is highly effective, is easily learned, and presents a technique that is useful in many situations (e.g., falling asleep at night).

To this point, we have focused on psychopathologies that can be treated effectively. In the next section, we will consider types that cannot be treated at present, progressively worsening until the person dies. Because they are initially noticed as a result of behavioral changes, they are appropriately considered to be psychopathological.

For older adults, being depressed may result in physical and social isolation. In general, the symptoms of depression in older adults differ in important ways from those seen in younger adults.

Dementia: Alzheimer's Disease

Arguably the most serious condition associated with aging is *dementia*, a family of diseases involving serious impairment of behavioral and cognitive functioning. As we saw in the Real People feature, dementia sometimes causes people to change from thinking, communicative human beings to confused, bedridden victims unable to recognize their family members and close friends. Roughly 4.5 million older adults in the United States (about 10% of people over age 65) have some type of dementia. Because of the rapidly increasing number of older adults, the number of cases is expected to double over the next several decades. However, it is clear that only a minority of older adults have dementia; the belief that dementia is an inevitable part of aging is erroneous.

The term *dementia* refers to a group of about a dozen related disorders, all of which are characterized by cognitive and behavioral deficits due to changes in the brain. Of these disorders, Alzheimer's disease is the most common.

WHAT ARE THE SYMPTOMS OF ALZHEIMER'S DISEASE?

Robert, in the fourth chapter-opening vignette, is unfortunately showing some of the key symptoms of *Alzheimer's disease*: gradual declines in memory, learning, attention, and judgment; confusion as to time and place; difficulties in communicating and finding the right words; decline in personal hygiene and self-care skills; inappropriate social behavior; and changes in personality. These symptoms may be vague in the beginning, but as the disease progresses, they become much more pronounced and are exhibited continuously.

By the middle stages of the disease, problems escalate further. Some victims begin to wander away from their homes and cannot remember how to return. Paranoid and other accusatory behaviors develop. Spouses become strangers. Victims may not even recognize themselves in a mirror; they wonder who is looking back at them. **In its advanced stages, Alzheimer's disease of-**

ten causes *incontinence* (the loss of bladder or bowel control) and total loss of mobility. Like the man in the photo, victims become completely dependent on others for care. It is at this point that many families seek out facilities such as adult day care centers, in order to provide a safe environment for their family member while the caregiver is at work.

The rate of deterioration in Alzheimer's disease is highly variable, although progression is usually faster the earlier in adulthood it is diagnosed (Bondareff, 1983). It is difficult to generalize about the level of a person's impairment based solely on time since diagnosis. Rather, the level of functioning should be assessed on an individual basis.

HOW IS ALZHEIMER'S DISEASE DIAGNOSED?

Absolute certainty that a person has Alzheimer's disease cannot be achieved while the individual is still alive. Definitive diagnosis must be based on an autopsy of the brain after death, because the defining criteria for diagnosing Alzheimer's disease involve documenting large numbers of structural changes in neurons that can only be observed under a microscope after brain tissue has been removed and specially prepared.

So how can it be determined whether a person probably has Alzheimer's disease while he or she is still alive? Although not definitive, the number and severity of behavioral changes lead clinicians to make fairly accurate diagnoses of *probable* Alzheimer's disease. But the accuracy depends on a broad-based and thorough series of medical and psychological tests, including complete blood tests, metabolic and neurological tests, and neuropsychological tests. A great deal of diagnostic work goes into ruling out virtually all other possible causes of the observed symptoms. This effort is essential. Because Alzheimer's disease is an incurable and fatal disease, every treatable cause of the symptoms must be explored first. In essence, the diagnosis of probable Alzheimer's disease is one of exclusion.

Differential diagnosis (recognizing the difference between one disease and another) of Alzheimer's disease is extremely important because many

other treatable diseases, sometimes called *pseudodementias*, can mimic the symptoms of early Alzheimer's disease. For example, severe depression and some types of vitamin deficiencies can cause serious memory impairments. Thyroid deficiencies, some brain tumors in the temporal lobe, and strokes in certain areas of the brain can cause behavioral outbursts. Without a complete battery of medical and neuropsychological tests, these conditions may be misdiagnosed as Alzheimer's disease and left untreated.

In an attempt to be as thorough as possible, clinicians usually interview family members about their perceptions of the observed behavioral symptoms. Most clinicians view this information as essential to understanding the history of the difficulties the person is experiencing. However, research indicates that spouses are usually inaccurate in their assessments of the level of their partner's impairment (McGuire & Cavanaugh, 1992). In part, this inaccuracy is due to lack of knowledge about the disease. Also, spouses wish to portray themselves as in control, either by denying that the symptoms are in fact severe or by exaggerating the severity to give the appearance that they are coping well in a very difficult situation. Still, some spouses provide highly accurate descriptions of their partner's symptoms. However, because of the potential for error, family reports should not be the only source of information about the person's ability to function.

A great deal of attention has been given to the development of more definitive tests for Alzheimer's disease while the person is still alive. **Much of this work has focused on *amyloid*, a protein that is produced in abnormally high levels in the Alzheimer's patients, perhaps causing the neurofibrillary tangles and neuritic plaques described earlier.** Research is progressing toward developing a way to measure amyloid concentrations in cerebrospinal fluid and blood. Additional work focuses on testing for the presence or absence of specific genes, a topic to which we now turn.

WHAT CAUSES ALZHEIMER'S DISEASE?

We do not know for sure what causes Alzheimer's disease. Over the years, several hypotheses have been offered, such as aluminum deposits in the brain and a slow-acting virus. Although some research found higher than normal concentrations of aluminum in the brains of some people with Alzheimer's disease, this was not true in all cases. Thus, aluminum deposits cannot be the only cause, or perhaps even one of the causes. No conclusive evidence about a virus has yet been reported.

Currently, most research is concentrating on identifying genetic links. The evidence is growing that at least some forms of Alzheimer's disease are inherited, based on studies of family trees, relatives, and identical twins. Indeed, several sites on various chromosomes have been tentatively identified as being involved in the transmission of Alzheimer's disease. If researchers can identify the gene(s) responsible for Alzheimer's disease, it would be possible to develop a test to see if people had the inheritance pattern.

One potential dilemma about such a test involves the possible inheritance patterns of the genes responsible for Alzheimer's disease. As noted in Chapter 2, genetic inheritance patterns vary from straightforward autosomal dominant patterns, in which inheriting one gene guarantees having the condition, to polygenic patterns, in which having the condition depends on having a complex set of interacting genes. In the case of autosomal dominant patterns, a positive test for the genetic marker means that the person is destined to get the disease. This situation already exists for some other diseases. **For example,** persons at risk for *Huntington's disease*, another type of dementia, can find out if they have the gene responsible for the disease through a blood test. Persons testing positive will get the disease, which usually strikes during young adulthood or middle age and is fatal. Thus, the development of genetic tests for Alzheimer's disease will provide not only a potential way to diagnose it, but also some difficult personal choices for people. For example, individuals who know they have the genes responsible for the disease may be faced with difficult decisions about having children. Genetic counseling programs, which currently focus mostly on diseases of childhood, would need to be expanded to help individuals face decisions about diseases occurring later in life.

WHAT CAN BE DONE FOR VICTIMS OF ALZHEIMER'S DISEASE?

Even though Alzheimer's disease is incurable, much can be done to alleviate its symptoms. Most of the research has been focused on drugs aimed at improving memory. **One such drug, *tacrine*, was approved by the U.S. Food and Drug Administration for use in persons with Alzheimer's disease.** In general, tacrine results in a modest (10–15%) improvement in performance on free recall tasks involving lists of words, but it has not been shown to be effective in real-world situations involving memory, such as remembering how to get home. Moreover, tacrine is ineffective in the majority of cases, and it has some serious side effects, such as liver toxicity, which may be fatal. Unfortunately, no drug currently available reverses the memory symptoms permanently (Abrams & Berkow, 1990).

In addition to memory drugs, medications to combat hostile behavior symptoms are widely used. **These drugs, such as *thioridazine* and *haloperidol*, are the same ones used to treat severe psychotic disorders in adults.** Additionally, antidepressants are effective in alleviating the depression that often accompanies Alzheimer's disease during its early stages. All of these medications must be used carefully, as older adults have a high risk of side effects such as severe motor impairment and increased cognitive impairment (Salzman, 1984).

Numerous effective behavioral and educational interventions have also been developed. **One behavioral intervention, based on the E-I-E-I-O approach to memory intervention discussed earlier in this chapter, involves using the implicit-internal memory intervention called *spaced retrieval*.** Adapted by Camp and colleagues (Camp & McKitrick, 1991), spaced retrieval involves teaching persons with Alzheimer's disease to remember new information by gradually increasing the time between retrieval attempts. How this is done is explained in the Spotlight on Research feature. This easy, almost magical technique has been used to teach names of staff members and other information; it holds considerable potential for broad application.

SPOTLIGHT ON RESEARCH

What's My Name? Memory Training in Alzheimer's Disease

Iris, an Alzheimer's disease victim, looked sternly at the researchers who had come to her day care center. "I know you're going to ask me for Jane's name." On the surface, this statement does not seem particularly meaningful. Yet only a month before, Iris could not remember Jane's name; in fact, she seemed incapable of learning it at all. What happened?

Iris learned Jane's name through a procedure called *spaced retrieval*. Adapted by Camp and colleagues (Camp & McKitrick, 1991), spaced retrieval is an example of an implicit-internal intervention that helps even people with severe cognitive impairment learn new information. How does it work?

The secret to spaced retrieval is progressively increasing the amount of time between the recall of the target information (e.g., a person's name). For example, the instructor shows the client a picture of a person and says the person's name. After an initial recall interval of 5 seconds, the instructor asks the client to remember the name. As long as the client remembers correctly, recall intervals are increased to 10, 20, 40, 60, 90, 120, 150 seconds, and so on. If the client forgets the target information, the correct answer is provided, and the next recall interval is decreased to the length of the last correct trial. During the interval, the instructor engages the client in conversation to prevent active rehearsal of the information.

Spaced retrieval works like magic, because even people who earlier could not retain information for more than 60 seconds can remember names taught through this technique for very long periods (e.g., 5 weeks or more). It appears that many types of information can be taught, making spaced retrieval a flexible intervention. Spaced retrieval can be used in virtually any setting, such as playing games or normal conversation, making it comfortable and nonthreatening to the client.

Although more work is needed to continue refining the technique, spaced retrieval is one of the most promising non-drug memory interventions for people with cognitive impairments.   ❧

CAMERON J. CAMP

"It is simply not enough to show that a person with dementia has a problem. We must become capable of helping them overcome it."

Most educational programs for caregivers of Alzheimer's victims teach techniques for improving self-care skills in persons with Alzheimer's disease, such as how to assist with toileting. Additionally, caregivers can be taught how to structure the environment to provide cognitive support, such as by labeling kitchen cabinets with their contents. These programs are very effective at reducing the stress caregivers experience, as well as helping to maintain the independence of persons with Alzheimer's disease as long as possible (Cavanaugh et al., 1994).

Dealing with persons who have Alzheimer's disease is highly stressful, as we will see in Chapter 14. Here, it should be noted that any intervention aimed at improving the victim's functioning may also have positive benefits for the caregiver. For example, research has indicated that caregivers are most stressed by problems that they are ill equipped to handle (Cavanaugh et al., 1994). Interventions that address these problems may have the additional benefit of lowering caregivers' stress.

In designing interventions for persons with Alzheimer's disease, the guiding principle should be optimizing the person's functioning. Regardless of the level of impairment, attempts should be made to help the person cope as well as possible with the symptoms. The key is helping all persons maintain their dignity as human beings. One of the best ways to find out about the latest medical and behavioral research, as well as about the educational and support programs available in your area, is to call the Alzheimer's Association number listed in the advertisement.

TEST YOURSELF

1. Compared to younger adults, older adults are less likely to label their feelings of sadness as _____.
2. A form of psychotherapy that focuses on people's beliefs about the self, the world, and the future is called _____.
3. Relaxation techniques are an effective therapy for _____.
4. The only way to definitively diagnose Alzheimer's disease is through _____.
5. Twisted fibers called _____ occur in the axon of neurons in persons with Alzheimer's disease.
6. After reading about the symptoms of Alzheimer's disease, what do you think would be the most stressful aspects of caring for a parent who has the disease? (You may want to refer back to the section on caring for aging parents in Chapter 12.)

Putting It All Together

Someone once observed that, all things considered, growing old is much better than the alternative. Based on what we have seen concerning the personal contexts of aging, it indeed is much better in many respects (though not totally rosy, to be sure). We began by wondering why people like Sarah live a long time and others do not, and we learned that many factors influence longevity. We saw how genetic and environmental factors interact (the biopsychosocial model strikes again!). We encountered Frank, the active 80-year old, who served as an example of how maintaining fitness throughout life has an important influence on health in the later years. We also discovered how physical changes that began in midlife continue to affect functioning as a person keeps growing older. Despite normative changes in recent memory ability and in some aspects of intelligence, some older people like Maria have gained wisdom through their experience in living. Cognitive changes in later life are not all a matter of decline. Finally, we saw that psychopathologies can exact a terrible toll among older adults; they must be properly diagnosed in order to separate treatable from untreatable conditions. People like Robert, who probably has Alzheimer's disease, must be examined carefully to identify the most likely cause of the problems.

Many of the stereotypes society holds about older adults are simply untrue. For one thing, only a minority of people ever get Alzheimer's disease, whereas the clear majority continue to demonstrate improvement in some cognitive functions such as wisdom. Old age does not imply the across-the-board decline that is often portrayed. Indeed, some segments of society are beginning to understand the beauty and importance of older adults.

Our initial foray into later life reveals the complexity of older adults. Just as it is impossible to characterize all children, adolescents, or young adults as being all alike, older adults are also a very diverse group of people. This diversity will continue to be in evidence in the next chapter.

Thinking about Development

1. How do the physical changes in old age reflect the interaction of nature and nurture (as discussed in Chapter 1)?

2. How does wisdom reflect postformal thinking (as discussed in Chapter 9)?

3. Using information on memory from Chapters 4, 6, 9, 12, and 13, try constructing a description of memory across the life span.

4. How does depression reflect the interaction of biological, psychological, social, and life-cycle forces?

Answers: (1) depression, (2) cognitive therapy, (3) anxiety disorders, (4) brain autopsy, (5) neurofibrillary tangles

Summary

What Are Older Adults Like?

The Demographics of Aging

■   The number of older adults is growing rapidly, especially the number of people over age 80. In the future, older adults will be more ethnically diverse and better educated than they are now.

How Long Will You Live?

■   *Average life expectancy* has increased dramatically in this century, due mainly to improvements in health care. *Useful life expectancy* refers to the number of years that a person is free from debilitating disease. *Maximum life expectancy* is the longest time any human can live. Genetic factors that can influence longevity include familial longevity and family history of certain diseases. Environmental factors include acquired diseases, toxins, pollutants, and lifestyle. Due to technological advances, there is a controversy regarding the quantity of life as against the quality. Women have a longer average life expectancy at birth than men. Ethnic group differences are complex; depending on how old people are, the patterns of differences change.

Physical Changes and Health

Biological Theories of Aging

■   There are four main biological theories of aging. Wear-and-tear theory postulates that aging is caused by body systems simply wearing out. Cellular theories focus on reactions within cells, involving free radicals and cross-linking. Metabolic theories focus on changes in cell metabolism. Programmed cell death theories propose that aging is genetically programmed. No single theory is sufficient to explain aging.

Physiological Changes

■   Three important structural changes in the neurons are neurofibrillary tangles, dendritic changes, and neuritic plaques. These have important consequences for functioning, because they reduce the effectiveness with which neurons transmit information.

■   The risk of cardiovascular disease increases with age. Normal changes in the cardiovascular system include buildup of fat deposits in the heart and arteries, a decrease in the amount of blood the heart can pump, a decline in heart muscle tissue, and stiffening of the arteries. Most of these changes are affected by lifestyle. Stroke and multi-infarct dementia cause significant cognitive impairment, depending on the location of the brain damage.

■   Strictly age-related changes in the respiratory system are hard to identify, due to the lifetime effects of pollution. However, older adults suffer shortness of breath, and the risk of chronic obstructive pulmonary disorder increases.

■   Parkinson's disease is caused by insufficient levels of dopamine, and it can be effectively managed with L-dopa. In a minority of cases, dementia develops.

■   Age-related declines in vision and hearing are well documented. However, similar changes in taste, smell, touch, pain, and temperature are not as clear.

Health Issues

■   Older adults have more sleep disturbances than younger adults. Nutritionally, most older adults do not need vitamin or mineral supplements. Cancer risk increases sharply with age.

Cognitive Processes

Information Processing

■   Older adults are much slower than younger adults at visual search, unless there is an advance signal. Age differences in divided-attention tasks depend on the level of difficulty; on easy tasks, there are no differences, but on hard tasks, younger adults do better. Older adults' reaction time is slower than younger adults'. However, the amount of slowing is lessened if older adults have practice or expertise in the task. Sensory and information-processing changes create problems for older drivers.

Memory

■   On laboratory memory tasks requiring free recall, older adults almost always do worse than younger adults. The difference is less on recognition memory tasks and on some real-world memory tasks. What people believe to be true about their memory is related to their performance. Beliefs about whether cognitive abilities are supposed to change may be most important. Differentiating memory changes associated with aging from memory changes due to disease should be accomplished through comprehensive evaluations. Memory training can be achieved in many ways. A useful framework is to combine explicit-implicit memory distinctions with external-internal types of memory aids.

Training Intellectual Abilities

■   Evidence from training studies indicates that performance on at least some intellectual abilities (e.g., inductive reasoning and spatial orientation) can be significantly improved.

Wisdom

■ Wisdom has more to do with being an expert in living than with age per se. Three factors that help people become wise are general personal conditions, specific expertise conditions, and facilitative life contexts.

Mental Health and Intervention

Depression

■ The key symptom of depression is persistent sadness. Other psychological and physical symptoms also occur, but the importance of these depends on the age of the person reporting them. Major causes of depression include imbalances in neurotransmitters and psychosocial forces such as loss and internal belief systems. Depression can be treated with medications, such as heterocyclic antidepressants and MAO inhibitors, and through psychotherapy, such as behavioral or cognitive therapy.

Anxiety Disorders

■ A variety of anxiety disorders afflict many older

adults. All of them can be effectively treated with either medications or psychotherapy.

Dementia: Alzheimer's Disease

■ Dementia is a family of diseases that cause severe cognitive impairment. Alzheimer's disease is the most common form of irreversible dementia. Symptoms of Alzheimer's disease include memory impairment, personality changes, and behavioral changes. These symptoms usually worsen gradually, with rates varying considerably among individuals. Definitive diagnosis of Alzheimer's disease can only be made following a brain autopsy. Diagnosis of probable Alzheimer's disease in a living person involves a thorough process through which other potential causes are eliminated. Most researchers are focusing on a probable genetic cause of Alzheimer's disease. Although Alzheimer's disease is incurable, various therapeutic interventions can improve the quality of the victim's life.

Key Terms

Alzheimer's disease   (471)
amyloid   (473)
anxiety disorders   (470)
average life expectancy   (449)
behavior therapy   (470)
cellular theories   (452)
cerebral vascular accidents   (454)
chronic obstructive pulmonary
    disease (COPD)   (455)
circadian rhythm   (456)
cognitive therapy   (470)
cross-linking   (452)
dementia   (471)
demographers   (447)
divided attention   (459)
dysphoria   (468)
explicit memory   (463)
external aids   (463)
free radicals   (452)

free recall   (461)
haloperidol   (474)
hemorrhage   (454)
heterocyclic antidepressants
    (HCAs)   (469)
Huntington's disease   (474)
implicit memory   (463)
incontinence   (472)
internal aids   (463)
internal belief systems   (469)
longevity   (449)
maximum life expectancy   (449)
metabolic theories   (452)
monoamine oxidase (MAO)
    inhibitors   (469)
multi-infarct dementia   (454)
neuritic plaques   (453)
neurofibrillary tangles   (453)
neurotransmitters   (453)

Parkinson's disease   (455)
population pyramid   (447)
presbycusis   (455)
programmed cell death
    theories   (452)
pseudodementias   (473)
reaction time   (459)
recognition   (461)
selective serotonin reuptake
    inhibitors (SSRIs)   (469)
selectivity   (459)
spaced retrieval   (474)
strokes   (454)
tacrine   (474)
thioridazine   (474)
useful life expectancy   (449)
wear-and-tear theory   (452)

If You'd Like to Learn More

BIRREN, J. E., ET AL. (Eds.) (1992). *Handbook of mental health and aging* (2nd ed.). San Diego, CA: Academic Press. This is perhaps the best one-volume overview of mental health issues in aging, covering numerous specific disorders and treatments.

CART, C. S., METRESS, E. K., & METRESS, S. P. (1992). *Biological bases of human aging and disease.* Boston: Jones and Bartlett. The authors provide a very readable overview of the major biological and physiological changes in aging.

HAYFLICK, L. (1994). *How and why we age.* New York: Ballantine. This excellent summary of the biology of aging is presented in a very readable and easy-to-understand format. It is probably the best comprehensive summary available at the introductory level.

KAUSLER, D. (1991). *Experimental psychology, cognition, and human aging.* New York: Springer-Verlag. This is one of the very best one-volume summaries of age-related differences in information processing and memory.

MARTZ, S. H. (Ed.). (1987). *When I am an old woman, I shall wear purple;* and (1992). *If I had my life to live over, I would pick more daisies.* Watsonville, CA: Papier-Mache Press. Both of these books are anthologies of poems and short stories about the personal meanings of aging to women.

WEST, R. L., & SINNOTT, J. D. (Eds.). (1991). *Everyday memory aging: Current research and methodology.* New York: Springer-Verlag. The book provides an overview of age differences in memory ability in real-world situations.

WHITBOURNE, S. K. (1985). *The aging body.* New York: Springer. This is an excellent scholarly discussion of physiological changes and their psychological impact.

ɞ Olive is a spry 88-year-old who spends more time thinking and reflecting about her past than she used to. She also tends to be much less critical now of decisions made years ago than she was at the time. Olive remembers her visions of the woman she wanted to become and concludes that she's come pretty close. Olive wonders if this process of reflection is something that most older adults go through.

ɞ Marcus is a 77-year-old retired construction worker who labored hard all of his life. He managed to save a little money, but he and his wife live primarily off of his monthly Social Security checks. Though not rich, they have enough to pay the bills. Marcus is largely happy with retirement, and he stays in touch with his friends. He thinks maybe he's a little strange, though—he has heard that retirees are supposed to be isolated and lonely.

ɞ Alma was married to Charles for 46 years. Even though he died 20 years ago, Alma still speaks about him as if he had only recently passed away. Alma still gets sad on special dates, such as their anniversary, or Charles' birthday, or the date on which he died. Alma tells everyone that she and Chuck, as she called him, had a wonderful marriage and that she still misses him terribly even after all these years.

ɞ Maria is an 82-year-old woman who still lives in the same neighborhood where she grew up. She had been in relatively good health for most of her life, but in the last year she has needed help with tasks, such as preparing meals and shopping for personal items. Maria wants very much to continue living in her own home. She dreads being placed in a nursing home, but her family wonders whether that might be the best option.

Social Aspects of Later Life

 What's it really like to be an older adult? As we saw in Chapter 13, aging brings with it both physical limits (such as increased likelihood of chronic disease) and psychological gains (such as increased expertise). Old age also brings social challenges. Older adults are sometimes stereotyped as marginal and powerless in society, much like children. Psychosocial issues confront older adults as well. How will you think about your life and bring some meaning and closure to it as you approach your death? What constitutes well-being for you? How will you use your time once you are no longer working full-time? Will you like being retired? What roles will your relationships with friends and family play in your life then? How will you cope if your partner is ill and requires care? What if your partner should die? Where will you live? What if you are frail?

These are a few of the issues we will examine in this chapter. As in Chapter 13, the main focus will be on the majority of older adults who are healthy and live in the community. Young-old people, 65–80 years old, make up the group of older adults about whom we know the most. Just as at other times in life, getting along in the environment is a complicated issue. We will begin by considering a few ideas about how to optimize our fit with the environment. Next, we will see how we bring the story of our lives to a culmination. After that, we will consider how interpersonal relationships and retirement provide contexts for life satisfaction. We will conclude by examining the social contexts of aging.

Theories of Psychosocial Aging

LEARNING OBJECTIVES

- *What are activity theory, disengagement theory, and continuity theory?*
- *What is the competence and environmental press model, and how do docility and proactivity relate to the model?*

Understanding how people grow old is not as simple as asking someone how old he or she is. As we saw in Chapter 13, aging is an individual process involving many variations in physical changes, cognitive functioning, and mental health. We must also recognize that, as Dennis the Menace notes, older

"WE HAVE A LOT IN COMMON, DON'T WE? I'M TOO YOUNG TO DO MOST EVERYTHING AND YOU'RE TOO OLD TO DO MOST EVERYTHING."

DENNIS THE MENACE® used by permission of Hank Ketcham and © by North America Syndicate.

adults are often marginalized in society. Psychosocial approaches to aging recognize these issues.

As a group, the theories we will consider show that there is more than one way to grow old successfully, depending on a person's life circumstances and resources. Let's consider two sets of theories—activity/disengagement/continuity and competence–environmental press—and examine research findings about how well they explain psychosocial aging. The first set expresses the common view that activity level alone determines how happy older people are. The second argues that it is more complicated than that.

Activity, Disengagement, and Continuity

When Sandy retired from her job as a secretary at an African American community center, she hardly slowed down. She continued singing in the gospel choir at her local Baptist church, got involved in the Black Women's Community Action Committee, and began volunteering at a local Head Start school. In contrast, her friend Levar decided that he wanted to take life easy after he retired from working on the assembly line. Levar stopped going to union meetings and functions of the Veterans of Foreign Wars and turned down the invitation to join a bowling team.

Sandy's life since she retired exemplifies *activity theory*, which states that people age better the more active they remain. Specifically, activity theory holds that people need to substitute new roles and activities for the ones they relinquish when they retire or when their partner or friends die. According to this view, being actively involved in roles that you find rewarding (spouse, worker, friend, etc.) keeps you happy in life. The more such roles you are able to maintain, the happier you are. The loss of such roles through death, retirement, or other cause results in lower life satisfaction, because aspects of your life seem empty.

Many older adults remain involved in personal and community activities. Activity theory postulates that doing so fosters well-being.

Levar's withdrawal from social contact is an example of *disengagement theory*, which holds that older adults voluntarily reduce the number of social activities and commitments they have—and are encouraged by society to do so. This withdrawal is viewed as necessary so that older people can maintain equilibrium in their lives and so that society can provide opportunities for younger people to take over the roles vacated by older adults (Cumming & Henry, 1961). Because social withdrawal is voluntary, the loss of roles through disengagement has no negative effects on life satisfaction, according to this theory.

Activity theory and disengagement theory appear to describe many people's lives in old age. However, research does not support either theory as an explanation for how *all* older adults behave. For example, a major review of the activity literature showed that life satisfaction is not affected very much by remaining engaged in activities (Okun et al., 1984). Also, an 8-year study demonstrated that activity level was unrelated to mortality in a group of Mexican Americans and a group of European Americans once age, health, and gender were taken into account (Lee & Markides, 1990). Indeed, some of the oldest old have few activities or friends (Poon, 1992).

Disengagement theory proposes that older adults disconnect from social involvement. However, it appears that such people, like this man, do not represent the majority of older adults.

Disengagement theory has little support either as a complete account of aging; few people withdraw willingly from personally meaningful activities or relationships (Carstensen, 1987). Indeed, some critics charge that disengagement theory provides society a way to legitimize stereotypes of older adults as inactive, withdrawn, and useless, on the grounds that that is really how they want to be (Palmore, 1990). Moreover, there is evidence that social isolation at any age lowers life satisfaction, impairs health, and shortens life (Antonucci, 1990).

What can we conclude about activity theory and disengagement theory? Current evidence suggests that satisfaction in old age does not depend either on substituting new roles for old ones or on totally withdrawing from them. It is not that simple. As we will see a bit later, satisfaction may depend more on the match between a person's level of competence and the specific demands the environment makes. But activity theory and disengagement theory served a very useful purpose. As a result of the research these theories sparked, we can reach the following conclusions about aging (Marshall, 1994). There is no one course of "normal" aging, but rather multiple courses; aging is a set of processes that occur at all levels, from biological to social, so aging cannot be predicted from only one perspective (such as exclusively biological forces); and there probably is no one "grand theory" of aging.

One way to recognize individual differences when thinking about how people respond to the complex world around them is to make a simple yet powerful observation: people tend to keep doing whatever works for them (Atchley, 1989). **According to *continuity theory*, people tend to cope with daily life in later adulthood in essentially the same ways they coped in earlier periods of life.** Essentially, the ways people respond to the world depend on five core personality traits, which, as we saw in Chapter 12, remain largely unchanged throughout adulthood. For example, someone who is extroverted and who seeks advice from others when she becomes ill as a middle-aged adult is likely to do the same thing when she feels ill in old age.

Continuity in behavior is supported by research in behavioral genetics, based on longitudinal studies of monozygotic and dizygotic twins. Genetic influences on behavior are clearly apparent; even the timing of a person's retirement has some connection to genetic influences (Plomin, DeFries, & McClearn, 1990). We are only beginning to explore and understand genetic influences in later life. But if much of our behavior in old age is simply a continuation of earlier behavior, it might be possible to make predictions about what a young adult or middle-aged person might be like in the future.

In sum, activity theory, disengagement theory, and continuity theory are useful in helping us appreciate the diversity of older adults. Certainly, some adults derive satisfaction from remaining active in late life; others are just as happy being by themselves. To understand people's level of satisfaction in old age, we must pay attention to whether or not they are able to do what they prefer and whether their responses are continuations of their behaviors earlier in life.

Competence and Environmental Press

Understanding psychosocial aging thus requires attention to individual's needs, rather than treating all older adults alike. One way of doing this is to focus on the relation between competence and environmental press. As we saw in the Chapter 1 summary reproduced in the table at the top of page 485, this approach is a good example of a theory that incorporates the elements of the biopsychosocial model (Lawton, 1982; Lawton & Nahemow, 1973).

M. POWELL LAWTON

"In one sense, all behavioral science may be seen as an effort to link behavior with the environment."

Perspective	Examples of Theories	Main Ideas	Emphases in Biopsychosocial Framework	Positions on Developmental Issues
Ecological and Systems	Competence–environmental press (Lawton and Nahemow)	Adaptation is optimal when ability and demands are in balance	Strong emphasis on biological, psychological, and social, moderate on life cycle	Nature–nurture interaction, continuity, context-specific

Competence **is defined as the upper limit of a person's ability to function in five domains: physical health, sensory-perceptual skills, motor skills, cognitive skills, and ego strength.** We discussed most of these domains in Chapter 13; ego strength, which is related to Erikson's concept of integrity, is discussed later in this chapter. These domains are viewed as underlying all other abilities and reflecting the biological and psychological forces. *Environmental press* **refers to the physical, interpersonal, or social demands that environments put on people.** Physical demands might include having to walk up three flights of stairs to one's apartment. Interpersonal demands include having to adjust one's behavior patterns to different types of people. Social demands include dealing with laws or customs that place certain expectations on people. These aspects of the theory reflect biological, psychological, and social forces. Both competence and environmental press change as people move through the life span; what you are capable of doing as a 5-year-old differs from what you are capable of doing as a 25-, 45-, 65-, or 85-year-old. Similarly, the demands put on you by the environment change as you age. Thus, the competence–environmental press framework reflects life-cycle factors as well.

The competence and environmental press model, depicted in the figure, shows how the two are related. Low to high competence is represented on the vertical axis, and weak to strong environmental press is represented on the horizontal axis. Points in the figure represent various combinations of the two. Most important, the shaded areas show that adaptive behavior and positive affect can result from many different combinations of competence and press levels. *Adaptation level* **is the area where press level is average for a particular level of competence; this is where behavior and affect are normal. Slight increases in press tend to improve performance; this area on the figure is labeled the** *zone of maximum performance potential.* **Slight decreases in press create the** *zone of maximum comfort,* **in which people are able to live happily without worrying about environmental demands.** Combinations of competence and environmental press that fall within either of these two zones result in adaptive behavior and positive affect, which translate into high quality of life.

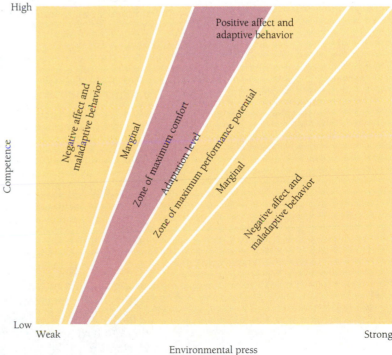

Lawton and Nahemow, 1973.

Making plans for the future is an important part of adaptation in late life. Such planning is an example of Lawton's notion of proactivity.

FORCES IN ACTION

As one moves away from these areas, behavior becomes increasingly maladaptive and affect becomes negative. Notice that these outcomes, too, can result from several different combinations, and for different reasons. For example, too many environmental demands on a person with low competence and too few demands on a person with high competence both result in maladaptive behaviors and negative affect.

What does this graph mean with regard to late life? Is aging merely an equation relating certain variables? The important thing to realize about the competence–environmental press model is that each person has the potential of being happily adapted to some living situations, but not to all. Whether people are functioning well depends on whether there is a good fit between what they are able to do and what the environment forces them to do. When the abilities match the demands, then people adapt. When there is a mismatch, people do not fare as well. In this view, aging is more than an equation, as the best fit must be determined on an individual basis.

How do people deal with changes in their particular combinations of environmental press (such as adjusting to a new living situation) and competence (perhaps due to illness)? People respond in two basic ways (Lawton, 1989). **When people choose new behaviors to meet new desires or needs, they exhibit** *proactivity* **and exert control over their lives. In contrast, when people allow the situation to dictate the options they have, they demonstrate** *docility* **and have little control.** Lawton (1989) argues that proactivity is more likely to occur in people with relatively high competence, and docility in people with relatively low competence.

The model has considerable research support. For example, the model accounts for why people choose the activities they do (Lawton, 1982), move to particular kinds of housing (Lawton, 1982), and need to exert some degree of control over their lives (Langer & Rodin, 1976). In short, there is considerable merit to the view that aging is a complex interaction between a person's competence level and environmental press, mediated by choice. This model can be applied in many different settings.

Finding Where You Fit

Lawton and Nahemow's competence–environmental press model is an excellent example of the biopsychosocial framework in action. Competence can be viewed as the result of the dual influence of biological and psychological forces. As we have seen, competence is reflected in physical capacity and in the breadth of a person's behavioral repertoire. For example, as a person's health deteriorates (and biological forces increase in importance), competence decreases accordingly. Or, as a person learns new coping strategies (and psychological forces increase in magnitude), competence improves. Similarly, environmental press reflects the influence of social forces. As we have seen, the demands of other people, the neighborhood, or society at large tax a person's physical and psychological abilities.

A person's position in the life span makes a difference in how relative increases and decreases in competence and environmental press are interpreted. Young children might be expected to have little competence, so we try to protect them from high levels of environmental demands. Young adults might be expected to be able to deal with much higher demands, because we expect them to have greater competence. Older adults may be experiencing declines in competence, so we may need to find ways to reduce the demands put on them.

In general, the competence–environmental press framework can be useful in helping people find the best fit that balances their abilities and the demands put on them. We could also view Lawton and Nahemow's framework as a way to help people balance the forces in the biopsychosocial framework.   ❧

TEST YOURSELF

1. Adding new roles to one's life in old age supports _____ theory, whereas withdrawing from social connections supports _____ theory.
2. A person's ability to function in several key domains is termed _____, whereas demands put on a person from external sources are termed _____.
3. How does continuity theory incorporate aspects of the biopsychosocial model?

Personality Development in Later Life

LEARNING OBJECTIVES

❧ *What is integrity in late life? How do people achieve it?*

❧ *How is well-being defined in adulthood? What developmental trends are there in the ways people view themselves?*

❧ *What role does religion play in late life?*

Think for a minute about the older adults you know well. Perhaps they are your grandparents, co-workers, or neighborhood acquaintances. What are they really like? How do they see themselves today? How do they visualize their lives a few years from now? How do they see themselves in the past?

These questions have intrigued authors for many years. A century ago, William James (1890), one of the early pioneers in psychology, wrote that a person's personality traits are set by young adulthood. Some researchers agree, as we saw in Chapter 12; some aspects of personality remain relatively stable through adulthood. But people also change in important ways, as Carl Jung (1960/1931) argued, by integrating opposite tendencies, such as masculine and feminine traits. Erik Erikson (1982) was convinced that personality development takes a lifetime; a reminder of his basic ideas can be seen in the table.

Perspective	Examples of Theories	Main Ideas	Emphases in Biopsychosocial Framework	Positions on Developmental Issues
Psychodynamic	Erickson's psycho-social theory	Personality develops through sequence of stages	Biological, social, and life-cycle forces crucial; less emphasis on psychological	Nature–nurture interaction, discontinuity, universal sequence but individual differences in rate

In this section, we will explore the final pieces in the personality puzzle, to see how important aspects of personality continue to evolve in later life.

Integrity versus Despair

As people enter late life, they begin the struggle of *integrity versus despair*. According to Erikson (1982), this struggle comes about as older adults like Olive, from the first chapter-opening vignette, try to understand their lives in terms of the future of their family and community. Thoughts of one's own death are balanced by the realization that one will live on through children, grandchildren, great-grandchildren, and the community as a whole. This realization produces what Erikson calls a "life-affirming involvement" in the present.

Taking stock of how one has lived life, called the life review, is a common activity in late life. It is also an important aspect of Erikson's stage of integrity versus despair.

The struggle of integrity versus despair requires people to engage in a *life review*. To achieve integrity, a person must come to terms with the choices and events that have made his or her life unique. There must also be an acceptance of the fact that life is drawing to a close. Looking back on life can resolve some of the second-guessing of one's own decisions that might have occurred earlier in adulthood (Erikson, Erikson, & Kivnick, 1986). People who were unsure whether they made the right choices concerning their children, for example, now feel satisfied that things eventually worked out well. In contrast, others feel bitter about their choices, blame themselves or others for their misfortunes, see their lives as meaningless, and greatly fear death. These people end up in despair rather than integrity.

Research shows a connection between engaging in a life review and achieving integrity. In one study, homebound older adults who were part of a program that assisted people in remembering and reviewing their lives showed significant improvements in life satisfaction, positive feelings, and depressive symptoms, compared to homebound older adults who did not participate (Haight, 1992). These improvements were still evident two months after the program ended.

Who reaches integrity? Erikson (1982) emphasizes that there is no one path. People from many backgrounds and cultures, who made many different choices and followed different lifestyles, all have the opportunity. Those who reach integrity become self-affirming and self-accepting; they judge their lives to have been worthwhile and good. They are glad to have lived the lives they did.

Well-Being and Possible Selves in Later Life

How do older adults view themselves? Traditionally, researchers addressed this question by having older adults tell them how they saw themselves at the moment (Lawton, 1984). From a life-span perspective, however, a better way to answer this question would be to have older adults report how they see themselves right now in comparison to how they remember themselves in the past and where they see themselves headed in the future.

This is exactly what Ryff (1991) did. In a fascinating series of studies, she redefined the meaning of well-being in adulthood and showed how adults' views of themselves are different at various points in adulthood. Based on the responses of hundreds of adults, Ryff (1989b, 1991) identified six dimensions of psychological well-being for adults and discovered that there are many important age and gender differences in well-being based on these components.

- *Self-acceptance*: having a positive view of oneself; acknowledging and accepting the multiple parts of oneself; and feeling positive about one's past.

- *Positive relation with others*: having warm, satisfying relationships with people; being concerned with their welfare; being empathic, affectionate, and intimate with them; and understanding the reciprocity of relationships.

- *Autonomy*: being independent and determining one's own life; being able to resist social pressures to think or behave in a particular way; evaluating one's life by internal standards.

- *Environmental mastery*: being able to manipulate, control, and effectively use resources and opportunities.

- *Purpose in life*: having goals and a sense of direction in one's life; feeling that one's present and past life have meaning; having a reason for living.

- *Personal growth*: feeling a need for continued personal improvement; seeing oneself as getting better and being open to new experiences; growing in self-knowledge and personal effectiveness.

Details of Ryff's research are presented in the Spotlight on Research feature. In general, older adults have a more positive view of themselves in the past than do young or middle-aged adults. In contrast, older adults have a less optimistic view of the future than the other two groups; they see the future primarily in terms of decline in most aspects of well-being.

Views of a Life—Well-Being and Aging

SPOTLIGHT ON RESEARCH

How people see themselves is an important part of their sense of well-being. As we have seen, Ryff discovered that well-being is a complex combination of six aspects of the self. How did she arrive at this conclusion? Previous research on well-being in late life had been conducted without theoretical guidance (Ryff, 1989a). Consequently, many researchers approached well-being from the perspective of loss; that is, researchers assumed that well-being, like physical prowess, was something that declined as people became older. Ryff (1989a) disagreed and set out to demonstrate her point. She thought that well-being could improve in late life.

In several large studies, conducted over many years with hundreds of adults, Ryff administered numerous self-report scales that measured many aspects of personality and well-being. The findings convinced her that a new approach was needed to describe the complex developmental patterns she was uncovering. This new approach drew from life-span developmental theories (such as those presented in this text), clinical theories of personal growth adapted from successful techniques in psychotherapy, and various definitions of mental health, yielding the most complete description yet of well-being in adulthood.

On the basis of her research and thinking, Ryff (1989b) developed a new measure of well-being that reflected the six-dimension model discussed in the text. This new measure allowed her to obtain people's ratings of how they view themselves right now, what they were like in the past, what they think they might be like in the future, and what they would most like to be like.

The most important discovery from Ryff's research is that young, middle-aged, and older adults have very different views of themselves, depending on whether they are describing their present, past, future, or ideal self-perceptions. The graph on the left, for example, shows that young and middle-aged adults are much more accepting of their ideal and future selves than they are of their present and past selves. For older adults, differences are much smaller. A similar pattern is evident in the graph on the right, which shows autonomy scores.

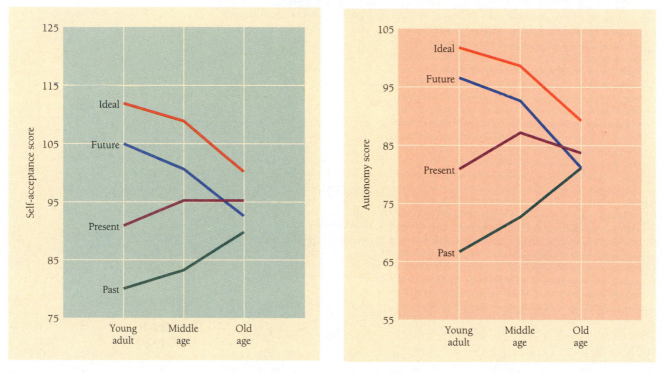

Ryff, 1991.

Perhaps the most interesting findings of Ryff's research concern the difference between people's ideal vision of themselves and what they thought they were really like. If you look carefully at the graphs, you will notice that the differences between the "ideal self" ratings and the "present self" ratings diminish with age. This finding implies that older adults see themselves as closer to really being the person they wanted to become than does any other age group. Ryff's data fit well with Erikson's (1982) idea of integrity. As people achieve integrity, they view their past less critically and become content with how they have lived their lives.

As Ryff (1991) notes, only by including all of these self-ratings will we understand people's sense of personal progress or decline over time from their goal of ideal functioning. Clearly, people judge themselves by many standards, and these differ with age.   ❧

Religiosity

When faced with the daily problems of living, what do most older adults do to help themselves cope? According to research, older adults use their religious faith more than anything else, including family or friends. When asked to describe their most frequent ways of dealing with problems in life, nearly half of the people surveyed in one study listed coping strategies associated with religion (Koenig, George, & Siegler, 1988). Of these, the most frequently used were placing trust in God, praying, and getting strength and help from God. These strategies can also be used to augment other ways of coping.

Reliance on religion in times of stress appears to be especially important for African Americans, who as a group are intensely involved in religious activities (Levin, Taylor, & Chatters, 1994). Churches offer considerable social support for the African American community, as well as serving an important function for the advocacy of social justice (Roberts, 1980). For example, the civil rights movement in the 1950s and 1960s was led by Dr. Martin Luther King, Jr., a Baptist minister, and contemporary congregations champion equal rights for all. The role of the church in African Americans' lives is central; indeed, one of the key predictors of life satisfaction among African Americans is regular church attendance (Coke, 1992).

Within the African American community, religion is especially important to women. The greater importance of the church in the lives of older African American women is supported by results from four national surveys of African American adults (Levin, Taylor, & Chatters, 1994). They are more active in church groups and attend services more frequently than African American men or either European American men or women. However, the gender differences diminish in people over age 70; religion becomes equally important for older African American men.

Religion is an important coping strategy for many people, especially among African American women.

Older persons of Mexican heritage adopt a different approach. Research indicates that they use *la fé de la gente* ("the faith of the people") as a coping strategy (Villa & Jaime, 1993). The notion of *fé* incorporates varying degrees of faith, spirituality, hope, cultural values, and beliefs. *Fé* does not necessarily imply that people identify with a specific religious community. Rather, they identify with a cultural value or ideology.

Among Native Americans, the spiritual elders are the wisdom-keepers, the repositories of the sacred ways and philosophies that extend indefinitely back in time (Wall & Arden, 1990). The wisdom-keepers also share dreams and visions, perform healing ceremonies, and may make apocalyptic prophecies. The place of the wisdom-keepers in the tribe is much more central than that of religious leaders in Western society.

Service providers would be well advised to keep in mind the self-reported importance of religion in the lives of many older adults when designing interventions to help them adapt to life stressors. For example, older adults may be more willing to talk with their minister about a personal problem than they would be to talk with a psychotherapist; when they seek help from a professional, it is more often with their family physician. However, when working with people of Mexican heritage, providers should realize that a major source of distress for this group is lack of familial interaction and support. Overall, many churches offer a wide range of programs to assist poor or homebound older adults in the community. Such programs may be more palatable to the people served than programs based in social service agencies. To be successful, service providers should try to view life as their clients see it.

TEST YOURSELF

1. The Eriksonian struggle that older adults face is termed _____.
2. According to Ryff, the six major aspects of well-being are _____.
3. The most commonly reported method for coping with life stress among older adults is _____.
4. Based on Ryff's research, discussed in this section, what do you think would be good areas to target for interventions designed to improve older adults' well-being?

I Used to Work at . . . : Living in Retirement

LEARNING OBJECTIVES

❧ *What does being retired mean?*

❧ *Why do people retire?*

❧ *How satisfied are retired people?*

❧ *What specific effects does retirement have on maintaining family and community ties?*

You probably take it for granted that some day, after working for many productive years, you will retire. But did you know that until 1935, when Social Security was inaugurated, retirement was rarely even considered by most Americans? Only since World War II has there been a substantial number of retired people in the United States (Elder & Pavalko, 1993). Today, the number is increasing rapidly, and the notion that people work a specified time and then retire is built into our expectations about work. As we noted in Chapter 11, an increasing number of middle-aged workers either retire early or are planning for retirement. In this section, we will consider what retirement is like for older adults.

What Does Being Retired Mean?

Take a moment to look at the photographs at the top of page 493. Can you pick out which of the people would claim that he or she is "retired"? It turns out that retirement is more difficult to define than just guessing from someone's age (Ekerdt & DeViney, 1990). One way is to equate retirement with complete withdrawal from the work force. But this definition is inadequate; many retired people continue to work part-time (Ruhm, 1990). Another possibility would be to define retirement as a self-described state. However, this definition will not work either, because some African Americans define themselves with labels other than "retired" in order to qualify for some social service programs (Gibson, 1991).

Part of the reason it is difficult to define retirement precisely is that the decision to retire involves the loss of occupational identity. As we saw in Chapter 11, what people do for a living is a major part of their identity; we introduce ourselves as postal workers, teachers, builders, or nurses as a way to tell people something about ourselves. Not doing those jobs anymore means that we either put that aspect of our lives in the past tense—"I used to work as a manager at the Hilton"—or say nothing at all. Loss of this aspect of ourselves can be difficult to face, so some look for a label other than "retired" to describe themselves.

A useful way to view retirement is as a complex process by which people withdraw from full-time participation in an occupation (Elder & Pavalko, 1993). The complexity of the retirement process must be acknowledged in order to understand what retirement means to people in different ethnic groups. For example, whereas middle-class European Americans often use a criterion of full-time employment to define themselves as retired or not, Mexican Americans use any of several different criteria, depending on how the question is asked (Zsembik & Singer, 1990). For example, Mexican Americans are most likely to claim that they are retired when asked directly ("Are you retired?") than when asked indirectly ("What are you doing these days?"). It may be that people want to appear active, so they choose some other descriptor. In contrast, European Americans are just as likely to call themselves retired no matter how they are asked. To learn how self-definitions vary from one group to another, complete the exercise in the See for Yourself feature.

Are You Retired?

As mentioned in the text, people who no longer work full-time may or may not label themselves as retired. To find out firsthand how people label themselves and how they occupy their time, try the following exercise. Interview several older adults who you believe may not work full-time anymore. Do not interview only your relatives; make sure that you have a diverse sample of older adults.

Begin your interview by asking them about the kinds of work (for pay or as a volunteer) they do now and the kinds they did in the past. Ask them if they call themselves retired. If so, why do they? If not, why not? How much do they miss not working in their old jobs? Ask also about how they keep themselves occupied now.

Gather the results of your interviews and see if you can draw any general conclusions. Are there certain characteristics common to people who call themselves retired? Or to those who do not? Are there similarities in how people keep themselves occupied? Bring the data to class and compare your results with other students' findings. See for yourself how people view retirement. 🐚

Why Do People Retire?

More workers retire by choice than for any other reason (Henretta, Chan, & O'Rand, 1992). Usually, these individuals retire when, considering projected income from Social Security, pensions, and personal savings, they feel financially secure. Of course, some are forced to retire because they lose their jobs (Henretta, Chan, & O'Rand, 1992). As corporations downsized in the early and mid-1990s, some older workers were offered buyout packages involving supplemental payments if they retired. Others were permanently furloughed, laid off, or dismissed.

Serious health problems also contribute to the decision to retire, especially in the case of early retirement (that is, retiring before one would normally be eligible for Social Security benefits). Health problems that cause functional impairment, such as serious cardiovascular disease or cancer, are the main reason European Americans, African Americans, and Hispanic Americans retire early (Stanford et al., 1991).

GENDER DIFFERENCES

Virtually everything we know about retirement decisions is based on research on men. What little data we have on women leads to contradictory conclusions. Some studies find that a married woman's decision to retire is related to her age and her husband's work status, not to the characteristics of her occupation (George, Fillenbaum, & Palmore, 1984). Other studies report that a woman's decision to retire is related not only to her husband's wages but also to her own financial status, independent of her husband's (Campione, 1988). These discrepant findings may be due to changing demographics. That is, only in the past few years have women remained in the work force long enough to make the decision to retire based on their own wage history and financial security. Clearly, there is a need for more research into women's retirement decisions. In light of gender differences in occupational selection and development (discussed in Chapter 11), it is possible that the reasons men retire may not generalize to women.

Both partners in this picture are retired. However, most of our knowledge about retirement comes from research on men; whether women's experiences are similar remains largely to be seen.

ETHNIC DIFFERENCES

Little research has been conducted on retirement decisions as a function of ethnicity. A few investigators have examined the characteristics of retired African Americans (e.g., Gibson, 1986, 1987; Jackson & Gibson, 1985). These studies show that African Americans tend to label themselves as retired or not based on subjective disability, work history, and source of income, rather than simply on whether or not they are currently employed. An important finding is that gender differences appear to be absent among African Americans; men and women base their self-labels on the same variables. Thus, findings based on European American samples must not be generalized to African Americans, and separate theoretical models for African Americans may be needed (Gibson, 1987). The same may be true for other ethnic groups as well.

Adjustment to Retirement

Researchers agree on one point: Retirement is an important life transition. New patterns of involvement must be developed in the context of changing roles and lifestyles (Antonovsky & Sagy, 1990). How do most people fare? As long as people have financial security, health, and a supportive network of relatives and friends, they appear to feel very good about being retired (Matthews & Brown, 1987). With regard to the theory discussed earlier in this chapter, high personal competence is associated with higher retirement satisfaction, probably because such people are able to optimize their level of environmental press.

For men, personal priorities are also important. Men who place more emphasis on family roles (e.g., as husband or grandfather) are happier retirees. Interestingly, women's morale in retirement does not appear to be related to an emphasis on any specific roles (Matthews & Brown, 1987).

One stereotype of retirement is that health begins to decline as soon as people stop working. Research findings do not support this belief; in fact, there is no evidence that retirement has any immediate negative effects on health (Ekerdt, 1987).

A second stereotype is that retirement dramatically reduces the number and quality of personal friendships. Again, there is no research support for this belief. In fact, several studies have shown that men like Marcus, from the second chapter-opening vignette, are typical; neither the number nor the quality of friendships declines as a result of retiring (Bossé et al., 1993). When friendships change during retirement, it is usually due to other factors, such as very serious health problems, that interfere with people's ability to maintain friendships.

Finally, some people believe that retired people become much less active overall. This stereotype, based on disengagement theory, is also not supported by research. Although the number of hours in paid work decreases on average with age, older adults are still engaged for hundreds of hours per year in productive activities such as unpaid volunteer work and helping others (Herzog et al., 1989). We will specifically consider volunteer activities in the next section.

Interpersonal Ties

Retirement rarely affects only a single individual. No matter how personal the joys and sorrows of retirement may be, retirees' reactions are shaped by the interpersonal relationships they have. Social ties help people deal with the stresses of retirement, as they do in other life transitions. In many cases, these ties involve friendships and other relationships formed earlier in adulthood.

Social relationships help cushion the effects of any life stress throughout adulthood. This support takes many forms: letting people know that they are loved, offering help if needed, providing advice, taking care of others' needs, and just being there to listen. As we noted earlier, retirees who have close and strong social ties tend to have an advantage in adjusting to the life changes that retirement brings.

We will consider general issues regarding social relationships in more detail later in this chapter. At this point, we will focus on two: what specific adjustments couples must make and how retirees maintain connections with their communities.

INTIMATE RELATIONSHIPS

Much attention has been focused on the role of intimate relationships in adjusting to retirement. Marriage has provided the framework for almost all of this research; gender differences have been noted. Marital status has little effect on older women's satisfaction with retirement (Fox, 1979). Indeed, we know relatively little about what does influence women's retirement satisfaction. This is primarily because most women in current older adult cohorts tended not to work outside the home.

For men, however, some evidence suggests that the never-married are as satisfied as married retirees. Perhaps never-married men prefer singlehood and become accustomed to it long before retirement. In contrast, divorced, separated, or widowed retired men are much less happy (Barfield & Morgan, 1978), which points to the stabilizing effects of marriage for men.

What about the impact of retirement on the marital relationship? Retirement has profound effects on intimate relationships, often disrupting long-established patterns of family interaction, forcing both partners (and others living in the house) to adjust. Simply being together more puts strain on the relationship. Daily routines need rearrangement, which may be stressful.

One change that confronts most retired couples (in traditional households in which only the husband was employed) is the division of household chores. Although retired men tend to do more work around the home than they did before retirement, this does not always lead to desirable outcomes (Ingraham, 1974). For example, an employed husband may compliment his wife on her domestic skills, but after retirement he may suddenly want to teach her how to do things "correctly." Part of the problem may be that such men are not used to taking orders. One retired executive remarked that before he retired, when he said, "Jump," highly paid employees wanted to know how high. "Now, I go home, I walk in the door and my wife says, 'Milton, take out the garbage.' I never saw so much garbage" (Quigley, 1979, p. 9). Finally, part of the problem may be in the perception of one's turf; after retirement men feel that they are thrust into doing things that they, and their partners, may have traditionally thought of as "women's work"

Being retired does not mean disconnecting from one's family. On the contrary, many people have increased interactions with children and grandchildren.

(Troll, 1971). As more dual-earner couples retire, it will be interesting to see how these issues are handled.

COMMUNITY TIES

Throughout adulthood, most people become and remain connected with their communities. Thus, an important consideration is whether the social environment aids retirees' ability to continue old ties and form new ones. The past few decades have witnessed the rapid growth of organizations devoted to providing such opportunities to retirees. National groups such as the American Association of Retired Persons provide the chance to learn, through magazines and pamphlets, about other retirees' activities and about services such as insurance and discounts. Many smaller groups exist at the community level, including senior centers and clubs. Several trade unions also have programs for their retired members. These activities help promote the notion of lifelong learning and help keep older adults cognitively active.

A common way for retired adults to maintain community ties is by volunteering. Older adults report that they volunteer to help them deal with life transitions (Adlersberg & Thorne, 1990) and to maintain social interactions and improve their communities (Morrow-Howell & Mui, 1989). There are many opportunities for retirees to help others. One federal agency, ACTION, administers four programs that have hundreds of local chapters: Foster Grandparents, Senior Companions, the Retired Senior Volunteer Program, and the Service Corps of Retired Executives. Nearly half of adults aged 65 to 74 volunteer their services in some way, with substantial participation rates even among people over age 80 (Chambré, 1993). These rates represent a more than 400% upsurge since the mid-1960s, when only about 1 in 10 older adults did volunteer work. What accounts for this tremendous increase?

Several factors are responsible (Chambré, 1993): improved public perception of the skills and wisdom older adults have to offer, a redefinition of the nature and merits of volunteer work, a more highly educated population of older adults, and greatly expanded opportunities for people to become involved in volunteer work that they enjoy. Given the demographic trends of increased numbers and educational levels of older adults (discussed in Chapter 13), even higher rates of voluntarism are expected during the next few decades (Chambré, 1993). This is a way for society to tap into the vast resources that older adults offer.

One way that older adults stay involved is by volunteering for any of a number of different organizations. Many organizations such as the American Red Cross rely on older volunteers in order to keep the number of services high and the relative costs low.

TEST YOURSELF

1. One useful way to view retirement is as a _____ .
2. The most common reason people retire is _____.
3. Overall, most retirees are _____ with retirement.
4. Many retirees keep contacts in their communities by _____.
5. Using the information from Chapter 11 on occupational development, create a developmental description of occupations, making sure that retirement is incorporated.

Answers: (1) complex process by which people gradually withdraw from employment, (2) by choice, (3) satisfied, (4) volunteering

Friends and Family in Late Life

LEARNING OBJECTIVES

❧ *What role do friends and family play in late life?*

❧ *What are older adults' marriages like?*

❧ *What is it like to care for one's spouse?*

❧ *How do people cope with widowhood? How do men and women differ?*

❧ *What special issues are involved in being a great-grandparent?*

We have seen throughout this text how our lives are shaped and shared by the company of others. **The term** *social convoy* **is used to suggest how a group of people journeys with us throughout our lives, providing us support in good and bad times.** Especially for older adults, the social convoy also provides a source of affirmation of who they are and what they mean to others (Antonucci, 1985).

Several studies have shown that the size of the social convoy and the amount of support it provides do not differ across generations, a result that generalizes to Hispanic American adults as well (Levitt, Weber, & Guacci, 1993b). The lack of age differences strongly supports the conclusion that friends and family are essential aspects of all adults' lives.

Friends and Siblings

By late life, some members of a person's social network have been friends for several decades. Research consistently finds that older adults' life satisfaction is hardly related at all to the number or quality of relationships with younger family members, but it is strongly correlated with the number and quality of their friendships (Essex & Nam, 1987).

The quality of late-life friendships is particularly important. Having at least one very close friend or confidant provides a buffer against the losses of roles and status that accompany old age, such as retirement or the death of a loved one (Antonucci, 1985). Patterns of friendship among older adults tend to mirror those in young adulthood (described in Chapter 10). That is, women have more numerous and more intimate friendships than men do. As noted previously, these differences help explain why women are in a better position to deal with the stresses of life. Widows, especially, take advantage of their friendship networks; research shows that they are involved with their friends more than married women, never-married women, or men (Hatch & Bulcroft, 1992).

Older adults tend to prefer the friends they have had for many years; they tend not to want to make new ones (Antonucci, 1985). Old friends can share aspects of the past that may be unknown to younger adults. Sadly, cherished friends die or become disabled, making it difficult to maintain contact (Rawlins, 1992). Many older adults turn to phone calls or letters to keep the friendships going.

Friendships are an important part of older adults' social network. In many cases, these friendships have lasted for decades and are closer than with some family members.

The preference for long-term friendships may explain older adults' desire to keep in touch with their siblings. Among people over age 60, 83% report that they feel close to at least one brother or sister (Dunn, 1984). Besides closeness, other dimensions of sibling friendships include involvement with each other, frequency of contact, envy, and resentment. Five types of relationships among older adult siblings have been identified (Gold, Woodbury, & George, 1990):

- *Intimate sibling relationships,* characterized by high levels of closeness and involvement but low levels of envy and resentment.
- *Congenial sibling relationships,* characterized by high levels of closeness and involvement, average levels of contact, and relatively low levels of envy and resentment.
- *Loyal sibling relationships,* characterized by average levels of closeness, involvement, and contact and relatively low levels of envy and resentment.
- *Apathetic sibling relationships,* characterized by low levels on all dimensions.
- *Hostile sibling relationships,* characterized by relatively high levels of involvement and resentment and relatively low levels on all other dimensions.

The relationships older adults have with their siblings is often the longest relationship of their lives. Although sisters tend to be closest, brothers also stay in touch.

The relative frequencies of these five types of sibling relationships are shown in the figure. As you can see, loyal and congenial relationships characterize nearly two-thirds of all older sibling pairs. Additionally, it appears that

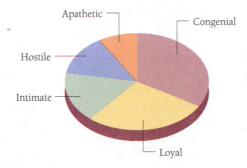

Gold et al., 1990.

older African American siblings have apathetic or hostile relationships with their siblings nearly five times less often than older European Americans do (4.5% for African Americans versus 22% for European Americans; Gold, 1990). Sometimes, hostile sibling relationships in late life date back to sibling rivalries in childhood (Greer, 1992).

When different combinations of siblings are considered separately, ties between sisters are typically the strongest, most frequent, and most intimate (Cicirelli, 1980; Lee, Mancini, & Maxwell, 1990). In contrast, brothers tend to maintain less frequent contact (Connidis, 1988). Little is known about brother–sister relationships. Even though many older adults end up providing care for or living with one of their siblings, we know virtually nothing about how well this works.

Clearly, there are major gaps in our understanding of sibling relationships. This is truly unfortunate, as our brothers and sisters play an important and meaningful role throughout our lives.

Marriage

"It's great to be 72 and still married," said Lucia. "Yeah, it's great to have Juan around to share old times with and have him know how I feel even before I tell him." Lucia and Juan are typical of most older married couples. Marital satisfaction improves once the children leave home and remains fairly high in older couples (Lee, 1988). One study found that 80% of couples married at least 50 years recollected their marriages as being happy from their wedding day to the present (Sporakowski & Axelson, 1984).

Older married couples show several specific differences from their middle-aged counterparts (Levenson, Carstensen, & Gottman, 1993). Older couples have a reduced potential for marital conflict and greater potential for pleasure, are more likely to be similar in terms of mental and physical health, and show fewer gender differences in sources of pleasure. In short, most older married couples have developed adaptive ways to avoid conflict and have grown more alike. In general, marital satisfaction among older couples remains high until health problems begin to interfere with the relationship (Gilford, 1984).

Caring for a Spouse

When most couples pledge their love to each other "in sickness and in health," most envision the sickness part to be no worse than an illness lasting a few weeks. For many couples, that may be the case, but for some, their pledge may be severely tested.

Francine and Ron were one such a couple. After 42 years of mainly good times together, Ron was diagnosed as having Alzheimer's disease. When first contacted by researchers, Francine had been caring for Ron for six years. "At times it's very hard, especially when he looks at me and doesn't have any idea who I am. Imagine, after all these years, not to recognize me. But I love him, and I know that he would do the same for me. But, to be perfectly honest, we're not the same couple we once were. We're just not as close; I guess we really can't be."

Francine and Ron are typical of couples in which one spouse cares for the other. Caring for a chronically ill spouse presents different challenges than caring for a chronically ill parent (see Chapter 12). The spousal caregiver assumes the new role after decades of shared responsibilities. Without warning, the division of labor that had worked for years must be readjusted. Such change inevitably puts stress on the relationship. This is especially true in cases involving Alzheimer's disease or other dementias, because of the cognitive and behavioral consequences of the disease (see Chapter 13).

Studies of people like those in the Real People feature, who are spousal caregivers of persons with Alzheimer's disease, show that marital satisfaction is much lower than for healthy couples (Kinney et al., 1993). Spousal caregivers report a loss of companionship and intimacy over the course of caregiving (Williamson & Schulz, 1990; Wright, 1991). Marital satisfaction is also an important predictor of spousal caregivers' reports of depressive symptoms; the better the perceived quality of the marriage, the fewer symptoms caregivers report (Kinney et al., 1993).

'Til Death Do Us Part: Spousal Caregiving

"To be perfectly honest, I never in a million years thought I would be in the position I'm in now. When I married Mike, I thought we would be happy and live out our lives with our families and friends. But now . . .."

Harriet's voice trailed off as her eyes filled with tears. Mike, 68 years old, had been diagnosed with Alzheimer's disease about six years earlier. Harriet, two years younger, dried her eyes and continued. "The worst part is when he gets aggressive with me. Sometimes he doesn't remember who I am and thinks I'm going to steal all of his clothes. All I want to do is the laundry. It's just so hard to keep telling myself that it's the disease. After 44 years of marriage, it's hard to accept that his mind is going and he just can't remember.

"Me, I just try to focus on all the good years we had. We've got three great kids, who help out as much as they can. But they have their own families, and jobs, and pressures. I know that. But sometimes I could really use a break; they're the best thing I have left.

"Why do I do what I'm doing? I promised Mike that I'd love him no matter what, and I've always kept my promises to him. It may sound strange, but I truly believe that somewhere inside he loves me as much as ever. I know I do. And that's what keeps me going. Besides, I couldn't afford to pay what it costs in a nursing home, and I don't think they would do as good a job as I'm doing. I'm biased, I guess, but he's my husband. To them, he'd only be another patient." ❧

Most spousal caregivers are forced to respond to an environmental challenge that they did not choose—their partner's illness. They adopt the caregiver role out of necessity. Once they adopt the role, caregivers assess their ability to carry out the duties required. Longitudinal research indicates that how caregivers perceive their ability to provide care at the outset of caregiving may be all-important (Kinney & Cavanaugh, 1993). Caregivers who perceive themselves as competent try to rise to the occasion; data indicate that they report fewer and less intense caregiving hassles than spousal caregivers who see themselves as less competent (Kinney & Cavanaugh, 1993).

This explanation fits with the docility component of the competence–environmental press model presented earlier, on pages 484–487 in this chapter. Caregivers attempt to balance their perceived competence with the environmental demands of caregiving. Perceived competence allows them to be proactive rather than merely reactive, which gives them a better chance to optimize their situation.

In any event, providing full-time care for a spouse is very stressful (Kinney & Cavanaugh, 1993). Coping with a spouse who may not remember the caregiver's name, who may act aggressively, and who has a chronic and fatal disease presents serious challenges even to the happiest of couples.

Widowhood

Bill and Edna had been married for 61 years when Bill died of cancer at age 87. Although Bill's illness had made it clear that Edna would some day be a widow, it still came as a shock. "There are lots of times when I feel him around. We were together for so long that you take it for granted that your husband is just there. And there are times when I just don't want to go on without him. But I suppose I'll get through it."

REAL PEOPLE

JENNIFER M. KINNEY
"... a general view of events as 'predictable' and 'working out as best as possible' are more important than are feelings of control over such events."

Traditional marriage vows proclaim that the union will last " 'til death do us part." Like Bill and Edna, virtually all older married couples will see their marriages end because one partner dies. For most people, the death of a spouse is one of the most traumatic events they will ever experience. Although widowhood may occur at any age, it is much more likely to occur in old age—and to women. More than half of all women over age 65 are widows, but only 15% of men the same age are widowers. The reasons for this discrepancy are related to biological and social forces: As we saw in Chapter 13, women have longer life expectancies. Also, women typically marry men older than themselves, as discussed in Chapter 10. Consequently, the average married woman can expect to live 10 to 12 years as a widow.

The loss of one's spouse is among the most traumatic losses in life. The loss of companionship is what many people find to be the hardest aspect of widowhood.

The impact of widowhood goes well beyond the ending of a long-term partnership. Widowed people may be left alone by family and friends who do not know how to deal with a bereaved person (see Chapter 15). As a result, widows and widowers often lose not only a spouse but also those friends and family who feel uncomfortable including a single person rather than a couple in social functions. Additionally, widowed individuals may feel awkward as the third party or may even view themselves as a threat to married friends (Field & Minkler, 1988). Because going to a movie or a restaurant alone may be unpleasant or unsatisfying to older widows or widowers, they may just stay home. Unfortunately, others may assume that they simply wish or need to be alone.

For both widows and widowers, the first few months alone can be very difficult. Newly widowed people are at risk for increased physical illness and report more symptoms of depression, lost status, economic hardship, and lower social support (Stroebe & Stroebe, 1983). But feelings of loss do not dissipate quickly, as the case of Alma in the third opening vignette shows clearly. As we will see in Chapter 15, feeling sad on important dates is a common experience, even many years after a loved one has died.

There are some important gender differences in how men and women react to widowhood. Widowers are at higher risk of dying themselves soon after their spouse, either by suicide or natural causes (Osgood, 1992). Some people believe that the loss of a wife presents a more serious problem for a man than the loss of a husband for a woman. Perhaps this is because a wife is often a man's only close friend and confidant, or because men are usually unprepared to live out their lives alone (Glick, Weiss, & Parkes, 1974; see Chapter 10). Older men are often ill equipped to handle such routine and necessary tasks as cooking, shopping, and keeping house, and they become emotionally isolated from family members. Although both widows and widowers suffer financial loss, widows often suffer more because survivor's benefits are usually only half of their husband's pensions (Smith & Zick, 1986). For many women, widowhood results in poverty.

An important factor to keep in mind about gender differences in widowhood is that men are usually older than women when they are widowed. To some extent, the difficulties reported by widowers may be partly due to this age difference. Indeed, if age is held constant, data over many years indicate that widows actually report higher anxiety than widowers (Atchley, 1975). Regardless of age, men have a clear advantage over women in the opportunity to form new heterosexual relationships, as there are fewer social restrictions on relationships between older men and younger women. Interestingly, though, older widowers are actually less likely to form new, close friendships than are widows. Perhaps this is simply a continuation of men's lifelong tendency to have few close friendships (see Chapter 10). Also, widows are more likely to join support groups, which foster the formation of new friendships (Vachon et al., 1980).

For many reasons, including the need for companionship and financial security, some widowed people remarry. One study examined remarriage as a coping response by older widows by interviewing 39 widows who had remarried, 192 who had considered remarriage, and 420 who had not considered it (Gentry & Schulman, 1988). Women who had remarried reported significantly fewer concerns than either of the other groups. Interestingly, the remarried widows were also the ones who recalled the most concerns about being alone and reported higher levels of emotional distress immediately after the death of their spouses. Apparently, remarriage helped these widows deal with the loss of their husbands by providing companionship and comfort.

Great-Grandparenthood

As discussed in Chapter 12, grandparenting is an important and enjoyable role for many adults. With increasing numbers of people, especially women, living to very old age, more people become great-grandparents. Age at first marriage and age at parenthood also play a role; people who reach these milestones at relatively younger ages are more likely to become great-grandparents. Most great-grandparents are women who married relatively young and had children and grandchildren who also married and had children relatively early in adulthood.

Although little research has been conducted on great-grandparents, their sources of satisfaction and meaning apparently differ from those of grandparents (Doka & Mertz, 1988; Wentkowski, 1985). Compared to grandparents, great-grandparents are much more similar in what they derive from the role, largely because they are less involved with the children than grandparents are. Three aspects of great-grandparenthood appear to be most important (Doka & Mertz, 1988).

First, being a great-grandparent provides a sense of personal and family renewal—important components for achieving integrity. Their grandchildren have produced new life, renewing their own excitement for life and reaffirming the continuance of their lineage. Seeing their families stretch across four generations may also provide psychological support, through feelings of symbolic immortality, to help them face death. They take pride and comfort in knowing that their families will live many years beyond their own lifetime.

Second, great-grandchildren provide new diversions in great-grandparents' lives. There are now new people with whom they can share their experiences. Third, becoming a great-grandparent is a major milestone, a mark of longevity that most people never achieve. The sense that one has lived long enough to see the fourth generation is perceived very positively.

Becoming a great-grandparent is not only a positive life transition but provides evidence that one's family will carry on for many years to come.

TEST YOURSELF

1. The two most common forms of sibling relationships in old age are loyal and _____.
2. In general, marital satisfaction in older couples is high until _____.

3. A key predictor of stress among spousal caregivers is _____.
4. _____ are at a higher risk of dying themselves soon after they lose their spouses.
5. Three aspects of being a great-grandparent that are especially important are personal and family renewal, diversion, and _____.
6. How do the descriptions of marital satisfaction and spousal caregiving presented here fit with the descriptions of marital satisfaction in Chapter 10 and caring for aging parents in Chapter 12? What similarities and differences are there?

Social Issues and Aging

LEARNING OBJECTIVES

🌿 *Who are frail older adults? How common is frailty?*

🌿 *Where do older adults live in the community?*

🌿 *Who are the most likely people to live in nursing homes? What are the characteristics of good nursing homes?*

🌿 *How do you know if an older adult is abused or neglected? Which people are most likely to be abused and to be abusers?*

As we have emphasized throughout this text, human development occurs in a social context. In late life, social contexts motivate creating specific programs to assist older adults, developing special living environments for them, and passing legislation to protect them from abusive individuals. In this section, we will consider these issues and how they affect the lives of older adults.

Frail Older Adults

In most of our discussion about aging to this point, we have focused on the majority of older adults who are healthy, cognitively competent, financially secure, and have secure family relationships. Some older adults, like the person in the photo, are not as fortunate. They have physical disabilities, are very ill, and may have cognitive or psychological disorders. **These *frail older adults* constitute a minority of the population over age 65, but a proportion that increases with age.**

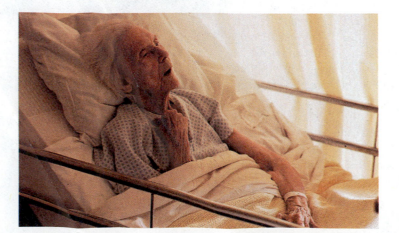

Frail older adults are people whose competence (in terms of the competence–environmental press model presented earlier) is declining. However, they do not have one specific problem that differentiates them from their active, healthy counterparts (Guralnick & Simonsick, 1993). **In general, they are unable to perform one or more basic self-care tasks such as eat-**

ing, bathing, toileting, walking, or dressing; collectively, these tasks are called *activities of daily living* or *ADLs.* A person could be considered frail if he or she needs help with one of these tasks.

Other tasks are also considered important for living independently. **These *instrumental activities of daily living (IADLs)* are actions that require some intellectual competence and planning.** Which actions constitute IADLs vary considerably from one culture to another (Katz, 1983). For example, for most older adults in Western culture IADLs would include shopping for personal items, paying bills, making telephone calls, taking medications appropriately, and keeping appointments. In other cultures, IADLs might include caring for animal herds, making bread, threshing grain, and tending crops.

PREVALENCE OF FRAILTY

How common are people like Maria, the 82-year-old woman in the fourth chapter-opening vignette who still lives in the same neighborhood in which she grew up? As you can see in the graph, several studies show that the number of

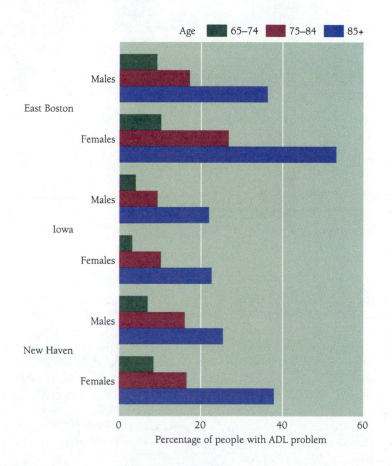

Percentage of people with ADL problem

older people needing help with ADLs increases dramatically with age (Guralnick & Wallace, 1991). Less than 10% of adults aged 65–74 need assistance, whereas as many as half of women over age 85 may need help. Poor health exacerbates the problem. One extensive study of people's functioning in the year prior to their death showed that over 70% of all older adults needed help with

ADLs; indeed, virtually everyone over age 85 needed some assistance, and half required help with all ADLs (Lentzner et al., 1992).

Similar results have been reported for IADLs. As you can see in the graph, the number of adults requiring assistance with IADLs also increases drastically after age 85 (Fulton et al., 1989).

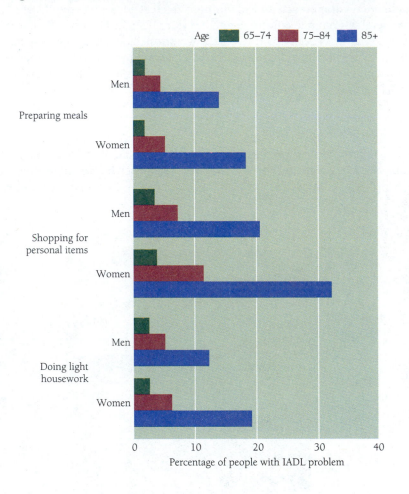

Why is the number of frail older adults increasing? First, the number of people living to very old age is increasing faster than any other segment of the population (see Chapter 13). Second, many older adults do not have access to medical interventions that could prevent some causes of frailty. For example, urinary incontinence can be treated effectively with behavioral interventions, which are unavailable to many older adults who are poor and members of an ethnic minority. Third, although the Older Americans Act provides much-needed assistance to thousands of older citizens through subsidized meals and social services, there are serious gaps in these programs. For example, many of the services require copayments, or transportation to the service delivery site, and they may be unavailable in rural areas.

Although frailty becomes more likely with increasing age, especially during the last year of life, there are many ways to help provide a supportive environment for frail older adults. We have already seen how many family members provide care. Later, we will consider the role that nursing homes play. The key to providing a supportive context for frail older adults is to create an optimal match between the person's competence and the environmental demands.

Living in the Community

Most older adults continue living in the community all of their lives, even if they need some assistance with ADLs. As shown in the figure, no less than 75% of women and 85% of men live in the community (Schneider & Guralnick, 1990). However, the number of older adults living at home who need assistance roughly doubles each decade over age 65. These increases parallel the age-related increases in the level of disability and dependence we described in the previous section.

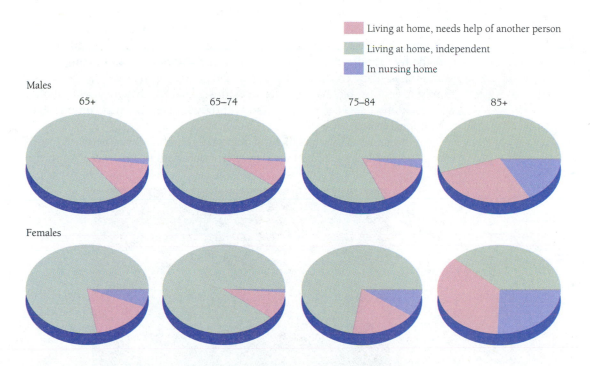

Where do all of these people live? **By far, most older adults live in *age-integrated housing*, where people of all ages live together and interact.** Most neighborhoods here and in other countries are age-integrated (Silverman, 1987). Young children and their parents live next to older adults, and all age groups see each other daily. **However, a growing number of older adults here and in other countries live in *age-segregated housing* (in which all residents are older adults), in other types of housing (such as resident hotels), or in no home at all.** Among such living arrangements are (Silverman, 1987):

- *Age-segregated apartment complexes for older adults,* some of which subsidize rents for less affluent residents.

- *Age-segregated retirement communities,* most of which cater to the needs of older adults.

- *Age-segregated communal housing* (sometimes called *assisted living*), which is an intermediate step between living independently and living in a nursing home.

- *Single-room-occupancy hotels,* which vary from skid row hotels for very poor residents to working-class or middle-class hotels that may even have organized activities for older residents.

- *Continuing care retirement communities,* which offer a continuum of care from independent housing through nursing homes.

Numerous studies on residents' satisfaction with their housing arrangements provide evidence for the competence–environmental press model presented at the beginning of the chapter. Research over several decades shows that the satisfaction of residents is not simply a matter of being all nearly the same age (or different ages). Only when the individual's needs (competence) match the demands of the environment (environmental press) are residents likely to be mostly satisfied with their living arrangements (Longino, 1982; Silverman, 1987).

For example, one study of an ethnically diverse, 400-resident, high-rise, age-segregated apartment complex found that healthy residents resented frail residents, ethnic tensions were high, and many residents were socially isolated, apathetic, and passive (Jacobs, 1975). In this study, healthy residents feared that the frail residents would want to turn the complex into a nursing home. Moreover, as many college students who live in large residence halls will attest, simply having people live together does not guarantee that they will interact with each other socially. For frail and withdrawn residents, this complex was not an ideal match.

Sadly, many older adults like the person in the photo have no place to call home. No one knows for certain how many homeless people there are in the

United States; estimates range as high as 3 million. Researchers estimate that between 25% and 30% of all homeless people are over age 60 (Cohen et al., 1988). Homeless older adults represent all ethnic groups, both men and women, as well as many different educational levels and prior occupations.

Older adults become homeless for varying reasons (Martin, 1990). Some people lose their jobs and income and have nowhere to go. Some are battered women. Some have serious untreated mental disorders or substance abuse problems. Unfortunately, we know so little about homeless older adults that we can say almost nothing about how to remedy the problem.

Living in Nursing Homes

As we have seen, the vast majority of older adults do not live in nursing homes. Most do not want to live in nursing homes; their families would also prefer some other solution. A nursing home is often viewed by older adults as a place where people go to die, and people who live there are considered abandoned by their families. Sometimes, though, placement in a nursing home is necessary because of the older person's needs or the family's circumstances.

Governmental regulations in the United States define two levels of care in nursing homes (Johnson & Grant, 1985). **Intermediate care consists of 24-hour care necessitating nursing supervision, but usually not at an intense level.** *Skilled nursing care* **consists of 24-hour care requiring fairly constant monitoring and provision of medical and other health services, usually by nurses.** Each state has specific regulations concerning each type of care.

WHO LIVES IN NURSING HOMES?

Look again at the pie charts on page 507. Notice that the proportion of 65–74-year-olds who live in nursing homes is very small. But this increases dramatically to 15% for men and 25% for women by the time they are over 85.

Beginning around age 75, women are nearly twice as likely to live in nursing homes than are men. Why is this the case? Usually, older men who need health or living assistance get help from their wives, whereas older women with similar needs are more likely to be widows or living alone for other reasons and have fewer caregiving options. Thus, these women are at higher risk for nursing home placement (Wolinsky et al., 1992).

In general, ethnic minority older adults have lower rates of nursing home placement than European Americans (Wolinsky et al., 1992). The reasons for these differences are not entirely clear. They may be due in part to different norms for caregiving: Some cultures may prefer to rely on family caregivers rather than institutions (Johnson & Barer, 1990). Also, groups have varying access to health care providers, including nursing homes, for financial reasons (Belgrave, Wykle, & Choi, 1993). Furthermore, members of some ethnic groups may lack knowledge about nursing homes as an option (Segall & Wykle, 1988–89).

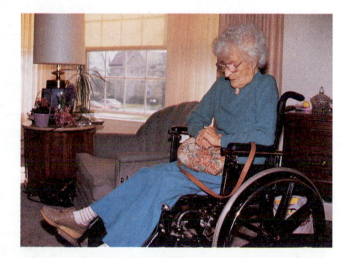

Contrary to popular belief, only about 5% of older adults live in nursing homes at any given point in time. The typical resident is a European American female who is in very frail health.

WHAT CHARACTERIZES A GOOD NURSING HOME?

Nursing homes vary a great deal in the amount and quality of care they provide. One useful way of evaluating them is by applying the competence–environmental press model. When applied to nursing homes, the goal is to find the optimal level of environmental support for people who have relatively low levels of competence.

Some researchers point out that congruence between the resident's needs and the ability of the nursing home to meet them is the crucial element for optimizing well-being (Kahana, 1982). An important part of meeting residents' needs is fostering family visitation. Research has shown that residents who were visited often by their families had significantly higher levels of psychosocial functioning (Greene & Monahan, 1982). Some tips on visiting people in nursing homes are presented in the You May Be Wondering feature.

How Do You Respond to a Nursing Home Resident?

The first time most people enter a nursing home, they are ill-prepared for what they experience: trying to talk to family members who are frail, have trouble remembering, and cannot get around very well. The hardest part is trying to figure out what to say.

However, visiting residents of nursing homes is a way to maintain social contacts and provide a meaningful activity. Even if the person you are visiting is frail or has a sensory impairment or some other type of disability, visits can be uplifting. As noted earlier in the chapter, high-quality social contacts help older adults maintain their life satisfaction. Listed below are several suggestions for making visits more pleasant (Papalia & Olds, 1995; adapted from Davis, 1985).

- Concentrate on the older adult's expertise and wisdom, as discussed in Chapter 13, by asking for advice on a life problem that he or she knows a lot about, such as dealing with friends, cooking, or crafts.
- Allow the older person to exert control over the visit: where to go (even inside the facility), what to wear, what to eat (if choices are possible).
- Listen attentively, even if the older person is repetitive. Avoid being judgmental, be sympathetic to complaints, and acknowledge feelings.
- Talk about things the person likes to remember, such as raising children, military service, growing up, work, courtship, and so on.
- Do a joint activity, such as putting a jigsaw puzzle together, arranging a photograph album, or doing arts and crafts.
- Record your visit on audiotape or videotape. This is valuable for creating a family history that you will be able to keep. The activity may facilitate a life review, as well as provide an opportunity for the older person to leave something of value for future generations by describing important personal events and philosophies.
- Bring children when you visit, if possible. Grandchildren are especially important, as most older adults are very happy to include them in conversations. Such visits also give children the opportunity to see their grandparents and learn about the diversity of older adults.
- Stimulate as many senses as possible. Wearing bright clothes and cologne, singing songs, reading books, and sharing foods (as long as they have been checked with the staff) help keep residents involved with their environment. Above all, though, hold hands. There's nothing like a friendly touch.

Always remember that your visits may be the only way that the residents have of maintaining social contacts with friends and family. By following these guidelines, you will be able to avoid difficulties and make your visits more pleasurable.   ❧

How nursing home residents are treated by staff is also a key to well-being. Most important, residents need to perceive that they have some degree of control in their lives (Langer, 1985). To demonstrate this point, Langer and Rodin (1976) conducted an ingenious experiment. One group of nursing home residents was told that staff members were there to care for them and to make decisions for them about their daily lives. In contrast, a second group of residents were encouraged to make their own decisions about meals, recreational activities, and so forth. Results showed that more than 90% of the second group showed significant improvement in well-being and activity level. But more than 70% of the passive group became weaker and more disabled, and they were more likely to have died 18 months later (Rodin & Langer, 1977).

An implication of these findings is that staff should provide help only when necessary, and repetitive routines should be avoided (Langer, 1985). These characteristics are most likely to be found in larger nonprofit facilities that have a high ratio of nurses to nurse's aides (Pillemer & Moore, 1989).

Elder Abuse and Neglect

Arletta, an 82-year-old woman in relatively poor health, has been living with her 60-year-old daughter Sally for the past two years. Recently, neighbors became concerned because they had not seen Arletta very much for several months. When they did, she looked rather worn and extremely thin, and as if she had not bathed in weeks. Finally, the neighbors decided that they should do something, so they called the local office of the department of human services. Upon hearing the details of the situation, a case worker immediately investigated. The case worker found that Arletta was severely malnourished, had not bathed in weeks, and appeared disoriented. Based on these findings, the agency concluded that Arletta was a victim of neglect. She was moved to a county nursing home temporarily.

Unfortunately, some older adults who need quality caregiving by family members or in nursing homes do not receive it. In some cases, older adults, like Arletta, are treated inappropriately. Arletta's case is representative of this sad but increasing problem: elder abuse and neglect. In this section, we will consider what elder abuse and neglect are, how often they happen, and what victims and abusers are like.

DEFINING ELDER ABUSE AND NEGLECT

Like child abuse (see Chapter 7) and spousal abuse (see Chapter 10), elder abuse is difficult to define precisely in practice. In general, researchers and public policy advocates describe several different categories of elder abuse (National Aging Resource Center on Elder Abuse, 1990): physical (such as beating or withholding care), psychological/emotional (such as verbal assaults and social isolation), sexual, material or financial exploitation (such as illegal or improper use of funds), and the violation of rights (such as being forced out of one's house or being denied privacy).

In addition to abuse, neglect of older adults is also a growing problem (NARCEA, 1990). Neglecting older adults can be either intended, such as refusing to fulfill basic caregiving obligations with the intention of inflicting harm, or unintended, such as not providing adequate medical care because of a lack of knowledge on the caregiver's part (Wolf, Godkin, & Pillemer, 1986).

Part of the problem in agreeing on a common definition of elder abuse and neglect is that perceptions differ among ethnic groups. For example, African American, Korean American, and European American older females used different criteria in deciding whether scenarios they read represented abuse (Moon & Williams, 1993). Specifically, older Korean American women were much less likely to judge a particular scenario as abusive and to indicate that help should be sought than women in either of the other two groups. Such ethnic differences may result in conflicts between social service workers using one set of definitions and clients using another, in deciding who should receive protective services.

PREVALENCE

Official estimates suggest that 3–4% of older adults in the United States are the victims of abuse or neglect. However, as is the case with child and spousal abuse, most researchers believe these estimates to be low (NARCEA, 1990). The most common forms are neglect, physical abuse, and financial or material exploitation. Thus, Arletta's case of neglect would be one of the most common types.

Abuse and neglect are not limited to older adults living in the community. In a study of 577 randomly selected nurses and nurse's aides who worked in intermediate care and skilled nursing facilities, Pillemer and Moore (1989) asked respondents about actions they had either performed themselves or had witnessed other staff commit. They reported that 10% of the respondents admitted to physically abusing a resident, and 40% admitted to psychologically abusing a resident at least once during the previous year. Additionally, 36% reported seeing acts of physical abuse, and 81% reported observing acts of psychological abuse over the same time period.

VICTIM AND ABUSER PROFILES

Relatively little research has focused on the characteristics of victims of elder abuse or neglect. Moreover, there is considerable controversy about the characteristics of abuse victims and perpetrators. One view is that victims tend to be overly dependent on others, and abuse is caused by the extreme stress associated with providing care (Steinmetz, 1993). Such victims are usually over age 80, female, excessively loyal to their caregiver, involved in frequent intergenerational conflict, burdened with a history of past abuse, socially isolated, and relatively unpleasant or demanding.

An alternative view is that the victim is not dependent; rather, it is the perpetrator who is dependent on the victim (Pillemer, 1993). That is, abuse is thought to be caused by the deviance and dependence of caregivers. In particular, perpetrators were dependent on victims in four areas: housing, financial assistance, household repair, and transportation.

These differing views of who gets abused and why represent very different theoretical positions. These positions are discussed more thoroughly in the Current Controversies feature.

CURRENT CONTROVERSIES

Which Older People Are Abused and Why?

One of the most controversial issues in aging is which older adults are at greatest risk for abuse and neglect. Sorting out this issue is important, in order to provide the most appropriate services to victims and to develop effective prevention strategies. As noted in the text, there are two competing views of who is at risk. At the heart of the debate is a deceptively simple question: Are abuse victims dependent on perpetrators, or are perpetrators dependent on abuse victims?

Most researchers and policymakers assume that abuse victims are dependent. Indeed, the typical picture is one of a victim who has been abused by his or her caregiver, who in turn is under considerable stress from having to provide care (Steinmetz, 1993). The stress, frustration, and burden caregivers experience are too much for some to take; they lash out and turn their emotions into abusive behavior. In this view, abuse and neglect of older adults have much in common with child abuse and neglect; both involve victims who are highly dependent on their perpetrators for basic care. This view is easy for people to understand, which is probably the reason why most prevention programs are based on a dependent-victim model.

Other researchers strongly disagree. Rather than the victims being dependent on caregiver-perpetrators, they see the perpetrators as being dependent on the victims (Pillemer, 1993). These perpetrators are not merely acting out their frustration; they are seen as deviant and suffering from mental disorders. In this approach, perpetrators depend on their victims for basic necessities, such as a place to live and financial assistance. Perpetrators also tend to be more violent in general, to have been arrested for other crimes, and to have been hospitalized for psychiatric disorders (Pillemer, 1993).

Which of these views is correct? The answer has profound implications for prevention and treatment. If victims are dependent, then programs are needed to provide basic services to caregivers to lower their stress. If perpetrators are deviant and have mental disorders, then programs need to identify individuals who are at risk for abusing older adults. Clearly, additional research is needed to provide the appropriate direction for policymakers and to settle the controversy.   ❧

Much more attention has been paid to identifying characteristics of abusers. Adult children are generally more likely to abuse older adults than are other people (NARCEA, 1990). In general, people who abuse or neglect older adults show higher rates of substance abuse and mental health problems, are inexperienced caregivers, have more economic problems, receive little help from other family members for caregiving, are hypercritical and insensitive to others, and are more likely to have been abused themselves (NARCEA, 1990; Pillemer, 1993).

An important exception to these general patterns is abuse of persons with dementia. Research has shown that in this case, the spouse is much more likely to actually become violent with the care-recipient, especially when the spousal caregiver has previously experienced violent or aggressive behavior from the care-recipient (Pillemer & Suitor, 1992). There is some reason for hope, however. Additional data suggest that spousal caregivers who have violent feelings report a greater likelihood that they will place the care-recipient in a nursing home in the near future (Pillemer & Suitor, 1992).

These characteristics fit with the family violence model as an explanation of abuse in general (see Chapter 10). Some authors argue that elder abuse and neglect can be likened to cases of spousal abuse when the perpetrator is a spouse, and likened to child abuse when the perpetrator is a family caregiver (Steinmetz, 1993). Other writers (Pillemer, 1993) deny any similarity between abuse of older adults and that of children, except in cases where mental disorders are present in both types of abusers. Although more research is needed to sort out these possible connections, abuse and neglect of older adults clearly could have aspects in common with other types of family violence. More research could lead to a general theoretical model of spousal and intergenerational abuse, which would allow us to know the circumstances most likely to give rise to abuse and neglect.

TEST YOURSELF

1. Activities of daily living (ADLs) include functioning in the areas of _____ .
2. Most older adults live in _____ .
3. Most people who live in nursing homes are _____ .
4. The group that most often abuses older adults is _____ .
5. How would the competence–environmental press framework, presented earlier in this chapter, apply specifically to the various types of housing and nursing homes discussed in this section?

Putting It All Together

From the moment our parents first thought about us, we have been involved in human relationships. We saw in this chapter that these involvements continue throughout old age. In a very real sense, people grow old within the broader social context of their environment and social network.

We discovered how the match between one's competence and the environmental demands one faces sets the stage for how well one adapts. How older people cope with daily life is typically a continuation of the ways they coped throughout their lives. We encountered people who, like Olive, spend time reflecting on their past in order to determine whether their lives have been well spent. We saw that the view of retirement as detrimental to health and as a cause of isolation is wrong; most people are like Marcus, who greatly enjoys retirement. Many older women, like Alma, are widows; such women are especially vulnerable to financial pressures. Also, like Maria, many people over 80 need assistance with their daily needs.

The general picture of older adults is characterized by continued activity for most. Still, we need to recognize that, especially among the oldest old, physical limitations are an important aspect of living. Although only a very small proportion of older adults are in nursing homes, many people over 80 need varying degrees of help to continue living independently.

Combined with Chapter 13, this chapter provides insight into the complexities of old age. So what do we know about a person if we know she is 85 years old? Not much more than the fact that she has celebrated 85 birthdays. That's not bad, either—it means that if you want to know something more than that, you'll need to get to know her.

We can now take a broader view of the biopsychosocial model as it relates to aging. In this chapter, we focused mainly on how sociocultural forces shape people's lives by setting the context for retirement and interpersonal relationships, as well as setting the agenda for social issues. How well people are able to face sociocultural forces (as exemplified by environmental press) is a function of their biological and psychological competence. Of course, this function is a dynamic one that changes as people grow older.

Thinking about Development

1. How does the competence–environmental press theory reflect biological, psychological, social, and life-cycle forces?

2. Connect the discussions of possible selves in this chapter and in Chapter 9 to create a description of adult development.

3. Now that all of Erikson's eight stages have been discussed, put them all together. Does this theory reflect a view of development based on continuity or discontinuity (as discussed in Chapter 1)? Why?

4. How are friendships and family and partner relationships in old age continuations of patterns established earlier in adulthood (discussed in Chapters 10 and 12)? How do they differ?

5. How do you think the social issues of aging discussed in the chapter will be affected by the projected increase in the number of older adults in the population?

Summary

Theories of Psychosocial Aging

Activity, Disengagement, and Continuity

■ Activity theory argues that older adults need to substitute new roles and activities for the ones they relinquish through retirement or the death of their partner or friends, and that they are more satisfied the more active they are. Disengagement theory claims that older adults normally withdraw from social contacts as they age. Research does not support a strong version of either activity or disengagement theory. Neither theory is sufficient to explain the aging process. Continuity theory is based on the view that people respond to daily life in old age in much the same way they responded in the past. There is support for this view from research in behavioral genetics.

Competence and Environmental Press

■ According to competence–environmental press theory, people's optimal adaptation occurs when there is a balance between their ability to cope and the level of environmental demands placed on them. When balance is not achieved, behavior becomes maladaptive. Several studies indicate that competence–environmental press theory can be applied to a variety of real-world situations.

Personality Development in Later Life

Integrity versus Despair

■ Older adults face the Eriksonian struggle of integrity versus despair, primarily through a life review. Integrity involves accepting one's life for what it is; despair involves bitterness about one's past. People who reach integrity become self-affirming and self-accepting, and they judge their lives to have been worthwhile and good.

Well-Being and Possible Selves in Later Life

■ Ryff has identified six aspects to well-being: self-acceptance, positive relation with others, autonomy, environmental mastery, purpose in life, and personal growth. Older adults view their past more positively than younger or middle-aged adults, and they see themselves as closer to their ideal selves.

Religiosity

■ Older adults use religion more often than any other strategy to help them cope with problems of life. This is especially true for African American women, who are more active in their church groups and attend services more frequently.

I Used to Work at . . .: Living in Retirement

What Does Being Retired Mean?

■ Retirement is a complex process by which people withdraw from full-time employment. No single definition is adequate for all ethnic groups; self-definition involves several factors, including eligibility for certain social programs.

Why Do People Retire?

■ People generally retire because they choose to, although some people are forced to retire or do so because of serious health problems, such as cardiovascular disease or cancer. However, there are important gender and ethnic differences in the reasons people retire and how they label themselves after retirement. Most of the research is based on European American men from traditional marriages.

Adjustment to Retirement

■ Retirement is an important life transition. Most people are satisfied with retirement. Most retired people maintain their health, friendship networks, and activity levels, at least in the years immediately following retirement. For men, personal life priorities are all-important; little is known about women's retirement satisfaction. Most retired people stay busy in activities such as volunteer work and helping others.

Interpersonal Ties

■ Retiring can disrupt long-held behavior patterns in marriages. Social relationships help buffer the stress of retirement. Readjusting to being home rather than at work is difficult for men in traditional marriages. Marriages are sometimes disrupted, but married men are generally happier in retirement than men who are not married. Participation in community organizations helps raise satisfaction. In particular, volunteer work can fill the void. Improved attitudes toward older adults in society also help.

Friends and Family in Late Life

Friends and Siblings

■ A person's social convoy is an important source of satisfaction in late life. Patterns of friendships among older adults are very similar to those among young adults. Sibling relationships are especially important in old age. Five types of sibling relationships have been identified: intimate, congenial, loyal, apathetic, and hostile. The loyal and congenial types are the most common. Ties between sisters are the strongest.

Marriage

■ Long-term marriages tend to be happy until one partner develops serious health problems. Older married couples show a lower potential for marital conflict and greater potential for pleasure. Overall, older married couples are more alike than younger married couples.

Caring for a Spouse

■ Caring for a spouse puts considerable strain on the relationship. The degree of marital satisfaction strongly affects how spousal caregivers perceive stress. Although caught off guard initially, most spousal caregivers are able to provide adequate care. Perceptions of competence among spousal caregivers at the outset of caregiving may be especially important.

Widowhood

■ Widowhood is a difficult transition for most people. Feelings of loneliness are hard to cope with, especially during the first few months following bereavement. Men generally have problems in social relationships and in household tasks; women tend to have more severe financial problems. Some widowed people remarry, partly to solve loneliness and financial problems.

Great-Grandparenthood

■ Becoming a great-grandparent is an important source of personal satisfaction for many older adults. Great-grandparents as a group are more similar to each other than grandparents are. Three aspects of great-grandparenthood are most important: sense of personal and family renewal; new diversions in life; and a major life milestone.

Social Issues and Aging

Frail Older Adults

■ The number of frail older adults is growing. Frailty is defined in terms of impairment in activities of daily liv-

ing (basic self-care skills) and instrumental activities of daily living (actions that require intellectual competence or planning). As many as half of the women over age 85 may need assistance with ADLs or IADLs. Supportive environments are useful in optimizing the balance between competence and environmental press.

Living in the Community

■ Most older adults live in the community in age-integrated housing. However, several other housing options exist, including age-segregated apartment complexes, retirement communities, communal housing, single-room occupancy hotels, and continuing care retirement communities. Regardless of the type of community, a match between people's needs and environmental demands is necessary for life satisfaction. Homelessness is a growing problem among older adults.

Living in Nursing Homes

■ Two levels of care are provided in nursing homes: intermediate care and skilled nursing care. Most residents of nursing homes are European American women who are in poor health. Ethnic minority older adults have a lower rate of placement in nursing homes than European Americans. Maintaining a resident's sense of control is an important component of good nursing homes.

Elder Abuse and Neglect

■ Abuse and neglect of older adults is an increasing problem, both in people living in the community and in nursing home residents. However, abuse and neglect are difficult to define precisely. Several categories are used, including physical, psychological/emotional, sexual, material or financial, and violation of rights. Most perpetrators are adult children of the victims. It is unclear whether older adult victims are dependent on their caregivers or the caregivers are dependent on the victims.

Key Terms

activities of daily living
   (ADLs) (505)
activity theory (483)
adaptation level (485)
age-integrated housing (507)
age-segregated housing (507)
competence (485)
continuity theory (484)

disengagement theory (483)
docility (486)
environmental press (485)
frail older adults (504)
instrumental activities of daily
   living (IADLs) (505)
integrity versus despair (488)
intermediate care (509)

life review (488)
proactivity (486)
skilled nursing care (509)
social convoy (498)
zone of maximum performance
   potential (485)
zone of maximum comfort (485)

If You'd Like to Learn More

BRUBAKER, T. H. (1990). *Family relationships in later life* (2nd ed.). Newbury Park, CA: Sage. This excellent introduction to family issues in older adults makes moderately difficult reading.

ERIKSON, E. H. (1982). *The life cycle completed: Review.* New York: Norton. By Erikson's own account, this short book represents a summary of his theory. It is moderately difficult reading.

JOHNSON, C. L. (1987). The institutional segregation of the elderly. In P. Silverman (Ed.), *The elderly as modern pioneers* (pp. 307–319). Bloomington, IN: University of Indiana Press. This easy-to-read chapter is an excellent introduction to issues in how older adults in nursing homes are treated.

MACE, N. L., & RABINS, P. V. (1991). *The 36-hour day* (2nd ed.). Baltimore: Johns Hopkins University Press. This is the best available overall guide to family caregiving for dementia patients.

MACNAB, F. (1994). *The 30 vital years.* New York: Wiley. This easy-to-read book discusses psychosocial aging and includes many anecdotes and case studies.

Greta, a college sophomore, was very upset when she learned that her roommate's mother had died suddenly. Her roommate was Jewish, and Greta had no idea what customs would be followed during the funeral. When Greta arrived at her roommate's house, she was surprised to find that all of the mirrors in the house were covered. Greta realized for the first time that death rituals vary in different religious traditions.

Donna and Carl have a 5-year-old daughter, Jennie, whose grandmother just died. Jennie and her grandmother were very close, as the two saw each other almost every day. Other adults have told her parents not to take Jennie to the funeral. Donna and Carl aren't sure what to do. They wonder whether Jennie will understand what happened to her grandmother, and they worry about how she will react.

Betty, 48 years old, was recently diagnosed with terminal ovarian cancer. She is having trouble dealing with the news. Betty wonders why she ended up with the disease rather than someone else, and she is very angry about it. Betty wonders if her feelings are normal.

After 67 years of marriage, Bertha lost her husband recently. At age 90, Bertha knew that neither she nor her husband was likely to live much longer, but the death was a shock just the same. Bertha thinks about him much of the time and often finds herself making decisions on the basis of "what John would have done" in the same situation.

Clare, 37, and her brother Alex, 41, lost their parents in an accident a few months ago. Since then, they have been thinking a lot about becoming the oldest generation in their family. Their experience has given both of them a new perspective on life and made them aware of their own mortality.

Dying and
Bereavement

We have a paradoxical relation-ship with death. Sometimes, we are fascinated by it. As tourists, we visit places where famous people died or are buried. We watch as television news-casts show people being killed in war. But when it comes to pondering our own death or that of people close to us, we have many problems. As La Rochefou-cauld, a French writer and reformer, wrote over 300 years ago, looking into the sun is easier than contem-plating our death. When death is personal, we become uneasy. Looking at the sun is hard indeed.

In this chapter, we will first consider definitional and ethical issues surrounding death. Next, we will ex-amine how people view death at different points in the life span. Third, we will look specifically at the process of dying. Dealing with grief is important for survivors, so we will consider this topic in the fourth section. In the fifth section, we will see how people cope with dif-ferent types of loss. Finally, we will try to make sense of near-death experiences.

Definitions and Ethical Issues

LEARNING OBJECTIVES

❧ *How is death defined?*

❧ *What legal and medical criteria are used to determine when death occurs?*

❧ *What are the ethical dilemmas surrounding euthanasia?*

Take a minute to look closely at the man visiting the grave of his deceased wife. His loss is obvious. Based on everyday experiences like this, death seems a very simple concept to define: the point at which a person is no longer alive. Simi-

larly, dying is simply the process of making the transition from being alive to being dead. It all seems clear enough, doesn't it? But death and dying are actually far more complicated and very hard to define. As we will see, the definition depends on the observer's perspective.

Sociocultural Definitions of Death

What comes to mind when you hear the word *death*? A driver killed in a traffic accident? A transition to an eternal reward? Black crepe paper? A cemetery? A car battery that doesn't work anymore? Each of these possibilities represents a way in which death can be considered in Western culture (Kalish, 1987). Other cultures have their own views. Among the Melanesians, the term *mate* includes the very sick, the very old, and the dead; the term *toa* refers to all other living people (Counts & Counts, 1985). Other South Pacific cultures believe that the life force may leave the body during sleep or illness; sleep, illness, and death are considered together. Thus, people "die" several times before experiencing "final death" (Counts & Counts, 1985).

Mourning rituals and states of bereavement also vary in different cultures (Simmons, 1945). Some cultures have formalized periods of time during which certain prayers or rituals are performed. For example, after the death of a close relative, Orthodox Jews recite ritual prayers and cover all the mirrors in the house. The men slash their ties as a symbol of loss. These are the customs that Greta, the college student we met in the first vignette, experienced. Thus, we must keep in mind that the experiences of our culture or particular group may not generalize to other cultures or groups.

Altogether, death can be viewed in at least ten ways (Kalish, 1987; Kastenbaum, 1985). Look at the list that follows and think about the examples of these different definitions. Then take another moment to think up some additional examples of your own.

The death of Emperor Hirohito in Japan was accompanied by nationwide mourning and rituals. The loss of prominent people and national leaders is captured by the notion of death as an event.

Death as an Image or Object

A flag at half-staff
Sympathy cards
Tombstone
Black crepe paper
Hearse
Monument or memorial

Death as a Statistic

Mortality rates
Number of AIDS patients who die
Murder and suicide rates
Life expectancy tables

Death as an Event

Funeral
Cemetery service
Family gathering
Memorial service
Viewing or wake

Death as a State of Being

Time of waiting
Nothingness
Transformation
Being happy with God all the time
State of being; pure energy

Death as an Analogy

Dead as a doornail
Dead letter box
Dead-end street
You're dead meat
In the dead of winter

Death as a Mystery

What is it like to die?
Will we meet family?
What happens after death?
Will I learn everything when I die?

Death as a Boundary

How many years do I have left?
You can't come back
What will happen to my family?
What do I do now?

Death as a Thief of Meaning

I feel so cheated
Why should I go on living?
Life doesn't mean much anymore

Death as Fear and Anxiety

Will dying hurt?
I worry about my family
I'm afraid to die
Who will care for the kids?

Death as Reward or Punishment

Live long and prosper
The wicked go to hell
Heaven awaits the just
Purgatory prepares you for heaven

Legal and Medical Definitions

Sociocultural approaches help us understand the different ways in which people view death. But they do not address a very fundamental question: How do we determine that someone has died? The medical and legal communities have grappled with this question for centuries and continue to do so today. Let us see what the current answers are.

Determining when death occurs has always been subjective. **For hundreds of years, people accepted and applied the criteria that now define** *clinical death*: **lack of heartbeat and respiration. Today, however, the most widely accepted criteria are those that characterize** *brain death*:

1. No spontaneous movement in response to any stimuli
2. No spontaneous respirations for at least one hour
3. Total lack of responsiveness to even the most painful stimuli
4. No eye movements, blinking, or pupil responses
5. No postural activity, swallowing, yawning, or vocalizing
6. No motor reflexes
7. A flat electroencephalogram (EEG) for at least 10 minutes
8. No change in any of these criteria when they are tested again 24 hours later

For a person to be declared brain dead, all eight criteria must be met. Moreover, other conditions that might mimic death—such as deep coma, hypothermia, or drug overdose—must be ruled out. Finally, according to most hospitals, the lack of brain activity must prevail both in the brainstem (which involves vegetative functions such as heartbeat and respiration) and in the cortex (which involves higher processes such as thinking). **It is possible for a person's cortical functioning to cease while brainstem activity continues; this is a** *persistent vegetative state,* **from which the person does not recover.** This condition can occur following a severe head injury or a drug overdose. Often, the person's relatives must make difficult ethical decisions.

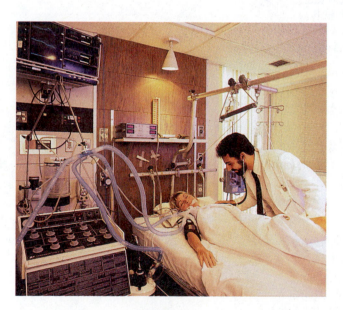

The decision to remove a person from a life support system presents a serious ethical dilemma to health care workers and family members alike. Situations like this help shape both health care policy and the very definition of death.

Ethical Issues

An ambulance screeches to a halt, and emergency personnel rush a woman into the emergency room. As a result of an accident at a swimming pool, she has no pulse and no respiration. Working rapidly, the trauma team reestablishes a heartbeat through electric shock. A respirator is connected. An EEG and other tests reveal extensive and irreversible brain damage. What should be done?

This is an example of the kinds of problems faced in the field of *bioethics,* **the study of the interface between human values and technological advances in health and life sciences. In the arena of death and dying, the most important bioethical issue is** *euthanasia*—**the practice of ending life for reasons of mercy.** The moral dilemma posed by euthanasia becomes apparent when we try to decide the circumstances under which a person's life should be ended. In our society this dilemma occurs most often when a person is being kept alive by machines or when someone is suffering from a terminal illness.

Euthanasia can be carried out in two different ways: active and passive. *Active euthanasia* **involves the deliberate ending of someone's life, which may be based on a clear statement of the person's wishes or a decision made by someone else who has the legal authority to do so.** Usually, this involves situations in which people are in a persistent vegetative state or suffer from the end stages of a terminal disease. Examples of active euthanasia would be administering a drug overdose, disconnecting a life-support system, or ending a person's life through so-called mercy killing. One widely reported example of active euthanasia involved Dr. Jack Kevorkian, a physician in Michigan shown in the photo, who created a suicide machine. In the early 1990s, Dr. Kevorkian's machine allowed several individuals with terminal diseases to give themselves lethal doses of medication or carbon monoxide.

The second form of euthanasia, *passive euthanasia*, **involves allowing a person to die by withholding available treatment.** For example, chemotherapy might be withheld from a cancer patient; a surgical procedure might not be performed; or food could be withdrawn. Again, these approaches are controversial. On the one hand, few would argue with a decision not to treat a newly discovered cancer in a person in the late stages of Alzheimer's disease, if treatment would do nothing but prolong and make even more agonizing an already certain death. On the other hand, many people might argue against withholding nourishment from a terminally ill person; indeed, such cases often end up in court. For example, in 1990 the U.S. Supreme Court took up the case of Nancy Cruzan, whose family wanted to end her forced feeding. The court ruled that unless clear and incontrovertible evidence is presented that an individual desires to have nourishment stopped (such as through a durable power of attorney or living will), a third party (such as a parent or partner) cannot decide to end it.

Euthanasia is a complex legal and ethical issue. In most jurisdictions, euthanasia is legal only when a person has made known his or her wishes concerning medical intervention. Unfortunately, many people fail to take this step, perhaps because it is difficult to think about such situations or because they do not know the options available to them. But without clear directions, medical personnel may be unable to take a patient's preferences into account.

There are two ways to make one's intentions known: living wills and durable power of attorney (like the one shown here). The purpose of

California Medical Association
DURABLE POWER OF ATTORNEY FOR HEALTH CARE DECISIONS
(California Probate Code Sections 4600-4753)

WARNING TO PERSON EXECUTING THIS DOCUMENT

This is an important legal document. Before executing this document, you should know these important facts:

This document gives the person you designate as your agent (the attorney-in-fact) the power to make health care decisions for you. Your agent must act consistently with your desires as stated in this document or otherwise made known.

Except as you otherwise specify in this document, this document gives your agent power to consent to your doctor not giving treatment or stopping treatment necessary to keep you alive.

Notwithstanding this document, you have the right to make medical and other health care decisions for yourself so long as you can give informed consent with respect to the particular decision. In addition, no treatment may be given to you over your objection, and health care necessary to keep you alive may not be stopped or withheld if you object at the time.

This document gives your agent authority to consent, to refuse to consent, or to withdraw consent to any care, treatment, service, or procedure to maintain, diagnose, or treat a physical or mental condition. This power is subject to any statement of your desires and any limitations that you include in this document. You may state in this document any types of treatment that you do not desire. In addition, a court can take away the power of your agent to make health care decisions for you if your agent (1) authorizes anything that is illegal, (2) acts contrary to your known desires or (3) where your desires are not known, does anything that is clearly contrary to your best interests.

This power will exist for an indefinite period of time unless you limit its duration in this document.

You have the right to revoke the authority of your agent by notifying your agent or your treating doctor, hospital, or other health care provider orally or in writing of the revocation.

Your agent has the right to examine your medical records and to consent to their disclosure unless you limit this right in this document.

Unless you otherwise specify in this document, this document gives your agent the power after you die to (1) authorize an autopsy, (2) donate your body or parts thereof for transplant or therapeutic or educational or scientific purposes, and (3) direct the disposition of your remains.

If there is anything in this document that you do not understand, you should ask a lawyer to explain it to you.

1. CREATION OF DURABLE POWER OF ATTORNEY FOR HEALTH CARE

By this document I intend to create a durable power of attorney by appointing the person designated below to make health care decisions for me as allowed by Sections 4600 to 4753, inclusive, of the California Probate Code. This power of attorney shall not be affected by my subsequent incapacity. I hereby revoke any prior durable power of attorney for health care. I am a California resident who is at least 18 years old, of sound mind, and acting of my own free will.

2. APPOINTMENT OF HEALTH CARE AGENT

(Fill in below the name, address and telephone number of the person you wish to make health care decisions for you if you become incapacitated. You should make sure that this person agrees to accept this responsibility. The following may not serve as your agent: (1) your treating health care provider; (2) an operator of a community care facility or residential care facility for the elderly; or (3) an employee of your treating health care provider, a community care facility, or a residential care facility for the elderly, unless that employee is related to you by blood, marriage or adoption. If you are a conservator under the Lanterman-Petris-Short Act (the law governing involuntary commitment to a mental health facility) and you wish to appoint your conservator as your agent, you must consult a lawyer, who must sign and attach a special declaration for this document to be valid.)

I, _____, hereby appoint:
(insert your name)

Name _____

Address _____

Work Telephone (_____)_____ Home Telephone (_____)_____

as my agent (attorney-in-fact) to make health care decisions for me as authorized in this document. I understand that this power of attorney will be effective for an indefinite period of time unless I revoke it or limit its duration below.

(Optional) This power of attorney shall expire on the following date: _____

© California Medical Association 1995 (revised)

both is to make known people's wishes about the use of life support, in the event they are unconscious or otherwise incapable of expressing them. A durable power of attorney has an additional advantage: It names an individual who has the legal authority to speak for the person if necessary. Although there is considerable support for both mechanisms, there are several problems as well. Many people fail to inform their relatives about their living will. Others do not tell the person named in a durable power of attorney where the document is kept. Obviously, this puts relatives at a serious disadvantage if decisions concerning the use of life-support systems need to be made.

Take a minute to reflect on the issues raised in the Current Controversies feature. The dilemmas posed there are difficult ones indeed. It is never easy deciding what to do in situations that quite literally involve life or death. If you find yourself feeling uncomfortable, you are certainly not alone. Most people find it difficult to decide how they feel about euthanasia. The belief that one person should not kill another is deeply rooted in society, so euthanasia is likely to be a much-debated topic for many years to come.

**CURRENT
CONTROVERSIES**

Bioethics and Euthanasia

There is no universally accepted definition of death that is free from problems. In fact, each time the legal or medical definition of death is changed, a host of ethical issues must be confronted. Most people in the United States now accept the brain death definition, but when this criterion was being implemented, it caused several problems. Perhaps most troublesome was the introduction of life-support technology, both to prolong life and to keep organs available for transplant surgery. Under the prevailing definition of death at the time—clinical death—the act of turning off a life-support system was considered murder, because death was defined solely in terms of pulse and respiration. When these bodily functions were present, even though artificially so, stopping them fell under the rubric of homicide in the criminal codes. Court decisions beginning in the 1970s refined the issues, and the criteria for brain death were adopted.

Relying on the criteria of brain death does not eliminate thorny ethical issues, however. Physicians must talk with families of people who are brain dead, presenting them with options. These essentially constitute methods of euthanasia (e.g., disconnecting life support, withholding drugs), which the physicians must be willing to carry out. Such actions are viewed as legal and permissible under current law. However, if the patient is not brain dead, the situation is considerably murkier. Should individuals have the right to information that will help them end their lives soon, before enduring horrible pain that will ultimately end in death anyway? Should physicians be permitted to give that information and provide assistance if the patient asks? What do you think?

Some countries, like the Netherlands, allow physicians to assist people who want to commit suicide (Cutter, 1991). In 1984, the Dutch Supreme Court eliminated prosecution of physicians who assist in suicide if five criteria are met:

1. The patient's condition is intolerable with no hope for improvement
2. No relief is available
3. The patient is competent

4. The patient makes a request repeatedly over time
5. Two physicians agree with the patient's request

It remains to be seen whether many other countries will follow the Netherlands' example and permit physician-assisted suicide. Bioethicists must make the dilemmas clear, and we must make ourselves aware of the issues. What is at stake is literally a matter of life and death. What do you think? 🖋

TEST YOURSELF

1. The phrase "dead as a doornail" is an example of the sociocultural definition of death as _____.
2. The difference between brain death and a persistent vegetative state is

   _____.
3. Withholding an antibiotic from a person who dies as a result is an example of _____.
4. Describe how people at each level of Kohlberg's theory of moral reasoning (described in Chapter 9) would deal with the issue of euthanasia.

Ideas about Death through the Life Span

LEARNING OBJECTIVES

🖋 *What do children understand about death? How should adults help them deal with it?*

🖋 *What concerns do adolescents have about death?*

🖋 *How do young adults view death?*

🖋 *What issues about death are most important for middle-aged adults?*

🖋 *How do older adults view death?*

Coming to grips with the reality of death is probably one of the hardest things we have to do in life. American society does not help much either, as it tends to distance itself from death through euphemisms ("passed away," "dearly departed") and by relocating many rituals from the home or church to the funeral parlor.

These trends make it difficult for people to learn about death in its natural context. Dying itself has been moved from the home to hospitals and other institutions such as nursing homes. The closest most people get to death is a quick glance inside a nicely lined casket at a corpse that has been made to look as if the person were still alive.

What, then, do people (especially children) understand about death? In this section, we will consider how our understanding of death changes through the life span.

Answers: (1) an analogy, (2) the brainstem still functions in a persistent vegetative state, (3) passive euthanasia

Childhood

Like the couple in the photograph, parents often take their children to funerals of relatives and close friends. But many of them wonder whether young children really know what death means. Young preschool-age children tend to believe that death is temporary and magical. They think it is something dra-

matic that comes to get you in the middle of the night like a burglar or a ghost (Dickinson, 1992). Not until 5 to 7 years of age do children realize that death is permanent, that it happens eventually to everyone, and that dead people no longer have any biological functions.

Why does this shift occur? Think back to Chapters 4 and 6, especially to the discussion of Piaget's theory of cognitive development. Take Jennie, the 5-year-old daughter of Donna and Carl in the second chapter-opening vignette. Where would she be in Piaget's terms? In this perspective, the ages 5 to 7 include the transition from preoperational to concrete-operational thinking. Therefore, Jennie will probably understand what happened to her grandmother.

FIRST EXPERIENCES

The first time a child experiences the death of a relative or a pet, they are very vulnerable. Children have no prior experience to help them come to terms with the event. Some find it highly traumatic, whereas others appear less affected. Many children feel afraid, alone, and upset. But some children try to cry and find they cannot. They are likely to ask adults many questions about death rituals. Like the boy in the cartoon, children feel the loss of relatives and miss them during special family times.

"I wish Granddad could've been at the reunion, too."

FAMILY CIRCUS, © 1993. Reprinted with special permission of King Features Syndicate.

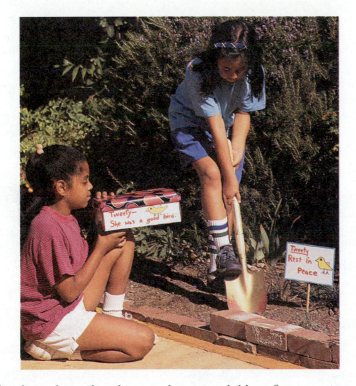

Like the girls in the photograph, many children first experience death when a pet dies (Dickinson, 1992). There seems to be little difference in children's reactions to the death of a relative and the death of a pet, as the following example shows.

> I had a cute little hamster. I think we had been talking about hibernation in school because when I came home and found the hamster lying there, I thought he was hibernating! My next door neighbor, Sharon, came over and said that if we warmed him up then he would come back to life. So I put him in my electric blanket to see if he would wake up. He never did and by that time my mom realized what had happened, so we had to bury him. My brother and I put him in the shoebox, put a blanket in there to keep him warm and a picture of us to keep him company. Then we buried him in the backyard. (Dickinson, 1992, p. 177)

Adults must be sensitive to children's needs at the time of a death, even that of a pet. How adults handle such situations could later help the child deal with the death of a relative (Dickinson, 1992).

Young adults, looking back on their first encounter with death as children, report having many of the feelings adults have: they're angry, confused, disbelieving, fearful, relieved, guilty, sad, and empty (Dickinson, 1992). One male college student recalled how, when he was 9, his father helped him deal with his feelings after his grandfather's death:

> The day of my grandfather's death my dad came over to my aunt and uncle's house where my brother and I were staying. He took us into one of the bedrooms and sat us down. He told us Grandaddy Doc had died. He explained to us that it was okay if we needed to cry. He told us that he had cried, and that if we did cry we wouldn't be babies, but would just be men showing our emotions. (Dickinson, 1992, pp. 175–176)

It is important for children to know that it is okay for them to feel sad, to cry, or to show their feelings in whatever way they want. Such reassurance may

GEORGE E. DICKINSON
". . . a child's experiences of death and loss may become life-long memories for the adult."

help children deal with their confusion at adults' explanations of death. Young adults remember feeling uncomfortable as children around dead bodies, often fearing that the deceased person would come after them. Still, children believe it is very important to attend the funeral of a relative. Even though they tend to remember few details immediately, their overall recovery is enhanced (Silverman & Worden, 1992).

Understanding death can be particularly difficult for children when adults are not open and honest with them, especially about the meaning of death. The use of euphemisms, such as "Grandma has gone away" or "Mommy is only sleeping," is unwise. Young children do not understand the deeper level of meaning in such statements; they are likely to take them literally.

When explaining death to children it is best to deal with them on their terms. Keep explanations simple, at a level they can understand. Try to allay their fears and reassure them that whatever reaction they have is okay. Providing loving support for the child will maximize the potential for a successful (though painful) introduction to one of life's realities.

Adolescence

By adolescence, children clearly understand the realities of death. With the onset of formal operational thinking, their understanding of death becomes even more adultlike. Because of this cognitive advance, some researchers believe that adolescents' attitudes toward death are the same as adults' views. However, adolescents may be more concerned with the quality of their lives than with how long they will live.

In general, adolescents are reluctant to discuss death and dying. As we saw in Chapter 8, adolescents have a sense that they are immortal, that nothing bad will happen to them. Even though they may come in contact with death through the loss of a friend or a friend's sibling or parent, adolescents tend to believe that nothing similar will happen to them. Therefore, they are unlikely to come forward to discuss their feelings and fears (Kastenbaum, 1985).

Young Adulthood

Because young adults are just beginning to pursue the family, career, and personal goals they have set, they tend to be more intense in their feelings toward death. When asked how they feel about death, young adults report a strong sense that those who die at this point in their lives would be cheated out of their future (Pattison, 1977).

Although not specifically addressed in research, the shift from formal-operational to postformal thinking could be an important one in young adults' contemplation of death. Presumably, this shift in cognitive development is accompanied by a lessening of the feeling of immortality, as young adults begin to integrate personal feelings and emotions with their thinking.

Middle Age

Midlife is the time when most people confront the death of their parents. Up until that point, people tend not to think much about their own death; the fact that their parents are still alive buffers them from reality. After all, in the normal course of events, our parents are supposed to die before we do.

Once their parents have died, people realize that they are now the oldest generation of their family—the next in line to die. Reading the obituary pages, they are reminded of this, as the ages of many of the people who have died get closer and closer to their own.

Probably as a result of this growing realization of their own mortality, middle-aged adults' sense of time undergoes a subtle yet profound change. It changes from an emphasis on how long they have already lived to how long they have left to live (Neugarten, 1969). This may lead to occupational change or other redirection such as improving relationships that had deteriorated over the years.

Late Adulthood

In general, older adults are less anxious about death and more accepting of it than any other age group (Keller, Sherry, & Piotrowski, 1984). For many older adults, the joy of living is diminishing (Kalish, 1987). More than any other group, they have experienced loss of family and friends and have come to terms with their own mortality. Older adults have more chronic diseases, which are not likely just to go away. They may feel that their most important life tasks have been completed.

As people grow older, death becomes more salient as family members and friends are lost. For some, reading the obituary page becomes part of their daily ritual.

Understanding Death

Understanding death is not a topic in which you might expect to see the biopsychosocial framework in action. Actually, the framework provides an excellent way to tie together several different threads. Most apparent is that life-cycle forces play a key role. We have seen that the same concept—death—has varied meanings, beyond the mere cessation of life, depending on people's age. Biological forces are equally important. As we will see in the next section, people who are facing their own imminent death experience certain stages based on their feelings at the time.

How a person's understanding of death develops is also the result of psychological forces. As the ability to think undergoes fundamental change, the view of death changes from a mostly magical approach to one that can be transcendent and transforming. Having gained experience through the deaths of friends and relatives, a person's level of comfort with death may increase. This experience may also come about by sharing rituals. People observe how others deal with death and how the culture sets the tone and prescribes behavior for survivors.

The combined action of forces determines how people face their own death, as well as how they cope with the grief that accompanies the loss of someone close. We will examine both of these topics in the remaining sections of this chapter. ❧

FORCES IN ACTION

TEST YOURSELF

1. In general, adults should avoid _____ when discussing death with children.
2. Adolescents are usually more concerned with _____ than _____.
3. Young adults faced with death feel _____.

4. An important concern of middle-aged adults is _____.
5. In general, older adults are _____ about death.
6. How do the different ways that adults view death relate to the stages of Erikson's theory discussed in Chapters 9, 11, 12, and 14?

The Process of Dying

LEARNING OBJECTIVES

🌿 *What is death anxiety?*

🌿 *What are the stages of dying?*

🌿 *How does the phase theory of dying differ from the stage theory?*

🌿 *How does dying differ through the life span?*

As we have seen, people are uncomfortable thinking about their own death; indeed, *death anxiety* **pervades society.** Completing the short exercise below might provide you with some interesting insights into your own anxieties about death.

A Self-Reflective Exercise on Death

1. In 200 words or less, write your own obituary. Be sure to include your age and cause of death. List your lifetime accomplishments. Don't forget to list your survivors.
2. Think about all the things you will have done that are not listed in your obituary. List some of them.
3. Think of all the friends you will have made and how you will have affected them.
4. Would you make any changes in your obituary now?

Well, how was it to think about your own death? Most people report feeling a little uncomfortable at first, but then getting more comfortable as they allow themselves to write their autobiography before it happens.

These exercises are preparation for asking the really tough questions: What is it like to die? How do terminally ill people feel about dying? Are people more concerned about dying as they grow older? To answer these questions, scholars have developed theories of dying, based on interviews and other methods. The theories show that dying is complex and that our thoughts, concerns, and feelings change as we move closer to death. We will examine two ways of conceptualizing the dying process: a stage approach and a phase approach. We will also consider how the feelings of dying people vary as a function of age.

The Stage Theory of Dying

One of the most influential theories of dying was proposed by Elisabeth Kübler-Ross, a physician in Chicago who wanted to help four seminary students conduct research on how people cope with impending death. In 1965, such research was quite controversial; her physician colleagues were initially outraged, and some even denied that their patients were terminally ill. Still,

Answers: (1) *euphemisms,* (2) *the quality of their lives; how long they will live,* (3) *cheated out of their lives,* (4) *their growing realization of their own mortality,* (5) *less anxious*

Kübler-Ross persisted and obtained permission to do the study. Eventually, she conducted over 200 interviews with terminally ill people. Kübler-Ross became convinced that most dying people follow a sequence of emotional reactions. Using her observations, she developed a sequence of five stages to describe the process of an appropriate death: denial, anger, bargaining, depression, and acceptance (Kübler-Ross, 1969).

When people like Betty, from the third opening vignette, are told that they have a terminal illness, their first reaction is likely to be shock and disbelief. Denial is a normal part of getting ready to die. Some people shop around for a more favorable diagnosis, and most feel that a mistake has been made. Others try to find reassurance in religion. Eventually, though, most people accept the diagnosis and begin to feel angry.

In the anger stage, people express hostility, resentment, and envy toward health care workers, family, and friends. Like Betty, they ask, "Why me?" and express a great deal of frustration. It seems so unfair that they are going to die when so many others will live. As the person deals with these feelings, they begin to diminish, and the person enters the bargaining stage.

In the bargaining stage, people look for a way out. Maybe a deal can be struck with someone (perhaps God) to allow survival. For example, a woman might promise to be a better mother if only she could live. Eventually, the individual becomes aware that such deals will not work.

When the illness can no longer be denied, perhaps due to surgery or pain, feelings of depression are very common. People report feeling deep loss, sorrow, guilt, and shame over their illness and its consequences. Kübler-Ross believes that discussing their feelings with others helps move them to an acceptance of death.

In the acceptance stage, the person accepts the inevitability of death. He or she often seems detached from the world and at complete peace. "It is as if the pain is gone, the struggle is over, and there comes a time for the 'final rest before the journey'" (Kübler-Ross, 1969, p. 100).

Although Kübler-Ross (1974) believes that these five stages represent the typical course of emotional development in the dying, she cautions that not everyone goes through all of them or progresses through them at the same rate or in the same order. Progression through the stages depends on people's physical health, their view of death, and many other factors. If we recognize that these individual differences are normal, Kübler-Ross's stages help people understand that feelings about dying change over time.

The Phase Theory of Dying

Kübler-Ross viewed dying as a series of discrete stages. In contrast, some writers view dying as a continuous process with three phases: an acute phase, a chronic living-dying phase, and a terminal phase (Pattison, 1977). These phases are represented in the diagram.

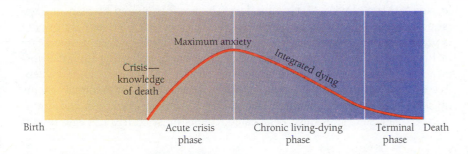

Birth | Acute crisis phase | Chronic living-dying phase | Terminal phase | Death

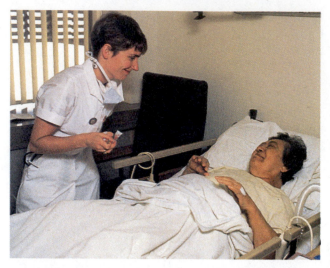

It is important for health care workers to feel comfortable talking with people about death. For many workers, this means confronting their own feelings and anxieties about the subject.

The acute phase begins when the individual becomes aware that his or her condition is terminal. This phase is marked by a high level of anxiety, denial, anger, and even bargaining. In time, the person adjusts to the idea of being terminally ill, and anxiety gradually declines. During this chronic living-dying phase, a person generally has many contradictory feelings that must be integrated. These include fear of loneliness, fear of the unknown, and anticipatory grief over the loss of friends, of body, of self-control, and of identity (Pattison, 1977). These feelings of fear and grief exist simultaneously or alternate with feelings of hope, determination, and acceptance (Shneidman, 1973). Finally, the terminal phase begins, and the individual starts to withdraw from the world. This last phase is the shortest, and it ends with death.

Theories of dying agree that how people deal with their own death is a complicated process. Denial and acceptance can take many forms and may even occur simultaneously. In the same time frame, people may take a last vacation and update their will. Clearly, the task of health care providers and mental health workers is to understand the unique responses and needs of terminally ill patients. People must stay in touch with the dying person's (and their own) feelings and be available for support. In this way, people can be helped to die with dignity.

Dying with dignity is an important right of every individual; ensuring this right is one of the goals of *hospice*. As described in the You May Be Wondering feature, hospice is a movement that began out of concern for terminally ill people. Focusing initially on pain management and control, hospice seeks to provide a supportive environment for dying people by keeping families engaged in caregiving and by providing professional assistance during this very stressful time.

? YOU MAY BE WONDERING

The Hospice Alternative

Consider how dying people should be treated and how they themselves face death. Clearly, the right to die with dignity is important. For many people, death with dignity means being with family and friends when they die, preferably at home. Hospice offers hope in this regard (Koff, 1981). The emphasis in a hospice is on the quality of life. The concern is to make the person as peaceful and comfortable as possible, not to delay an inevitable death. Although medical care is available at a hospice, it is aimed primarily at controlling pain and restoring normal functioning, whereas medical care at a hospital usually aims to cure the disease.

Modern hospices are modeled after St. Christopher's Hospice in England, founded in 1967 by Dr. Cicely Saunders. The services offered by a hospice are requested only after the person or physician believes that no treatment or cure is possible. Thus, the hospice program is markedly different from hospital care or home care. The differences are evident in the principles that underlie hospice care: Clients and their families are viewed as a unit; clients should be kept free of pain; emotional and social impoverishment must be minimal; clients must be encouraged to maintain competencies; conflict resolution and fulfillment of realistic desires must be assisted; clients must be free to begin or end relationships; and staff members must seek to alleviate pain and fear (Saunders, 1977).

Two types of hospices exist: inpatient and outpatient. Inpatient hospices provide all care for clients; outpatient hospices provide services to clients who remain in their own homes. The latter variation is becoming increasingly popular, largely because more clients can be served at a lower cost.

Researchers have documented important differences between inpatient hospices and hospitals (VandenBos, DeLeon, & Pallack, 1982). In contrast to hospitals, the primary aim of the hospice is comfort care; hospitals usually use more aggressive treatment approaches. A person is admitted to a hospice only after the diagnosis of a terminal disease, which usually means that the person is given less than six months to live by two physicians. Hospice clients are more mobile, less anxious, and less depressed; spouses visit hospice clients more often and participate more in their care; and hospice staff members are perceived as more accessible. In addition, most hospice clients who had been in hospitals before coming to a hospice strongly prefer the care at the hospice (Walsh & Cavanaugh, 1984).

Although hospice is a valuable alternative for many people, it may not be appropriate for everyone. Some disorders require treatments or equipment not available at inpatient hospices, and some people may find that a hospice does not meet their needs or fit with their personal beliefs. The perceived needs of hospice clients, their families, and the staff do not always coincide. Often, the staff and family members emphasize pain management, whereas many of the clients want more attention paid to personal issues, such as talking directly about death or about their religious beliefs (Walsh & Cavanaugh, 1984). Staff and family members should ask clients what they need, rather than making assumptions about what they need.

Although a hospice offers an important alternative to a hospital or other institution as a place to die, it is not always available. For example, older adults who are slowly dying but whose time of death is uncertain may not be eligible, as many hospices are only able to take in clients who have six months or less to live. Meeting the needs of these other dying individuals will be a challenge for future health care providers. 🖾

A Life-Span Developmental Perspective on Dying

Take a look at the four people in the photographs. Think for a minute what your reaction would be to the news that each of these people had died. How would you feel? Would your feelings be different for the different individuals?

In this section, we will briefly examine how the age of a dying person changes the way death is viewed and experienced.

Intellectually, we realize that dying is not something that happens only to one age group. But most of us tend not to think about it, because we are used to associating dying with old age. Death knows no age limits, yet one person's death often seems more acceptable than another's (Kastenbaum, 1985). The death of a 95-year-old woman is considered natural; she has lived a long, full life. But the death of an infant is considered to be a tragedy. Whether or not such feelings are justified, they point to the fact that death is viewed and experienced differently depending on age.

Children die from acute diseases and accidents; young adults die mainly from accidents (although in some locations AIDS is now the primary cause of death); and the old die mainly from chronic diseases such as heart disease and cancer (Kalish, 1987). Because people of different ages die in different ways, their dying processes differ (Kalish, 1985). Most notably, the elderly take longer to die and are more likely to die in isolation than any other age group.

Many of the concerns of dying individuals have to do with how old they are (Kalish, 1987). The most obvious difference comes in the extent to which people feel cheated. Younger people feel cheated in that they are losing what they might attain; older adults feel cheated that they are losing what they have. Beyond these general differences, not much is known about how people of various ages differ in how they face death.

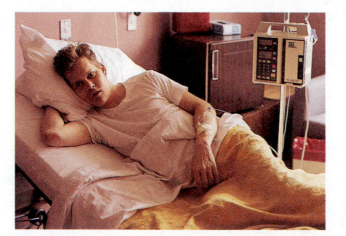

In some communities, AIDS has become the leading cause of death among segments of the young adult population.

One important factor that affects dying older adults is that their deaths are viewed by the community as less tragic than the deaths of younger people (Kalish & Reynolds, 1976; Kastenbaum, 1985). Consequently, older adults receive less intense life-saving treatment and are perceived as less valuable and not as worthy of a large investment of time, money, or energy. "The terminally aged may be as helpless as a child, but they seldom arouse tenderness" (Weisman, 1972, p. 144). Many dying older adults reside in long-term care facilities, where contacts with family and friends are fewer. The elderly, especially the ill and those with diminished functional competence, offer less to their communities. Consequently, when their death occurs, the emotional pain is not as great, because the resulting losses are viewed as less significant and meaningful (Kalish, 1987).

TEST YOURSELF

1. Feeling uncomfortable thinking about your own death is a manifestation of _____.
2. The five stages of dying are _____.
3. When an individual begins withdrawing from the world, he or she has entered the _____ phase of dying.
4. Older adults mainly die from _____.
5. How would being in a hospice facilitate people's coming to terms with their death?

Answers: (1) death anxiety, (2) denial, anger, bargaining, depression, and acceptance, (3) terminal, (4) chronic diseases

Surviving the Loss: The Grieving Process

LEARNING OBJECTIVES

❧ *What stages do people experience during the grief process?*

❧ *What feelings do grieving people have?*

❧ *How does grief affect people?*

❧ *What is the difference between normal and abnormal grief?*

Each of us suffers many losses over a lifetime. Whenever we lose someone close to us through death or other separation, we experience grief and mourning. *Grief* **is the sorrow, hurt, anger, guilt, confusion, and other feelings that arise after suffering a loss.** *Mourning* **concerns the ways in which we express our grief.** For example, you can tell that the woman in the photograph is in mourning because of her black dress and the veil covering her face. Mourning is highly influenced by culture. For some, mourning may involve wearing black, attending funerals, and observing an official period of grief; for others, it means drinking, wearing white, and marrying the deceased spouse's sibling. Grief corresponds to the emotional reactions following loss, whereas mourning is the culturally approved

behavioral manifestations of those feelings. Even though mourning rituals may be fairly standard within a culture, how people grieve varies, as we will see next.

Stages of Grief

How do people grieve? What do they experience? The process of grieving is a complicated and personal one. Just as there is no right way to die, there is no right way to grieve. Recognizing that there are plenty of individual differences, we will consider these patterns in this section.

The grieving process is often described as a set of phases. Like the stages and phases of dying, the phases of grieving are not clearly demarcated, nor does one pass from one to another cleanly. When someone close to us dies, we must reorganize our lives, establish new patterns of behavior, and redefine relationships with family and friends. Although there is an apparent sequence to the phases, keep in mind that progress through them is not always even or predictable.

The grieving process can be divided into three main phases: initial phase, intermediate phase, and recovery phase (Parkes, 1972). Each phase has certain characteristics, and particular issues are more important at some points than others.

When the death occurs, the survivor's reaction is shock, disbelief, and numbness. People often report feeling empty, cold, and confused, which serves to protect them from the pain of bereavement. The shock and disbelief typically continue for several days following the death and then give way to several weeks of sorrow and sadness, which are expressed mainly through crying.

One of the difficulties encountered in the first phase is that people are expected to begin recovering from these feelings, but they face anxieties as they attempt to do so. As a result of pressure from friends, employers, and others, survivors may suppress emotions. Unfortunately, suppression of feelings is often interpreted as a sign of recovery, which it certainly is not. Along with learning how to deal with sorrow, survivors must handle feelings of not being able to go on with life. Fortunately, most people eventually realize that such anxieties are not well-founded and are actually hindering their own recovery.

The intermediate phase begins several weeks after the death, when people begin to realize what life without the deceased person means. Researchers point to three behavior patterns that characterize the intermediate phase. First, the bereaved person thinks about the death a great deal; feelings of guilt or responsibility are common. Second, survivors try to understand why the person

The loss of someone close to us is difficult to handle. It is common for people to think about close friends and relatives who have died, and to keep the memories of them fresh in their minds.

died. They search for some reason for the death, to try to put it in a meaningful context. Finally, people search for the deceased. They feel the person's presence and dream or even converse with him or her. Such behavior demonstrates a longing to be with the deceased, and it is often a reaction to feelings of loneliness and despair. Eventually, these feelings and behaviors diminish, and the bereaved person moves to the final phase.

Entry into the recovery phase of grief often results from a conscious decision that continued dwelling on the past is pointless and that life needs to move forward. Once this is recognized, recovery can begin. Behaviorally, the process takes many forms; increased socializing is one common example. It is not unusual to see marked improvement in the survivor's self-confidence. Emerging from a bereavement experience is an achievement. People are often more capable and stronger as a result of coping with such a tragic event. Survivors may need to develop new skills—cooking, balancing a checkbook, or home repair—which used to be done by the deceased individual.

In considering these phases of grief, we must avoid making several mistakes. First, grieving ultimately is an individual experience. The process that works well for one person may not be the best for someone else. Second, we must not underestimate the amount of time people need to progress from the initial shock to recovery. To a casual observer, this may seem to occur over a few weeks. Actually, it takes much longer to resolve the complex emotional issues that are faced during bereavement. Researchers and therapists alike agree that a person needs at least one year following the loss to begin recovery, and two years is not uncommon. Finally, *recovery* may be a misleading term. It is probably more accurate to say that we learn to live with our loss rather than that we recover from it. The impact of the loss of a loved one lasts a very long time, perhaps for the rest of one's life.

EXPECTED VERSUS UNEXPECTED DEATH

When death is expected, people respond differently than when death is unexpected. When death is anticipated, people go through a period of anticipatory grief before the death. This supposedly serves to buffer the impact of the loss when it does come, as well as facilitating recovery. The opportunity for anticipatory grieving results in a lower likelihood of psychological problems such as depression one year after the death of a spouse (Ball, 1976–1977; Parkes, 1972), greater acceptance by parents following the death of a child (Binger et al., 1969), and more rapid recovery of effective functioning and subsequent happiness (Glick, Weiss, & Parkes, 1974). However, anticipating the death of someone close does produce considerable stress in itself (Norris & Murrell, 1987).

The reasons why recovery from anticipated deaths is quicker are not yet fully understood. We know that the long-term effects of stressful events are generally less problematic if they are expected, so the same principle probably holds for death. Perhaps it is helpful that there is an opportunity to envision life without the dying person and a chance to make appropriate arrangements. In practicing, we may realize that we need support, may feel lonely and scared, and may take steps to get ourselves ready. Moreover, if we recognize that we are likely to have certain feelings, they may be easier to understand and deal with when they come.

Also an anticipated death is often less mysterious. Most of the time, we understand why the person died. An unexpected death leaves us with many questions: Why *my* loved one? Why now? Survivors may feel vulnerable; what happened to their loved one could just as easily happen to them. Understanding the real reason why someone dies makes adjustment easier.

These findings do not mean that people who experience the anticipated death of a loved one fail to grieve. One study revealed that widows whose husbands had been ill for at least one month prior to their deaths grieved just as intensely as did widows whose husbands died unexpectedly, as the graph shows (Hill, Thompson, & Gallagher, 1988).

Automobile accidents are an example of unanticipated death. The grief associated with such deaths is typically intense.

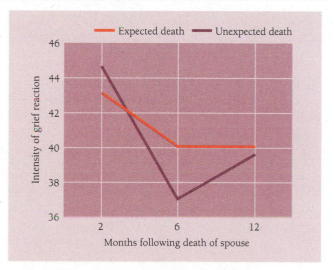

Normal Grief Reactions

The feelings experienced during grieving are intense, which not only makes it difficult to cope but also can make a person question her or his own reactions. The feelings involved usually include sadness, denial, anger, loneliness, and guilt. A summary of these feelings is presented in the following list (Vickio,

Cavanaugh, & Attig, 1990). Take a minute to read through them to see if they agree with what you might expect.

Disbelief	Denial	Shock
Sadness	Anger	Hatred
Guilt	Fear	Anxiety
Confusion	Helplessness	Emptiness
Loneliness	Acceptance	Relief
Happiness	Lack of enthusiasm	Absence of emotion

Many authors refer to the psychological side of coming to terms with bereavement as *grief work*. Even without personal experience of the death of close family members, people recognize the need to give survivors time to deal with their many feelings. One study asked college students to describe the feelings they thought were typically experienced by a person who had lost particular loved ones (such as a parent, child, sibling, friend). The students were well aware of the need for grief work, recognized the need for at least a year to do it, and were very sensitive to the range of emotions and behaviors demonstrated by the bereaved (Vickio, Cavanaugh, & Attig, 1990).

In the time following the death of a loved one, dates that have personal significance may reintroduce feelings of grief. For example, holidays such as Thanksgiving or birthdays that were spent with the deceased person may be difficult times. The actual anniversary of the death can be especially troublesome. **The term** *anniversary reaction* **refers to changes in behavior related to feelings of sadness on this date.** Personal experience and research show that recurring feelings of sadness or other examples of the anniversary reaction are very common in normal grief (Bornstein & Clayton, 1972).

LONGITUDINAL RESEARCH FINDINGS

Most research on how people react to the death of a loved one is cross-sectional. Norris and Murrell (1987) conducted a longitudinal study of older adults' grief work; three interviews were conducted before the death and one after. The fascinating results of their research are described in more detail in the Spotlight on Research feature. The results of this study fit nicely with the earlier discussion on expected versus unexpected death. They also have important implications for interventions. That is, interventions aimed at reducing stress or promoting health may be more effective if performed before the death. Additionally, because health problems increased only among those in the bereaved group who felt no stress before the death, it may be that the stress felt before the death is a product of anticipating it. Lundin (1984) also found it to be the case that health problems increased only for those experiencing sudden death.

SPOTLIGHT ON RESEARCH

Family Stress and Adaptation Before and After Bereavement

What happens to a family that experiences the death of a loved one? Norris and Murrell (1987) sought to answer this question by tracking families before and after bereavement. As part of a very large normative longitudinal study, they conducted detailed interviews approximately every six months. The data concerning grief reactions compared 63 older adults in families experiencing the death of an immediate family member with 387 older adults in families who had not experienced such a death in order to document the extra stress people feel due to grief.

The researchers obtained extensive information on physical health, including functional abilities and specific ailments, psychological distress, and family stress. The psychological distress measure tapped symptoms of depression. The family stress measure assessed such things as new serious illness of a family member, having a family member move in, additional family responsibilities, new family conflict, or new marital conflict.

The results were enlightening. Among bereaved families, overall family stress increased before the death and then decreased. The level of stress experienced by these families was highest in the period right around the death. Moreover, bereavement was the only significant predictor of family stress, meaning that the anticipation and experience of bereavement caused stress.

Even more interesting were the findings concerning the relationship between health and stress. Bereaved individuals who reported stress before the death were in poorer health before the death than were bereaved persons who were not experiencing stress. However, bereaved individuals reporting prior stress showed a significant drop in physical symptoms six months after the death; bereaved persons reporting no prior stress reported a slight increase. The net result was that both groups ended up with about the same level of physical symptoms six months after bereavement. Note also that bereaved people reported less stress six months after their loss than a group of nonbereaved people. Both sets of results are shown in the graphs.

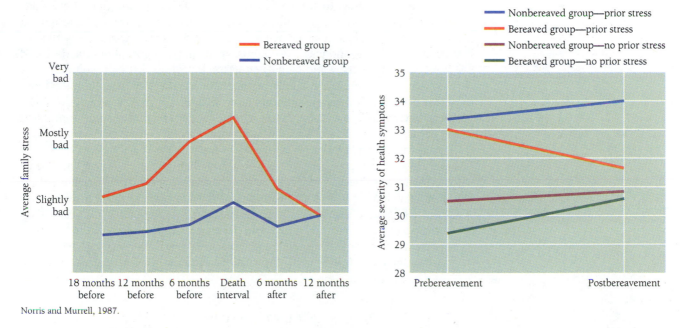

Norris and Murrell, 1987.

The Norris and Murrell study has two major implications. First, bereavement does not appear to cause poor health; the bereaved groups were not much different from the group of nonbereaved people in nonstressful families. Second, bereavement appears to increase psychological distress substantially. In sum, marked changes in psychological distress following bereavement are normal, but marked changes in physical health are not. 🙟

Effects of Normal Grief on Adults' Health

Many people have assumed that losing a close loved one must have obvious negative effects on the health of the survivor, especially if the survivor is elderly. As the Norris and Murrell study showed, however, such health effects are not inevitable.

Additional research supports this point. Middle-aged adults are most likely to report physical health problems following bereavement; younger and older adults report few health problems. Younger adults may be able to deal with their losses because they are better equipped overall to handle stress. Older adults have more experience with such losses and anticipate them, and they may draw on their background in order to cope physically. In contrast, middle-aged adults have less experience, and they are also in the midst of dealing with their own mortality. As a result, the loss of a close family member is an emotionally unsettling reminder of their own fate (Perkins & Harris, 1990).

Abnormal Grief Reactions

Not everyone is able to move through the phases of grief and begin rebuilding a life. Sometimes the feelings of hurt, loneliness, and guilt are so overwhelming that they become the focus of the survivor's life. Thus, what distinguishes normal from abnormal grief is not the kind of reaction but rather its intensity and duration (Schulz, 1985).

Overall, the most common manifestation of abnormal grief is excessive guilt and self-blame. In some people, guilt results in a disruption of everyday routines and a diminished ability to function. People begin to make judgment errors, may reach a state of agitated depression, may experience problems sleeping or eating, and may have intense recurring thoughts about the deceased person. Many of these individuals either seek professional help voluntarily or are referred by concerned family members or friends. Unfortunately, the long-term prognosis for people suffering abnormal grief responses is not good unless they obtain professional help (Schulz, 1985). The most common problem is depression, which can become severe and chronic. Other problems include social withdrawal, with a resulting loss of the person's social network.

How long intense grief needs to continue before it is considered abnormal is a matter of subjective judgment. As we have seen, several research studies indicate that it takes at least one year for survivors to begin to move forward with their lives, and in many cases it may take longer. Consequently, clinicians tend to suspect that the person's grief is interfering with his or her daily life if intense grief reactions are still present more than two years after the loss. However, such judgments must be made on a case-by-case basis; no set period of time is used as a firm criterion.

TEST YOURSELF

1. People who experience the anticipated death of a loved one recover _____ than people who experience an unexpected death.
2. Feeling sad on the date when your grandmother died the previous year is an example of an _____.
3. _____ show the most negative effects following bereavement.
4. The most common manifestations of abnormal grief are _____.
5. If you were to create a brochure listing the five most important things to do and not to do in connection with losing a close family member or friend through death, what would you include? Why?

Answers: (1) more quickly, (2) anniversary reaction, (3) middle-aged adults, (4) guilt and self-blame

Dealing with Different Types of Loss

LEARNING OBJECTIVES

❧ *Why does the death of a parent cause surviving children to redefine their role as parents?*

❧ *How do people deal with the death of a child?*

❧ *Why is the death of a partner usually so traumatic?*

❧ *How do people deal with different types of losses?*

Our society tends to view some deaths as more tragic or as easier to accept than others. For example, people typically consider the death of a child to be extremely tragic, unless it occurs at birth. Also, a young person whose parent dies is considered to suffer a greater loss than a middle-aged person who loses an aged parent. The point is that our society in a sense makes judgments about how much grief a person should have following different types of loss. We have noted that death is always a traumatic event for survivors. But unfortunately the survivors are not always encouraged to express their grief over a period of time, or even to talk about their feelings. For example, most employers in the United States expect workers to return within three to five days after a funeral and to resume their normal duties immediately. Society thus tries to impose arbitrary time limits on the grieving process, even though this is contrary to virtually all the evidence we have.

Death of One's Parent

Most parents die after their children are grown. But whenever parental death occurs, it hurts. We lose not only a key relationship but also an important psychological buffer between ourselves and death. We, the children, are now next in line. Indeed, the death of a parent often leads the surviving children to redefine the meaning of parenthood and the importance of time together (Malinak, Hoyt, & Patterson, 1979). Clare and Alex, the surviving adult children in the last opening vignette, are examples of this redefinition.

As for the woman in the photo, the death of a parent deprives people of many important things: a source of guidance and advice, a source of love, and a model for their own parenting style. It also cuts off the opportunity to improve aspects of their relationship with the parent. Expressing feelings toward a parent before he or she dies is important. The loss of a parent is perceived as a very significant one; society allows us to grieve for a reasonable length of time.

Death of One's Child

The couple in the photo experienced what many people believe is the worst type of loss: the death of a child. Because children are not supposed to die before their parents, it is as if the natural order of things has been violated. Unexpected loss is especially traumatic, as in sudden infant death syndrome or au-

tomobile accidents. But parents of terminally ill children still suffer a great deal, even with the benefit of anticipatory grieving. Mourning is always intense, and some parents never recover or attempt to reconcile themselves to the death of their child.

Some of the most overlooked losses are those that happen through stillbirth, miscarriage, abortion, or neonatal death (Borg & Lasker, 1981). Attachment to the child begins before birth, so the loss hurts deeply. Yet parents who experience this type of loss are expected to recover very quickly. If such societal expectations are not met, the parents may be subjected to unfeeling comments. A personal story of one couple's experience of miscarriage is in the Real People feature.

The Grief of Miscarriage

REAL PEOPLE

As noted in the text, one of the most overlooked types of loss is through miscarriage. Unfortunately, many people react to miscarriages by telling the grieving couple that they "can have more children," "It's not that bad, because you really didn't know the baby," "It probably would have been deformed anyway, so it's good that it happened this way," and similar insensitive statements.

One of the authors personally experienced this type of loss. He and his wife had undergone extensive treatment for infertility, and they were elated at the news of the pregnancy. When they lost their baby, they were devastated. All the statements listed above were actually said to them. Their grief was worse because they knew that it would be difficult to get pregnant again. The poem at the top of page 543 was written the night the miscarriage happened, and serves as testimony to the grief couples in this situation experience.

Last night
  as I sat holding your hand
  in the emergency room,
  watching helplessly as the life we had created
  come to an end,
I felt more alone and powerless
  than in my whole life.
Your look of fear, your trembling, the
  lack of control over events, my own
  ocean of grief
All swept over me like a tidal wave.
I became too intimately familiar with
  the deepest pit of my stomach,
  too closely acquainted with utter helplessness.
Intellectually, the event is over now.
Gone. In the past. Life goes on.
But I know that from time to time
  for the rest of my life
I'll see him or her in every child I'll
  ever meet.
I'll never really forget.
How could I?   ❧

Finally, grandparents' feelings can easily be overlooked. They, too, feel the pain and loss when their grandchild dies. Moreover, they grieve not only for the grandchild but also for their own child's loss (Hamilton, 1978). Grandparents must also be included in whatever rituals or support groups the family chooses.

Death of One's Partner

The death of a partner differs from other losses. It clearly represents a deep personal loss, especially when the couple has had a long and close relationship. In a very real way, when one's partner dies, a part of oneself dies, too. Bertha, the widow in the fourth opening vignette, is a good case in point. She and her husband had formed a strong partnership, and the loss of her longtime companion hurt Bertha deeply.

There is pressure from society to mourn the loss of one's partner for a period of time. Typically, this pressure is manifested if the survivor begins to show interest in finding another mate before an "acceptable" period of mourning has passed. Although Americans no longer specify the length of the period, many feel that about a year is appropriate. The fact that such pressure and negative commentary usually do not accompany other losses is another indication of the seriousness with which most people take the death of a partner.

Responses to the loss of a spouse vary with the age of the survivor. Young adult spouses tend to grieve more intensely immediately following the death than do older spouses. However, the situation 18 months later is reversed. At that time, older spouses report more grief than do younger spouses (Sanders, 1980–1981). Indeed, older bereaved spouses may grieve for at least 30 months (Thompson et al., 1991). The differences seem to be related to four factors. The death of a young spouse is more unexpected; there are fewer role models of the same age for young widows and widowers; older widows feel greater loss of a long-term companion, while younger widows feel a loss of the future; and the

The death of one's husband is a relatively common event among older women. As a result, other widows provide a support network for this woman, who only recently lost her husband.

opportunities for remarriage are greater for younger survivors. Older widows anticipate fewer years of life and prefer to cherish the memory of their deceased spouse rather than attempting a new marriage (Raphael, 1983).

Social support plays a significant role in the outcome of the grieving process during the first two years after the death of a partner. Particularly important is the quality of the support system for the grieving widow, rather than simply the number of friends. Survivors who have a few friends or relatives with whom they have strong, close relationships are better off than survivors who have many acquaintances (Dimond, Lund, & Caserta, 1987).

One study of spousal bereavement measured how the surviving spouse rated the marriage. Bereaved older adults rated their relationships at 2, 12, and 30 months after the death of their spouses. Nonbereaved older adults served as a comparison group. The results are summarized in the graphs. Bereaved widows and widowers gave their marriages more positive ratings than nonbereaved older adults. A marriage lost through death left a positive bias in memory. However, bereaved spouses' ratings were related to depression in an interesting way. The more depressed the bereaved spouse, the more positive the marriage's rating. In contrast, depressed nonbereaved spouses gave their marriages negative ratings. This result suggests that depression following bereavement signifies positive aspects of a relationship; whereas depression not connected with bereavement indicates a troubled relationship (Futterman et al., 1990).

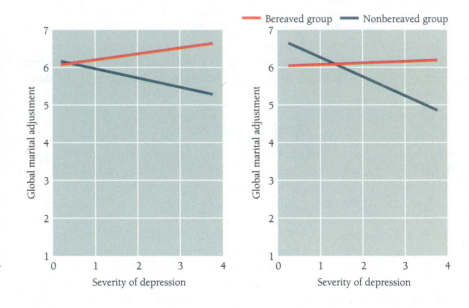

Comparisons of Types of Loss

There has been little research comparing people's grief reactions from different types of loss. Typically, bereaved parents show higher levels of depression and other grief reactions than bereaved spouses or adult children (Owen, Fulton, & Markusen, 1982). Other research reveals that the intensity of depression following loss is related specifically to how important the survivor considers the relationship with the deceased person (Murphy, 1988). Survivors are more often depressed (and more seriously so) following the deaths of people who were particularly important to them.

One study compared the grief reactions of 255 middle-aged women who had experienced the loss of a spouse, a parent, or a child within the preceding two years. Bereaved mothers reported significantly higher levels of depression than widows, who in turn reported significantly greater depression than adult children. In fact, over 60% of the bereaved mothers had depression scores in the moderate to severe depression range (Leahy, 1993).

We must be careful in our interpretation of these data. As noted earlier, there are many aspects of grief other than depression. Until researchers provide evidence on the other aspects, it is premature to conclude that some types of loss result in greater grief than others. All we can say at this point is that following some types of loss, some people tend to report more depressive symptoms, at more serious levels. Meanwhile, you can see for yourself how individual differences in dealing with loss provide clues to aspects of grief besides depression.

Individual Differences in Grief

The text describes different reactions that people have when a loved one dies. Sometimes, we make assumptions about how people are supposed to feel based on what we read or hear from other sources. Keep in mind that people are unique and have their own ways of dealing with losses. You may have experienced the loss of a friend or family member yourself. If so, you already know that your reaction differed somewhat from the descriptions here. It is instructive to talk to other people as well, to appreciate the wide range of experiences people have following loss. Check with your friends and family members. Talk to them about their experiences and jot down some notes based on what they say. Can you discover several different ways for dealing with losses through death? When you do, compile a list of feelings and behaviors and see how well they fit with the discussions in the text. ❧

SEE FOR YOURSELF

TEST YOURSELF

1. The death of a parent deprives people of _____.
2. Some of the most overlooked losses are the loss of a child through _____.
3. Shortly after the death of a spouse, _____ widows grieve more intensely than _____ widows.
4. In a study comparing different types of loss, _____ reported the highest level of depression.
5. What insights into the quality of relationships can we get by observing grief following loss?

Near-Death Experiences

Near-Death Experiences

LEARNING OBJECTIVES

❧ *What is a near-death experience?*

Most people believe that death does not mark the end of being. Exactly what is believed to come after death varies widely among individuals and cultures,

Answers: (1) a key relationship and a psychological buffer against death, (2) stillbirth, miscarriage, abortion, or neonatal death, (3) younger; older, (4) grieving mothers

but many themes are held in common. Such beliefs and themes have been part of human culture for thousands of years. Many of the artifacts found in ancient burial sites, like the one shown in the photograph from King Tutankhamen's tomb, were meant to be used by the deceased in an afterlife.

From a modern perspective, we can examine these themes with two questions in mind. Is the belief in something following death just wishful thinking? Is there any scientific reason to suspect another type of existence?

These were the questions that prompted Moody (1975, 1988) to interview children and adults who had had close calls with death—that is, near-death experiences. **In *near-death experiences* people who have been declared clinically dead, or have come very close to dying, recover and report certain types of experiences and feelings.** On the basis of interviews, Moody identified several aspects common to people of all ages, although individual experiences differed somewhat. The common aspects of the experiences include:

1. An awareness of a buzzing or drumming sound, or possibly hearing oneself declared dead
2. Feeling oneself moving out of one's body and then quickly down a tunnel, funnel, or cave toward an intense light
3. Seeing or feeling the presence of dead relatives, who are there to help one make the transition from this life
4. Sensing the light as a power or presence, sometimes interpreted or experienced as love, that makes one review one's own life rather than be judged
5. "Seeing" one's life pass in front of one's eyes in a kaleidoscopic view of thoughts and deeds
6. Being instantly able to tap into knowledge of any sort
7. Being aware or being told that the time for one's death has not yet come and that one must return to finish the normal life span

Some of the people whom Moody interviewed resented having survived. For them, the near-death experience was extraordinarily pleasant, and they felt cheated. For most people, the close encounter with death gave them a new and more positive outlook on life. Many people changed their life styles, and some acquired a deep spiritual commitment. Most no longer feared death; knowing what it would be like had removed the mystery and doubt.

Moody makes no claims that these experiences prove the existence of life after death. Nevertheless, he does believe that these data are significant, if for no other reason than that the participants' experiences were so remarkably similar. Subsequent verifications of these reports have been offered (Moody, 1977; Siegel, 1980). Many people see the consistency of the reports as evidence that there is life after death. Because belief in some form of an afterlife is so widespread, this is not very surprising.

There are also critics, however. Siegel (1980) uses evidence from several sources to refute claims that the near-death reports reflect experiences of an afterlife. According to Siegel, each of the common themes in these reports can be explained by known processes. For example, Siegel points out that the feeling of moving down a tunnel is sometimes reported by people who are recovering from anesthesia. Reports of bright lights or cities on a cloud occur as drug-induced hallucinations. Many people report feeling the presence of deceased loved ones at various times. In short, Siegel argues that it is more likely that the experiences reflect neurological processes we do not yet fully understand than actual experiences of an afterlife.

Whose interpretation is correct? Unfortunately, the question is currently unanswerable and is likely to stay that way. But the belief in an afterlife may help people adapt in this life. Some might use death as a stimulus for personal growth if they think that something might follow it. Additionally, without the concept of an afterlife, some people would feel a devastating fear of total non-being. A belief in an afterlife may be nothing more than a way of denying the reality and the finality of death. But the adaptive value of this belief is potentially great; the fact that so many different cultures throughout human history have believed in it gives some credence to this view.

TEST YOURSELF

1. For some people, the near-death experience is evidence of _____.
2. How might people at different stages of cognitive development interpret the research on near-death experiences?

Putting It All Together

As we've discovered in this chapter, thinking about death isn't easy. We aren't taught how to deal with it very well. Like Greta, we encounter different rituals and customs concerning funerals and mourning and we do not fully understand them. You may have been in a situation like that of Donna and Carl, facing the dilemma of whether to bring young children to a funeral. You may know someone like Betty who has just been diagnosed with a terminal disease, or someone like Bertha who just lost a spouse. Like Clare and Alex, you may have experienced the loss of a close relative or friend.

Death is not as pleasant a topic as children's play or occupational development. It's not something we can go to college to master. What it represents to many people is the end of their existence, and that is a very scary prospect. But because we all share in this fear at some level, each of us is equipped to provide support and comfort for grieving survivors.

Confronting our own death will be the final developmental milestone we encounter. Does it in fact put an end to the voyage we started when our lives began? We decide individually what to believe about that. Death is the last life-cycle force we encounter, the ultimate triumph of biological forces that limit the length of life. People deal with death, either their own or someone else's, through an interaction of psychological forces (such as coping skills and intellectual and emotional understanding of death) and the sociocultural forces expressed in a particular society's traditions and rituals.

Now we come to the end of our journey. In a way, we have ended as we began, discussing an issue that science cannot resolve, that we must face alone. Just as science cannot state precisely when life begins, neither can it say exactly when death occurs. We must face the beginning of life by ourselves, and we likewise cross the threshold to death on our own. But death may turn out to be the most incredible journey we will ever take.

Answers: (1) an afterlife

Thinking about Development

1. To what extent do the definitions of death reflect universal aspects of development (as discussed in Chapter 1)? To what extent do they reflect diversity?

2. How are the bioethical issues concerning death similar to or different from bioethical issues concerning birth (such as abortion, neonatal intensive care, genetic counseling, and the like)?

3. How could a parent use Piaget's theory to good advantage when talking to children of different ages about death?

4. How are the theories of dying and the stages of grief related?

5. How do biological, psychological, social, and life-cycle factors come into play in understanding how people deal with different types of loss?

Summary

Definitions and Ethical Issues

Sociocultural Definitions of Death

■ Death is a difficult concept to define precisely. Different cultures have different meanings for death. Among the meanings in Western culture are images, statistics, events, state of being, analogy, mystery, boundary, thief of meaning, basis for anxiety, and reward or punishment.

Legal and Medical Definitions

■ For many centuries, a clinical definition of death was used: the absence of a heartbeat and respiration. Currently, brain death is the most widely used definition. It is based on several highly specific criteria, including brain activity and responses to specific stimuli.

Ethical Issues

■ Two types of euthanasia are distinguished. Active euthanasia consists of deliberately ending someone's life, such as turning off a life support system. Passive euthanasia is ending someone's life by withholding some type of intervention or treatment (for example, by stopping nutrition). It is essential that people make their wishes known, either through a durable power of attorney or a living will.

Ideas about Death through the Life Span

Childhood

■ Children do not fully understand the permanence, universality, and lack of functioning in death until around the ages of 5 to 7. Their first experiences are likely to be with pets. Adults must exercise patience and avoid the use of euphemisms when discussing death with children. Given proper support, children are capable of attending funerals and other rituals.

Adolescence

■ Adolescents tend to not talk about death, although their understanding approaches that of adults. However, they have feelings of immortality—a tendency to believe that death affects other people but not themselves.

Young Adulthood

■ Young adults tend to believe that their peers who die are cheated out of their future. Cognitive developmental changes involving postformal thought may help integrate feelings and thoughts about death.

Middle Age

■ Middle-aged adults come to realize that they are next in line to die, usually at the point when they experience the loss of their parents. It is common for middle-aged adults to change their perception of time from the amount of time they have lived to the amount of time they have left.

Late Adulthood

■ Older adults are least concerned about dying. They may even look forward to it, for a variety of reasons. This is due in part to the achievement of integrity in Erikson's framework.

The Process of Dying

The Stage Theory of Dying

■ Kübler-Ross's theory includes five stages: denial, anger, bargaining, depression, and acceptance. People do not necessarily go through all of them or go through them in order.

The Phase Theory of Dying

■ A second view states that dying occurs in three phases: an acute phase, a chronic living-dying phase, and a terminal phase. Feelings and emotions vary according to the specific phase an individual is in.

A Life-Span Developmental Perspective on Dying

■ Older adults take longer to die and are more likely to die alone than any other group. Age differences in the dying experience and in the social definition of loss help put the meaning of dying into perspective. The goal of hospice is to maintain the quality of life and to manage the pain of terminal patients. Hospice clients are typically better off psychologically than hospital patients.

Surviving the Loss: The Grieving Process

Stages of Grief

■ People normally deal with their grief in various ways. Three main phases of grief have been identified: the initial phase, the intermediate phase, and the recovery phase. Progress through these stages depends on several factors, such as the type of loss and the support the individual receives. When death is expected, survivors go through anticipatory grief; unexpected death is usually more difficult for people to handle.

Normal Grief Reactions

■ Dealing with grief, called *grief work*, usually takes at least one to two years. Grief is equally intense for both expected and unexpected death, but it may begin before the actual death when the patient has a terminal illness. Normal grief reactions include sorrow, sadness, denial, disbelief, guilt, and anniversary reactions.

Effects of Normal Grief on Adults' Health

■ In terms of dealing with normal grief, middle-aged adults have the most difficult time. Poor copers tend to have low self-esteem before losing a loved one.

Abnormal Grief Reactions

■ Excessive guilt and self-blame are common signs of abnormal grief. Intense grief reactions that impair normal functioning more than two years after the loss are often viewed as abnormal.

Dealing with Different Types of Loss

Death of One's Parent

■ The death of a parent reminds people of their own mortality and deprives them of a very important person in their lives. The transition to being the oldest generation in one's family is sometimes a difficult one.

Death of One's Child

■ The death of a child is thought to be the most tragic type of loss. Miscarriage, abortion, stillbirth, and neonatal death are also highly traumatic. For most people, losing a child violates the natural order of things; children are not supposed to die before their parents.

Death of One's Partner

■ The death of a partner is the loss of a lover and companion. Bereaved spouses tend to view their marriages in a positive light. The loss of a spouse does not significantly impair a person's physical health, although it does increase psychological stress.

Comparisons of Types of Loss

■ Little research has been done comparing different types of loss. What we know reveals that bereaved mothers report more depressive symptoms than widows, who report more symptoms than bereaved adult daughters.

Near-Death Experiences

■ Many people report near-death experiences having several similar components. Whether these experiences reflect life after death is open to debate.

Key Terms

active euthanasia   (523)
anniversary reaction   (538)
bioethics   (522)
brain death   (522)
clinical death   (522)

death anxiety   (530)
euthanasia   (522)
grief   (535)
grief work   (538)
hospice   (532)

mourning   (535)
near-death experiences   (546)
passive euthanasia   (523)
persistent vegetative state   (522)

If You'd Like to Learn More

KALISH, R. A. (1981). *Death, grief, and caring relationships.* Pacific Grove, CA: Brooks/Cole. This easy-to-read classic gives clear, concise discussions of the topics covered in this chapter.

KASTENBAUM, R. (1985). Death and dying: A life-span approach. In J. E. Birren and K. W. Schaie (Eds.), *Handbook of the psychology of aging* (2nd ed., pp. 619–643). New York: Van Nostrand Reinhold. Moderately difficult reading, this chapter presents a summary of the research literature. Some familiarity with the issues and terminology is assumed.

KUSHNER, H. S. (1981). *When bad things happen to good people.* New York: Schocken. This is easy reading but contains very thought-provoking material. The book was written by a rabbi after the death of his son.

NULAND, S. B. (1994). *How we die: Reflections on life's final chapter.* New York: Knopf. This is a good discussion of the actual things that happen when people die. It is excellent for countering myths about death.

STEPHENSON, J. S. (1985). *Death, grief, and mourning: Individual and social realities.* New York: Free Press. The reading level is moderately easy to difficult, depending on the topic and how much background you have. Mainly, the book presents a historical and philosophical discussion.

TAYLOR, N. (1993). *A necessary end.* New York: Nan A. Talese. The author tells how he dealt with the death of his parents and found meaning in it.

abusive relationship when one partner in a relationship becomes violent or aggressive toward the other.

accommodation according to Piaget, changing existing knowledge based on new knowledge.

achievement the identity status in Marcia's theory in which adolescents have explored alternative identities and are now secure in their chosen identities.

active euthanasia the deliberate ending of someone's life.

activities of daily living (ADLs) self-care tasks such as eating, bathing, toileting, walking, or dressing.

activity the dimension of temperament defined by the tempo and vigor of a child's activity.

activity theory the view that people age better the more active they remain.

adaptation level the area where environmental press is average for a particular level of competence.

addiction physical dependence on a particular substance, such as alcohol.

adolescent egocentrism the self-absorption that is characteristic of teenagers as they search for identity.

aerobic exercise exercise that places a moderate stress on the heart by maintaining a pulse rate between 60% and 90% of the maximum heart rate.

age discrimination denying a job or promotion to someone solely on the basis of age.

age effects differences between individuals that are the result of biological, psychological, or sociocultural processes in the biopsychosocial model.

age integrated housing where people of all ages live together and interact.

age of viability the age at which a fetus can survive because most of its bodily systems function adequately; typically at 7 months after conception.

age segregated housing where all residents are of the same age.

agreeableness a dimension of personality associated with being accepting, willing to work with others, and caring.

alienation when workers feel that what they are doing is meaningless, that their efforts are devalued, or

when they do not see the connection between what they do and the final product.

alleles variations of genes.

altruism prosocial behavior such as helping and sharing in which the individual does not benefit directly from his or her behavior.

Alzheimer's disease a disease associated with aging characterized by gradual declines in memory, learning, attention, and judgment; confusion as to time and where one is; difficulties in communicating and finding the words one wants to use; declines in personal hygiene and self-care skills; inappropriate social behavior; and changes in personality.

amniocentesis a prenatal diagnostic technique that involves withdrawing a sample of amniotic fluid through the mother's abdomen using a syringe.

amnion an inner sac in which the developing child will rest.

amyloid a protein that is produced in abnormally high levels in Alzheimer's disease and which may be responsible for the neurofibrillary tangles and neuritic plaques.

animism crediting inanimate objects with life and life-like properties such as feelings.

anniversary reaction changes in behavior related to feelings of sadness on the actual anniversary of a death.

anorexia nervosa a persistent refusal to eat, accompanied by an irrational fear of being overweight.

anoxia lack of oxygen during delivery, typically because the umbilical cord becomes pinched or tangled during delivery.

anxiety disorders problems such as feelings of severe anxiety for no apparent reason, phobias to specific things or places, and obsessive-compulsive disorders in which thoughts or actions are repeatedly performed.

appraisal an evaluation of a situation to determine if it exceeds a person's resources and is, therefore, stressful.

artistic personality in Holland's theory, the type of person who likes to express himself through unstructured tasks.

assimilation   according to Piaget, taking in information that is compatible with what one already knows.

attachment   an enduring social-emotional relationship between infants and their caregivers.

attention   processes that determine which information will be processed further by an individual.

authoritarian parents   parents who show high levels of control and low levels of warmth toward their children.

authoritative parents   parents who use a moderate degree of control and who are warm and responsive to their children.

autosomes   the first 22 pairs of chromosomes.

average life expectancy   the age at which half of the people born in a particular year will have died.

avoidant attachment   a relationship in which infants turn away from their mothers when they are reunited following a brief separation.

axon   a tube-like structure that emerges from the cell body and transmits information to other neurons.

babbling   speechlike sounds that consist of vowel-consonant combinations.

basal metabolic rate   the speed with which the body consumes calories.

basic cry   a cry that starts softly and gradually becomes more intense; often heard when babies are hungry or tired.

battered woman syndrome   a situation in which a woman believes that she cannot leave an abusive situation.

behavior therapy   an explanation of depression that says that depressed people experience too few rewards or reinforcements from their environment.

bioethics   the study of the interface between human values and technological advances in health and life sciences.

biological forces   all genetic and health-related factors that affect development.

biopsychosocial framework   a view that integrates biological, psychological, sociocultural, and life cycle forces on development.

blended family   a family consisting of a biological parent, a stepparent, and children.

brain death   the most widely accepted definition of death, including no heartbeat, respiration, responsiveness, reflexes, and brain activity.

burnout   a depletion of a person's energy and motivation.

cardinality principle   the counting principle that the last number name denotes the number of objects being counted.

career plateauing   either a lack of promotional opportunity from the organization or a person's decision not to seek advancement.

caregiver speech   speech that adults use with babies that is slow, loud, and has exaggerated changes in pitch.

cell body   the center of the neuron that keeps the neuron alive.

cellular theory   a theory of aging that focuses on processes that occur within individual cells that cause the build-up of harmful substances over one's lifetime.

cephalocaudal   the principle that growth occurs from the head first and then down the spine.

cerebral cortex   the wrinkled surface of the brain that regulates many functions that are distinctly human.

cerebral vascular accident   *see* stroke.

chorion   an outer sac in which the developing child will rest during prenatal development.

chorionic villus sampling   a prenatal diagnostic technique that involves taking a sample of tissue from the chorion.

chromosomes   threadlike structures in the nuclei of the sperm and egg that contain genetic material.

chronic obstructive pulmonary disease (COPD)   the most common form of incapacitating respiratory disease among older adults; examples are asthma and emphysema.

circadian rhythm   the sleep-wake cycle.

climacteric   the loss of ability to bear children, which usually begins in the 40s and is complete by age 50 or 55.

clinical death   death defined by a lack of heartbeat and respiration.

clique   a small group of friends who are similar in age, sex and race.

cognitive therapy   an approach to depression that is based on the idea that maladaptive beliefs or cognitions about oneself are responsible for depression.

cohabitation   two or more unrelated adults living together.

cohort effects   differences between individuals that are the result of experiences and circumstances that are unique to a person's particular generation.

comparable worth   equating pay in occupations that are determined to be equivalent in importance but differ in terms of the gender distribution of the people in them.

competence the upper limit of a person's ability to function in five domains: physical health, sensory-perceptual skills, motor skills, cognitive skills, and ego strength.

cones specialized neurons in the back of the eye that sense color.

confounding when two or more variables may be responsible for the behaviors that are observed and the influence of each cannot be separated.

conscientiousness a dimension of personality associated with being hardworking, ambitious, energetic, scrupulous, and persevering.

continuity theory the view that people tend to cope with daily life in late adulthood in essentially the same ways they coped in earlier periods of life.

continuity versus discontinuity an issue concerned with whether a developmental phenomenon follows a smooth progression throughout the life span or a series of abrupt shifts.

conventional level the second level of reasoning in Kohlberg's theory, where moral reasoning is based on society's norms.

conventional personality in Holland's theory, the sort of person who likes to apply verbal and quantitative skills to structured, well-defined tasks.

convergent thinking using information to arrive at one standard, correct answer.

cooing early vowel-like sounds that babies produce.

cooperative play play that is organized around a theme, with each child taking on a different role; begins at about 2 years of age.

coping attempts to deal with stress.

corpus callosum a thick bundle of neurons that connects the two hemispheres of the brain.

correlation coefficient a statistic that reveals the strength and direction of the relation between two variables.

corticoids hormones that become more numerous in response to stress.

cross-linking a theory of aging in which some proteins interact randomly with certain body tissues, such as muscles and arteries.

cross-sectional design a research design in which people of different ages are compared at one point in time.

cross-sequential design a research design consisting of two or more cross-sectional studies that are conducted at two or more times of measurement.

crowd a large group including many cliques that have similar attitudes and values.

crowning the appearance of the top of the baby's head during labor.

crystallization the first phase in Super's theory of career development, in which adolescents use their emerging identities for ideas about careers.

crystallized intelligence knowledge that has been acquired through experience and education in a particular culture.

cultural conservator a style in which grandparents request that their grandchildren be allowed to live with them in order to ensure that the grandchildren learn the native ways.

culture the knowledge, attitudes, and behavior associated with a group of people.

culture-fair intelligence tests intelligence tests devised using items that are common to many cultures.

date (acquaintance) rape when someone is forced to have sexual intercourse with someone that they know.

death anxiety refers to the fact that people are uncomfortable thinking about their own death.

deductive reasoning drawing conclusions from facts; characteristic of formal operational thought.

dementia a family of diseases involving serious impairment of behavioral and cognitive functioning.

demographers people who study population trends.

dendrite the end of the neuron that receives information; it looks like a tree with many branches.

deoxyribonucleic acid (DNA) a molecule composed of four nucleotide bases that is the biochemical basis of heredity.

dependent variable the behavior that is observed after other variables are manipulated.

depression a disorder characterized by pervasive feelings of sadness, irritability, and low self-esteem.

developmental theories theories that organize knowledge to provide testable explanations of human behavior and how that behavior changes over time.

differentiation distinguishing and mastering individual motions.

diffusion the identity status in Marcia's theory in which adolescents do not have an identity and are doing nothing to achieve one.

disengagement theory the view that older adults voluntarily reduce the number of social activities and commitments they have, and are encouraged by society to do so.

disorganized (disoriented) attachment   a relationship in which infants don't seem to understand what's happening when they are separated and later reunited with their mothers.

dispenser of family wisdom   a grandparent who assumes an authoritarian position and provides information and advice.

dispositional praise   praise that links a child's altruistic behavior to an underlying altruistic disposition.

distant grandparenting   grandparents who have little contact except on holidays, birthdays, or other family celebrations.

divergent thinking   thinking in novel and unusual directions.

divided attention   performing more than one task at a time.

dizygotic twins   twins that are the result of the fertilization of two separate eggs by two sperm; also called fraternal twins.

docility   when people allow the situation to dictate the options they have.

dominance hierarchy   an ordering of individuals within a group in which group members with lower status defer to those with greater status.

dominant   the form of an allele whose chemical instructions are followed.

dream   as related to vocational development, a vision of one's career.

dysphoria   feeling sad or down; the most prominent symptom of depression.

ecological theory   a view that human development cannot be separated from the environmental contexts in which development occurs.

ectoderm   the outer layer of the embryo that will become the hair, outer layer of skin, and the nervous system.

ego   according to Freud, the rational component of the personality; develops during the first few years of life.

egocentrism   difficulty in seeing the world from another's point of view; typical of children in the preoperational period.

electroencephalogram (EEG)   a pattern of brain waves recorded from electrodes that are placed on the scalp.

emotionality   the aspect of temperament that refers to the strength of the infant's emotional response to a situation, the ease with which that response is triggered, and the ease with which the infant can be returned to a nonemotional state.

empathy   experiencing another person's feelings.

encapsulated   result of the processes of thinking becoming connected with the products of thinking.

endoderm   the inner layer of the embryo, which will become the lungs and the digestive system.

enterprising personality   in Holland's theory, the type of person who likes to use verbal skill in positions of power or leadership.

environmental press   the number and type of physical, interpersonal, or social demands that environments put on people.

epigenetic principle   the view in Erikson's theory that each psychosocial stage has its own period of importance.

erythrocytes   the red blood cells that carry oxygen and carbon dioxide to and from the body.

ethnic identity   feeling a part of one's ethnic group and knowing the unique elements of the group's culture and heritage.

ethology   a branch of biology concerned with adaptive behaviors that are characteristic of different species.

eugenics   the effort to improve the human species by letting only people who have characteristics that are valued by a society mate and pass along their genes.

euthanasia   the practice of ending a life for reasons of mercy.

exchange theory   a view that marriage is based on each partner contributing something to the relationship that the other would be hard-pressed to provide.

exosystem   according to Bronfenbrenner, social settings that influence one's development even though one does not experience them firsthand.

experiment   a systematic way of manipulating factors that a researcher thinks cause a particular behavior.

explicit memory   the conscious and intentional recollection of information.

expressive style   a style of language learning that describes children whose vocabularies include many social phrases that are used like one word.

extended family   a family in which grandparents and other relatives live with parents and children.

external aids   memory aids that rely on environmental resources, such as notebooks or calendars.

extinction   the phenomenon in which a behavior ultimately stops when it is no longer reinforced.

extraversion   a dimension of personality that refers to the extent that individuals thrive on social interaction, like to talk, take charge easily, readily express their opinions and feelings, like to keep busy, have seemingly unending energy, and prefer stimulating and challenging environments.

extremely low birth weight   newborns who weigh less than 1000 grams (2 pounds).

familial mental retardation   a form of mental retardation that does not involve biological damage but represents the low end of the normal distribution of intelligence.

family life cycle   a series of relatively predictable changes that families experience.

fast mapping   the fact that children make connections between new words and referents so quickly that they can't be considering all possible meanings.

fetal alcohol syndrome   a disorder affecting babies whose mothers consumed large amounts of alcohol while they were pregnant.

fictive grandparenting   a style that allows adults to fill in for missing or deceased biological grandparents, functionally creating the role of surrogate grandparent.

filial obligation   a sense of responsibility to care for a parent if necessary.

fine motor skills   motor skills associated with grasping, holding, and manipulating objects.

fluid intelligence   abilities such as thinking in a flexible, adaptive manner, drawing inferences, and understanding relations between concepts.

foreclosure   the identity status in Marcia's theory in which adolescents have an identity that was chosen based on advice from adults, rather than one that was a result of personal exploration of alternatives.

formal grandparenting   grandparents who see their role in traditional terms, expressing a strong interest in the grandchild, but maintaining a hands-off attitude toward child rearing.

frail older adults   older adults who have physical disabilities, are very ill, and may have cognitive or psychological disorders.

free radicals   chemicals produced randomly during normal cell metabolism that bond easily to other substances inside cells; may cause cellular damage associated with aging.

free recall   a memory task in which people are simply asked to report everything they can remember about the material they learned.

frontal cortex   a brain region that regulates personality and goal-directed behavior.

fun seeking grandparenting   grandparents who see themselves as a primary source of fun for their grandchildren and avoid more serious types of interaction.

gender identity   a sense of oneself as male or female.

gender stereotypes   beliefs and images about males and females that are not necessarily true.

gene   a group of nucleotide bases that provide a specific set of biochemical instructions.

generativity   according to Erikson, being productive by helping others to ensure the continuation of society by guiding the next generation.

genetic counseling   constructing a family tree to determine the likelihood that a couple's child would inherit a disorder that runs in the family.

genotype   a person's hereditary makeup.

gifted   traditionally, individuals with intelligence test scores of at least 130.

glass ceiling   the level to which women and minorities may rise in a company but beyond which they may not go.

grammatical morphemes   words or endings of words that make a sentence grammatical.

grief   the sorrow, hurt, anger, guilt, confusion, and other feelings that arise after suffering a loss.

grief work   the psychological side of coming to terms with bereavement.

habituation   becoming unresponsive to a stimulus that is presented repeatedly.

haloperidol   a medication used to treat severe psychotic disorders in adults.

hassles   day-to-day events that upset and annoy people.

hemispheres   the right and left halves of the cortex.

hemorrhage   a break in any blood vessel that leads to loss of blood.

heterocyclic antidepressants (HCAs)   a type of medication used to treat depression.

heterozygous   when the alleles differ from each other.

high density lipoproteins (HDLs)   lipoproteins that help clear arteries.

homogamy   similarity of values and interests.

homozygous   when the chromosomes in a pair are the same.

hope   according to Erikson, an openness to new experience tempered by wariness that occurs when trust and mistrust are in balance.

hormone replacement theory   a treatment for symptoms accompanying the climacteric in which women take low doses of estrogen and progesterone.

hospice   a movement that seeks to provide a supportive environment for dying people by keeping families engaged in caregiving and by providing professional assistance during this very stressful time.

human development   the multidisciplinary scientific study of how people change and how they stay the same.

Huntington's disease   a progressive and fatal type of dementia.

id   according to Freud, the element of personality that wants immediate gratification of bodily wants and needs; present at birth.

imaginary audience   adolescents' feeling that their behavior is constantly being watched by their peers.

implementation   the third phase in Super's theory of career development, in which individuals now enter the work force.

implicit memory   effortless recollection of information.

incomplete dominance   the situation in which one allele does not completely dominate another.

incontinence   the loss of bladder or bowel control.

independent variable   the factor that is manipulated by the researcher in an experiment.

index offense   acts that are illegal regardless of the age of the perpetrator.

indifferent-uninvolved parents   parents who are neither warm nor controlling and who try to minimize the amount of time spent with their children.

indulgent-permissive parents   parents who are warm and caring but exert little control over their children.

information processing theory   a view that human cognition consists of mental hardware and software.

insecure attachment   a relationship in which infants act as if they do not perceive the mother to be dependable.

instrumental activities of daily living (IADLs)   acts that require some intellectual competence and planning, such as cooking and doing the laundry.

instrumental orientation   characteristic of Kohlberg's Stage 2, in which moral reasoning is based on the aim of looking out for one's own needs.

integration   linking individual motions into a coherent, coordinated whole.

integrity versus despair   according to Erikson, a struggle that comes about as older adults try to integrate their lives with a view of their family's and community's futures.

intelligence quotient   a mathematical representation of how a person scores on an intelligence test in relation to how other people of the same age score.

interindividual variability   patterns of change in a domain (e.g., intelligence) that are different for different people.

intermediate care   a facility that provides 24-hour care, but not involving intensive skilled nursing.

internal aids   memory aids that rely on mental processes, such as imagery.

internal belief systems   what one tells oneself about why certain things are happening.

internal working model   an infant's understanding of how responsive and dependable the mother is; thought to influence close relationships throughout the child's life.

interpersonal norms   characteristic of Kohlberg's Stage 3, in which moral reasoning is based on winning the approval of others.

intimacy versus isolation   according to Erikson, the psychosocial conflict of young adulthood.

intonation   a pattern of rising and falling pitch that appears around the age of 7 months in infants' babbling.

investigative personality   in Holland's theory, the type of personality associated with being task-oriented and thinking abstractly.

in vitro fertilization   the technique of fertilizing eggs with sperm in a petri dish and then transferring several of the fertilized eggs to the mother's uterus where they might implant in the lining of the wall of the uterus.

job satisfaction   the positive feeling that results from an appraisal of one's work.

joint custody   when, following divorce, both parents retain legal custody of their children.

juvenile delinquency   when adolescents commit illegal acts that are destructive toward themselves or others.

kinkeepers   the people who gather the family together for celebrations and keep family members in touch with each other.

learned helplessness   the feeling that one is always at the mercy of external events and that one does not have any control over one's own destiny.

learning disability   when a child with normal intelligence has difficulty mastering at least one academic subject.

life cycle force   differences in how the same event may affect people of different ages.

life review   a process of reviewing one's life.

life-span construct   a unified sense of the past, present, and future that is based on one's experiences and input from others.

life span perspective   the view that development is determined by many biological, psychological, and social factors and that all parts of the life span are interrelated.

life story   the second manifestation of the life-span construct, a personal narrative that organizes past events into a coherent sequence.

locomotion   the ability to move around in the world.

longevity   the number of years that a person will live.

longitudinal design   a research design in which a single cohort is studied over multiple times of measurement.

longitudinal sequential design   a research design consisting of two or more longitudinal designs that include two or more cohorts.

long-term memory   a permanent storehouse for memories that has unlimited capacity.

low birth weight   newborns who weigh less than 2500 grams (5 pounds).

low density lipoproteins (LDLs)   lipoproteins that cause fatty acids to accumulate in arteries, which impedes the flow of blood.

macrosystem   according to Bronfenbrenner, the cultural and subcultural settings in which the microsystems, mesosystems, and exosystems are embedded.

mad cry   a more intense version of a basic cry.

maximum life expectancy   the oldest age to which any person lives.

menarche   the onset of menstruation.

menopause   the cessation of menstruation.

mental age   in intelligence testing, a measure of children's performance corresponding to the chronological age of those whose performance equals the child's.

mental operations   cognitive actions that can be performed on objects or ideas.

mesoderm   the middle layer of the embryo; becomes the muscles, bones, and circulatory system.

mesosystem   according to Bronfenbrenner, the interrelations between different microsystems.

metabolic theory   a theory of aging that focuses on aspects of the body's metabolism as a reason why people age.

metabolism   the energy required for bodily functions.

microsystem   according to Bronfenbrenner, the people and objects that are present in one's immediate environment.

midlife crisis   a time of psychological questioning during which people reevaluate their lives.

monoamine oxidase (MAO) inhibitors   a type of medication used to treat depression.

monozygotic twins   twins that result when a single fertilized egg splits to form two new individuals; also called identical twins.

moral reasoning   the ethical rules that people use to explain what they think is right or wrong behavior in a particular situation.

moratorium   the identity status in Marcia's theory in which adolescents are still examining different alternatives and have yet to find a satisfactory identity.

motor skills   coordinated movements of the muscles and limbs.

mourning   the culturally approved ways in which people express their grief.

multidimensional theories   approaches to intelligence that identify different areas of intellectual abilities.

multidirectionality   refers to the fact that some aspects of intelligence improve and other aspects decline across adulthood.

multi-infarct dementia   a disease caused by numerous small cerebral vascular accidents.

nature versus nurture   an issue concerning the manner in which genetic and environmental factors influence development.

near-death experiences   experiences in which people who had been declared clinically dead, or had come very close to dying, recovered and reported certain types of experiences or feelings.

neural plate   a flat group of cells present in prenatal development that becomes the brain and spinal cord.

neuritic plaques   damaged and dying neurons that collect around a core of protein.

neurofibrillary tangles   abnormal filaments found in large numbers of neurons in persons with Alzheimer's disease.

neuron   the basic cellular unit of the brain and nervous system that specializes in receiving and transmitting information.

neuroticism   a dimension of personality that refers to the extent that individuals tend to be anxious, hostile, self-conscious, depressed, impulsive, and vulnerable.

niche-picking   the process of deliberately seeking environments that are compatible with one's genetic makeup.

nonexperimental method   research methods that do not involve the manipulation of variables but involve observation of phenomena.

nonnormative influences   forces that affect only a few people.

nonREM sleep sleep in which heart rate, breathing, and brain activity are steady.

norepinephrine a neurotransmitter that helps control arousal; low levels are related to depression.

normative age-graded influences forces that affect all people at certain points in the life span.

normative history-graded influences forces that affect people in a certain generation at a particular point in history.

nuclear family a family consisting of parent(s) and child(ren).

obedience orientation characteristic of Kohlberg's Stage 1, in which moral reasoning is based on the belief that adults know what is right and wrong.

observational studies careful investigations of people that provide useful, detailed information.

occupational priorities what people want from their employment.

one-to-one principle the counting principle that states that there must be one and only one number name for each object counted.

openness to experience a dimension of personality that refers to people who tend to have a vivid imagination and dream life, appreciation of art, and a strong desire to try anything once.

operant conditioning a view of learning, proposed by B. F. Skinner, that emphasizes reward and punishment.

optimally exercised ability the level of performance a normal, healthy adult would demonstrate under the best conditions of training or practice.

organic mental retardation mental retardation that can be traced to a specific biological or physical problem.

organization a key principle in Piaget's theory, according to which all schemes are linked to each other.

osteoporosis a disease in which bones become porous like honeycombs and are extremely easy to break.

overextension when children define words more broadly than adults do.

pain cry a cry that begins with a sudden, long burst, followed by a long pause and gasping.

parallel play when children play alone but are aware of and interested in what another child is doing.

Parkinson's disease a common disease among older adults that results in motor problems, including slow walking, difficulty getting into and out of chairs, and hand tremors.

passive euthanasia allowing a person to die by withholding an available treatment.

perception the processes by which the brain receives, selects, modifies, and organizes incoming nerve impulses that are the result of physical stimulation.

period of the fetus the longest period of prenatal development, extending from the 9th until the 38th week after conception.

persistent vegetative state a state in which a person's cortical functioning ceases while brainstem activity continues.

personal control beliefs beliefs about the degree to which one's performance in a situation is within one's control.

personal fable the feeling of many adolescents that their feelings and experiences are unique and have never been experienced by anyone else before.

personality-type theory a view proposed by Holland that people find their work fulfilling when the important features of a job or profession fit the workers' personalities.

phenotype the physical, behavioral, and psychological features that are the result of the interaction between one's genes and environment.

phenylketonuria (PKU) an inherited disorder in which babies are born lacking a liver enzyme.

phonemes unique speech sounds that can be used to create words.

phonological processing understanding and using sounds in written and oral language.

placenta the structure through which nutrients and wastes are exchanged between the mother and the developing child.

plasticity refers to the fact that an ability can be modified by certain conditions or experiences.

polygenic inheritance when phenotypes are the result of the combined activity of many separate genes.

population pyramid a graphic technique used by demographers to illustrate population trends.

positron emission tomography a procedure that shows the amount of activity in various regions of the brain by monitoring levels of radioactive glucose.

possible selves a representation of what one could become, what one would like to become, and what one is afraid of becoming.

postconventional level the third level of reasoning in Kohlberg's theory, in which morality is based on a personal moral code.

postformal thought   thought characterized by the realization that the correct answer may vary from situation to situation, that problem solutions must be realistic, that most situations are ambiguous, and that emotion and other subjective factors are an important part of thought.

power assertion   punishment that relies upon parents having greater power than their children.

practical intelligence   skills and knowledge necessary for people to function in everyday life.

preconventional level   the first level of reasoning in Kohlberg's theory, where moral reasoning is based on external forces.

prenatal development   the many changes that turn a fertilized egg into a newborn human.

presbycusis   loss in the ability to hear high-pitched tones.

preterm (premature)   babies born before the 36th week after conception.

primary circular reaction   according to Piaget, when infants accidentally produce pleasant events that are centered on the body and then try to recreate the events.

primary mental abilities   groups of related intellectual skills, such as spatial skill and mathematical skill.

private speech   comments that are not intended for others but serve the purpose of helping children regulate their behavior.

proactivity   when people choose new behaviors to meet new desires or needs.

processes   information processing, memory, fluid intelligence.

products   an outcome of thinking; expertise.

programmed cell death theories   theories that suggest that aging is genetically programmed.

prosocial behavior   any behavior that benefits another person.

proximodistal   the principle that growth occurs first from the center of the body and then out to the extremities.

pseudodementias   treatable diseases that can mimic the symptoms of early Alzheimer's disease or related disorders.

psychodynamic theory   a theory in which human behavior is guided by motives and drives that are internal and often unconscious.

psychological forces   all internal perceptual, cognitive, emotional, and personality factors that affect development.

psychosocial theory   a theory proposed by Erik Erikson in which personality development is the result of the interaction of maturation and societal demands.

puberty   a collection of physical changes that marks the onset of adolescence, such as growth of breasts or testes and the growth spurt.

punishment   applying an aversive stimulus (e.g., a spanking) or removing an attractive stimulus (e.g., TV viewing).

purpose   according to Erikson, balance between individual initiative and the willingness to cooperate with others.

rapid eye movement (REM) sleep   sleep in which an infant's eyes will dart rapidly beneath the eyelids.

reaction range   the phenomenon that a particular genotype can interact with various environments to produce a range of phenotypes.

reaction time   the speed with which a person can make a particular response.

realistic personality   in Holland's theory, the type of personality that is well suited for physical labor and solving concrete problems.

reasonable woman standard   the appropriate legal criterion for determining whether sexual harassment has occurred; based on whether a reasonable woman would view a behavior as harassing.

recessive   an allele whose instructions are ignored when it is combined with a dominant allele.

recognition   a memory task requiring the selection of the correct item from a list of correct and incorrect choices; an example is a multiple-choice test.

referential style   a style of language learning that describes children whose vocabularies are dominated by names of objects, persons, or actions.

reflective judgment   a way in which adults reason about dilemmas that is characterized by the realization that the search for truth is an ongoing, never-ending journey.

reflexes   unlearned responses that are triggered by specific stimulation.

reinforcement   a consequence that increases the likelihood that a behavior will be repeated in the future.

reliability   as applied to tests, when test scores are consistent from one testing time to another.

resistant attachment   a relationship in which, after a brief separation, infants want to be held but are difficult to console.

retinal disparity   a way to infer depth based on differences in the retinal images in the left and right eyes.

returning adult students college students over the age of 25 years.

rites of passage rituals that mark the initiation in-to a new phase of development, such as adulthood.

role conflict the feeling that one is being pulled in multiple directions by incompatible demands.

role transitions assuming new responsibilities and du-ties when a person moves from one phase of devel-opment (e.g., adolescence) to another (e.g., adult-hood).

sandwich generation middle-aged adults between two generations (their parents and children) that put demands and pressures on them.

scaffolding a teaching style in which adults adjust the amount of assistance that they offer, based on the learner's needs.

scenario the first manifestation of the life-span con-struct that consists of expectations about the future.

scheme according to Piaget, a mental structure that organizes information and regulates behavior.

scientific method a method of study that involves systematic observation, testing alternative hypothe-ses, and sharing results with the scientific com-munity.

scripts the means by which people remember com-mon events consisting of sequences of activities.

secondary circular reaction according to Piaget, when infants accidentally produce interesting events with objects and then try to repeat those events.

secondary mental abilities broad categories of related primary mental abilities.

secular growth trends the fact that people in indus-trialized societies are larger and are maturing earlier than in previous generations.

secure attachment a relationship in which infants have come to trust and depend on their mothers.

selective serotonin reuptake inhibitors (SSRIs) a type of medication used to treat depression that alters the balance of serotonin in the brain.

selectivity as applied to attention, the ability to pick out important from irrelevant information in the environment.

self-efficacy the belief that one is capable of perform-ing a certain task.

sensorimotor period the first of Piaget's four stages of cognitive development, which lasts from birth to approximately 2 years.

severe malnourishment when children weigh less than 60% of average body weight for their age.

sex chromosomes the 23rd pair of chromosomes; these determine the sex of the child.

sex discrimination denying a job to someone solely on the basis of whether the person is a man or woman.

sickle-cell trait a disorder in which individuals show signs of mild anemia only when they are seriously deprived of oxygen; occurs in individuals who have one dominant allele for normal blood cells and one recessive sickle-cell allele.

simple social play play that begins at about 15–18 months; toddlers engage in similar activities as well as talk and smile at each other.

skilled nursing care 24-hour care requiring fairly constant monitoring and provision of medical and other health services, usually by nurses.

sociability the dimension of temperament defined by preference for being with other people.

social clock refers to the fact that adults often associ-ate future events with a time or age by which they expect to complete them.

social contract characteristic of Kohlberg's Stage 5, in which moral reasoning is based on the belief that laws are for the good of all members of society.

social convoy a group of people who journey together throughout their lives and provide each other sup-port in good and bad times.

socialization the process of teaching children the val-ues, roles, and behaviors of their culture.

social learning theory a view that thinking as well as direct reinforcement and punishment plays an im-portant part in shaping behavior.

social personality in Holland's theory, someone who is skilled verbally and interpersonally and likes to use those skills.

social role a set of cultural guidelines about how one should behave, especially with other people.

social systems morality characteristic of Kohlberg's Stage 4, in which moral reasoning is based on maintenance of order in society.

sociocultural forces all interpersonal, societal, cul-tural, and ethnic factors that influence development.

spaced retrieval a memory intervention that involves teaching persons with Alzheimer's disease to re-member new information by gradually increasing the time between retrieval attempts.

specification the second phase in Super's theory of ca-reer development, in which adolescents learn more about specific lines of work and begin training.

stable-order principle the counting principle that states that number names must always be counted in the same order.

stagnation according to Erikson, a state in which people are not able to deal with the needs of their children or are unable to provide mentoring to younger adults.

status offense acts that are not crimes if they are committed by an adult, such as truancy and running away from home.

stress and coping paradigm the dominant framework used to study stress.

stroke an interruption in the flow of blood in the brain due to a blockage in a cerebral artery.

superego according to Freud, the moral component of the personality that has incorporated adult standards of right and wrong.

surrogate parents grandparents who assume all of the normal roles of a parent.

tacrine a drug designed to alleviate the memory loss associated with Alzheimer's disease.

telegraphic speech speech used by young children that contains only the words that are necessary to get a message across.

temperament a consistent style or pattern of behavior.

teratogen an agent that causes abnormal prenatal development.

tertiary circular reaction according to Piaget, repeating old schemes with new objects.

thioridazine a medication used to treat severe psychotic disorders in adults.

time of measurement effects differences due to the social, environmental, historical, or other events that have occurred at the time the data are collected.

time-out punishment that involves removing children who are misbehaving from a situation to a quiet, unstimulating environment.

toddlers young children who have learned to walk.

type A behavior pattern a person who is intensely competitive, angry, hostile, restless, aggressive, and impatient.

type B behavior pattern a person who is noncompetitive, calm, unaggressive, and patient.

ultrasound a prenatal diagnostic technique that involves bouncing sound waves off the fetus to generate an image of the fetus.

umbilical cord a structure containing veins and arteries that connects the developing child to the placenta.

underextension when children define words more narrowly than adults do.

unexercised ability the level of performance a person would exhibit without practice or training.

universal ethical principles characteristic of Kohlberg's Stage 6, in which moral reasoning is based on moral principles that apply to all.

universal versus context-specific development the issue of whether there is one path of development or several.

useful life expectancy the number of years that a person has that are free from debilitating chronic disease and impairment.

validity as applied to tests, the extent to which the test measures what it is supposed to measure.

very low birth weight newborns who weigh less than 1500 grams (3 pounds).

visual acuity the smallest pattern that one can distinguish reliably.

visual cliff a glass-covered platform that appears to have a "shallow" side and "deep" side; used to study infants' depth perception.

vocational maturity the degree of congruity between a person's age and the person's occupational behaviors.

wear-and-tear theory a theory of aging that suggests that the body, much like a machine, gradually deteriorates over time and finally wears out.

Wernicke-Korsakoff syndrome a syndrome that is an indirect result of long-term alcoholism; symptoms include memory loss, severe disorientation, confusion, and visual problems.

will according to Erikson, a young child's understanding that he or she can act on the world intentionally, which occurs when autonomy, shame, and doubt are in balance.

working memory a type of memory in which a small number of items can be stored briefly.

zone of maximum comfort in environmental press theory, the area where slight decreases in press allow people to live happily without worrying about environmental demands.

zone of maximum performance in environmental press theory, the area in which slight increases in press tend to improve performance.

zone of proximal development the difference between what children can do with assistance and what they can do alone.

zygote the fertilized egg.

R E F E R E N C E S

AAMIDOR, A. (1993, August 18). Following the pack. *The Indianapolis Star,* p. C1.

ABBEY, A. (1991). Acquaintance rape and alcohol consumption on college campuses: How are they linked? *Journal of American College Health, 39,* 165–169.

ABEL, Z. L. (1980). Fetal alcohol syndrome: Behavioral teratology. *Psychological Bulletin, 87,* 29–50.

ABRAMS, W. B., & BERKOW, R. (1990). *The Merck manual for geriatrics.* Rahway, NJ: Merck, Sharp, & Dohme Research Laboratories.

ACKERMAN, B. P. (1993). Children's understanding of the speaker's meaning in referential communication. *Journal of Experimental Child Psychology, 55,* 56–86.

ADAMS, R. D. (1980). Morphological aspects of aging in the human nervous system. In J. E. Birren & R. B. Sloane (Eds.), *Handbook of mental health and aging* (pp. 149–160). Englewood Cliffs, NJ: Prentice-Hall.

ADAMS, R. J. (1989). Newborns' discrimination among mid- and long-wavelength stimuli. *Journal of Experimental Child Psychology, 47,* 130–141.

ADAMS, R. S. (1969). Location as a feature of instructional interaction. *Merrill-Palmer Quarterly, 15,* 309–321.

ADELMAN, C. (1991). *Women at thirtysomething: Paradoxes of attainment.* Washington, DC: U.S. Department of Education, Office of Educational Research, Office of Research.

ADLER, N. (1994). *Adolescent sexual behavior looks irrational—But looks are deceiving.* Washington, DC: Federation of Behavioral, Psychological, and Cognitive Sciences.

ADLER, S., & ARANYA, N. (1984). A comparison of the work needs, attitudes, and preferences of professional accountants at different career stages. *Journal of Vocational Behavior, 25,* 574–580.

ADLERSBERG, M., & THORNE, S. (1990). Emerging from the chrysalis: Older women in transition. *Journal of Gerontological Social Work, 16,* 4–8.

AHRONS, C., & WALLISCH, L. (1986). The relationship between former spouses. In D. Perlman & S. Duck (Eds.), *Intimate relationships: Development, dynamics, and deterioration* (pp. 269–296). Newbury Park, CA: Sage.

AINSWORTH, M. D. S. (1978). The development of infant-mother attachment. In B. M. Caldwell & H. N. Ricciuti (Eds.), *Review of child development research* (Vol. 3). Chicago: University of Chicago Press.

AINSWORTH, M. S. (1993). Attachment as related to mother-infant interaction. *Advances in Infancy Research, 8,* 1–50.

AITKEN, M., BENNETT, S. N., & HESKETH, J. (1981). Teaching styles and pupil progress: A re-analysis. *British Journal of Educational Psychology, 51,* 187–196.

ALES, K. L., DRUZIN, M. L., & SANTINI, D. L. (1990). Impact of advanced maternal age on the outcome of pregnancy. *Surgery, Gynecology & Obstetrics, 171,* 209–216.

ALEXANDER, J. F., WALDRON, H. B., BARTON, C., & MAS, C. H. (1989). The minimizing of blaming attributes and behaviors in delinquent families. *Journal of Consulting and Clinical Psychology, 57,* 19–24.

ALLEN, K. R., & CHIN-SANG, V. (1990). A lifetime of work: The context and meanings of leisure for aging black women. *Gerontologist, 30,* 734–740.

ALLEN, M. C. (1984). Developmental outcome and follow-up of the small for gestational age infant. *Seminars in Perinatology, 8,* 123–156.

ALLGEIER, A. R., & ALLGEIER, E. R. (1995). *Sexual interactions* (4th ed.). Lexington, MA: Heath.

ALWIN, D. F., CONVERSE, P. E., & MARTIN, S. S. (1985). Living arrangements and social integration. *Journal of Marriage and the Family, 47,* 319–334.

AMATO, P. R., & KEITH, B. (1991). Parental divorce and the well-being of children: A meta-analysis. *Psychological Bulletin, 110,* 26–46.

AMERICAN ASSOCIATION OF RETIRED PERSONS. (1993). *Aging of the U.S. Population.* Washington, DC: Author.

AMERICAN HEART ASSOCIATION. (1990). *The healthy American diet.* Dallas, TX: Author.

AMERICAN PSYCHIATRIC ASSOCIATION. (1987). *Diagnostic and statistical manual of mental disorders* (3rd ed., rev.). Washington, DC: Author.

AMERICAN PSYCHOLOGICAL SOCIETY. (1993). Vitality for life. *APS Observer,* December.

ANAND, K. J., & HICKEY, P. R. (1987). Pain and its effect in the human neonate and fetus. *New England Journal of Medicine, 31,* 1321–1329.

ANASTASI, A. (1988). *Psychological testing* (6th ed.). New York: Macmillan.

ANASTOPOULOS, A. D., GUEVREMONT, D. C., SHELTON, T. L., & DUPAUL, G. J. (1992). Parenting stress among families of children with attention deficit hyperactivity disorder. *Journal of Abnormal Child Psychology, 20,* 503–520.

ANASTOPOULOS, A. D., SHELTON, T. L., DUPAUL, G. J., & GUEVREMONT, D. C. (1993). Parent training for attention-deficit hyperactivity disorder: Its impact on parent functioning. *Journal of Abnormal Child Psychology, 21,* 581–596.

ANDERSON, K. E., LYTTON, H., & ROMNEY, D. M. (1986). Mothers' interactions with normal and conduct-disordered boys: Who affects whom? *Developmental Psychology, 22,* 604–609.

ANGLIN, J. M. (1993). Vocabulary development: A morphological analysis. *Monographs of the Society for Research in Child Development, 58*(10, Serial No. 238).

ANTONARAKIS, S. E., & THE DOWN SYNDROME COLLABORATIVE GROUP. (1991). Parental origin of the extra chromosome in trisomy 21 as indicated by analysis of DNA polymorphisms. *New England Journal of Medicine, 324,* 872–876.

ANTONOVSKY, A., & SAGY, S. (1990). Confronting developmental tasks in the retirement transition. *Gerontologist, 30,* 362–368.

ANTONUCCI, T. C. (1985). Personal characteristics, social support, and social behavior. In R. H. Binstock & E. Shanas (Eds.), *Handbook of aging and the social sciences* (2nd ed., pp. 94–128). New York: Van Nostrand Reinhold.

ANTONUCCI, T. C. (1990). Attachment, social support, and coping with negative life events. In E. M. Cummings, A. L. Greene, & E. H. Karraker (Eds.), *Life-span developmental psychology: Vol. 11. Stress and coping across the life-span.* Hillsdale, NJ: Erlbaum.

APGAR, V. (1953). A proposal for a new method of evaluation of the newborn infant. *Current Researches in Anesthesia and Analgesia, 32,* 260–267.

APGAR, V., & BECK, J. (1974). *Is my baby all right?* New York: Pocket Books.

ARBONA, C. (1990). Career counseling research and Hispanics: A review of the literature. *Counseling Psychologist, 18,* 300–323.

ARNETT, J., & TABER, S. (1994). Adolescence terminable and interminable: When does adolescence end? *Journal of Youth and Adolescence, 23,* 517–537.

ARYEE, S. (1993). Dual-earner couples in Singapore: An examination of work and nonwork sources of their experienced burnout. *Human Relations, 46,* 1441–1468.

ASLIN, R. N. (1987). Visual and auditory discrimination in infancy. In J. D. Osofsky (Ed.), *Handbook of infant development* (2nd ed.). New York: Wiley.

ATCHLEY, R. C. (1975). The life course, age grading, and age-linked demands for decision making. In N. Datan & L. H. Ginsberg (Eds.), *Life-span developmental psychology: Normative life crises* (pp. 261–278). New York: Academic Press.

ATCHLEY, R. C. (1989). A continuity theory of normal aging. *Gerontologist, 29,* 183–190.

ATTIE, I., BROOKS-GUNN, J., & PETERSEN, A. C. (1990). A developmental perspective on eating disorders and eating problems. In M. Lewis & S. M. Miller, (Eds.), *Handbook of developmental psychopathology.* New York: Plenum.

ATWATER, E. (1992). *Adolescence.* Englewood Cliffs, NJ: Prentice-Hall.

AU, T. K., & GLUSMAN, M. (1990). The principle of mutual exclusivity in word learning: To honor or not to honor? *Child Development, 61,* 1474–1490.

AZRIN, N. H., & FOXX, R. M. (1974). *Toilet training in less than a day.* New York: Simon and Schuster.

BACHMAN, J. (1983). Premature affluence: Do high school students earn too much? *Economic Outlook USA* (Summer), 64–67.

BACHMAN, J. G., & SCHULENBERG, J. (1993). How part-time work intensity relates to drug use, problem behavior, time use, and satisfaction among high school seniors: Are these consequences or merely correlates? *Developmental Psychology, 29,* 220–235.

BAILEY, J. M., BOBROW, D., WOLFE, M., & MIKACH, S. (1995). Sexual orientation of adult sons of gay fathers. *Developmental Psychology, 31,* 124–129.

BAILLARGEON, R. (1987). Object permanence in $3\frac{1}{2}$- and $4\frac{1}{2}$-month-old infants. *Developmental Psychology, 23,*655–664.

BAILLARGEON, R. (1994). How do infants learn about the physical world? *Current Directions in Psychological Science, 3,* 133–140.

BAKER, T. B. (1988). Models of addiction. *Journal of Abnormal Psychology, 97,* 115–117.

BALL, J. F. (1976-1977). Widow's grief: The impact of age and mode of death. *Omega: Journal of Death and Dying, 7,* 307–333.

BALTES, M. M., & BALTES, P. B. (EDS.). (1986). *The psychology of control and aging.* Hillsdale, NJ: Erlbaum.

BALTES, P. B. (1993). The aging mind: Potential and limits. *Gerontologist, 33,* 580–594.

BALTES, P. B., DITTMANN-KOHLI, F., & DIXON, R. A. (1984). New perspectives on the development of intelligence in adulthood: Toward a dual-process conception and a model of selective optimization with compensation. In P. B. Baltes & O. G. Brim, Jr. (Eds.), *Life-span development and behavior* (Vol. 6, pp. 33–76). New York: Academic Press.

BALTES, P. B., & STAUDINGER, U. M. (1993). The search for a psychology of wisdom. *Current Directions in Psychological Science, 2,* 75–80.

BALTIMORE SCHOOL CLINICS TO OFFER BIRTH CONTROL BY SURGICAL IMPLANT. (1992, December 4). *The New York Times,* pp. A1, A28.

BANCROFT, J., AXWORTHY, D., & RATCLIFFE, S. (1982). The personality and psychosexual development of boys with 47-XXY chromosome constitution. *Journal of Child Psychology and Psychiatry, 23,* 169–180.

BANDURA, A. (1977). *Social learning theory.* Englewood Cliffs, NJ: Prentice-Hall.

BANDURA, A. (1986). *Social foundations of thought and action: A social-cognitive theory.* Englewood Cliffs, NJ: Prentice-Hall.

BANDURA, A., ROSS, D., & ROSS, S. A. (1963). Imitation of film-mediated aggressive models. *Journal of Abnormal and Social Psychology, 66,* 3–11.

BANKS, M. D., & DANNEMILLER, J. L. (1987). Infant visual psychophysics. In P. Salapatek & L. Cohen (Eds.), *Handbook of infant perception* (Vol. 1). Orlando, FL: Academic Press.

BARFIELD, R. E., & MORGAN, J. N. (1978). Trends in satisfaction with retirement. *Gerontologist, 18,* 19–23.

BARKLEY, R. A. (1990). Attention deficit disorders: History, definition, and diagnosis. In M. Lewis & S. M. Miller, (Eds.), *Handbook of developmental psychopathology.* New York: Plenum.

BARON, J. N., & BIELBY, W. T. (1985). Organizational barriers to gender equality: Sex segregation of jobs and opportunities. In A. S. Rossi (Ed.), *Gender and the life course* (pp. 233–251). New York: Aldine.

BARR, H. M., STREISSGUTH, A. P., DARBY, B. L., & SAMPSON, P. D. (1990). Prenatal exposure to alcohol, caffeine, tobacco, and aspirin: Effects on fine and gross motor performance in 4-year-old children. *Developmental Psychology, 26,* 339–348.

BARTON, M. E., & TOMASELLO, M. (1991). Joint attention and conversation in mother-infant-sibling triads. *Child Development, 62,* 517–529.

BARTON, P. E., & KIRSCH, I. S. (1990). *Workplace competencies: The need to improve literacy and employment readiness.* Washington, DC: U.S. Government Printing Office.

BARUCH, G. K. (1984). The psychological well-being of women in the middle years. In G. K. Baruch & J. Brooks-Gunn (Eds.), *Women in midlife* (pp. 161–180). New York: Plenum.

BASKETT, L. M. (1985). Sibling status effects: Adult expectations. *Developmental Psychology, 21,* 441–445.

BATES, E., BRETHERTON, I., & SNYDER, L. (1988). *From first words to grammar: Individual differences and dissociable mechanisms.* New York: Cambridge University Press.

BATES, J. E. (1987). Temperament in infancy. In J. D. Osofsky (Ed.), *Handbook of infant development* (2nd ed.). New York: Wiley.

BAUMRIND, D. (1975). *Early socialization and the discipline controversy.* Morristown, NJ: General Learning Press.

BAUMRIND, D. (1991a). Effective parenting during the early adolescent transition. In P. A. Cowan & E. M. Hetherington (Eds.), *Family transitions.* Hillsdale, NJ: Erlbaum.

BAUMRIND, D. (1991b). Parenting styles and adolescent development. In R. M. Lerner, A. C. Petersen, & J. Brooks-Gunn (Eds.), *Encyclopedia of adolescence.* New York: Garland.

BAYLEY, N. (1969). *Bayley scales of infant development: Manual.* New York: The Psychological Corporation.

BEAL, C. R., & BELGRAD, S. L. (1990). The development of message evaluation skills in young children. *Child Development, 61,* 705–712.

BEAN, F., & TIENDA, M. (1987). *The Hispanic population in the United States.* New York: Russell Sage Foundation.

BECK, A. T. (1967). *Depression: Clinical, experimental, and theoretical aspects.* New York: Harper & Row.

BECK, A. T., RUSH, J., SHAW, B., & EMERY, G. (1979). *Cognitive therapy of depression.* New York: Guilford.

BECK, M. (1994). How far should we push Mother Nature? *Newsweek* (January 17), 54–57.

BECKER, B. J. (1986). Influence again: An examination of reviews and studies of gender differences in social influence. In J. S. Hyde & M. C. Linn (Eds.), *The psychology of gender differences. Advances through meta-analysis.* Baltimore, MD: Johns Hopkins University Press.

BELGRAVE, L. L., WYKLE, M. L., & CHOI, J. M. (1993). Health, double jeopardy, and culture: The use of institutionalization by African-Americans. *Gerontologist, 33,* 379–385.

BELL, A. P., WEINBERG, M. S., & HAMMERSMITH, S. K. (1981). *Sexual preference: Its development in men and women.* New York: Simon & Schuster.

BELSKY, J. (1993). Etiolo gy of child maltreatment: A developmental-ecological analysis. *Psychological Bulletin, 114,* 413–434.

BELSKY, J., STEINBERG, L., & DRAPER, P. (1991). Childhood experience, interpersonal development, and reproductive strategy: An evolutionary theory of socialization. *Child Development, 62,* 647–670.

BENGTSON, V. L. (1985). Diversity and symbolism in grandparental roles. In V. L. Bengtson & J. F. Robertson (Eds.), *Grandparenthood* (pp. 11–25). Newbury Park, CA: Sage.

BENGTSON, V. L., & ROBERTSON, J. F. (EDS.). (1985). *Grandparenthood.* Newbury Park, CA: Sage.

BENGTSSON, H., & JOHNSON, L. (1992). Perspective taking, empathy, and prosocial behavior in late childhood. *Child Study Journal, 22,* 11–22.

BENIN, M. H., & AGOSTINELLI, J. (1988). Husbands' and wives' satisfaction with the division of labor. *Journal of Marriage and the Family, 50,* 349–361.

BERG, W. K., & BERG, K. M. (1987). Psychophysiological development in infancy: State, startle, and attention. In J. D. Osofsky (Ed.), *Handbook of infant development* (2nd ed.). New York: Wiley.

BERK, L. E. (1992). Children's private speech: An overview of theory and the status of research. In R. M. Diaz & L. E. Berk (Eds.), *Private speech: From social interaction to self-regulation.* Hillsdale, NJ: Erlbaum.

BERK, L. E. (1994). *Child development* (3rd ed.). Needham Heights, MA: Allyn & Bacon.

BERKO, J. (1958). The child's learning of English morphology. *Word, 14,* 150–177.

BERKOW, R. (ED.). (1987). *The Merck manual of diagnosis and therapy* (15th ed.). Rahway, NJ: Merck, Sharp, & Dohme Research Laboratories.

BERNDT, T. J., & PERRY, T. B. (1990). Distinctive features and effects of adolescent friendships. In R. Montemeyer,

G. R. Adams, & T. P. Gullotta, (Eds.), *From childhood to adolescence: A transition period?* London, UK: Sage.

BERRY, R. E., & WILLIAMS, F. L. (1987). Assessing the relationship between quality of life and marital and income satisfaction: A path analytical approach. *Journal of Marriage and the Family, 49,* 107–116.

BERTENTHAL, B. I., CAMPOS, J. J., & KERMOIAN, R. (1994). An epigenetic perspective on the development of self-produced locomotion and its consequences. *Current Directions in Psychological Science, 3,* 140–145.

BEST, D. L., WILLIAMS, J. E., CLOUD, J. M., DAVIS, S. W., ROBERTSON, L. S., EDWARDS, J. R., GILES, H., & FOWLES, J. (1977). Development of sex-trait stereotypes among young children in the United States, England, and Ireland. *Child Development, 48,* 1375–1384.

BETZ, E. L. (1984). A study of career patterns of women college graduates. *Journal of Vocational Behavior, 24,* 249–263.

BETZ, N. E., HEESACKER, R. S., & SHUTTLEWORTH, C. (1990). Moderators of the congruence and realism of major and occupational plans in college students: A replication and extension. *Journal of Counseling Psychology, 37,* 269–276.

BINGER, C. M., ABLIN, A. R., FEUERSTEIN, R. C., KUSHNER, J. H., ZOGER, S., & MIKKELSON, C. (1969). Childhood leukemia—Emotional impact on patient and family. *New England Journal of Medicine, 280,* 414.

BIRCH, L. L. (1991). Obesity and eating disorders: A developmental perspective. *Bulletin of the Psychonomic Society, 29,* 265–272.

BIRNHOLZ, J. C., & BENACERRAF, B. R. (1983). The development of human fetal hearing. *Science, 222,* 516–518.

BIRREN, J. E., & RENNER, V. J. (1977). Research on the psychology of aging. In J. E. Birren & K. W. Schaie (Eds.), *Handbook of the psychology of aging* (pp. 3–38). New York: Van Nostrand Reinhold.

BLANCHARD-FIELDS, F. (1986). Reasoning on social dilemmas varying in emotional saliency: An adult developmental study. *Psychology and Aging, 1,* 325–333.

BLASS, J. P., & BARCLAY, L. L. (1985). New developments in the diagnosis of dementia. *Drug Development Research, 5,* 39–58.

BLUMENTHAL, J. A., EMERY, C. F., COX, D. R., WALSH, M. A., KUHN, C. M., WILLIAMS, R. B., & WILLIAMS, R. S. (1988). Exercise training in healthy Type A middle-aged men: Effects on behavioral and cardiovascular responses. *Psychosomatic Medicine, 50,* 418–433.

BLUMSTEIN, P., & SCHWARTZ, P. (1983). *American couples.* New York: Morrow.

BOGATZ, G. A., & BALL, S. (1972). *The second year of "Sesame Street": A continuing evaluation.* Princeton, NJ: Educational Testing Service.

BOHANNON, J. N., MACWHINNEY, B., & SNOW, C. (1990). No negative evidence revisited: Beyond learnability or who has to prove what to whom. *Developmental Psychology, 26,* 221–226.

BONDAREFF, W. (1983). Age and Alzheimer's disease. *Lancet, 1,* 1447.

BOOTH, A., & JOHNSON, E. (1988). Premarital cohabitation and marital success. *Journal of Family Issues, 9,* 387–394.

BOOTZIN, R. R., & ENGLE-FRIEDMAN, M. (1987). Sleep disturbances. In L. L. Carstensen & B. A. Edelstein (Eds.), *Handbook of clinical gerontology* (pp. 238–251). New York: Pergamon.

BORG, S., & LASKER, J. (1981). *When pregnancy fails.* Boston: Beacon.

BORK, A. (1985). *Personal computers for education.* New York: Harper & Row.

BORNSTEIN, P. E., & CLAYTON, P. J. (1972). The anniversary reaction. *Diseases of the Nervous System, 33,* 470–472.

BOSSÉ, R., ALDWIN, C. M., LEVENSON, M. R., SPIRO, A., III, & MROCZEK, D. K. (1993). Change in social support after retirement: Longitudinal findings from the Normative Aging Study. *Journal of Gerontology: Psychological Sciences, 48,* 210–217.

BOSSÉ, R., & EKERDT, D. J. (1981). Change in self-perception of leisure activities with retirement. *Gerontologist, 21,* 650–653.

BOUCHARD, T. J., & MCGUE, M. (1981). Familial studies of intelligence: A review. *Science, 212,* 1056.

BOUZA, A. V. (1990). *The police mystique: An insider's look at cops, crime, and the criminal justice system.* New York: Plenum.

BOWLBY, J. (1969). *Attachment and loss* (Vol. 1). New York: Basic Books.

BOYER, C. B., & HEIN, K. (1991). AIDS and HIV infection in adolescents: The role of education and antibody testing. In R. M. Lerner, A. C. Petersen, & J. Brooks-Gunn (Eds.), *Encyclopedia of adolescence* (Vol. 1). New York: Garland.

BOZETT, F. W. (1988). Gay fatherhood. In P. Bronstein & C. P. Cowan (Eds.), *Fatherhood today: Men's changing role in the family* (pp. 214–235). New York: Wiley.

BRABECK, M. M., & WEISGERBER, K. (1989). College students' perceptions of men and women choosing teaching and management: The effects of gender and sex role egalitarianism. *Sex Roles, 21,* 841.

BRADLEY, R. H., CALDWELL, B. M., & ROCK, S. L. (1988). Home environment and school performance: A ten-year follow-up and examination of three models of environmental action. *Child Development, 59,* 852–867.

BRADLEY, R. H., CALDWELL, B. M., ROCK, S. L., RAMEY, C. T., BARNARD, K. E., GRAY, C., HAMMOND, M. A., MITCHELL, S., GOTTFRIED, A. W., SIEGEL, L., & JOHNSON, D. L. (1989). Home environment and cognitive development in the first 3 years of life: A collaborative study involving six sites and three ethnic groups in North America. *Developmental Psychology, 25,* 217–235.

BRADY, J. E., NEWCOMB, A. F., & HARTUP, W. W. (1983). Context and companion's behavior as determinants of cooperation and competition in school-age children. *Journal of Experimental Child Psychology, 36,* 396–412.

BRAINE, M. D. S. (1976). Children's first word combinations. *Monographs of the Society for Research in Child Development, 41*, Serial No. 164.

BRAND, E., CLINGEMPEEL, W. G., & BOWEN-WOODWARD, D. (1988). Family relationships and children's psychological adjustment in stepmother and stepfather families. In E. M. Hetherington & J. D. Arasten (Eds.), *Impact of divorce, single parenting and step parenting on children* (pp. 299–324). Hillsdale, NJ: Erlbaum.

BRANDSTÄDTER, J. (1989). Personal self-regulation of development: Cross-sequential analyses of development-related control beliefs and emotions. *Developmental Psychology, 25,* 96–108.

BRAUNGART, J. M., PLOMIN, R., DEFRIES, J. C., & FULKER, D. W. (1992). Genetic influence on tester-rated infant temperament as assessed by Bayley's Infant Behavior Record: Nonadoptive and adoptive siblings and twins. *Developmental Psychology, 28,* 40–47.

BRAY, D. W., & HOWARD, A. (1983). The AT&T longitudinal studies of managers. In K. W. Schaie (Ed.), *Longitudinal studies on adult psychological development* (pp. 266–312). New York: Guilford.

BRAZELTON, T. B. (1984). *Brazelton Behavior Assessment Scale* (rev. ed.). Philadelphia: Lippincott.

BRAZELTON, T. B., NUGENT, J. K., & LESTER, B. M. (1987). Neonatal behavioral assessment scale. In J. D. Osofsky (Ed.), *Handbook of infant development* (2nd ed). New York: Wiley.

BRETHERTON, I. (1992). The origins of attachment theory: John Bowlby and Mary Ainsworth. *Developmental Psychology, 28,* 759–775.

BRIGHAM, J. C., & SPIER, S. A. (1992). Opinions held by professionals who work with child witnesses. In H. Dent & R. Flin (Eds.), *Children as witnesses.* New York: Wiley.

BRIM, O. G., JR., & KAGAN, J. (1980). Constancy and change: A view of the issues. In O. G. Brim, Jr. & J. Kagan (Eds.), *Constancy and change in human development* (pp. 1–25). Cambridge, MA: Harvard University Press.

BRODY, E. M. (1981). Women in the middle and family help to older people. *Gerontologist, 21,* 471–480.

BRODY, E. M. (1990). *Women in the middle: Their parent-care years.* New York: Springer.

BRODY, E. M., JOHNSEN, P. T., FULCOMER, M. C., & LANG, A. M. (1983). Women's changing roles and help to aging parents: Attitudes of three generations of parents. *Journal of Gerontology, 38,* 597–607.

BRODY, G. H., STONEMAN, Z., & MCCOY, J. K. (1994). Forecasting sibling relationships in early adolescence from child temperaments and family processes in middle childhood. *Child Development, 65,* 771–784.

BRODY, N. (1992). *Intelligence* (2nd ed.). San Diego, CA: Academic Press.

BRODZINSKY, D. M., & RIGHTMYER, J. (1980). Individual differences in children's humor development. In P. McGhee & A. Chapman (Eds.), *Children's humour.* Chichester, UK: Wiley.

BROMAN, C. L. (1988). Household work and family life satisfaction of blacks. *Journal of Marriage and the Family, 50,* 743–748.

BRONFENBRENNER, U. (1979). Contexts of child rearing: Problems and prospects. *American Psychologist, 34,* 844–850.

BRONFENBRENNER, U. (1989). Ecological systems theory. In R. Vasta (ed.), *Annals of child development: Vol. 6. Theories of child development: Revised formulations and current issues.* Greenwich, CT: JAI Press.

BRONSON, G. W. (1991). Infant differences in rate of visual encoding. *Child Development, 62,* 44–54.

BROOKS, L., & BETZ, N. E. (1990). Utility of expectancy theory in predicting occupational choices in college students. *Journal of Counseling Psychology, 37,* 57–64.

BROOKS-GUNN, J. (1988). Antecedents and consequences of variations in girls' maturational timing. *Journal of Adolescent Health Care, 9,* 1–9.

BROOKS-GUNN, J. (1991). How stressful is the transition to adolescence for girls? In M. E. Colten & S. Gore (Eds.), *Adolescent stress: Causes and consequences. Social institutions and social change* (pp. 131–149). New York: Aldine de Gruyter.

BROOME, M. E., & KOEHLER, C. (1986). Childbirth education: A review of effects on the woman and her family. *Family and Community Health, 9,* 33–44.

BROPHY, J. E., & GOOD, T. L. (1986). Teacher behavior and student achievement. In M. C. Wittrock (Ed.), *Handbook of research on teaching* (3rd ed.). New York: Macmillan.

BROWN, B. B., & LOHR, M. J. (1987). Peer-group affiliation and adolescent self-esteem: An integration of ego-identity and symbolic-interaction theories. *Journal of Personality and Social Psychology, 52,* 47–55.

BROWN, B. B., LOHR, M. J., & MCCLENAHAN, E. L. (1986). Early adolescents' perceptions of peer pressure. *Journal of Early Adolescence, 6,* 139–154.

BROWN, B. B., MOUNTS, N., LAMBORN, S. D., & STEINBERG, L. (1993). Parenting practices and peer group affiliation in adolescence. *Developmental Psychology, 64,* 467–482.

BROWN, J. R., & DUNN, J. (1992). Talk with your mother or your sibling? Developmental changes in early family conversations about feelings. *Child Development, 63,* 336–349.

BROWNE, A., & WILLIAMS, K. R. (1993). Gender, intimacy, and lethal violence: Trends from 1976 to 1987. *Gender and Society, 7,* 78–98.

BRYAN, J. H., & WALBEK, N. B. (1970). Preaching and practicing generosity: Children's actions and reactions. *Child Development, 41,* 329–353.

BRYANT, B. K. (1992). Conflict resolution strategies in relation to children's peer relations. *Journal of Applied Developmental Psychology, 13,* 35–50.

BRYANT, B. K., & CROCKENBERG, S. B. (1980). Correlates and dimensions of prosocial behavior: A study of female siblings with their mothers. *Child Development, 51,* 529–554.

BUHRMESTER, D., & FURMAN, W. (1987). The development of companionship and intimacy. *Child Development, 58,* 1101–1113.

BUHRMESTER, D., & FURMAN, W. (1990). Perceptions of sibling relationships during middle childhood and adolescence. *Child Development, 61,* 1387–1398.

BULLOCK, W. A., & DUNN, N. J. (1988, August). *Aging, sex, and marital satisfaction.* Paper presented at the meeting of the American Psychological Association, Atlanta.

BUMPASS, L. L., SWEET, J. A., & CHERLIN, A. (1991). The role of cohabitation in declining rates of marriage. *Journal of Marriage and the Family, 53,* 913–927.

BUREAU OF LABOR STATISTICS. (1992). *Occupational Outlook Handbook* (1992–1993 Ed.). Washington, DC: Author.

BURKE, R. J. (1991a). Organizational treatment of minority managers and professionals: Costs to the majority? *Psychological Reports, 68,* 439–449.

BURKE, R. J. (1991b). Work experiences of minority managers and professionals: Individual and organizational costs of perceived bias. *Psychological Reports, 69,* 1011–1023.

BURNS, A. (1992). Mother-headed families: An international perspective and the case of Australia. *Society for Research in Child Development: Social Policy Report, 6,* 1–22.

BURRUS-BAMMEL, L. L., & BAMMEL, G. (1985). Leisure and recreation. In J. E. Birren & K. W. Schaie (Eds.), *Handbook of the psychology of aging* (2nd ed., pp. 848–889). New York: Van Nostrand Reinhold.

BURSUCK, W. D., & ROSE, E. (1992). Community college options for students with mild disabilities. In F. R. Rusch, L. DeStefano, J. Chadsey-Rusch, L. A. Phelps, & E. Szymanski (Eds.), *Transition from school to life* (pp. 71–91). Sycamore, IL: Sycamore.

BUSCH, J. W. (1985). Mentoring in graduate schools of education: Mentors' perceptions. *American Educational Research Journal, 22,* 257–265.

BUSS, A. H., & PLOMIN, R. (1984). *Temperament: Early developing personality traits.* Hillsdale, NJ: Erlbaum.

BUSS, D. M. (1994). *The evolution of desire.* New York: Basic Books.

BUSS, D. M., ET AL. (1990). International preferences in selecting mates: A study of 37 cultures. *Journal of Cross-Cultural Psychology, 21,* 5–47.

CAHAN, L. S., FILBY, N. N., MCCUTCHEON, G., & KYLE, D. W. (1983). *Class size and instruction.* New York: Longman.

CAMARA, K. A., & RESNICK, G. (1988). Interparental conflict and cooperation. Factors moderating children's post-divorce adjustment. In E. M. Hetherington & J. D. Arasten (Eds.), *Impact of divorce, single parenting and step parenting on children.* Hillsdale, NJ: Erlbaum.

CAMP, C. J., FOSS, J. W., STEVENS, A. B., REICHARD, C. C., MCKITRICK, L. A., & O'HANLON, A. M. (1993). Memory training in normal and demented elderly populations: The E-I-E-I-O model. *Experimental Aging Research, 19,* 277–290.

CAMP, C. J., & MCKITRICK, L. A. (1991). Memory interventions in Alzheimer's-type dementia populations: Methodological and theoretical issues. In R. L. West & J. D. Sinnott (Eds.), *Everyday memory and aging: Current research and methodology* (pp. 155–172). New York: Springer-Verlag.

CAMPBELL, A. (1981). *The sense of well-being in America: Recent patterns and trends.* New York: McGraw-Hill.

CAMPBELL, F. A., & RAMEY, C. T. (1994). Effects of early intervention on intellectual and academic achievement: A follow-up study of children from low-income families. *Child Development, 65,* 684–698.

CAMPIONE, W. A. (1988). Predicting participation in retirement preparation programs. *Journal of Gerontology, 43,* 91–95.

CAMPOS, J. J., HIATT, S., RAMSAY, D., HENDERSON, C., & SVEJDA, M. (1978). The emergence of fear on the visual cliff. In M. Lewis & L. Rosenblum (Eds.), *The origins of affect.* New York: Plenum.

CAMPOS, R. G. (1989). Soothing pain-elicited distress in infants with swaddling and pacifiers. *Child Development, 60,* 781–792.

CAPALDI, D. M., & PATTERSON, G. R. (1991). Relation of parental transitions to boys' adjustment problems: I. A linear hypothesis. II. Mothers at risk for transitions and unskilled parenting. *Developmental Psychology, 27,* 489–504.

CAREY, S. (1978). The child as a word learner. In M. Halle, J. Bresnan, & G. Miller (Eds.), *Linguistic theory and psychological reality.* Cambridge, MA: MIT Press.

CAREY, S. (1985). *Conceptual change in childhood.* Cambridge, MA: MIT Press.

CARLSON, C. L, PELHAM, W. E., MILICH, R., & DIXON, J. (1992). Single and combined effects of methylphenidate and behavior therapy on the classroom performance of children with attention-deficit hyperactivity disorder. *Journal of Abnormal Child Psychology, 20,* 213–232.

CARSTENSEN, L. L. (1987). Age-related changes in social activity. In L. L. Carstensen & B. A. Edelstein (Eds.), *Handbook of clinical gerontology* (pp. 222–237). New York: Pergamon.

CASCARDI, M., & O'LEARY, K. D. (1992). *Gender specific trends in spousal homicide across a decade.* Unpublished manuscript, State University of New York, Stony Brook.

CASCARDI, M., VIVIAN, D., & MEYER, S. (1991). *Context and attributions for marital violence in discordant couples.* Paper presented at the annual meeting of the Association for the Advancement of Behavior Therapy, New York.

CAVANAUGH, J. C. (1981). Early developmental theories: A brief review of attempts to organize developmental data prior to 1925. *Journal of the History of the Behavioral Sciences, 17,* 38–47.

CAVANAUGH, J. C. (1991). On the concept of development: Contextualism, relative time, and the role of dialectics. In P. van Geert & L. Mohs (Eds.), *Annals of theoretical psychology: Vol. 6. Developmental psychology* (pp. 325–333). New York: Plenum.

CAVANAUGH, J. C. (In press). Memory self-efficacy as a key to understanding cognitive aging. In F. Blanchard-Fields & T. M. Hess (Eds.), *Perspectives on cognitive changes in adulthood and aging.* New York: McGraw-Hill.

CAVANAUGH, J. C., FELDMAN, J. M., & HERTZOG, C. (1995). *Memory self-efficacy as a moderator of memory change.* Unpublished manuscript, University of Delaware.

CAVANAUGH, J. C., GRADY, J. G., & PERLMUTTER, M. (1983). Forgetting and use of memory aids in 20 to 70 year olds' everyday life. *International Journal of Aging and Human Development, 17,* 113–122.

CAVANAUGH, J. C., KINNEY, J. M., DUNN, N. J., MCGUIRE, L. C., & NOCERA, R. (1994). Caregiver-patient dyads: Documenting the verbal instructions caregivers provide in joint cognitive tasks. *Journal of Adult Development, 1,* 27–36.

CAVANAUGH, J. C., KRAMER, D. A., SINNOTT, J. D., CAMP, C. J., & MARKLEY, R. J. (1985). On missing links and such: Interfaces between cognitive research and everyday problem solving. *Human Development, 28,* 146–168.

CECI, S. J. (1990). *On intelligence . . . more or less: A bioecological treatise on intellectual development.* Hillsdale, NJ: Erlbaum.

CENTERS FOR DISEASE CONTROL. (1992). *Setting the national agenda for injury control in the 1990s.* Washington, DC: United States Department of Health and Human Services, Public Health Service.

CERNOCH, J. M., & PORTER, R. H. (1985). Recognition of maternal axillary odors by infants. *Child Development, 56,* 1593–1598.

CHAMBERLAIN, M. C., NICHOLS, S. L., & CHASE, C. H. (1991). Pediatric AIDS: Comparative cranial MRI and CT scans. *Pediatric Neurology, 7,* 357–362.

CHAMBRÉ S. M. (1993). Voluntarism by elders: Past trends and future prospects. *Gerontologist, 33,* 221–228.

CHAO, P. (1983). *Chinese kinship.* London, UK: Kegan Paul International.

CHAPMAN, P. D. (1988). *Schools as sorters: Lewis M. Terman, applied psychology, and the intelligence testing movement, 1890–1930.* New York: New York University Press.

CHARNESS, N., & BOSMAN, E. A. (1990). Expertise and aging: Life in the lab. In T. M. Hess (Ed.), *Aging and cognition: Knowledge organization and utilization* (pp. 343–385). Amsterdam, The Netherlands: North-Holland.

CHASE-LANSDALE, P. L., & HETHERINGTON, E. M. (1990). The impact of divorce on life-span development: Short and long term effects. In P. B. Baltes, B. L. Featherman, & R. M. Lerner, (Eds.), *Life-span development and behavior* (Vol. 10). Hillsdale, NJ: Erlbaum.

CHASSIN, L., PRESSON, C. C., MONTELLO, D., SHERMAN, S. J., & MCGREW, J. (1986). Changes in peer and parent influence during adolescence: Longitudinal versus cross-sectional perspectives on smoking initiation. *Developmental Psychology, 22,* 327–334.

CHERLIN, A. J., & FURSTENBERG, F. F., JR. (1986). *The new American grandparent: A place in the family, a life apart.* New York: Basic Books.

CHERLIN, A. J., FURSTENBERG, F. F., JR., CHASE-LANSDALE, P. L., KIERNAN, D. E., ROBINS, P. K., MORRISON, D. R., & TEITLER, J. O. (1991). Longitudinal studies of effects of divorce on children in Great Britain and the United States. *Science, 252,* 1386–1389.

CHILMAN, C. S. (1983). *Adolescent sexuality in a changing American society* (2nd ed.). New York: Wiley.

CHINEN, A. B. (1989). *In the ever after.* Willmette, IL: Chiron.

CHISHOLM, J. S. (1983). *Navajo infancy: An ethological study of child development.* New York: Aldine.

CHOMSKY, N. (1959). Review of B. F. Skinner's "Verbal Behavior." *Language, 35,* 26–129.

CHOMSKY, N. (1982). *Lectures on government and binding.* New York: Foris.

CHRISTIANSEN, B. A., & GOLDMAN, M. S. (1983). Alcohol-related expectancies versus demographic/background variables in the prediction of adolescent drinking. *Journal of Consulting and Clinical Psychology, 51,* 249–257.

CHUGANI, H. T., & PHELPS, M. E. (1986). Maturational changes in cerebral function in infants determined by 18FDG positron emission tomography. *Science, 231,* 840–843.

CICIRELLI, V. G. (1980). Sibling relationships in adulthood: A life-span perspective. In L. W. Poon (Ed.), *Aging in the 1980s* (pp. 455–474). Washington, DC: American Psychological Association.

CIPANI, E. (1991). Educational classification and placement. In J. L. Matson & J. A. Mulick (Eds.), *Handbook of mental retardation* (2nd ed.). New York: Pergamon.

CLARKE, A. M., & CLARKE, A. D. (1989). The later cognitive effects of early intervention. *Intelligence, 13,* 289–297.

CLARKE-STEWART, K. A. (1989). Infant day care: Maligned or malignant? *American Psychologist, 44,* 266–273.

CLARKE-STEWART, K. A., & FEIN, G. G. (1983). Early childhood programs. In P. H. Mussen (Ed.), *Handbook of child psychology* (Vol. 2). New York: Wiley.

CLEEK, M. B., & PEARSON, T. A. (1985). Perceived causes of divorce: An analysis of interrelationships. *Journal of Marriage and the Family, 47,* 179–191.

CLEMONS, A. W., & AXELSON, L. J. (1985). The not-so-empty nest: The return of the fledgling adult. *Family Relations, 34,* 259–264.

CLIFTON, R., PERRIS, E., & BULLINGER, A. (1991). Infants' perception of auditory space. *Developmental Psychology, 27,* 187–197.

CLIFTON, R. K. (1992). The development of spatial hearing in human infants. In L. A. Werner & E. W. Rubel (Eds.), *Developmental psychoacoustics* (pp. 135–157). Washington, DC: American Psychological Association.

COHEN, C., TERESI, J., HOLMES, D., & ROTH, E. (1988). Survival strategies of older homeless men. *Gerontologist, 28,* 58–65.

COHEN, G. D. (1990). Psychopathology and mental health in the mature and elderly adult. In J. E. Birren & K. W. Schaie

(Eds.), *Handbook of the psychology of aging* (3rd ed., pp. 359–371). San Diego, CA: Academic Press.

COHEN, S., LICHTENSTEIN, E., PROCHASKA, J. O., ROSSI, J. S., GUTZ, E. R., CARR, C. R., ORLEANS, C. T., SCHOENBACH, V. J., BIENER, L., ABRAMS, D., DICLEMENTE, C., CURRY, S., MARLATT, G. A., CUMMINGS, K. M., EMONT, S. L., GROVINO, G., & OSSIP-KLEIN, D. (1989). Debunking myths about self-quitting: Evidence from 10 prospective studies of persons who attempt to quit smoking by themselves. *American Psychologist, 44,* 1355–1365.

COKE, M. M. (1992). Correlates of life satisfaction among elderly African Americans. *Journal of Gerontology: Psychological Sciences, 47,* 316–320.

COLBY, A., KOHLBERG, L., GIBBS, J. C., & LIEBERMAN, M. (1983). A longitudinal study of moral development. *Monographs of the Society for Research in Child Development, 48* (Whole #200).

COLEMAN, M., & GANONG, L. H. (1990). Remarriage and stepfamily research in the 1980s: Increased interest in an old family form. *Journal of Marriage and the Family, 52,* 925–940.

COMMONS, M. L., SINNOTT, J. D., RICHARDS, F. A., & ARMON, C. (EDS.). (1989). *Adult development: Vol. 1. Comparisons and applications of adolescent and adult developmental models.* New York: Praeger.

CONNIDIS, I. (1988, November). *Sibling ties and aging.* Paper presented at the Gerontological Society of America, San Francisco.

CONSULTING PSYCHOLOGISTS PRESS, INC. (1994). *Strong Interest Inventory of the Strong Vocational Interest Blanks, Form T317.* Palo Alto, CA: Stanford University Press.

COONEY, T. M., PEDERSEN, F. A., INDELICATO, S., & PALKOVITZ, R. (1993). Timing of fatherhood: Is "on-time" optimal? *Journal of Marriage and the Family, 55,* 205–215.

COONEY, T. M., SMYER, M. A., HAGESTAD, G. O., & KLOCK, R. (1986). Parental divorce in young adulthood: Some preliminary findings. *American Journal of Orthopsychiatry, 56,* 470–477.

COONEY, T. M., & UHLENBERG, P. (1990). The role of divorce in men's relations with their adult children after mid-life. *Journal of Marriage and the Family, 52,* 677–688.

CORDES, C. L., & DOUGHERTY, T. W. (1993). A review and integration of research on job burnout. *Academy of Management Review, 18,* 621–656.

CORNISH, N. (1994, Sept. 12). Over the hill? *Wilmington (DE) News-Journal,* pp. D10–D11.

CORNWELL, K. S., HARRIS, L. J., & FITZGERALD, H. E. (1991). Task effects in the development of hand preference in 9-, 13-, and 20-month-old infant girls. *Developmental Neuropsychology, 7,* 19–34.

CORRIGAN, P. W., HOLMES, E. P., LUCHINS, D., BUICHAN, B., ET AL. (1994). Staff burnout in a psychiatric hospital: A cross-lagged panel design. *Journal of Organizational Behavior, 15,* 65–74.

COSBY, A. (1974). Occupational expectations and the hypothesis of increasing realism of choice. *Journal of Vocational Behavior, 5,* 53–65.

COSTA, P. T., JR., & MCCRAE, R. R. (1978). Objective personality assessment. In M. Storandt, I. C. Siegler, & M. F. Elias (Eds.), *The clinical psychology of aging* (pp. 119–143). New York: Plenum.

COSTA, P. T., JR., & MCCRAE, R. R. (1988). Personality in adulthood: A six-year longitudinal study of self-reports and spouse ratings on the NEO Personality Inventory. *Journal of Personality and Social Psychology, 54,* 853–863.

COSTA, P. T., JR., MCCRAE, R. R., & ARENBERG, D. (1980). Enduring dispositions in adult males. *Journal of Personality and Social Psychology, 38,* 793–800.

COSTA, P. T., JR., MCCRAE, R. R., & HOLLAND, J. L. (1984). Personality and vocational interests in an adult sample. *Journal of Applied Psychology, 42,* 390–400.

COSTIN, S. E., & JONES, D. C. (1992). Friendship as a facilitator of emotional responsiveness and prosocial interventions among young children. *Developmental Psychology, 28,* 941–947.

COTTON, S., ANTHILL, J. K., & CUNNINGHAM, J. D. (1989). The work motivations of mothers with preschool children. *Journal of Family Issues, 10,* 189–210.

COUNCIL ON ETHICAL AND JUDICIAL AFFAIRS. (1990). Black-white disparities in health care. *Journal of the American Medical Association, 263,* 2344–2346.

COUNTS, D., & COUNTS, D. (EDS.). (1985). *Aging and its transformations: Moving toward death in Pacific societies.* Lanham, MD: University Press of America.

COWAN, C. P., & COWAN, P. A. (1992). *When partners become parents.* New York: Basic Books.

COX, M. J., OWEN, M. T., HENDERSON, V. K., & MARGAND, N. A. (1992). Prediction of infant-father and infant-mother attachment. *Developmental Psychology, 28,* 474–483.

CRATON, L. G., & YONAS, A. (1988). Infants' sensitivity to boundary flow information for depth at an edge. *Child Development, 59,* 1522–1529.

CRICK, N. R., & DODGE, K. A. (1994). A review and reformulation of social information-processing mechanisms in children's social adjustment. *Psychological Bulletin, 115,* 74–101.

CROOK, C. (1987). Taste and olfaction. In P. Salapatek & L. Cohen (Eds.), *Handbook of infant perception* (Vol. 1). Orlando, FL: Academic Press.

CROSS, S., & MARKUS, H. (1991). Possible selves across the life span. *Human Development, 34,* 230–255.

CULP, R. E., APPELBAUM, M. I., OSOFSKY, J. D., & LEVY, J. A. (1988). Adolescent and older mothers: Comparison between prenatal maternal variables and newborn interaction measures. *Infant Behavior and Development, 11,* 353–362.

CUMMING, E., & HENRY, W. H. (1961). *Growing old: The process of disengagement.* New York: Basic Books.

CUNNINGHAM, F. G., MACDONALD, P. C., & GANT, N. F. (1989). *Williams obstetrics* (18th ed.) London, UK: Appleton & Lange.

CURCIO, C. A., BUELL, S. J., & COLEMAN, P. D. (1982). Morphology of the aging central nervous system: Not all downhill. In J. A. Mortimer, F. J. Pirozzola, & G. I. Maletta (Eds.), *Advances in neurogerontology: Vol 3. The aging motor system* (pp. 7–35). New York: Praeger.

CUTLER, S. J., & HENDRICKS, J. (1990). Leisure and time use across the life course. In R. H. Binstock & L. K. George (Eds.), *Handbook of aging and the social sciences* (3rd ed., pp. 169–185). San Diego, CA: Academic Press.

CUTTER, M. A. G. (1991). Euthanasia: Reassessing the boundaries. *Journal of NIH Research, 3*(5), 59–61.

DAMON, W. (1988). *The moral child.* New York: Free Press.

DAVIDSON, K. M., RICHARDS, D. S., SCHATZ, D. A., & FISHER, D. A. (1991). Successful in utero treatment of fetal goiter and hypothyroidism. *New England Journal of Medicine, 324,* 543–546.

DAVIS, B. W. (1985). *Visits to remember: A handbook for visitors of nursing home residents.* University Park, PA: Pennsylvania State University Cooperative Extension Service.

DECASPER, A. J., & SPENCE M. J. (1986). Prenatal maternal speech influences newborn's perception of speech sounds. *Infant Behavior and Development, 9,* 133–150.

DEFRANK, R., & IVANCEVICH, J. M. (1986). Job loss: An individual level review and model. *Journal of Vocational Behavior, 19,* 1–20.

DEKOVIC, M., & JANSSENS, J. M. (1992). Parents' child-rearing style and child's sociometric status. *Developmental Psychology, 28,* 925–932.

DELLAS, M., & JERNIGAN, L. P. (1990). Affective personality characteristics associated with undergraduate ego identity formation. *Journal of Adolescent Research, 5,* 306–324.

DEMARIS, A., & RAO, K. V. (1992). Premarital cohabitation and subsequent marital stability in the United States: A reassessment. *Journal of Marriage and the Family, 54,* 178–190.

DENNEY, N. W. (1982). Aging and cognitive changes. In B. B. Wolman (Ed.), *Handbook of developmental psychology* (pp. 807–827). Englewood Cliffs, NJ: Prentice-Hall.

DENNEY, N. W. (1989). Everyday problem solving: Methodological issues, research findings, and a model. In L. W. Poon, D. C. Rubin, & B. A. Wilson (Eds.), *Everyday cognition in adulthood and late life* (pp. 330–351). Cambridge, UK: Cambridge University Press.

DENNEY, N. W. (1990). Adult age differences in traditional and practical problem solving. In E. A. Lovelace (Ed.), *Aging and cognition: Mental processes, self-awareness, and interventions* (pp. 329–349). Amsterdam, The Netherlands: North-Holland.

DENNEY, N. W., & PEARCE, K. A. (1989). A developmental study of practical problem solving in adults. *Developmental Psychology, 11,* 521–522.

DENNEY, N. W., PEARCE, K. A., & PALMER, A. M. (1982). A developmental study of adults' performance on traditional and practical problem-solving tasks. *Experimental Aging Research, 8,* 115–118.

DENNIS, W., & DENNIS, M. G. (1940). The effects of cradling practices upon the onset of walking in Hopi children. *Journal of Genetic Psychology, 56,* 77–86.

DIAMOND, J. (1986). I want a girl just like the girl . . . *Discover, 7*(11), 65–68.

DIBLASIO, F. A., & BENDA, B. B. (1990). Adolescent sexual behavior: Multivariate analysis of a social learning model. *Journal of Adolescent Research, 5,* 449–466.

DICKINSON, G. E. (1992). First childhood death experiences. *Omega, 25,* 169–182.

DIELMAN, T., SCHULENBERG, J., LEECH, S., & SHOPE, J. T. (1992, March). *Reduction of susceptibility to peer pressure and alcohol use/misuse through a school-based prevention program.* Paper presented at the meeting of the Society for Research on Adolescence, Washington, DC.

DIMOND, M., LUND, D. A., & CASERTA, M. S. (1987). The role of social support in the first two years of bereavement in an elderly sample. *Gerontologist, 27,* 599–604.

DIPRETE, T. A., & SOULE, W. T. (1988). Gender and promotion in segmented job ladder systems. *American Sociological Review, 53,* 26–40.

DISHION, T. J. (1990). The family ecology of boys' peer relations in middle childhood. *Child Development, 61,* 874–892.

DITTMANN-KOHLI, F., & BALTES, P. B. (1990). Toward a neofunctionalist conception of adult intellectual development: Wisdom as a prototypical case of intellectual growth. In C. Alexander & E. Langer (Eds.), *Higher stages of human development: Perspectives on adult growth* (pp. 54–78). New York: Oxford University Press.

DIXON, R. A. (1992). Contextual approaches to adult intellectual development. In R. J. Sternberg & C. A. Berg (Eds.), *Intellectual development* (pp. 350–380). New York: Cambridge University Press.

DIXON, R. A., KRAMER, D. A., & BALTES, P. B. (1985). Intelligence: A life-span developmental perspective. In B. B. Wolman (Ed.), *Handbook of intelligence: Theories, measurements, and application* (pp. 301–350). New York: Wiley.

DOBASH, R. P., & DOBASH, R. E. (1992). *Women, violence, and social change.* New York: Routledge.

DOCKRELL, J., & MCSHANE, J. (1993). *Children's learning difficulties: A cognitive approach.* Cambridge, UK: Blackwell Publishers.

DODGE, K. A., BATES, J. E., & PETTIT, G. S. (1990). Mechanisms in the cycle of violence. *Science, 250,* 1678–1683.

DOHRENWEND, B. P. (1979). Stressful life events and psychopathology: Some issues of theory and method. In J. E. Barrett, B. M. Rose, & G. L. Klerman (Eds.), *Stress and mental disorder* (pp. 1–15). New York: Raven Press.

DOKA, K. J., & MERTZ, M. E. (1988). The meaning and significance of great-grandparenthood. *Gerontologist, 28,* 192–197.

DOMINO, G. (1992). Cooperation and competition in Chinese and American children. *Journal of Cross Cultural Psychology, 23,* 456–467.

DOWNEY, J., ELKIN, E. J., EHRHARDT, A. A., MEYER-BAHLBURG, H. F. L., BELL, J. J., & MORISHIMA, A. (1991). Cognitive ability and everyday functioning in women with Turner's syndrome. *Journal of Learning Disabilities, 24,* 32–39.

DRABMAN, R. S., & THOMAS, M. H. (1976). Does watching violence on television cause apathy? *Pediatrics, 52,* 329–331.

DRYFOOS, J. G. (1990). *Adolescents at risk: Prevalence and prevention.* New York: Oxford University Press.

DUARA, R., LONDON, E. D., & RAPOPORT, S. I. (1985). Changes in structure and energy metabolism of the aging brain. In C. E. Finch & E. L. Schneider (Eds.), *Handbook of the biology of aging* (2nd ed., pp. 595–616). New York: Van Nostrand Reinhold.

DUBOIS, D. L., & HIRSCH, B. J. (1990). School and neighborhood friendship patterns of black and whites in early adolescence. *Child Development, 61,* 524–536.

DUNN, J. (1983). Sibling relationships in early childhood. *Child Development, 54,* 787–881.

DUNN, J. (1984). Sibling studies and the developmental impact of critical incidents. In P. B. Baltes & O. G. Brim, Jr. (Eds.), *Life-span development and behavior* (Vol. 6). New York: Academic Press.

DUNN, J., & KENDRICK, C. (1981). Social behavior of young siblings in the family context: Differences between same-sex and different-sex dyads. *Child Development, 52,* 1265–1273.

DUNN, J., SLOMKOWSKI, C., & BEARDSALL, L. (1994). Sibling relationships from the preschool period through middle childhood and early adolescence. *Developmental Psychology, 30,* 315–324.

DUVALL, E. M. (1977). *Marriage and family development* (5th ed.). Philadelphia: Lippincott.

DUVALL, E. M., & MILLER, B.C. (1985). *Marriage and family development* (6th ed.). New York: Harper & Row.

DWYER, J. W., & COWARD, R. T. (1991). A multivariate comparison of the involvement of adult sons versus daughters in the care of impaired parents. *Journal of Gerontology: Social Sciences, 46,* 259–269.

DYK, P. H., & ADAMS, G. R. (1990). Identity and intimacy: An initial investigation of three theoretical models using cross-lag panel correlations. *Journal of Youth and Adolescence, 19,* 91–110.

EARNSHAW, A. R., AMUNDSON, N. E., & BORGEN, W. A. (1990). The experience of job insecurity for professional women. *Journal of Employment Counseling, 27,* 2–18.

EATON, W. O., CHIPPERFIELD, J. G., & SINGBEIL, C. E. (1989). Birth order and activity level in children. *Developmental Psychology, 25,* 668–672.

EATON, W. O., & ENNS, L. R. (1986). Sex differences in human motor activity level. *Psychological Bulletin, 100,* 19–28.

ECKHARDT, M. J., HARFORD, T. C., KAELBER, C. T., PARKER, E. S., ROSENTHAL, L. S., RYBACK, R. S., SALMOIRAGHI, G. C., VANDERVEEN, E., & WARREN, K. R. (1981). Health hazards associated with alcohol consumption. *Journal of the American Medical Association, 246,* 648–666.

EDELSTEIN, S. (December 1990–January 1991). Do grandparents have rights? *Modern Maturity,* 40–42.

EDWARDS, C. A. (1994). Leadership in groups of school-age girls. *Developmental Psychology, 30,* 920–927.

EISDORFER, C., & WILKIE, F. (1977). Stress, disease, aging, and behavior. In J. E. Birren & K. W. Schaie (Eds.), *Handbook of the psychology of aging* (pp. 251–275). New York: Van Nostrand Reinhold.

EISENBERG, N. (1988). The development of prosocial and aggressive behavior. In M. H. Bornstein & M. E. Lamb (Eds.), *Developmental psychology: An advanced textbook* (2nd ed., pp. 461–495). Hillsdale, NJ: Lawrence Erlbaum Associates, Inc.

EISENBERG, N., FABES, R. A., SCHALLER, M., CARLO, G., & MILLER, P. A. (1991). The relations of parental characteristics and practices to children's vicarious emotional responding. *Child Development, 62,* 1393–1408.

EISENBERG, N., & MILLER, P. A. (1987). The relation of empathy to prosocial and related behaviors. *Psychological Bulletin, 101,* 91–119.

EISENBERG, N., & SHELL, R. (1986). Prosocial moral judgement and behavior in children: The mediating role of cost. *Personality and Social Psychology Bulletin, 12,* 426–433.

EKERDT, D. J. (1987). Why the notion persists that retirement harms health. *Gerontologist, 27,* 454–457.

EKERDT, D. J., & DEVINEY, S. (1990). On defining persons as retired. *Journal of Aging Studies, 4,* 211–229.

ELDER, G. H., JR., & PAVALKO, E. K. (1993). Work careers in men's later years: Transitions, trajectories, and historical change. *Journal of Gerontology: Social Sciences, 48,* 180–191.

ELICKER, J., ENGLUND, M., & SROUFE, L. A. (1992). Predicting peer competence and peer relationships in childhood from early parent-child relationships. In R. D. Parke & G. W. Ladd (Eds.), *Family-peer relationships: Modes of linkage.* Hillsdale, NJ: Erlbaum.

ELKIND, D. (1978). *The child's reality: Three developmental themes.* Hillsdale, NJ: Erlbaum.

ELKIND, D., & BOWEN, R. (1979). Imaginary audience behavior in children and adolescents. *Developmental Psychology, 15,* 38–44.

ELLIS, W. K., & RUSCH, F. R. (1991). Supported employment: Current practices and future directions. In J. L. Matson & J. A. Mulick (Eds.), *Handbook of mental retardation* (2nd ed.). New York: Pergamon.

ELLISON, C. G. (1990). Family ties, friendships, and subjective well-being among black Americans. *Journal of Marriage and the Family, 52,* 298–310.

ELLISON V. BRADY, 924 F.2d 871 (9th Circuit 1991).

ENNS, J. T. (1990). Relations between components of visual attention. In J. T. Enns (Ed.), *The development of attention: Reserach and theory.* Amsterdam: Elsevier.

EPSTEIN, L. H., & CLUSS, P. A. (1986). Behavioral genetics of childhood obesity. *Behavior Therapy, 17,* 324–334.

EPSTEIN, L. H., McCURLEY, J., WING, R. R., & VALOSKI, A. (1990). Five-year follow-up of family-based behavioral treatments for childhood obesity. *Journal of Consulting and Clinical Psychology, 58,* 661–664.

EPSTEIN, L. H., & WING, R. R. (1987). Behavioral treatment of childhood obesity. *Psychological Bulletin, 101,* 331–342.

ERICKSON, M. T. (1987). *Behavior disorders of children and adolescents.* Englewood, Cliffs, NJ: Prentice-Hall.

ERICSSON, K. A., & SMITH, J. (EDS.). (1991). *Toward a general theory of expertise: Prospects and limits.* New York: Cambridge University Press.

ERIKSON, E. H. (1968). *Identity: Youth and crisis.* New York: Norton.

ERIKSON, E. H. (1982). *The life cycle completed: Review.* New York: Norton.

ERIKSON, E. H., ERIKSON, J. M., & KIVNICK, H. Q. (1986). *Vital involvement in old age.* New York: Norton.

ERVIN-TRIPP, S. (1970). Discourse agreement: How children answer questions. In J. R. Hayes (Ed.), *Cognition and the development of language.* New York: Wiley.

ESSEX, M. J., & NAM, S. (1987). Marital status and loneliness among older women. *Journal of Marriage and the Family, 49,* 93–106.

ESTES, R. J., & WILENSKY, H. L. (1978). Life cycle squeeze and the morale curve. *Social Problems, 25,* 277–292.

FAGOT, B. I. (1985). Changes in thinking about early sex role development. *Developmental Review, 5,* 83–98.

FALBO, T., & POLIT, E. F. (1986). Quantitative review of the only child literature: Research evidence and theory development, *Psychological Bulletin, 100,* 176–186.

FALBO, T., & POSTON, D. L., JR. (1993). The academic, personality, and physical outcomes of only children in China. *Child Development, 64,* 18–35.

FALKNER, J., & TANNER, J. M., (Eds.). (1962). *Human growth: A comprehensive treatise, Vol. 2: Postnatal growth, neurobiology* (2nd ed.). New York: Plenum.

FARRELL, M. P., & ROSENBERG, S. D. (1981). *Men at midlife.* Boston: Auburn House.

FARVER, J. M., & BRANSTETTER, W. H. (1994). Preschoolers' prosocial responses to their peers' distress. *Developmental Psychology, 30,* 334–341.

FELDMAN, D. H., & GOLDSMITH, L. T. (1991). *Nature's gambit.* New York: Teachers College Press.

FELNER, R. D., & ADAN, A. M. (1988). The School Transitional Environment Project: An ecological intervention and evaluation. In R. H. Price, E. L. Cowan, R. P. Lorion, & J. Ramos-McKay (Eds.), *14 ounces of prevention: A casebook for practitioners.* Washington, DC: American Psychological Association.

FELTEY, K. M., AINSLIE, J. J., & GEIB, A. (1991). Sexual coercion attitudes among high school students: The influence of gender and rape education. *Youth and Society, 23,* 229–250.

FEMINIST MAJORITY FOUNDATION. (1991). *Empowering women in business.* Washington, DC: Author.

FENSON, L., DALE, P. S., REZNICK, J. S., BATES, E., THAL, D. J., & PETHICK, S. J. (1994). Variability in early communicative development. *Monographs of the Society for Research in Child Development, 59* (5, Serial No. 242).

FIELD, D., & MINKLER, M. (1988). Continuity and change in social support between young-old and old-old or very-old age. *Journal of Gerontology: Psychological Sciences, 43,* 100–106.

FIELD, T. M. (1990). *Infancy.* Cambridge, MA: Harvard University Press.

FIELD, T. M., & WIDMAYER, S. M. (1982). Motherhood. In B. J. Wolman (Ed.), *Handbook of developmental psychology,* (pp. 681–701). Englewood Cliffs, NJ: Prentice-Hall.

FIELDS, R. (1992). *Drugs and alcohol in perspective.* Dubuque, IA: William C. Brown.

FINGERHUT, L. A., & KLEINMAN, J. C. (1990). International and interstate comparisons of homicide among young males. *Journal of the American Medical Association, 263,* 3292–3295.

FINN, J. D., & ACHILLES, C. M. (1990). Answers and questions about class size: A statewide experiment. *American Educational Research Journal, 27,* 557–577.

FISCHER, K. W. (1983). Developmental levels as periods of discontinuity. In K. W. Fischer (Ed.), *Levels and transitions in children's development.* San Francisco: Jossey-Bass.

FISHER, C. B., & BRONE, R. J. (1991). Eating disorders in adolescence. In R. M. Lerner, A. C. Petersen, & J. Brooks-Gunn (Eds.), *Encyclopedia of adolescence* (Vol. 1). New York: Garland.

FISHER, H. E. (1987). The four-year itch. *Natural History, 96*(10), 22–33.

FISHER, H. E. (1994). The nature of romantic love. *Journal of NIH Research, 6*(4), 59–64.

FITZGERALD, L. F., & ORMEROD, A. J. (1991). Perceptions of sexual harassment: The influence of gender and academic context. *Psychology of Women Quarterly, 15,* 281–294.

FITZGERALD, L. F., & SHULLMAN, S. L. (1993). Sexual harassment: A research analysis and agenda for the 1990s. *Journal of Vocational Behavior, 42,* 5–27.

FITZGERALD, L. F., SHULLMAN, S. L., BAILEY, N., RICHARDS, M., SWECKER, J., GOLD, Y., ORMEROD, A. J., & WEITZMAN, L. (1988). The incidence and dimensions of sexual harassment in academia and the workplace. *Journal of Vocational Behavior, 32,* 152–175.

FITZPATRICK, M. A. (1984). A topological approach to marital interaction—Recent theory and research. *Advances in Experimental Sociology, 18,* 1–47.

FIVUSH, R. (1993). Scripts and gender: A new approach for examining gender-role development. *Developmental Review, 13,* 126–146.

FLAKS, D. K., FILCHER, I., MASTERPASQUA, F., & JOSEPH, G. (1995). Lesbians choosing motherhood: A comparative study of lesbian and heterosexual parents and their children. *Developmental Psychology, 31,* 105–114.

FLAVELL, J. H. (1985). *Cognitive development* (2nd ed.). Englewood Cliffs, NJ: Prentice-Hall.

FLAVELL, J. H., GREEN, F. L., & FLAVELL, E. R. (1986). Development of knowledge about the appearance-reality distinction. *Monographs of the Society for Research in Child Development, 51* (Serial No. 212).

FOX, A. (1979, January). Earnings replacement rates of retired couples: Findings from the Retirement History Study. *Social Security Bulletin, 42,* 17–39.

FOX, N. A., & DAVIDSON, R. J. (1988). Patterns of brain electrical activity during facial signs of emotion in 10-month-old infants. *Developmental Psychology, 24,* 230–236.

FRANKENBURG, W. K., & DOBBS, J. B. (1969). The Denver Developmental Screening Test. *Journal of Pediatrics, 71,* 181–191.

FRENCH, D. C. (1988). Heterogeneity of peer-rejected boys: Aggressive and nonaggressive subtypes. *Child Development, 53,* 976–985.

FRENCH, D. C. (1990). Heterogeneity of peer-rejected girls. *Child Development, 61,* 2028–2031.

FRIEDMAN, M., & ROSENMAN, R. H. (1974). *Type A behavior and your heart.* New York: Random House.

FRIEND, M., & DAVIS, T. L. (1993). Appearance-reality distinction: Children's understanding of the physical and affective domains. *Developmental Psychology, 29,* 907–914.

FROMAN, L. (1994). Adult learning in the workplace. In J. D. Sinnott (Ed.), *Interdisciplinary handbook of adult lifespan learning* (pp. 203–217). Westport, CT: Greenwood Press.

FRY, P. S. (1986). *Depression, stress, and adaptation in the elderly.* Rockville, MD: Aspen.

FULTON, J. P., KATZ, S., JACK, S. S., & HENDERSHOT, G. E. (1989). *Physical functioning of the aged: United States, 1984.* Hyattsville, MD: National Center for Health Statistics.

FURSTENBERG, F. F., JR. (1982). Conjugal succession: Reentering marriage after divorce. In P. B. Baltes & O. G. Brim, Jr. (Eds.), *Life-span development and behavior* (Vol. 5, pp. 108–146). New York: Academic Press.

FURSTENBERG, F. F., BROOKS-GUNN, J., & MORGAN, S. P. (1987). *Adolescent mothers in later life.* New York: Cambridge University Press.

FURSTENBERG, F. F., JR., & NORD, C. W. (1985). Parenting apart: Patterns of childbearing after marital disruption. *Journal of Marriage and the Family, 47,* 893–912.

FUTTERMAN, A., GALLAGHER, D., THOMPSON, L. W., LOVETT, S., & GILEWSKI, M. (1990). Retrospective assessment of marital adjustment and depression during the first two years of spousal bereavement. *Psychology and Aging, 5,* 277–283.

GABLE, S., & ISABELLA, R. A. (1992). Maternal contributions to infant regulation of arousal. *Infant Behavior and Development, 15,* 95–107.

GAGE, N. (1978). The yield of research on teaching. *Phi Delta Kappan, 59,* 229–235.

GAILEY, C. W. (1987). Evolutionary perspectives on gender hierarchy. In B. B. Hess & M. M. Feree (Eds.), *Analyzing gender* (pp. 32–67). Newbury Park, CA: Sage.

GAJAR, A. H. (1992). University-based models for students with learning disabilities: The Pennsylvania State University model. In F. R. Rusch, L. DeStefano, J. Chadsey-Rusch, L. A. Phelps, & E. Szymanski (Eds.), *Transition from school to life* (pp. 51–70). Sycamore, IL: Sycamore.

GALLER, J. R., & RAMSEY, F. (1989). A follow-up study of the influence of early malnutrition on development: Behavior at home and at school. *Journal of the American Academy of Child and Adolescent Psychiatry, 28,* 254–261.

GALLER, J. R., RAMSEY, F., & FORDE, V. (1986). A follow-up study of the influence of early malnutrition on subsequent development: IV. Intellectual performance during adolescence. *Nutrition and Behavior, 3,* 211–222.

GARBARINO, J., & KOSTELNY, K. (1992). Child maltreatment as a community problem. *Child Abuse and Neglect, 16,* 455–464.

GARDNER, H. (1983). *Frames of mind: The theory of multiple intelligences.* New York: Basic Books.

GARLAND, A. F., & ZIGLER, E. (1993). Adolescent suicide prevention: Current research and social policy implications. *American Psychologist, 48,* 169–182.

GARLAND, C., BARRETT-CONNOR, E., SUAREZ, L., CRIQUI, M. H., & WINGARD, D. L. (1985). Effects of passive smoking on ischemic heart disease mortality of nonsmokers: A prospective study. *American Journal of Epidemiology, 121,* 645–650.

GARN, S. M. (1975). Bone loss and aging. In R. Goldman & M. Rockstein (Eds.), *The physiology and pathology of aging.* New York: Academic Press.

GARNER, P. W., JONES, D. C., & PALMER, D. J. (1994). Social cognitive correlates of preschool children's sibling caregiving behavior. *Developmental Psychology, 30,* 905–911.

GARVEY, C., & BERNINGER, G. (1981). Timing and turn taking in children's conversations. *Discourse Processes, 4,* 27–59.

GATZ, M., & SIEGLER, I. C. (1981, August). *Locus of control: A retrospective.* Paper presented at the meeting of the American Psychological Association, Los Angeles.

GAYLORD, S. A., & ZUNG, W. W. K. (1987). Affective disorders among the aging. In L. L. Carstensen & B. A. Edelstein (Eds.), *Handbook of clinical gerontology* (pp. 76–95). New York: Pergamon.

GELMAN, R., & MECK, E. (1986). The notion of principle: The case of counting. In J. Hiebert (Ed.), *Conceptual and procedural knowledge: The case of mathematics.* Hillside, NJ: Erlbaum.

GENTRY, M., & SCHULMAN, A. D. (1988). Remarriage as a coping response for widowhood. *Psychology and Aging, 3,* 191–196.

GEORGE, L. K., FILLENBAUM, G., & PALMORE, E. (1984). Sex differences in the antecedents and consequences of retirement. *Journal of Gerontology, 39,* 364–371.

GERBNER, G. (1993). *Women and minorities on television (a report to the Screen Actors Guild).* Philadelphia: University of Pennsylvania, Annenberg School for Communication.

GIACONIA, R. M., & HEDGES, L. V. (1982). *Identifying features of open education.* Stanford, CA: Stanford University Press.

GIBRAN, K. (1923). *The prophet.* New York: Knopf.

GIBSON, E. J. (1969). *Principles of perceptual learning and development.* New York: Appleton-Century-Crofts.

GIBSON, E. J., & WALK, R. D. (1960). The "visual cliff." *Scientific American, 202,* 64–71.

GIBSON, R. C. (1986). *Blacks in an aging society.* New York: Carnegie Corporation.

GIBSON, R. C. (1987). Reconceptualizing retirement for black Americans. *Gerontologist, 27,* 691–698.

GIBSON, R. C. (1991). The subjective retirement of black Americans. *Journal of Gerontology: Social Sciences, 46,* 204–209.

GILFORD, R. (1984). Contrasts in marital satisfaction throughout old age: An exchange theory analysis. *Journal of Gerontology, 39,* 325–333.

GILL, J. S., ZEZULKA, A. V., SHIPLEY, M. J., GILL, S. K., & BEEVERS, D. G. (1986). Stroke and alcohol consumption. *New England Journal of Medicine, 315,* 1041–1046.

GILLIGAN, C. (1982). *In a different voice: Psychological theory and women's development.* Cambridge, MA: Harvard University Press.

GILLIGAN, C. (1985, March). *Remapping development.* Paper presented at the biennial meeting of the Society for Research in Child Development, Toronto.

GILLIS, J. J., GILGER, J. W., PENNINGTON, B. F., & DEFRIES, J. C. (1992). Attention deficit disorder in reading-disabled twins: Evidence for a genetic etiology. *Journal of Abnormal Child Psychology, 20,* 303–315.

GILMORE, D. (1990). *Manhood in the making: Cultural components of masculinity.* New Haven, CT: Yale University Press.

GINOTT, H. G. (1969). *Between parent and teenager.* New York: Macmillan.

GLAMSER, F., & HAYSLIP, B., JR. (1985). The impact of retirement on participation in leisure activities. *Therapeutic Recreation Journal, 19,* 28–38.

GLENN, N. D. (1991). The recent trend in marital success in the United States. *Journal of Marriage and the Family, 53,* 261–270.

GLENN, N. D., & MCLANAHAN, S. (1981). The effects of offspring on the psychological well-being of older adults. *Journal of Marriage and the Family, 43,* 409–421.

GLENN, N. D., & MCLANAHAN, S. (1982). Children and marital happiness: A further specification of the relationship. *Journal of Marriage and the Family, 44,* 63–72.

GLENN, N. D., & SUPANCIC, M. (1984). The social and demographic correlates of divorce and separation in the United States: An update and reconsideration. *Journal of Marriage and the Family, 46,* 563–575.

GLENN, N. D., & WEAVER, C. N. (1978). The marital happiness of remarried divorced persons. *Journal of Marriage and the Family, 40,* 269–282.

GLICK, I. O., WEISS, R. S., & PARKES, C. M. (1974). *The first year of bereavement.* New York: Wiley.

GLICK, P. C. (1989). The family life cycle and social change. *Family Relations, 38,* 123–129.

GLICK, P. C., & LIN, S. (1986). Recent changes in divorce and remarriage. *Journal of Marriage and the Family, 48,* 737–747.

GLICK, P. C., & NORTON, A. J. (1979). Marrying, divorcing, and living together in the U.S. today. *Population Bulletin, 32,* 1–41.

GOFF, S. J., MOUNT, M. K., & JAMISON, R. L. (1990). Employer supported child care, work/family conflict, and absenteeism: A field study. *Personnel Psychology, 43,* 793–809.

GOLD, D. T. (1990). Late-life sibling relationships: Does race affect typological distribution? *Gerontologist, 30,* 741–748.

GOLD, D. T., WOODBURY, M. A., & GEORGE, L. K. (1990). Relationship classification using grade of membership analysis: A typology of sibling relationships in later life. *Journal of Gerontology: Social Sciences, 45,* 43–51.

GOLDMAN, S. R. (1989). Strategy instruction in mathematics. *Learning Disability Quarterly, 12,* 43–55.

GOLDSMITH, H. H., BUSS, A. H., PLOMIN, R., & ROTHBART, M. K. (1987). What is temperament? Four approaches. *Child Development, 58,* 505–529.

GOLDSTEIN, E. (1979). Effect of same-sex and cross-sex role models on the subsequent academic productivity of scholars. *American Psychologist, 34,* 407–410.

GOLEMAN, D. (1990, April 24). Anger over racism is seen as a cause of blacks' high blood pressure. *The New York Times,* p. C3.

GOODE, W. J. (1956). *After divorce.* Glencoe, IL: Free Press.

GOODNOW, J. J. (1992). *Parental belief systems: The psychological consequences for children.* Hillsdale, NJ: Erlbaum.

GORDON, C., GAITZ, C. M., & SCOTT, J. (1976). Leisure and lives: Personal expressivity across the life span. In R. H. Binstock & E. Shanas (Eds.), *Handbook of aging and the social sciences* (2nd ed., pp. 310–341). New York: Van Nostrand Reinhold.

GOTTESMAN, I. I. (1963). Genetic aspects of intelligent behavior. In N. R. Ellis (Ed.), *Handbook of mental deficiency* (p. 255). New York: McGraw-Hill.

GOTTLIEB, L. N., & MENDELSON, M. J. (1990). Parental support and firstborn girls' adaptation to the birth of a sibling. *Journal of Applied Developmental Psychology, 11,* 29–48.

GOTTMAN, J. M. (1986). The world of coordinated play: Same- and cross-sex friendships in children. In J. M. Gottman and Jeffrey G. Parker (Eds.), *Conversations of friends.* New York: Cambridge University Press.

GOULD, R. L. (1978). *Transformation: Growth and change in adult life.* New York: Simon and Schuster.

GRABER, J. A., BROOKS-GUNN, J., PAIKOFF, R. L., & WARREN, M. P. (1994). Prediction of eating problems: An 8-year study of adolescent girls. *Developmental Psychology, 30,* 823–834.

GREEN, A. L., & BOXER, A. M. (1986). Daughters and sons as young adults. In N. Datan, A. Greene, & H. W. Reese (Eds.), *Life-span developmental psychology: Intergenerational relations* (pp. 125–150). Hillsdale, NJ: Erlbaum.

GREENBERG, B. S., FAZEL, S., & WEBER, M. (1986). *Children's view on advertising.* New York: Independent Broadcasting Authority Research Report.

GREENBERG, M. T., & CRNIC, K. A. (1988). Longitudinal predictors of developmental status and social interaction in premature and full-term infants at age two. *Child Development, 59,* 554–570.

GREENBERGER, E., & STEINBERG, L. (1983). Sex differences in early work experience: Harbinger of things to come? *Social Forces, 62,* 467–486.

GREENE, V. L., & MONAHAN, D. J. (1982). The impact of visitation on patient well-being in nursing homes. *Gerontologist, 22,* 418–423.

GREENHAUS, J. H., PARASURAMAN, S., & WORMLEY, W. M. (1990). Effects of race on organizational experiences, job performance evaluations, and career outcomes. *Academy of Management Journal, 33,* 64–86.

GREENWOOD, J., LOVE, E. R., & PRATT, O. E. (1983). The effects of alcohol or of thiamine deficiency upon reproduction in the female rat and fetal development. *Alcohol and Alcoholism, 18,* 45–51.

GREER, J. (1992). *Adult sibling rivalries.* New York: Crown.

GROSSMAN, H. J. (ED.). (1983). *Classification in mental retardation.* Washington, DC: American Association on Mental Deficiency.

GRUNAU, R. V. E., JOHNSTON, C. C., & CRAIG, K. D. (1990). Neonatal facial and cry responses to invasive and non-invasive procedures. *Pain, 42,* 295–305.

GUELZOW, M. G., BIRD, G. W., & KOBALL, E. H. (1991). An exploratory path analysis of the stress process for dual-career men and women. *Journal of Marriage and the Family, 53,* 151–164.

GUERRA, N. G., & SLABY, R. G. (1990). Cognitive mediators of aggression in adolescent offenders: 2. Intervention. *Developmental Psychology, 26,* 269–277.

GUILFORD, J. P. (1967). *The nature of human intelligence.* New York: McGraw-Hill.

GUNTER, N. C., & GUNTER, B. G. (1990). Domestic division of labor among working couples: Does androgyny make a difference? *Psychology of Women Quarterly, 14,* 355–370.

GURALNICK, J. M., & SIMONSICK, E. M. (1993). Physical disability in older Americans. *The Journals of Gerontology, 48* (Special Issue), 3–10.

GURALNICK, J. M., & WALLACE, R. B. (1991). The conceptualization and design of intervention studies on frailty in the older population: Insights from observational epidemiologic studies. In R. Weindruch, E. C. Hadley, & M. G. Ory (Eds.), *Reducing frailty and falls in older persons* (pp. 29–43). Springfield, IL: Charles C Thomas.

GUTEK, B. A., SEARLE, S., & KLEPA, L. (1991). Rational versus gender role explanations for work-family conflict. *Journal of Applied Psychology, 76,* 560–568.

GUTMANN, D. L. (1987). *Reclaimed powers: Toward a new psychology of men and women in later life.* New York: Basic Books.

GUTTMACHER, A. F., & KAISER, I. H. (1986). *Pregnancy, birth, and family planning.* New York: New American Library.

HAAN, N., MILSAP, R., & HARTKA, E. (1986). As time goes by: Change and stability in personality over fifty years. *Psychology and Aging, 1,* 220–232.

HAAS, L. (1990). Gender equality and social policy: Implications of a study of parental leave in Sweden. *Journal of Family Issues, 11,* 401–423.

HAGESTAD, G. O. (1978). *Patterns of communication and influence between grandparents and grandchildren.* Paper presented at the World Conference on Sociology, Helsinki, Finland.

HAGESTAD, G. O., & NEUGARTEN, B. L. (1985). Age and the life course. In R. H. Binstock & E. Shanas (Eds.), *Handbook of aging and the social sciences* (2nd ed., pp. 35–61). New York: Van Nostrand Reinhold.

HAHN, W. (1987). Cerebral lateralization of function: From infancy through childhood. *Psychological Bulletin, 101,* 376–392.

HAIGHT, B. K. (1992). Long-term effects of a structured life review process. *Journal of Gerontology: Psychological Sciences, 47,* 312–315.

HALL, G. S. (1904). *Adolescence.* New York: Appleton.

HALLINAN, M. T., & TEIXEIRA, R. A. (1987). Opportunities and constraints: Black-white differences in the formation of interracial friendships. *Child Development, 58,* 1358–1371.

HALPERN, D. F. (1986). *Sex differences in cognitive abilities.* Hillsdale, NJ: Erlbaum.

HALPERN, J. (1987). *Helping your aging parents.* New York: McGraw-Hill.

HALPERN, J. J., & LURIA, Z. (1989). Labels of giftedness and gender-typicality: Effects on adults' judgments of children's traits. *Psychology in the Schools, 26,* 301–310.

HAMER, D. H., HU, S., MAGNUSON, V. L., HU, N., & PATTATUCCI, A. M. (1993). A linkage between DNA markers on the X chromosome and male sexual orientation. *Science, 261,* 321–327.

HAMILTON, J. (1978). Grandparents as grievers. In J. O. Sahler (Ed.), *The child and death.* St. Louis: C. V. Mosby.

HAMMILL, D. D. (1990). On defining learning disabilities: An emerging consensus. *Journal of Learning Disabilities, 23,* 74–84.

HAMON, R. R., & BLIESZNER, R. (1990). Filial responsibility expectations among adult child-older parent pairs. *Journal of Gerontology: Psychological Sciences, 45,* 110–112.

HAMOND, N. R., & FIVUSH, R. (1991). Memories of Mickey Mouse: Young children recount their trip to Disney World. *Cognitive Development, 6,* 433–448.

HARRINGER, C. (1994). Adults in college. In J. D. Sinnott, (Ed.), *Interdisciplinary handbook of adult lifespan learning* (pp. 171–185). Westport, CT: Greenwood Press.

HARRIS, L. J. (1983). Laterality of function in the infant: Historical and contemporary trends in theory and research. In G. Young, S. J. Segalowitz, C. M. Corter, & S. E. Trehub (Eds.), *Manual specialization and the developing brain.* New York: Academic Press.

HARRIS, M. B., & TURNER, P. H. (1986). Gay and lesbian parents. *Journal of Homosexuality, 12,* 101–113.

HARRIS, P. L., & KAVANAUGH, R. D. (1993). Young children's understanding of pretense. *Monographs of the Society for Research in Child Development, 58* (Serial No. 231).

HART, D. A. (1992). *Becoming men: The development of aspirations, values, and adaptational styles.* New York: Plenum.

HARTER, S. (1990). Self and identity development. In S. S. Feldman & G. R. Elliott (Eds.), *At the threshold: The developing adolescent.* Cambridge, MA: Harvard University Press.

HARTUP, W. W. (1983). Peer relations. In R. H. Mussen (Ed.), *Handbook of child psychology* (Vol. 4). New York: Wiley.

HARTUP, W. W. (1992a). Friendships and their developmental significance. In H. McGurk (Ed.), *Contemporary issues in childhood social development.* London, UK: Routledge.

HARTUP, W. W. (1992b). Peer relations in early and middle childhood. In V. B. Van Hasselt & M. Hersen (Eds.), *Handbook of social development: A lifespan perspective* (pp. 257–281). New York: Plenum.

HARTUP, W. W., & MOORE, S. G. (1990). Early peer relations: Developmental significance and prognostic implications. *Early Childhood Research Quarterly, 5,* 1–17.

HASKETT, M. E., & KISTNER, J. A. (1991). Social interactions and peer perceptions of young physically abused children. *Child Development, 62,* 979–990.

HASS, A. (1979). *Teenage sexuality.* New York: Macmillan.

HATCH, L. R., & BULCROFT, C. (1992). Contact with friends in later life: Disentangling the effects of gender and marital stability. *Journal of Marriage and the Family, 54,* 222–232.

HAURI, P. (1982). *The sleep disorders.* Kalamazoo, MI: Upjohn.

HAVIGHURST, R. J. (1982). The world of work. In B. B. Wolman (Ed.), *Handbook of developmental psychology* (pp. 771–787). Englewood Cliffs, NJ: Prentice-Hall.

HAWKINS, J., SHEINGOLD, K., GEARHART, M., & BERGER, C. (1982). Microcomputers in schools: Impact on the social life of elementary classrooms. *Journal of Applied Developmental Psychology, 3,* 361–373.

HAYFLICK, L. (1994). *How and why we age.* New York: Ballantine.

HEANEY, R. P., GALLAGHER, J. C., JOHNSTON, C. C., NEER, R., PARFITT, A. M., & WHEDON, G. D. (1982). Calcium nutrition and bone health in the elderly. *American Journal of Clinical Nutrition, 36,* 987–1013.

HEAROLD, S. (1986). A synthesis of 1,043 effects of television on social behavior. In G. Comstock (Ed.), *Public communications and behavior* (Vol. 1, pp. 65–133). New York: Academic Press.

HEDGES, L. V., & STOCK, W. (1983, Spring). The effects of class size: An examination of rival hypotheses. *American Education Research Journal,* 63–85.

HELSON, R., & MOANE, G. (1987). Personality change in women from college to midlife. *Journal of Personality and Social Psychology, 52,* 1176–1186.

HENDERSON, K. A. (1990). The meaning of leisure for women: An integrative review of the research. *Journal of Leisure Research, 22,* 228–243.

HENNON, C. B. (1983). Divorce and the elderly: A neglected area of research. In T. H. Brubaker (Ed.), *Family relationships in later life* (pp. 149–172). Newbury Park, CA: Sage.

HENRETTA, J. C., CHAN, C. G., & O'RAND, A. M. (1992). Retirement reason versus retirement process: Examining the reasons for retirement typology. *Journal of Gerontology: Social Sciences, 47,* 1–7.

HENSHAW, S. K. (1993). Teenage abortion, birth and pregnancy statistics by state, 1988. *Family Planning Perspectives, 25,* 122–126.

HERZOG, A. R., KAHN, R. L., MORGAN, J. N., JACKSON, J. S., & ANTONUCCI, T. C. (1989). Age differences in productive activities. *Journal of Gerontology: Social Sciences, 44,* 129–138.

HETHERINGTON, E. M. (1989). Coping with family transitions: Winners, losers and survivors. *Child Development, 60,* 1–14.

HETHERINGTON, E. M. (1993). An overview of the Virginia Longitudinal Study of Divorce and Remarriage with a focus on early adolescence. *Journal of Family Psychology, 7,* 39–56.

HETHERINGTON, S. E. (1990). A controlled study of the effect of prepared childbirth classes on obstetric outcomes. *Birth, 17,* 86–90.

HILL, C. D., THOMPSON, L. W., & GALLAGHER, D. (1988). The role of anticipatory bereavement in older women's adjustment to widowhood. *Gerontologist, 28,* 792–796.

HOBART, C. (1988). The family system in remarriage: An exploratory study. *Journal of Marriage and the Family, 50,* 649–661.

HOFF-GINSBERG, E. (1990). Maternal speech and the child's development of syntax: A further look. *Journal of Child Language, 17,* 85–99.

HOFF-GINSBERG, E. (1991). Mother-child conversation in different social classes and communicative settings. *Child Development, 62,* 782–796.

HOFFMAN, M. L. (1970). Moral development. In P. H. Mussen (Ed.), *Carmichael's manual of child psychology* (3rd ed.) (Vol. 2). New York: Wiley.

HOFFMAN, M. L. (1988). Moral development. In M. H. Bornstein & M. E. Lamb (Eds.), *Developmental psychology : An advanced textbook* (2nd ed.). Hillsdale, NJ: Erlbaum.

HOGAN, D. P., & ASTONE, N. M. (1986). The transition to adulthood. *Annual Review of Sociology, 12,* 109–130.

HOLDEN, G. W. (1988). Adults' thinking about a child-rearing problem: Effects of experience, parental status and gender. *Child Development, 59,* 1623–1632.

HOLLAND, J. L. (1973). *Making vocational choices: A theory of careers.* Englewood Cliffs, NJ: Prentice-Hall.

HOLLAND, J. L. (1985). *Making vocational choices: A theory of vocational personalities and work environments* (2nd ed.). Englewood Cliffs, NJ: Prentice-Hall.

HOLLAND, J. L. (1985) *Self-directed search professional manual.* Lutz, FL: Psychological Assessment Resources, Inc.

HOLLAND, J. L. (1987). Current status of Holland's theory of careers: Another perspective. *Career Development Quarterly, 36,* 24–30.

HOLYROAD, K. A., APPEL, M. A., & ANDRASIK, F. (1983). A cognitive-behavioral approach to psychophysiological disorders. In D. Meichenbaum & M. E. Jarenko (Eds.), *Stress reduction and prevention.* New York: Plenum.

HORN, J. L. (1970). Organization of data on life-span development of human abilities. In L. R. Goulet & P. B. Baltes (Eds.), *Life-span developmental psychology: Research and theory* (p. 463). New York: Academic Press.

HORN, J. L. (1982). The aging of human abilities. In B. B. Wolman (Ed.), *Handbook of developmental psychology* (pp. 847–870). Englewood Cliffs, NJ: Prentice-Hall.

HORN, J. L., & HOFER, S. M. (1992). Major abilities and development in the adult period. In R. J. Sternberg & C. A. Berg (Eds.), *Intellectual development* (pp. 44–99). Cambridge, UK: Cambridge University Press.

HOROWITZ, F. D., & O'BRIEN, M. (1986). Gifted and talented children: State of knowledge and directions for research. *American Psychologist, 41,* 1147–1152.

HOWARD, A. (1992). Work and family crossroads along the career. In S. Zedeck (Ed.), *Work, families, and organizations* (p. 375). San Francisco: Jossey-Bass.

HOWARD, A., & BRAY, D. W. (1980, August). *Career motivation in mid-life managers.* Paper presented at the meeting of the American Psychological Association, Montreal.

HOWARD, M., & MCCABE, J. B. (1990). Helping teenagers postpone sexual involvement. *Family Planning Perspectives, 22,* 21–26.

HOWE, N., & ROSS, H. S. (1990). Socialization perspective taking and the sibling relationship. *Developmental Psychology, 26,* 160–165.

HOWES, C., & MATHESON, C. C. (1992). Sequences in the development of competent play with peers: Social and social pretend play. *Developmental Psychology, 28,* 961–974.

HOWES, C., UNGER, O., & SEIDNER, L. B. (1990). Social pretend play in toddlers: Parallels with social play and with solitary pretend. *Child Development, 60,* 77–84.

HUDSON, J. (1988). Children's memory for atypical actions in script-based stories: Evidence for a disruption effect. *Journal of Experimental Child Psychology, 46,* 159–173.

HUESMANN, L. R. (1986). Psychological processes promoting the relation between exposure to media violence and aggressive behavior by the viewer. *Journal of Social Issues, 42,* 125–139.

HUSTON, A. C., WATKINS, B. A., & KUNKEL, D. (1989). Public policy and children's television. *American Psychologist, 44,* 424–433.

HUSTON, A. C., & WRIGHT, J. C. (1994). Educating children with television: The forms of the medium. In D. Zillmann, J. Bryant, A. C. Huston (Eds.), *Media, children, and the family:* *Social scientific, psychodynamic, and clinical perspectives* (pp. 73–84). Hillsdale, NJ: Lawrence Erlbaum Associates, Inc.

HUYCK, M. H. (1982). From gregariousness to intimacy: Marriage and friendship over the adult years. In T. M. Field, A. Huston, H. C. Quay, L. Troll, & G. E. Finley (Eds.), *Review of human development* (pp. 471–484). New York: Wiley.

HUYCK, M. H. (1990). Gender differences in aging. In J. E. Birren & K. W. Schaie (Eds.), *Handbook of the psychology of aging* (3rd ed., pp. 124–132). San Diego, CA: Academic Press.

HYDE, J. S., FENNEMA, E., & LAMON, S. J. (1990). Gender differences in mathematics performance: A meta-analysis. *Psychological Bulletin, 107,* 139–155.

HYDE, J. S., & LINN, M. C. (1988). Gender differences in verbal ability. *Psychological Bulletin, 104,* 53–69.

INGRAHAM, M. (1974). *My purpose holds: Reactions and experiences in retirement of TIAA-CREF annuitants.* New York: Educational Research Division, Teachers Insurance and Annuity Association College Retirement Equities Fund.

INHELDER, B., & PIAGET, J. (1958). *The growth of logical thinking from childhood to adolescence.* New York: Basic Books.

IVANCEVICH, J. M., & MATTESON, M. T. (1988). Type A behavior and the healthy individual. *British Journal of Medical Psychology, 61,* 37–56.

JACKSON, B., TAYLOR, J., & PYNGOLIL, M. (1991). How age conditions the relationship between climacteric status and health symptoms in African American women. *Research in Nursing and Health, 14,* 1–9.

JACKSON, J. S., & GIBSON, R. C. (1985). Work and retirement among the black elderly. In Z. Blau (Ed.), *Current perspectives on aging and the life cycle* (pp. 193–222). Greenwich, CT: JAI.

JACKSON, N. E., & BUTTERFIELD, E. C. (1986). A conception of giftedness designed to promote research. In R. J. Sternberg & J. E. Davidson (Eds.), *Conceptions of giftedness.* Cambridge, UK: Cambridge University Press.

JACOBS, J. (1975). *Older persons and retirement communities.* Springfield, IL: Charles C Thomas.

JACOBS, J. E., & ECCLES, J. S. (1992). The impact of mothers' gender-role stereotypic beliefs on mothers' and children's ability perceptions. *Journal of Personality and Social Psychology, 63,* 932–944.

JACOBSON, J. L., JACOBSON, S. W., & HUMPHREY, H. E. B. (1990). Effects of in utero exposure to polychlorinated biphenyls and related contaminants on cognitive functioning in young children. *Journal of Pediatrics, 116,* 38–45.

JACOBSON, J. L., JACOBSON, S. W., PADGETT, R. J., BRUMITT, G. A., & BILLINGS, R. L. (1992). Effects of prenatal PCB exposure on cognitive processing efficiency and sustained attention. *Developmental Psychology, 28,* 297–306.

JACOBSON, S. W., GEIN, G. G., JACOBSON, J. L., SCHWARTZ, P. M., & DOWLER, J. K. (1985). The effect of intrauterine PCB exposure on visual recognition memory. *Child Development, 56,* 853–860.

JAEGER, E., & WEINRAUB, M. (1990). Early nonmaternal care and infant attachment: In search of process. In K. McCartney (Ed.), *Child care and maternal employment: A social ecology approach*. San Francisco: Jossey-Bass.

JAMES, L. R., & JONES, A. P. (1980). Perceived job characteristics and job satisfaction: An examination of reciprocal causation. *Personnel Psychology, 33,* 97–135.

JAMES, W. (1890). *The principles of psychology*. New York: Holt.

JENSEN, M. D., BENSON, R. C., & BOBACK, I. M. (1981). *Maternity care*. St. Louis, MO: C. V. Mosby.

JOHNSON, C. L. (1988). Active and latent functions of grandparenting during the divorce process. *Gerontologist, 28,* 185–191.

JOHNSON, C. L., & BARER, B. M. (1990). Family and networks among inner city blacks. *Gerontologist, 30,* 726–733.

JOHNSON, C. L., & GRANT, L. (1985). *The nursing home in American society*. Baltimore, MD: Johns Hopkins University Press.

JOHNSON-LAIRD, P. N. (1988). *The computer and the mind: An introduction to cognitive science*. London, UK: Fontana.

JOHNSTON, J. A. (1993, July 4). The cost of kids. *Sunday News Journal* (Wilmington, DE), p. E1.

JOHNSTON, L. D., O'MALLEY, P. M., & BACHMAN, J. G. (1993). *National survey results on drug use from Monitoring the Future Study, 1975–1992* (Vol. 1). Rockville, MD: National Institute on Drug Abuse.

JOHNSTONE, B., FRAME, C. L., & BOUMAN, D. (1992). Physical attractiveness and athletic and academic ability in controversial-aggressive and rejected-aggressive children. *Journal of Social and Clinical Psychology, 11,* 71–79.

JONES, L. Y. (1980). *Great expectations: America and the baby boom generation*. New York: Coward, McCann, & Geoghegan.

JONES, M. C. (1965). Psychological correlates of somatic development. *Child Development, 36,* 899–911.

JONES, M. C., & BAYLEY, N. (1950). Physical maturing among boys as related to behavior. *Journal of Educational Psychology, 41,* 1–148.

JORDAN, B. (1980). *Birth in four cultures*. Montreal, CN: Eden.

JUNG, C. J. (1960/1931). The stages of life. In G. Adler, M. Fordham, & H. Read (Eds.), *The collected works of C. J. Jung: Vol. 8. The structure and dynamics of the psyche*. London, UK: Routledge & Kegan Paul.

JUSCZYK, P. W. (1981). The processing of speech and nonspeech sounds by infants: Some implications. In R. N. Aslin, J. R. Alberts, & M. R. Peterson (Eds.), *Development of perception* (Vol. 1). New York: Academic Press.

KAHANA, B., & KAHANA, E. (1970). Grandparenthood from the perspective of the developing grandchild. *Developmental Psychology, 3,* 98–105.

KAHANA, E. (1982). A congruence model of person-environment interaction. In M. P. Lawton, P. G. Windley, & T. O. Byerts (Eds.), *Aging and the environment: Theoretical approaches* (pp. 97–121). New York: Springer.

KAIL, R. (1990). *The development of memory in children* (3rd ed.). New York: W. H. Freeman.

KAIL, R., & BISANZ, J. (1992). The information-processing perspective on cognitive development in childhood and adolescence. In R. J. Sternberg & C. A. Berg (Eds.), *Intellectual development*. New York: Cambridge University Press.

KAIL, R. V., & SALTHOUSE, T. A. (1994). Processing speed as a mental capacity. *Acta Psychologica, 86,* 199–225.

KAIL, R. V., & WICKS-NELSON, R. (1993). *Developmental psychology* (5th ed.). Englewood Cliffs, NJ: Prentice-Hall.

KALISH, R. A. (1975). *Late adulthood*. Pacific Grove, CA: Brooks/Cole.

KALISH, R. A. (1985). The social context of death and dying. In R. H. Binstock & E. Shanas (Eds.), *Handbook of aging and the social sciences* (2nd ed., pp. 149–170). New York: Van Nostrand Reinhold.

KALISH, R. A. (1987). Death and dying. In P. Silverman (Ed.), *The elderly as modern pioneers* (pp. 320–334). Bloomington: Indiana University Press.

KALISH, R. A., & REYNOLDS, D. (1976). *Death and ethnicity: A psychocultural study*. Los Angeles: University of Southern California Press.

KANDEL, D. B. (1978). Homophily, selection, and socialization in adolescent friendships. *American Journal of Sociology, 84,* 427–436.

KANEKAR, S., KOLSAWALLA, M. B., & NAZARETH, T. (1989). Occupational prestige as a function of occupant's gender. *Journal of Applied Social Psychology, 19,* 681–688.

KANTER, R. M. (1976, May). Why bosses turn bitchy. *Psychology Today*, pp. 56–59.

KANTROWITZ, B. (1993, August 2). Murder and mayhem, guns and gangs: A teenage generation grows up dangerous—and scared. *Newsweek*, 40–46.

KARNIOL, R. (1989). The role of manual manipulative states in the infant's acquisition of perceived control over objects. *Developmental Review, 9,* 205–233.

KASTENBAUM, R. (1985). Dying and death: A life-span approach. In J. E. Birren & K. W. Schaie (Eds.), *Handbook of the psychology of aging* (2nd ed., pp. 619–643). New York: Van Nostrand Reinhold.

KATZ, S. (1983). Assessing self-maintenance: Activities of daily living, mobility, and instrumental activities of daily living. *Journal of the American Geriatrics Society, 31,* 721–727.

KAZDIN, A. E. (1982). Applying behavioral principles in the schools. In C. R. Reynolds & T. B. Gutkin (Eds.), *The handbook of school psychology*. New York: Wiley.

KAZDIN, A. E. (1990). Childhood depression. *Journal of Child Psychology and Psychiatry and Allied Disciplines, 31,* 121–160.

KEANE, S. P., BROWN, K. P., & CRENSHAW, T. M. (1990). Children's intention-cue detection as a function of maternal social behavior: Pathways to social rejection. *Developmental Psychology, 26,* 1004–1009.

KEARNS, D. (1989, December 17). Improving the workforce: Competitiveness begins at school. *New York Times*, sec. 3, p. 2.

KEGAN, R. (1982). *The evolving self.* Cambridge, MA: Harvard University Press.

KEITH, J. (1990). Age in social and cultural context: Anthropological perspectives. In R. H. Binstock & L. K. George (Eds.), *Handbook of aging and the social sciences* (3rd ed., pp. 91–111). San Diego, CA: Academic Press.

KEITH, J. (1994). Conclusion. In J. Keith, et. al., *The aging experience: Diversity and commonality across cultures.* Newbury Park, CA: Sage Publications.

KELLER, H. (1965). *Helen Keller: The story of my life.* New York: Airmont.

KELLER, J. W., SHERRY, D., & PIOTROWSKI, C. (1984). Perspectives on death: A developmental study. *Journal of Psychology, 116,* 137–142.

KELLY, J. B. (1982). Divorce: The adult perspective. In B. B. Wolman (Ed.), *Handbook of developmental psychology* (pp. 734–750). Englewood Cliffs, NJ: Prentice-Hall.

KELLY, J. R., STEINKAMP, M. W., & KELLY, J. R. (1987). Later-life satisfaction: Does leisure contribute? *Leisure Sciences, 9,* 189–200.

KENDALL, P. C. (1987). Cognitive processes and procedures in behavior therapy. In G. T. Wilson, C. M. Franks, P. C. Kendall, and J. P. Foreyt (Eds.), *Review of behavior therapy: Theory and practice* (11th ed.). New York: Guilford.

KENNEY, R. A. (1982). *Physiology of aging: A synopsis.* Chicago: Yearbook Medical.

KENRICK, D. T. (1987). Gender, genes, and the social environment. In P. C. Shaver & C. Hendrick (Eds.), *Review of Personality and Social Psychology: Vol. 7. Sex and gender.* (pp. 14–43). Newbury Park, CA: Sage.

KIMBALL, M. M. (1986). Television and sex-role attitudes. In T. M. Williams (Ed.), *The impact of television* (pp. 265–301). New York: Academic Press.

KIMBALL, M. M. (1989). A new perspective on women's math achievement. *Psychological Bulletin, 105,* 198–214.

KINGSTON, P. W., & NOCK, S. L. (1987). Time together among dual-earner couples. *American Sociological Review, 52,* 391–400.

KINNEY, J. M. (1993, August). *Sense of coherence and mastery among spousal caregivers.* Paper presented at the meeting of the American Psychological Association, Toronto.

KINNEY, J. M., & CAVANAUGH, J. C. (1993, November). *Until death do us part: Striving to find meaning while caring for a spouse with dementia.* Paper presented at the annual meeting of the Gerontological Society of America, New Orleans.

KINNEY, J. M., HAFF, M., ISACSON, A., NOCERA, R., CAVANAUGH, J. C., & DUNN, N. J. (1993, November). *Marital satisfaction and caregiving hassles among caregivers to spouses with dementia.* Paper presented at the annual meeting of the Gerontological Society of America, New Orleans.

KINSBOURNE, M. (1989). Mechanisms and development of hemisphere specialization in children. In C. R. Reynolds & E. Fletcer-Janzen (Eds.), *Handbook of clinical child neuropsychology.* New York: Plenum.

KIRASIC, K. C., & ALLEN, G. L. (1985). Aging, spatial performance, and spatial competence. In N. Charness (Ed.), *Aging and human performance* (pp. 191–223). Chichester, UK: Wiley.

KIRSCH, I. S., JUNGEBLUT, A., JENKINGS, L., & KOLSTAD, A. (1993). *Adult literacy in America.* Washington, DC: U.S. Government Printing Office.

KITCHENER, K. S., & KING, P. M. (1989). The reflective judgment model: Ten years of research. In M. L. Commons, C. Armon, L. Kohlberg, F. A. Richards, T. A. Grotzer, & J. D. Sinnott (Eds.), *Adult development: Vol. 2. Models and methods in the study of adolescent and adult thought* (pp. 63–78). New York: Praeger.

KITSON, G. L., & SUSSMAN, M. B. (1982). Marital complaints, demographic characteristics, and symptoms of mental distress in divorce. *Journal of Marriage and the Family, 44,* 87–101.

KIVETT, V. R. (1991). Centrality of the grandfather role among older rural black and white men. *Journal of Gerontology: Social Sciences, 46,* 250–258.

KIVNICK, H. Q. (1982). *The meaning of grandparenthood.* Ann Arbor, MI: UMI Research.

KLAPPER, J. T. (1968). The impact of viewing "aggression": Studies and problems of extrapolation. In O. N. Larsen (Ed.), *Violence and the mass media.* New York: Harper and Row.

KLEIMAN, G. M. (1984). *Brave new schools: How computers can change education.* Reston, VA: Reston.

KLEIN, N. K., HACK, M., & BRESLAU, N. (1989). Children who were very low birth weight: Developmental and academic achievement at nine years of age. *Journal of Developmental and Behavioral Pediatrics, 10,* 32–37.

KLIGMAN, L. H., GROVE, G. L., & BALIN, A. K. (1985). Aging of human skin. In C. E. Finch & E. L. Schneider (Eds.), *Handbook of the biology of aging* (2nd ed., pp. 820–841). New York: Van Nostrand Reinhold.

KLINE, D. W., & SCHIEBER, F. (1985). Vision and aging. In J. E. Birren & K. W. Schaie (Eds.), *Handbook of the psychology of aging* (2nd ed., pp. 296–331). New York: Van Nostrand Reinhold.

KLINE, R. B., CANTER, W. A., & ROBIN, A. (1987). Parameters of teenage alcohol use: A path analytic conceptual model. *Journal of Consulting and Clinical Psychology, 55,* 521–528.

KNOWLES, M. (1984). *The adult learner: A neglected species.* Houston, TX: Gulf.

KOENIG, H. G., GEORGE, L. K., & SIEGLER, I. C. (1988). The use of religion and other emotion-regulating coping strategies among older adults. *Gerontologist, 28,* 303–310.

KOFF, T. H. (1981). *Hospice: A caring community.* Cambridge, MA: Winthrop.

KOGAN, N. (1983). Stylistic variation in childhood and adolescence: Creativity, metaphor, and cognitive style. In P. H. Mussen (Ed.), *Handbook of child psychology* (Vol. 3, pp. 630–706). New York: Wiley.

KOHLBERG, L. (1969). Stage and sequence: The cognitive-developmental approach to socialization. In D. Goslin (Ed.), *Handbook of socialization theory and research* (pp. 347–480). Chicago: Rand McNally.

KOHLBERG, L. (1984). *Essays on moral development: Vol. II. The psychology of moral development.* San Francisco: Harper & Row.

KOHLBERG, L. (1987). The development of moral judgment and moral action. In L. Kohlberg (Ed.), *Child psychology and childhood education: A cognitive-developmental view* (pp. 259–328). New York: Longman.

KOLATA, G. (1990a). *The baby doctors.* New York: Delacorte.

KOLATA, G. (1990b, February 6). Rush is on to capitalize on test for gene causing cystic fibrosis. *New York Times,* p. C3.

KOLB, B. (1989). Brain development, plasticity, and behavior. *American Psychologist, 44,* 1203–1212.

KOPP, C. B., & KRAKOW, J. B. (1982). *The child: Development in a social context.* Reading, MA: Addison-Wesley.

KORNHABER, A. (1985). Grandparenthood and the "new social contract." In V. L. Bengtson & J. F. Robertson (Eds.), *Grandparenthood* (pp. 159–172). Newbury Park, CA: Sage.

KOTRE, J. (1984). *Outliving the self: Generativity and the interpretation of lives.* Baltimore, MD: Johns Hopkins University Press.

KOWALSKI, R. M. (1992). Nonverbal behaviors and perceptions of sexual intentions: Effects of sexual connotativeness, verbal response, and rape outcome. *Basic and Applied Social Psychology, 13,* 427–445.

KRAM, K. E. (1980). *Mentoring processes at work: Developmental relationships in managerial careers.* Unpublished doctoral dissertation, Yale University, New Haven, CT.

KRAM, K. E. (1985). *Mentoring at work: Developmental relationships in organizational life.* Glenview, IL: Scott, Foresman.

KRAMER, D. A. (1989). A developmental framework for understanding conflict resolution processes. In J. D. Sinnott (Ed.), *Everyday problem solving: Theory and applications* (pp. 138–152). New York: Praeger.

KRAMER, D. A. (1990). Conceptualizing wisdom: The primacy of affect-cognition relations. In R. J. Sternberg (Ed.), *Wisdom: Its nature, origins, and development* (pp. 279–313). Cambridge, UK: Cambridge University Press.

KRAMER, D. A., ANGIULD, N., CRISAFI, L., & LEVINE, C. (1991, August). *Cognitive processes in real-life conflict resolution.* Paper presented at the annual meeting of the American Psychological Association, San Francisco.

KRAMER, D. A., & BACELAR, W. T. (1994). The educated adult in today's world: Wisdom and the mature learner. In J. D. Sinnott (Ed.), *Interdisciplinary handbook of adult lifespan learning* (pp. 31–50). Westport, CT: Greenwood Press.

KRAUSE, N. (1991). Stress and inoculation from close ties in later life. *Journal of Gerontology: Social Sciences, 46,* 183–194.

KROUT, J. A. (1988). Rural versus urban differences in elderly parents' contacts with their children. *Gerontologist, 28,* 198–203.

KÜBLER-ROSS, E. (1969). *On death and dying.* New York: Macmillan.

KÜBLER-ROSS, E. (1974). *Questions and answers on death and dying.* New York: Macmillan.

KURDEK, L. A. (1991a). Predictors of increases in marital distress in newlywed couples: A 3-year prospective longitudinal study. *Developmental Psychology, 27,* 627–636.

KURDEK, L. A. (1991b). The relations between reported well-being and divorce history, availability of a proximate adult, and gender. *Journal of Marriage and the Family, 53,* 71–78.

KURTZ, P. D., GAUDIN, J. M., WODARSKI, J. S., & HOWING, P. T. (1993). Maltreatment and the school-age child: School performance consequences. *Child Abuse and Neglect, 17,* 581–589.

LABOUVIE-VIEF, G. (1985). Intelligence and cognition. In J. E. Birren & K. W. Schaie (Eds.), *Handbook of the psychology of aging* (2nd ed., pp. 500–530). New York: Van Nostrand Reinhold.

LACHMAN, M. E. (1985). Personal efficacy in middle and old age: Differential and normative patterns of change. In G. H. Elder, Jr. (Ed.), *Life-course dynamics: Trajectories and transitions, 1968–1980* (pp. 188–213). Ithaca, NY: Cornell University Press.

LACROIX, A. Z., LANG, J., SCHERR, P., WALLACE, R. B., CORNONI-HUNTLEY, J., BERKMAN, L., CURB, J. D., EVANS, D., & HENNEKENS, C. H. (1991). Smoking and mortality among older men and women in three communities. *New England Journal of Medicine, 324,* 1619–1625.

LAFRENIERE, P., STRAYER, F. F., & GAUTHIER, R. (1984). The emergence of same-sex affiliative preferences among preschool peers: A developmental/ethnological perspective. *Child Development, 55,* 1958–1965.

LAJER, M. (1982). Unemployment and hospitalization among bricklayers. *Scandinavian Journal of Social Medicine, 10,* 3–10.

LAMB, M. E., & OPPENHEIM, D. (1989). Fatherhood and father-child relationships: Five years of research. In S. H. Cath, A. Gurwitt, & L. Gunsberg (Eds.), *Fathers and their families.* Hillsdale, NJ: Erlbaum.

LAMB, M. E., STERNBERG, K. J., & PRODROMIDIS, M. (1992). Nonmaternal care and the security of infant-mother attachment: A reanalysis of the data. *Infant Behavior and Development, 15,* 71–83.

LAMBORN, S. D., MOUNTS, N. S., STEINBERG, L., & DORNBUSCH, S. M. (1991). Patterns of competence and adjustment among adolescents from authoritative, authoritarian, indulgent, and neglectful families. *Child Development, 62,* 1049–1065.

LANGER, E. J. (1985). Playing the middle against both ends: The usefulness of older adult cognitive activity as a model for cognitive activity in childhood and old age. In S. Yussen (Ed.), *The growth of reflection in children* (pp. 267–285). New York: Academic Press.

LANGER, E. J., & RODIN, J. (1976). The effects of choice and enhanced personal responsibility for the aged: A field experiment in an institutional setting. *Journal of Personality and Social Psychology, 34,* 191–198.

LAROSSA, R. (1988). Fatherhood and social change. *Family Relations, 34,* 451–457.

LARSON, R. W., RAFFAELLI, M., RICHARDS, M. H., HAM, M., & JEWELL, L. (1990). Ecology of depression in late childhood and early adolescence: A profile of daily states and activities. *Journal of Abnormal Psychology, 99,* 92–102.

LARUE, A., DESSONVILLE, C., & JARVIK, L. F. (1985). Aging and mental disorders. In J. E. Birren & K. W. Schaie (Eds.), *Handbook of the psychology of aging* (2nd ed., pp. 664–702). New York: Van Nostrand Reinhold.

LATACK, J. C. (1984). Career transitions within organizations: An exploratory study of work, nonwork, and coping strategies. *Organizational Behavior and Human Performance, 34,* 296–322.

LAUER, J., & LAUER, R. (1985). Marriages made to last. *Psychology Today, 19,* 22–26.

LAURSEN, B., & COLLINS, W. A. (1994). Interpersonal conflict during adolescence. *Psychological Bulletin, 115,* 197–209.

LAWTON, M. P. (1982). Competence, environmental press, and the adaptation of old people. In M. P. Lawton, P. G. Windley, & T. O. Byerts (Eds.), *Aging and the environment: Theoretical approaches* (pp. 33–59). New York: Springer-Verlag.

LAWTON, M. P. (1984). The varieties of well-being. In C. Z. Malatesta & C. E. Izard (Eds.), *Emotion in adult development* (pp. 67–84). Newbury Park, CA: Sage.

LAWTON, M. P. (1989). Environmental proactivity in older people. In V. L. Bengtson & K. W. Schaie (Eds.), *The course of later life: Research and reflections* (pp. 15–23). New York: Springer.

LAWTON, M. P., MOSS, M. S., & FULCOMER, M. (1986–1987). Objective and subjective uses of time by older people. *International Journal of Aging and Human Development, 24,* 171–188.

LAWTON, M. P., & NAHEMOW, L. (1973). Ecology of the aging process. In C. Eisdorfer & M. P. Lawton (Eds.), *The psychology of adult development and aging* (pp. 619–674). Washington, DC: American Psychological Association.

LAZARUS, R. S., & FOLKMAN, S. (1984). *Stress, appraisal, and coping.* New York: Springer.

LEAHY, J. M. (1993). A comparison of depression in women bereaved of a spouse, a child, or a parent. *Omega, 26,* 207–217.

LEANA, C. R., & FELDMAN, D. C. (1991). Gender differences in responses to unemployment. *Journal of Vocational Behavior, 38,* 65–77.

LEANA, C. R., & FELDMAN, D. C. (1992). *Coping with job loss.* New York: Lexington Books.

LEE, D. J., & MARKIDES, K. S. (1990). Activity and aging among persons over an eight year period. *Journal of Gerontology: Social Sciences, 45,* 39–42.

LEE, G. R. (1985). Kinship and social support in the elderly: The case of the United States. *Aging and Society, 5,* 19–38.

LEE, G. R. (1988). Marital satisfaction in later life: The effects of nonmarital roles. *Journal of Marriage and the Family, 50,* 775–783.

LEE, G. R., SECCOMBE, K., & SHEHAN, C. L. (1991). Marital status and personal happiness: An analysis of trend data. *Journal of Marriage and the Family, 53,* 839–844.

LEE, T. R., MANCINI, J. A., & MAXWELL, J. W. (1990). Sibling relationships in adulthood: Contact patterns and motivation. *Journal of Marriage and the Family, 52,* 431–440.

LEICHTMAN, M. D., & CECI, S. L. (1995). The effects of stereotypes and suggestions on preschoolers' reports. *Developmental Psychology, 31,* 568–578.

LEMARE, L. J., & RUBIN, K. H. (1987). Perspective taking and peer interaction: Structural and developmental analyses. *Child Development, 58,* 306–315.

LEMIRE, R. J., LOESER, J. D., LEECH, R. W., & ALVORD, E. C., JR. (1975). *Normal and abnormal development of the nervous system.* Philadelphia, PA: Lippincott.

LENNON, R., EISENBERG, N., & CARROLL, J. (1986). The relation between nonverbal indices of empathy and preschoolers' prosocial behavior. *Journal of Applied Developmental Psychology, 7,* 219–224.

LENTZNER, H. R., PAMUK, E. R., RHODENHISER, R. R., & POWELL-GRINER, E. (1992). The quality of life in the year before death. *American Journal of Public Health, 82,* 1093–1098.

LEON, G. R. & DINKLAGE, D. (1989). Obesity and anorexia nervosa. In T. H. Ollendick & M. Hersen (Eds.), *Handbook of child psychopathology* (2nd ed.). New York: Plenum.

LEON, G. R., GILLUM, B., GILLUM, R., & GOUZE, M. (1979). Personality stability and change over a 30-year period: Middle to old age. *Journal of Consulting and Clinical Psychology, 47,* 517–524.

LEPPER, M. R., & GURTNER, J. (1989). Children and computers. *American Psychologist, 44,* 170–178.

LEVENSON, R. W., CARSTENSEN, L. L., & GOTTMAN, J. M. (1993). Long-term marriage: Age, gender, and satisfaction. *Psychology and Aging, 8,* 301–313.

LEVIN, J. S., TAYLOR, R. J., & CHATTERS, L. M. (1994). Race and gender differences in religiosity among older adults: Findings from four national surveys. *Journal of Gerontology: Social Sciences, 49,* 137–145.

LEVINSON, D. (1988). Family violence in cross cultural perspective. In V. B. Van Hasselt, R. L. Morrison, A. S. Bellack, & M. Hersen (Eds.), *Handbook of family violence* (pp. 435–456). New York: Plenum.

LEVINSON, D. J., DARROW, C., KLINE, E., LEVINSON, M., & MCKEE, B. (1978). *The seasons of a man's life.* New York: Knopf.

LEVITT, A. G., & UTMAN, J. A. (1992). From babbling towards the sound systems of English and French: A longitudinal two-case study. *Journal of Child Language, 19,* 19–49.

LEVITT, M. J., GUACCI-FRANCO, N., & LEVITT, J. L. (1993a). Convoys of social support in childhood and early adolescence: Structure and function. *Developmental Psychology, 29,* 811–818.

LEVITT, M. J., WEBER, R. A., & GUACCI, N. (1993b). Convoys of social support: An intergenerational analysis. *Psychology and Aging, 8,* 323–326.

LEVY, G. D. (1989). Developmental and individual differences in preschoolers' recognition memories: The influences of gender schematization and verbal labeling of information. *Sex Roles, 21,* 305–324.

LEVY, J. (1976). A review of evidence for a genetic component in the determination of handedness. *Behavior Genetics, 6,* 429–453.

LEWIN, T. (1992, Dec. 4). Baltimore school clinics to offer birth control by surgical implant. *New York Times,* pp. A1, A28.

LEWINSOHN, P. (1974). A behavioral approach to depression. In R. J. Friedman & M. M. Katz (Eds.), *The psychology of depression: Contemporary theory and research.* Washington, DC: V. H. Winston.

LEWINSOHN, P. M. (1975). The behavioral study and treatment of depression. In M. Hersen, R. M. Eisler, & P. M. Miller (Eds.), *Progress in behavior modification* (Vol. 1, pp. 19–64). New York: Academic Press.

LIBEN, L. S., & SIGNORELLA, M. L. (1993). Gender-schematic processing in children: The role of initial interpretations of stimuli. *Developmental Psychology, 29,* 141–149.

LIEBERT, R. M., & SPRAFKIN, J. (1988). *The early window: Effects of television on children and youth.* New York: Pergamon.

LIEBERT, R. M., SPRAFKIN, J. N., & POULOS, R. W. (1975). Selling cooperation to children. In W. S. Hale (Ed.), *Proceedings of the 20th annual conference of the Advertising Research Foundation* (pp. 54–57). New York: Advertising Research Foundation.

LIEBOWITZ, M. (1983). *The chemistry of love.* Boston: Little, Brown.

LIN, C. C., & FU, V. R. (1990). A comparison of childrearing practices among Chinese, immigrant Chinese, and Caucasian-American parents. *Child Development, 61,* 429–433.

LINDEN, M. G., BENDER, B. G., HARMON, R. J., MRAZEK, D. A., & ROBINSON, A. (1988). 47, XXX: What is the prognosis? *Pediatrics, 82,* 619–630.

LINDSAY, P. (1984). High school size, participation in activities, and young adult social participation: Some enduring effects of schooling. *Educational Evaluation and Policy Analysis, 6,* 73–83.

LINN, M. C., & PETERSON, A. C. (1985). Emergence and characterization of sex differences in spatial ability: A meta-analysis. *Child Development, 56,* 1479–1498.

LIST, N. D. (1988). Cancer screening in the elderly. In R. Chernoff & D. A. Lipschitz (Eds.), *Health promotion and disease prevention in the elderly* (pp. 113–129). New York: Raven Press.

LOGAN, R. D. (1986). A reconceptualization of Erikson's theory: The repetition of existential and instrumental themes. *Human Development, 29,* 125–136.

LOMRANZ, J., BERGMAN, S., EYAL, N., & SHMOTKIN, D. (1988). Indoor and outdoor activities of aged women and men as related to depression and well-being. *International Journal of Aging and Human Development, 26,* 303–314.

LONGINO, C. F. (1982). American retirement communities and residential relocation. In M. A. Warnes (Ed.), *Geographical perspectives on the elderly* (pp. 239–262). London, UK: Wiley.

LOURENCO, O. M. (1993). Toward a Piagetian explanation of the development of prosocial behaviour in children: The force of negational thinking. *British Journal of Developmental Psychology, 11,* 91–106.

LOVETT, M. W., BORDEN, S. L., DELUCA, T., LACERENZA, L., BENSON, N. J., & BRACKSTONE, D. (1994). Treating the core deficits of developmental dyslexia: Evidence of transfer of learning after phonologically- and strategy-based reading programs. *Developmental Psychology, 30,* 805–822.

LOWENTHAL, M., THURNHER, M., & CHIRIBOGA, D. (1975). *Four stages of life.* San Francisco: Jossey-Bass.

LÖWIK, M. R. H., WEDEL, M., KOK, F. J., ODINK, J., WESTENBRINK, S., & MEULMEESTER, J. F. (1991). Nutrition and serum cholesterol levels among elderly men and women (Dutch nutrition surveillance system). *Journal of Gerontology: Medical Sciences, 46,* 23–28.

LUNDGREN, B. K., STEEN, G. B., & ISAKSSON, B. (1987). Dietary habits in 70- and 75-year-old males and females: Longitudinal and cohort data from a population study. *Näringsforskning.*

LUNDIN, T. (1984). Morbidity following sudden and unexpected bereavement. *British Journal of Psychiatry, 144,* 84–88.

LUTHAR, S. S., ZIGLER, E., & GOLDSTEIN, D. (1992). Psychosocial adjustment among intellectually gifted adolescents: The role of cognitive-developmental and experiential factors. *Journal of Child Psychology and Psychiatry and Allied Disciplines, 33,* 361–373.

LYONS-RUTH, K., ALPERN, L., & REPACHOLI, B. (1993). Disorganized infant attachment classification and maternal psychosocial problems as predictors of hostile-aggressive behavior in the preschool classroom. *Child Development, 64,* 572–585.

LYTTON, H. (1980). *Parent-child interaction: The socialization process observed in twin and singleton families.* New York: Plenum Press.

LYTTON, H., & ROMNEY, D. M. (1991). Parents' differential socialization of boys and girls: A meta-analysis. *Psychological Bulletin, 109,* 267–296.

MACCOBY, E. E. (1980). *Social development: Psychological growth and the parent-child relationship.* San Diego, CA: Harcourt Brace Jovanovich.

MACCOBY, E. E. (1990). Gender and relationships: A developmental account. *American Psychologist, 45,* 513–520.

MACCOBY, E. E., BUCHANON, C. M., MNOOKIN, R. H., & DORNBUSCH, S. M. (1993). Postdivorce roles of mothers and fathers in the lives of their children. *Journal of Family Psychology, 7,* 24–38.

MACCOBY, E. E., DEPNER, C. E., & MNOOKIN, R. H. (1990). Coparenting in the second year after divorce. *Journal of Marriage and the Family, 52,* 141–155.

MACCOBY, E. E., & JACKLIN, C. N. (1974). *The psychology of sex differences.* Stanford, CA: Stanford University Press.

MACCOBY, E. E., & MARTIN, J. A. (1983). Socialization in the context of the family: Parent-child interaction. In P. H. Mussen (Ed.), *Handbook of child psychology* (Vol. 4). New York: Wiley.

MACKLIN, E. D. (1988). Heterosexual couples who cohabit nonmaritally: Some common problems and issues. In C. S. Chilman, E. W. Nunnally, & F. M. Cox (Eds.), *Variant family forms* (pp. 56–72). Newbury Park, CA: Sage.

MADDOX, G. L., & CAMPBELL, R. T. (1985). Scope, concepts, and methods in the study of aging. In R. H. Binstock & E. Shanas (Eds.), *Handbook of aging and the social sciences* (2nd ed., pp. 3–31). New York: Van Nostrand Reinhold.

MAIN, M., & CASSIDY, J. (1988). Categories of response to reunion with the parent at age 6: Predictable from infant attachment classifications and stable over a 1-month period. *Developmental Psychology, 24,* 415–426.

MALINAK, D. P., HOYT, M. F., & PATTERSON, V. (1979). Adults' reactions to the death of a parent: A preliminary study. *American Journal of Psychiatry, 136,* 1152–1156.

MALINOSKY-RUMMELL, R., & HANSEN, D. J. (1993). Long-term consequences of childhood physical abuse. *Psychological Bulletin, 114,* 68–79.

MARCIA, J. E. (1980). Identity in adolescence. In J. Adelson (Ed.), *Handbook of adolescent psychology.* New York: Wiley.

MARCIA, J. E. (1991). Identity and self-development. In R. M. Lerner, A. C. Petersen, & J. Brooks-Gunn (Eds.), *Encyclopedia of adolescence* (Vol. 1). New York: Garland.

MARCIANO, T. D. (1985). Homosexual marriage and parenthood should not be allowed. In H. Feldman & M. Feldman (Eds.), *Current controversies in marriage and family* (pp. 293–302). Newbury Park, CA: Sage.

MARGOLIN, L., & WHITE, J. (1987). The continuing role of physical attractiveness in marriage. *Journal of Marriage and the Family, 49,* 21–27.

MARKOVITS, H., & VACHON, R. (1989). Reasoning with contrary-to-fact propositions. *Journal of Experimental Child Psychology, 47,* 398–412.

MARKUS, H., & NURIUS, P. (1986). Possible selves. *American Psychologist, 41,* 954–969.

MARQUIS, K. S., & DETWEILER, R. A. (1985). Does adopted mean different? An attributional analysis. *Journal of Personality and Social Psychology, 48,* 1054–1066.

MARSH, H. W. (1991). Employment during high school: Character building or a subversion of academic goals? *Sociology of Education, 64,* 172–189.

MARSHALL, V. W. (1994). Sociology, psychology, and the theoretical legacy of the Kansas City studies. *Gerontologist, 34,* 768–774.

MARSHALL, W. A., & TANNER, J. M. (1970). Variations in the pattern of pubertal changes in boys. *Archives of Disease in Childhood, 45,* 22.

MARSIGLIO, W. (1993). Attitudes toward homosexual activity and gay friends: A national survey of heterosexual 15- to 19-year old males. *Journal of Sex Research, 30,* 12–17.

MARTIN, C. L., & HALVERSON, C. F. (1981). A schematic processing model of sex typing and stereotyping in children. *Child Development, 52,* 1121.

MARTIN, C. L., & HALVERSON, C. F. (1987). The roles of cognition in sex roles and sex typing. In D. B. Carter (Ed.), *Current conceptions of sex roles and sex typing: Theory and research.* New York: Praeger.

MARTIN, C. L., & LITTLE, J. K. (1990). The relation of gender understandings to children's sex-typed preferences and gender stereotypes. *Child Development, 61,* 1427–1439.

MARTIN, M. A. (1990). The homeless elderly: No room at the end. In Z. Harel, P. Ehrlich, & R. Hubbard (Eds.), *The vulnerable aged* (pp. 149–166). New York: Springer.

MARTIN, T. R., & BRACKEN, M. B. (1986). Association of low birth weight with passive smoke exposure in pregnancy. *American Journal of Epidemiology, 124,* 633–642.

MARTORELL, R. MENDOZA, F., & CASTILLO, R. (1988). Poverty and stature in children. In J. C. Waterlow (Ed.), *Linear growth retardation in less developed countries.* New York: Raven.

MASHETER, C. (1991). Postdivorce relationships between ex-spouses: The roles of attachment and interpersonal conflict. *Journal of Marriage and the Family, 53,* 103–110.

MASLOW, A. H. (1968). *Toward a psychology of being* (2nd ed.). Princeton, NJ: Van Nostrand.

MATSUI, T., IKEDA, H., & OHNISHI, R. (1989). Relation of sex-typed socializations to career self-efficacy expectations of college students. *Journal of Vocational Behavior, 35,* 1–16.

MATTHEWS, A. M., & BROWN, K. H. (1987). Retirement as a critical life event: The differential experiences of men and women. *Research on Aging, 9,* 548–571.

MATTHEWS, K., WING, R., KULLER, L., MEILAHN, E., KELSEY, S., COSTELLO, E., & CAGGIULA, A. (1990). Influences of natural menopause on psychological characteristics and symptoms of middle-aged healthy women. *Journal of Consulting and Clinical Psychology, 58,* 345–351.

MATTHEWS, R., & MATTHEWS, A. M. (1986). Infertility and involuntary childlessness: The transition to nonparenthood. *Journal of Marriage and the Family, 48,* 641–649.

MATULA, K. E., HUSTON, T. L., GROTEVANT, H. D., & ZAMUTT, A. (1992). Identity and dating commitment among women and men in college. *Journal of Youth and Adolescence, 21,* 339–356.

MAURER, D., & ADAMS, R. J. (1987). Emergence of the ability to discriminate a blue from gray at one month of age. *Journal of Experimental Child Psychology, 44,* 147–156.

MAYO CLINIC. (1992). *Mayo Clinic family health book* (Interactive edition). Rochester, MN: Mayo Foundation for Medical Education and Research. (CD ROM published by Interactive Ventures, Inc.)

MCCALL, R. B. (1979). *Infants.* Cambridge, MA: Harvard University Press.

MCCLOSKEY, L. A., & COLEMAN, L. M. (1992). Difference without dominance: Children's talk in mixed- and same-sex dyads. *Sex Roles, 27,* 241–257.

MCCORD, C., & FREEMAN, H. P. (1990). Excess mortality in Harlem. *New England Journal of Medicine, 322,* 173–177.

MCCORMICK, C. M., & MAURER, D. M. (1988). Unimanual hand preferences in 6-month-olds: Consistency and relation to familial-handedness. *Infant Behavior and Development, 11,* 21–29.

MCDOWD, J. M., & CRAIK, F. I. M. (1988). Effects of aging and task difficulty on divided attention performance. *Journal of Experimental Psychology: Human Perception and Performance, 14,* 267–280.

MCGEE, R., STANTON, W. R., & SEARS, M. R. (1993). Allergic disorders and attention deficit disorder in children. *Journal of Abnormal Child Psychology, 21,* 79–88.

MCGEE, R., WILLIAMS, S., & FEEHAN, M. (1992). Attention deficit disorder and age of onset of problem behaviors. *Journal of Abnormal Child Psychology, 20,* 487–502.

MCGHEE, P. E. (1976). Children's appreciation of humor: A test of the cognitive congruency principle. *Child Development, 47,* 420–426.

MCGILLY, K., & SIEGLER, R. S. (1990). Conditional reasoning, representation, and level of abstraction. *Developmental Psychology, 26,* 931–941.

MCGIVERN, J. E., LEVIN, J. R., PRESSLEY, M., & GHATALA, E. S. (1990). A developmental study of memory monitoring and strategy selection. *Contemporary Educational Psychology, 15,* 103–115.

MCGUIRE, J. M., NORLANDER, K. A., & SHAW, S. F. (1990). Postsecondary education for students with learning disabilities: Forecasting challenges for the future. *Learning Disabilities Focus, 5,* 69–74.

MCGUIRE, L. C., & CAVANAUGH, J. C. (1992, August). *Objective measures versus spouses' perceptions of cognitive status in dementia patients.* Paper presented at the biennial Cognitive Aging Conference, Atlanta.

MCMANUS, I. C., SIK, G., COLE, D. R., KLOSS, J., MELLON, A. F., & WONG, J. (1988). The development of handedness in children. *British Journal of Developmental Psychology, 6,* 257–273.

MCNALLY, S., EISENBERG, N., & HARRIS, J. D. (1991). Consistency and change in maternal child-rearing practices and values: A longitudinal study. *Child Development, 62,* 190–198.

MCNAUGHTON, S., & LEYLAND, J. (1990). The shifting focus of maternal tutoring across different difficulty levels on a problem solving task. *British Journal of Developmental Psychology, 8,* 147–155.

MCNEAL, E. T. & CIMBOLIC, P. (1986). Antidepressants and biochemical theories of depression. *Psychological Bulletin, 99,* 361–374.

MEIER, D. E. (1988). Skeletal aging. In B. Kent & R. Butler (Eds.), *Human aging research: Concepts and techniques* (pp. 221–244). New York: Raven Press.

MEILMAN, P. W. (1979). Cross-sectional age changes in ego identity status during adolescence. *Developmental Psychology, 15,* 230–231.

MENAGHAN, E. G., & LIEBERMAN, M. A. (1986). Changes in depression following divorce: A panel study. *Journal of Marriage and the Family, 48,* 319–328.

MERVIS, C. B., & JOHNSON, K. E. (1991). Acquisition of the plural morpheme: A case study. *Developmental Psychology, 27,* 222–235.

MEYER, B. J. F., & RICE, G. E. (1989). Prose processing in adulthood: The text, the reader, and the task. In L. W. Poon, D. C. Rubin, & B. Wilson (Eds.), *Everyday cognition in adulthood and late life* (pp. 157–194). Cambridge, UK: Cambridge University Press.

MILLER, J. G., & BERSOFF, D. M. (1992). Culture and moral judgment: How are conflicts between justice and interpersonal responsibilities resolved? *Journal of Personality and Social Psychology, 62,* 541–554.

MILLER, S. S., & CAVANAUGH, J. C. (1990). The meaning of grandparenthood and its relationship to demographic, relationship, and social participation variables. *Journals of Gerontology: Psychological Sciences, 45,* 244–246.

MILLS, R. S. L., & GRUSEC, J. E. (1989). Cognitive, affective, and behavioral consequences of praising altruism. *Merrill-Palmer Quarterly, 35,* 299–326.

MINUCHIN, P. P., & SHAPIRO, E. K. (1983). The school as a context for social development. In E. M. Hetherington (Ed.), *Handbook of child psychology: Vol. 4. Socialization, personality, and social development* (4th ed.). New York: Wiley.

MIURA, I. T., KIM, C. C., CHANG, C. M., & OKAMOTO, Y. (1988). Effects of language characteristics on children's cognitive representation of number: Cross-national comparisons. *Child Development, 59,* 1445–1450.

MIZE, J., & LADD, G. W. (1990). A cognitive social-learning approach to social skill training with low-status preschool children. *Developmental Psychology, 26,* 388–397.

MOATS, L. C., & LYON, G. R. (1993). Learning disabilities in the United States: Advocacy, science, and the future of the field. *Journal of Learning Disabilities, 26,* 282–294.

MOBILY, K. E., LEMKE, J. H., & GISIN, G. J. (1991). The idea of leisure repertoire. *Journal of Applied Gerontology, 10,* 208–223.

MODELL, J. (1989). *Into one's own: From youth to adulthood in the United States, 1920–1975.* New York: Holt, Rinehart, & Winston.

MOLFESE, D. L., & BURGER-JUDISCH, L. M. (1991). Dynamic temporal-spatial allocation of resources in the human brain: An alternative to the static view of hemisphere differences. In F. L. Ketterle (Ed.), *Cerebral laterality: Theory and research. The Toledo symposium.* Hillsdale, NJ: Erlbaum.

MOLLER, L. C., HYMEL, S., & RUBIN, K. H. (1992). Sex typing in play and popularity in middle childhood. *Sex Roles, 26,* 331–353.

MONCZUNSKI, J. (1991). That incurable disease. *Notre Dame Magazine, 20*(1), 37.

MONEY, J. (1987). Sin, sickness, or status? Homosexual gender identity and psychoneuroendocrinology. *American Psychologist, 42,* 384–389.

MONTGOMERY, G. T. (1992). Comfort with acculturation status among students from south Texas. *Hispanic Journal of Behavioral Sciences, 14,* 201–223.

MOODY, R. A., JR. (1975). *Life after life.* Atlanta, GA: Mockingbird.

MOODY, R. A., JR. (1977). *Reflections on life after life.* New York: Bantam.

MOODY, R. A., JR. (1988). *The light beyond.* New York: Bantam.

MOON, A., & WILLIAMS, O. (1993). Perceptions of elder abuse and help-seeking patterns among African-American, Caucasian American, and Korean-American elderly women. *Gerontologist, 33,* 386–395.

MOORE, B. S., UNDERWOOD, B., & ROSENHAN, D. L. (1973). Affect and altruism. *Developmental Review, 8,* 99–104.

MOORE, K. L., & PERSAUD, T. V. N. (1993). *Before we are born* (4th ed.). Philadelphia: Saunders.

MORGAN, B., & GIBSON, K. R. (1991). Nutritional and environmental interactions in brain development. In K. R. Gibson and A. C. Peterson (Eds.), *Brain maturation and cognitive development: Comparative and crosscultural perspectives.* New York: Aldine De Gruyter.

MORGANE, P. J., AUSTIN-LAFRANCE, R., BRONZINO, J. D., TONKISS, J., DIAZ-CINTRA, S., CINTRA, L., KEMPER, T., & GALLER, J. R. (1993). Prenatal malnutrition and development of the brain. *Neuroscience and Biobehavioral Reviews, 17,* 91–128.

MORISON, R., & MASTEN, A. S. (1991). Peer reputation in middle childhood as a predictor of adaptation in adolescence: A seven-year follow-up. *Child Development, 62,* 991–1007.

MORRIS, J. N., & SHERWOOD, S. (1984). Informal support resources for vulnerable elderly persons: Can they be counted on, why do they work? *International Journal of Aging and Human Development, 18,* 1–17.

MORRISON, A. M., WHITE, R. P., VAN VELSOR, E., & THE CENTER FOR CREATIVE LEADERSHIP. (1992). *Breaking the glass ceiling: Can women reach the top of America's largest corporations?* (Updated ed.). Reading, MA: Addison-Wesley.

MORRONGIELLO, B. A., & FENWICK, K. D. (1991). Infants' coordination of auditory and visual depth information. *Journal of Experimental Child Psychology, 52,* 277–296.

MORRONGIELLO, B. A., FENWICK, K. D., & CHANCE, G. (1990). Sound localization acuity in very young infants: An observer-based testing procedure. *Developmental Psychology, 26,* 75–84.

MORROW, P. C., & MCELROY, J. C. (1987). Work commitment and job satisfaction over three career stages. *Journal of Vocational Behavior, 30,* 330–346.

MORROW-HOWELL, N., & MUI, A. (1989). Elderly volunteers: Reasons for initiating and terminating service. *Journal of Gerontological Social Work, 13,* 21–34.

MORTIMER, J. T. (1991). Employment. In R. M. Lerner, A. C. Petersen, & J. Brooks-Gunn (Eds.), *Encyclopedia of adolescence* (Vol. 1). New York: Garland.

MORTIMER, J. T., FINCH, M. D., & KUMKA, D. (1982). Persistence and change in development: The multidimensional self-concept. In P. B. Baltes & O. G. Brim, Jr. (Eds.), *Life-span development and behavior* (Vol. 4, pp. 263–313). New York: Academic Press.

MUEHLENHARD, C. L. (1988). "Nice women" don't say yes and "Real men" don't say no: How miscommunication and the double standard can cause sexual problems. *Women and Therapy, 7,* 95–108.

MURPHY, C. (1986). Taste and smell in the elderly. In H. L. Meiselman & R. S. Rivlin (Eds.), *Clinical measurement of taste and smell* (pp. 343–371). New York: Macmillan.

MURPHY, S. (1988). Mental distress and recovery in a high-risk bereavement sample three years after untimely death. *Nursing Research, 37,* 30–35.

MURRELL, A. J., FRIEZE, I. H., & FROST, J. L. (1991). Aspiring to careers in male- and female-dominated professions: A study of black and white college women. *Psychology of Women Quarterly, 15,* 103–126.

MYERS, R. (1983). *D.E.S.: The bitter pill.* New York: Putnam.

NACHTIGALL, L. E., & NACHTIGALL, L. B. (1990). Protecting older women from their growing risk of cardiac disease. *Geriatrics, 45*(5), 24–34.

NATHANSON, C. A., & LORENZ, G. (1982). Women and health: The social dimension of biomedical data. In J. Z. Giele (Ed.), *Women in the middle years* (pp. 37–87). New York: Wiley.

NATIONAL AGING RESOURCE CENTER ON ELDER ABUSE. (1990). *Elder abuse and neglect: A synthesis of research.* Washington, DC: Author.

NATIONAL CENTER FOR EDUCATIONAL STATISTICS. (1991). *Preliminary data: Participation in adult education, 1991.* Washington, DC: Government Printing Office.

NATIONAL CENTER FOR EDUCATIONAL STATISTICS. (1993). *Preliminary data: Participation in adult education, 1993.* Washington, DC: Government Printing Office.

NATIONAL CENTER FOR HEALTH STATISTICS. (1993). *Vital statistics of the United States, 1989: Vol. II. Mortality, part A.* Washington DC: Public Health Service.

NATIONAL RESEARCH COUNCIL. (1987). *Risking the future: Adolescent sexuality, pregnancy, and childbearing* (Vol. 1). Washington, DC: National Academy Press.

NATIONAL RESEARCH COUNCIL (1989). *Recommended dietary allowances* (10th ed.). Washington, DC: National Academy Press.

NEISSER, U., & WINOGRAD, E. (EDS.). (1988). *Remembering reconsidered.* New York: Cambridge University Press.

NELSON, K. (1973). Structure and strategy in learning to talk. *Monographs of the Society for Research in Child Development, 38,* No. 149.

NEUGARTEN, B. L. (1969). Continuities and discontinuities of psychological issues into adult life. *Human Development, 12,* 121–130.

NEUGARTEN, B. L., & WEINSTEIN, K. K. (1964). The changing American grandparent. *Journal of Marriage and the Family, 26,* 299–304.

NEWCOMB, A. F., BUKOWSKI, W. M., & PATTEE, L. (1993). Children's peer relations: A meta-analytic review of popular, rejected, neglected, controversial, and average sociometric status. *Psychological Bulletin, 113,* 99–123.

NEWMAN, B. S., & MUZZONIGRO, P. G. (1993). The effects of traditional family values on the coming out process of gay male adolescents. *Adolescence, 28,* 213–226.

NIELSON, A. C. (1990). *Annual Nielsen report on television: 1990.* New York: Nielson Media Research.

NOCK, S. L. (1981). Family life transitions: Longitudinal effects on family members. *Journal of Marriage and the Family, 43,* 703–714.

NOLEN-HOEKSEMA, S. (1988). Life-span views on depression. In P. B. Baltes & R. M. Lerner (Eds.), *Life-span development and behavior* (Vol. 9, pp. 203–241). Hillsdale, NJ: Erlbaum.

NOLEN-HOEKSEMA, S., & GIRGUS, J. S. (1994). The emergence of gender differences in depression during adolescence. *Psychological Bulletin, 115,* 424–443.

NORBECK, J. S., & TILDEN, V. P. (1983). Life stress, social support, and emotional disequilibrium in complications of pregnancy: A prospective, multivariate study. *Journal of Health and Social Behavior, 24,* 30–46.

NORRIS, F. N., & MURRELL, S. A. (1987). Older adult family stress and adaptation before and after bereavement. *Journal of Gerontology, 42,* 606–612.

NORTON, A. J., & MOORMAN, J. E. (1987). Current trends in marriage and divorce among American women. *Journal of Marriage and the Family, 49,* 3–14.

NYDEGGER, C. N. (1986). Asymmetrical kin and the problematic son-in-law. In N. Datan, A. L. Greene, & H. W. Reese (Eds.), *Life-span developmental psychology: Intergenerational relations* (pp. 99–123). Hillsdale, NJ: Erlbaum.

OAKES, J., GAMORAN, A., & PAGE, R. N. (1992). Curriculum differentiation: Opportunities, outcomes, and meanings. In P. W. Jackson (Ed.), *Handbook of research on curriculum.* New York: Macmillan.

OCHS, A. L., NEWBERRY, J., LENHARDT, M. L., & HARKINS, S. W. (1985). Neural and vestibular aging associated with falls. In J. E. Birren & K. W. Schaie (Eds.), *Handbook of the psychology of aging* (2nd ed., pp. 378–399). New York: Van Nostrand Reinhold.

OFFER, D., OSTROV, E., HOWARD, K. I., & ATKINSON, R. (1988). *The teenage world: Adolescents' self-image in ten countries.* New York: Plenum.

OFFERMANN, L. R., & GROWING, M. K. (1990). Organizations of the future: Changes and challenges. *American Psychologist, 45,* 95–108.

OGLETREE, R. J. (1993). Sexual coercion experience and help-seeking behavior of college women. *Journal of American College Health, 41,* 149–153.

OKAGAKI, L., & STERNBERG, R. J. (1993). Parental beliefs and children's school performance. *Child Development, 64,* 36–56.

OKUN, M. A., STICK, W. A., HARING, M. J., & WITTER, R. A. (1984). The social activity/subjective well-being relation: A quantitative synthesis. *Research on Aging, 6,* 45–65.

OLDHAM, J. M., & LIEBERT, R. S. (EDS.). (1989). *The middle years.* New Haven, CT: Yale University Press.

O'LEARY, K. D. (1993). Through a psychological lens: Personality traits, personality disorders, and levels of violence. In R. J. Gelles & D. R. Loseke (Eds.), *Current controversies on family violence* (pp. 7–30). Newbury Park, CA: Sage.

O'LEARY, K. D., BARLING, J., ARIAS, I., ROSENBAUM, A., MALONE, J., & TYREE, A. (1989). Prevalence and stability of physical aggression between spouses: A longitudinal analysis. *Journal of Consulting and Clinical Psychology, 57,* 263–268.

OLIAN, J. D., CARROLL, S. J., GIANNANTONIA, C. M., & FEREN, D. B. (1988). What do proteges look for in a mentor? Results from three experimental studies. *Journal of Vocational Behavior, 33,* 15–37.

OLLER, D. K. (1986). Metaphonology and infant vocalizations. In B. Lindblom & R. Zetterstrom (Eds.), *Precursors of early speech.* Basingstoke, UK: Macmillan.

OLLER, D. K., & EILERS, R. E. (1988). The role of audition in infant babbling. *Child Development, 59,* 441–449.

OLSON, D. H., & MCCUBBIN, H. (1983). *Families: What makes them work.* Newbury Park, CA: Sage.

ORLICK, T., ZHOU, Q. Y., & PARTINGTON, J. (1990). Co-operation and conflict within Chinese and Canadian kindergarten settings. *Canadian Journal of Behavioural Science, 22,* 20–25.

ORWOLL, L., & PERLMUTTER, M. (1990). The study of wise persons: Integrating a personality perspective. R. J. Sternberg (Ed.), *Wisdom: Its nature, origins, and development* (pp. 160–177). Cambridge, UK: Cambridge University Press.

OSGOOD, N. J. (1992). *Suicide in later life.* Lexington, MA: Lexington Books.

OTTEN, M. W., TEUTSCH, S. M., WILLIAMSON, D. F., & MARKS, J. S. (1990). The effect of known risk factors on the excess mortality of black adults in the United States. *Journal of the American Medical Association, 263,* 845–850.

OVIATT, S. L. (1982). Inferring what words mean: Early development in infants' comprehension of common object names. *Child Development, 53,* 274–277.

OWEN, E. H. (1991). *Trends in academic progress.* Washington, DC: U.S. Government Printing Office.

OWEN, G., FULTON, R., & MARKUSEN, E. (1982). Death at a distance: A study of family survivors. *Omega, 13,* 191–225.

PACIFICI, C., & BEARISON, D. J. (1991). Development of children's self-regulations in idealized and mother-child interactions. *Cognitive Development, 6,* 261–277.

PACY, B. (1993, Spring). Plunged into flux. *Notre Dame Magazine, 22,* 34–38.

PADGHAM, J. J., & BLYTH, D. A. (1991). Dating during adolescence. In R. M. Lerner, A. C. Petersen, & J. Brooks-Gunn (Eds.), *Encyclopedia of adolescence* (Vol. 1). New York: Garland.

PALMORE, E. B. (1990). *Ageism: negative and positive.* New York: Springer.

PAPALIA, D. E., & OLDS, S. W. (1995). *Human development* (6th ed.). New York: McGraw-Hill.

PARAZZINI, F., LUCHINI, L., LA VECCHIA, C., & CROSIGNANI, P. G. (1993). Video display terminal use during pregnancy and reproductive outcome-a meta-analysis. *Journal of Epidemiology and Community Health, 47,* 265–268.

PARK, D. C., MORRELL, R. W., FRIESKE, D. A., BLACKBURN, A. B., & BIRCHMORE, D. (1991). Cognitive factors and the use of over-the-counter medication organizers by arthritis patients. *Human Factors, 33,* 57–67.

PARK, K. A., & WATERS, E. (1989). Security of attachment and preschool friendships. *Child Development, 60,* 1076–1081.

PARKE, R. D. (1990). In search of fathers: A narrative of an empirical journey. In I. Sigel & G. Brody (Eds.), *Methods of family research.* Hillsdale, NJ: Erlbaum.

PARKE, R. D., & BAHVNAGRI, N. P. (1989). Parents as managers of children's peer relationships. In D. Belle (Ed.), *Children's social networks and social supports.* New York: Wiley.

PARKE, R. D., & SLABY, R. G. (1983). The development of aggression. In E. M. Hetherington (Ed.), *Handbook of child psychology: Vol. 4. Socialization, personality, and social development* (4th ed.). New York: Wiley.

PARKER, J. G., & ASHER, S. R. (1987). Peer relations and later personal adjustment: Are low-accepted children at risk? *Psychological Bulletin, 102,* 357–389.

PARKES, C. M. (1972). *Bereavement.* New York: International Universities Press.

PARROT, A., & ELLIS, M. J. (1985). Homosexuals should be allowed to marry and adopt or rear children. In H. Feldman & M. Feldman (Eds.), *Current controversies in marriage and family* (pp. 303–312). Newbury Park, CA: Sage.

PARTEN, M. (1932). Social participation among preschool children. *Journal of Abnormal and Social Psychology, 27,* 243–269.

PASCUAL-LEONE, J. (1990). An essay on wisdom: Toward organismic processes that make it possible. In R. J. Sternberg (Ed.), *Wisdom: Its nature, origins, and development* (pp. 244–278). Cambridge, UK: Cambridge University Press.

PASLEY, K., & IHINGER-TALLMAN, M. (1987). *Remarriage and stepparenting.* New York: Guilford.

PATTERSON, C. J. (1992). Children of lesbian and gay parents. *Child Development, 63,* 1025–1042.

PATTERSON, G. R., DEVARYSHE, B. D., & RAMSEY, E. (1989). A developmental perspective on antisocial behavior. *American Psychologist, 44,* 329–335.

PATTERSON, S. J., SOCHTING, I., & MARCIA, L. E. (1992). The inner space and beyond: Women and identity. In G. R. Adams, T. P. Gullotta, & R. Montemayor (Eds.), *Adolescent identity formation* (Advances in adolescent development, Vol. 4, pp.). Newbury Park, CA: Sage.

PATTISON, E. M. (ED.). (1977). *The experience of dying.* Englewood Cliffs, NJ: Prentice-Hall.

PEARLIN, L. I., & JOHNSON, J. (1977). Marital status, life strains, and depression. *American Sociological Review, 42,* 704–715.

PEGG, J. E., WERKER, J. F., & MCLEOD, P. J. (1992). Preference for infant-directed over adult-directed speech: Evidence from 7-week-old infants. *Infant Behavior and Development, 15,* 325–345.

PELLEGRINO, J. W., & KAIL, R. V. (1982). Process analysis of spatial aptitude. In R. J. Sternberg (Ed.), *Advances in the psychology of human intelligence, Vol. 1* (p. 316). Hillsdale, NJ: Lawrence Erlbaum Associates, Inc.

PENNINGTON, B. F., GROISSER, D., & WELSH, M. C. (1993). Contrasting cognitive deficits in attention deficit hyperactivity disorder versus reading disability. *Developmental Psychology, 29,* 511–523.

PEPLAU, L. A. (1991). Lesbian and gay relationships. In J. C. Gonsiorek & J. D. Weinrich (Eds.), *Homosexuality: Research implications for public policy* (pp. 177–196). Newbury Park, CA: Sage.

PEPLAU, L., & GORDON, S. L. (1985). Women and men in love: Sex differences in close heterosexual relationships. In V. O'Leary, R. K. Unger, & B. S. Wallston (Eds.), *Women, gender, and social psychology* (pp. 257–292). Hillsdale, NJ: Erlbaum.

PERKINS, H. W., & HARRIS, L. B. (1990). Familial bereavement and health in adult life course perspective. *Journal of Marriage and the Family, 52,* 233–241.

PERRY, W. I. (1970). *Forms of intellectual and ethical development in the college years.* New York: Holt, Rinehart & Winston.

PERSHAGEN, G., HRUBEC, Z., & SVENSSON, C. (1987). Passive smoking and lung cancer in Swedish women. *American Journal of Epidemiology, 125,* 17–24.

PETERSON, L. (1983). Role of donor competence, donor age, and peer presence on helping in an emergency. *Developmental Psychology, 19,* 873–880.

PETRUS, J. J., & VETROSKY, D. T. (1990, April). Cancer: Risk factors, prevention, and screening. *Physician Assistant,* 21–38.

PETTIT, G. S., BAKSHI, A., DODGE, K. A., & COIE, J. D. (1990). The emergence of social dominance in young boys' play groups: Developmental differences and behavioral correlates. *Developmental Psychology, 26,* 1017–1025.

PFOST, K. S., & FIORE, M. (1990). Pursuit of nontraditional occupations: Fear of success or fear of not being chosen? *Sex Roles, 23,* 15–24.

PHILLIS, D. E., & STEIN, P. J. (1983). Sink or swing? The lifestyles of single adults. In E. R. Allgeier & N. B. McCormick (Eds.), *Changing boundaries: Gender roles and sexual behavior* (pp. 202–225). Palo Alto, CA: Mayfield.

PHINNEY, J. (1989). Stage of ethnic identity in minority group adolescents. *Journal of Early Adolescence, 9,* 34–49.

PHINNEY, J. (1990). Ethnic identity in adolescents and adults. *Psychological Bulletin, 108,* 499–514.

PHINNEY, J. S. (1993). Multiple group identities: Differentiation, conflict, and integration. In J. Kroger (Ed.), *Discussions on ego identity* (pp. 46–73). Hillsdale, NJ: Lawrence Erlbaum Associates, Inc.

PHINNEY, J. S., & CHAVIRA, V. (1992). Ethnic identity and self-esteem: An exploratory longitudinal study. *Journal of Adolescence, 15,* 271–281.

PIAGET, J. (1929). *The child's conception of the world.* New York: Harcourt, Brace.

PIAGET, J., & INHELDER, B. (1956). *The child's conception of space.* Boston: Routledge & Kegan Paul.

PICKENS, J. (1994). Perception of auditory-visual distance relations by 5-month-old infants. *Developmental Psychology, 30,* 537–544.

PILLEMER, K. (1993). The abused offspring are dependent. In R. J. Gelles & D. R. Loseke (Eds.), *Current controversies on family violence* (pp. 237–249). Newbury Park, CA: Sage.

PILLEMER, K., & MOORE, D. W. (1989). Abuse of patients in nursing homes: Findings from a survey of staff. *Gerontologist, 29,* 314–320.

PILLEMER, K., & SUITOR, J. J. (1992). Violence and violent feelings: What causes them among family caregivers? *Journal of Gerontology: Social Sciences, 47,* 165–172.

PINCUS, T., CALLAHAN, L. F., & BURKHAUSER, R. V. (1987). Most chronic diseases are reported more frequently by individuals with fewer than 12 years of formal education in the age 18–64 United States population. *Journal of Chronic Diseases, 40,* 865–874.

PLAN FOR WIDER USE OF NORPLANT BY GIRLS DIVIDING BALTIMORE. (1993, Feb. 16). *New York Times,* p. B16.

PLOMIN, R. (1984). Childhood temperament. In B. Lahey & A. Kazdin (Eds.), *Advances in clinical child psychology* (Vol. 6). New York: Plenum.

PLOMIN, R. (1990). *Nature and nurture.* Pacific Grove, CA: Brooks/Cole.

PLOMIN, R., DEFRIES, J. C., & MCCLEARN, G. E. (1990). *Behavioral genetics: A primer* (2nd ed.). New York: W. H. Freeman.

PLUDE, D. J., & DOUSSARD-ROOSEVELT, J. A. (1989). Aging, selective attention, and feature integration. *Psychology and Aging, 4,* 98–105.

POLIT, D. (1984). The only child in single-parent families. In T. Falbo (Ed.), *The single-child family* (pp. 178–210). New York: Guilford.

POON, L. W. (1992). *The Georgia centenarian study.* Amityville, NY: Baywood.

PORTER, R. H., MAKIN, J. W., DAVIS, L. B., & CHRISTENSEN, K. M. (1992). Breast-fed infants respond to olfactory cues from their own mother and unfamiliar lactating females. *Infant Behavior and Development, 15,* 85–93.

POSNER, J. D., GORMAN, K. M., GITLIN, L. N., ET AL. (1990). Effects of exercise training in the elderly on the occurrence and time to onset of cardiovascular diagnoses. *Journal of the American Geriatrics Association, 38,* 205–210.

POST, F. (1987). Paranoid and schizophrenic disorders among the aging. In L. L. Carstensen & B. A. Edelstein (Eds.), *Handbook of clinical gerontology* (pp. 43–56). New York: Pergamon.

POULIN-DUBOIS, D., SERBIN, L. A., KENYON, B., & DERBYSHIRE, A. (1994). Infants' intermodal knowledge about gender. *Developmental Psychology, 30,* 436–442.

POULSON, C. L., KYMISSIS, E., REEVE, K. F., ANDREATOS, M., & REEVE, L. (1991). Generalized vocal imitation in infants. *Journal of Experimental Child Psychology, 51,* 267–279.

PRATT, M. W., SCRIBNER, S., & COLE, M. (1977). Children as teachers: Developmental studies of instructional communication. *Child Development, 48,* 1475–1481.

QUIGLEY, M. W. (1979, June 19). Executive corps: Free advice pays off for both sides. *Newsday,* p. 9.

RAGLAND, O. R., & BRAND, R. J. (1988). Type A behavior and mortality from coronary heart disease. *New England Journal of Medicine, 318,* 65–69.

RAGOZIN, A. S., BASHAM, R. B., CRNIC, K. A., GREENBERG, M. T., & ROBINSON, N. M. (1982). Effects of maternal age on parenting role. *Developmental Psychology, 18,* 627–634.

RAMEY, C. T., & CAMPBELL, F. A. (1991). Poverty, early childhood education, and academic competence: The Abecedarian experiment. In A. Huston (Ed.), *Children reared in poverty.* New York: Cambridge University Press.

RAMEY, C. T., & RAMEY, S. L. (1990). Intensive educational intervention for children of poverty. *Intelligence, 14,* 1–9.

RAMOS-FORD, V., & GARDNER, H. (1991). Giftedness from a multiple intelligence perspective. In N. Colangelo & G. A. Davis (Eds.), *Handbook of gifted education.* Boston: Allyn and Bacon.

RAPAPORT, J. L., & ISMOND, D. R. (1990). *DSM-III-R training guide for diagnosis of childhood disorders.* New York: Brunner/Mazel.

RAPHAEL, B. (1983). *The anatomy of bereavement.* New York: Basic Books.

RAPOPORT, R., & RAPOPORT, R. N. (1975). *Leisure and the family life cycle.* London, UK: Routledge & Kegan Paul.

RATHUNDE, K. R., & CSIKSZENTMIHALYI, M. (1993). Undivided interest and the growth of talent: A longitudinal study of adolescents. *Journal of Youth and Adolescence, 22,* 385–405.

RAUDENBUSCH, S. W. (1984). Magnitude of teacher expectancy effects on pupil IQ as a function of credibility of expectancy induction: A synthesis from 18 experiments. *Journal of Educational Psychology, 76,* 85–97.

RAWLINS, W. K. (1992). *Friendship matters.* Hawthorne, NY: Aldine de Gruyter.

REEDY, M. N., BIRREN, J. E., & SCHAIE, K. W. (1981). Age and sex differences in satisfying love relationships across the adult life span. *Human Development, 24,* 52–66.

REICH, P. A. (1986). *Language development.* Englewood Cliffs, NJ: Prentice-Hall.

REID, D. H., WILSON, P. G., & FAW, G. D. (1991). Teaching self-help skills. In J. L. Matson & J. A. Mulick (Eds.), *Handbook of mental retardation* (2nd ed.). New York: Pergamon.

REUBENS, B., HARRISON, J., & KUPP, K. (1981). *The youth labor force, 1945–1995: A cross-national analysis.* Totowa, NJ: Allanheld, Osmun.

RHODES, J. E., & JASON, L. A. (1990). A social stress model of substance abuse. *Journal of Consulting and Clinical Psychology, 58,* 395–401.

RHYNE, D. (1981). Basis of marital satisfaction among men and women. *Journal of Marriage and the Family, 43,* 941–955.

RICCIUTI, H. N. (1993). Nutrition and mental development. *Current Directions in Psychological Science, 2,* 43–46.

RICE, M. L., HUSTON, A. C., TRUGLIO, R., & WRIGHT, J. (1990). Words from "Sesame Street": Learning vocabulary while viewing. *Developmental Psychology, 26,* 421–428.

RICH, C. L., SHERMAN, M., & FOWLER, R. C. (1990, Winter). San Diego suicide study: The adolescents. *Adolescence,* pp. 855–865.

RIGGS, D. S., & O'LEARY, K. D. (1992). *Violence between dating partners: Background and situational correlates of courtship aggression.* Unpublished manuscript, State University of New York, Stony Brook.

RILEY, M. W. (1979). Introduction. In M. W. Riley (ed.), *Aging from birth to death: Interdisciplinary perspectives* (pp. 3–14). Boulder, CO: Westview.

RILEY, V. (1981). Psychoneuroendocrine influence on immunocompetence and neoplasia. *Science, 212,* 1100–1109.

ROBERTS, J. D. (1980). *Roots of a black future: Family and church.* Philadelphia: Westminster.

ROBERTS, P., & NEWTON, P. M. (1987). Levinsonian studies of women's adult development. *Psychology and Aging, 2,* 154–163.

ROBERTSON, J. F. (1976). Significance of grandparents: Perceptions of young adult grandchildren. *Gerontologist, 16,* 137–140.

ROBERTSON, J. F. (1977). Grandmotherhood: A study of role concepts. *Journal of Marriage and the Family, 39,* 165–174.

ROBINSON, B., & THURNHER, M. (1979). Taking care of aged parents: A family cycle transition. *Gerontologist, 19,* 586–593.

ROCHE, A. F. (1979). Secular trends in stature, weight, and maturation. *Monographs of the Society for Research in Child Development, 44* (Serial No. 179).

RODEHEAVER, D., & THOMAS, J. L. (1986). Family and community networks in Appalachia. In N. Datan, A. Greene, & H. W. Reese (Eds.), *Life-span developmental psychology: Intergenerational relations* (pp. 77–98). Hillsdale, NJ: Erlbaum.

RODGERS, J. L., & ROWE, D. C. (1993). Social contagion and adolescent sexual behavior: A developmental EMOSA model. *Psychological Review, 100,* 479–510.

RODIN, J., & LANGER, E. J. (1977). Long-term effects of a control-relevant intervention with the institutionalized aged. *Journal of Personality and Social Psychology, 35,* 897–902.

ROFFWARG, H. P., MUZIO, J. N., & DEMENT, W. C. (1966). Ontogenetic development of the human sleep-dream cycle. *Science, 152,* 604–619.

ROGERS, J., & BLOOM, F. E. (1985). Neurotransmitter metabolism and function in the aging central nervous system. In C. E. Finch & E. L. Schneider (Eds.), *Handbook of the biology of aging* (2nd ed., pp. 645–691). New York: Van Nostrand Reinhold.

ROOPNARINE, J. (1992). Father-child play in India. In K. MacDonald (Ed.), *Parent-child play.* Albany: State University of New York Press.

ROSCOE, B., DIANA, M. S., & BROOKS, R. H. (1987). Early, middle, and late adolescents' views on dating and factors influencing partner selection. *Adolescence, 22,* 59–68.

ROSE, S. A., & ORLIAN, E. K. (1991). Asymmetries in infant cross-modal transfer. *Child Development, 62,* 706–718.

ROSENBERG, E. B. (1992). *The adoption life cycle.* Lexington, MA: Lexington Books.

ROSENBERG, L., PALMER, J. R., & SHAPIRO, S. (1990). Decline in the risk of myocardial infarction among women who stop smoking. *New England Journal of Medicine, 322,* 213–217.

ROSENFIELD, P., LAMBERT, N. M., & BLACK, A. (1985). Desk arrangement effects on pupil classroom behavior. *Journal of Educational Psychology, 77,* 101–108.

ROSENSTEIN, D., & OSTER, H. (1988). Differential facial responses to four basic tastes in newborns. *Child Development, 59,* 1555–1568.

ROSENTHAL, D. A., & FELDMAN, S. S. (1992). The relationship between parenting behaviour and ethnic identity in Chinese-American and Chinese-Australian adolescents. *International Journal of Psychology, 27,* 19–31.

ROSIN, H. M., & KORABIK, K. (1990). Marital and family correlates of women managers' attrition from organizations. *Journal of Vocational Behavior, 37,* 104–120.

ROSIN, H. M., & KORABIK, K. (1991). Workplace variables, affective responses, and intention to leave among women managers. *Journal of Occupational Psychology, 64,* 317–330.

ROSKIES, E., & LOUIS-GUERIN, C. (1990). Job insecurity in managers: Antecedents and consequences. *Journal of Organizational Behavior, 11,* 345–359.

ROSS, J. M. (1989). Recruiting and retaining adult students in higher education. *New Directions for Continuing Education* (Vol. 41, pp. 49–62). San Francisco: Jossey-Bass.

ROTENBERG, K. J., & MAYER, E. V. (1990). Delay of gratification in native and white children: A cross-cultural comparison. *International Journal of Behavioral Development, 13,* 23–30.

ROTH, W. F. (1991). *Work and rewards: Redefining our work-life reality.* New York: Praeger.

ROTHBAUM, F., & WEISZ, J. R. (1994). Parental caregiving and child externalizing behavior in nonclinical samples: A meta-analysis. *Psychological Bulletin, 116,* 55–74.

ROVEE-COLLIER, C. (1987). Learning and memory in infancy. In J. D. Osofsky (Ed.), *Handbook of infant development* (2nd ed.). New York: Wiley.

RUBENFELD, M. I., & GILROY, F. D. (1991). Relationship between college women's occupational interests and a single-sex environment. *Career Development Quarterly, 40,* 64–70.

RUBINSTEIN, R. L. (1987). Never-married elderly as a social type: Reevaluating some images. *Gerontologist, 27,* 108–113.

RUBLE, T. L. (1983). Sex stereotypes: Issues of changes in the 1970s. *Sex Roles, 9,* 397–402.

RUHM, C. J. (1990). Career jobs, bridge employment, and retirement. In P. Doeringer (Ed.), *Bridges to retirement: Older workers in a changing labor market* (pp. 92–107). Ithaca, NY: ILR Press.

RUSCH, F. R., SZYMANSKI, E. M., & CHADSEY-RUSCH, J. (1992). The emerging field of transition services. In F. R. Rusch, L. DeStefano, J. Chadsey-Rusch, L. A. Phelps, & E. Szymanski (Eds.), *Transition from school to life* (pp. 5–15). Sycamore, IL: Sycamore.

RUTTER, M., & GILLER, H. (1984). *Juvenile delinquency: Trends and perspectives.* New York: Guilford.

RUTTER, M., MAUGHAN, B., MORTIMORE, P., & OUSTON, J. (1979). *Fifteen thousand hours: Secondary schools and their effects on children.* Cambridge, MA: Harvard University Press.

RYBASH, J. M., HOYER, W. J., & ROODIN, P. A. (1986). *Adult cognition and aging.* New York: Pergamon.

RYFF, C. D. (1989a). Beyond Ponce de Leon and life satisfaction: New directions in quest of successful aging. *International Journal of Behavioral Development, 12,* 35–55.

RYFF, C. D. (1989b). Happiness is everything, or is it? Explorations on the meaning of psychological well-being. *Journal of Personality and Social Psychology, 57,* 1069–1081.

RYFF, C. D. (1991). Possible selves in adulthood and old age: A tale of shifting horizons. *Psychology and Aging, 6,* 286–295.

RYFF, C. D., LEE, Y. H., ESSEX, M. J., & SCHMUTTE, P. S. (1994). My children and me: Mid-life evaluations of grown children and of self. *Psychology and Aging, 9,* 195–205.

RYKKEN, D. E. (1987). Sex in the later years. In P. Silverman (Ed.), *The elderly as modern pioneers* (pp. 125–144). Bloomington, IN: University of Indiana Press.

SAFILIOS-ROTHSCHILD, C. (1977). *Love, sex, and sex roles.* Englewood Cliffs, NJ: Prentice-Hall.

SALGANIK, L. H., PHELPS, R. P., BIANCHI, L., NOHARA, D., & SMITH, T. M. (1993). *Education in states and nations: Indicators comparing U.S. states with the OECD countries in 1988.* Washington, DC: U.S. Government Printing Office.

SALTHOUSE, T. A. (1984). Effects of age and skill in typing. *Journal of Experimental Psychology: General, 113,* 345–371.

SALZMAN, C. (1984). *Clinical geriatric psychopharmacology.* New York: McGraw-Hill.

SANDERS, C. M. (1980–1981). Comparison of younger and older spouses in bereavement outcome. *Omega: Journal of Death and Dying, 11,* 217–232.

SANSON, A., PRIOR, M., SMART, D., & OBERKLAID, F. (1993). Gender differences in aggression in childhood: Implications for a peaceful world. *Australian Psychologist, 28,* 86–92.

SAUNDERS, C. (1977). Dying they live: St. Christopher's Hospice. In H. Feifel (Ed.), *New meanings of death* (pp. 153–179). New York: McGraw-Hill.

SAXE, G. B. (1988). The mathematics of child street vendors. *Child Development, 59,* 1415–1425.

SCARR, S. (1992). Developmental theories for the 1990s: Development and individual differences. *Child Development, 63,* 1–19.

SCARR, S., & MCCARTNEY, K. (1983). How people make their own environments: A theory of genotype environment effects. *Child Development, 54,* 424–435.

SCHAFFER, H. R., & EMERSON, P. E. (1964). The development of social attachments in infancy. *Monographs of the Society for Research in Child Development, 29* (Serial no. 3).

SCHAIE, K. W. (1977). Quasi-experimental designs in the psychology of aging. In J. E. Birren & K. W. Schaie (Eds.), *Handbook of the psychology of aging* (pp. 38–58). New York: Van Nostrand Reinhold.

SCHAIE, K. W. (1984). Historical time and cohort effects. In K. A. McCluskey & H. W. Reese (Eds.), *Life-span developmental psychology: Historical and generational effects* (pp. 1–45). New York: Academic Press.

SCHAIE, K. W. (1994). The course of adult intellectual development. *American Psychologist, 49,* 304–313.

SCHIEDEL, D. G., & MARCIA, J. E. (1985). Ego identity, intimacy, sex role orientation, and gender. *Developmental Psychology, 21,* 149–160.

SCHLEGEL, A., & BARRY, H. (1991). *Adolescence: An anthropological inquiry.* New York: Free Press.

SCHMITT, B., SEEGER, J., KREUZ, W., ENENKEL, S., & JACOBI, G. (1991). Central nervous system involvement of children with HIV infection. *Developmental Medicine and Child Neurology, 33,* 535–540.

SCHNEIDER, E. L., & GURALNICK, J. M. (1990). The aging of America: Impact on health care costs. *Journal of the American Medical Association, 263,* 2335–2340.

SCHNORR, T. M., GRAJEWSKI, B. A., HORNUNG, R. W., THUN, M. J., EGELAND, G. M., MURRAY, W. E., CONOVER, D. L., & HALPERIN, W. E. (1991). Video display terminals and the risk of spontaneous abortion. *The New England Journal of Medicine, 324,* 727–733.

SCHRAMM, W., LYLE, J., & PARKER, E. B. (1961). *Television in the lives of our children.* Stanford, CA: Stanford University Press.

SCHUCKET, M. A. (1987). Biological vulnerability to alcoholism. *Journal of Consulting and Clinical Psychology, 55,* 301–309.

SCHULZ, R. (1985). Emotion and affect. In J. E. Birren & K. W. Schaie (Eds.), *Handbook of the psychology of aging* (2nd ed., pp. 531–543). New York: Van Nostrand Reinhold.

SCHWARTZ, F. (WITH J. ZIMMERMAN). (1992). *Breaking with tradition: Women and work, the new facts of life.* New York: Warner Books.

SCOTT, R. B., & MITCHELL, M. C. (1988). Aging, alcohol, and the liver. *Journal of the American Geriatrics Society, 36,* 255–265.

SCOZARRO, P. P., & SUBICH, L. M. (1990). Gender and occupational sex-type differences in job outcome factor perceptions. *Journal of Vocational Behavior, 36,* 109–119.

SEARS, P. S., & BARBEE, A. H. (1978). Career and life satisfaction among Terman's gifted women. In J. C. Stanley, W. C. George, & C. H. Solano (Eds.), *The gifted and the creative: Fifty year perspective* (pp. 28–66). Baltimore, MD: Johns Hopkins University Press.

SEGALL, M., & WYKLE, M. L. (1988–89). The black family's experience with dementia. *Journal of Applied Social Science, 13,* 170–191.

SELIGMAN, M. E. P. (1989, August). *Why is there so much depression today?* G. Stanley Hall Lecture presented at the annual meeting of the American Psychological Association, New Orleans.

SELTZER, J. A. (1991). Relationships between fathers and children who live apart: The father's role after separation. *Journal of Marriage and the Family, 53,* 79–102.

SERBIN, L. A., POWLISHTA, K. K., & GULKO, J. (1993). The development of sex typing in middle childhood. *Monographs of the Society for Research in Child Development, 58* (Serial no. 232).

SHAINESS, N. (1984). *Sweet suffering: Woman as victim.* Indianapolis, IN: Bobbs-Merrill.

SHATZ, M., & GELMAN, R. (1977). Beyond syntax: The influence of conversational constraints on speech modifications. In C. E. Snow & C. A. Ferguson (Eds.), *Talking to children: Language input and acquisition.* Cambridge, UK: Cambridge University Press.

SHEEHY, G. (1992). *The silent passage: Menopause.* New York: Random House.

SHELTON, B. A., & JOHN, D. (1993). Ethnicity, race, and difference: A comparison of white, black, and Hispanic men's household labor time. In J. C. Hood (Ed.), *Men, work, and family* (pp. 131–150). Newbury Park, CA: Sage.

SHEPHARD, R. J. (1978). *Physical activity and aging.* Chicago: Yearbook Medical.

SHERROD, K. B., O'CONNOR, S., VIETZE, P. M., & ALTEMEIER, W. A. III (1984). Child health and maltreatment. *Child Development, 55,* 1174–1183.

SHIRLEY, M. M. (1931). *The first two years: A study of twenty-five babies: Vol. 1. Postural and locomotor development.* Westport, CT: Greenwood Press.

SHIROM, A., & MAZEH, T. (1988). Periodicity in seniority-job satisfaction relationship. *Journal of Vocational Behavior, 33,* 38–49.

SHNEIDMAN, E. S. (1973). *Deaths of man.* New York: Quadrangle/New York Times.

SHOTLAND, R. L., & GOODSTEIN, L. (1992). Sexual precedence reduces the perceived legitimacy of sexual refusal: An examination of attributions concerning date rape and consensual sex. *Personality and Social Psychology Bulletin, 18,* 756–764.

SIEGEL, R. K. (1980). The psychology of life after death. *American Psychologist, 35,* 911–931.

SIEGLER, I. C., GEORGE, L. K., & OKUN, M. A. (1979). A cross-sequential analysis of adult personality. *Developmental Psychology, 15,* 350–351.

SIEGLER, R. S. (1981). Developmental sequences within and between concepts. *Monographs of the Society for Research in Child Development, 46* (Serial No. 189).

SIEGLER, R. S., & ROBINSON, M. (1982). The development of numerical understandings. In H. W. Reese & L. P. Lipsitt (Eds.), *Advances in child development and behavior* (Vol. 16). New York: Academic Press.

SIGNORIELLI, N., & LEARS, M. (1992). Children, television, and conceptions about chores: Attitudes and behaviors. *Sex Roles, 27,* 157–170.

SILVERMAN, P. (1987). Community settings. In P. Silverman (Ed.), *The elderly as modern pioneers* (pp. 185–210). Bloomington: Indiana University Press.

SILVERMAN, P. R., & WORDEN, J. W. (1992). Children's understanding of funeral ritual. *Omega, 25,* 319–331.

SIMMONS, L. W. (1945). *Role of the aged in primitive society.* New Haven, CT: Yale University Press.

SIMMONS, R., & BLYTH, D. (1987). *Moving into adolescence.* New York: Aldine de Gruyter.

SIMMONS, R. G., & BLYTH, D. A. (1987). *Moving into adolescence: The impact of pubertal change and school context.* New York: Aldine De Gruyter.

SIMONS, R. L., WHITBECK, L. B., CONGER, R. D., & CHYI-IN, W. (1991). Intergenerational transmission of harsh parenting. *Developmental Psychology, 27,* 159–171.

SIMONTON, D. K. (1990). Creativity and wisdom in aging. In J. E. Birren & K. W. Schaie (Eds.), *Handbook of the psychology of aging* (3rd ed., pp. 320–329). San Diego, CA: Academic Press.

SIMPSON, E. L. (1974). Moral development research: A case study of scientific cultural bias. *Human Development, 17,* 81–106.

SINNOTT, J. D. (1986). Sex roles and aging: Theory and research from a systems perspective. *Contributions to human development* (Vol. 15). New York: Karger.

SINNOTT, J. D. (1994). The future of adult lifespan learning: Learning institutions face change. In J. D. Sinnott (Ed.), *Interdisciplinary handbook of adult lifespan learning* (pp. 449–465). Westport, CT: Greenwood Press.

SINNOTT, J. D. (ED.). (1994). *Interdisciplinary handbook of adult lifespan learning.* Westport, CT: Greenwood Press.

SIPERSTEIN, G. N. (1988). Students with learning disabilities in college: The need for a programmatic approach to critical transitions. *Journal of Learning Disabilities, 21,* 431–436.

SLABY, R. G., & GUERRA, N. G. (1988). Cognitive mediators of aggression in adolescent offenders: 1. Assessment. *Developmental Psychology, 24,* 580–588.

SLATE, J. R., JONES, C. H., & DAWSON, P. (1993). Academic skills of high school students as a function of grade, gender, and academic track. *High School Journal, 76,* 245–251.

SLOANE, J. H., KELLERMAN, A. L., REAY, D. T., FERRIS, J. A., KOEPSELL, T., & RIVARA, F. P. (1988). Handgun regulation, crime, assault and homicide: A tale of two cities. *New England Journal of Medicine, 319,* 1256–1262.

SMART, J. C. (1989). Life history influences on Holland vocational type development. *Journal of Vocational Behavior, 34,* 69–87.

SMITH, A. B., & INDER, P. M. (1993). Social interaction in same and cross gender pre-school peer groups: A participant observation study. *Educational Psychology, 13,* 29–42.

SMITH, E. L., & SERFASS, R. C. (1981). *Exercise and aging: The scientific basis.* Hillsdale, NJ: Erlbaum.

SMITH, J., & BALTES, P. B. (1990). Wisdom-related knowledge: Age/cohort differences in responses to life-planning problems. *Developmental Psychology, 26,* 494–505.

SMITH, K. R., & ZICK, C. D. (1986). The incidence of poverty among the recently widowed: Mediating factors in the life course. *Journal of Marriage and the Family, 48,* 619–630.

SMITH, M., COLLIGAN, M., HORNING, R. W., & HURRELL, J. (1978). *Occupational comparisons of stress-related disease incidence.* Cincinnati, OH: National Institute for Occupational Safety and Health.

SNAREY, J. R. (1985). Cross-cultural universality of social-moral development: A critical review of Kohlbergian research. *Psychological Bulletin, 97,* 202–232.

SNEDEKER, B. (1982) *Hard knocks: Preparing youth for work.* Baltimore, MD: Johns Hopkins University Press.

SNOW, M. E., JACKLIN, C. N., & MACCOBY, E. E. (1983). Sex-of-child differences in father-child interaction at one year of age. *Child Development, 54,* 227–232.

SNYDER, C. J., & BARRETT, G. V. (1988). The Age Discrimination in Employment Act: A review of court decisions. *Experimental Aging Research, 14,* 3–47.

SOKOLOV, J. L. (1993). A local contingency analysis of the fine-tuning hypothesis. *Developmental Psychology, 29,* 1008–1023.

SOLNICK, R. L., & CORBY, N. (1983). Human sexuality and aging. In D. S. Woodruff & J. E. Birren (Eds.), *Aging: Scientific perspectives and social issues* (2nd ed., pp. 202–224). Pacific Grove, CA: Brooks/Cole.

SOMMER, R. (1969). *Personal space.* Englewood Cliffs, NJ: Prentice-Hall.

SONG, M. J., & GINSBURG, H. P. (1988). The effect of the Korean number system on young children's counting: A natural experiment in numerical bilingualism. *International Journal of Psychology, 23,* 319–332.

SORENSON, R. (1973). *Adolescent sexuality in contemporary society.* New York: World Book.

SPARROW, S., BALLA, D., & CICCHETTI, D. (1984). *Vineland Adaptive Behavior Scales.* Circle Pines, MN: American Guidance Services.

SPENCE, J. T. (1985). Achievement American style: The rewards and costs of individualism. *American Psychologist, 40,* 1285–1295.

SPETNER, N. B., & OLSHO, L. W. (1990). Auditory frequency resolution in human infancy. *Child Development, 61,* 632–652.

SPITZER, M. E. (1988). Taste acuity in institutionalized and noninstitutionalized elderly men. *Journals of Gerontology: Psychological Sciences, 43,* 71–74.

SPORAKOWSKI, M. J., & AXELSON, L. J. (1984). Long-term marriages: A critical review. *Lifestyles: A Journal of Changing Patterns, 7*(2), 76–93.

SROUFE, L. A., & FLEESON, J. (1986). Attachment and the construction of relationships. In W. W. Hartup and Z. Rubin (Eds.), *Relationships and development.* Hillsdale, NJ: Erlbaum.

STANFORD, E. P., HAPPERSETT, C. J., MORTON, D. J., MOLGAARD, C. A., & PEDDECORD, K. M. (1991). Early retirement and functional impairment from a multi-ethnic perspective. *Research on Aging, 13,* 5–38.

STANFORD, E. P., & LOCKERY, S. A. (1984). Aging and social relations in the black community. In W. H. Quinn & G. A. Hughston (Eds.), *Independent aging: Family and social systems perspectives* (pp. 164–181). Rockville, MD: Aspen.

STANOVICH, K. E. (1993). Dysrationalia: A new specific learning disability. *Journal of Learning Disabilities, 26,* 501–515.

STARK, E. (1992, May). *From dependency to empowerment: Framing and reframing the battered woman.* Paper presented at the Second Annual Conference: Domestic Violence: The Family/Community Connection, State University of New York Division of Nursing, Stony Brook, NY.

STARKO, A. J. (1988). Effects of the Revolving Door Identification Model on creative productivity and self-efficacy. *Gifted Child Quarterly, 32,* 291–297.

STEEN, B. (1987). Nutrition and the elderly. In M. Bergener (Ed.), *Psychogeriatrics* (pp. 349–361). New York: Springer.

STEIN, P. (1978). The lifestyles and life changes and the never married. *Marriage and Family Review, 1,* 1–11.

STEINBERG, L. (1990). Autonomy, conflict, and harmony in the family relationship. In S. S. Feldman & G. R. Elliott (Eds.), *At the threshold: The developing adolescent.* Cambridge, MA: Harvard University Press.

STEINBERG, L., & DORNBUSCH, S. M. (1991). Negative correlates of part-time employment during adolescence: Replication and elaboration. *Developmental Psychology, 27,* 304–313.

STEINBERG, L., FEGLEY, S., & DORNBUSCH, S. M. (1993). Negative impact of part-time work on adolescent adjustment: Evidence from a longitudinal study. *Developmental Psychology, 29,* 171–180.

STEINBERG, L., LAMBORN, S. D., DORNBUSCH, S. M., & DARLING, N. (1992). Impact of parenting practices on adolescent achievement: Authoritative parenting, school involvement, and encouragement to succeed. *Child Development, 63,* 1266–1281.

STEINMETZ, S. K. (1993). The abused elderly are dependent. In R. J. Gelles & D. R. Loseke (Eds.), *Current controversies on family violence* (pp. 222–236). Newbury Park, CA: Sage.

STELMACH, G. E., GOGGIN, N. L., & GARCIA-COLERA, A. (1987). Movement specification time with age. *Experimental Aging Reseach, 13,* 42.

STERN, M., & KARRAKER, K. H. (1989). Sex stereotyping of infants: A review of gender labeling studies. *Sex Roles, 20,* 501–522.

STERNBERG, R. J. (1985). *Beyond IQ: A triarchic theory of human intelligence.* Cambridge, UK: Cambridge University Press.

STERNBERG, R. J. (1986). A triangular theory of love. *Psychological Review, 93,* 119–135.

STEVENSON, H. W. (1988). Culture and schooling: Influences on cognitive development. In E. M. Hetherington, R. M. Lerner, & M. Perlmutter (Eds.), *Child development in life-span perspective* (pp. 241–258). Hillsdale, NJ: Lawrence Erlbaum Associates, Inc.

STEVENSON, H. W., & LEE, S. (1990). Contexts of achievement. *Monographs of the Society for Research in Child Development, 55* (Serial No. 221).

STEVENSON, H. W., & STIGLER, J. W. (1992). *The learning gap.* New York: Summit.

STEWARD, R. J., & KRIESHOK, T. S. (1991). A cross-cultural study of vocational identity: Does a college education mean the same for all persisters? *Journal of College Student Development, 32,* 562–563.

STEWART, L., & PASCUAL-LEONE, J. (1992). Mental capacity constraints and the development of moral reasoning. *Journal of Experimental Child Psychology, 54,* 251–287.

STEWART, R. B., MOBLEY, L. A., VAN TUYL, S. S., & SALVADOR, W. A. (1987). The firstborns' adjustment to the birth of a sibling: A longitudinal assessment. *Child Development, 58,* 341–355.

STIFTER, C. A., & FOX, N. A. (1990). Infant reactivity: Physiological correlates of newborn and 5-month temperament. *Developmental Psychology, 26,* 582–588.

STOCKER, C. M., & MCHALE, S. M. (1992). The nature and family correlates of preadolescents' perceptions of their sibling relationships. *Journal of Social and Personal Relationships, 9,* 179–195.

STRAUS, M. A., GELLES, R. J., & STEINMETZ, S. K. (1980). *Behind closed doors: Violence in the American family.* Garden City, NY: Anchor/Doubleday.

STRAUS, M. A., & KANTOR, G. K. (1987). Stress and child abuse. In R. E. Helfer & R. S. Kempe (Eds.), *The battered child* (4th ed.). Chicago: University of Chicago Press.

STROEBE, M. S., & STROEBE, W. (1983). Who suffers more? Sex differences in health risks of the widowed. *Psychological Bulletin, 93,* 279–301.

STUNKARD, A. J., SORENSEN, T. I. A., HANIS, C., TEASDALE, T. W., CHAKRABORTY, R., SCHULL, W. J., & SCHULSINGER, F. (1986). An adoption study of human obesity. *New England Journal of Medicine, 314,* 193–198.

SULLIVAN, L. W. (1987). The risks of the sickle-cell trait: Caution and common sense. *New England Journal of Medicine, 317,* 830–831.

SULS, J., & WILLS, T. A. (1991). *Social comparison: Contemporary theory and research.* Hillsdale, NJ: Erlbaum.

SUPER, C. M. (1981). Cross-cultural research on infancy. In H. C. Triandis and A. Heron (Eds.), *Handbook of cross-cultural psychology: Vol. 4. Developmental psychology.* Boston: Allyn and Bacon.

SUPER, C. M., HERRERA, M. G., & MORA, J. O. (1990). Long-term effects of food supplementation and psychosocial intervention on the physical growth of Colombian infants at risk of malnutrition. *Child Development, 61,* 29–49.

SUPER, D. E. (1957). *The psychology of careers.* New York: Harper & Row.

SUPER, D. E. (1976). *Career education and the meanings of work.* Washington, DC: U.S. Offices of Education.

SUPER, D. E. (1980). A life span, life space approach to career development. *Journal of Vocational Behavior, 16,* 282–298.

SWANSON, J. L. (1992). Vocational behavior, 1989–1991: Life-span career development and reciprocal interaction or work and nonwork. *Journal of Vocational Behavior, 41,* 101–161.

SWENSON, C. H., ESKEW, R. W., & KOHLHEPP, K. A. (1981). Stages of the family life cycle, ego development, and the marriage relationship. *Journal of Gerontology, 43,* 841–853.

TANNEN, D. (1990). *You just don't understand.* New York: Morrow.

TANNER, J. M. (1970). Physical growth. In P. H. Bussen (Ed.), *Carmichael's manual of child psychology* (3rd ed.). New York: Wiley.

TANNER, J. M. (1978). *Fetus into man: Physical growth from conception to maturity.* Cambridge, MA: Harvard University Press.

TAYLOR, M., CARTWRIGHT, B. S., & CARLSON, S. M. (1993). A developmental investigation of children's imaginary companions. *Developmental Psychology, 29,* 276–285.

TAYLOR, M., & GELMAN, S. A. (1989). Incorporating new words into the lexicon: Preliminary evidence for language hierarchies in two-year-old children. *Child Development, 60,* 625–636.

TEACHMAN, J. (1986). First and second marital dissolution: A decomposition exercise for whites and blacks. *Sociological Quarterly, 27,* 571–590.

TERKEL, S. (1974). *Working.* New York: Pantheon.

THELEN, E., & ULRICH, B. D. (1991). Hidden skills. *Monographs of the Society for Research in Child Development, 56* (Serial No. 223).

THELEN, E., ULRICH, B. D., & JENSEN, J. L. (1989). The developmental origins of locomotion. In M. H. Woollacott & A. Shumway-Cook (Eds.), *Development of posture and gait across the life span.* Columbia, SC: University of South Carolina Press.

THOMAE, H. (1976). *Patterns of aging.* Basel: Karger.

THOMAE, H. (1980). Personality and adjustment to aging. In J. E. Birren & R. B. Sloane (Eds.), *Handbook of mental health and aging* (pp. 285–301). Englewood Cliffs, NJ: Prentice-Hall.

THOMAS, D. A. (1990). The impact of race on managers' experiences of developmental relationships (mentoring and sponsorship): An intra-organizational study. *Journal of Organizational Behavior, 11,* 479–492.

THOMAS, G. S., & RUTLEDGE, J. H. (1986). Fitness and exercise for the elderly. In K. Dychtwald (Ed.), *Wellness and health promotion for the elderly* (pp. 165–178). Rockville, MD: Aspen.

THOMAS, J. L. (1986). Age and sex differences in perceptions of grandparenthood. *Journal of Gerontology, 41,* 417–423.

THOMAS, J. L. (1988). Predictors of satisfaction with children's help for younger and older elderly parents. *Journal of Gerontology: Social Sciences, 43,* 9–14.

THOMAS, J. L., BENCE, S. L., & MEYER, S. M. (1988, August). *Grandparenting satisfaction: The roles of relationship meaning and perceived responsibility.* Paper presented at the meeting of the American Psychological Association, Atlanta.

THOMAS, N. G., & BERK, L. E. (1981). Effects of school environments on the development of young children's creativity. *Child Development, 52,* 1152–1162.

THOMPSON, A. D. (1978). Alcohol and nutrition. *Clinics in Endocrinology and Metabolism, 7,* 405–428.

THOMPSON, L., & WALKER, A. J. (1989). Gender in families: Women and men in marriage, work, and parenthood. *Journal of Marriage and the Family, 51,* 845–871.

THOMPSON, L. W., & GALLAGHER, D. (1986). Treatment of depression in elderly outpatients. In G. Maletta & F. J. Pirozzolo (Eds.), *Advances in neurogerontology: Vol. 4. Assessment and treatment of the elderly patient.* New York: Praeger.

THOMPSON, L. W., GALLAGHER-THOMPSON, D., FUTTERMAN, A., GILEWSKI, M. J., & PETERSON, J. (1991). The effects of late-life spousal bereavement over a 30-month interval. *Psychology and Aging, 6,* 434–441.

THOMSON, E., & COLELLA, U. (1992). Cohabitation and marital stability: Quality or commitment? *Journal of Marriage and the Family, 54,* 259–267.

THORNBERRY, T. P., KROHN, M. D., LIZOTTE, A. J., & CHARD-WIERSCHEM, D. (1993). The role of juvenile gangs in facilitating delinquent behavior. *Journal of Research in Crime and Delinquency, 30,* 55–87.

TIZARD, B., & HODGES, J. (1978). The effect of early institutional rearing on the development of eight-year-old children. *Journal of Child Psychology and Psychiatry, 19,* 99–118.

TODA, S., & FOGEL, A. (1993). Infant response to the still-face situation at 3 and 6 months. *Developmental Psychology, 29,* 532–538.

TOFFLER, A. (1970). *Future shock.* New York: Random House.

TOLSON, J. M., & URBERG, K. A. (1993). Similarity between adolescent best friends. *Journal of Adolescent Research, 8,* 274–288.

TOPPING, K., & WHITELEY, M. (1993). Sex differences in the effectiveness of peer tutoring. *School Psychology International, 14,* 57–67.

TREBOUX, D., & BUSCH-ROSSNAGEL, N. A. (1990). Social network influence on adolescent sexual attitudes and behaviors. *Journal of Adolescent Research, 5,* 175–189.

TRICKETT, P. K., ABER, J. L., CARLSON, V., & CICCHETTI, D. (1991). Relationship of socioeconomic status to the etiology and developmental sequelae of physical child abuse. *Developmental Psychology, 27,* 148–158.

TRICKETT, P. K., & KUCZYNSKI, L. (1986). Children's misbehaviors and parental discipline strategies in abusive and nonabusive families. *Developmental Psychology, 22,* 115–123.

TROLL, L. E. (1971). The family of later life: A decade review. *Journal of Marriage and the Family, 33,* 263–290.

TROLL, L. E., & BENGTSON, V. (1982). Intergenerational relations throughout the life span. In B. B. Wolman (Ed.), *Handbook of developmental psychology* (pp. 890–911). Englewood Cliffs, NJ: Prentice-Hall.

TRUJILLO, K. M., WALSH, D. M., & BROUGHAM, R. R. (1991, June). *Age differences in exercise motivation.* Paper presented at the annual meeting of the American Psychological Society, Washington, DC.

TURNER, B. F. (1982). Sex-related differences in aging. In B. B. Wolman (Ed.), *Handbook of developmental psychology* (pp. 912–936). Englewood Cliffs, NJ: Prentice-Hall.

TURPIN, B. (1993). "Mom, please!" *Notre Dame Magazine, 22,* 41–43.

UHLENBERG, P., COONEY, T. M., & BOYD, R. (1990). Divorce for women after midlife. *Journal of Gerontology: Social Sciences, 45,* 3–11.

UNIFORM CRIME REPORTS FOR THE UNITED STATES. (1992). Washington, DC: U.S. Government Printing Office.

UNITED STATES ADVISORY BOARD ON CHILD ABUSE AND NEGLECT. (1995). *A nation's shame: Fatal child abuse and neglect in the United States.* Washington, DC: U.S. Department of Health and Human Services.

UNITED STATES BUREAU OF THE CENSUS. (1991). *Statistical abstract of the United States.* Washington, DC: U.S. Government Printing Office.

UNITED STATES DEPARTMENT OF HEALTH AND HUMAN SERVICES. (1984). *Vital statistics of the United States, 1981: Vol. 2. Mortality* (Part A). Hyattsville, MD: U.S. Public Health Service.

UNITED STATES DEPARTMENT OF HEALTH AND HUMAN SERVICES. (1988). *Vital statistics of the United States, 1985: Vol. 2. Mortality* (Part A). Hyattsville, MD: U.S. Public Health Service.

UNITED STATES DEPARTMENT OF HEALTH AND HUMAN SERVICES. (1990). *Health United States 1989* (DHHS Publication No. PHS 90–1232). Washington, DC: U.S. Government Printing Office.

UNITED STATES DEPARTMENT OF HEALTH AND HUMAN SERVICES. (1991). *Vital statistics of the United States, 1988: Vol. 2. Mortality* (Part A). Hyattsville, MD: U.S. Public Health Service.

UNITED STATES DEPARTMENT OF HEALTH AND HUMAN SERVICES. (1993). *Mortality surveillance system.* Hyattsville, MD: U.S. Public Health Service.

UNITED STATES DEPARTMENT OF HEALTH AND HUMAN SERVICES. (1994). *Vital statistics of the United States, 1991: Vol. 2. Mortality* (Part A). Hyattsville, MD: U.S. Public Health Service.

UNITED STATES DEPARTMENT OF LABOR. (1991). *A report on the glass ceiling initiative.* Washington, DC: Author.

UNITED STATES DEPARTMENT OF LABOR. (1995). *Bureau of Labor Statistics Report.* Washington, DC: Author.

VACHON, M. L. S., LYALL, W. A. L., ROGERS, J., FREEDMAN-LETOFSKY, K., & FREEMAN, S. J. A. (1980). A controlled study of self-help intervention for widows. *American Journal of Psychiatry, 137,* 1380–1384.

VAILLANT, G. E. (1977). *Adaptation to life.* Boston: Little, Brown.

VALKENBURG, P. M., & VAN DER VOORT, T. H. A. (1994). Influence of TV on daydreaming and creative imagination: a review of research. *Psychological Bulletin, 116,* 316–339.

VANDENBOS, G. R., DELEON, P. H., & PALLACK, M. S. (1982). An alternative to traditional medical care for the terminally ill. *American Psychologist, 37,* 1245–1248.

VAN GENNEP, A. (1909). *Les rites de passage.* Paris: E. Nourry. (Trans. as *The rites of passage* by M. B. Vizedom & G. L. Caffee (1960). Chicago: University of Chicago Press.)

VAN HOOSE, W. H., & WORTH, M. R. (1982). *Adulthood in the life cycle.* Dubuque, IA: William C. Brown.

VAN IJZENDOORN, M., GOLDBERG, S., KROONENBERG, P. M., & FRENKEL, O.J. (1992). The relative effects of maternal and child problems on the quality of attachment: A meta-analysis of attachment in clinical samples. *Child Development, 63,* 840–858.

VAN IJZENDOORN, M. H., & KROONENBERG, P. M. (1988). Cross-cultural patterns of attachment: A meta-analysis of the strange situation. *Child Development, 59,* 147–156.

VAN LOOSBROEK, E., & SMITSMAN, A. W. (1990). Visual perception of numerosity in infancy. *Developmental Psychology, 26,* 916–922.

VAN MAANEN, J., & SCHEIN, E. H. (1977). Career development. In R. J. Hackman & J. L. Suttle (Eds.), *Improving life at work* (pp. 30–95). New York: Goodyear.

VERHAEGHEN, MARCOEN, A., & GOOSENS, L. (1993). Facts and fiction about memory aging: A quantitative integration of research findings. *Journal of Gerontology: Psychological Sciences, 48,* 157–171.

VERMA, I. M. (1990). Gene therapy. *Scientific American, 263,* 68–84.

VICKIO, C. J., CAVANAUGH, J. C., & ATTIG, T. (1990). Perceptions of grief among university students. *Death Studies, 14,* 231–240.

VILLA, R. F., & JAIME, A. (1993). *La fé de la gente.* In M. Sotomayor & A. Garcia (Eds.), *Elderly Latinos: Issues and solutions for the 21st century.* Washington, DC: National Hispanic Council on Aging.

VINOVSKIS, M. A. (1988). The historian and the life course: Reflections on recent approaches to the study of American family life in the past. In P. B. Baltes, D. L. Featherman, & R. M. Lerner (Eds.), *Life-span development and behavior* (Vol. 8, pp. 33–59). Hillsdale, NJ: Erlbaum.

VOLLING, B., & BELSKY, J. (1992). The contribution of mother-child and father-child relationships to the quality of sibling interaction: A longitudinal study. *Child Development, 63,* 1209–1222.

VORHEES, C. V., & MOLLNOW, E. (1987). Behavior teratogenesis: Long-term influences on behavior. In J. D. Osofsky (Ed.). *Handbook of infant development* (2nd ed.). New York: Wiley.

VYGOTSKY, L. S. (1978). *Mind in society: The development of higher psychological processes* (M. Cole, V. John-Steiner, S. Scribner, & E. Soubermen, Eds.). Cambridge, MA: Harvard University Press.

VYGOTSKY, L. S. (1986). *Thought and language* (A. Kozulin, Trans.). Cambridge, MA: MIT Press. (Original work published in 1934.)

WACHS, T. D. (1983). The use and abuse of environment in behavior-genetic research. *Child Development, 54,* 396–407.

WACHS, T. D. (1987). Specificity of environmental action as manifest in environmental correlates of infant's mastery motivation. *Developmental Psychology, 23,* 782–790.

WAGNER, N. E., SCHUBERT, H. J. P., & SCHUBERT, D. S. P. (1985). Family size effects: A revision. *Journal of Genetic Psychology, 146,* 65–78.

WAGNER, R. K., & STERNBERG, R. J. (1986). Tacit knowledge and intelligence in the everyday world. In R. J. Sternberg & R. K. Wagner (Eds.), *Practical intelligence* (pp. 51–83). Cambridge, UK: Cambridge University Press.

WALBERG, H. J. (1986). Synthesis of research on teaching. In M. C. Wittrock (Ed.), *Handbook of research on teaching* (3rd ed.). New York: Macmillan.

WALKER, L. E. A. (1984). *The battered woman syndrome.* New York: Springer.

WALKER, L. J. (1989). A longitudinal study of moral reasoning. *Child Development, 60,* 157–166.

WALKER, L. J., & TAYLOR, J. H. (1991). Family interactions and the development of moral reasoning. *Child Development, 62,* 264–283.

WALL, S., & ARDEN, H. (1990). *Wisdomkeepers: Meetings with Native American spiritual elders.* Hillsboro, OR: Beyond Words Publishing.

WALLERSTEIN, J. S., & BLAKESLEE, S. (1989). *Second chances: Men, women, and children a decade after divorce.* New York: Ticknor & Fields.

WALLERSTEIN, J. S., & KELLY, J. B. (1980). *Surviving the breakup: How children and parents cope with divorce.* New York: Basic Books.

WALSH, E. K., & CAVANAUGH, J. C. (1984, November). *Does hospice meet the needs of dying clients?* Paper presented at the meeting of the Gerontological Society of America, San Antonio.

WANTZ, M. S., & GAY, J. E. (1981). *The aging process: A health perspective.* Cambridge, MA: Winthrop.

WARD, R., LOGAN, J., & SPITZE, G. (1992). The influence of parent and child needs on coresidence in middle and later life. *Journal of Marriage and the Family, 54,* 209–221.

WARD, S. L., & OVERTON, W. F. (1990). Semantic familiarity, relevance, and the development of deductive reasoning. *Developmental Psychology, 26,* 288–493.

WATERS, H. F. (1993, July 12). Networks under the gun. *Newsweek,* 64–66.

WECHSLER, D. (1991). *Manual for the Wechsler Intelligence Test for Children–III.* New York: The Psychological Corporation.

WEIBEL-ORLANDO, J. (1990). Grandparenting styles: Native American perspectives. In J. Sokolovsky (Ed.), *The cultural context of aging* (pp. 109–125). New York: Bergin & Garvey.

WEISHAUS, S., & FIELD, D. (1988). A half century of marriage: Continuity or change? *Journal of Marriage and the Family, 50,* 763–774.

WEISMAN, A. D. (1972). *On dying and denying.* New York: Behavioral Publications.

WEISNER, T. S., & WILSON-MITCHELL, J. E. (1990). Nonconventional family lifestyles and sex typing in six-year-olds. *Child Development, 61,* 1915–1933.

WEITZMAN, L. J. (1985). *The divorce revolution: The unexpected social and economic consequences for women and children in America.* New York: Free Press.

WELSH, M. C., PENNINGTON, B. F., & GROISSER, D. B. (1991). A normative-developmental study of executive function: A window on prefrontal function in children. *Developmental Neuropsychology, 7,* 131–149.

WENTKOWSKI, G. (1985). Older women's perceptions of great-grandparenthood: A research note. *Gerontologist, 25,* 593–596.

WENTZEL, K. R., & ERDLEY, C. A. (1993). Strategies for making friends: Relations to social behavior and peer acceptance. *Developmental Psychology, 29,* 819–826.

WERKER, J. F., & LALONDE, C. E. (1988). Cross-language speech perception: Initial capabilities and developmental change. *Developmental Psychology, 24,* 672–683.

WERNER, E. E. (1989). Children of Garden Island. *Scientific American, 260,* 106–111.

WERNER, E. E., & SMITH, R. S. (1992). *Overcoming the odds: High risk children from birth to adulthood.* Ithaca, NY: Cornell University Press.

WERNER, H. (1948). *Comparative psychology of mental development.* Chicago: Follet.

WERTSCH, J. V. (1985). *Vygotsky and the social formation of mind.* Cambridge, MA: Harvard University Press.

WERTSCH, J. V., & TULVISTE, P. (1992). L. S. Vygotsky and contemporary developmental psychology. *Developmental Psychology, 28,* 548–557.

WEST, R. L. (1986). Everyday memory and aging. *Developmental Neuropsychology, 2,* 323–344.

WHITBOURNE, S. K. (1985). *The aging body.* New York: Springer.

WHITBOURNE, S. K. (1986). *The me I know: A study of adult identity.* New York: Springer-Verlag.

WHITBOURNE, S. K. (1987). Personality development in adulthood and old age: Relationships among identity style, health, and well-being. In K. W. Schaie (Ed.), *Annual review of gerontology and geriatrics* (Vol. 7, pp. 189–216). New York: Springer.

WHITBOURNE, S. K., & TESCH, S. A. (1985). A comparison of identity and intimacy statuses in college students and alumni. *Developmental Psychology, 21,* 1039–1044.

WHITE, A. T., & SPECTOR, P. E. (1987). An investigation of age-related factors in the age-job satisfaction relationship. *Psychology and Aging, 2,* 261–265.

WHITING, B. B., & EDWARDS, P. E. (1988). *Children of different worlds.* Cambridge, MA: Harvard University Press.

WHITNEY, E. N., CATALDO, C. B., & ROLFES, S. R. (1987). *Understanding normal and clinical nutrition* (2nd ed.). St. Paul, MN: West.

WICKS-NELSON, R., & ISRAEL, A. C. (1991). *Behavior disorders of childhood* (2nd ed.). Englewood Cliffs, NJ: Prentice-Hall.

WIDOM, C. S. (1989). Does violence beget violence? A critical examination of the literature. *Psychological Bulletin, 106,* 3–28.

WIENS, A. N., & MENUSTIK, C. E. (1983). Treatment outcome and patient characteristics in an aversion therapy program for alcoholism. *American Psychologist, 38,* 1089–1096.

WILK, C. (1986). *Career, women, and childbearing: A psychological analysis of the decision process.* New York: Van Nostrand Reinhold.

WILLIAMS, J. E., & BEST, D. L. (1990). *Measuring sex stereotypes: A thirty-nation study* (rev. ed.). Newbury Park, CA: Sage.

WILLIAMSON, D. F., KAHN, H. S., REMINGTON, P. L., & ANDA, R. F. (1990). The 10-year incidence of overweight and major weight gain in U.S. adults. *Archives of Internal Medicine, 150,* 665–672.

WILLIAMSON, G. M., & SCHULZ, R. (1990). Relationship orientation, quality of prior relationship, and distress among caregivers of Alzheimer's patients. *Psychology and Aging, 5,* 502–509.

WILLIS, S. L., & SCHAIE, K. W. (In press). Cognitive training in the normal elderly. In F. Boller (Ed.), *Cerebral plasticity in human aging.* New York: Springer-Verlag.

WILSON, J. G. (1977). Current status of teratology. In J. G. Wilson & F. C. Fraser (Eds.), *Handbook of teratology* (Vol. 1). New York: Plenum.

WINER, G. A., CRAIG, R. K., & WEINBAUM, E. (1992). Adults' failure on misleading weight-conservation tests: A developmental analysis. *Developmental Psychology, 28,* 109–120.

WITELSON, S. F. (1987). Neurobiological aspects of language in children. *Child Development, 58,* 653–688.

WOLF, R. S., GODKIN, M. A., & PILLEMER, K. A. (1986). Treatment of the elderly: A comparative analysis. *Journal of Long Term Home Health Care, 5*(4), 10–17.

WOLFE, D. A. (1985). Child-abusive parents: An empirical review and analysis. *Psychological Bulletin, 97,* 462–482.

WOLFF, P. H. (1987). *The development of behavioral states and the expression of emotions in early infancy.* Chicago: University of Chicago Press.

WOLFSON, C., HANDFIELD-JONES, R., GLASS, K. C., MCCLARAN, J., & KEYSERLINGK, E. (1993). Adult children's perceptions of their responsibility to provide care for dependent elderly parents. *Gerontologist, 33,* 315–323.

WOLINSKY, F. D., CALLAHAN, C. M., FITZGERALD, J. F., & JOHNSON, R. L. (1992). The risk of nursing home placement and subsequent death among older adults. *Journal of Gerontology: Social Sciences, 47,* 173–182.

WOLRAICH, M. L., LINDGREN, S. D., STUMBO, P. J., STEGINK, L. D., APPELBAUM, M. I., & KIRITSY, M. C. (1994). Effects of diets high in sucrose or aspartame on the behavior and cognitive performance of children. *New England Journal of Medicine, 330,* 301–307.

WOODRUFF-PAK, D. S. (1988). *Psychology and Aging.* Englewood Cliffs, NJ: Prentice-Hall.

WOOLLACOTT, M. H., SHUMWAY-COOK, A., & WILLIAMS, H. (1989). The development of balance and locomotion in children. In M. H. Woollacott, & A. Shumway-Cook (Eds.), *Development of posture and gait across the life span.* Columbia, SC: University of South Carolina Press.

WRIGHT, L. K. (1991). The impact of Alzheimer's disease on the marital relationship. *Gerontologist, 31,* 224–237.

XIAOHE, X., & WHYTE, M. K. (1990). Love matches and arranged marriages. *Journal of Marriage and the Family, 52,* 709–722.

YANKELOVICH, D. (1981). *New rules: Searching for self-fulfillment in a world turned upside down.* New York: Random House.

YLLÖ, K. A. (1993). Through a feminist lens: Gender, power, and violence. In R. J. Gelles & D. R. Loseke (Eds.), *Current controversies on family violence* (pp. 47–62). Newbury Park, CA: Sage.

YONAS, A., & OWSLEY, C. (1987). Development of visual space perception. In P. Salapatek and L. Cohen (Eds.), *Handbook of infant perception* (Vol. 2). Orlando, FL: Academic Press.

ZAHN-WAXLER, C., RADKE-YARROW, M., WAGNER, E. & CHAPMAN, M. (1992). Development of concern for others. *Developmental Psychology, 28,* 126–136.

ZASLOW, M. J., & HAYES, C. D. (1986). Sex differences in children's responses to psychosocial stress: Toward a cross-context analysis. In M. E. Lamb, A. L. Brown, & B. Rogoff (Eds.), *Advances in developmental psychology* (Vol. 4). Hillsdale, NJ: Erlbaum.

ZELAZO, N. A., ZELAZO, P. R., COHEN, K. M., & ZELAZO, P. D. (1993). Specificity of practice effects on elementary neuromotor patterns. *Developmental Psychology, 29,* 686–691.

ZELAZO, P. R. (1993). The development of walking: New findings and old assumptions. *Journal of Motor Behavior, 15,* 99–137.

ZICK, C. D., & MCCULLOUGH, J. L. (1991). Trends in married couples' time use: Evidence from 1977-78 and 1987-88. *Sex Roles, 24,* 459–488.

ZIGLER, E., & HALL, N. W. (1989). Physical child abuse in America: Past, present, and future. In D. Cicchetti & V. Carlson (Eds.), *Child maltreatment: Theory and research on the causes and consequences of child abuse and neglect.* New York: Cambridge University Press.

ZIMBERG, S. (1985). Principles of alcoholism psychotherapy. In S. Zimberg, J. Wallace, & S. B. Blume (Eds.), *Practical approaches to alcoholism psychotherapy* (pp. 3–22). New York: Plenum.

ZSEMBIK, B. A., & SINGER, A. (1990). The problem of defining retirement among minorities: The Mexican Americans. *Gerontologist, 30,* 749–757.

ZURAIVIN, S. J. (1991). Research definitions of child physical abuse and neglect: Current problems. In R. H. Starr, Jr., & D. A. Wolfe (Eds.), *The effects of child abuse and neglect.* New York: Guilford.

N A M E I N D E X

This page constitutes an extension of the copyright page. We have made every effort to trace the ownership of all copyrighted material and to secure permission from copyright holders. In the event of any question arising as to the use of any material, we will be pleased to make the necessary corrections in future printings. Thanks are due to the following authors, publishers, and agents for permission to use the material indicated.

Figure Credits

CHAPTER 1

20: Adapted from *The Child: Development in a Social Context,* by Claire B. Kopp & Joanne B. Krakow, p. 648. Copyright © 1982 Addison-Wesley Publishing Co., Inc. Used with permission of the publisher.

CHAPTER 2

49: From "Genetic Aspects of Intelligent Behavior," by I. I. Gottesman. In N. R. Ellis (Ed.), *Handbook of Mental Deficiency,* p. 255. Copyright © 1963 Norman R. Ellis. Reprinted with permission.

55: From *Before We Are Born,* Fourth Edition, by K. L. Moore & T. V. N. Persaud, p. 130. Copyright © 1993 W. B. Saunders. Reprinted with permission.

61: From *Before We Are Born,* Fourth Edition, by K. L. Moore and T. V. N. Persaud, p. 130. Copyright © 1993 W. B. Saunders. Reprinted with permission.

70: Adapted from *Child Development,* Third Edition, by L. E. Berk, p. 131. Copyright © 1994 Allyn and Bacon. Used with permission.

CHAPTER 3

85: From *Normal and Abnormal Development of the Nervous System,* by R. J. Lemire, J. D. Loeser, R. W. Leech, & E. C. Alvord, Jr., p. 236. Copyright © 1975 by J. B. Lippincott Company. Reprinted with permission.

95: From "Specificity of Practice Effects," by N. A. Zelazo et al., 1993, *American Psychologist, 49,* 686–691. Copyright © American Psychological Association. Reprinted with permission.

101: Adapted from "Pattern Perception in Infancy," by P. Salapatek. In L. B. Cohen & P. Salapatek (Eds.), *Infant Cognition: From Sensation to Perception.* Copyright © 1975 Academic Press Inc. Adapted by permission.

CHAPTER 4

119: From R. V. Kail & R. Wicks-Nelson, *Developmental Psychology, 5/E,* © 1993, p. 195. Reprinted by permission of Prentice-Hall, Upper Saddle River, New Jersey.

136: From "The Child's Learning of English Morphology," by J. Berko, 1958, *Word, 14,* p. 150, International Linguistics Corp.

CHAPTER 5

167: From "Process Analysis of Spatial Aptitude," by J. W. Pellegrino and R. V. Kail. In R. J. Sternberg (Ed.) *Advances in the Psychology of Human Intelligence, Vol. 1,* p. 316. Copyright © 1982 Lawrence Erlbaum Associates, Inc. Reprinted with permission.

169: From "A Schematic Processing Model of Sex Typing and Stereotyping in Children," by C. L. Martin & C. F. Halverson, 1981, *Child Development, 52,* p. 1121. Copyright © 1981 Society for Research in Child Development, Inc. Reprinted with permission.

CHAPTER 7

237: From "Strategies for Making Friends: Relations to Social Behavior and Peer Acceptance," by K. R. Wentzel & C. A. Erdley, 1993, *Developmental Psychology, 19,* 819–826. Copyright © 1993 American Psychological Association. Reprinted with permission.

CHAPTER 8

253: Adapted from "Variations in the Pattern of Pubertal Changes in Boys," by W. A. Marshall & J. M. Tanner, 1970, *Archives of Disease in Childhood, 45,* p. 22. Copyright © 1970 British Medical Association. Used with permission.

253: From "Puberty," by W. A. Marshall & J. M. Tanner. In J. Falkner & J. M. Tanner (Eds.), *Human Growth: A Comprehensive Treatise, Second Edition, Vol. 2: Postnatal Growth, Neurobiology,* p. 196. Copyright © 1962 Plenum Publishing Corporation. Reprinted with permission.

270: Adapted and reproduced by special permission of the publisher, Psychological Assessment Resources, Inc., 16204 North Florida Avenue, Lutz, FL 33549 from the *Self-Directed Search Professional Manual* by John L. Holland, Ph.D. Copyright © 1985 by PAR, Inc. Further reproduction is prohibited without permission from PAR, Inc.

271: Modified and reproduced by special permission of the publisher, Consulting Psychologists Press, Inc., Palo Alto, CA 94303 from the Strong Interest Inventory of the Strong Vocational Interest Blanks, Form T317. Copyright © 1994 by The Board of Trustees of the Leland Stanford Junior University. All rights reserved. Printed under license from the Stanford University Press, Stanford, CA 94305. Further reproduction is prohibited without the publisher's written consent.

CHAPTER 9

312: From "The Course of Adult Intellectual Development," by K. W. Schaie, 1994, *American Psychologist, 49;* 304–313. Copyright © American Psychological Association. Reprinted with permission.

314: From "Organization of Data on Life-Span Development of Human Abilities," by J. L. Horn. In L. R. Goulet & P. B. Baltes (Eds.), *Life-Span Developmental Psychology: Research and Theory,* p. 463. Copyright © 1970 Academic Press. Reprinted with permission.

319: From "Reasoning on Social Dilemmas Varying in Emotional Saliency: An Adult Developmental Study," by F. Blanchard-Fields, 1986,

Psychology and Aging, 1, 325–333. Copyright © 1986 American Psychological Association. Reprinted with permission.

328: From *The Me I Know: A Study of Adult Identity,* by S. K. Whitbourne. Copyright © 1986 Springer-Verlag Publishing. Reprinted with permission.

CHAPTER 10

340: From "Age and Sex Differences in Satisfying Love Relationships across the Adult Life Span," by M. N. Reedy, J. E. Birren, & K. W. Schaie, 1981, *Human Development, 24,* 52–66. Copyright © 1981 S. Karger AG, Basel. Reprinted with permission.

343: From "International Preferences in Selecting Mates: A Study of 37 Cultures," by D. M. Buss et al., 1990, *Journal of Cross-Cultural Psychology, 21,* 5–47. Copyright © 1990 by Sage Publications, Inc. Reprinted by permission of Sage Publications, Inc.

344: From "Through a Psychological Lens: Personality Traits, Personality Disorders, and Levels of Violence," by K. D. O'Leary. In R. J. Gelles & D. R. Loseke (Eds.), *Current Controversies on Family Violence,* pp. 7–30. Copyright © 1993 by Sage Publications, Inc. Reprinted by permission of Sage Publications, Inc.

344: From "Through a Psychological Lens: Personality Traits, Personality Disorders, and Levels of Violence," by K. D. O'Leary. In R. J. Gelles & D. R. Loeske (Eds.), *Current Controversies on Family Violence,* pp. 7–30. Copyright © 1993 by Sage Publications, Inc. Reprinted by permission of Sage Publications, Inc.

357: From "Relationships between Fathers and Children Who Live Apart: The Father's Role after Separation," by J. A. Seltzer, 1991, *Journal of Marriage and the Family, 53,* p. 79. Copyrighted © 1991 National Council on Family Relations, 3989 Central Ave. NE, Suite 550, Minneapolis, MN 55421. Reprinted by permission.

361: From *Marriage and Family Development,* 6th Edition, by E. M. Duvall & B. C. Miller. Copyright © 1985 Harper & Row, Publishers, Inc. Reprinted by permission of HarperCollins Publishers, Inc.

362: From *Career, Women, and Childbearing: A Psychological Analysis of the Decision Process,* by C. Wilk. Copyright © 1986 Van Nostrand Reinhold. Reprinted with permission.

CHAPTER 11

375: From *Career Motivation in Mid-life Managers,* by A. Howard & D. W. Bray. Paper presented at the meeting of the American Psychological Association, Montreal, August 1990.

CHAPTER 12

410: From "Bone Loss and Aging," by S. M. Garn. In R. Goldman & M. Rockstein (Eds.), *The Physiology and Pathology of Aging.* Copyright © 1975 Academic Press. Reprinted with permission.

418: From "Aging and Cognitive Changes," by N. W. Denney. In B. B. Wolman (Ed.), *Handbook of Developmental Psychology,* p. 821. Copyright © 1982. Reprinted by permission of Prentice-Hall, Inc., Englewood Cliffs, N.J.

CHAPTER 13

460: From "Movement Specification Time with Age," by G. E. Stelmach, N. L. Goggin, & A. Garcia-Colera, 1987, *Experimental Aging Research, 13,* p. 42. Copyright © 1987 Beech Hill Enterprises, Inc. Reprinted with permission of Dr. Jeffrey Elias.

462: From "Aging, Spatial Performance, and Spatial Competence," by K. C. Kirasic & G. L. Allen. In N. Charness (Ed.), *Aging and Human Performance,* pp. 191–223. Copyright © 1985 John Wiley & Sons, Ltd. Reprinted by permission of John Wiley & Sons, Inc.

CHAPTER 14

485: From "Ecology of the Aging Process," by M. P. Lawton & L. Nahemow. In C. Eisdorfer & M. P. Lawton (Eds.), *The Psychology of Adult Development and Aging,* pp. 619–674. Copyright © 1973 American Psychological Association. Reprinted with permission.

490: From "Possible Selves in Adulthood and Old Age: A Tale of Shifting Horizons," by C. D. Ryff, 1991, *Psychology and Aging, 6,* 286–295. Copyright © 1991 American Psychological Association. Reprinted with permission.

499: From "Relationship Classification Using Grade of Membership Analysis: A Typology of Sibling Relationships in Later Life," by D. T. Gold, M. A. Woodbury, & L. K. George, 1990, *Journal of Gerontology: Social Sciences, 45,* pp. 43–51. Copyright © 1990 Gerontological Society of America. Reprinted with permission.

505: Modified from "The Conceptualization and Design of Intervention Studies on Frailty in the Older Population," by J. M. Guralnick & R. B. Wallace. In R. Weindruch, E. C. Hadley, & M. G. Ory (Eds.), *Reducing Frailty and Falls in Older Persons,* pp. 29–43. Copyright © 1991. Used courtesy of Charles C. Thomas, Publisher, Springfield, Illinois.

506: From Fulton et al., for the National Center on Health Statistics, 1989.

507: Modified from "The Aging of America: Impact on Health Care Costs," by E. L. Schneider & J. M. Guralnick, 1990, *Journal of the American Medical Association, 263,* 2335–2340. Copyright © 1990 American Medical Association. Used with permission.

CHAPTER 15

523: Copyright © 1995 California Medical Association. Reprinted with permission.

531: From *Adult Development and Aging,* Second Edition, by J. C. Cavanaugh, Brooks/Cole Publishing, 1993.

537: From "The Role of Anticipatory Bereavement in Older Women's Adjustment to Widowhood," by C. D. Hill, L. W. Thompson, & D. Gallagher, 1988, *The Gerontologist, 28,* 792–796. Copyright © 1990 Gerontological Society of America. Reprinted with permission.

539: From "Older Adult Family Stress and Adaptation Before and After Bereavement," by F. N. Norris & S. A. Murrell, 1987, *Journal of Gerontology: Social Sciences, 42,* pp. 606–612. Copyright © 1990 Gerontological Society of America. Reprinted with permission.

544: From "Retrospective Assessment of Marital Adjustment and Depression during the First Two Years of Spousal Bereavement," by A. Futterman, D. Gallagher, L. W. Thompson, S. Lovett, & M. Gilewski, 1990, *Psychology and Aging, 5,* 277–283. Copyright © 1990 American Psychological Association. Reprinted with permission.

Photo Credits

CHAPTER 1

3: M. Siluk/The Image Works; **4:** Mathias Oppersdorff/Photo Researchers; **6:** Mary Kate Denny/PhotoEdit; **7:** American Stock Photography; **8:** (top) O'Rourke/The Image Works; (bottom) MacDuff Everton/The Image Works; **9:** (top) Tom Lyle/Medichrome; (bottom) Cleo Photo/Jeroboam; **10:** Esbin-Anderson/The Image Works; **12:** The Bettmann Archive; **13:** UPI/Bettmann; **14:** Cleo Photo/Jeroboam; **15:** (top and bottom) The Bettmann Archive; **16:** (top) Tony Freeman/PhotoEdit; (bottom) Chuck Painter/News and Publications Service, Stanford University; **17:** The Bettmann Archive; **18:** Michael Newman/PhotoEdit; **19:** Michael Newman/PhotoEdit; **22:** Michael Hayman/Stock Boston; **27:** Suzanne Arms-Wimberley/Jeroboam; **29:** Amy C. Etra/PhotoEdit

CHAPTER 2

38: Merritt Vincent/PhotoEdit; **40:** (left) Ken Edward/Science Source/Photo Researchers; (right) Francis Leroy/Custom Medical Stock; **41:** Biophoto Associates/Science Source/Photo Researchers; **45:** David M. Grossman; **48:** (top) Myrleen Ferguson Cate/PhotoEdit; (bottom)

Courtesy the University of London, Institute of Psychiatry, Plomin/Dunn Research Group; **49:** © D. W. Cunningham 1995; **50:** Robert Kail; **53:** (top and bottom) Lennart Nilsson, A CHILD IS BORN, Dell Publishing Company; **54:** (top and bottom left, bottom right) Lennart Nilsson, A CHILD IS BORN, Dell Publishing Company; **58:** David M. Grossman; **63:** Richard Hirneisen/Medichrome; **68:** Robert Kail; **70:** Innervisions

CHAPTER 3

78: David Young-Wolff/PhotoEdit; **83:** Stock Boston; **84:** PhotoEdit; **86:** (top) Alexander Tsiaras/Stock Boston; (bottom) Reprinted with permission from SCIENCE, "Maturational Changes in Cerebral Function in Infants Determined by FDG Positron Emission Tomography." Copyright 1986 American Association for the Advancement of Science.; **87:** Peter Menzel/Stock Boston; **90:** Dexter Gormley; **91:** Felicia Martinez/PhotoEdit; **92:** Erika Stone/Photo Researchers; **93:** Robert Brenner/PhotoEdit; **94:** (top) Rick Browne/Stock Boston; (bottom) Mitch Reardon/ Photo Researchers; **98:** Dion Ogust/The Image Works; **99:** Michael Tamborrino/Medichrome; **102:** Innervisions; **103:** American Stock Photography

CHAPTER 4

108: Robert Brenner/PhotoEdit; **111:** Shmuel Thaler/Jeroboam; **113:** Innervisions; **115:** Tom McCarthy/PhotoEdit; **116:** (top) Tony Freeman/PhotoEdit; (bottom) Tony Freeman/PhotoEdit; **122:** Ann Chwatsky/Jeroboam; **123:** (top) Courtesy, Dr. Carolyn Rovee-Collier; (bottom) Mike Mazzaschi/Stock Boston; **124:** Tony Freeman/PhotoEdit; **125:** George E. Jones/Photo Researchers; **127:** David Young-Wolff/PhotoEdit; **129:** Eric A. Wessman/Stock Boston; **130:** Michael Newman/ PhotoEdit; **133:** UPI/Bettmann; **134:** Lawrence Migdale/Stock Boston; **135:** © 1994 Don Perdue/Children's Television Workshop; **138:** Susan Johns/Photo Researchers; **139:** Amy C. Etra/PhotoEdit

CHAPTER 5

144: Myrleen Ferguson Cate/PhotoEdit; **149:** PhotoEdit; **150:** Innervisions; **153:** Charles Gupton/Stock Boston; **155:** Boulton-Wilson/Jeroboam; **157** (top) David M. Grossman;(bottom) Tony Freeman/PhotoEdit; **158:** David Young-Wolff/PhotoEdit; **160:** Mary Kate Denny/PhotoEdit; **161:** Frank Siteman; **162:** Charles Harbutt/Actuality; **163:** Dion Ogust/The Image Works; **164:** © Conley, 1991, courtesy the Arizona State University News Bureau; **166:** David Young-Wolff/PhotoEdit; **168:** David Young-Wolff/PhotoEdit; **169:** Crews/The Image Works; **171:** Gale Zucker/Stock Boston

CHAPTER 6

178: Mary Kate Denny/PhotoEdit; **182:** Richard Hutchings/Photo Researchers; **185:** David Young-Wolff/PhotoEdit; **187:** Tony Freeman/PhotoEdit; **188:** The Bettmann Archive; **190:** Will & Deni McIntyre/Photo Researchers; **191:** M. Siluk/The Image Works; **192:** David M. Grossman; **193:** David M. Grossman; **195:** News and Publications Service, Stanford University; **196:** Frank Siteman; **201:** Okoniewski/The Image Works; **203:** Becky Huffman/Resources and Residential Alternatives, Inc.; **204:** Russell D. Curtis/Jeroboam; **205:** Tony Freeman/PhotoEdit; **209:** Richard Hutchings/PhotoEdit; **211:** Courtesy of the University of Michigan, photo by D. C. Goings

CHAPTER 7

216: Bob Daemmrich/The Image Works; **220:** James L. Shaffer/PhotoEdit; **224:** Myrleen Ferguson Cate/PhotoEdit; **226:** Bill Bachmann/PhotoEdit; **227:** Billy E. Barnes/Jeroboam; **229:** Dennis MacDonald/PhotoEdit; **232:** David Young-Wolff/PhotoEdit; **234:** Richard Hutchings/PhotoEdit; **235:** Frank Siteman; **238:** David Young-Wolff/PhotoEdit; **240:** Ray Ellis/Photo Researchers;

242: © Peter Iovino/Touchstone Television; **243:** Tony Freeman/PhotoEdit; **244:** Courtesy of the University of Kansas; **245:** The Bettmann Archive; **246:** © Richard Termine/Children's Television Workshop

CHAPTER 8

250: Richard Hutchings/PhotoEdit; **254:** (left) Bob Daemmrich/The Image Works; (right) David Young-Wolff/PhotoEdit; **255:** (top) © Mark Sherman; (bottom) Douglas/The Image Works; **257:** Tony Freeman/PhotoEdit; **260:** Richard Hutchings/PhotoEdit; **261:** Tom McCarthy/PhotoEdit; **262:** Myrleen Ferguson Cate/PhotoEdit; **265:** David Young-Wolff/PhotoEdit; **268:** PhotoEdit; **270:** Michael Newman/PhotoEdit; **271:** Consulting Psychologists Press; **272:** (left) The Bettman Archive; (center) The Bettmann Archive; (right) Billy E. Barnes/Jeroboam; **276:** U.S. Department of Health & Human Services; **277:** Rape Treatment Center, Santa Monica Hospital; **280:** Richard Hutchings/PhotoEdit; **281:** Dennis McDonald/Photo Edit

CHAPTER 9

292: Bob Daemmrich/The Image Works; **294:** PhotoEdit; **296:** Patrick Ward/Stock Boston; **297:** Bob Daemmrich/The Image Works; **298:** Michael Newman/PhotoEdit; **300:** Cleo Photo/Jeroboam; **301:** AP/Wide World Photos, Inc.; **303:** M. Bernsau/The Image Works; **304:** Billy E. Barnes/Stock Boston; **305:** Spencer Grant/Photo Researchers; **306:** David Young-Wolff/PhotoEdit; **307:** (left) Ogust/The Image Works; (right) Grecco/Stock Boston; **308:** Bob Daemmrich/Stock Boston; **310:** Richard Pasley/Stock Boston; **311:** (left) John Coletti/Stock Boston; (right) Amy C. Etra/PhotoEdit; **315:** Michael Newman/PhotoEdit; **326:** Courtesy of the University of Massachusetts, photo by Steve Long; **328:** Amy C. Etra/PhotoEdit; **330:** Steve Skjold/PhotoEdit

CHAPTER 10

336: Esbin-Anderson/The Image Works; **339:** (top) M. Antman/ The Image Works; (bottom) Bob Daemmrich/The Image Works; **340:** (top) T. Prettyman/PhotoEdit; (bottom) Myrleen Ferguson Cate/PhotoEdit; **341:** Michael Newman/PhotoEdit; **342:** Tony Freeman/PhotoEdit; **346:** Los Angeles Commission on Assaults Against Women; **348:** Laima Druskis/Jeroboam; **350:** Bill Aron/PhotoEdit; **352:** Frank Siteman; **353:** Frank Siteman; **356:** Tony Freeman/PhotoEdit; **357:** David Young-Wolff/PhotoEdit; **359:** Ron Davis/Shooting Star; **360:** Tony Freeman/PhotoEdit; **364:** Spencer Grant/Stock Boston; **366:** PhotoEdit; **367:** PhotoEdit

CHAPTER 11

372: Tony Freeman/PhotoEdit; **374:** David M. Grossman; **376:** Charles Harbutt/Actuality; **377:** AP/Wide World Photos, Inc.; **379:** Jim Pickerell/Stock Boston; **380:** Laima Druskis/Stock Boston; **384:** Tom McCarthy/PhotoEdit; **385:** (top) David Young-Wolff/PhotoEdit; (bottom) Michael Newman/PhotoEdit; **386:** Bob Daemmrich/The Image Works; **387:** Charles Harbutt/Actuality; **388:** (left) AP/Wide World Photos, Inc.; (right) AP/Wide World Photos, Inc.; **389:** (top left) AP/Wide World Photos, Inc.; (top right) AP/Wide World Photos, Inc.; (bottom) John Coletti/Stock Boston; **391:** Bob Daemmrich/Stock Boston; **395:** Rob Crandall/Stock Boston; **396:** Frank Siteman; **397:** Frank Siteman; **402:** Bob Daemmrich/Stock Boston

CHAPTER 12

406: Michael Newman/PhotoEdit; **409:** David Young-Wolff/PhotoEdit; **412:** Suzanne Arms-Wimberley/Jeroboam; **413:** Peter Southwick/Stock Boston; **415:** Melanie Brown/PhotoEdit; **416:** Tom McCarthy/PhotoEdit; **418:** Michael Newman/PhotoEdit; **419:** (top) The Bettmann Archive; (bottom) Reuters/Bettmann; **420:** (left) John Coletti/Stock Boston; (right) Stephen McBrady/PhotoEdit;

TO THE OWNER OF THIS BOOK:

We hope that you have enjoyed *Human Development* as much as we have enjoyed writing it. We'd like to know your thoughts and experiences about the book as a student. In what ways did it help you, and how can we make it bettter for future readers?

School and address: _____

Department: _____

Instructor's name: _____

1. What did you like most about *Human Development?* _____

_____

_____

2. How might it be improved? _____

_____

_____

5. Were all of the chapters of the book assigned for you to read?　　Yes _____　No _____

If not, which ones weren't? _____

_____

_____

6. In the space below, or on a separate sheet of paper, please let us know any additional reactions that you may have regarding your experience using this book.

_____

_____

_____

_____

_____

_____

_____

_____

Optional:

Your name: _____ Date: _____

May Brooks/Cole quote you, either in promotion for *Human Development,* or in future
publishing ventures?

Yes: _____ No: _____

Sincerely,

Robert V. Kail
John C. Cavanaugh

FOLD HERE

BUSINESS REPLY MAIL
FIRST CLASS   PERMIT NO. 358   PACIFIC GROVE, CA

POSTAGE WILL BE PAID BY ADDRESSEE

ATT: *Robert V. Kail, John C. Cavanaugh*

Brooks/Cole Publishing Company
511 Forest Lodge Road
Pacific Grove, California 93950-9968

NO POSTAGE
NECESSARY
IF MAILED
IN THE
UNITED STATES

FOLD HERE